D0471326

THE UNITED STATES
AND
WORLD ORGANIZATION
1920-1933

Wide World

WOODROW WILSON
From a portrait by F. Graham Cootes

THE UNITED STATES AND WORLD ORGANIZATION

1920-1933

BY

DENNA FRANK FLEMING

AMS Press, Inc.
New York
1966

Reprinted 1966
with Permission of Columbia University Press

AMS Press, Inc.
New York, N.Y. 10003

Manufactured in The United States of America

TO

THOSE IN EVERY NATION WHO HAVE SOUGHT, AND
TO THOSE WHO IN THE FUTURE WILL SEEK, "THE REIGN OF
LAW BASED ON THE CONSENT OF THE GOVERNED
AND SUSTAINED BY THE ORGANIZED
OPINION OF MANKIND"

PREFACE

IT IS now eighteen years since the United States completed her original refusal to assist in the building of the League of Nations. This volume attempts to record what followed that epochal decision.

The contrast between the world's aspirations in 1920 and its condition in 1938 is both alarming and challenging. The writer is far from believing that all participants in war are so defeated that it makes little difference who wins, but he is still unable to discover any reason for disbelieving that the one enduring gain which any nation could have salvaged from the Great War was a reasonably dependable assurance that its stupendous follies would not be repeated.

Yet at the beginning of 1938 the world situation appears to be far worse than it was in early 1914. Then, one or two great empires were suspected of aggressive designs. Now, three of the "Great Powers" have proclaimed their aggressive purposes from the housetops so insistently, and have demonstrated their abilities at conquest so repeatedly, that the world is engaging in the maddest scramble for arms which has ever occurred. The pre-1914 arms race was a sane and orderly waste of economic resources as compared to the uneconomic spending for destructive apparatus which is going forward at present.

How is it possible that today fear of wars of conquest should be driving nearly all the world's peoples before it, and paralyzing at the same time a large part of their productive processes? How is it possible that the League of Nations, which was created expressly to prevent the return of international anarchy, has been pushed into the background—apparently helpless to protect its members from conquest or to prevent the world from being plunged into war again?

What has been responsible for such an incredible relapse? What leaders, what policies, what omissions have almost killed the greatest promise ever held out to man—at the same time loosing far greater destructive forces than any previously known? What consequences, in particular, have flowed from the decision of the United States again to entrust its prosperity and security to neutrality and aloofness from the world's political troubles?

The writer does not suppose that he has recorded with final exactness all the explanations of the downfall of the structure of "Normalcy" which was erected in 1920, or of the perilous descent toward another world war which is still in progress. He has tried to trace the main threads of that great collapse down to the spring of 1933, by following, as simultaneously as possible, the unfolding of developments in both hemispheres. The book attempts to describe the chief events of world politics during this period, as they centered around the League of Nations and the United States. It has been intended to include some record of the varied activities of the League, with extended accounts of the crises in its life.

This volume is the result of an award by the University of Pennsylvania of a Penfield Traveling Scholarship for the year 1932-1933, which, with the cordial assistance of Vanderbilt University enabled me to spend six months in Geneva during the last phases of the Disarmament Conference and while the Lytton report on the Manchurian War was being debated. Leave of absence was again granted by Chancellor James H. Kirkland for the autumn of 1935, making possible the writing of additional chapters and a visit to London and Geneva during the consideration of the Ethiopian war by the League Council and Assembly. My warmest thanks are given to both universities for providing the major part of the time necessary for this study, and I am equally grateful to many individuals who have generously helped to bring it to completion. For courteous and constructive assistance, I am deeply indebted, especially to Hon. Roland S. Morris,

Dr. William C. Binkley, Dr. James T. Shotwell, Mr. Whitney H. Shepardson, Hon. Norman H. Davis, Mrs. Charles E. Simonson, Hon. Newton D. Baker, President Isaiah Bowman, Admiral Cary T. Grayson, Dean Luther P. Eisenhart, Senator James P. Pope, Dr. William E. Dodd, Dr. Manley O. Hudson, Hon. Albert Rathbone, Dr. Charles G. Fenwick, Dr. James W. Garner, Mr. Clark E. Eichelberger, and Miss Esther G. Ogden.

I have endeavored to record in the footnotes my indebtedness to the work of other writers, particularly to the many monographs on topics in this period, without which a survey of this scope could hardly have been written. In each chapter the first citation of an authority contains full bibliographical data.

D. F. F.

Nashville, Tennessee
January 15, 1938

CONTENTS

I. THE CREATION OF THE LEAGUE OF NATIONS 3
II. THE ABSTENTION OF THE UNITED STATES 26
III. SEPARATE PEACE 42
IV. NON-RECOGNITION 60
V. WASHINGTON PEACE CONFERENCE 79
VI. ISOLATION PERFECTED 112
VII. ENDING THE WAR 148
VIII. THE SEARCH FOR SECURITY 180
IX. NORMALCY 219
X. PROSPERITY 278
XI. COLLAPSE 317
XII. DISARMAMENT 361
XIII. MANCHURIA 393
XIV. FOR AND AGAINST THE LEAGUE 457
XV. TOWARD THE FUTURE 495
INDEX 551

ILLUSTRATIONS

WOODROW WILSON *Frontispiece*

THE LEAGUE OF NATIONS SECRETARIAT BUILDING 40

THE SECRETARIAT WING OF THE NEW LEAGUE BUILDING 40

SIR ERIC DRUMMOND 56

AMERICAN SECRETARIES OF STATE, 1921-1929 76

VISCOUNT CECIL OF CHELWOOD 156

PREMIERS AND FOREIGN MINISTERS OF THE GREAT POWERS WHO PLAYED ACTIVE PARTS IN THE LEAGUE OF NATIONS 216

Aristide Briand, Gustav Stresemann, Sir Austen Chamberlain, Ramsay MacDonald, Edouard Herriot, Sir John Simon

OUTSTANDING OFFICIALS OF THE LEAGUE OF NATIONS SECRETARIAT 234

Sir Arthur Salter, Salvador de Madariaga, M. R. Haas, Dr. Ludwig Rajchman, Paul Mantoux, Sir Herbert Ames

LEADING OPPONENTS OF AMERICAN MEMBERSHIP IN THE LEAGUE OF NATIONS 250

William E. Borah, Hiram Johnson, William Randolph Hearst, John Bassett Moore, Edwin M. Borchard, George Holden Tinkham

LEADING AMERICAN ADVOCATES OF INTERNATIONAL ORGANIZATION 292

Nicholas Murray Butler, James T. Shotwell, Newton D. Baker, William E. Dodd, Manley O. Hudson

AMERICAN MEMBERS OF THE LEAGUE SECRETARIAT 314

Raymond B. Fosdick, Arthur Sweetser, Whitney H. Shepardson, Benjamin Gerig, Howard Huston

THE INTERNATIONAL LABOR OFFICE BUILDING 346

THE NEW LEAGUE OF NATIONS LIBRARY 346

PRINCIPAL NEGOTIATORS FOR THE UNITED STATES AT GENEVA 390

NORMAN H. DAVIS, STEPHEN G. PORTER, HUGH WILSON, HUGH GIBSON, PRENTISS GILBERT

DISTINGUISHED REPRESENTATIVES OF THE SMALLER NATIONS AT GENEVA 428

PAUL HYMANS, EDUARD BENES, GIUSEPPE MOTTA, FRIDTJOF NANSEN, NICOLAS POLITIS, EAMON DE VALERA

THE LYTTON COMMISSION OF INQUIRY 436

THE LEAGUE ASSEMBLY WHICH CONSIDERED THE LYTTON REPORT 448

HENRY L. STIMSON 456

THE NEW HALL OF THE LEAGUE OF NATIONS ASSEMBLY 528

SENATOR JAMES P. POPE 544

THE UNITED STATES AND WORLD ORGANIZATION 1920-1933

CHAPTER I

THE CREATION OF THE LEAGUE OF NATIONS

IN THE early summer of 1914 a world war was the last thing which the American people thought about. They had been told often that the bankers would never permit a great war to occur again, and the internationalization of trade and finance had gone far enough to make it seem reasonable that the international bankers would simply refuse credit to any nation which threatened to disrupt the channels of commerce.

Our government was also uninterested in the balance-of-power politics which preceded the war. President Wilson, it is true, had become sufficiently uneasy to arrange a mediatory mission of Colonel House to Europe in mid-May, 1914. But Wilson was intent upon the reorganization of our own life. He had come to power as a result of the inability of the Republican party to keep the stream of progress moving. At length, in 1912, that party had split into two fairly equal parts on the issues of reform, presenting to Wilson and his party their opportunity. They had seized it at once, opening a session of Congress on April 7, 1913, which was to merge into the regular session and continue its labors until 565 days had passed.

The United States Absorbed in Her Own Affairs

An Era of Reform. Never before had any President or any party been as zealous and effective in patiently constructing conservative reforms. First the Payne-Aldrich Tariff, worst liability of the defeated Republicans, was attacked and after six months of steady labor actually revised downward. For the first and last time in many years tariff revision had not meant a rise in the rates. The Underwood Tariff Act of October 3, 1913, had also included the first income-tax law in our history. This measure, which was to transfer the chief burden of Federal taxation from the consumers of tariff-protected goods to the recipients of large incomes, was framed by Representative Cordell Hull, of Tennessee, a statesman who twenty years later was to take up again the task of reducing tariffs and restoring world trade, after another long period of Republican rule.

Late in December, 1913, the Federal Reserve Act was enacted, creating for the first time a strong, supervised organization of our banking resources. Within a month, on January 20, 1914, President Wilson had called upon Congress to modernize the antitrust laws and to create a Federal Trade Commission to combat the unfair practices of trade and finance which the Pujo committee had so strikingly exposed in its report of February 28, 1913.[1] The discussion of these laws consumed additional months. The Federal Trade Commission Act did not pass the Senate until August 5, 1914, as the last declarations of war were being issued in Europe. It did not become law until September 26, three weeks before the Clayton Antitrust Act was signed.[2]

Caribbean Issues Composed. These weighty measures and others, such as the Smith-Lever Act of May 8, 1914, providing for agricultural education, left little time for the contemplation of foreign affairs.[3] Yet questions of foreign policy had been continually to the fore. In an address on March 11, and again at

[1] The testimony before the committee "confirmed the impression," says a recent historian, "that the men who had fought or tricked their way to the control of finance and business exercised a dominance over the life of the individual that was inconsistent with any theory of democratic control of public policy." Frederic L. Paxson, *American Democracy and the World War: Pre-War Years, 1913-1917*, Boston, 1936, p. 86.

[2] These laws had been opposed strenuously by Republican interests. The *New York Tribune* tried repeatedly to induce the Congress to bolt President Wilson's leadership. On May 25, 1914, its leading editorial was headed: "Drop the Anti-Trust Bills and Let the Country Have a Rest." On July 7, the *Tribune's* leader proclaimed: "It Is Not Patriotism But Cowardice Which Keeps Congress in Session."

[3] "It would have taxed the ingenuity and temper of any government, working in a vacuum, to offer, sift, and pass as many basic laws as came from the first two sessions of the Sixty-Third Congress." Paxson, *American Democracy and the World War: Pre-War Years, 1913-1917*, p. 107.

Mobile on October 27, 1913, the President held out his hand to Latin America in cordiality, resisting constantly the strong pressure upon him to intervene in the Mexican civil war. But on April 10, 1914, the arrest of an American officer and several marines by Mexicans at Tampico led him to back the demand for a salute to our flag and to occupy Vera Cruz on April 22, partly to prevent the German steamer *Ypiranzí* from docking with arms for the Mexican dictator, General Huerta. Three days later, however, Wilson accepted an offer of mediation from Argentina, Brazil, and Chile, and during weeks of conferences at Niagara Falls, Canada, the mediators paved the way for the exit of Huerta, on July 16, 1914.

Four days earlier another major international conflict was brought to a close by the passage in the Senate of the Panama Canal Tolls Repeal Bill, which had been approved by the House of Representatives April 1, after being denounced by Speaker Champ Clark as "this stupendous folly, this unspeakable humiliation of the American Republic." The President had asked for repeal of the preferential tolls granted to our own ships as contrary to our treaties with Great Britain. He won the tolls battle but could not secure the approval of two-thirds of the Senate for a treaty of April 10, 1914, awarding Colombia $25,000,000 damages for the seizure of Panama by Theodore Roosevelt.

War in Europe. The intent of the Wilson Administration to live on terms of forbearance and friendship with our neighbors was clearly established when the events in Europe between July 23 and August 5, 1914, suddenly revealed that the civilized Christian nations of the world were living in a state of fundamental anarchy, a century and a half after the Industrial Revolution had begun to weave their interests into a single fabric. It had been supposed that the organization of the great powers into two balancing alliances was a guaranty of peace. Then it developed that nothing could prevent the sudden plunging into war of all the great powers and many lesser ones. The debacle of 1914 was so pitiful and so complete that in every country men of heart and head were compelled to begin working for stronger international organization against war. The ancient balance-of-power device for securing national safety had collapsed so tragically before their eyes that they were compelled to seek something more effective to replace it or demonstrate a total blindness in the human race, such as would not entitle it to survive.

The Failure of Neutrality

Nowhere did the outbreak of the war cause greater astonishment than in the United States. A century of freedom from world wars had encouraged a belief that they were no longer likely to shatter an interdependent world. Then it happened.

The first effects were disconcerting enough. A hundred thousand American tourists, suddenly become refugees, were repatriated from Europe with difficulty. Stock exchanges closed, foreign trade halted and had to seek new channels. Our domestic economy was sufficiently dislocated to make the winter a hard one before the war boom from Entente purchases began.

An Irritating Blockade. As it grew, British restrictions upon neutral trade that might reach Germany and her allies, even indirectly, multiplied beyond all previously accepted rules, arousing constant protest from American shippers. The British, however, paid liberally for the cargoes seized, and steadily increased their own orders as they gradually throttled all trade with the Central Empires. Everything became contraband of war, largely under pretext of reprisals, but in reality because a war of attrition, in which virtually all civilians engage in war effort, makes victory depend upon the weakening of the support behind the lines—even if starvation must be employed.

Sympathy for the Allies. This process was countenanced the more readily by us because we wanted the Allies to win the war. Ties of many kinds predisposed us to the cause of Britain and France. Kinship, language, commercial and social intercourse, common systems of law, and belief in democracy, all inclined us to support the France which had suddenly been attacked by Germany or the Britain which had gone, though not for reasons of chivalry alone, to the rescue of Belgium. The role of autocratic Russia did not disturb this feeling seriously, in the face of the plainly observed assault of Austria-Hungary upon Serbia.

The rapid German invasion of Belgium and North France, climaxed by the heroic stand of the French and British at the Marne won further sympathy for the Allies, and when stories of atrocities began to pour out of the war zone the German cause was further damaged. Some of these reports were fabricated, some of them misrepresented what had been justified reprisals; others were greatly exaggerated by the burning emotions aroused from unpleasant contacts with the invading troops. There was some truth in a fraction of the tales. At the time nearly all of them were believed, while German accounts of atrocities committed by the Belgians did not receive much credence. The ever-present fact that the Germans had seized and held captive some eight or ten million people, while the Western Allies had not, made the denials and countercharges of the Germans of little avail.

The German-Americans and the German Government fought a propaganda campaign in the United States more stubborn than it was wise, but they could not make headway. Their cause was lost at the start of the war. After it began, events steadily made their position more hopeless before American opinion.

Appalling New Weapons. Unable to crush France swiftly, as they had so confidently dreamed of doing, and gripped in the stranglehold of the British blockade, the Germans called science to their aid. They lashed out with new weapons which kept us shocked and confirmed us in thinking them ruthless. Poison gas spread its terror beyond the first British troops that succumbed to it. Zeppelins over London dramatized to great city populations everywhere a possible fate for themselves that was not relished. The use of submarines drove home further the unwelcome fact that civilians were now subject to destruction in wartime, on both land and sea. The starving pressure of the Allied blockade upon

Germany was much more in accordance with tradition, and it was not so instantly destructive.

Germany could hope to break the blockade only by relentless use of the submarine, a strange weapon that was too weak to enforce its will except by torpedoes loosed under the sea. On the ocean surface it could not face a small cannon such as all ships would soon carry rather than be sent to the bottom, for sinking was all that the submarine could do with any enemy merchantman encountered. Worse still, the submarine could not safely risk a visit to ascertain whether a ship was neutral or belligerent. No such distinction, moreover, could be made if the campaign was to succeed. Any ship which appeared to be carrying a cargo toward English coasts had to be sunk.

Warnings were often ventured, sometimes at the cost of the prey escaping, and in any event the comparatively few men aboard a freighter generally escaped to her boats after a torpedo struck. The submarine commanders then usually towed the boats nearer shore or risked a radio broadcast of their location [4]—a practice which submarines will probably abandon in the future, since the wholesale destruction of crews may well be the final thing necessary to weaken decisively both the enemy's will and his ability to carry on.

Submarine warfare involved not only the destruction of neutral ships, but also the killing of American citizens, accustomed to traveling primarily on foreign ships. Any large freighter may be a considerable passenger carrier, and passenger liners are also huge cargo boats. Whereas the British extensions of the usual rules of blockade had caused us great irritation and some loss, the German extensions involved the closing of the seas to us without possibility of compensation. The British trampled on our long-established rights when they herded our ships into their ports and detained, at a liberal price, what they supposed might reach the enemy; the Germans were able only to destroy our goods and our citizens who were not lucky enough to escape. The

[4] Admiral William S. Sims, *New York Tribune*, April 4, 15, 1923.

enforcement of one illegal blockade still permitted us to enjoy a great war-trade prosperity; the other threatened to end it.

A Long Diplomatic Duel. Faced not with an abuse of its rights upon the high seas, but with their extinction, the American Government protested promptly against the first German proclamation of a submarine war zone around the British Isles, saying, on February 10, 1915, that it would hold the German Government to "a strict accountability" for injury to the lives and property of Americans.[5]

It was, then, only a question of time until a crisis would arise. The first of our ships, the *Gulflight*, had already been lost with four American lives when, on May 7, 1915, the English liner *Lusitania* was sunk without warning, with a loss of 1,153 lives out of 1,918 on board, including 114 Americans—men, women and children.

News of the tragedy sent throughout the nation a wave of wrath which was only a little more intense than the horror of other neutral countries. The reaction was so terrific that it produced a cleavage of opinion in Germany as to the wisdom of the campaign, a division that continued up until the final decision, in January, 1917, to risk everything upon unrestricted use of the submarines.[6]

The *Lusitania* negotiations, complicated by the sinking without warning of the White Star liner *Arabic*, on August 19, 1915, and by other factors, had been brought to a climax by the torpedoing of the unarmed French channel-steamer *Sussex*, April 10, 1916, involving the wounding of three Americans. To President Wilson's demand, on April 18, that the German Government abandon "its present methods of submarine warfare" on pain of

[5] *Foreign Relations of the United States, 1915 Supplement*, pp. 98-100. Up to this time a considerable number of neutral vessels had been destroyed by German mines or submarines. A British statement at the time alleged a total of thirty-six ships, all belonging to the four small neighbors of Germany. J. B. McMaster, *The United States and the World War*, New York, 1918, Vol. I, p. 65.

[6] One of the fullest, if perhaps one-sided, accounts of the internal struggle in Germany is to be found in Admiral Alfred von Tirpitz, *My Memoirs*, New York, 1919.

a severance of diplomatic relations, Germany had replied with a clear promise to observe "the general principles of visit and search" and to avoid sinkings "without warning and without saving human lives, unless these ships attempt to escape or to offer resistance." [7]

The revocation of this pledge, on January 31, 1917, gave the United States no choice but to sever relations with Germany. War could now be no longer postponed, if American rights upon the sea were to be defended against the submarine. To abandon all right to traverse the high seas was not compatible with national self-respect, nor with national safety in the future, particularly in the probable event of German victory. Our fortunes had gradually become merged with those of the Allies until their defeat must, in considerable degree, be ours.

If Germany Won. This development lent weight to the conclusion that a tremendous German-controlled empire, extending from the English Channel to the Persian Gulf, would be able to challenge us when no allies remained. The depth of German hatred aroused by our munitions trade with the Allies was known. It had deepened with each halt in the submarine campaign caused by our protests.

The fall of the Tsarist Government in March had also removed the taint of autocracy from the cause of the Allies at the same time that the domination of Central Europe by the German militarists had become undisputed. It is now much easier to speak cynically of a war for democracy than it was when the proud German military caste bestrode half of Europe. Triumphant since their great victory over Napoleon at Leipzig, Prussian generals were close to excelling his greatest conquests, and no one had reason to doubt the arrogance with which they would rule Europe.

Unthinkable as it had seemed to all Americans two years before, the United States entered the Great War, on April 6, 1917. Affecting us deeply from its first day, the war had steadily en-

[7] *Foreign Relations of the United States, 1916 Supplement*, pp. 232, 257-60.

croached upon our rights as a neutral until none remained—except the right to send one luridly painted ship a week to England, down a narrow lane marked out by the German navy. The conflict had sucked our interests, our sympathies, and our ideals into its vortex, until our neutrality had ceased to exist. The stubborn efforts of a pacifist President had only postponed the opening date of our belligerency.

The Movement for a League of Nations

To Woodrow Wilson the war was a tragedy that could be alleviated only by the subsequent creation of some organization of the nations capable of preventing its repetition. His mind had turned to that compelling necessity in the early months of the war,[8] along with those of many other leaders of national thought.

A League to Enforce Peace. In January, 1915, a group of some thirty statesmen and students of public affairs began a series of meetings in New York City to work out a program for the future. Their deliberations resulted in the calling of a conference in Independence Hall, Philadelphia, on June 17, 1915, attended by three hundred distinguished citizens, at which the League to Enforce Peace was formed. The list of its twenty-two Vice-Presidents and other officials reads like a roster of national leaders in business, the professions, and public life.[9] The gathering perfected an organization fit to be headed by William H. Taft, ex-President and future Chief Justice of the United States. The platform adopted called for a world court for the adjudication of justiciable questions, a conciliation commission for the hearing of all disputes not recognized as submissible to a court, and combined action by the nations against a member which went to war without first using one agency or the other.

It is difficult to see how less could have been attempted by men of any courage or vision, or how they could have stood

[8] See the account of his brother-in-law, Dr. Stockton Axson, in the *New York Times*, February 4, 1924.

[9] *The League to Enforce Peace*, New York, 1915, pp. 1-2.

apathetically before a disastrous collapse of world order without making an effort to organize the peoples of the world against its repetition. To dismiss them as "visionary" is to do them high honor. They demonstrated that ability to see ahead which is the very essence of statesmanship. The League of Nations might sometime split into two warring halves, said President A. Lawrence Lowell of Harvard University in 1915, but "each case where it can be made obvious that a nation would have gone to war with its neighbor if it had not been for such a League of Peace discourages every other nation from trying it." Both the decisions of the Court, added William H. Taft, and the "ever recurring congresses of the League" would widen the scope and application of international law.[10]

A Year before Our Entry. Be it to the credit of the American people that in the period during which the preservation of their neutrality seemed possible they rallied to the leadership of men who refused to admit that every nation must retain the power to bring civilization to the point of extinction whenever it chooses. The rebellion against such a counsel of despair grew so rapidly that when the second national convention of the League to Enforce Peace was held in Washington, on May 17, 1916, it was greeted by the *Washington Star* as "the largest and most distinguished gathering of a voluntary character that ever assembled in this city." [11]

Two days before the opening date of the conference more than 2,000 delegates from every state in the Union and the territories across the seas had registered, with more arriving on every train. Assembled, the best intellect of the nation heard, in clear, cold sentences, conclusions stated by the greatest students of human society, statements which their own common sense verified. Said Franklin H. Giddings: "In only one way has the area of peace been widened as the centuries have passed. The lawbreaker and the war-maker have been restrained by authority armed

[10] *Ibid.*, pp. 17, 25.
[11] *Enforced Peace*, New York, 1916, p. 10.

and employing force. History offers us no suggestion of any other possibility. In a federation of nations desiring peace, and adequately organized to prevent war, rests our hope of the further material and moral progress of mankind." To which was added the voice of Herbert Spencer, speaking through Oscar S. Straus, saying that nothing less could "put an end to the rebarbarization which is continually threatening civilization." [12]

In soberly endorsing that statement did a great outpouring of able men subscribe to an idle delusion? If so, the same conviction had the support of the "hard-headed" business men of the nation. Mr. R. G. Rhett, President of the Chamber of Commerce of the United States, reported to the Conference the results of a national referendum of Chambers of Commerce on the program of the League to Enforce Peace. By a vote of ninety-six per cent the Chambers had voted "that this country take the initiative in forming a league of nations," while seventy-seven per cent had voted in favor of enforcing the decisions of the proposed court and conciliation committee by economic pressure.[13]

Sixty-four per cent of the chambers were for military enforcement of mediatory decisions, sixteen votes short of the two-thirds majority necessary to commit the National Chamber of Commerce.[14]

Lodge and Wilson in Agreement. The same conference found Senator Henry Cabot Lodge declaring that he did "not believe that when Washington warned us against entangling alliances he meant for one moment that we should not join with the other civilized nations of the world if a method could be found to diminish war and encourage peace." On the future preservation

[12] *Ibid.*, pp. 34, 175. The 1918 Convention in Philadelphia was attended by 3,500 officially accredited delegates. On November 1, 1919, the League to Enforce Peace had on its lists 13,000 volunteer speakers and had expended $783,163. *League to Enforce Peace Bulletin* No. 87, May 25, 1918; No. 163, November 1, 1919.

[13] Even in Austria the distinguished jurist Henry Lammasch had come to the conclusion that neutral nations should forbid their citizens to trade with a belligerent which had refused mediation. Theodore Marburg, *The Development of the League of Nations Idea*, New York, 1932, Vol. II, p. 787.

[14] *Enforced Peace*, p. 16.

of international order he had said a year before "not failure but low aim is crime," and he still held that "if we cannot solve it in this way it can be solved in no other." [15]

After this firm affirmation, nothing could have been more fitting, from the twin standpoints of history and of the tragedy in progress, than that President Wilson should close the conference with a statement of his belief that the people of the United States would wish their Government to favor at the close of the war a universal association of nations to preserve the freedom of the seas and "to prevent any war begun either contrary to treaty covenants or without full warning and full submission of the causes to the opinion of the world." [16]

Similar Efforts Abroad. While the League to Enforce Peace mobilized American opinion behind the establishment of some security against future war, equally able groups labored in England and on the Continent, studying plans and principles, sifting them down and rallying the peoples to support the idea. The Central Organization for a Durable Peace, started at the Hague April 5, 1915, led the neutrals, and had the cooperation of representatives from nearly all the belligerent nations.

Shortly afterwards the British League of Nations Society was formed, May 3, 1915, and English committees headed by Viscount Bryce and L. S. Woolf elaborated widely discussed schemes. In September, 1916, Lord Cecil stimulated the British Cabinet to set up the Phillimore Committee, which worked out the draft that ultimately became the chief basis of the Covenant of the League of Nations.[17]

[15] Henry Cabot Lodge, *The Senate and the League of Nations*, New York, 1925, pp. 131-32.

[16] Albert Shaw, (ed.) *Messages and Papers of Woodrow Wilson*, New York, 1924, Vol. I, p. 275.

Wilson had not committed himself to the cause of a league of nations until nearly two years had passed. He had waited until he could speak with authority. His open advocacy was therefore antedated a few days by that of Sir Edward Grey. Marburg, *The Development of the League of Nations Idea*, Vol. II, p. 763.

[17] Felix Morley, *The Society of Nations*, Washington, 1932, pp. 7-11; C. K. Webster and S. Herbert, *The League of Nations in Theory and Practice*, Boston, 1933, pp. 31-32. The Report of the French Ministerial Commission was made on June 8, 1918.

Since many of the best minds of the modern world were at work on the problem during two or three years, there is no justification for the charge, of which so much was made later, that the Covenant was hastily framed. Parts of its structure had been hammered out, in many countries and well in advance, by men who faced the reality of the problem as none coming after them could ever do. That a supreme effort to achieve a real beginning in international organization should be made was as inevitable as it was right. The necessities of the war, moreover, just as certainly presaged some of the outlines of the future League of Nations. The Allied Governments were compelled to form international organizations, such as the Inter-Allied Shipping Board, which developed international secretariats of proved efficiency and achieved such results that the lessons learned were certain to impress the makers of the Covenant.[18]

Steady Advocacy by the President. In the United States, President Wilson had done much to advance the idea of a league of nations before our period of neutrality ended. Standing for it continuously throughout his campaign for re-election, in 1916, he had advanced the principle in his peace note sent soon afterwards to all the warring powers and had stimulated the Allies into formally committing themselves in its favor in their reply of January 10, 1917.[19] Mediation between the warring nations was not to be the role of Wilson, but before the last hope of that solution vanished with the German proclamation of January 31, 1917, he had once more declared his own allegiance to a league of nations, before the Senate on January 22, 1917.[20]

Then without warning the war came to America. The President did not rush to meet it. He waited two months for the overt

[18] Webster and Herbert, *The League of Nations in Theory and Practice*, See on pp. 28-30 the enumeration of nine streams of thought which converged into the demand for a permanent league of nations.

[19] Webster and Herbert, *The League of Nations in Theory and Practice*, p. 33; C. P. Howland, *Survey of American Foreign Relations, 1928*, New Haven, 1928, p. 238.

[20] Marburg, *The Development of the League of Nations Idea*, Vol. II, p. 763. Shaw, *Messages and Papers of Woodrow Wilson*, Vol. I, pp. 348-56.

act which would send him to the Congress to call the United States to its defense. That he could no longer avoid. But he did more. In calling for war he lifted the eyes of the nation to the only objective that could conceivably compensate humanity for the wounds it had already suffered and for the sapping of its heritage that must still ensue. He demanded "such a concert of free peoples as shall bring peace and safety to all nations and make the world itself free."

Woodrow Wilson did not fail to grasp the situation which faced humanity, appalling as it was, and he rose to meet it. In the succeeding months he attained a height of leadership such as no man had ever dreamed of. It was his privilege to open the road which, under the impulsion of the uncontrollable effects of modern warfare, the nations of the future must travel.

From this supreme task he never turned aside, even in the months later when he was stricken to the earth. "A concert of free peoples" was an objective difficult to attain, but it was not an ambitious goal. Within those five small words lay the minimum values of liberty and security from arbitrary attack which the race must attain or lose as a unit. In the year 1938 there is strong probability that both may be lost throughout the world, but there is little to indicate that half of the earth can be free and secure while the remainder lives without liberty or under the oppressive fear of attack.

Wilson's message of hope in "a concert of free peoples," sent to the faltering Russian people on May 26, 1917, came too late to prevent the wiping out of everything which existed in that greatest of land areas. In the succeeding months the same call was reiterated by the leaders of American opinion until even the peoples of deepest Asia had heard it.[21] As the final campaign of the war neared, the President made the best effort of which he was capable to outline a peace settlement that would last. Ines-

[21] Note the account of Dr. William T. Ellis in the *Literary Digest*, February 16, 1924, p. 1.

The Central Powers assented to the principle of a league of nations in their replies to the Papal note of August 16, 1917.

capably, he crowned his Fourteen Points, on January 8, 1918, with the League of Nations, and in another address to Congress, February 11, 1918, warned that unless a new order was created "the world will be without peace, and human life will lack tolerable conditions of existence and development."

"The Most Essential Part of the Peace." At the climax of the war he rephrased the issue at Washington's tomb, July 4, 1918, in an immortal sentence: "What we seek is the reign of law based on the consent of the governed and sustained by the organized opinion of mankind." [22] When the end of the war was at hand, the President went to New York to plead in a powerful analysis of Allied war aims for impartial justice in the coming settlement, and for a league of nations to be made "the most essential part of the peace settlement itself."

The Drive to Postpone the League

The President's Leadership Challenged. When this statement was made, on September 27, 1918, the congressional election of 1918 was but a month away. It found the leaders of the Republican party determined to capture control of the Congress, as a step essential to regaining the Presidency in 1920. Their situation was difficult and, they believed, dangerous in the extreme. If to Wilson's triumphs in domestic legislation and in war leadership were added a crowning achievement in the Peace Conference, his party would probably be entrenched in power for a generation.

To prevent this catastrophe, a swift return to partisanship was necessary, and in the patriotic enthusiasm attendant upon the final victories of the war it was a difficult and dangerous thing to bring about. Yet without it the President seemed certain at least to retain control of the Senate and of the all-important machinery that would direct consideration of the treaty of peace. The safest

[22] Returning from this address the President had requested Colonel House, on July 8, to prepare a draft of a league covenant. From the document submitted, Wilson completed his own first draft on August 15, 1918. Charles Seymour, ed. *The Intimate Papers of Colonel House*, New York, 1928, Vol. IV, p. 24.

method of arousing the normally Republican voters to desert the President was to goad him into a party appeal. For this purpose, Will H. Hays, Chairman of the Republican National Committee, and others, inspired ex-President Theodore Roosevelt to issue, on October 13, a violent, highly provocative attack upon the President and his leadership.[23]

While the President hesitated to reply and to yield to the pleas of Democratic Congressmen for his aid in their re-election, Roosevelt, on October 24, directed to the Senate, the most vulnerable place in Wilson's armor, a bitter demand that the conduct of the peace negotiations be taken out of his hands. Urging the Senators to repudiate "in their entirety" the President's Fourteen Points, he cried out to them to "pass some resolution demanding the unconditional surrender of Germany as our war aim, and stating that our peace terms have never yet been formulated or accepted by our people." [24]

Perhaps this sudden challenge to the President's great program for a permanent peace, acclaimed by the nation without dissent up to this time, should have been ignored.[25] His famous appeal for an undivided leadership issued the next day, October 25, is almost universally credited with having lost him control of the Senate, by the smallest possible margin. With the aid of the tainted vote of Truman H. Newberry, of Michigan, whose seat had been purchased by an expenditure of money so huge that it later forced him and other Senators who supported him out of the Senate, the

[23] John McCook Roots, *The Treaty of Versailles in the United States Senate.* A prize thesis, unpublished, in the Library of Harvard University, p. 12.

[24] *New York Times*, October 25, 1918. At the close of the Spanish-American war Roosevelt had joined conspicuously in a wide campaign to preserve a Republican Congress to support President McKinley in making peace. When himself President, in 1906, Roosevelt had combated the election of a Democratic Congress as merely causing "purposeless confusion," Joseph Tumulty, *Woodrow Wilson as I Know Him*, New York, 1921, p. 328.

[25] Even the *Saturday Evening Post* uttered on August 11, 1917, a sentiment which presumably it would now consider treasonable, saying then: "We consider it a great thing in this war to hold up the idea that American soldiers are fighting for something bigger even than the United States."

new Senate was organized and its Foreign Relations Committee packed with irreconcilable foes of the President.[26]

Notice to the Allies. The election over, demands were at once raised that the President refrain from going to the Peace Conference. Fear of his success was still so great that Roosevelt pressed the narrow advantage won in the election in a proclamation to "our Allies and our enemies and Mr. Wilson himself," which declared that the President had "no authority whatever to speak for the American people at this time." [27]

No Practical League. A week later, December 3, 1918, Senator Lodge outlined in a letter to former Senator A. J. Beveridge the plan of campaign that was to be used to defeat the President's effort to create a league of nations. It would be a mistake, he wrote, either to admit that the league was a good thing or to meet it with a flat denial. The thing to do was "to show up the impossibility of any of the methods proposed." His own judgment was that "the whole thing will break up in the conference." There might be "some vague declarations of the beauties of peace," but if "any practical League" resulted, "then our issue is made up and we shall win." They would begin by pointing out the dangers.[28]

Adept as Lodge was in the art of pointing out the dangers, it would be much easier for him to ridicule or arouse doubts as to the wisdom of whatever league-of-nations agreement came out of the Conference if it could be separated from the treaty of peace.

[26] If 4,000 voters in Michigan who voted for Newberry had supported his opponent, Henry Ford, the casting vote of Vice-President Marshall would have enabled the Democrats to organize the Senate. Changes of less than 1,000 votes in Delaware or New Hampshire would have produced the same result. The story of the Newberry case, including his conviction in the courts, is given in the author's *The United States and the League of Nations, 1918-1920*, New York, 1932, p. 401. The Republicans won the House of Representatives by a majority of 45.

[27] *Kansas City Star*, November 26, 1918.

[28] Claude G. Bowers, *Beveridge and the Progressive Era*, Boston, 1932, pp. 500-501. Beveridge had responded to a letter of Theodore Roosevelt, of October 16, 1918, saying that it would not be best to "totally reject the idea" by asking, "as a matter of practical party politics, if we are to abandon the issue of Nationalism versus Internationalism, as exemplified in Mr. Wilson's League of Nations scheme, what issue have we?" (Page 499.)

To block the latter for a long period would be most inconvenient, not to say dangerous. To forestall such a development, and to weaken the President before he arrived in Paris, Senator Knox introduced a resolution in the Senate, on December 3, declaring that any project for a league of nations should be postponed for consideration, "if and when at some future time general conferences on those subjects might be deemed useful." [29]

It is doubtful if a more brazen, presumptuous demand has ever been made by a group of politicians in any country. After the life of the whole world had been disrupted by a breakdown of international order that was stupid and inexcusable, even if it was not criminally planned as was then generally believed, the new Senate leaders could think of nothing better to do than to forbid any immediate effort to organize against a similar calamity. After they had read during long years of the death or mutilation, of the physical and mental agony of hundreds of millions of their own race, they could be guilty of thinking only of schemes to defeat the President of their own nation to whom the stricken multitudes of every land looked for assurance against a return of the scourge. While devoted men everywhere strained to catch the opportunity to build some foundations for a safer world, before the nations should be turned away from any high endeavor by their renewed dissensions, disorganization, and daily cares, the Senators could only urge that any effort to advance be halted until a Republican President had been elected. When those twin leeches of human failure, the tendencies to forget and to put off what can be postponed, had already begun to drain attention away from the chance of a century, the enemies of Wilson advanced and coolly warned the world that no action must be taken until "if and when at some future time general conferences on those subjects might be deemed useful"—deemed by the Olympian cynics who regressed from one gloomy, bitter prognostication to another until they had repudiated even the poor promise of their "if and when," "after the election" gesture. What they demanded was nothing less than

[29] *Congressional Record*, Vol. 57, Pt. 1, p. 23.

that the whole of outraged humanity should make no advance upon the path of international organization, upon which it had already proceeded far before the war, until they should give the word and assume the leadership. The historian may search long before he comes upon an equal example of upstart effrontery.[30]

Strategy Adopted. The determination of the ruling Republican leaders to prevent Wilson from being credited with the creation of a league of nations having been clearly revealed, Roosevelt and Lodge held a conference in New York City a few days later, at which the plan of campaign in mind was elaborated. It was agreed that if the President secured a league of nations along the lines explained to the country throughout the preceding three years it should be attacked by reservations which would make it of little value to him. Various reservations were actually formulated, though only tentatively, of course.[31] The two knew from their experience in emasculating the Taft arbitration treaties of 1911 exactly how to proceed, though it might take a long time.[32]

The Peace Conference Addressed. The campaign was publicly opened by Knox and Lodge in Senate speeches of December 14 and 21, 1918. Knox ignored all necessity that a beginning be

[30] It is the judgment of one of the most thorough students of the period "that every expression of American public opinion during the previous five-year period had been emphatically for the incorporation of the proposed League in the peace settlement." C. A. Berdahl, *The Policy of the United States with Respect to the League of Nations*, Geneva, 1932, p. 49.

The testimony of Secretary of State Lansing, who followed the President on the League with great reluctance, is equally clear. "With popular sentiment overwhelmingly in favor of some sort of world union which would to an extent insure the nations against another tragedy like the one which in November, 1918, had left the belligerents wasted and exhausted and the whole world a prey to social and industrial unrest, there was beyond question a demand that out of the great international assembly at Paris there should come some common agency devoted to the prevention of war. To ignore this all-prevalent sentiment would have been to misrepresent the peoples of the civilized world and would have aroused almost universal condemnation and protest."—Robert Lansing, *The Peace Negotiations, a Personal Narrative*, New York, 1921, p. 31.

[31] For accounts of this conference, see *New York Times*, October 29 and 30, 1920; Corinne Roosevelt Robinson, *My Brother, Theodore Roosevelt*, New York, 1921, pp. 361-62; Fleming, *The United States and the League of Nations, 1918-1920*, pp. 72-76.

[32] The successful campaign of Roosevelt and Lodge in 1911 is described in the author's *Treaty Veto of the American Senate*, New York, 1930, pp. 90-109.

made while the enormity of the war was fresh in men's minds and argued that nothing could be done now except to give Europe a consultative pact. Lodge, too, was totally unmoved by the world-wide sweep of the war. He actually protested against "trying to provide against wars which may never be fought" and warned that if any "extraneous provision" were "unwisely added" to the treaty, such provisions "would surely be stricken out or amended, no matter how many signatures might be added to a treaty. Protracted opposition and amendments mean long delays, and delay is only less fortunate than rejection." [33]

This warning was plainly and admittedly directed at the leaders of the Allied Powers in the hope that they would ignore Wilson.[34] The leaders of the United States Senate, by grace of a majority of two, served notice upon the congress of nations then gathering that no advance in international organization would be permitted at that time, "no matter how many" nations desired it. Whatever was attempted would be obstructed as long as might be necessary.

Lodge had already sent a long memorandum to leaders of the Peace Conference by one of the President's own peace commissioners, which the Senator hoped might "*be very important to them in strengthening their positions*"—a missive which Henry White was too honorable even to consider presenting to any of the European diplomats to whom it was addressed.[35]

[33] *Congressional Record*, Vol. 57, Pt. 1, pp. 603-5, 724.

[34] *Selections from the Correspondence of Theodore Roosevelt and Henry Cabot Lodge*, New York, 1925, Vol. II, p. 550.

[35] Allan Nevins, *Henry White*, New York, 1930, pp. 352-53. If the President could have included in his delegation "Regular" Republicans strong enough to split the Republican Party, and who would have resisted the band of implacables which had seized control of it to the point of splitting the party, such appointments would have been justified. Any Republican member of the delegation who supported Wilson in framing the League would have had to choose between his party standing and the League. The reader of the following pages may judge as to whether Taft, Hughes, and Root, who had elevated Roosevelt to control of the Party to achieve victory in 1918, would have undone their work in 1920.

What the controlling leaders of the Senate would have done, had Wilson taken them to Paris, does not need elaboration. And if anyone was entitled to go as a Republican, Lodge was the man.

The League Covenant Drawn Up. Not only did this maneuver fail, but the President's progress in Europe was exactly what had been feared. The account of his reception written by Lincoln Steffens is typical of all the others. While the President's train proceeded from Brest to Paris, peasant families knelt beside the track, here and there all along the way, praying for him and his mission. In Paris, London, and Rome such multitudes cheered him as had never greeted any conqueror. "We could see and hear and feel that the American President was making himself the world leader of all democracies, the hope of the race. He succeeded in that. When he returned to Paris to go to work with the premiers and peace delegates, Woodrow Wilson was the spokesman of public opinion and the potential ruler of Europe. Whether he realized it or no, we newspaper men knew it, and we knew, too, that the statesmen of Europe knew it and feared it." [36]

As the President gathered strength, the chance that the Peace Conference would heed the demands of the Republican Senate leaders that the League of Nations be postponed indefinitely decreased correspondingly. It even became very doubtful that

[36] *The Autobiography of Lincoln Steffens*, New York, 1931, Vol. II, p. 779. Another keen observer who attended the Conference wrote: "When he went abroad at the close of the war, no American, and probably no human being, ever held such a position of influence among the nations of the earth. Although the current had already turned against him in America, the enthusiasm that greeted him as one saw it in France passed all bounds. The common people looked to him as the leader of the world, the smaller nations regarded him as a sort of Messiah. No one could have believed that in a few short months he would be abandoned by his people, discredited, hated, slandered, hounded by his enemies, even to the very last when he lay helpless and broken."—J. H. Denison, *Emotional Currents in American History*, New York, 1932, p. 279. The book is a study of national psychology which makes illuminating reading for the whole of this and other periods in our history.

A former editor of the *London Times* has written lately that Wilson's power of putting into words the aspirations and ideals of the great majority of the Allied peoples "gradually won for President Wilson the moral leadership of the Allied cause" and enabled him to come to Europe "as the First Citizen of what, it was fondly hoped, would truly be a new world."—Henry Wickham Steed, *Vital Peace*, New York, 1936, p. 116.

Lord Cecil's record is that no foreign statesmen or potentate was ever received as Wilson was greeted throughout Europe, "not only for himself but because he embodied the passionate aspiration of the world for peace."—Viscount Cecil, *The Way of Peace*, London, 1928, p. 235.

they could force its separation from the Treaty of Peace. If that much could be accomplished, the League could be handled with comparative ease, but to hold up the Treaty of Peace itself until the election of 1920 could be won might cause the Republican chiefs to lose what had been gained in 1918. To keep the world unsettled by holding up the peace for a year and a half was a grave undertaking.

When, therefore, the President actually succeeded in hammering out a draft of a Covenant of a League of Nations and in securing its adoption by the Conference on February 14, the rage of the Senatorial ring was foreordained. Their consternation was almost equally great, also, for the "Republican senators were swamped with telegrams and communications from anxious constituents deploring their lack of support of the League project and urging them to cooperate with the President." Senator Lodge's secretary, Charles F. Redmond, often delivered to him a large basketful in a single day. Approval of the Covenant was so strong that only a few Senators dared to oppose it directly and openly. Lodge was afraid for Borah to risk a trial meeting in Boston. The Irishmen of Boston, however, saw to its success.[37]

[37] Roots, *The Treaty of Versailles in the United States Senate*, MS, pp. 37-38. Mr. Roots interviewed many Senators and other political leaders in 1925.

After Borah's attack on the Covenant in the Senate, February 21, 1919, Lodge said to him: "My dear fellow, I agree with you absolutely, absolutely, but we can't beat the thing. Eighty-five per cent of the Senate are for it. The best we can do is to get changes that will emasculate it as much as possible" (p. 86, Borah quoted).

Lodge also wrote to Beveridge, on January 30, that caution had to be exercised until the new Senate had been organized and control of the Foreign Relations Committee secured. Bowers, *Beveridge and the Progressive Era*, p. 502.

When Lodge asked Senator James E. Watson, of Indiana, to direct the organization of the Senate against the League, Watson thought the League could not be defeated. "Senator," he said to Lodge, "I don't see how we are ever going to defeat this proposition. It appears to me that eighty per cent of the people are for it. Fully that percentage of the preachers are right now advocating it, churches are very largely favoring it, all the people who have been burdened and oppressed by this awful tragedy of war and who imagine this opens a way to world peace are for it, and I don't see how it is possible to defeat it." Lodge replied: "Ah, my dear James, I do not propose to try to beat it by direct frontal attack, but by the indirect method of reservations." "What do you mean by that?" Watson asked. "Illustrate it to me."

Lodge illustrated and "then went on for two hours to explain other reserva-

An Ultimatum to the Conference. The support of the Covenant by the country was so nearly unanimous that a desperate move to sidetrack it abroad seemed to be preferable to the risks involved in a long war of attrition against it at home. After several preliminary blasts in the Senate, Lodge argued at great length about "the uncertainties which cloud this instrument from end to end," and dismissed the possibility of creating a league of nations at that time. Knox followed him, on March 1, 1919, with the demand: "Let us have an end of this!" [38]

This ultimatum was then put by Knox into written form, and after the signatures of slightly more than one-third of the incoming Senate, all Republicans, had been secured, it was published in the form of a proposed Senate resolution. The Round Robin demanded openly that the Peace Conference put aside the Covenant until after the peace treaty had been made. After that, the proposal for a league of nations might "then be taken up for careful consideration"—a contingency that need not be feared after the spoils had all been divided and after the Conference had worn itself out in months of contention over the territorial settlements.[39]

The issuance of this manifesto was a bold step. It might have succeeded had not Taft stood with Wilson on the same platform at a meeting in New York, as he was again sailing for Paris, giving him complete support. With Roosevelt lately dead and Taft at the head of a great wing of his party, it did not seem probable that the Senate leaders would win.

---

tions, going into the details of the situation that would thus be evolved, until I became thoroughly satisfied that the Treaty could be beaten in that way."—Watson, *As I Knew Them*, Indianapolis, 1936, pp. 190-91.

[38] *Congressional Record*, Vol. 57, Pt. 5, pp. 4520-28, 4569-72.

[39] *Congressional Record*, Vol. 57, Pt. 5, p. 4974. If any doubt as to the purpose of the document existed it was set at rest by the statement of Senator Boies Penrose, on March 5, that it was "a notice to the people in Paris."—*New York Times*, March 5, 1919.

CHAPTER II

THE ABSTENTION OF THE UNITED STATES

IN THE months after March 4, 1919, the men who had fathered the Round Robin knew that much time would be required to wear down the public support which the League commanded. On April 29, Lodge told Borah again that any attempt to defeat the treaty and the League by a straight vote would still be "hopeless." They agreed that "there was only one thing to do and that was to proceed in the discussion of the treaty by way of amendment and reservation." [1]

During May two important objectives were obtained. A war chest that was "both deep and full" was obtained from the strong boxes of two multimillionaire friends of Knox, Henry C. Frick and Andrew Mellon.[2] "All anxiety respecting sinews of war was dispelled," and the indispensable organization of the Senate was at last perfected. A filibuster designed to compel the President to call the Senate into session had defeated the appropriation bills at the close of the short session in March. Congress now had to meet in advance of the end of the fiscal year, which fell on July 1.

Renewed Defiance. With the Senate floor again under them, the amendments made to the Covenant in answer to their objections were spurned, the Monroe Doctrine was waved aloft, and shortly before the Peace Conference adjourned a final demand that the Peace Conference divorce the Treaty from the League was made by Knox, on June 10, 1919. Protests by Taft against the packing of the Foreign Relations Committee against the League Covenant were of no avail.[3]

[1] H. C. Lodge, *The Senate and the League of Nations*, New York, 1925, p. 147.

[2] George Harvey, *Henry Clay Frick the Man*, New York, 1928, pp. 293, 325-26, 329-30.

[3] *Congressional Record*, Vol. 58, Pt. 1, pp. 63, 161, 791-92, 796, 894; Vol. 58, Pt. 2, pp. 1221, 1430. The clique went so far as to violate the sacred rule of

When President Wilson sailed for home, July 1, 1919, the cries of defiance from his enemies became louder, though their confidence did not increase proportionately. Chairman Will H. Hays wrote to the impatient Beveridge that the Party was "split this way and that way." It had been impossible to persuade forty-nine Senators to take a united position. If they did not represent forty-nine different positions, the situation was almost that bad.[4]

When the man who had ruled them so long was nearing shore, with such an epochal achievement as a League of Nations compact in his pocket, the ranks of his opponents needed some support. In the emergency the chief attorney for the Republican party had come to the rescue of the sorely beset leaders. After spending "six or seven hours" with Knox, Elihu Root issued a letter advising that certain reservations be concentrated upon,[5] a draft which appeared to hold all Republican Senators in line.

The Campaign for Reservations

This unifying solvent, so exactly in accord with his original plans, was a great relief to Lodge, and also to Beveridge, though both were still most uneasy. Beveridge wrote, on July 7, that "If Wilson gets this thing through, especially if he gets it through with Republican support, I think our chances of winning, which three months ago seemed to be a certainty, will be gravely dimin-

seniority in appointing members of the Committee. Senator Frank B. Kellogg, friendly to the League, was passed over in favor of Senator George H. Moses, a newcomer who was an Irreconcilable. The number of bitter-enders on the Committee was increased from four to seven—half of the total number of them in the Senate. On the basis of their voting strength they would have been entitled to not more than two members out of the seventeen. The addition of Harding and New, "strong reservationists," to Chairman Lodge, virtually increased the Committee strength of the Irreconcilable block to ten. See the analysis by C. A. Berdahl, *The Policy of the United States with Respect to the League of Nations*, Geneva, 1932, pp. 50-51.

[4] Claude G. Bowers, *Beveridge and the Progressive Era*, Boston, 1932, p. 506. Hays unhesitatingly declared to newspaper men at the time that he was for "a league of nations." The country seemed to want it, and conditions of unrest throughout the world argued for it. *New York Times*, June 27, 1919.

[5] Bowers, *Beveridge and the Progressive Era*, p. 506; *New York Times*, June 22, 1919.

ished." [6] Lodge himself, with the Treaty at last in his grasp on July 10, dared not risk an immediate vote, nor did he need to.[7] He had in his hands the indispensable power to delay a vote as long as it should be necessary.

After considering the Treaty for six weeks, the Foreign Relations Committee adopted fifty amendments and, on August 21, decided to open a peace conference of its own, to which all who had been disappointed at Paris might come, though all the Committee could do was to air their grievances. The purpose to delay action upon the Treaty until the resentments and fears left by the war could be mobilized now became wholly clear. The German-, Irish-, and Italian-Americans were known to be disappointed over decisions of the Paris Conference. If their emotions could be capitalized, and sufficient appeals made to the isolationist traditions of the native majority, the success of the opposition strategy was plainly indicated.

Wilson's Appeal to the People. As the Committee showed every disposition to sit astride the Treaty indefinitely, President Wilson came to the conclusion that his cause was lost, unless the country could be aroused to demand approval unmistakably. The situation he had feared in issuing his appeal for a Democratic Congress a year before had come to pass, but he believed that the American people would compel approval of the League.

Already worn from six months of intense strain in Paris, the President made thirty-seven addresses in twenty-two days, traveling eight thousand miles to the Pacific coast and back to Kansas before his strength gave way. Within sight of the end of his tour, he was compelled to hasten back to the White House where he

[6] Bowers, *Beveridge and the Progressive Era,* p. 506.

[7] All the leaders of the struggle whom John M. Roots interviewed agreed that if a vote upon the Covenant had been taken in July or even in August it would have been approved with very mild reservations, "or none at all." Roots, *The Treaty of Versailles in the United States Senate*, Ms. p. 51.

This is also the judgment of a bitter opponent of the League, Dr. David Jayne Hill, who has recorded that "the whole country" was favorable to ratification. See Hill, *The Problem of a World Court,* New York, 1927, p. 88.

struggled precariously for life itself during the decisive months of the campaign against the League.

The Pro-League Republicans Held. Totally unable to capitalize the fears of going too far which had revived in some Republican leaders during his tour, he was unable to come to a timely compromise with the seven or eight Republican Senators who were strongly for the League and wanted only minor changes in the Covenant. While his cause was leaderless, the Senate leaders held the mild-reservationist Republicans in line by a campaign to adopt many amendments to the Treaty. This course the pro-League Republicans would not stand for, but during October, in the process of voting down their leaders on the amendments, they all pledged themselves publicly to support reservations—which would accomplish the purposes of Lodge and Knox just as well.

It was Lodge's task to keep his entire party strength together, no matter how slow was his progress. Attempting to reassure Beveridge, August 4, 1919, he explained that "the votes to defeat the treaty directly are not there, for the simple reason that the League is tied on to the treaty of peace, and we cannot get votes to separate them." But "strong and effective reservations" had been agreed upon. "Any that go on will be effective, and Mr. Wilson's maneuver will be without result." The situation was "one of extreme difficulty," but "in addition to having all the Republicans practically united on strong reservations along the lines indicated by Mr. Root," he had "a good deal more than a third who would vote down the treaty if the reservations were not adopted." [8]

Eventually fourteen reservations were safely voted by a majority of the Senate. The President's Fourteen Points should be exactly matched. The vote to ratify the Treaty with the reservations, November 19, 1919, failed 39 to 55, the Irreconcilable Republicans joining the pro-League Democrats.[9]

[8] Bowers, *Beveridge and the Progressive Era*, p. 507.

[9] *Congressional Record*, Vol. 58, Pt. 9, pp. 8786-87, 8803. "Be it remembered," says Senator James E. Watson, who acted as Senate whip for Lodge, "that a

Compromise Rejected. Such an end to a great endeavor seemed incredible to so many people that compromise negotiations could not safely be resisted.[10] They failed. Wilson's slim hold upon life made it impossible for his friends and those of the League to persuade him to yield. His spirit unbroken, he believed that any concession would only lead to further demands,[11] and he still clung to his confidence that the people would give victory to his cause. He had repeatedly agreed to accept interpretative reservations, first in his second conference with the Foreign Relations Committee, August 19, 1919, and later in a public statement of January 26, 1920. The Hitchcock reservations, which he endorsed on the later date, had been written by his own hand before he started on his Western tour. But no reservations of other than Senate Republican authorship stood a chance of acceptance, particularly while the great power of his personal leadership flickered low in a sickroom.[12]

His opponents had gone too far to retreat, even if they had wanted to do so. After a terrific hue and cry had filled the land for a whole year, the people would want to know, after the coming election, who had won the struggle over the Treaty. The League could not now be permitted to pass in any form without an unmistakably large Republican label attached to it. Any final concession that would permit the Democrats to claim authorship

---

reservation can be adopted by a majority vote, and thus fastened on the treaty, while it requires a two-thirds majority of the Senate to confirm the treaty. And in that way all the Lodge reservations were voted through, and then most of those who voted for the reservations voted against the Treaty itself, because they were opposed to it, with or without reservations, and that did it."—James E. Watson, *As I Knew Them*, Indianapolis, 1936, p. 199.

[10] Lodge, *The Senate and the League of Nations*, pp. 192-93.

[11] William G. McAdoo, *Crowded Years*, Boston and New York, 1931, pp. 514-15.

[12] Wilson's belief that his enemies would not compromise with him on any fair basis needs little substantiation beyond the pages of the book by Senator Lodge, which Mark Sullivan has characterized as "a last thrust of malevolence." Lodge emphasizes repeatedly the care with which he studied Wilson, with a view to predicting his reactions, and proclaims on the final page of his apologia that as the contest over the League ended "I made no mistake in my estimate of what President Wilson would do under certain conditions."—Lodge, *The Senate and the League of Nations*, pp. 212, 218-19, 226; Mark Sullivan, "America and the League: Six Years After," *World's Work*, January, 1926, Vol. 51, p. 289.

of some of the "reservations," or all of them, might be fatal. Why all the tremendous uproar over a few fine points of interpretation? Defeating the League entirely, and the Treaty of Peace with it, was now a lesser risk than that of having the Republican claim that they had saved the country clouded. The chiefs of the opposition knew that the intellectual leadership of the nation still held to the League, but they also knew that the reaction of large masses against Wilson and the rigors of the war was more important politically.[13]

If Senator Lodge had had any doubt as to the wisdom of continuing on the course he had laid down before the Covenant was written, it was removed, at the crisis of the compromise negotiations, by his Irreconcilable wing. Called from the conference room to Senator Hiram Johnson's office to face eight of the bitter-enders, Lodge found himself confronted with the loss of his leadership in the Senate, if he made any concession whatever.[14]

Of all things, a new bolt of the Roosevelt Republicans, who had put the party out of power during eight momentous years, could not be permitted. Hence the Treaty with the Lodge reservations attached failed of approval finally on March 19, 1920, this time by a vote of 49 to 35, seven votes short of the required two-thirds majority.[15] The votes of fifteen Irreconcilables added

[13] Lodge wrote in 1925 that the clergy, the university teachers, the newspaper editors, and all others who addressed the public were overwhelmingly in favor of the Covenant, "as it stood."

George Harvey testified in his book, in 1928, that the business world was for the League. "Bankers noticeably and capitalists, though less aggressively, seemed to be literally unanimous in their advocacy." He thought that "of all classes none was so zealous, so determined and so active as the moneyed element of New York"—the industrial capital of the country.

There was thus no one left to oppose the League except "The man in the street, to use a common expression," who, says Lodge, "didn't understand the treaty at all." It was, of course, the business of Lodge and his confederates to enlighten him—by way of his suspicions, prejudices, fears, and hatreds. Lodge, *The Senate and the League of Nations*, pp. 147-48; Harvey, *Henry Clay Frick the Man*, p. 325.

[14] D. F. Fleming, *The United States and the League of Nations, 1918-1920*, New York, 1932, pp. 402-16.

Lodge had written to Beveridge, on January 3, 1920, "Don't be disturbed about the talk of compromises in the newspapers." Bowers, *Beveridge and the Progressive Era*, p. 509.

[15] *Congressional Record*, Vol. 59, Pt. 5, pp. 27-28.

to twenty of Wilson's supporters kept from the President the onus of rejecting what he regarded as the emasculated remains of the Covenant.

The rejection of the Lodge reservations also appeared to leave the Democrats their best chance of escaping defeat in the midst of the reactions of grievance and discontent which had already succeeded the high emotions and stern discipline of the war. Of all the impulses of the war years surely the universal determination to prevent a repetition of the calamity could be depended on to hold. The Democratic party by standing unequivocally for the League might hope to escape the accumulated resentments it had incurred in eight crowded years.[16]

The Republican Victory of 1920

That hope was vain. It could be realized only if a great segment of habitual Republican voters bolted on the League issue. This schism did not occur, because, in the first place, the reservations did not appear to most Republicans to negative the League. At least a doubt as to the necessity of reservations had been created, and that was all that was needed. Republican voters were sure to censure Wilson for failing to permit their ruling leaders to make at least a few little changes in the Covenant. The strategy adopted by Lodge and his associates in the beginning was fundamentally sound. Never-ending questioning can remodel or defeat any treaty that may be negotiated hereafter, so long as a two-thirds vote for treaties is required in the Senate.

[16] The first demand that the issue be carried into the campaign of 1920 had been made by Lodge, immediately after the Treaty with his reservations had failed in November. Two days later, he endorsed the often-repeated plea of the Irreconcilables as follows: "There is no room for further compromise between Americanism and the supergovernment presented by the League. All I ask now is that we may have the opportunity to lay those reservations before the American people. To that great and final tribunal alone I would appeal. I wish to carry those reservations into the campaign."

It was not until January 8, 1920, that Wilson accepted the challenge and called also for "a solemn referendum." *New York Times,* November 22, 1919, and January 9, 1920.

A Broad Platform. The danger of a Republican split was further removed by the usual device of straddling the issue. The Republican National Convention would have stood openly for the League with the reservations. The Republican National Committeee, the Advisory Platform Committee itself,[17] and "a clear majority of the Republican leaders who were present" were all in favor of ratifying the Treaty with the reservations, while powerful leaders such as Murray Crane, of Massachusetts, were not disposed to insist upon the reservations.[18]

Indeed an all-night session of the Platform Committee produced such a strongly pro-League plank that the Irreconcilable Senator Medill McCormick, of Illinois, stormed out of the committee room uttering words that could only be paraphrased. Others of the terrible dozen joined in the kind of offensive for which they were already noted, Lodge himself having complained that no man of his age should be "obliged to hear" such language. Senator Frank B. Brandegee, of Connecticut—in whom gloom, pessimism, and hatred combined as combustibly as in Knox, McCormick, and Johnson—took the warpath.[19]

When Borah, Brandegee, and McCormick, led by their vindictive mentor, George Harvey, cornered Crane, Lodge, and Ogden L. Mills in a hotel room, the outcome could be foretold without prophetic powers. Lodge declared that he would fight on the Convention floor against any approval of the League with his reservations; Mills drew from his pocket a compromise plank, thoughtfully prepared for the emergency by Elihu Root three weeks before, which would mean all things to all men and nothing too definitely. Crane, always delicate in health, could not continue the battle longer. Before the Convention adjourned, his fight for

[17] For an excellent account of the action of the various committees, and of the Convention, see Berdahl, *The Policy of the United States with Respect to the League of Nations*, pp. 59-60. Also *New York Times*, May 12 and June 9, 1920.

[18] Mark Sullivan, "The Big Issue for 1924," *World's Work*, November, 1923, Vol. 47, pp. 98-99.

[19] *Ibid.*; also the same author's "America and the League," *World's Work*, January, 1926, Vol. 51, p. 291.

the League brought about a collapse, which hastened his death a few months later.[20]

A handful of violent men had again dominated the party. They now proceeded to consolidate their hold on it by dictating the nomination of an ideal presidential candidate for their objective. Harvey, Brandegee, McCormick and Lodge, together with three other Senators invited in, chose Senator Warren G. Harding, of Ohio, and handed him down to the Convention.[21]

[20] *New York Tribune*, June 11, 1920; *New York Times*, June 11, 1920; *Springfield Republican*, October 3, 1920. See also the article by William H. Taft in the *Boston Transcript*, and other papers, June 16, 1920. Taft stated that "good judges were of the opinion" that but for the introduction of the Root compromise the League with the Lodge reservations would have been approved outright. As events turned out, Taft stated flatly that: "The Republican platform means that the United States will enter the League with the Lodge reservations."

Senator Watson has a different version of the framing of the League plank. Lodge, desiring to be temporary chairman, wished to have Watson as chairman of the committee on resolutions. "So we both started out on the warpath and were both elected to the positions we sought." Watson then "appointed a subcommittee of seven with great care, having in mind the previous attitude of its members toward the League."

After a first meeting in the room of Senator Crane, who was "a very sick man at that time," Watson asked George Harvey to frame a resolution, from two or three considered. At another meeting the next afternoon Crane still stood for the Treaty without reservation. Whereupon Borah attacked him "making many pointed observations with reference to Senator Crane and the motives that prompted the latter to advocate ratification. He caustically mentioned Senator Crane's association with the House of Morgan" and threatened to bolt the ticket and fight it. Senator Brandegee, in tears, declared that he would do the same. Harvey was then called upon to produce his plank, and after a few suggested alterations Watson records that "I took the proposed plank, thrust it into my pocket and bolted for the door, saying as I went: Gentlemen, this is the resolution that will be adopted by the committee tomorrow, and so far as I am concerned this ends all conferences on the subject."

"In these ways history is made," says Watson himself, "and a policy adopted which is of incalculable significance to the future of the nation."—James E. Watson, *As I Knew Them*, Indianapolis, 1936, pp. 215-16.

[21] Before the final decision was made, doubts as to his "availability" were resolved as follows. George Harvey called Harding in at two o'clock in the morning and told him that "before finally acting, we think you should tell us, on your conscience and before God, whether there is anything which might be brought up against you that would embarrass the party, any impediment that might disqualify you or make you inexpedient, either as candidate or as President."

Harding, rather stunned, asked for a little time alone, and after ten minutes came out to say that there was no impediment. It was not until 1927 that the book by Nan Britton, *The President's Daughter*, published, in a detailed mass of dates and places, the story of her long liaison with Harding, beginning in

A Perfect Candidate. Amiable, "regular," with no deep convictions on the League issue, Harding steered a difficult course through the campaign by alternating condemnations of the League with promises of projecting a new association of nations, or of revising and using the existing one. Each faction in the party thus clutched hopefully at the utterances which it favored, thinking to hold the candidate to them.

The Pro-League Wing Preponderant? In this rivalry all surface indications pointed to the eventual supremacy of the pro-League Republicans. If leadership means anything at all they represented by far the larger section of the party.[22] Of all the candidates for the Republican nomination only Hiram Johnson was totally opposed to the League. Frank O. Lowden, Leonard Wood, Herbert Hoover, Nicholas Murray Butler all favored going into it upon some basis of reservations. Having an immense preponderance of preconvention support back of them, these leaders were supported during the campaign by the voices of such prominent and respected leaders as William H. Taft, A. Lawrence Lowell, Elihu Root, Charles E. Hughes, George W. Wickersham, Jacob G. Schurman, W. Murray Crane and the Vice-Presidential candidate, Calvin Coolidge—all urging support of Harding as the way into the League. Charles G. Dawes, later Vice-President, had also issued a strong statement urging unconditional ratification of the Treaty.[23]

Into the League with Harding. Should it be cause for wonder that the pro-League Republican voters believed them? The grave heart-searchings which immense numbers still had, as they listened

---

1916, and including the birth of a child in 1919 and visits from Harding at Chicago during the Republican national convention of 1920. Mark Sullivan, *Our Times*, New York, Vol. VI, 1935, pp. 63-64, 357-61.

[22] One of the pro-League Republicans says: "At first less than a fourth of the party had even patience with the Lodge reservations. The three-fourths regarded them as too severe in tone and more drastic than was necessary, while only a negligible few would reject the League of Nations altogether." Samuel Colcord, *The Great Deception*, New York, 1921, p. 23.

[23] *Ibid.*, pp. 26, 75. The statements of Wood, Lowden, Hoover, and Coolidge are quoted in detail, pp. 125-32. See also the *Chicago Tribune*, September 1, 1919, for Dawes's stand.

to Harding's contradictory speeches, must have been ended by the statement of the Thirty-One, issued on October 14 as the campaign neared its close. Signed by so many of the greatest leaders in national life—all Republicans—this appeal assured the troubled consciences of those who felt it would be the tragedy of a century if the world started blundering aimlessly off toward catastrophe again, that "Mr. Harding is willing to follow" the course of "changing the terms of this treaty rather than by beginning anew."

The authority of the Thirty-One was not beyond question, for their assurance to the voters rested upon a quotation from one of Harding's speeches. The authorship of the manifesto, moreover, promised more for the salvation of the Republican Party than it did for that of the League of Nations. It was composed by that able elder statesman who served the cause of the League by compromising with the League's enemies on three crucial occasions. While he doubtless hoped to save both, the net result of his efforts was to be the success of the Party and the loss of the League. It is not possible to be on both sides of a question, especially if it be an immense issue, great both morally and materially.

Elihu Root had gathered all the divergent elements in the Republican Senate membership together in June for the start of the struggle in the Senate. From Borah to McCumber there had been the widest differences of deep conviction that men could conceivably have, yet his mediation had held them all together, each expecting to see his view triumph essentially or wholly. Again at the Republican National Convention, Root had had his formula ready, composing all differences of earnest belief under a blanket of harmonizing words that enabled every man still to look forward to the realization of his dearest hopes or his bitterest hates. Now, at the end of the campaign Root's voice came to the Republican voters themselves, assuring multitudes of them that the intense pain of seeing a great aspiration totally lost might still be avoided by voting for the candidate of the small group of men who had started out to defeat that aspiration two years before and whose determination had only increased as they fought the personal object of their deepest hatred. When supported, too, by thirty of the great, including Hughes and Hoover, the final endeavor of Root must have carried far.

There is no reason to doubt that millions of Republican voters believed they were voting for entry into the League of Nations. They were continually told throughout the campaign that Harding would give them a revised League, whereas Cox would continue to be powerless to muster two-thirds of the Senate for the unamended Covenant.[24]

The Cabal in Control. The widespread assurance of the eminent and nationally respected Republicans of the day did not, however, prevail against the violence of the bitter-enders. In any great national crisis the moderate men are likely to be suppressed by others who act without restraint. Those who attempt to compromise any great issue need not be surprised if they are crushed between the opposing views. The Irreconcilables were few, but, having dominated the organization politicians throughout the struggle, they knew that they could continue to rule them.

In order to supervise Harding's first utterance on the League, George Harvey, vitriolic leader of the anti-Wilson League "cabal," to use Harvey's own term,[25] went to the nominee's home and "all but slept with him for nine days." [26] Since Harvey had been the directing will of the ring during most of the long battle and its open leader in the Republican Convention, Harding was not likely to defy him. The nominee could only assure the pro-League leaders, when they came to see him, that they could tell their friends everywhere, personally but not publicly, that he would move strongly to secure revision of the League.[27]

[24] The *Woman Citizen*, polling its readers in July, 1921, found that four-fifths of the Republicans, replying liberally from every state in the Union, believed they had voted for entry into the League. Colcord, *The Great Deception*, pp. 43-44.

[25] Harvey, *Henry Clay Frick the Man*, pp. 328-29.

[26] Bowers, *Beveridge and the Progressive Era*, p. 519.

[27] See the testimony of Professor Irving Fisher, of Yale University. *New York Times*, September 3, 1923.

Whenever Harding ventured to reassure his pro-League following too positively in public, he could be sure that his masters would bear down upon him. Thinking he might dare to support Root in promising at least our entry into the World Court, which Root was assisting the League to create, he found himself pounded by the Irreconcilables with "smashing" telegrams and letters. Lodge joined in, and there was such a "descent in force" upon the candidate that he subsided.[28]

Irish and German Shock Troops. On the platform the anti-League faction resoundingly attacked the League, root and branch. In most large cities they could be sure of a huge anti-Wilson audience that would shake the roof. The Irish, indignant that Wilson in the Peace Conference had not ended British control of Ireland, and fearing that the League would somehow perpetuate British rule, were sure to be there. The German-Americans, too, could be counted upon. Bitter because of our entry into the war, with their love of the Fatherland suppressed until it was a bursting volcano, enraged by the severe and humiliating terms imposed upon Germany, they struck at the League as something designed to fasten the "unjust" settlement upon her. Likewise the Italians were disgruntled that Italy had not received Fiume.

In the regions where these elements were numerous, immense crowds rewarded the assaults of the "battalion of death" Senators with such terrific acclaim that those embattled gentlemen were lifted to new heights of belief in the correctness and the invincibility of their views. Did not they receive much louder shouts of applause than any League speaker could command?[29]

They did, for where the Germans and Irish were in a minority at Republican gatherings they acted as cheer leaders and made noise out of all proportion to their numbers. Samuel Colcord, who observed this drive throughout the campaign and who repeatedly gained the confidence of the leaders of demonstrations after meetings, securing invitations to attend all the rallies he could, has

[28] Bowers, *Beveridge and the Progressive Era*, p. 521.

[29] Such meetings had been held during many months preceding the campaign of 1920.

described how the process worked in a gathering at Carnegie Hall, New York, where both sides were represented. "An able and eloquent speaker in making the opening address voiced sentiments strongly in favor of the League. An irreconcilable United States Senator in his address opposed and strongly condemned it. The first address was supported throughout with apparently sincere but not demonstrative applause from about half of the audience. The sallies of the Senator, not half so convincing, were greeted with demonstrations of hand-clapping and shouts which would appear excessive in volume if they came from an entire audience of twice the size." [30]

With these elements making it "a point to be present in impressive numbers and more impressive demonstration at every Republican rally, so dominating such occasions as often as to seem the unanimous expression of the spirit of the assembly," [31] it was not strange that great numbers of indifferent voters should conclude that there must be something dangerous about the League and themselves join eventually in the clamor against it.

It was equally inevitable that the lesser Republican orators should respond to the loudest applause and that they should attack the whole League idea in order to make sure of defeating the clear stand of the enemy for it. It is not feasible to explain to an electoral audience the merits of a long set of complicated and questionable reservations, especially when the listeners have been tired out for a long year with interminable discussions of them. Reasoning, chiefly in the form of questioning continually the wisdom of the Covenant, had long since exhausted its possi-

[30] Colcord, *The Great Deception*, p. 79. Mr. Colcord's book was written in 1921 in defense of the pro-League view that the Republican voters of 1920 had cast their ballots in favor of the League, expecting it to be revised and entered. While the book is not in the best historical form, it is written fresh from the conflict and gives a good view of it.

Still hoping for constructive action from Harding, Colcord feared that "the gravest menace of the great deception" was the influence upon the President's mind of "the German-Irish inspired and directed exhibition of hostility to the League of Nations," which the new Chief Executive had felt in his own campaign meetings (p. 99).

[31] *Ibid.*, p. 79.

bilities. Those who had been held in the Party by promises of the League with reservations could not now be increased. There remained only the less reflective multitudes to be gathered in by capitalizing the passions which the war and two years of attack upon the President had stirred. No one who lived through the campaign of 1920 should be able to forget the hatred that was vented upon the head of the broken man in the White House, whose Cabinet could not prepare him for the blow that was about to fall. Instead, he insisted upon reassuring them, maintaining stoutly on election day that when a great moral issue was involved the people could and would see it.[32]

Had it ever been possible to hold the "solemn referendum" which Wilson had demanded, his faith might have been justified, but it was not possible to prevent the accumulated grievances of the racial minorities and of many economic groups from being vented. Facing a deeply jealous majority party, Wilson could not draw enough support from it to stem the tide.

The Anti-League Verdict. To such an extent did other forces contribute to the seven million majority obtained by Harding and Coolidge that the latter said soon after the election: "I doubt if any particular mandate was given in the last election on the question of the League of Nations and if it was the preponderant issue." [33] Coolidge's knowledge of the extent of pro-League belief in his own party may be presumed to have contributed to his judgment. One could find the percentage of voters who believed in the League of Nations only by subtracting the anti-League Democrats who held to their party in 1920, and adding to the remainder the pro-League Republicans who stood by their own party. That the resulting figure would show a majority vote for the League could not be asserted. On the other hand it is equally clear that the Republican majority was by no means a measure of the actual anti-League strength. The proportion of Republicans who really wanted the League was too great to justify that claim.

[32] David F. Houston, *Eight Years with Wilson's Cabinet*, New York, 1926, Vol. II, pp. 94-95.

[33] *New York Times*, November 23, 1920.

Boesch

THE LEAGUE OF NATIONS SECRETARIAT BUILDING, 1920–1936

The Wilson tablet in the foreground was installed by the city of Geneva.

Boesch

THE SECRETARIAT WING OF THE NEW LEAGUE BUILDING—END VIEW

This vast structure was erected (1929–1937) out of the regular League budgets at a cost of $9,000,000. From 1920 to 1933 the League's members paid $57,293,000 (pre-devaluation) into its treasury—a considerable investment in international organization. Yet the first amount would scarcely build a first-class cruiser, or the second one a superdreadnought.

And the position of their party had been so veiled in reservations and campaign assurances designed to hold League support that any future attitude toward the League of Nations was open to it, except acceptance without reservations.

It remained to be seen which wing of the Party would prevail. After the election the pro-League leaders went to Harding to do what they could. Hughes and Hoover and Taft, Senator Porter J. McCumber and Oscar S. Straus conferred with him, but with George Harvey hovering in Harding's home most of the time and with Senator Knox coming last in the procession of "the best minds" whom the President-elect had promised to consult, the immediate result could not be in much doubt.[34]

Senator Lodge announced in Boston that the people had declared against "Mr. Wilson's League of Nations which he brought home from Paris and laid before the Senate. So far as the United States is concerned that League is dead." [35]

[34] *New York Times*, December 11, 14, 25, 30, and 31, 1920.
[35] *New York Times*, November 21, 1920.

CHAPTER III

SEPARATE PEACE

THE NEW President continued to sustain the hopes of his League supporters a little while longer. The announcement of his cabinet raised them distinctly. Two of the greatest of the pro-League Republicans were included, Herbert Hoover as Secretary of Commerce and Charles E. Hughes as Secretary of State. With Hughes directing our foreign affairs surely the Treaty would be ratified in some form.

As throughout the campaign, however, equal assurance was held out to the Irreconcilables. One of the sternest of the bitter-enders, Senator Albert B. Fall, of New Mexico, was named Secretary of the Interior. Andrew W. Mellon, one of the two men who had financed the national campaign against the League, was appointed Secretary of the Treasury. With Mellon and Fall in the Cabinet, the anti-League element did not need to be alarmed, even if they had not felt themselves fully able to dominate our foreign policy from the Senate.

No Supergovernment. Harding's inaugural address once more gave comfort to both camps. It first conformed with the expectations of the battalion of death, with the words: "America can be a party to no permanent military alliance. It can make no political commitments." Was that not enough? Besides the usual argument by innuendo, "permanent military alliance," there was the flat barring of any "political commitment."

But fair assurances followed. The new President was "sure our people will not misunderstand nor will the world misconstrue. We have no thought to impede the paths to closer relationship. We wish to promote understanding. We want to do our part in making offensive warfare so hateful that governments who resort to it must prove the righteousness of their cause or stand as outlaws before the bar of civilization."

The world would not mind our pulling out of the movement upon which its hopes were centered. It would not "misconstrue" the really deep yearning which the Republicans had been compelled to smother in scotching the "Wilson League." We were just as eager as they, said Harding, to make aggressive war "hateful," and we were "ready to associate ourselves with the nations of the world, great and small, for conference, for counsel, to seek the expressed views of world opinion, to recommend a way to approximate disarmament."

Did not such association with the nations promise much? Moreover, we had kind feelings toward arbitration, mediation, and conciliation and "would gladly join" in that "expressed conscience of progress" which sought to establish "a world court." Might not the League itself be altered a bit and called an "Association"? Perhaps, but "Since freedom impelled and independence inspired and nationally exalted, a world supergovernment is contrary to everything we cherish and can have no sanction by our republic." [1]

Contrary Interpretations. The term *supergovernment* seemed to damn the League completely. Yet the editor of the Republican *New York Tribune* thought not. "He closes no door to future entry," said the *Tribune* of March 5. The *New York Times* felt that he scarcely needed to do so. In its opinion: "The Senators who quibbled against the Treaty were really against it in any form. They did not want to alter the League; they meant to kill it, and now having tasted blood, they are ready to kill also Mr. Harding's 'association.' " [2]

Peace by Resolution. Aside from the fate of the League, it was incumbent upon the new administration to find some way to end

[1] *New York Tribune*, March 5, 1921. The address did not mention the name of the League of Nations.

[2] *New York Times*, April 8, 1921. Senator Lodge had complained against a similar charge while campaigning. "This argument that opposition to this League means that we are against any league," he said, "is the most preposterous statement ever made. The great and beautiful cause of peace is not bound up within the four corners of the ill-omened thing Mr. Wilson brought back from Paris." *New York Times*, October 20, 1920.

the state of war which still existed. Several previous attempts by way of Congressional resolution had failed.[3] The last of these, the Porter resolution, had passed the House of Representatives, April 9, 1920, by a vote of 242 to 150. For the possibility that the German Government might not take similar action, it provided that, if within 45 days from the enactment of the resolution Germany did not make a like statement and renounce "on behalf of itself and its nationals any claim, demand, right or benefit against the United States or its nationals, that it or they would not have had the right to assert had the United States ratified the Treaty of Versailles," all commercial intercourse should be prohibited and no financial assistance or supplies might be sent to the German Government or its citizens.[4]

Some doubts evidently arose as to the sufficiency of this threat, for on April 30 the Senate Foreign Relations Committee reported a substitute resolution by Senator Knox. This draft provided that the property of German nationals (valued at several hundred million dollars) which had been seized and was still held by the United States Government, should be kept until Germany had made treaties with the United States satisfying all American claims against Germany for losses due to her acts, waiving all claims against us due to war acts, and granting most-favored-nation treatment to our nationals. All "rights, privileges, indemnities, reparations or advantages" which we would have had under the Treaty of Versailles were also claimed.[5]

The Knox resolution was adopted by the Senate on May 15, 1920, and by the House of Representatives on May 21. Six days later it was vetoed by President Wilson on the ground that "a peace in which none of the essential interests which we had at heart when we entered the war are safeguarded is, or ought to be, inconceivable, as inconsistent with the dignity of the United

[3] Senator Lodge had introduced a brief resolution on November 19, 1919, declaring the war at an end. This was abandoned for a resolution by Senator Knox, of December 12, and this in turn for a second resolution by the same author. *Current History*, June, 1920, Vol. 12, p. 376.

[4] *Congressional Record*, Vol. 59, Pt. 6, p. 5480.

[5] *Current History*, June, 1920, Vol. 12, pp. 372-73.

States, with the rights and liberties of her citizens, and with the very fundamental conditions of civilization." The day following, May 28, 1920, a motion to override the veto was lost in the House by a vote of 220 to 152.[6]

"The" League Definitely Rejected. The events of a year having removed the Wilson veto, President Harding ventured to suggest a method of terminating the war, in the course of a special message which he delivered to Congress on April 12, 1921. Once more he sought to avoid what his conservative colleagues in the Senate had dreaded since the closing weeks of the war, the rejection of the Treaty of Peace. To salvage the Treaty, if possible, he now threw the League overboard bodily, declaring outright:

In the existing League of Nations, world governing with its superpowers, this Republic will have no part. There can be no misinterpretation, and there will be no betrayal of the deliberate expression of the American people in the recent election; and, settled in our decision for ourselves, it is only fair to say to the world in general, and to our associates in the war in particular, that the League Covenant can have no sanction by us . . . we can have no part in a committal to an agency of force in unknown contingencies; we can recognize no super-authority.

"A" League Assured. "The" League having been finally disposed of, Harding hastened at once to renew his promise of "a" league. "In rejecting the League covenant and uttering that rejection to our own people and to the world," he continued, "we make no surrender of our hope and aim for an association to promote peace in which we would most heartily join." After all, his pro-League supporters would not mind the passing of the League if another of pure Republican pedigree could be organized. Harding's assurance of it was positive: we would "relinquish no effort to bring the nations of the world into such fellowship."

Ratification of the Treaty Proposed. With "the" League exorcised, the President then proposed the ratification of the Treaty of Versailles, warning that "It would be idle to declare for separate treaties of peace with the Central Powers on the assumption

[6] *Congressional Record,* Vol. 59, Pt. 7, pp. 7102, 7429; Pt. 8, p. 7808.

that these alone would be adequate, because the situation is so involved that our peace engagements cannot ignore the Old World relationships and the settlements already effected. . . . The wiser course would seem to be . . . to engage under the existing treaty, assuming, of course, that this can be satisfactorily accomplished by such explicit reservations and modifications as will secure our absolute freedom from inadvisable commitments and safeguard all our essential interests."

Thus would a perfectly safe and pure "association" be inaugurated. "With the super-government league definitely rejected and with the world so informed, and with the status of peace proclaimed at home, we may proceed to negotiate the covenanted relationships so essential to the recognition of all rights everywhere of our own nation and obey our full part in joining the peoples of the world in pursuits of peace once more." [7]

The Treaty Abandoned. "Covenanted relationships" under the Treaty, even though modified by many "explicit reservations," carried no appeal to the Irreconcilables. The process of compromising with them ended, as always, in their complete victory. Secretary Hughes was soon able to relate that "it became perfectly clear, after the most careful consideration that the re-submission of the Treaty of Versailles, with suggested reservations, would have no other result than the renewal of the former controversy." [8]

With the renewed thunder of the band, the submission of Harding was foreordained. Hughes's approval may have been justified by some lingering hope that he would be able somehow to redeem the often-made pledge of "an association of nations" during the course of the naval disarmament conference which Senator

[7] *New York Tribune*, April 13, 1921. Should the reader be somewhat nonplused by the meaning of this final declaration, he will appreciate the comment of the editor of the *Tribune* upon the message. He thought that Harding's "careful and continuous effort to be accurate" did not "make for ease of reading," but added that the Monroe Doctrine had been "announced in singularly colorless phraseology" and both the Constitution and the Declaration of Independence made "hard reading."

[8] *New York Times*, July 16, 1922.

Borah had forced upon the administration and which would meet in Washington in the autumn.

Our Declaration of War Repealed. The state of war was at length ended, inside the United States, by repealing the resolution of April 6, 1917, which had declared the war. The Knox draft was rejected by the House as possibly reflecting upon our declared motives in entering the conflict. In conference the Senate receded from its position on this point and the Knox-Porter resolution was approved by the President July 2, 1921.[9]

This step formally terminated much of the war legislation in the United States, and it laid down conditions under which any treaty of peace with Germany must be negotiated. The resolution, of course, could not establish peace with Germany without her consent. She must now be approached, reluctant though the new American government was. Our refusal to accept the Treaty of Versailles had given the Germans great comfort and made it probable that they would grant us any terms we desired. That, however, could not make the asking pleasant to a mighty nation which had lately proclaimed its solidarity with the Allied nations on so many public forums and battlefields.

A Separate Treaty

No Senators were candidates for the honor of negotiating the treaty. Senator Lodge, who had declared repeatedly during the war that "no peace that satisfied Germany in the least degree can ever satisfy us," did not desire to go to Berlin now. "It cannot be a negotiated peace," he had continued on August 23, 1918. "It must be a dictated peace, and we and our allies must dictate it." He had been in favor of making peace in Berlin, regardless of the cost in men and money. "In one word," he said, "we must go to Berlin and there dictate peace." [10] To have asked the Germans—in Berlin—for a treaty of peace, after the bitter demands he had

[9] *Congressional Record,* Vol. 61, Pt. 4, p. 3299; *Current History,* October, 1921, Vol. 15, p. 58.

[10] *Congressional Record,* Vol. 56, Pt. 9, p. 9394.

made for their complete subjugation, would not have been pleasant. Nor would the successful conclusion of a separate treaty have squared well with the Senator's demands after the Armistice that everything be done in harmony with our allies. Sensing some opposition abroad to the President's peace plans, Lodge had warned, on December 21, 1918, that

> nothing can be accomplished unless we work in complete harmony with those who are associated with us in the war against the central powers. I know very well that technically we had no treaty of alliance with the allies by whose side we fought, but technicalities are of no consequence in the presence of facts. . . . To attempt in any way to separate us from our allies now or to prevent perfect unity of action is as harmful as such efforts were when we were fighting in northern France and on the plains of Flanders. To encourage or even permit any serious differences to arise between the United States and Great Britain, or with France, or Italy, or Belgium, would be a world calamity of the worst kind.[11]

None of Lodge's colleagues, who had felt the tie of brotherhood in arms so strongly until a brotherhood for peace had been established, now had time to negotiate a separate treaty of peace with Germany, so the task was left to Mr. E. L. Dresel, who concluded a treaty with the Germans, after many parleys, on August 25, 1921.[12] The treaty was signed in the German Foreign Office without any pomp or ceremony, or even any speeches. "The ceremony began at 5:20 and closed at 5:22 p.m. The signers of the treaty stood up." Since the American commissioner was suffering from a physical disability which prevented him from sitting comfortably, the German diplomat also stood. "Dresel signed both copies, shoved them across the desk and Rosen signed. One journalist was present." [13] Neither side wished to recall the signature of the Treaty of Versailles.

Based upon the Treaty of Versailles. Yet the whole treaty was based upon that document. After the terms laid down in the

[11] *Congressional Record,* Vol. 57, Pt. 1, p. 725.
[12] *Current History,* October, 1921, Vol. 15, p. 58.
[13] George Seldes, *World Panorama: 1918-1933,* Boston, 1933, p. 196.

Knox-Porter resolution had been conceded, Germany agreed to accord us all the rights and privileges stipulated for our benefit in the Treaty of Versailles, "notwithstanding the fact that such treaty has not been ratified by the United States."

Articles 2 and 3 then proceeded to specify the parts of the Treaty of Versailles under which the United States claimed advantages and the parts for which it would assume no responsibility. The rights and advantages which the United States should have and enjoy were "those defined in Section 1 of Part IV. and Parts V., VI., VIII., IX., X., XI., XII., XIV., and XX." of the Versailles Treaty.

The United States should not be bound by the provisions of Part I, dealing with the Covenant of the League of Nations, nor by any of the provisions of the Treaty which related to the Covenant, nor by any action taken by the League of Nations, unless it expressly assented to such action. No obligation was assumed under Part II (Boundaries of Germany), Part III (Political Clauses for Europe), Sections 2 to 8 of Part IV (German Rights and Interests Outside Germany), or Part XIII (International Labor Organization). The right to sit on the Reparation Commission under the terms of Part XIII was reserved, but the United States was not to be bound to participate unless it elected to do so.[14]

We thus claimed all the rights and advantages that the Treaty of Versailles gave us without assuming any responsibility for its enforcement, and without accepting any of its obligations. Legally, this action of the United States could not be questioned. As Senator Lodge had said: "technically we had no treaty of alliance with the allies by whose side we fought." The policy was defensible morally also, perhaps, on the ground that after all we had fought for our own individual reasons, and that we had contributed enough to the victory to justify our taking any course we pleased. It should not be considered strange, however, that a good deal of bitterness was voiced in England and France at this

[14] *Congressional Record*, Vol. 61, Pt. 6, p. 5769.

deliberate skimming of the cream from the Versailles compact, which had been drawn with such difficulty.

To many Americans, said the *New York Globe,* (Ind. Rep.), "the treaty today is a sharp deal; tomorrow it will be the memory of shame," but the *Baltimore Sun* (Ind. Dem.) concluded that "the American people will not now weep over the spilt milk of the Versailles pact." [15]

A Committee Reservation. The treaty did not prove to be wholly satisfactory to the Senate Foreign Relations Committee. It was reported from this body to the Senate, on September 24, with a reservation specifying that American nationals should have all the rights claimed in the Treaty of Versailles and that the United States should not be represented or participate in any body, agency, or commission authorized by the Treaty, nor should any person so represent the United States "unless and until an act of the Congress of the United States shall provide for such representation or participation." [16]

Advantages without Obligations. With this reservation it might have been thought that the treaty "disentangled" us from European affairs as completely as could be desired. The thing was not so simple, however, to Borah. When he examined it with the Treaty of Versailles, it became "the most involved and complex instrument" with which he had ever had to deal. Moreover, he did not like its implications. "We especially provide," he said, "that whatever comes to us must come free, without the discharge of any responsibility or obligation whatever, upon our part. The execution of the Versailles Treaty, whether it be expensive in treasure or blood, we step from under." It was his opinion that "to go into Europe for the purpose of securing some moiety of trade, some advantage in business, some material compensation, some right or privilege under this treaty, and to refuse to stay to perform any obligations connected with its realization is a position that is indefensible in morals, and we will not long stand to it

[15] *Literary Digest,* September 10, 1921, pp. 12-13.
[16] *Congressional Record,* Vol. 61, Pt. 6, 5769.

before the world." [17] How could we ever have the hardihood to claim any rights under a treaty whose burdens we rejected? He said in all seriousness that his country would never stoop to such a policy.

He was not in favor of claiming any advantages under the Treaty of Versailles which could be enjoyed only because the French troops held the Rhine. Moreover there was no way to obtain any of the supposed benefits except to go into conference with the Allies. All that Germany had granted us was the privilege to sit with these powers to determine what our rights should be. If that did not constitute an alliance, a combination tied together by interest, he did not know what would.

Strangely enough, Lodge was no longer moved by such perils. He had only admiration for the treaty, saying on September 26: "We receive all that is desirable for the United States and we are not called upon to make any embarrassing concessions." [18] After this Borah directed his assault particularly against the probable appointment of an American to the Reparations Commission under the treaty. When compared with this Commission, the League was an infantile conception. The Commission was a government, having legislative, executive, and judicial powers all combined in its hands. With a representative on the Commission, we should have to send troops to suppress the German people if they rebelled against it.[19]

To Senator Williams the proposed treaty was an "ignominious postscript to one of the most glorious chapters in the history of the world." [20]

A Proper Assertion of Our Rights. Consideration of the treaty having been resumed on October 5, Senator Morris Sheppard gave a five-hour review of the activities and accomplishments of the League of Nations, after which Senator Moses found himself glad to support the treaty because "the finest advantage which this

[17] *Ibid.*, pp. 5777-78.
[18] *Ibid.*, p. 5791.
[19] *Ibid.*, pp. 5794-5802.
[20] *Ibid.*, p. 5805.

treaty provides for is that, in definite form of words and with unmistakable language, it cuts us loose at once and, I hope, forever, from that body of death known as the League of Nations." Compared to the Allies, we had been most generous in asking nothing for ourselves, and all that we now asked was the restoration of certain rights freely accorded to us before the war, the actual cost of our army of occupation and reparation for our people who had suffered directly as a consequence of the war. In addition, we naturally desired to safeguard ourselves against an adverse application of mandatory provisions for the former enemy colonies, to which we had a one-fifth interest title.[21]

Ratified by Agreement. Senator Walsh, of Montana, opposed the treaty, on October 12, on the ground that it assumed responsibility for Part V of the Treaty of Versailles, dealing with the disarmament of Germany, without giving us any vote in the councils of the League, which would determine the fact of any renewed German aggression. Moreover, we pledged ourselves to keep Germany disarmed without contributing in any degree to the guarantees of protection which the League afforded her. Following up this contention, he offered an amendment saying that so long as Germany observed the obligations of Part V, the United States would join the other signatories of the Treaty of Versailles in any steps that might be agreed upon to protect her from invasion. This amendment was defeated 71 to 6, and a similar one, agreeing to use our good offices in case disarmed Germany should be attacked, was rejected by a similar vote. Senator Lenroot denied that we assumed any responsibility under Part V; we only reserved the right to claim advantages under it.[22]

Senator Hitchcock, of Nebraska, leader of the fight for the League Covenant, argued that no good could come from the defeat of the treaty. It was a choice between this treaty or none.

[21] *Ibid.*, pp. 6006-60.

[22] *Ibid.*, pp. 6248-54, 6361, 6364, 6367. Senator Johnson, of California, could not see why we should be guilty of any wrong in claiming our rights under the Treaty of Versailles (p. 6409).

Any settlement that restored diplomatic relations with Germany and enabled us to exert some stabilizing influence on European conditions was better than continued doubt and uncertainty. The Democratic Senators had decided in conference that the treaty should not be made a party question. Senator Hitchcock was personally in favor of bowing to the decision that a separate peace be concluded.[23] The same position was taken by Senator Pomerene, of Ohio, and other Democratic senators.[24]

Fourteen of them voted for the treaty, on October 18, 1921, giving it a legal majority of eight votes. The poll was 66 to 20. The minority was composed of seventeen Democrats and three Irreconcilables, Reed, Borah, and La Follette.[25] Though unacknowledged by them, it was a day of triumph for the leaders of the bitter-enders, and for all the reservationists. In their opposition to the League they had also killed all American participation in executing the Treaty. Such an immediate schism in the ranks of the conquerors could not but encourage the Germans, especially the proud German industrialists, in the belief that the burdens of the Treaty might be evaded. Inevitably, Gustav Strese-

[23] *Congressional Record,* Vol. 61, Pt. 6. pp. 6410-11. Senator Williams added that the decision of the Democratic caucus had not been due to a majority in favor of the treaty; the situation was otherwise (p. 6413).

[24] *Ibid.,* p. 6421.

[25] *Ibid.,* p. 6438. There was little reference in the debate to the stipulation which forbade representation on any commission or other agency operating under the treaty, unless and until Congress had passed an act providing for such representation. This provision was intended to prevent the President, under the assumed influence of Secretary Hughes, from appointing a representative on the Reparations Commission. It appeased the fears of the Irreconcilables that we should be wholly involved in European affairs through the Commission at the same time that it asserted again a right of the Senate to control our foreign affairs. This part of the resolution was, in the opinion of former Attorney General G. W. Wickersham, an unconstitutional invasion of the executive power by the Senate. The constitution, he observed, makes treaties the supreme law of the land and it charges the President with the execution of our laws. The Senate is without authority to tell the President that he may not discharge a constitutional duty unless authorized by act of Congress.

The Administration accepted the prohibition, however, and confined its efforts toward a solution of the reparations problem to indirect attempts to secure agreement. G. W. Wickersham, "The Senate and Foreign Relations," *Foreign Affairs,* December 15, 1923, Vol. II, pp. 180, 188. The reservation is a repetition of No. 7 of the Lodge reservations to the Treaty of Versailles.

mann hailed the separate peace with the United States as "an important step toward shaking the whole edifice of the Treaty of Versailles." [26] It was an important step, one which made it impossible for the United States to do more than make futile gestures during the swift descent of the reparations quarrel into the tragedy of the French invasion of the Ruhr, little more than two years later. By that time Senator Borah was trying to induce President Harding to summon all the powers quickly to Washington, to do something about it.

After Three Years. Before the Armistice in 1918 any proposal to make a separate peace with Germany would have been regarded by both the Government and people of the United States as the most monstrous sort of treason. An advocate of such a step would have been fortunate to escape with his life. Three years later the thing had occurred. Armistice Day itself was celebrated by the final exchange of ratifications of the treaty, in Berlin.[27] Separate peace had not come about purposely, but as the end result of an effort to whittle away the one positive, enduring gain that the nation had looked forward to throughout the struggle—reasonable security against future outbreaks of world madness.

No people could have justified its claim to be called civilized if it had not yearned at least, striven mightily at best, toward that objective. And those Americans who had seen the Covenant splendidly meet the plain need for an advance in human organization, now could not avoid a sense of having witnessed a betrayal fraught with the most tragic consequences for the whole of humanity. Deprived of the material and moral support of the most powerful of all nations, the failure of the League to cope with a great emergency could not be doubted. Could it therefore live at all? Real faith was required to avoid accepting the confident

[26] *New York Times*, October 3, 1921.

[27] S. F. Bemis, ed., *American Secretaries of State and Their Diplomacy*, New York, 1929, Vol. X, p. 228. Similar treaties of peace were concluded with Austria and Hungary in August, 1921, based upon the Treaties of Saint-Germain and Trianon respectively.

belief of the League's American foes that they had strangled it at birth.[28]

The League Lives

Yet, strange to relate, by the time the United States had concluded her separate peace with Germany the League had just finished the second annual meeting of its Assembly, at which the membership of forty-eight nations was recorded. More surprising still, every one of the neutral nations invited to join the League had accepted. Most astonishing of all, two years of strident outcry against the Covenant in the United States had attracted the surprised attention of all the nations, without leading a single one to reject the League as a dangerous "super-government," or to qualify its membership with any of the fears perpetually expressed by the leaders of the United States Senate.

The survival of the League must be credited in large degree to the faithfulness to it of some leaders in many lands. Others, more powerful, would have abandoned it had they been able to get its charter out of the Treaty or to administer the peace settlement without its aid. Both groups did unite in believing that President Wilson's world leadership could hardly be finally repudiated in his own country.

The Secretariat Organized. Wilson had been able to watch over the League's first feeble steps himself. After having secured with painful effort important amendments to the Covenant, in order to satisfy its American critics, he had seen the revised draft unanimously approved by the Peace Conference, on April 28, 1919. A week later the organization of the Secretariat was begun, under the direction of Sir Eric Drummond, who had been selected for the leadership of the League's permanent organization at the special request of the President.[29] From that time until the

[28] The death of the League and the severing of all ties with the Allies was "a matter of pride with the Senate especially, which killed the League in order to kill Wilson."—Philip Gibbs, *More That Must Be Told*, New York, 1921, p. 348.

[29] *The League of Nations Chronicle*, July, 1933. Wilson had become acquainted with Sir Eric while he was acting as private secretary to Lord Balfour during the latter's visit to the United States in 1917.

first failure of the Senate to approve the Covenant, on November 19, the League's constitution was subjected to unremitting fire in the United States. The perils portrayed here, however, did not prevent the congresses of six Latin American countries from ratifying it in October and November, 1919—in every case without important opposition.

Early Sessions of the Council. By January 10, 1920, when the League came officially into existence, it had twenty-three members. President Wilson then called the League Council to hold its first meeting in Paris on January 16. In the course of the year the Council held eleven sessions. No month passed without a meeting. The great issues of the day were reserved by the Great Powers to the Supreme Council. Then, too, some of the tasks referred to the infant League Council should hardly have been put upon it. A proposed inquiry into labor conditions in Russia could scarcely be productive, and it gained the League no good will. The Powers that did not care to assume a mandate over Armenia need not have asked the League to do so.

There was, however, useful work to be done. Among the dozens of items on agendas of the Council may be noted the appointment of Commissioners for the Saar Valley and for Danzig, the naming of the Mandates Commission and of jurists to draw up the Statute of the Permanent Court of International Justice, the conciliation of the Aaland Islands dispute between Sweden and Finland, the first efforts to prevent war between Poland and Lithuania over Vilna, and the initial steps toward making effective the provisions of the Peace Treaties for the protection of minorities.

Growing Membership. By the time the Senate came to its second deadlock over the precise terms of our entry into the League, March 19, 1920, ten additional nations had ratified the Covenant without qualification, including all the American nations asked to join. Likewise, the five small neutrals of Western Europe, which had more to lose than any distant people could have from any dangerous involvement, adhered to the Covenant with negligible opposition in their Parliaments, except in Sweden, where the

Boesch

SIR ERIC DRUMMOND, NOW THE EARL OF PERTH

Secretary-General of the League of Nations, 1919–1933.

vote was two to one in favor of entry. In Switzerland, where the only direct popular referendum undertaken anywhere was held, the division was closer, but decisively in favor of the League.[30]

The First Assembly. A week after the election of Harding, President Wilson convened the first Assembly of the League in Geneva, a bitter-sweet duty indeed. Meeting in the gloom which succeeded the tornado of hatred against its principal founder, the League's opening Assembly "surprised even its warmest advocates." [31] Woodrow Wilson was not there to open it, but Lord Cecil was present. A loyal and powerful second to Wilson in the creation of the League, Cecil was to be, through all its early years, the greatest personal force—aside from the Secretary-General—operating to sustain and guide it with a clear-sighted, practical-minded devotion that will leave him a unique figure in its annals. Behind him Benes of Czechoslovakia, Motta of Switzerland, Branting of Sweden, Nansen of Norway, and others worked as earnestly. Hymans of Belgium, the first President of the Assembly, sagaciously helped to develop it into a world forum such as few had dared hope for. The quiet determination evinced by the Assembly that the acts of the Council should be discussed made it easy for succeeding Assemblies to extend the range of its review; the equally unheralded decision to meet annually lifted the Assembly to an influence that the League's founders had not anticipated.

Commencing with a membership of forty-two states, the Assembly considered the applications of fourteen others for admission to the League and granted six, leaving the others for future action. The reception of two states from the Central Empires coalition, Austria and Bulgaria, offered some hope of the essential

[30] The vote was 416,870 to 328,719. President Motta stated to the First Assembly that Switzerland would have had less difficulty in joining if Germany had not been excluded, *Journal of the First Assembly*, p. 256.

The main debate, however, was over the effects of League membership upon Switzerland's neutralized status.

[31] C. K. Webster and S. Herbert, *The League of Nations in Theory and Practice*, Boston, 1933, p. 65.

A message of sympathy was sent to President Wilson by the Assembly, at its second sitting. The President returned an expression of confidence in its future.

universality which the abstention of the United States so greatly imperiled.

Reconstruction Advanced. In the succeeding year, while the United States drifted toward a treaty of peace with Germany that would leave her almost as isolated politically as the humiliated enemy, the first of a long line of great conferences on specialized subjects began.[32] The Transit Conference at Barcelona, attended by forty-three states, March 10 to April 20, 1921, drew up two important conventions, one on freedom of transit, another on the regime of navigable waterways. Together they did much to open the world's highways. A conference on the white-slave traffic—one of the subjects so jealously reserved by the Lodge reservations—met in Geneva in July. Composed of representatives of thirty-four countries, it proposed a treaty for the suppression of the traffic in women and children, without the participation of the American Government. We were not in a position to countenance the attacking of a world evil by international action.

First moves toward disarmament were made, while the Council, with varied success, struggled with the boundary disputes already before it and received new ones. Especially notable was the reference to it of the Upper Silesian dispute, which had divided the Allied Supreme Council and had created a dangerous situation. The division of the territory proposed by the League Council was not ideal, but its acceptance by the Allies, after their own failure, raised the prestige of the League considerably.

A World Court Created. The Second Assembly, meeting from September 5 to October 5,1921, admitted the four new Baltic Republics to membership and successfully achieved, with the Council, the election of eleven judges and four deputy judges of the new World Court.[33] The American and other delegations to the Second Hague Conference, in 1907, had made earnest efforts to

[32] The Brussels Financial Conference, had met from September 24 to October 8, 1920. It was attended by an American observer in "an unofficial capacity."—"American Cooperation With the League of Nations," *Geneva Special Studies,* July, 1931, Vol. II, No. 7, p. 7.

[33] The Permanent Court of International Justice.

create such a court at that time, but had been unable to agree upon a method of electing the judges. The small states would not yield their right to an equal vote and the Great Powers, with their immense interests, would not grant it. In 1920, Elihu Root, continuing his life-long labor to create a true world tribunal, served on the commission of jurists which drew up the court statute. When the usual deadlock over the method of electing the judges developed, Root suggested that the mutually acceptable nature of the representation of large and small states in the Assembly and Council provided a solution of the problem. His insight was rewarded by the smooth manner in which the first election, and all succeeding ones, passed off.[34]

Time for Appraisal. By the time that the United States formally refused any responsibility in the League of Nations, that response to the cry of mankind in its hour of anguish had perfected its organization and gave promise of survival in the immediate future. Although the abstention of the United States had everywhere weakened the hope that the League would achieve its prime objective, enough important international chores had been successfully performed to indicate the great value of an institution working steadily to promote the common welfare. If a breathing space could be had, too, the United States might come to accept a share in the League's work, making eventual success probable.

[34] In the first election, nine of the judges chosen on the first balloting in the Assembly were similarly elected in the Council. Dr. John Bassett Moore, of the United States, received 21 votes on the second ballot, a bare majority of those voting, and was declared elected. It was only on the election of the last deputy judge that the Assembly and Council disagreed, whereupon a conference committee selected a compromise name, which was accepted. *Records of the Second Assembly, Plenary Meetings*, pp. 235-50.

CHAPTER IV

NON-RECOGNITION

WHILE the League struggled to find a footing it cannot be said that it received any aid from the Government of the United States. Installed as Ambassador to Great Britain, George Harvey promptly announced to a distinguished audience that the United States would not associate with the League in the slightest degree. Expatiating three different times upon the majority of 7,000,000 by which Harding had been elected, he averred that "anybody could see that it follows then inevitably and irresistibly that our present Government could not without betrayal of its creators and masters and will not, I can assure you, have anything whatsoever to do with the League or with any commission or committee appointed by it or responsible to it, directly or indirectly, openly or furtively." [1] Speaking to the Prime Minister and many other high officials of a nation that was a member of the League, he explained how "absurd" it was that "by hook or by crook, unwillingly and surely unwittingly" we might be beguiled into the League.

Proclaiming that "I came to London as an unalloyed American," Harvey insisted that our war aims had been wholly selfish. He dismissed the ordering of millions of American youths to European battlefields as lightly as he had issued his countless diatribes against the League. "We sent them solely to save the United States of America," he declared, and added that if the war had lasted three years longer "we" would have sent 5,000,000 or 10,000,000. No price would have been too great to "save" the United States—without getting the faintest assurance of security against a repetition of the necessity of future "salvation." [2]

[1] *New York Times*, May 20, 1921.

[2] These utterances started a wave of public protest in the United States which did not stop for months. More than a column is required in the *New York Times Index* to list the rebukes to Harvey published in that paper. Many

Neither President Harding nor Secretary Hughes could be induced to comment upon this remarkable utterance of an official whose normal function was to serve as their mouthpiece. President Harding satisfied the public interest concerning his reaction in his usual manner. Into his Memorial Day address, ten days later, he inserted a paragraph strongly supporting Harvey's interpretation of our war aims and another repudiating just as decisively the "to save our own skins" idea.[3]

Higher Aims Attested by Hughes. Two weeks later, Hughes ventured, in the course of an address to Brown University Alumni, to contradict his Ambassador. Our soldiers had "offered their lives and all the energies of the country were harnessed in the supreme effort because we loved the institutions of liberty and intended to maintain them, because we hated tyranny and the brutality and ruthlessness which found expression in the worship of force, and because we found our fate linked with that of the free peoples who were struggling for the preservation of the essentials of freedom. With them we made common cause, as from one end of the country to the other rang appeals in the name of civilization itself." [4]

Yet the League Was Taboo. Unfortunately Hughes did not repudiate the more important part of Harvey's address. After he had acknowledged with some vehemence that we fought for high purposes, he proceeded to act upon Harvey's dictum that the League was untouchable. In spite of his long advocacy of a league of nations and his prominent part in issuing the Appeal of the Thirty-one, Hughes acquiesced to a surprising degree in the desire of the Republican Senate leaders that the League be treated as non-existent and, if possible, killed by chilly scorn. The op-

people, like President Henry N. MacCracken, of Vassar College, cited appeals to American youth and public of a far different character from Harvey's "fighting to save your own skins" formula. Others joined General John F. O'Ryan in testifying that many of our soldiers at least had been animated by purposes very much higher. *New York Times*, June 5, 1921.

[3] *New York Times*, May 31, 1921.

[4] *New York Times*, June 16, 1921. Hughes's hearers "wildly cheered" this and similar utterances, repeatedly forcing him to stop his address.

ponents of Wilson had so completely transferred their hatred of him to the League that they were unable to wish it well, if it could do some good without them. So confident had they been that our abstention would kill the League that its very survival was an offense. Moreover, the prospect of its permanent establishment gave them a distinctly unpleasant outlook. If it actually proved to be the menacing superstate which the whole Republican campaign against it had either alleged or implied, the situation of the United States would be uncomfortable, if not positively dangerous. When we refused to grant the right of the League to live, we could hardly complain if in an emergency it aligned many nations against us.

On the other hand, if the League should succeed in keeping the peace and in promoting international cooperation, without placing undue burdens upon its members, its success was likely to make the loudly professed fears of its American opponents ridiculous. Whether the League developed in one direction or the other, it would be better for its American opponents that it should not develop at all.

For Secretary Hughes the problem of refusing any relationship with the League, or of finding a satisfactory one, was acute from the day he took office. The Wilson Administration had been pursuing for four months the usual policy of a defeated Government, that of deferring all action in foreign affairs that could be postponed. Thus an invitation to attend the Barcelona Conference on Transit and Communications, which would meet six days after the inauguration of Harding, was courteously declined, January 3, 1921. The reason given by Acting Secretary of State Norman H. Davis was that his Government, not being a member of the League, did not find it practicable to appoint a representative. Altogether, a total of fifteen communications received from the League had been acknowledged or disposed of by March 4, while eighteen remained to be answered.[5]

[5] The address by Secretary Hughes in Baltimore, October 23, 1924.

No Discussion of Mandates. Among the items of League business still to be attended to was the settlement of the terms of the mandates for the former German and Turkish colonies. The Council of the League was in process of fixing the final terms of the mandates when it received a strong protest from Secretary Colby, on February 21, against the taking of final action without the consent of the United States. Upon receipt of that message the Council at once adjourned its discussions and invited the United States to be represented at its April session, when it was hoped the final decisions could be taken. The President of the Council observed in his letter that: "A problem so intricate and involved as that of mandates can hardly be handled by the interchange of formal notes." [6]

The Council's cordial invitation was not honored by Hughes with a rejection. No reply whatever was made, while the Council waited from month to month and the need for a settlement of the status of the territories grew, especially from the standpoint of preserving the supervisory influence of the League over them. Finally, in August, 1921, Hughes began the very process of negotiation with the four Powers who were our co-legatees that the Council had feared. Notes were written to Great Britain, France, Italy, and Japan, just as if the League Council did not exist. Negotiations with each concerning the territories they were to administer went slowly forward, though all of the agreements reached would have to be referred to the Council since the Powers must act through it.

Although the negotiations dragged on for years the changes which resulted in the terms of the earlier mandates were slight, and the later treaties include, verbatim, the terms of the later mandates as fixed in the Council.[7] Our refusal to negotiate with the Powers through the Council simply complicated, for all con-

[6] *Council Minutes,* Twelfth Session, pp. 70-76.

[7] C. A. Berdahl, "Relations of the United States with the Council of the League of Nations," *American Political Science Review,* June, 1932, Vol. 26, pp. 497-98; Raymond B. Fosdick, "Secretary Hughes and the League of Nations," *New York Times,* October 19, 1924.

cerned, the making of the many treaties with the mandatory powers which our refusal to enter the League had made necessary, if we were to enjoy equal rights with the members of the League in the mandated territories.

Health Organization Obstructed. In the process perhaps the League suffered more than the United States. Certainly that was the case in the creation of its now universally acclaimed health service. In 1920 the spread of pestilence demonstrated clearly the need for an effective international health agency. Aside from the collection and dissemination of information with regard to epidemic disease on a world scale, the necessity for standardizing vital statistics, for developing port sanitation, and for promoting international sanitary agreements was evident.

A beginning had been made in the Rome Treaty of 1907, which established an *Office Internationale d'Hygiene Publique* in Paris, but some important nations did not belong to the *Office* and its finances were wholly inadequate. Therefore, after a long study by experts, "the League decided that this old machinery ought to become the technical basis of the new health organization of the League. The advantages of this plan were so obvious that it was approved without reserve, not only by the public health officers of France, Great Britain, Italy and many other nations, but by the representatives of all the Red Cross Societies." [8]

With such unanimity of opinion expressed, no one supposed that there would be any objection to the making of certain minor changes that would be necessary in the treaty of 1907, until Hughes bluntly vetoed the plan. He did not say that he himself was jealous and suspicious of any growth in usefulness or prestige which the League might have. He did not reply that, in spite of his many affirmations of the need for a league of nations, he would not now venture to displease the Senate chiefs by so small a request as was asked of him. He did not even give a sign that though he himself recognized the reasonableness of the proposal the men-

[8] Fosdick's article in the *New York Times,* October 19, 1924, reprinted and slightly expanded in pamphlet form, from which the facts in this section are taken.

tality of the Senate leaders was such that they would vent their hatred of the League upon a request so patently in order. Hughes made no move to place the responsibility where it belonged—on the Senate; he assumed it himself without vouchsafing to the French Government the slightest word of explanation or extenuation.[9]

His own attitude was in fact revealed by the defense that: "The interests of health had not suffered by maintaining the international office at Paris intact." [10] He offered no evidence to meet the contrary conclusion at which the rest of the nations had arrived after much technical study and attached no significance to the fact that his action now compelled them to maintain two international health organizations, with two sets of officials, two offices, and excessive overhead expense.[11]

Consent to Opium Regulation Refused. The same spirit was also shown toward the assumption by the League of the warfare upon the opium traffic. A treaty of 1912, largely made abortive by the war, had vested administrative duties in the Netherlands Government. Again, after the remaining nations of the world had agreed to the transfer of important responsibility to the League, the United States alone objected. Hughes was not willing to vex the Senate with a request that the Hague Treaty of 1912 be modi-

[9] The consternation which Hughes's arbitrary blocking of the League's health plans caused in the League has been described by a member of the Faculty of the Yale Medical School who represented the League of Red Cross Societies in the health conference. C. E. A. Winslow, *The Nation's Health*, Vol. III, p. 594.

[10] *New York Times*, July 17, 1922.

[11] This attitude was exemplified again in 1922 when Assistant Surgeon General Blue was permitted to attend, at the expense of the League, a conference on the standardization of anti-toxin serums. Although his invitation came direct from the League's Health Section it was accepted in the following form: "Public Health Service glad collaborate with *Office Internationale d'Hygiene Publique* in standardization." Thus it was found possible to permit Dr. Blue to attend a League conference duly accredited to an organization that was not conducting the conference.

Later communiqués from the State Department took pains to represent our cooperation as being with the *Office Internationale* when in fact the League's Health Section was acting. See, for example, the State Department announcement of September 27, 1924.

fied in a manner which every other nation agreed would increase its effectiveness.

His reply to a note of the Netherlands Government commented upon the resolutions concerning the opium traffic adopted by the Second Assembly of the League without making any reference whatever to the League. From his letter, one would never have suspected that the League existed. He did, however, suggest a way of preventing the United States from falling completely out of the campaign against the drug traffic—an effort in which it had always been the chief leader, not from altruism alone, but because of the fearful havoc which the narcotic habit wrought among its citizens. Unable to abandon all effort to achieve control of the trade in dangerous drugs, Hughes stated that the American Government would, through the Netherlands Government, communicate to the Powers signatory to the opium convention an annual report covering statistics on the production, manufacture, and sale of narcotic drugs within the United States. By taking this method of answering a request for this information which had come to the State Department from the League, the Secretary of State avoided the taint of direct communication with it.

Thereafter when an organization speaking in the name of nearly fifty nations wanted information from the Government of the United States upon the subject of opium, it wrote a letter to the Netherlands Government. The Hague would then soberly write to Washington, being careful not to mention the League of Nations, and would receive an equally grave reply which would be transmitted to Geneva, where the desired information was merged with the replies coming in from the other Governments. In this fashion did a mighty nation conserve its dignity and prestige in the eyes of its fellows.[12]

[12] Fosdick, in *New York Times,* October 19, 1924. Some communications on opium continued to follow the circuitous route through Holland down to 1932. Berdahl, in *American Political Science Review,* June, 1932, Vol. 26, p. 102.

By January, 1923, however, Hughes had unbent enough to send a representative to sit with the League's Opium Committee in a consultative capacity. The delegate arrived after the session had begun, sat in a doubtful capacity, and

Economic Statistics Anonymously Contributed. Nor was the method adopted for supplying information to the Monthly Bulletin of Statistics published by the League's Economic Section more creditable. To the League's request for information, made in May, 1921, no reply came until January, 1922, when the American consul in Geneva began to appear at the League Secretariat each month to leave the desired data unobtrusively upon the desk of a League official. In this dangerous operation the State Department covered its tracks completely. It is not recorded that the consul came only at dusk and departed in haste, but he was careful never to write a letter. To use Fosdick's descriptive phrase, he left only a "memorandum, without letter-head, beginning or end—a typewritten piece of paper, which anybody might have written and for which nobody was responsible." If a Senator should thunder, the State Department would be in a position to deny all complicity in the nefarious business of compiling international statistics which would be of use to business men everywhere.

Yet the Secretary of State continued to be uneasy. The League's reports to Washington about the developments following the Barcelona Conference on Transit and Communications led the American consul to call on the Secretary General of the League, early in 1922, to inform him "orally and unofficially" that, since the United States had no relations with the League of Nations, no reply would be made to such communications. The obvious implication was that Hughes wished to keep both his files and his wastebaskets as clear of League documents as he could.

Cooperation on Arms-Traffic Regulation Withheld. The same desire was reflected more churlishly still in the way the State Department handled the League's effort to secure ratifications of the Saint-Germain Arms Traffic Control Treaty. This treaty, signed in 1919 by three American representatives at the Peace Conference, sought to curb the arms trade by a system of licensing and publicity. In attempting to get the treaty into operation, the

naturally contributed little, aside from the testimony by his presence that the United States could not suppress its interest in one subject with which the League was struggling.

Secretary-General inquired, on March 8, 1921, whether the United States was prepared to ratify the treaty and said that the Council "would highly appreciate an early reply." None came.

On November 21, 1921, the Secretary-General again asked the same question, without result. Once more, on June 13, 1922, he ventured to write, but without eliciting an answer until July 28, 1922, nearly a year and a half after his first inquiry. On the latter date, Secretary Hughes merely refused to ratify the Convention, withholding his reasons, although at the same time he dispatched a note to the British Government explaining his position.

Evidently the Secretary, in addressing the League at all, had done as much as he could bring himself to do, and hoped the British Government would inform the League of his objections to the treaty. If that government took it upon itself to spare Hughes embarrassment, the League apparently was not satisfied with the reasons given for the inactivity of the United States. Nor, if one may judge from the defense made by Hughes in a speech at Baltimore, should it have been.

In that address he gave three reasons for not ratifying the treaty. It was "not a provision for a general limitation of armament," to which the obvious reply was that no one had supposed it to be. "Particular objection" was made to the provision "by which the contracting parties were prohibited from selling arms and munitions to states not parties to the convention." This would prevent the shipment of military supplies to several Latin-American countries, which, it was "understood," had not signed or adhered to the treaty, "to wit: Argentina, Colombia, Costa Rica, Dominican Republic, Honduras, Mexico, Paraguay, Uruguay and Salvador, however desirable it might be to permit such shipments." These countries "might not desire to adhere to the convention." Or they might wish to do so. If not, Hughes was apparently solicitous of retaining the right to ship arms to one faction or another during future revolutions in Mexico and other American states.

If these objections did not carry conviction, Hughes's last reason was conclusive. "Finally, it was noted that the provisions of the convention relating to the League of Nations were so intertwined with the whole as to make it impracticable for this Government to ratify as it was not a member of the League." [13]

He explained his failure to give any explanation to the League on the ground that "the League was not a party to the convention," which clearly meant that the representatives of forty nations acting together had no right to consideration. But the matter "had been taken up with us by the British Government, which was a party" and "we supposed it would advise its co-signatories of our decision. This was later done."

For some reason these nations did not abandon the effort to achieve a regulation of the arms traffic when the British Government whispered the attitude of the United States to them. The 1922 Assembly had the hardihood to adopt a resolution which said "the Assembly considers it highly desirable that the Government of the United States should express the objections which it has to formulate to the provisions of the Convention of St. Germain, as well as any proposals which it may care to make as to the way in which these objections can be overcome." [14]

Another six months having passed, the Council authorized a letter to Secretary Hughes, on April 21, 1923, asking "whether the Government of the United States would be disposed to state its views as to the manner in which it would be willing to co-operate with other Governments in the control of the traffic in arms and the private manufacture of arms." [15]

No answer to its letter of May 1 having been received when the Council met to consider the question in July, a postponement was taken.[16] Eventually, however, when the Assembly was coming together again, and might consider publicly the lack of results of its 1922 request, Hughes did send to the Council the identical reply which he had given to Great Britain more than a year

[13] *New York Times,* October 24, 1924.
[14] *Monthly Summary of the League of Nations,* Vol. II, No. 9, pp. 212, 228.
[15] League of Nations, *Official Journal,* 1923, p. 587.
[16] *Ibid.,* p. 873.

earlier. A year's effort had not drawn from him any constructive ideas.

No Mail Acknowledged for Six Months. During the early months of the new Administration the State Department developed an extraordinary capacity for mislaying mail from Geneva. Among the many documents from the League's headquarters that were lost was a questionnaire of February, 1921, asking for information as to legislation dealing with the traffic in women and girls. Later an invitation to attend the July conference on the same subject followed the questionnaire into hiding. To the American Social Hygiene Association the State Department stoutly denied all knowledge of either. Shortly before the conference met, however, the American consul in Geneva informed the League that the missing papers had been found, but he could not say what the attitude of the United States toward the conference was.

In fact up to this time the State Department had not been able to reply to any communications from Geneva whatsoever. It was not until June 30, 1921, that the American consul called at the Secretariat and said to Sir Eric Drummond: "I am instructed to say verbally and *unofficially* that the American Government has received your communications of November 18 and May 22, but inasmuch as the American Government has no relations with the League of Nations there will be no reply to them." [17]

Someone in the Secretariat having thought of the idea of sending all messages to Washington by registered mail, the American Consul turned up again to say that he was instructed to say "unofficially and orally" that the State Department had been receiving its registered mail, "but inasmuch as the American Government did not recognize the existence of the League, it would not reply." [18]

When, however, dispatches from Europe began to describe the mass of mail from Geneva that was accumulating in the State

[17] *New York Times,* September 30, 1921; *Yearbook of the League of Nations,* 1922, p. 168.

[18] Edwin L. James, in *New York Times,* July 18, 1921.

Department, listing the important and varied nature of the subjects dealt with, this policy could not be maintained. Criticism of the Department's discourtesy became so caustic that on August 15 the Department began to write answers to the League's letters. By August 29, fifteen replies had been prepared and were forwarded to Geneva in a single shipment. They were all nearly identical, "exceedingly lawyer-like in tone," and each ended with the following sentence or one similar to it: "The Secretary of State has taken note of this information for any purpose of relevancy to the United States as a state not a member of the League of Nations." [19]

This quantity method for disposing of the unwanted messages from the League was used by Hughes during the remainder of 1921. On November 3, 1921, another batch of nine such acknowledgments was received from Washington and on December 20 a further consignment of eleven. In both cases the Secretary did not even trouble to date any of the letters.[20]

The desire of the State Department was apparently to withhold the slightest hint of recognition from the League that would aid it to survive, or indicate that any of its labors could be good. No other explanation has been authoritatively advanced. An inspired, though not official, statement in the *New York Times* of October 3, 1921, related the surprise of the Department on learning that it had been receiving mail from the League of Nations. Investigation was made and it was discovered that the clerk who opened the mail had thought them all "mere routine notices requiring no acknowledgment" or any other sort of attention. He had "simply placed them on file without calling them to the attention of any official," and without meaning any offense at all. They all looked alike to him—questionnaires, requests for specific information, invitations to great international conferences, reports on half a dozen important subjects.

If, after living through the months of furious controversy over

[19] Fosdick, in *New York Times*, October 19, 1924.
[20] *Ibid.*

the League of Nations, the Department's mail clerk could summon no curiosity as to what the League might be saying to the United States, it is to be wondered that any business at all came to the attention of Department officials in the first months of the Harding Administration.

Nominations to the World Court Restrained. The ability of the State Department to file away letters calling for specific action was nowhere better illustrated than in the case of the invitations to make nominations for judges of the Permanent Court of International Justice. These invitations were sent June 4, 1921, to the Department with the request that they be forwarded to the four men who constituted the American panel of the old Hague Arbitration Tribunal: Elihu Root, Oscar Straus, John Bassett Moore, and George Gray. When the invitations did not arrive, one of the members let the fact be known and the Secretary-General of the League cabled the four officials, on August 13, 1921, at a cost of several hundred dollars.

Root then approached the State Department, and the four original invitations were forwarded in time to permit the panel to meet and agree upon nominations. It was agreed that, as a matter of courtesy, Root should consult Secretary Hughes, with the result that Root reported shortly to his three associates "that Hughes objected to nominations being made by Americans on the ground that it would involve serious risk of immediate controversy which might be very injurious to the success of important policies the Government was then pursuing." [21]

This objection was greatly regretted by Straus and Judge Gray, both of whom wrote in protest to Root on September 13. Judge Gray failed to see how the Government could be embarrassed by that action and thought "this interposition of the Administration most unfortunate." It would "certainly be viewed by a large number of our people as evidence that their country had been prevented by partisan and personal considerations from giving its sympathy to a hopeful effort to attain an object which the

[21] Fosdick, in *New York Times*, October 19, 1924.

good and intelligent the world over have so long desired." Similarly, Straus felt it to be "too bad that home politics and anti-Wilsonism have had such an influence upon our attitude or rather that of the Senate." [22] However, after consultation they both yielded and a cablegram was sent to Geneva declining to make nominations on the ground that they could not exercise this new function "under another treaty to which the United States is not a party." Judge Gray pressed for the inclusion of a sentence placing the responsibility upon Secretary Hughes, but was overruled.

Some months later Hughes himself denied his responsibility, saying positively on July 13, that: "The American Hague Judges acted in accordance with their own views of propriety." Pressed further, Hughes reiterated the excuse of insufficient authority which the four judges had so reluctantly advanced as a reason for their inactivity.[23] How weighty this technical objection really was may be judged from the fact that he did not raise it when another year had passed and a vacancy in the Court was to be filled. The American group made its nomination, in July, 1923, and saw its candidate elected.[24]

Must All International Organization Be Abandoned? Hughes's disinclination to countenance either the Court or the League did not arise because he failed to realize the need for international organization to keep the peace. His speech accepting the Republican nomination for the Presidency in 1916 showed an awareness of what must be done which was as complete as that demonstrated by Taft and Wilson. Not only must there be "development of international organization in order to provide international justice," but behind it "the cooperation of the nations to prevent resort to hostilities before the appropriate agencies of peaceful settlement have been utilized. If the peace of the world is to be maintained it must be through the preventive power of a common

[22] *Ibid.*

[23] *New York Times,* July 15 and 20, 1922.

[24] When John Bassett Moore received notice of his election to the Court, in 1921, he accepted without consulting Secretary Hughes.

purpose." In such common action also, Hughes proposed that his country have a full part, saying: "If at the close of the present war the nations are ready to undertake practicable measures in the common interest in order to secure international justice, we cannot fail to recognize our international duty. The peace of the world is our interest, as well as the interest of others, and in developing the necessary agencies for the prevention of war we shall be glad to have an appropriate share." [25]

Strong Reservations Endorsed. On this solid ground Hughes stood, until his sober conception actually began to take living form in the Covenant, and until the opposition of the Senate leaders became pronounced. Then he lost most of his conviction. In a speech to the Union League Club in New York City, March 26, 1919, he made six criticisms of the original draft of the Covenant, five of which were soon dealt with by amendments adopted at Wilson's insistence. Only his objection to Article 10 went unanswered, but the changes made did not satisfy him. He proposed further reservations, in a letter of July 24, 1919, to Senator Frederick Hale, concerning withdrawal, domestic questions, and the Monroe Doctrine. He now wished to eliminate [26] Article 10 altogether.

By the time, therefore, that the campaign of the Republican Senate leaders against the League had fully developed, Hughes had given the drive his full support. He was still able to urge the election of Harding as the way into the League, but he had abandoned every thought of giving the League any power to keep the peace. All idea of "the preventive power of a common purpose" was lost in his effort to restrict the operation of the League in this hemisphere and to limit our own responsibility

[25] *New York Times,* August 1, 1916. Shortly before this Hughes expressed his "emphatic approval" of the program of the League to Enforce Peace to a committee from that organization. Theodore Marburg, *The Development of the League of Nations Idea,* New York, 1932, Vol. I, p. 139.

[26] Felix Morley, *The Society of Nations,* Washington, 1932, p. 179; C. C. Hyde, in S. F. Bemis, ed., *American Secretaries of State and Their Diplomacy,* New York, 1929, Vol. X, p. 363.

anywhere. The kind of league that he continued to support nominally was exactly the harmless makeshift that Lodge had expected, before the Covenant was written, to be able to ridicule away without serious trouble. Far from fighting the devitalization of the Covenant, as Taft had done until the first vote in the Senate, Hughes had aided the process in its early stages. He had in reality become one of Lodge's most effective assistants.

The League Repudiated. Accordingly, he felt no great wrench when he discovered that Harding was quite willing to abandon the League and that the powers in the Senate wished the very name to be ignored. When the prominence of his own name in the Manifesto of the Thirty-One led to expressions of disappointment over his attitude toward the League he resented them warmly.[27] Shortly afterward, when Henry Cabot Lodge was about to be re-elected to the Senate by a greatly reduced majority,[28] Hughes went to Boston, where he justified Lodge's war of attrition against Wilson and cast the League wholly into outer darkness. It had been "patent," he said, "that the American people would never consent to assume any obligations, moral or legal, which would fetter their appropriate freedom of action in unknown contingencies."

The worst opponent of the League, or of any league, could not have said more. A stronger affirmation of the totally lawless character of the national state could not have come from the narrowest nationalist. Issuing from a former Justice of the Supreme Court, it had the effect of destroying every vestige of hope that a semblance of law could be established internationally—for if the nations will not assume the slightest common responsibility for the peace, they must remain forever at the mercy of

[27] See his letter to Hamilton Holt, saying he could not "see any reason why you should address me in the manner you have chosen," and demanded that no more open letters be written him. *New York Times*, July 20, 1920.

[28] Lodge, 413,363; Gaston, 405,138. In 1920 the Republicans had carried Massachusetts by more than 350,000. Lodge was seated after a recount failed to shake his slim margin. *New York Times*, November 9, 1922; *World Almanac*, 1922, p. 457.

those who are strong enough to set upon them, or disrupt their lives by the indirect effects of such lawlessness.[29]

Equally astonishing was Hughes's statement that: "This American opinion, easily discerned and emphatically expressed in the Senate, was disregarded through a preference for ambiguous phrases which were tenaciously clung to, although most injurious if they promised what was feared here and hoped for elsewhere." In this fashion he denied the existence of overwhelming American support for the Covenant, so irresistible that by the testimony of Lodge himself he did not dare to risk a vote in the Senate until the autumn of 1919.[30] What might not Woodrow Wilson have accomplished if he had but listened to the "opinion" so "easily discerned and emphatically expressed in the Senate"! [31]

Assuredly the war President would have achieved less than he did had he accepted Hughes's analysis of what could be done. Hughes diagnosed correctly the fundamental problems of Europe as political, "involving national hopes and fears; deep-rooted convictions as to national safety and opportunity; national ambitions, in some cases long cherished, in others recently awakened." What our cooperation did not mean was also defined in the best terms of the Irreconcilables. It did not mean "that we should embroil ourselves in controversies not growing out of our interests, but growing out of age-long rivalries and conflicting interests. . . . There is no reason why we should fritter away our helpful influence by becoming a partisan of either party to such controversies, much less to make the fatal mistake of attempting to assume the role of dictator."

With such an attitude of mind toward our share in the League's responsibilities, it was not surprising that Hughes should be convinced that the Great Powers would never permit their vital interests to be "decided upon in any large group." For our

[29] Later in the address he again assumed the perpetuation of an anarchy of "sovereign" states, stating that in Europe "each major difficulty centers in the self-determined action of independent states and is beyond external control."

[30] See above, the beginning of Chapter II.

[31] Hughes did not fail to heed that mighty opinion. "To revive the old controversy in any phase," he said, "would have been easy but disastrous."

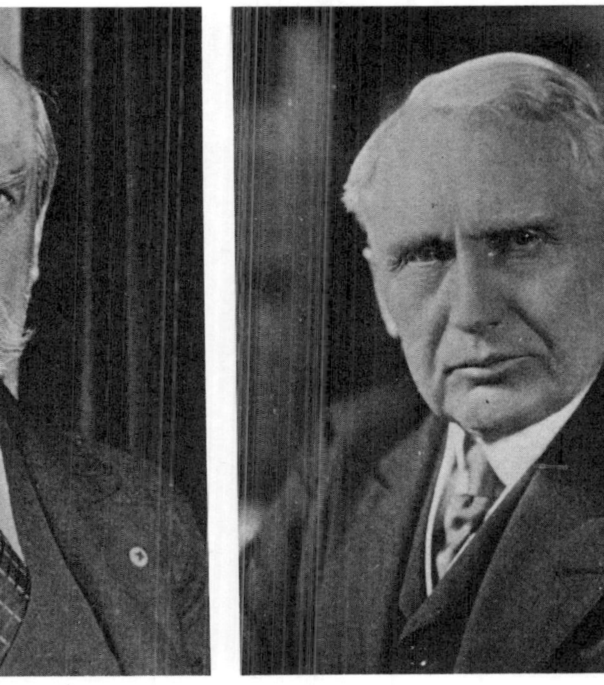

Wide World
CHARLES EVANS HUGHES

Underwood & Underwood
FRANK B. KELLOGG

AMERICAN SECRETARIES OF STATE
1921–1929

own part, we might adhere to the World Court, if a way could be found to help elect the judges, but there was nothing pressing about it. In alluding to the Court "which has been set up," in referring to our attendance at sanitary conferences abroad, and to our participation in "efforts to prevent disease, to curtail commerce in narcotics, and to cooperate in the prevention of traffic in women and children," the Secretary of State was careful to avoid mentioning that these five important activities were being promoted by the League of Nations. In his entire address at Boston the name of the League was not uttered.

It was fitting that he should close with an appeal that the people of Massachusetts should not fail to re-elect Senator Lodge. It might not matter so much to Massachusetts, but it would be "an irreparable loss to the nation." [32]

Salvage Attempted. The sentiments expressed by Hughes in Boston make it clear why he did not feel that his advocacy of the League of Nations had been of such a character as to require his resignation when he found that the promise of a Republican way into the League was not fulfilled. "On the contrary," says a sympathetic biographer, "he felt that his abandonment of the Administration in the circumstances would amount to unworthy conduct which he could not condone." [33]

To his determination not to resign most of his contemporaries very probably agreed, though many undoubtedly felt that, out of deference to the very large number of people who regarded his leadership prior to the election as pro-League, he might have condoned the League somewhat more graciously than he did in the first year of his incumbency. The kind of courage that will face a popular and partisan fury which has been stirred to white heat is not required when defiance would serve no constructive pur-

[32] *New York Times*, October 31, 1922. All credit for the approval of the Washington Conference treaties by the Senate was given to the "leadership and unremitting attention" of Senator Lodge, whereas the Four Power Treaty, the key to them all, was passed through the influence of Senator Underwood, as will appear in the next chapter.

[33] C. C. Hyde, in S. F. Bemis, ed., *American Secretaries of State and Their Diplomacy*, Vol. X, p. 367.

pose. Little positive aid to the League was possible in the early part of Harding's term, had there been a desire to give it. If, moreover, Hughes had lost all faith in the possibility of a league of nations he was entitled to change his ground.

Certainly, it was his duty to give first consideration to the dangerous situation in which the rejection of the League left his country. On him lay the responsibility of extricating the United States, if he could. Furthermore, the naval disarmament conference offered a chance to achieve a settlement of the most pressing of the political problems left by the failure of the United States to enter the League of Nations. It was imperative that the most should be made of this opportunity and Hughes devoted himself unsparingly to it.

CHAPTER V

WASHINGTON PEACE CONFERENCE

AT ABOUT the same time that the separate treaty of peace with Germany became assured, the new Administration decided to attempt a renewal of association with our former allies that would signify good will and prevent immediate and dangerous rivalries from springing up. The United States was headed for trouble with them in both the oceans which composed her frontiers. Having repudiated the treaty of peace drawn by her associates and by her own President and having refused to assume any responsibility for the maintenance of the peace in the future, she was at the same time engaged in a great naval building program which would make her navy equal if not superior to that of Great Britain, and thus able to challenge English control of the seas or to frustrate any naval measures upon which the League might agree in order to deal with an outbreak of war.[1] It was true that Great Britain was so impoverished by the war that she could ill afford to undertake a new naval rivalry, yet she could hardly be expected to relinquish without a struggle her century-old control of the seas—a control which had but yesterday saved her very life and upon which the existence of her empire depended daily, if unrestrained force was to continue to rule the world.

Rivalry in the Pacific. The situation in the Pacific was more disquieting. American public opinion, favorable to Japan while the little brown men were fighting great Russia, had changed soon afterward and, aided by fear of Japanese penetration on the Pacific coast, had become distinctly hostile. It was stirred further by the steady, aggressive pressure of Japan upon China during the war and by the apparent intent of Japan to establish an

[1] See statistics on comparative naval strengths and authorized building in the report of the Secretary of the Navy, *Current History*, February, 1921, Vol. 13, Pt. 2, p. 189.

Asiatic Monroe Doctrine which might seriously limit American enterprise in the Far East. This was an important matter to many large business interests in the United States, well represented in the new Administration. The markets of the East had almost limitless possibilities if the Open Door could be preserved, a case which seemed unlikely if Japan dominated the region unchecked. She had already practically denied us access to the former German cable at the island of Yap, which station, in the atmosphere left by the defeat of the Treaty, we had vainly asked for ourselves.[2] Japanese control of hundreds of other ex-German islands, even though they could not be legally fortified, seemed to menace our hold upon the Philippines. Japan had added to her strength during the war and seemed quite under the control of her militaristic elements.

Furthermore, the Japanese had a close working alliance with Great Britain which had stood the test of two wars, and, while there was no sentiment in England for invoking it against the United States and much opinion favorable to its dissolution, the alliance stood as a potential means of uniting the British and Japanese fleets against the United States.

Some move to bring the United States back into working relations with the Great Powers, particularly the naval powers, appeared imperative. The change was demanded, moreover, by domestic considerations. There was a strong sense of defeat and disappointment in the minds of myriads of Americans, Republican and Democratic alike, due to the negative attitude taken towards world peace and order. Liberal promises had been made to them that the United States would be brought into some kind of association with the nations, and the moral compulsion to take some

[2] D. Y. Thomas, *One Hundred Years of the Monroe Doctrine*, New York, 1923, p. 472.

Dr. Sidney L. Gulick, a serious student of Far Eastern affairs, states that Japan was making feverish war preparations based upon fear of war with the United States. They had seen in this country a rising tide of war talk and of insistence that there must be a war with Japan. They had noted our moving a large fleet into the Pacific, observed our huge building program, and responded to their militaristic elements as they would not have done otherwise. *Congressional Record*, Vol. 62, Pt. 4, p. 4171.

constructive step was supported by every healthy instinct of statesmanship. The developing rivalry in both the Atlantic and the Pacific indicated what direction it should take.

Pressure for a Naval Conference. The way had also been prepared by groups outside the Administration. After the defeat of the League the retiring Secretaries of War and of the Navy had logically advanced great programs of defense. If the United States would stand aloof from the world she should be prepared to defend herself against it. Secretary Daniels advocated a navy second to none, at the same time calling repeatedly for a conference on disarmament that would spare us the expensive and dangerous rivalry involved in competitive arming. Several Democratic members of Congress offered resolutions proposing such a conference but were unable to get them considered.[3]

The leader of the Irreconcilables, too, favored some mitigation of the logical consequences of splendid isolation, once it had been successfully re-established. Senator Borah offered a joint resolution, on December 14, 1920, requesting the President to enter into negotiations with Great Britain and Japan to reduce naval expenditures, and on February 15, 1921, he proposed an amendment to the naval appropriation bill authorizing the President to call the two powers to a naval disarmament conference and insisted on its adoption. The Republican leaders in the Senate opposed the move, and the bill went over to the new session.[4] Borah reintroduced the resolution in the new Congress, April 13, and again offered the amendment on May 4. The latter was ably supported by Democratic Senators, like King of Utah, who pleaded for a policy of leadership and accommodation.[5] The Administration at first opposed the idea of a conference but, after it had sounded the other Governments, withdrew its opposition and the

[3] Thomas, *One Hundred Years of the Monroe Doctrine*, p. 468; *Current History*, February, 1921, Vol. 13, Pt. 2, p. 189; *Congressional Record*, Vol. 61, Pt. 4, p. 3225.

[4] *Congressional Record*, Vol. 60, Pt. 1, p. 310; Pt. 3, p. 3171; Pt. 4, p. 3225.

[5] *Ibid.*, Vol. 61, Pt. 1, pp. 188, 1006; Pt. 2, pp. 1420, 1968.

proposal passed both houses, the Senate by unanimous vote and the House, after the President had requested its approval, by a vote of 330 to 4 on June 29.[6]

The call for the conference was issued by President Harding on July 10 and it sat in Washington from November 12, 1921, to February 6, 1922.[7] The United States, Great Britain, Japan, France, and Italy carried on the naval limitation discussions. China, Holland, Portugal, and Belgium were represented in the deliberations on Pacific questions.

The Problem of the Anglo-Japanese Alliance. Naval reduction and Pacific problems were found to be closely related. The United States keenly desired the abrogation of the Anglo-Japanese Alliance, and many people in Britain did not like to consider even the potential union of the British and Japanese fleets against the United States, though it was generally known that the 1911 renewal of the Alliance excepted its application against the United States.

The British Dominions—those emerging nations whose votes in the League Assembly had been represented as always marshaled against the United States—were divided. Canada insisted strongly that the alliance be canceled.[8] The Australians, however, objected

[6] *Ibid.*, Vol. 61, Pt. 4, pp. 3223, 3226, 3523.

[7] Our representatives in the conference were: Secretary Charles E. Hughes, Henry Cabot Lodge, Elihu Root, and Oscar W. Underwood.

[8] The role of Arthur Meighen, Canadian Prime Minister, was first described by Grattan O'Leary, who represented the Canadian press at the Premiers' Conference in London, June, 1921, and who was known to be very close to Premier Meighen, in an article in *MacLean's Magazine*.

According to this account Meighen communicated with the British Government on February 14, 1921, objecting to the renewal of the Anglo-Japanese Alliance and urging the calling of a conference on Pacific affairs between the United States, Britain, and Japan.

Arriving in London for the Premiers' conference in June, Meighen is said to have found Australia, New Zealand, and Britain strongly in favor of a renewal of the Alliance. Meighen, nevertheless, emphatically opposed its continuance on the ground that it had outlived its purpose, the curbing of Russia and Germany, and could now only lead to an armament race with the remaining great power, the United States.

Pressing his proposal of a conference, Meighen secured a sounding of the Japanese and United States embassies in London a week before the invitation to the conference was issued by President Harding. William Slavens McNutt,

to breaking the alliance abruptly, thereby incurring Japanese enmity. They preferred to preserve some kind of entente with Japan that would, if possible, give them some assurance against Japanese expansion without binding them to support it elsewhere. The British Government recognized the wisdom of this policy from the imperial standpoint and also felt itself without moral justification for brusquely terminating an alliance which had served Britain well and which the other party did not desire to end.

The obvious solution seemed to be the inclusion of the United States in the alliance and its alteration to remove all obligatory provisions. If the United States and Japan could be brought into an entente which would guarantee the basic interests of each, mutual distrust would be removed and no new ill will would be directed against the Empire. British leaders, therefore, began publicly to advance this idea as soon as the conference seemed likely to develop, and continued to advocate it in the conference.[9]

Thus the Administration whose militant sponsors denounced all "political" association with other nations found itself compelled to face the fact that political relationships not only existed, but were the dominating factors in international affairs. Secretary Hughes electrified the world and gained a great strategical advantage for his cause of naval reduction by the sweeping, detailed proposals which he publicly laid before the conference at its opening session. Then, as the inevitable private discussions developed, and as Pacific issues were opened up, he and his colleagues were continually confronted by the fact that the association between Britain and Japan did exist; that it dominated the Pacific Ocean—where the advance and the safeguarding of American commerce were keenly desired; that if it were to be destroyed some new working agreement, some new assurance of stability in the Pacific, would have to take its place; and finally that the new

"Canada's Part in the Washington Conference," *Literary Digest*, November 19, 1921, p. 48.

While it is to be doubted that the Canadian initiative was responsible for the calling of the Washington Conference, its effect upon the British attitude is generally accepted.

[9] *Congressional Record*, Vol. 62, Pt. 4, pp. 3552, 3608.

understanding would be meaningless—even impossible—unless the United States became a party to it.

The adjustment had to be made cautiously. Senator Borah had not asked the Administration to confer on any Pacific problems at all. He had merely urged the naval powers to stop building ships, and other dominant Senators had assumed such strong positions against "involvements" and "entanglements" in opposing Mr. Wilson's League that they could hardly abandon them so soon. The problem was therefore discussed very quietly and informally among the chief delegates in the early weeks of the conference, until the Americans became convinced that the risk must be taken. Then Secretary Hughes proposed the arrangement which was substantially embodied in the Four Power Treaty, and Senator Lodge presented it to a surprised public in an address to the conference on December 10, 1921.[10]

Four Power Treaty

Article I of this treaty provided for an adjustment of relations between the four signatory powers—the United States, the British Empire, France, and Japan—as follows:

> The high contracting parties agree as between themselves to respect their rights in relation to their insular possessions and insular dominions in the region of the Pacific Ocean.
>
> If there should develop between any of the high contracting parties a controversy arising out of any Pacific question and involving their said rights which is not satisfactorily settled by diplomacy and is likely to affect the harmonious accord now happily subsisting between them, they shall invite the other high contracting parties to a joint conference to which the whole subject will be referred for consideration and adjustment.

[10] *Ibid.* A Japanese observer described Lodge's presentation as "the most flowery speech delivered during the entire conference." Introduced by Secretary Hughes "with an unusual sign of enthusiasm," he talked of "Sprinkled isles, Lily on lily that o'erlace the sea" until "the prosaic pact was made a thing of poetic beauty."—Yamato Ichihashi, *The Washington Conference and After*, Palo Alto, 1928, p. 114.

Article II took account of any possible disturbance of the existing order in the Pacific by other powers, saying:

If the said rights are threatened by the aggressive action of any other power the high contracting parties shall communicate with one another fully and frankly in order to arrive at an understanding as to the most efficient measures to be taken, jointly or separately, to meet the exigencies of the particular situation.

Article III set ten years as the minimum life of the agreement, after which time it might be terminated by any of the signatories on twelve months' notice. Article IV specifically stated that upon ratification of the treaty the Anglo-Japanese Alliance as renewed in London on July 13, 1911, should terminate.[11]

Secretary Hughes later refuted with some warmth the imputation raised in the Senate that in the making of this treaty the American delegates had been imposed upon or had furtively agreed "to accept some plan cunningly contrived by others." He reminded the Senators that "the views of this Government as to the importance of the termination of the Anglo-Japanese Alliance had been communicated long before the conference met, and it had also been clearly stated that this Government could enter into no alliance or make any sort of commitment to the use of arms, or which would impose any sort of obligation as to its decisions in future contingencies." The matter of the Anglo-Japanese Alliance naturally could not be placed upon the agenda, but the American delegates had reviewed the whole matter thoroughly, and Hughes had himself drafted the Four Power Treaty.

There was not the slightest mystery about it; it was a straightforward document which attained "one of the most important objects the American Government has had in view" and it was of the highest importance to the maintenance of friendly relations in the Far East upon a sound basis. "Its failure," he said in conclusion, "would be nothing short of a national calamity."[12]

[11] *Congressional Record*, Vol. 62, Pt. 1, p. 276.
[12] *Ibid.*, Pt. 4, p. 3712, a letter of March 11, 1922, to Senator Underwood.

President Harding's Plea for Approval. President Harding, in submitting the treaties to the Senate, on February 10, 1922, was no less concerned for the fate of the Four Power Treaty. He went before that body four days after the conference adjourned to present the treaties agreed upon and to "invite your prompt approval of all of them." Knowing full well what arguments could resound in the Senate against any possible association with other nations, he devoted almost the whole of his address, after the treaties had been enumerated, to a plea that the fate of the League in the Senate be not visited upon the Four Power Pact.

There was no "alliance, entanglement or involvement," no "commitment to armed forces, no alliance, no written or moral obligation to join in defense, no expressed or implied agreement to arrive at any agreement except in accordance with our constitutional methods." Yet the treaty meant something. If a solemn plighting of faith by leading nations of the earth was valueless, then, indeed, there was "little on which to hang our faith in advancing civilization or the furtherance of peace." But the older nations were not so treacherous and dangerous as they had been painted, he told the Senators by implication. He was "ready to assume the sincerity and the dependability of the assurances of our neighbors of the Old World" that they would respect our rights. He believed there was an inviolable national honor. It was necessary both to believe in it and to pledge it.

"Frankly, Senators," he said, "if nations may not safely agree to respect each other's rights, and may not agree to confer if one party to the compact threatens trespass, or may not agree to advise if one party to the pact is threatened by an outside power, then all concerted efforts to tranquilize the world and stabilize peace must be flung to the winds. Either these treaties must have your cordial sanction, or every proclaimed desire to promote peace and prevent war becomes a hollow mockery."

It is doubtful if any American executive will ever utter a more anxious appeal to the Senate to cease from obstruction while the Republic undertakes its share of the task of promoting international order. Woodrow Wilson in his travail, had he ever ventured to speak to the Senate so plainly, could hardly have uttered a more intense cry for cooperation and agreement. And well might his successor fear the impact of the forces which had been Mr. Wilson's undoing. He had seen them formed and marshaled. Then, it is true, their triumph had been held to be a patriotic victory. Now, though statements about the full preservation of complete national sovereignty were often on his lips, the responsibility of living in a world thickly settled by other peoples weighed upon him almost as heavily, it seemed, as it had upon the broken figure who silently watched from a nearby street the effort of his successor to find a place for their country in a disordered world—a place of safety, if not one of leadership.

The new President had now served in the roles both of critic and of governor and he had discovered how much easier the one part was than the other. Alluding to his experience as a Senator, he said, late in his address: "Since that experience I have come to know the viewpoint and inescapable responsibility of the Executive. To the Executive comes the closer view of world relationship and a more impressive realization of the menaces, the anxieties, and the apprehensions that are to be met."

Yet he had by no means forgotten the Senators and the lengths to which they might go in opposing executive policy, for he had said only a moment before: "I had occasion to learn of your very proper jealousy of the Senate's part in contracting foreign relationships. Frankly, it was in my mind when I asked representatives of both the majority and minority to serve on the American delegation. It was designed to have you participate. And you were ably represented."

Harding felt that he had done what he could. He had appointed the official leaders of the two parties in the Senate, Lodge and Underwood, as his delegates to the conference and had thus practically assured himself of their support for the treaties, for they could hardly oppose in the Senate what they had agreed to in the conference. In thus preventing the two leaders from exercising their expected function as Senators by making them his agents, he had apparently violated a clear provision of the Constitution, but he no doubt felt that the risk of failing to insure powerful advocates for the treaties in the Senate was great enough to justify the policy.[13]

The results of another effort of American statesmanship were

[13] Senator Robinson's objection to the practice was "that when the President reaches into the Senate and takes the most influential factors there to assist in negotiating a treaty he deprives the Senate of the unbiased judgment and expression of opinion on the part of those Senators, who, for the time being, have become Executive Agents rather than Senators." *Congressional Record*, Vol. 62, Pt. 4, pp. 4242-43.

President McKinley used Senators as his negotiators in making the treaty of peace with Spain, on the Alaskan Boundary Commission, and in other cases until a strong protest arose in the Senate against such employment of Senators. On different occasions the Senate was about to pass a resolution condemning it, but hesitated to embarrass Senate members acting as negotiators. Finally the chairman of the Judiciary Committee, Senator Hoar, was instructed to see the President and arrange for a cessation of the custom, a mission in which he was successful. George F. Hoar, *The Autobiography of Seventy Years*, New York, 1903, Vol. II, pp. 49-50.

The Constitution provides, in Article I, sec. 6: "No Senator or Representative shall, during the time for which he was elected, be appointed to any civil office under the authority of the United States, which shall have been created, or the emoluments whereof shall have been increased, during such time; and no person holding any office under the United States shall be a member of either House during his continuation in office."

Senator Hoar thought it "beyond dispute that the intention of that provision was to protect the members of the legislative branch of the Government from Executive influence. . . . He was to preserve his independence of Executive influence and to approach all questions in which he might have to deal with matters which concern the Executive power, or Executive action, absolutely free from any bias."

He also rejected as cavil the suggestion that the negotiators of treaties were not officers. "To say that the President cannot appoint a Senator or Representative postmaster in a country village—because that would put an improper temptation in the way of the legislator to induce him to become the tool of the Executive will, and then permit the President to send him abroad; to enable him to maintain the distinction and enjoy the pleasures of a season at a foreign capital as the representative of the United States, with all expenses paid, and a large compensation added, determined solely by the Executive will; and to hold that the framers of the Constitution would for a moment have tolerated that seems to me utterly preposterous."

Even though the power be unconstitutional, the President seems to have saved two important treaties by making Senators his agents in drafting them. The treaty of peace with Spain was ratified with two votes to spare, and the Four Power Treaty, as we shall see, with a margin not much wider. In either case, if leading Senators had not helped frame the treaties and had not exerted their influence for them in the Senate, it seems unlikely that they would have commanded the two-thirds majority.

now before the Senate, and the President submitted to his former colleagues in reservation-making "that if we cannot join in making effective these covenants for peace, and stamp this conference with America's approval, we shall discredit the influence of the Republic, render future efforts futile or unlikely, and write discouragement where today the world is ready to acclaim new hope." The urgency, the almost despairing appeal of this plea, could hardly be accentuated unless in the sentence in which he had just said: "If to these understandings for peace, if to these advanced expressions of the conscience of leading powers, if to these concords to guard against conflict and lift the burdens of armament, if to all of these the Senate will not advise and consent, then it will be futile to try again." [14]

A Committee Reservation. The Four Power Treaty was reported from the Foreign Relations Committee on March 1, with the inevitable reservation saying that "The United States understands that under the statement in the preamble or under the terms of this treaty there is no commitment to armed force, no alliance, no obligation to join in any defense." [15] The President's assurance that none of these things were true could hardly be sufficient to the Irreconcilable gentlemen who had been placed upon the Committee in the spring of 1918 to make sure that Wilson's League should be properly reserved and amended. After having defended the ramparts with such complete abandon then they could hardly forsake them now. The new agreement seemed to provide only for conference and nothing more, but people were calling it an alliance; it certainly replaced one. Therefore the Senate had better make sure as usual that it didn't do any of the things that people said it might. Senator Brandegee fathered the reservations.[16]

In the opinion of Senator Spencer, of Missouri, the reservation was far more likely to produce than to eliminate misunderstanding, for the reservation itself was in greater need of explanation

[14] *Congressional Record,* Vol. 62, Pt. 3, pp. 2391-92. Besides the two Senators, the American delegates to the conference were Secretary Hughes and Elihu Root.
[15] *Congressional Record,* Vol. 62, Pt. 3, pp. 2391-92.
[16] *Ibid.,* Pt. 4, p. 3784.

than the treaty it attempted to explain. He regarded it as a gross imposition on a treaty the terms of which were perfectly clear, but would vote for it to advance ratification. Senator Lenroot agreed that there was not the slightest reason for the reservation, but since refusing to adopt it would perhaps leave a question that would otherwise never have been raised, he, too, would vote for it. This was substantially the position of Senator Kellogg. He also believed it unnecessary and would not vote for it if he did not think it essential to get the votes for ratification. Senator Colt, of Rhode Island, on the other hand, felt compelled to conclude that there was an implied moral obligation, in Article 2, to use force and, since it was at least arguable that this was the case, the reservation should be adopted.[17]

Senator Lodge for the Treaty. In opening the general defense of the treaty, on March 8, Senator Lodge vigorously combated the use of the broad definition of the word "alliance" which made it practically synonymous with "treaty." An alliance in international law meant an agreement binding the parties to support each other with force. The Anglo-Japanese Alliance had been such a contract and among the purposes of the conference he put its abrogation first. It was the most dangerous element in our relations with the Orient. Without its abrogation, disarmament could not be accomplished, and the defeat of the Four Power Treaty would mean the failure of the conference. "Let there be no illusion on that point."

Lodge did not want this conference to fail. It was interesting to hear him plead for trust and tolerance. He was even inspired to feel that the conference of 1921 might be providing the compensation for the Great War. "The misery and the horrors of the Great War must never come again," he said, "if we can do anything to stop it. We must try our best to secure this beneficent result. We who have passed through the valley of the shadow in these last years must leave nothing undone that we can do to save our children and our children's children from the awful calamity

[17] *Ibid.*, p. 3910; Pt. 5, pp. 4308, 4316, 4333.

which we of this generation have been compelled to endure. It was with this hope, with this purpose that the conference met."

Then, apparently bethinking himself that the results of the conference might not comprise the widest possible effort to prevent the next catastrophe, he added that it was only a beginning. He did not seem aware that any other beginning had been made, but he wanted this one to be received in a kindly manner. If we "continue[d] to preach suspicion and hatred of other nations," if we declined to deal with them and felt in our hearts "that they were all actuated by the basest of motives," nothing whatever could be done. If we had learned the lesson of the war, then the door would now stand open "for further attempts to breed a larger kindliness and a more forbearing spirit among the nations of the earth" that would result in further, more assured and steady steps in the same direction. The world's peace could be maintained in this way "without alliances or penalties or the sanction of force lurking in the background."

Having said these things, the Massachusetts Senator appealed for the approval of the treaty because of its American origin. "We called this conference," he reminded the Senate, "we proposed the treaties, agreements and declarations in which the conference culminated. Are we now to stumble and fall at the threshold of the undertaking which we designed and brought to fulfillment? Are we to sink back into a sullen solitude, a prey to dark suspicions, a hermit nation armed to the teeth and looking forward always to wars as inseparable from the existence of mankind upon the earth?" [10]

[18] Mr. Paul D. Cravath, a prominent Republican of New York City, expressed his opinion of the desirability of upholding American negotiators in even stronger fashion in an address to the Council on Foreign Relations, February 17, 1922. He said: "One of the chief arguments that influenced me in advocating our acceptance of the Treaty of Versailles and the League of Nations, in spite of all the objections that I saw, was this: It seemed to me that it would be a disgrace to our country if a treaty negotiated by our President in the greatest international conference ever held, at the end of the greatest war the world had ever seen, would not be accepted by the United States Senate, and in spite of all the objections to it I think it was an eternal disgrace to this country that the treaty was rejected. For the same reason, it seems to me that unless

A dozing Senator might have thought that he heard someone pleading for our acceptance of the obligations of the League of Nations, but Lodge hastened to add that we had believed we could best help the world by maintaining our own strength and complete independence, "untrammeled and unhampered, free from the hatreds and rivalries of Europe." If we could not do this, then the clouds of war would "again settle heavily over the future of civilization. This must not be," he declaimed. "The United States has never yet permitted failure or defeat to be written in her history. She will not permit it now. Under her lead a beginning has been made to secure the world's peace in the coming years. Let us not blight or wither this new hope," he said in conclusion. "Can we not say now, as we have always said, to a doubting, weary, and waiting world:

" 'And not by eastern windows only,
When daylight comes, comes in the light,
In front the sun climbs slow, how slowly,
But westward, look, the land is bright.' "[19]

What a different course the world's history might have taken if Lodge had been able to urge "a larger kindliness and a more forbearing spirit" when the preaching of "suspicion and hatred of other nations," which he now deprecated, first broke loose in full chorus, when all "dark suspicions" were nourished, when the "lesson of the war" was more painfully apparent to all than it could ever be again, even to aged men who "passed through the valley of the shadow" in the regulated precincts of the Senate chamber! Or, to put it otherwise, how different the turn of events might have been if Wilson had not refused to permit Lodge and his associates any share in framing the great legislation of 1919! The result of this policy had been that the Senators could not feel that there was enough of real simon-pure American origin about the League to justify even the admission that it constituted

the objections to these treaties are absolutely overwhelming, it will be another disgrace, a crowning disgrace, if the Senate should fail to ratify this series of treaties or any of them." *Congressional Record*, Vol. 62, Pt. 4, p. 4166.

[19] *Congressional Record*, Vol. 62, Pt. 4, pp. 3551-52.

a beginning in keeping the world's peace. It was merely Wilson's League.

Nor was the point to be left to implication, if it were disputed, for when Senator Reed began at once to deny that the Four Power Treaty had originated with the American people or the American Congress—which was true enough—and to call upon the Senators to smite it as they had smitten the proposal of a recent Democratic President, he was interrupted by Senator New, of Indiana, who said: "The Senator has just concluded a statement to the effect that another enterprise which was called by an American president was resisted by the Senator from Massachusetts [Mr. Lodge]. I call attention to the fact that the other enterprise, the League of Nations, to which the Senator undoubtedly refers, was not an American proposal and it was not called by an American president at all. True, an American president participated, but the proposition did not originate with us at all."

When Senator Reed expressed astonishment at these statements, New insisted: "But it was never an American proposition at all." [20] What does constitute an American proposition was not threshed out, but evidently it was considered to be a proposition which Republican Senators had assisted in framing.

With this introduction to the debate, some partisan attack upon the treaty by Democratic Senators was perhaps to be expected. There was much temptation for it on general principles. The memories of the defeat of the Covenant were still fresh enough to suggest that it might be well to save the country from the possible perils of a pact sponsored by the very individuals who had managed the campaign which nullified Wilson's effort. The consequences of saving the country a second time by the same devices might indeed be serious, but they could not be more serious than those of the salvation in 1919 and 1920.

New Balance of Power. To the Irreconcilable foes of any positive commitment to future action of any kind the new agreement was no more palatable than the old. Indeed, they freely said

[20] *Ibid.*, p. 3556.

that it had all the vices of the League and none of its virtues. It made no difference to Senator Reed that we had agreed to do nothing except talk. In his judgment the treaty would be construed to mean that we were to talk, to come to a conclusion, and to act upon the conclusion.

The very existence of the treaty, moreover, would, he thought, tend to furnish opportunities for us both to talk and to act. All history proved that combinations produced counter-combinations; such was the law of self defense. The law held for individuals. It had brought people together in tribes, and the combinations of tribes had produced opposing groups. Combinations between nations had always had the same result. There was no exception to the rule in all history, and there would be none in this instance. There had never been a quadruple alliance formed that had not brought forth another one. Russia and Germany (and China, other Senators added) would inevitably conclude that an agreement of the four powers to rule the Pacific which left them out was inimical to their interests. These great giants, whose potential power was incalculable, would not always remain prostrate and powerless, and as they rose again they would be driven into each others' arms.[21]

Reed did not go on, of course, to the conclusion that since combinations of powers had always produced counterbalancing groups and war, the logical course was to make a great effort to get all the nations into one great union, instead of starting on the old road again. On the contrary, he still favored remaining wholly free to enter future wars on our own terms.

Senator Borah, too, saw in the treaty only the old balance-of-power system and apparently abhorred it as much as he did the alternative to it. "I trust I am for peace," he said. "God knows I want to serve that cause if I can find out the way to do so. I do not want to err in that vital soul-absorbing question. But when I look back over the bloody past, with its dead and diseased and

[21] *Ibid.*, pp. 3557-58.

insane, and recognize as the most prolific source of all this unspeakable misery, this system of political grouping, this system of the balance of power, I have not the courage to tell the people of my country that to continue that system means peace. From my view it would be a cowardly falsehood, a shameless deception, a brazen betrayal."[22]

How one could feel so strongly about the failure of the old method of regulating international rivalries and at the same time oppose the creation of some machinery for adjusting international relations is one of the problems for the future to explain. The effort to gather the nations into one great organization, designed to adjust the frictions sure to arise and to remove the fear of aggression from all, might fail, but what other reasonable hope for stable civilized international relations, short of the millennium, was there? That those who refused the solution to which all logic pointed were sometimes uneasy is not to be wondered at.

Comparisons with the League Covenant. Borah held, however, to his position that no organization, no commitment, was wise and objected to the Four Power Pact for the same reason that he had objected to the League. He agreed that Article 10 of the League Covenant had left our Congress and Government legally free to decide what we should do about future wars, and he freely acknowledged that we would have the same legal freedom under the new treaty, but he contended, as did Senators who believed in the League, that "Article 2 of this treaty and Article 10 of the League of Nations Covenant contained the same moral obligations exactly."[23] In all international agreements the effective force was the moral obligation, not the legal tie, which could not be enforced.

Senator Johnson, of California, likewise insisted that the two articles had the same meaning. He placed them side by side on the wall of the Senate and in the *Record*, and asked the Senate

[22] *Ibid.*, p. 3797.
[23] *Ibid.*, Pt. 5, pp. 4317-20.

to note the likeness.[24] The obligation to follow the advice of the Council, which we did not specifically agree to follow, was no more binding than the obligation to execute the "efficient measures" which we ourselves agreed to determine. He thought it strange that "the same gentlemen when they were engaged in the delicate task of safeguarding American rights under the League of Nations" had demanded a reservation to Article 10 by which the final determination of any action should be with Congress. Then, they had said there would be no means of escape from action by Congress, except by breach of faith, although we were not pledged to action and Lodge had declared that "legislation by Congress under those circumstances would be a mockery of independent action." Now, with substantially the same obligation, the ground was shifted and they talked of constitutional obligations taking precedence so that even "though we were guilty of a breach of faith constitutional sanctions would save our honor." As Senator Lodge, when told that nothing warlike would be done without the assent of Congress, had replied, "If that is true let us say so in the covenant," so Johnson now said: "If that is true let us say so in the treaty." [25]

[24] *From the Four Power Treaty:*

With a view to the preservation of the general peace and the *maintenance of their rights* in relation to their insular possessions, etc., have determined to conclude a treaty to the effect, etc.

I. The high contracting parties agree as between themselves to respect their *rights* in relation to their insular *possessions,* etc.

II. If the said rights are threatened by the aggressive action of any other power, the high contracting parties shall communicate with one another fully and frankly in order to arrive at an understanding as to *the most efficient measures to be taken, jointly or saparately, to meet the exigencies of a particular situation.*

From the League Covenant:

The high contracting parties, in order to promote international cooperation and to achieve international peace and security, agree, etc.

Article 10. The members of the league undertake to respect and preserve as against external aggression the territorial integrity and existing political independence of all members of the league. *In case of any such aggression the council shall advise upon the means by which the obligation shall be fulfilled.*

The italics are Mr. Johnson's. *Congressional Record,* Vol. 62, Pt. 4, p. 3782.

[25] *Congressional Record,* Vol. 62, Pt. 4, p. 3782. All the bitterest opponents of the League now agreed that the Covenant had not impaired the right of Congress to declare war.

Senator Reed was also astonished to find that "while at that time there were on the other side of this Chamber a certain determined body of men" who declared that the language of Article 10 was an exact obligation, and that it must be redeemed, and that they would never give their consent to the making of any kind of obligation which bound us in honor to enter into conflicts originating between other nations than ourselves "the same men were now asserting that similar language did not bind us."[26]

The regular Republicans, of course, maintained that there was a vital difference between the two documents, that under Article 10 we were committed to a guaranty of territorial integrity, before the Council ever met to "advise upon the means by which" the obligation should be fulfilled, whereas there was no such definite obligation stated in Article 2 of the Four Power Treaty. Senator Borah countered this reasoning not only by denying that there was any essential difference in the two articles but also by showing that Article 2 of the treaty under debate also included the sum and substance of Article 11 of the League Cov-

---

Senator Reed maintained that "it was as true then as it is now that the President can not declare war; that the League of Nations could not declare war; that no power on earth could declare war except the Congress of the United States. If that fact be a protection against this treaty and this agreement, it was equally a protection against the League of Nations; so why not join the League of Nations and say we will make war or we will keep the peace just as the Congress determines, because you are powerless by any league of nations or by any compact to drag us into war without the voluntary act of Congress" (p. 4345).

Even Senator Poindexter was equally emphatic on the point, saying: "Now I lay down the proposition that a nation cannot be bound to perform the act which holds more of good or evil fortune for its people than any other governmental act which it can perform, namely, the act of making war, unless it is provided for in the clearest and most express terms. It seems to me contrary to any rule of interpretation of instruments, even those between private parties, to hold that there may be read between the lines and by implication an agreement to bind a power to lead its people into war. I deny that there is any such principle of construction of treaties or agreements between nations. Mr. President, the entire course of diplomatic history negatives that proposition" (p. 4174).

[26] *Congressional Record*, Vol. 62, Pt. 4, p. 3798. Senator Williams, of Mississippi, added his opinion that if a Republican President had sent the Treaty of Versailles to the Senate three-fourths of the Republicans would have voted for it and that if Wilson had sent the Four Power Treaty, two-thirds of the Democrats would be for it (p. 3855).

enant, which was broader in scope than Article 10, and under which—rather than under Article 10—the League had moved to compose disputes. The old Article 11 declared that any threat of war was of concern to all and that the league should "take any action that may be deemed wise and effectual to safeguard the peace of nations"; the new Article 2 would have the parties "communicate with one another fully and frankly in order to arrive at an understanding as to the most efficient measures to be taken" to protect their rights. What was the difference? Were we not morally bound to support the measures advised to meet the emergency in the one case as well as in the other? [27]

Many Democratic Senators naturally felt even more strongly on this point. They pointed out that the new commitment was even broader in scope than the old. Article 10 guaranteed only the vital principle of territorial independence. Article 2 guaranteed the "rights" of the contracting parties in the Pacific. Who, asked Senator Robinson, might accurately define the "rights" of Japan in the Pacific Ocean?

That question was not, however, the real point of Robinson's objection. He thought the treaty made necessary the use of force to uphold it, but he believed in putting force behind the peace. What he objected to was the limited, exclusive, selfish nature of the proposed league. It was a provocative grouping which would be ineffective in keeping the peace. If you would put the force of enough nations behind the peace it would be a reality, "instead of a menacing little imitation league, a four-ply alliance, destined to involve us in distress and humiliation, if not in war." [28]

The treaty was one result of our failure to enter the League, said Senator Pittman. The other three Powers were members of

[27] *Congressional Record,* Vol. 62, Pt. 5, p. 4320. Borah thought, too, that the executive would be able to create situations that left Congress little choice as to whether to use force or not under the proposed treaty about as effectively as through the League. He argued that England was not legally bound to go to the aid of France in 1914. The English Parliament was legally free to go into the war or stay out, but he maintained that the cabinet had entered into so many understandings with the French, practically naval understandings, that the Parliament had little to do except to order them supported by war (p. 4329).

[28] *Congressional Record,* Vol. 62, Pt. 5, pp. 4325-26.

the League and could act through it. We were not a member of the League. Therefore they had got up this regional understanding to enable us to participate in maintaining the peace of the Pacific. If the Four Power Pact was not a substitute for the League, as far as the Pacific was concerned, what was the peaceful use of it at all? If the League was the body to prevent war in the Pacific, then this instrument was unnecessary, and if a dispute threatening war was taken to the League Council, we would have no influence in settling it because we were not represented there. If the treaty did not in fact constitute an alliance, why were the other Pacific powers, notably China and Russia, not included?

This point was pressed by Norman H. Davis, in a debate in New York City which was frequently discussed in the Senate. Even if the rights of the excluded Pacific powers were scrupulously respected, he reasoned, their mere exclusion from this treaty and from conferences over questions affecting their rights would inevitably cause suspicion and tend to create another group of powers to counterbalance the big four. Nine nations were asked to join in the treaty on Chinese integrity. Why were the same nations not included in this treaty? If the whole proposal did not lead us back into the system of alliances, what was to be gained by trying to segregate the world's problems into different compartments? What would be the relation of one compartment to the other? If the Far East was to be put in one compartment, the Near East in another, Europe in another, and South America in another, would it not be necessary to define how the relations between them were to be maintained? How many of these groups were we to join, and if a nation joined more than one, to what extent would it be a free agent and to what group would it owe most allegiance?

Davis was opposed to breaking the world up into parts to accomplish particular purposes and he thought it of doubtful wisdom to join any combination which ignored the moral rights of weaker nations at the start by excluding them from the group. Alliances or special agreements between a certain group of nations either originated from moral or material objectives not in harmony with those of other nations or else inevitably developed conflicting objectives. We had learned by experience that even a so-called diplomatic agreement between two Powers relating to a particular question or territory resulted almost invariably in their acting in concert on questions outside the scope of the agreement. He thought that this Four Power Treaty grew out of about the same kind of situation which had produced other alliances and that we had no guarantee that it would end differently.[29]

Senator Caraway, of Arkansas, also rebelled against the selfish and exclusive character of the proposed grouping. He did not characterize the United States as a predatory power because of its continued holding of the Philippines, but he objected to going into a combination with three other Powers, each of whom held Pacific territory that did not belong to them and never did rightfully belong to them, in order to stabilize conditions as they were in the Pacific Ocean. Why was it necessary unless to gain selfish ends or avoid the consequences of our abstention from the League? The Treaty of Versailles had provided that all the peoples of the earth should enter into agreement to guarantee the peace of the world by having each respect the rights of the others. If that agreement could not be depended on, what was to be expected from the new one? Were Senators going to be content to say, "My prayers and my hopes and my love of humanity are confined to the Pacific Ocean, and to the Pacific Ocean only, and I do not care what happens to all the rest of the earth?" [30]

Senator McCumber, of North Dakota, the lone Republican Senator who had championed the League Covenant even to the extent of voting for it unreserved and unamended, saw gain in the proposed treaty because it, like the League, provided for conference and discussion in which the better conscience of the peoples might be registered. He too, however, asked pointedly about all of the Washington agreements:

[29] *Ibid.*, Pt. 4, p. 4165.
[30] *Ibid.*, Pt. 5, p. 4314.

If these treaties mark a vast forward step in international understanding among those nations which border upon and have possessions within the Pacific, why should we not bring within the fold the great nations of Continental Europe? Why should we stop the good work? Why should we make no attempt to extend to all great nations the principles agreed to with reference to humane rules of warfare, with reference to disarmament, and with reference to the pledge to recognize at all times the political and administrative integrity of other nations, and, above all, the principles of open discussion of all disputes before resorting to the arbitrament of arms? Why should these principles be bounded by the shores of the Pacific Ocean only? [31]

An Entangling Alliance. It was inevitable that many who believed in the League should regard the proposed association as a backward step and not a gracious one. Senator Harris, of Georgia, could find no way to compare a league of all nations with a league of four nations. In his judgment the latter was one of the kinds of entangling alliances which George Washington had warned against and which Woodrow Wilson had all but given his life to end.

He felt, moreover, that Democratic Senators were entitled to oppose it without being automatically charged with partisanship. He thought the course of the Democrats contrasted strongly with that of the Republicans in 1919 and 1920. The Democrats had not sought to embarrass the Washington Conference, whereas the Republicans had done everything within their power to destroy President Wilson's influence while he was negotiating for a League of Nations to keep the peace. The Democrats had sincerely supported the purpose for which the Washington Con-

[31] *Ibid.*, Pt. 4, p. 3839. McCumber submitted a detailed plan for a proposed association of nations, which seems to be one of the forebears of the Briand-Kellogg Peace Pact of 1928.

Senator Colt in supporting the treaties also called attention once more to the fact that associations of nations for the settlement of political disputes were vitally necessary. Arbitration and a world court were needed for the adjudication of disputes of a legal nature, but it was manifest that the really dangerous causes of war were of a political nature and must be dealt with by political machinery. Lord Bryce had lately analyzed the sixteen European wars between 1815 and 1915 and had found that two, or possibly three, of them were susceptible of arbitration by a court on legal principles (Pt. 5, p. 4309).

ference had been called—disarmament—and had given every encouragement to it. Surely they were entitled to oppose this unexpected fruit of the conference which seemed plainly to conflict with our century-old policy of avoiding entanglements. At least the Republicans who had raised the cry of entangling alliances against a League Covenant designed to dissolve all alliances should not now cast reflection upon their brethren for opposing what seemed very much nearer an entangling alliance.[32]

Furthermore, the Democratic Senators believed they had more tangible things to view with alarm than had the Republicans in 1919. The latter had condemned the failure of the Peace Conference to force Japan out of Shantung in peremptory fashion and had daily warned that if the Chinese rose against the Japanese, we might have to fight the Japanese as aggressors under the League. Japan was also in possession of Eastern Siberia and of the northern half of the island of Sakhalin when the Four Power Treaty was signed and when it was debated. Here, said the critics of that treaty, was a likely situation. Russia would not always remain helpless, and when she moved to assert her lawful right to the territories seized by Japan, we should become involved the moment the Russians crossed the narrow strait which separates Siberia from Sakhalin.

Where now was the acute Republican conscience of 1919, they asked? How shameful would be our position bound by this treaty to give moral if not military support to Japan against Russia! And what did this treaty accomplish, continued Senator Robinson, if not to bind the United States, England, and France to the establishment of Japanese supremacy throughout the Orient? [33]

This point was developed more fully in the New York debate previously referred to, in which Norman H. Davis maintained that the treaty tended to tie our hands and protect the Japanese rear, leaving her free to prosecute aggressive policies on the Asi-

[32] *Congressional Record,* Vol. 62, Pt. 5, p. 4336.
[33] *Ibid.,* Pt. 4, p. 3610.

atic mainland all the more vigorously.[34] This unintended effect of the treaty seemed to Roland S. Morris, former American Ambassador to Japan, of fundamental importance. Our effort to support the Open Door in China had been largely futile because the innocent and simple words of the Anglo-Japanese Alliance had acted as a screen behind which nations desiring to violate the Open Door could do so. He had hoped that this alliance would be abrogated by the Conference without our joining the alliance. He submitted that whether or not the Four Power Treaty was an alliance was to be judged not only by what it included but by its exclusive character and by the limitations it put upon our freedom to support the vast Pacific nations now submerged but sure to rise.[35]

The Robinson Amendment. The principal effort of the critics of the treaty in 1922 was aimed at adding an amendment which provided that nations outside the Four-Power circle should be called into conference whenever their rights were involved in a controversy with one of the Four Powers. Such an amendment would have the effect of bringing all Pacific Powers into the proposed league for the purpose of settling disputes. As proposed by Senator Robinson, the amendment read:

> Each of the high contracting parties will respect the rights and possessions of all other nations and refrain from all acts of aggression against any other power or powers. If there should develop between any of the high contracting parties and any other power or powers, a controversy relating to said insular rights and possessions or to any far eastern questions which is not satisfactorily settled by diplomacy and is likely to affect the harmonious accord subsisting between any party or parties to this compact and any other power or powers, the high contracting parties shall invite all powers claiming an interest in the controversy to a joint conference to which the whole subject shall be referred for consideration and adjustment.

The majority of the Democrats and the Irreconcilables throughout the debate supported this broadening of the pact,

[34] He envisaged, however, a check on Japanese militarism from the growth of liberalism in that country.

[35] *Congressional Record*, Vol. 62, Pt. 4, pp. 4163, 4170.

first as a reservation and later as an amendment. Three votes were taken upon it, in slightly different form; on the day the treaty was ratified, March 24, 1922, 36 Senators were mustered for it while the opposition varied from 55 to 59. Twenty additional amendments were defeated by larger majorities.[36]

Ratified by Democratic Votes. The Treaty itself was ratified by a vote of 67 to 27, 2 not voting. The minority was composed of 23 Democrats—including Reed, of Missouri—and four Republicans, Borah, France, Johnson, and La Follette. The majority was made up of 55 Republicans and 12 Democrats.[37] If 5 of these 12 Democrats had not followed the leadership of Underwood in supporting the treaty it would have been defeated. If the Democrats had emulated the unanimity of the Republicans of 1919, by insisting that the Four Power Treaty be perfected by reservations fundamentally altering its character, that treaty would have been lost, and with it, according to the Republican leaders, the entire work of the Washington Conference. If the minority had insisted in 1922, as the Republicans did in 1919, on forestalling all the possible entanglements and undesirable involvements which they thought they foresaw, the Washington Treaties would have fared as the Treaty of Versailles did.

Perhaps the Democrats do not deserve great credit for refusing to take vengeance upon the Republicans for the failure of 1920. The Republican action had apparently been heavily indorsed by the people in the election of 1920. The people counted, too, upon the benefits of naval reduction and they might not respond again to the cry of entanglement, disregarding the conservative value of the treaty proposals. They expected to gain immediately this time, and in dollars. The risk of defeating again so soon another American effort to stabilize a distracted world was in itself appalling to contemplate. Outraged as the Democrats may have felt over what appeared to them the defective, if not

[36] *Ibid.*, Pt. 5, pp. 4486-97.
[37] *Congressional Directory*, February, 1922, pp. 157-58.

dangerous, application of the principle they had fought for, it was well that they did not unite to demand all that might be attained, or complete insurance against all the unpleasant contingencies which might arise under the treaty.

It seemed to the Democrats that there was "no comparison between the obvious danger of misunderstandings under this four-power pact and misunderstandings under a league of nations in which there are a great many neutral nations, disinterested nations, nations which have never sought other people's territory, nations whose whole course has been fair and honorable and high." [38] The powers which we were joining were in fact the very ones held up in the League debate as the chief predatory nations most likely to rob or impose upon us. Even if this imputation had been accepted, however, an understanding with these same Powers, apart from the great body of neutral opinion, was better than a state of misunderstanding with all the nations, as a third of the Democratic Senators eventually concluded.

The Supplementary Treaties. As originally drawn, the Four Power Treaty had been so worded as to include apparently the entire Japanese archipelago in its scope. When this caused protest in this country and also in Japan, where it was felt that national pride suffered from the protection thus unequally given, a supplementary treaty was signed excluding the home islands of Japan, but including Formosa and the south half of Sakhalin.

Efforts were made to amend this treaty by removing Sakhalin from its protection, and to attach some of the old Lodge reservations to it, but without success. Senator Lodge himself was not now solicitous about multiplying reservations. Another supplementary agreement had been signed by the four powers saying that the Four Power Treaty should not be deemed to be an assent of the United States to the mandates over Pacific islands given by the League and that controversies to be considered under the treaty should not include "questions which according to princi-

[38] Senator Pittman, in *Congressional Record*, Vol. 62, Pt. 5, p. 4617.

ples of international law lie exclusively within the domestic jurisdiction of the respective powers." [39]

Lodge did not want the Senate to pass upon this one of the supplementary agreements. He thought such consideration was unnecessary and resisted it for some time until overborne with the usual argument that if it was not included in the bond after having been brought up in debate the Japanese could say it was not binding.[40] Senator Pittman then offered verbatim the Lodge reservation of 1919 to the League Covenant on the subject of domestic questions "out of the same abundance of caution which moved the Senator from Massachusetts." The press reported that the reservation was so involved that it caused merriment in the Senate galleries when read, and it aroused none of the old fervor on the floor of the Senate. Even Senator Lodge had cooled to it. He voted against it, as did most of the Senators who had stood with him two years before. The reservation was defeated 49 to 21, with 26 not voting.[41] It no longer seemed necessary to enumerate all the domestic affairs of which we retained control, including the traffic in women and children, in opium and other dangerous drugs, when associating ourselves with other nations.

As the French Saw It. The attaching of the Brandegee reservation to the Treaty had the effect of putting the French under severe temptation to add reservations of their own, inserting into the treaties by this means concessions they were unable to gain in the conference. The naval and Four Power treaties were not ratified by the French Parliament until July 8, 9, and 12, 1923, some sixteen months after ratification here. There was no objection to the Four Power Treaty on the ground that it was an alliance. On the other hand it was welcomed because of the opportunity for political association with England, Japan, and the United States which it gave. Some French editors had felt that it was effectively weakened as an alliance by the Senate reservation. The Paris *Journal* had declared that the reservation morally viti-

[39] *Congressional Record,* Vol. 62, Pt. 5, p. 4617.
[40] *Ibid.,* p. 4614.
[41] *Ibid.,* pp. 4541, 4615, 4620.

ated the treaty just as earlier ones had emasculated the Treaty of Versailles. The Pacific Treaty "was not concluded for truisms, but to substitute for the Anglo-Japanese Alliance mutual assurances for the nations bordering on the Pacific." Now America said again that she wanted the assurances but not the risks. A writer in *Action Française* was equally positive that the Senate, according to its habit, had "emptied the treaty of its contents." [42]

Briand, who had headed the French delegation to the conference, did not agree that the compact had been made worthless. Speaking for it in the Chamber of Deputies, he believed that: "When peoples threatened by war can meet and talk the thing over freely there is a large chance that war will be avoided." He hoped that similar regional groupings would be formed and that the thing would end in "vast compacts among all nations." [43]

The Protection of China

Two political agreements of great importance to China were concluded at the Washington Conference. A treaty between Japan and China restored Shantung to China and a Nine Power Treaty guaranteed her against future interference from Japan. The Wilson Administration, believing that Japan was trying to seize control of the national life of China while the war raged in Europe, had offered determined and persistent diplomatic support to China against Japanese demands, notably the famous Twenty-One Demands of January 18, 1916.[44]

[42] Thomas, *One Hundred Years of the Monroe Doctrine*, pp. 488-89; *New York Times*, March 27, 1922, July 9, 10, and 13, 1923.

[43] *New York Times*, July 10, 1923. Briand expressed his appreciation of Secretary Hughes's action in insisting that France be admitted to the treaty. No doubt this was a wise step from the standpoint of its ratification here as well. If France had not been included, the treaty would have appeared to Senators more exclusive still. It was a little more palatable also to those cordially disliking England or Japan.

[44] Paul S. Reinsch, *An American Diplomat in China*, Garden City, New York, 1922, pp. 64, 126 ff. The results of Minister Reinsch's work in China seem to have been considerably offset by the Lansing-Ishii agreement, concluded in Washington, November 2, 1922, which recognized that Japan had "special interests in China, particularly in that part to which her possessions are contiguous." Washington's explanation to the Chinese that only economic interests

At Paris, however, Wilson had consented to the cession of the German rights in Shantung to Japan, with a written understanding that political control would be handed back to China by Japan. This "immoral surrender" had been assailed by Wilson's opponents in the United States for many months with great violence, while China refused to concede to Japan the economic properties and privileges in Shantung which she had seized from Germany. When, therefore, Hughes and Balfour succeeded at Washington in inducing the Japanese and Chinese to agree upon terms for the retrocession of Shantung, the achievement was real.

The Shantung Treaty, signed February 6, 1922, provided that "Japan shall restore to China the former German leased territory of Kiao-Chau," together with all public property, except that which was needed for the use of the Japanese consulate and schools. The former German railroad from Tsingtao to Tsinanfu was to be turned over to China, but she was required to pay Japan for its assessed value. The ex-German mines were to be operated by a company in which Japanese capital could not exceed the amount of Chinese capital.

Of still greater significance was the Nine Power Treaty, signed by Japan with the other Pacific powers (excepting Russia) which guaranteed in the most explicit terms the territorial integrity and independence of China and the Open Door. In Article I the contracting powers, other than China, agreed:

(1) To respect the sovereignty, the independence, and the territorial and administrative integrity of China;

(2) To provide the fullest and most unembarrassed opportunity to China to develop and maintain for herself an effective and stable government;

(3) To use their influence for the purpose of effectually establishing and maintaining the principle of equal opportunity for the commerce and industry of all nations throughout the territory of China;

(4) To refrain from taking advantage of conditions in China in

---

were referred to did not appease the Chinese. Nor did it conform with Japan's ideas of what her interests on the mainland were. Robert L. Jones, *History of the Foreign Policy of the United States*, New York, 1933, pp. 422-23.

order to seek special rights or privileges which would abridge the rights of subjects or citizens of friendly States, and from countenancing action inimical to the security of such States.

In other articles the parties agreed: (1) not to make any treaties in the future which would "infringe or impair the principles stated in Article I"; (2) not to seek or support "any arrangement which might purport to establish in favor of their interests any general superiority of rights with respect to commercial or economic development in any designated region of China"; and (3) "fully to respect China's rights as a neutral in time of war to which China is not a party"—a provision which would prevent Japan from again going into China to drive out some other power, as in the Shantung case.

Article VII also provided in positive terms for consultation among the signatories in case there should be a violation of the treaty or a threat of violation.[45]

This treaty closed the long campaign of the Republican Senators to discredit Wilson, under guise of deep indignation about the rape of Shantung.[46] Throughout the long war on Wilson the Senators had charged, openly or by implication, that Japan could not be trusted to keep her agreement to restore Shantung. Now another Japanese promise to respect the integrity of China was freely accepted by Senator Lodge and his associates.

It was true that several other nations witnessed Japan's bond of future good behavior toward China, but it was also true that before signing it Japan had achieved secure naval control of the

[45] Article VII stated: "The Contracting Powers agree that, whenever a situation arises which in the opinion of any one of them involves the application of the stipulations of the present Treaty, and renders desirable discussion of such application, there shall be full and frank communication between the Contracting Powers concerned."

The full text of the Nine Power Treaty may be found in *Current History*, March, 1922, Vol. 15, pp. 1026-28; in Henry L. Stimson, *The Far Eastern Crisis*, New York, 1936, p. 267; and in the Department of State *Treaty Series*, No. 723.

[46] The insincerity of this campaign was never more clearly characterized than by Senator Porter J. McCumber in assailing the Shantung amendment gesture of his Republican colleagues on the Senate Foreign Relations Committee. He did not hesitate to term the Shantung weapon a poisoned dagger. *Congressional Record*, Vol. 58, Pt. 5, pp. 4345-48.

Orient. The 5-5-3 ratio awarded to her in the Five Power Naval Limitation Treaty was avowedly aimed at giving Britain, the United States, and Japan superiority over any other navy in their own waters. But in Japan's case her control of the Orient was buttressed by an agreement that neither Britain nor the United States would add to their existing fortifications north of Singapore or west of Hawaii. Control of all Chinese waters was turned over to Japan, and the possibility of recovering it from her practically abolished.

The solicitude of the Senate Republicans for China's future had borne strange fruit. Japan's proud imperialists had been called upon the international carpet, in Washington, compelled to disgorge some of their seizures, obliged to swear never to interfere with China again, and then presented with the power to do so without fear of future interference.[47]

Nor was there a moment's thought of strengthening the only control which thereafter could prevent Japan from becoming the absolute master of China's destiny, the League of Nations. Had the United States thrown its whole weight into establishing the authority of the League, the naval agreements would not have destroyed the safety of any people. In the absence of any effort to establish the League firmly, while there was time, full sway was guaranteed to that Japanese militarism about whose encroachments in China such indignation had been professed.

Within ten years we were to find ourselves hoping against hope that the League of Nations, with its authority and obligations weakened from the day of our repudiation of them, would do something strenuous to save China from Japanese invasion.

Naval Limitation outside the League

The political gains of the United States in the conference were more substantial. The Anglo-Japanese Alliance was dissolved, an

[47] Public statements were exchanged between Baron Shidehara and Secretary Hughes on the subject of Japan's continued occupation of Russian territory, in which Hughes stressed his understanding that Japan would evacuate. *Current History*, March, 1922, Vol. 15, pp. 1000-1006.

event which gave deep satisfaction to our diplomats. Our claim to full naval parity with Great Britain was also conceded, though it was to be nearly two decades before full equality was to be approached in fact. And, not least in importance, the Washington Conference achieved the first successful limitation of armaments. The limitation extended only to one powerful arm, dreadnoughts, but it turned naval rivalry into less expensive channels and opened the way for future efforts at disarmament. The date upon which unfinished warships were ordered scrapped was an important one in human history. The economies achieved were also large. The many people to whom the destruction of ships on the ways and the actual sinking of others seemed a sinful waste, did not look ahead to the great cost of completing and operating these huge craft.

Durable world disarmament, especially upon land, would have to come through the League of Nations, if at all. The gains made at Washington, or through the League, would be temporary, unless the League had power and energy enough to deal with the great political issues which give rise to armaments. It was unfortunate in the extreme that the Washington Conference was not a League conference and that its many treaties were not negotiated under the Covenant. Joined together, the treaties and the Covenant would have strengthened each other mutually, building a fine foundation for further achievements. As the first great success of a world-wide League of Nations they might well have averted that disintegration of the League, and of the Washington Treaties, which afterward took place. It was something to have the United States engage in sporadic good works, as Senatorial resolutions might direct, but it was of far greater moment that the world should feel the tremendous power and authority of the United States continuously behind the new effort of all the nations to organize and consolidate the peace through the League.

It was upon the League that the peace and security of all depended. If it went down, all lesser arrangements would disappear also.

CHAPTER VI

ISOLATION PERFECTED

IT WAS natural that after the close of the war there should be a letdown from the high level of endeavor which had been maintained until the Armistice. It was natural that hundreds of thousands of Americans suddenly picked up from their homes and sent to Europe on crowded transports should object to obedience to the army law of deference to officers, many of whom obviously had no particular fitness to command,[1] and that the Americans should too quickly look down upon a strange people who did not have much modern plumbing. It was equally certain that our own evaluation of our contribution to the common cause would not coincide with that of the French and English. We rightly felt it to be decisive and most expensive; the others could not forget the long agony of the years before we came, their huge casualty lists, and proportionately greater sacrifice of wealth.[2]

It was inevitable, too, that the effort of the American President to frame a peace of appeasement, without too much victory in it, should partially fail. There were too many hot war-passions still flowing in scarcely controllable tides. Most certain of all was stern resistance to a lenient peace by France, four times invaded by German armies within a century. Deeply seared by the interminable strain of the German pressure during the eternity that

[1] "Like all sons of frontiersmen they hated discipline and had little of the Teutonic willingness to obey an order simply because it was an order. War was as hateful to them because it meant loss of liberty as because it meant loss of life." Preston W. Slosson, *The Great Crusade and After*, New York, 1930, p. 34.

See also, concerning the backwash from the war, J. H. Denison, *Emotional Currents in American History*, New York, 1932, pp. 281-82.

[2] "Truly war is long! The loophole through which one peered at the ragged sandbanks of a Boche trench; the firing bank where one sat in the mud while a comrade watched; the icy water in which one's feet froze; the slimy shelter where straw rotted; then billets in desolated villages; inspections and reviews; all the burdens of barrack life,—such with death at the end was the lot of all—officers and men alike."—André Tardieu, *The Truth about the Treaty*, Indianapolis, 1921, p. 30.

began in August, 1914, spurred by the knowledge that she could never hope to withstand alone the superior industrial and man power of Germany, France's drive for security might be deflected, but not stopped.

Europe Left to Its Fate

Wilson and Lloyd George did manage to prevent France from seizing strategic security by permanently detaching the Saar Valley and the left bank of the Rhine from Germany, but only at the price of signing a treaty guaranteeing France against unprovoked attack by Germany until the League Council should decide by majority vote that the League offered sufficient protection to France. And when, as a move in an internal political struggle, the United States Senate refused even to consider approving this treaty, the effect upon all future European politics was certain to be profound. "France," pleaded one of her leading journalists, "has nothing to do with Republicans and Democrats in America; she recognizes and can only recognize Americans. If she is refused the guarantees asked for, because such guarantees are a source of displeasure to some; if she is refused the guarantees that the President of the United States offered her personally, because they do not suit others, what *are* the guarantees she is to have or take?" [3]

The predicament of the French was acute. It was conceivable, and seemed probable to many, that they might have achieved security by a generous peace to Germany, but France's almost fatal wounds of war would have prohibited her from taking that course, if older memories had not precluded it. Instead, she accepted the guarantee of temporary occupations of German territory on her eastern frontier and sought to establish as quickly as possible the liberated nations east and south of Germany. Thus she had a peace neither of reconciliation nor of conquest. Should she rely upon the infant League of Nations, or use the Rhine-Saar

[3] Stephen Lauzanne, "France and the Treaty," *North American Review*, November, 1919, Vol. 210, pp. 610-11.

occupations and the reparations bond to throttle Germany down as long as possible?

It is easy for us in remote physical security to urge the wisdom of the first course, but all possibility of France's espousing it in the first years after 1918 was removed by our repudiation of the League and the Anglo-American guaranty treaty.

No one could be more fully aware than the writer of the facts that we kept our war with Germany legally separate from the cause of the Allies, that a provision of our Constitution—unique among all civilized governments—gives one-sixteenth of our national legislature the power to defeat any treaty which the President may sign, and that, especially after the League had been rejected, we came to feel that our "Allies" had been too grasping after the war. No one could escape knowledge, either, of the deep offense which the American people took in later years when all reparation and war-debt payments ceased, as they were bound to cease long before sixty years had passed, even if the League could succeed in preventing new wars from sweeping the earth and devouring its resources.

Nevertheless, there can be no clear understanding of the tragic relapses of the post-war period toward war without an appreciation of the terrific blow which our abstention from the League gave to war-stunned Europe. America had waited long before intervening, but when she did move she came with a power and a purpose which thrilled all humanity with hope. Never before had a nation stepped upon a world stage with as decisive effect and as high aim. The peoples of the old world were too bound by old fears and new hatreds to follow any foreign leader for a long period. Indeed, they could not be expected to lose sight of all national objectives or fail to answer the rallying calls of their own leaders. Still, no candid student of the late war and post-armistice period can doubt that Wilson's call for a beginning in world government stirred the nations of all continents as no human call had ever done before. In all nations, too, many of the finest spirits clung to his objective as essential to the future of civilization, even though their compatriots returned to the search for older and more tangible rewards and safeguards.[4]

"Mr. Wilson may have been an unexpert negotiator," said a leading English publicist, in 1921:

He may have antagonized the Republican Party in his own country. He may have committed this or that minor error in tactics. But all that is dust in the balance compared to the main fact, that he had vision where the others had passion; that he looked to the future, while they looked to the past; that he drew his inspiration from reason and truth, while they drew their expertness from hatred, greed and fear. Nor is it only on the statesmen of Europe on whom the blame must be laid. It falls also on the peoples to whose passions they appealed, and who responded to the appeal. Their electorates were behind them urging them on even had they wished to halt.

The prophet lies sick and broken now, and every dog barks at him. Would that my voice were strong and authoritative enough to bear to him, while he yet lives, that verdict of posterity which will acclaim him as the first statesman who ever came to an international conference of victory to put humanity above country, the interests of the peoples above that of their rulers, reason above passion, justice above revenge, and reconciliation and peace above all. The powers of this world defeated him, and men will pay, and are paying, dearly for it. But if there is to be any continuing civilization for mankind, if there is to be any movement toward a better and juster society, his name will live when those of his adversaries are lost in ignominy; his star will shine from the heaven of our fixed lights when their marsh fires are vanished, together with the swamp on which they fed.[5]

Mr. G. Lowes Dickinson's record of the effect of the entry of the United States into the war under Wilson's leadership is that:

When America entered the war, although we saw that she would thereby prolong it, we ventured to believe that that evil would be

[4] "There was never a more popular figure in Europe than President Wilson. His clean, smiling face, squarely chiselled, stirred the emotions of men from London to Athens, from Moscow to Rome. Out of the fiery furnace the common people came with strong determination that never again should war devastate the world. They rejoiced in the advent of Mr. Wilson. He represented for them their aspiration. He was the embodiment of a universal demand."—Sisley Huddleston, *Europe in Zigzags*, London, 1929, pp. 337-38.

[5] G. Lowes Dickinson, "SOS—Europe to America," *Atlantic Monthly*, February, 1921, Vol. 127, p. 246.

justified by the results. There had stepped into the arena, like a champion of medieval legend, a nation that had no ends of her own to gain, a nation that stood, for the first time in all the long course of history, for Right, for humanity and for nothing else. Every successive utterance of the President renewed and enhanced our faith. That grave voice, sounding majestically above the shrill rhetoric of our own statesmen, carried with it the promise of a new world. And all that was young, all that was hopeful, all that was faithful in Europe turned to America as to the sun rising on a shipwrecked world.[6]

It was unavoidable that the complete abandonment of the League of Nations by the United States in 1920 should strike the peoples of Europe as an incredible event, so unbelievable that for years they continued to think that the domestic quarrel which gave rise to it would soon be adjusted. It seemed impossible to believe that a world leadership such as no nation had ever before held would be suddenly and voluntarily abandoned. It seemed impossible to conclude that the greatest moral leadership ever established should be followed at once by no leadership at all.

Sir John Foster Fraser has acknowledged the power of our leadership thus: "There would have been no League of Nations if it had not been for the moral force of the United States in favor of such a League. I was in America in 1918," added Sir John, "when the whole country, irrespective of party politics, was enthusiastically favorable to a League. When the formation began it was regarded as the glory of America, something that could never have been attempted except by a nation with the lofty principles of the United States." [7]

The disillusionment and sense of despair was universal, but nowhere deeper than in the defeated nations. The United States had sealed their doom. She had removed their last hope of a negotiated peace and had then hurled her tremendous economic and military power at them with such breath-taking speed that they were soon crushed. Surrendering to the United States, they had hoped too much that Wilson's principles would save them

[6] *Ibid.*, p. 245.
[7] *Current Opinion*, July, 1921, Vol. 71, p. 581.

from the consequences of defeat, and they had not appreciated how much his influence had ameliorated the terms imposed upon them. But American participation in the administration of the peace treaties was counted upon by everyone, especially the Germans. The very detachment of the United States from the national complexes which dominated Europe was assurance that the settlements would be administered under the influence of some second thought. After our election in 1920 a German editor cried out, with foreboding despair: "First the Americans make a scrap heap of Europe and then withdraw with a noble gesture of duty, leaving Europe to its misery." [8]

This is a charge from which we instinctively shrink. Our part in a world war, we say, was only that of avenging a private quarrel against one of the many participants in the war, and when we had smashed his resistance our job was done. Let his other enemies do as they please with him.

This defense, too, might be accepted, if nothing was to be done to prevent or mitigate wars of mutual extermination. In that event, all sense of responsibility toward a beaten enemy could be disclaimed. Yet our power had also led to the swift and complete dissolution of two other great empires, the Austrian and the Turkish. The nations newly sprung from them struggled to find a footing, with some assurance of continued existence in the future, struggled without any sustaining hand from the world's greatest nation, except as its loans and charity reached out to tide over the worst threats of famine and communism. At the very best it did not lie in us to condemn them too harshly when they

[8] *Täglische Rundschau,* as quoted in the *Literary Digest,* December 6, 1920, p. 22.

From the Antipodes the comment was equally bitter. The Australian *Sydney Bulletin* said: "Another Germany may arise, and go mad, and tear President Wilson's Fourteen Points to pieces, and throw mud upon Senator Lodge's seven concrete terms and utterly defy the Covenant of the League. Congress reserves to the United States the right to go on trading with such a nation—presumably even to sell it munitions. . . . Of course the United States may interfere. . . . But only after profound conviction has satisfied Congress that interference is for the best from the United States' standpoint. It will enter the International business as a partner when a 15% dividend is reasonably certain."—*Literary Digest,* June 12, 1920, p. 31.

began hastily to make alliances with France and among themselves. Nor should we be totally unable to comprehend the continuing cries, to us among others, of an excessively mutilated Hungary for a mitigation of her fate and a tolerable national existence.

If in recent years the European nations have appeared to us as an aggregation of ungrateful peoples who will not pay their war debts, it is only just to recall that all over the Continent we were first remembered as the Great Power which smashed Europe to bits, promising a better and safer future for all, and then departed, leaving many sorely wounded nations to apply or disregard our prescription for future salvation as they chose. An inseparable part of that legacy is the memory of 1920, suggesting to men in every part of Europe that our form of government does not permit us to have a foreign policy.[9]

The War Debts Funded

Having elected to follow the anti-League wing of the Republican party, or to bow to the strength of the post-war reaction which its Senate leaders had stimulated and led, the Harding Government turned, in its domestic program, to the business of shutting out European goods and collecting our share of the war debts due from our former war associates.

Inter-Allied war debts had been contracted in large volume before we entered the war. In its early years Great Britain had not been militarily prepared to bear the brunt of the fighting, but she could and did finance those who held the lines. Before our own entry, Britain had loaned close to $6,000,000,000 to her allies, who in turn had loaned to each other about $2,000,000,000. These sums had been spent almost entirely in the country making

[9] It is not to be supposed that many Europeans know how small is the number of determined men which can defeat a treaty in the United States Senate. Legions of Americans do not know. When adherence to the World Court was defeated by a vote of 52 to 36, January 29, 1935, it was widely assumed here at home that a minority of the Senators favored accepting the Court, whereas the majority voted for it.

the loan, to finance the export of goods and supplies. This practice was necessary, if the Allies were to help each other effectively, because they could not otherwise raise the abnormal amounts of foreign exchange which would be necessary to move the unusual quantities of goods needed for unproductive purposes.[10]

When we entered the war we conformed to the already established practice, and for the same reasons. We could stiffen the resistance of the Allies by huge shipments of goods, while we trained and shipped our armies. It seemed to us the best kind of business, not only because it kept our farms and factories running profitably at high speed; the ranking leaders of Congress indicated that they were strongly inclined to regard the supplies as a gift to the common cause.[11]

Representative Claude Kitchin, Chairman of the House Ways and Means Committee, said, before the first great loans were approved in Congress: "You will understand that they will be fighting with our money their battles and will be fighting with our money our battles." Representative John J. Fitzgerald, Chairman of the Appropriations Committee, declared: "I have little sympathy with the suggestion that possibly we will not get our money back. I care not so much if we do, if American lives be preserved by the granting of the money." Congressman Henry T. Rainey, later chosen Speaker of the House, also stressed that we were not making these loans as an investment, but to "further our interests primarily in this world war. . . . Every blow struck at Germany by any of her enemies was struck also in our interest." Representative Martin B. Madden also, Republican "watch-dog of the Treasury," soon to be Chairman of the House Appropriations Committee, reminded the House that: "Everyone

[10] The most authoritative account of the creation of the war debts is that by Albert Rathbone, "Making War Loans to the Allies," *Foreign Affairs*, April, 1925, Vol. V, pp. 1-28. Mr. Rathbone was Assistant Secretary of the Treasury in charge of making the war loans from 1918 to 1920.

[11] Representatives Andrew Montague, of Virginia, and George Graham, of Pennsylvania, thought that large sums should be advanced to France as a free return for her help in financing the American Revolution. *Congressional Record*, Vol. 55, Pt. 1, pp. 672, 677.

knows that we will not have an army in the field for a year or more than a year, and our duty to posterity and to liberty is to do everything we can do to win the victory for the American people and for the liberty of the world." Referring to the loans, he "would not care whether they were repaid or not." [12]

In the Senate, also, similar sentiments were expressed. Senator Reed Smoot, the coming Republican Chairman of the Finance Committee, believed that every dollar of the loans would be spent to uphold the principles in which we believed and for the benefit of the United States "whether spent by us or by the Allies." Senator Albert B. Cummins was for outright gifts. He would vote the necessary billions to the Allied nations "with never a thought of its repayment at any time under any circumstances." He warned that "in the years to come the fact that the United States has in its possession bonds of these great countries, which when they emerge from the war will all be bankrupt, will create an embarrassment from which the men of these days will find it difficult to escape." [13]

[12] *Ibid.*, p. 670. Representative Campbell, of Kansas, thought it a waste of time to talk about whether the loans would be repaid. James R. Mann, of Illinois, thought it "our highest duty" to give aid to those fighting our enemy. Joseph W. Fordney, of Michigan, emphasized that the loans were not an investment. Their sole purpose was to aid the Allies in fighting "our battle." Both Mann and Fordney hoped that the sending of the money would prevent any American boys from crossing the ocean.

Former Speaker Joseph G. Cannon, of Illinois, did not think of the loans as a gift, and J. Hampton Moore, of Pennsylvania, wanted the expectation of repayment understood.

In reply, James W. Collier, of Mississippi, described the "exorbitant" interest rates which the Allies had to pay because of their strained credit and felt that to strengthen that credit was to strike a severe blow at "the common enemy," a sentiment that was shared by Nicholas Longworth, of Ohio, a future Speaker of the House. "The cause of the Allies is now our cause," said Longworth. "Let us do everything possible to promote it. Their victory will be our victory; their defeat may mean our defeat." He closed by saying: "Above all, we act with the belief that the debt we are about to incur, stupendous though it is, is no greater than this, the greatest Republic of all time, owes to human civilization" (pp. 640, 647, 658, 668, 669).

See also the excellent memorandum of the *Foreign Policy Association, Information Service*, "The United States and the War Debts," by Lewis W. Jones, Vol. III, Spec. Supp. No. 1.

[13] *Congressional Record*, Vol. 55, Pt. 1, pp. 757, 762. Senator Borah also feared "the chain of evil consequences to flow from this peculiar and particular kind of transaction."

By 1921, the Republican leaders of Congress had been driven by their opposition to Wilson to attack the League, and by their opposition to the League to attack the Treaty, and by their opposition to the Treaty to deny that any common cause with the Allies had ever existed, or any high goal ever pursued together. Hence it was logical that on February 9, 1922, five days after the former Allies had left the Washington Conference, a law should go into effect calling upon them to surrender bonds bearing 4¼ per cent interest, payable within twenty-five years, to cover the goods advanced to them during the war.[14]

The Debt Funding Commission, however, consisting of Secretaries Mellon, Hughes, and Hoover, Senator Smoot, and Representative Burton,[15] negotiated funding agreements conceding lower and different rates of interest to the various debtors. The Commission found the total of the debts to be, with accrued interest at five per cent, $11,600,073,934.96 and succeeded in funding practically the whole amount. Thus it received bonds of United Kingdom, on July 5, 1923, to the amount of $4,600,000,000, to bear interest at 3 per cent to 1932 and 3½ per cent thereafter. The length of time required to liquidate the debt was also advanced to sixty-two years. This was done partly to meet the

In introducing the bill in the Senate, Chairman Simmons, of the Finance Committee, thought there was little else which we could do then to help "our allies." There would be long weary months before we could help them in the field. Senator Hoke Smith, of Georgia, also spoke of "our allies" and Senator Porter J. McCumber thought Americans should understand that even a $7,000,000,000 loan was not a large contribution to the cost of "the Great War in which we are now engaged." It had already cost Great Britain alone $40,000,000,000, and she was spending 140,000 lives a month (pp. 757, 747, 760).

14 Shortly before the election of 1920, on August 5, President Wilson had informed Lloyd George that it was "highly improbable that either Congress or popular opinion in this country will ever permit a cancellation of any part of the debt of the British Government to the United States."—United States Treasury, *Annual Report on State of Finances, 1925-26*, p. 72.

15 Senator Thomas J. Walsh, of Montana, contested the constitutionality of the Smoot and Burton appointments on the ground that whenever commissions are vested with power to deal finally with a matter they become officers of the United States. The Senate judiciary committee sustained this contention, declaring the two Congressmen ineligible to serve. After Attorney General Daugherty had pronounced this ruling erroneous, it was reversed by a vote of 9 to 7. *Congressional Record*, Vol. 62, Pt. 3, p. 2894; *New York Times*, February 23 and 27, March 7, 9, and 16, 1922.

objection of the British Government that it could not pay so large a sum in twenty-five years and partly to make it impossible for poorer governments to refuse to fund.

To facilitate further settlements, the principle of capacity to pay was adopted and liberally interpreted, especially in favor of the Fascist government of Benito Mussolini. Italy's settlement on November 14, 1925, called for no interest on her $2,000,000,000 debt until 1930, one eighth of one per cent until 1940, and one quarter of one per cent until 1950. Principal payments were likewise small, beginning with $5,000,000. Settlement with France was not reached until April 29, 1926. On her $4,000,000,000, France was to pay interest at 1 per cent for ten years beginning in 1930 and rising to an eventual 3½ per cent.

None of the settlements recorded any cancellation of the principal. Assuming the collection of 5 per cent interest on principal payments extending over sixty-two years, the various interest rates granted represented handsome "cancellations," ranging from 30 per cent to 80 per cent in the case of Italy.[16] These adjustments seemed fair to the Funding Commission. To many they seemed unfair to Great Britain, a heavy creditor to the other Allies and the first to assume her debt to the United States. The capacity of the nations to pay was also quickly to be proved a highly variable thing. The time was soon to come when Britain's inability to pay would become quite clear, at a moment when the gold reserves of France were enormous and her economic condition still good.

In 1926, with sixty years stretching out before him, each to bring several hundred million dollars back from Europe to the United States Treasury, Secretary Andrew W. Mellon could say confidently that our financial policies toward Europe were "directed not toward ameliorating merely present hardships but

[16] Estonia, Finland, Great Britain, Hungary, Latvia, Lithuania and Poland, 30 per cent; Czechoslovakia and Rumania, 37 per cent; Belgium and France, 60 per cent; Greece, 72 per cent; Austria, 74 per cent; Jugoslavia, 76 per cent; Italy, 80 per cent. Erik Achorn, *European Politics and Civilization since 1815*, New York, 1934, pp. 648-50.

toward laying the foundations for a prosperity that will be permanent."[17]

American Tariffs Raised

The effort of the Harding Government to collect the war debts was apparently successful. Yet from its beginning it was accompanied by a simultaneous campaign to make repayment impossible, as every economist, banker, or citizen who had some knowledge of international trade well knew. For with one hand the Congress elected in 1920 demanded payment of the war debts and with the other it enthusiastically erected tariff barriers to keep the demanded payments from entering the country.

Our New Creditor Position. Before the war the Department of Commerce did not make as careful an effort to keep a balance of our international payments as it did after Herbert Hoover became its Secretary in 1921. Everyone knew, nevertheless, that the United States was a debtor country and always had been. From colonial days down to 1914 European capital had come to the United States to build our canals and railways, to develop our mines and erect great industries. These huge investments, accelerating our development greatly as they came, were repaid chiefly out of the abundant raw materials, especially cotton, which we produced. We always had an ample export surplus of goods with which to meet our debts. The industrial equipment which the older industrial countries shipped to us was returned with interest in cotton and copper, meat and wheat. From the standpoint of our debtor position, too, our capacity to pay was properly protected, particularly after 1860, by tariffs which insured a permanent "favorable" balance of trade, that is, one sufficiently unfavorable in the exchange of valuable products to enable us to meet our debts.

This debtor position had been headed toward liquidation be-

[17] Andrew W. Mellon, "Our Best Customer," *Saturday Evening Post,* June 19, 1926, p. 82. For the details of the various debt settlements, see the *United States World War Foreign Debt Commission Reports,* Government Printing Office, Washington, 1927.

fore the war. In 1914, our net debt to the Old World was but $3,000,000,000,[18] and it did not take it long to disappear after the avalanche of war supplies began to leave our shores. During the first half of 1915 alone, United States railway securities worth $480,972,000 were returned to us from abroad, in part payment for the torrent of goods required by the Allies. It is estimated that Great Britain had sent back $1,100,000,000 in American securities before January 1, 1916, when the British Dollar Securities Commission was formed. That Commission mobilized a further $1,-322,000,000 worth of our bonds and stocks for use in 1916.[19] As the securities ran out, too, gold came to our shores in increasing volume. From early 1915 to the close of 1921 our supply of gold was doubled, increasing by more than $1,500,000,000.[20] Finally, all these resources being insufficient to finance the vast fleets of heavily laden ships moving from our shores to Europe, we purchased $6,779,000,000 worth of foreign securities, during the war period.

According to the conservative estimates of George N. Peek, the war had changed the United States from a $3,000,000,000 debtor into a $6,000,000,000 creditor, aside from the $10,000,-000,000 of war debts.[21] The latter, in fact, represented the financing of the stream of our goods to Europe after all other means had practically dried up. So mighty was that current, indeed, that the Treasury had kept on financing it for months after the guns stopped firing, fearing that to block it would produce swift disaster to our farms and factories alike.

Not all of these figures were available to the lawmakers of 1921-1922. But no one who had been at all aware of the economic

[18] George N. Peek, *Letter to the President on International Credits for Foreign Trade and Other Purposes, 1896-1933*, Government Printing Office, Washington, 1934, p. 2.

[19] United States Department of Commerce Trade Information Bulletin No. 552, *Balance of International Payments of the United States in 1927*, p. 23.

[20] *Statesman's Year-Book*, 1933, p. 475.

The stock of gold in the United States increased from $1,818,188,000 in 1912 to $3,784,652,000 in 1921. The increase of $1,966,464,000 was more than 100 per cent. *Statistical Abstract of the United States*, 1933, p. 402.

[21] *Letter to the President*, cited above.

effects of the war (as what business man was not?) could doubt that the United States had been changed from a debtor to a heavy creditor. Nor was it possible to doubt that the vast credits now in our hands represented goods which had been shipped from our ports in countless thousands of ships, toward which endless trains had converged through every hamlet for five years.

The quantity of real wealth which had left the country was almost inconceivable to any mortal mind, but the first thing which the Republican leaders did was to move to prevent any compensating return flow of usable goods. The ancient cry that the "pauper labor" of Europe would get us now was at once raised, and the Republican Congresses made haste to frame higher tariffs, lest a Europe impoverished and ruined to the point of social dissolution should suddenly overwhelm us with a vast flood of things to eat and to wear and to enjoy. It almost seemed that having made war upon Europe with our goods, during her helplessness, we must now quickly arm ourselves to repulse her retaliation.

Wilson's Last Veto. This first effort of the architects of "Normalcy" was halted by President Wilson's veto of the proposed emergency tariff. His veto message was read to the House of Representatives shortly after midnight, on the morning of March 4, 1921. Conscious that it was hearing the last of a long succession of state papers which had influenced American and world history as the utterances of few preceding Presidents had, the House listened with unusual quiet.

"Very little reflection," said the President, "would lead anyone to conclude that the measure would not furnish in any substantial degree the relief sought by producers of most of the staple commodities which it covers." It was obvious that, except for sugar and wool, "actual relief can come only from the adoption of constructive measures of a broader scope, from the restoration of peace everywhere in the world, the resumption of normal industrial pursuits, the recovery particularly of Europe." What the farmers needed most of all was larger foreign markets.

It was "not a little singular that a measure which strikes a blow at our foreign trade should follow so closely" the action of Congress to renew the activities of the War Finance Corporation in aid of foreign marketing. It was equally remarkable that we had been "vigorously building up a great merchant marine and providing for the improvement of marketing in foreign countries, by the passage of an export trade law and by the promotion of banking agencies in foreign countries." Now it appeared "that we propose to render these measures abortive in whole or in part."

Certainly, the time was not one in which to fear foreign competition, "with our principal competitors in varying degrees sadly stricken and laboring under conditions from which they will not recover for many years." Nor was it a moment in which to obstruct Europe's payment of her great debts to us. With Europe now owing us in excess of $9,000,000,000 in war debts and more than $4,000,000,000 in commercial debts, there were only three ways in which she could repay us, "namely by establishing private credits, by the shipment of gold, or of commodities."

The first two methods were not available. Accordingly: "If we wish to have Europe settle her debts, governmental or commercial, we must be prepared to buy from her." And if we wished

> to assist Europe and ourselves by the export either of food or raw materials or of finished products, we must be prepared to welcome commodities which we need and which Europe will be prepared, with no little pain, to send us. Clearly this is no time for the erection here of high trade barriers. It would strike a blow at the large and successful efforts which have been made by many of our great industries to place themselves on an export basis. It would stand in the way of the normal readjustment of business conditions throughout the world, which is as vital to the welfare of this country as to that of all the other nations. The United States has a duty to itself as well as to the world, and it can discharge this duty by widening, not by contracting, its world markets.

The logic of Wilson's final warning was inescapable. There was no way by which a great creditor nation could continue playing the role of a debtor, unless temporarily by the method of constantly plunging the world deeper into its debt, an expedient so dangerous that the President does not seem to have considered it possible.

The steepness of the proposed rates disturbed him, not only because of their profoundly grave international implications, but because they indicated a return to "a policy of legislation for selfish interests which will foster monopoly and increase the disposition to look upon the Government as an instrument for private gain, instead of an instrument for the promotion of the general well being."

Noting that the proposed rates were as high or higher than the Payne-Aldrich Tariff, Wilson could not believe that "the sober judgment of the masses," or even of the special classes favored, would sanction such a reversion. But Wilson's parting admonition was no more effective than Christ's farewell cry to Jerusalem. The interests with a stake in high duties were converging upon Washington, and the Congressional leaders who had endured in bitterness eight years of unaccustomed absence from the seats of power were ready to welcome them. Wilson's veto was sustained in the expiring Congress by a vote of 132 for it to 201 for overriding. But in the special session immediately following, the bill was reintroduced, April 11, 1921, passed with embellishments, and signed by President Harding on May 27, to become effective at once.

The Fordney-McCumber Tariff of 1922. Then the really serious business of restoring "protection" began. By July 7, Chairman Fordney was able to report a general tariff revision to the House of Representatives, and to secure its passage July 21. The Senate Finance Committee opened its hearings on November 7 and received a new stream of pleas for protection on everything from matches to church statuary. Industrial giants, grown enormous on war profits, vied with weaker manufacturers, all pleading that the world be not permitted to retaliate upon them for what they had just done to it.

These pleas fell upon sympathetic ears. It was December 31 before they could all be heard and April 11, 1922, before they could be digested into the Fordney-McCumber Bill. It required 2,057 amendments to partially appease the fears of struggling industries.[22] Then the Senate itself took over the task and wrestled with it fitfully until late August, adding about 400 additional amendments.

The knowledge of the Senators about the defense needs of thousands of products proved to be all-embracing, sufficient to every end. They argued over the proper rate for acetic acid, voted a duty on ammonium nitrate after a long session, rejected an increased duty on citrate of lime, adopted higher duties on paint products, refused to restore cement to the free list or to cut the duty on quarry tiles, defeated a move of the farm bloc to increase the duty on quicksilver, and acted on casein and carbon. Drawing upon deep wells of economic wisdom, they increased the duty on steel wire in one vote and rejected a cut in the proposed rate for light bulbs in another. They wrangled over the rates on glass products and fixed at just the right point the rates on firearms and bicycles. One ballot restored brick and cement to the free list and another removed sewing machines and cash registers from it.[23]

The Fordney-McCumber Tariff was signed by the President on September 21, 1922. In it the new masters of the world's greatest creditor nation doubled the rates on plate glass and chrome; increased the duties on toys from 35 per cent ad valorem to 70 per cent, on laces from 60 per cent to 90 per cent and on silks 45 per cent to 55 per cent; lifted cutlery rates from 25 per cent to as high as 175 per cent, clocks from 30 per cent to 50 per cent, furniture from 25 per cent to 60 per cent and gloves (cotton) from 35 per cent to 75 per cent. With the world owing us $16,-000,000,000, the tariff makers of 1922 raised the duty on sugar from 1 to 1.76 cents a pound and on lemons from 14 per cent to 88 per cent; taxed beef 3 cents a pound; took wool from the free list, giving it 31 cents a pound protection, and levied a new tariff

[22] *New York Times,* April 19, 1922.
[23] *New York Times,* May 3, 12, 15, 18, 20, 22, 23, and 28, June 1 and 9, 1922.

of 30 to 42 cents a bushel on wheat, of which we had a perennial surplus. The wheat farmers could then be told that they, too, had protection, though the milling industry, the railroads, and ports which had formerly handled large quantities of Canadian wheat in transit to Europe suffered losses which did the growers of a surplus commodity no good.[24]

While the bill was in process of enactment, there were warnings from financial leaders that Europe could not pay its debts if the bill passed, but no one in power paid any attention. The long delay in enacting the bill was not due to any sober second thought on the part of the men who had declared immediately after our decisive intervention in the world's greatest political disturbance that we could have nothing to do with world politics. The delay was long because no one knew, or could find out, just what rates would bar the dreaded European goods. One could not be sure that a given rate would keep Swiss watches from leaping to the wrists of American men who would like them. It was chiefly because of this dread with respect to hundreds of desirable commodities, that the bill gave to the President the right to raise or lower duties 50 per cent. The rates established were higher than those of the Payne-Aldrich Tariff of 1909, which had had such an important part in preparing the last Republican downfall, but in case they were not high enough to keep the wily British from slipping English tweeds upon our backs, the genial Senator who had been selected to occupy the President's chair could be relied on to defeat them by a swift proclamation.

The flexible tariff provision was, however, a first confession by Congress that it could not fix 4,000 tariff rates by any rule of reason or logic. The method of tariff making by logrolling was flayed in the strongest terms by Senators Simmons, of North Carolina, and Walsh, of Montana, in a statement issued September 1, 1922. They charged that "Congress has maintained for months a

[24] *A Comparison of the Tariff Acts of 1909, 1913 and 1922*, Government Printing Office, Washington, 1924; *New York Herald Commercial and Financial Chronicle*, September 23, 1922, p. 1389; "The Tariff in an Unbalanced World," *Chase Economic Bulletin*, November 19, 1923, Vol. III, No. 5, p. 151.

bargain counter where tariff duties were sold to organized cliques and combines whose joint strength could command a majority of votes." Looking beyond the approaching Congressional election, the two Senators asked: "In view of the indefensible, scandalous pork-barrel character of this legislation, how much longer can our law-making body retain the confidence and respect of the American public?" [25]

The elections which occurred a month later showed a strong recoil from the great wave of partisan, racial, and sectional fury with which the Senate cabal [26] and the reactions from the war had overwhelmed Wilson. The Republican majority in the House fell sharply from one hundred and fifty to fifteen, the slender new majority including several radical Republicans. In the Senate the party's margin dropped from twenty-two to ten, including again several liberals who could not be counted upon to support the party's economic policies.

But, incontestably, "Normalcy" had arrived. The United States had suddenly abandoned a world leadership such as no other nation had ever had or could exercise. After the most stupendous of political interventions in the affairs of Europe and Asia, she had covered a precipitate retreat with strident assertions of the virtues of the Monroe Doctrine, which no nation dreamed of challenging. After carrying a new world league of all the nations through the vital stage of organization, she had surrendered the one positive gain which she could possibly get from the disaster of the World War—reasonable security against another—and retired to the insistent repetition of Washington's precepts as the only true means of salvation, immediately after the inextricable entanglement of all nations had been proved beyond all possibility of questioning.

After having expanded her commerce swiftly from the Rio Grande to Cape Horn, having extended it throughout the Orient

[25] *New York Times*, September 1, 1922.

[26] The term used by George Harvey, the organizer of the group. George Harvey, *Henry Clay Frick the Man*, New York, 1928, p. 329.

and covered all Europe with a heavy blanket of obligations to her, the United States had hastily sought the shelter of William McKinley's economics, simultaneously demanding that the nations render to us their dues. Having become the world's premier gold holder and creditor, with no chance whatever of recovering her war "investments" except in the form in which they had been made —goods and services—she deliberately added unprecedented heights to her fiscal barriers.

"Business as usual" was the slogan of the reaction. In the world's political affairs, no responsibility; in its economic life an old-fashioned, bouncing, "favorable" balance of trade, with the world still and always obliged to take more of our wealth than it returned. Nothing had changed. The eloquence of Borah had moved the political clock back to 1794 and the political skill of Henry Cabot Lodge had retarded the economic dial to 1896. Let nothing now interfere with business!

Reparations Payments Enforced

There is no ground for believing that if the United States had taken the part in reorganizing the world which was implicit in her leadership during the war, everything would have developed differently, that political stability in Europe would have been quickly achieved, the worst errors of the new map rapidly revised, and the reparations nightmare easily resolved before it ran into tragedy.

The Great Illusion had possessed all the nations before the war and it still held them in its grip. A few men, notably Norman Angell, had explained that no future large-scale war could be made to pay for itself by anything that could be exacted from the defeated enemy.[27] But the peoples would not believe. Was the levying of indemnities not as old as war? And had they not been collected from France by Germany, with great ease and profit, as

[27] Norman Angell, *The Great Illusion*, London, 1914. Angell's warning was even generally and persistently twisted into an assertion that there would never be any important wars in the future.

late as 1870? Now Germany should pay for the war which it was believed she had deliberately begun.

The Basis of Reparations. At the insistence of the Allies, President Wilson's proposal of compensation for damage done in the occupied regions was expanded in the armistice terms to say that "compensation will be made by Germany for all damage done to the civilian population of the Allies and their property by the aggression of Germany, by land, by sea, and from the air." Under this formula, too, the British, led by Premier Hughes of Australia, and supported by France, Serbia, and others, argued in the Peace Conference for the inclusion of all war costs as "damage done to the civilian population."

This contention was consistently and successfully opposed by the American delegation. A variant of it, however, that the damages to civilians must include war pensions was eventually accepted by Wilson, after the arguments in favor of inclusion had been very persuasively presented by General Jan Smuts, of South Africa, in a memorandum of March 31, 1919. His argument that the people who had lost husbands and fathers were just as much entitled to reparation as those who had lost houses and livestock, was difficult to controvert, but it doubled the claims which were to be laid upon Germany.[28]

The amount to be claimed was so huge, in fact, that the only question left was, how much of it could Germany pay? Partly because no one knew and partly because the Allied publics expected such fantastic sums, Lloyd George and Clemenceau refused to fix the reparation total, leaving it to the Reparations Commission to extract all that was possible. It was stipulated only that Germany should pay $5,000,000,000 by May 1, 1921.

Early Claims and Deliveries. It was not until two days before that date that the Reparations Commission announced that the

[28] Thomas W. Lamont, in E. M. House and Charles Seymour, *What Really Happened in Paris*, New York, 1921, pp. 260-63, 268-72, 275. The Smuts memorandum is given in H. W. V. Temperley, *A History of the Peace Conference*, Vol. V, pp. 272-74.

The American experts estimated the pension item as $15,000,000,000, and the physical damage chargeable to the Germans as an equal sum.

reparation total would be $32,000,000,000. Three months earlier, the Allied Governments had demanded $56,000,000,000, which in turn was a considerable reduction from the $120,000,000,000 talked of in Lloyd George's 1918 election campaign. But the $32,000,000,000 figure left Germany no hope of escape. The $500,000,000 (plus certain sums) required of Germany annually did not even represent interest on the total fixed, so that the total must continue to grow.

It is not remarkable, therefore, that Germany lacked the will to pay. Especially was this true of the wealthy German industrialists, who busily sent as much of their funds out of the country as they could, lest they be taxed for reparations. It was not strange, either, that the Germans should feel that they had paid the initial $5,000,000,000 required of them in kind (coal, rolling stock, etc.) before the Reparations Commission figures so indicated. Disagreement over this calculation led to the Allied occupation of Düsseldorf, Duisburg, and Ruhrort, industrial centers on the right bank of the Rhine, on March 8, 1921. This action, coupled with a threat to occupy the whole Ruhr district, compelled Germany to assume the burden laid down by the Commission.

She managed, too, to make one payment of $250,000,000 on August 31, 1921, but obtained a partial moratorium for 1922, in March, reducing her monthly payments to $12,500,000. These were met until August 14, when the Reparations Commission was compelled to accept treasury bills "taking into account the fact that the German state had lost its credit both internal and external, and that the mark had depreciated continuously down to three one-thousandths of its normal value." [29]

The Reparations Dilemma. The reparations conflict had reached a complete deadlock. The Allies had always been compelled to choose between assisting Germany to become again a great industrial and commercial power, or the loss of their reparations claims. If they chose the first course, Germany would

[29] F. Lee Benns, *Europe since 1914,* New York, 1934, p. 262. Pages 256-90 contain an excellent account of the reparations struggle.

quickly become their competitor in all the world's markets, including their own. Even more alarming to France, Germany would at once become potentially a powerful military factor. Was the result of the war to be that the enemy which had lately bled them white must rapidly become again the strongest power in Europe? Frenchmen could not accept that result. Nor could they believe that the all-powerful Germany of yesterday could be too poor to pay reparations today.

But the horns of the dilemma which Norman H. Davis had clearly stated at Paris[30] were implacable. The Allies could not collect reparations from Germany without permitting her to become an industrial giant, encroaching upon their foreign markets. Also the bulk of the wealth of Germany was immovable. It could not be carted out of the country. Rolling stock, cattle, machinery, coal, and timber could be and were moved to France and Belgium in large quantities, as they had been transported into Germany during the war. Yet these commodities could not be obtained or used without limit. They competed with French products and threw British miners out of work in great numbers. The protests of injured domestic industries were by no means inaudible.

Gold could be taken while Germany's supply lasted, but as it soon gave out the Reich Government had no choice but to print paper money. In January, 1921, the mark, already inflated, stood at 45 to the dollar. A year later the quotation was 162, and as the reparations payments continued, fitfully and inadequately from the standpoint of the Allies, it fell to 435 to the dollar in July, 1922, when the Commission recognized that cash payments must cease. The decline of the mark, however, did not halt. By September a dollar would buy 1,303 marks, and by December, 6,865.[31]

Suspicion would not down that the Germans, particularly the industrialists, were deliberately pushing the inflation of the mark.

[30] See S. J. Woolf, "Norman Davis Talks War and Peace." *New York Times Magazine*, November 17, 1935, p. 3.

[31] R. L. Buell, *Europe: A History of Ten Years*, New York, 1929, pp. 51, 53.

The declining mark enabled German exporters momentarily to leap over all tariff barriers abroad and to expand their physical holdings at home. The inflation furnished evidence to the world, also, that Germany could not pay reparations, while it brought in sizable returns from all those Americans who would gamble in marks.[32] Still, the heavy pressure on Germany of unlimited claims for reparation could hardly be doubted. Like her enemies, Germany had been impoverished by the war, but, unlike them, had been starved by the blockade. To attempt to recover she had to import great quantities of raw materials—and foodstuffs—thus acquiring a large "unfavorable" balance of trade.

But the payment of reparations required a large surplus of exports, a "favorable" balance. There was no other way by which reparations could continue to be paid, just as there was no way for the war debts to be paid, except by a flow of goods and services into the United States and Britain. There was no such thing as international money. The huge intergovernmental claims left by the war could be satisfied only by such streams of goods and services as would provide sufficient foreign exchange to record the transfers on the books of banks and governments. "Money" of any kind was wholly inadequate to the demand, even gold, which could be shipped about. The gold could accumulate in the vaults of the chief creditor nations, as it had already begun to do, in such quantities as to undermine both the international exchange of goods and the currency systems of debtor countries, but these results could only impede and bring toward extinction that perpetual transfer of governmental debts which had been planned to continue for several generations.

Deadlock. It was an almost hopeless entanglement in which all the nations which had fought were involved, and from which they could not be extricated until they had come by very slow degrees to see that no nation, unless it be little Belgium, could

[32] A *New York World* inquiry in 1922 estimated that $960,000,000 had been "invested" in German marks since the Armistice. Some 80,000,000,000 marks had been bought at $12.00 to the thousand and other billions at 70 cents a thousand. *Annual Register*, London, 1922, p. 288.

recover its war losses in important measure—and then only by subordinating its current economic interests to the transfer of goods based upon the past destruction of wealth. In 1922 no nation was ready to recognize the choices which must be made, least of all the French, who had incurred a fresh debt of several billion dollars to cover the reconstruction of their devastated regions in anticipation of the payment by Germany of vast reparations. Was France now to carry this new burden while she bound up her enemy's wounds and helped to set him on his feet, re-establishing his vanished credit by supplying him with new funds and by greatly scaling down her reparation claims against him?

Either that had to be done, or France had to attempt forcible foreclosure on the physical property of a great nation. She chose to make the latter uncharted attempt. The Germans should be compelled to pay, in spite of some difficulty in establishing a legal default on their part. The Reparations Commission had estopped Poincaré from claiming a default in cash payments, but he eventually discovered the matter of telegraph poles. The Germans had delivered only 59,000 of the 200,000 poles specified in the Treaty. In defense, they protested that this default was not voluntary. The collapse of the mark had disrupted their contracts with the timber companies.[33]

The plea was at least plausible, but it did not deter that French statesman who was even more stern against Germany than Clemenceau. Poincaré demanded authority from the Reparations Commission to seize the industrial heart of Germany and got the mandate, by a vote of three to one, only Great Britain protesting. For Britain such a venture could only mean partial economic paralysis in Europe and an aggravation of the grave unemployment existing in her own land, which she had promised would be "fit for heroes." It would be much easier to start the armies marching again than to liquidate the losses and hatreds which they would create.

[33] Buell, *Europe: A History of Ten Years*, pp. 54-55.

The United States Apart. At no point in the post-war years was the loss of American participation in the peace settlements felt more keenly. When the Reparations Commission was created, everyone had taken it for granted that the United States would occupy its seat, along with Great Britain, France, Italy and one nation to be selected from the other Allies. Belgium was made the fifth member.

It had been the intention of Lloyd George that this Commission by determining Germany's capacity to pay should prevent her from being overloaded. His calculation was that Great Britain and the United States would have the controlling influence. This was a reasonable certainty, not only because of the predominant economic power of the Anglo-Saxon Powers, but because, as the guarantors of France's security, they would have a large measure of control over her policy. The possibility of the three continental Allies outvoting the British and American representatives on the Commission existed, but it was not a strong probability. Security was France's main concern. With it she could be open to reason; without it the prevention of German recovery "was sure to be the controlling purpose of French policy."[34] And if unallayed and uninformed national passion had been too strong in France to be easily deflected, it is hardly likely that Italy and Belgium would have overruled the vote of the greatest economic power among the nations in order to insist that the enduring tragedy of the Ruhr occupation be enacted. It is impossible in any great international body, even in the Council of the League itself, to prevent the voice of a mighty nation from carrying much greater weight than that of a weaker one.

The element of impartiality, the ability to consider calmly facts and violently opposed positions, was needed in the Reparations Commission most of all. Again, it is not to be inferred that the relatively detached reasoning of the United States delegate would have prevailed in all cases. Assuredly, there was no reason

[34] F. H. Simonds and Brooks Emeny, *The Great Powers in World Politics*, New York, 1935, p. 235. See also pp. 233-34, 241.

why our view should have dominated throughout, deeply concerned as France and her allies were. Nor is it to be presumed that the United States would have been continually convulsed by European enmity or compelled to assume all Europe's financial and economic burden, as some allege. As events did develop, the United States found herself without voice or vote to defend either her own great claims to Europe's future wealth or her more important stake in reciprocal commercial intercourse with a settled, peaceful Europe. The balance expected in the Reparations Commission did not exist. Instead, the British were isolated and were unable to forward a settlement that would advance prosperity for everybody.[35]

International Action Demanded by Borah. The American Government was by no means unaware of the gravity of the crisis of 1922. Even Senator Borah was acutely conscious of it. For ten days, in December, 1922, he pushed for the calling, in Washington, of a world economic conference that would also limit the armies and all naval vessels below the battleship class.[36]

Against his proposal to regulate thus all outstanding world problems—and incidentally to disarm France—Senator Borah's associates in the defeat of the League and the Treaty levied both argument and ridicule. Lodge reminded him that when we acted as host to a conference we could not veto freely any proposition

[35] Writing in 1921, Thomas W. Lamont, a leading banker and one of the American financial experts at the Peace Conference, said concerning our absence from the Reparations Commission: "This omission has, in my judgment, been, in considerable measure, responsible for the lamentable delay that has occurred in fixing the amount of the German indemnity. The Americans were always a moderating influence throughout the Peace Conference. There was no reason why they should not continue as such in the post-treaty deliberations. They would have occupied a position of peculiar impartiality by reason of the fact that, under the action of the reparations commission itself, the United States expected to receive little or no compensation. Our failure to name a delegate for this commission has been not merely a great disappointment to our former associates in the war, but has, I believe, been largely responsible for the continued unsettlement in Europe, with its unfortunate reflex upon our own industrial and commercial business."—House and Seymour, *What Really Happened in Paris*, p. 285.

[36] For the text of Borah's proposed amendment to the naval appropriation, see *Congressional Record*, Vol. 64, Pt. 1, p. 84.

which might be made. He joined with Senator Hiram Johnson in suggesting that the war debts and our participation in the Reparations Commission could not be kept out of such a conference. Johnson was so shocked that he was moved to prefer "a League of Nations with some rules of procedure, with the members bound by some preliminary agreement, to this general omnibus endeavor which has neither limitations nor specifications." But he ridiculed the whole idea of trying to settle things by conferences.[37]

But these protests did not deter Borah. In beginning the debate he maintained that a crisis had been reached in the affairs of Europe which closely affected our own affairs. We were "further into the affairs of Europe now than we were on the 4th day of March 1921," and getting in deeper and deeper all the time. He scouted the suggestion that our "observer" in the Reparations Commission was not really active, and before giving up his drive a week later, cried out: "Talk about not being in Europe! That does not rise even to the level of sophistry. Talk about not being involved, and getting deeper day by day so long as the reparations question is unsettled, for that unsettles all Europe."

From his passionate concern about the situation one would never suppose that Borah had been one of those most responsible for our severing all connection with the pacification of Europe and the rest of the world after the war. That, however, he also explained. He had always believed in conferences. Not all of them had been ridiculous. There was the Portsmouth Peace Conference, ending the Russo-Japanese war, which President Theodore Roosevelt had called to settle a purely foreign question, "if any question can be a foreign question," yet peace had been won without our underwriting it or departing from the "doctrine of no entanglement."

[37] *Ibid.*, pp. 925-26; Pt. 2, p. 1046. Borah's Republican colleague from Oregon, Senator Charles McNary, in supporting him said: "I shall always think that much of the unrest and hatred existing among the nations at this time would not have occurred if that treaty containing the Covenant of the League of Nations, with the Lodge reservations, had been ratified" (p. 989).

Again, the Second Hague Conference had been called at the instance of President Roosevelt. True it did not prevent the Great War, but it did adjust many difficulties, and we had participated in it fully and vigorously, with a reservation which properly guarded our traditional policy, as we had in the Algeciras Conference, the success of which he also credited to Roosevelt. At Algeciras "it was through the leadership of the American representatives or their dominance at the conference that many of the different questions which at one time seemed insoluble were finally adjusted." Only four nations were directly concerned in the affairs of Morocco out of sixteen attending the conference, and every kind of question concerning the government of Morocco was considered and arranged. War had been prevented and the United States had signed with the rest, saying that we did so "without assuming obligation or responsibility for the enforcement thereof."

Finally the Great War had come suddenly, without conference. Did Borah shrink from that? Not at all. He said: "It has always been contended, and I think with some degreee of effectiveness, that had the nations of the earth been permitted to have a conference between the first day of July and the first day of August, 1914, and had the masses of the people been advised of the fact that war was at hand, a different condition of affairs would have resulted on the 4th day of August, 1914." [38]

At no point in his argument did Borah pause to say that no conference was held in 1914 precisely because the moral authority of one great nation, Great Britain, was not sufficient to draw the nations into conference. He did not suggest that the Hague Conferences were of no avail in 1914 because they had developed no permanent secretariat, no perpetual sequence of conferences among the powers which would make it difficult for any nation to abstain from conference in the hour of need and impossible to prevent the others from conferring at once. Nor did Borah mention that the Hague Conferences had imposed not the slightest

[38] *Congressional Record*, Vol. 64, Pt. 2, pp. 931, 1055, 1053, 1052.

obligation upon the nations to take some common action when a tragedy of monstrous magnitude threatened.

On the contrary, the success of the Washington Conference had confirmed him in the belief that we ourselves could continue to be the unfettered arbiter of all world affairs, however vast and complicated they might be. He had said many times that he "had no doubt as to the responsibility and as to the obligation of this Government with reference to effecting peace throughout the world." He had objected only to "a permanent alliance or a permanent league." The Round Robin of March 4, 1919, had only declared against the League of Nations "in the form now proposed," and in the Republican Convention of 1920 he had pressed earnestly, he declared, for the promise of an "association of nations" which "shall secure instant and general international conference whenever peace shall be threatened by political action." He still knew of no other way to meet these emergencies, "unless we propose to go into a permanent league."

Now, with Europe again drifting to a new collision which would leave some deeper scars than the war itself, did Borah admit that a permanent League, laboring incessantly to anticipate and adjust the crises which by his own enumeration had been frequent enough since 1905, might have enough to keep it very busy? Instead, he closed his plea for summoning the nations to Washington again, less than a year after they had been there, with the following burst of true but futile insight: "When shall we escape from the spell of war? When shall we loosen the grip of the monster? This is the most stupendous problem in the world today. Beside this question all other questions are subsidiary and incidental. Without a solution, and a favorable solution of this riddle, human progress becomes a misfortune, the inventions of the human mind a curse, and civilization, so called, an alluring trap into which men and women are ensnared to a death of unspeakable torture."

What was the answer to the "most stupendous problem in the world"? The remedy was certainly not to be found in one all-seeing, supremely eloquent, and wise Senator, standing in his impregnable tower of irresponsibility on Capitol Hill and prodding the President of the United States, at just the right moment, to summon the nations of the world to Washington to compose each crisis as it arises—always without obligation on the part of the United States.

No man, unless it be Lodge himself, has done more to confuse and distract American public opinion concerning its relation to world affairs than Senator Borah. His apparently boundless broad-mindedness, his deep sympathy for afflicted humanity, make even his insistence that there shall be no organized, sustained attack upon the world's problems seem like probable wisdom. His position was clear-cut in 1919; in the succeeding period his impressive joustings at world problems should entitle him to rank as the great confusionist.[39] Nor should his immediate responsibiltiy for the defeat of the Treaty of Versailles in the United States be forgotten, since it strongly encouraged the Germans to believe they could evade the Treaty, while our abstention steeled the French to enforce it.

In attempting to persuade Senator Borah from pressing his new conference, Senators Lodge, McCormick, and Watson all agreed, in the words of the latter, that the Administration had been holding informal conversations for two or three months concerning "just how far we could go, how far we might be asked to go, how far other nations would be willing to go, in the adjustment of the situation." [40]

Aside from this revealing statement, none of the three Senators

[39] *Ibid.*, pp. 1054, 1057. Replying to an unctuous statement of Lodge in the debate under review, Senator John Sharp Williams agreed that the League had not counted to the full. "Why? Because you took its right arm; you left it fightless; you left it almost ambitionless, but if you think the common people of America have been stupefied and annihilated by what you did you are mistaken. Long after you and I have gone out of public life there will be the common sense and conscience of the common people behind the idea of preserving and enforcing—mark you, enforcing—the peace of the world" (p. 928). Perhaps Senator Williams was right, but hardly so in the absence of clear-cut leadership.

[40] *New York Times*, December 30, 1922; *Congressional Record*, Vol. 64, Pt. 2, p. 1059.

explained further how delicate was that task, in the wake of the repudiation of the Treaty itself, to which their war on Wilson's League had carried them. They did not add that France, left without the protection either of her Treaty of Guarantee or of a strong League of Nations, was now going her bitter way, not disposed to listen to the men whom she regarded as her betrayers, and who were now advising that her claims upon Germany be moderated when enforcement might give her financial solvency and military security as well. But the American Government felt that it must do something to avert a tragedy for all the peoples concerned, even though it had surrendered its position of leadership and authority. Secretary Hughes could at least make a public appeal to France and propose a solution, unofficially of course.

Hughes's New Haven Address. This he did in an address to the American Historical Association at New Haven, on December 29, 1922. "There is not the slightest desire," said Hughes, "that France shall lose any part of her just claims. On the other hand, we do not desire to see a prostrate Germany. There can be no economic recuperation in Europe unless Germany recuperates." The "first condition of a satisfactory settlement is that the question should be taken out of politics," Hughes urged. But to this French spokesmen at once replied that it was a political question and nothing could make it otherwise. But to Hughes the alternative, forcible measures, was not attractive. "No one," he cautioned, "can foretell the extent of the serious consequences which might ensue from such a course. Apart from the political results, I believe the opinion of experts is that such measures will not produce reparation payments, but might tend to destroy the basis of those payments, which must be found in economic recuperation."

To work out a settlement, he proposed an independent commission of "men of the highest authority in finance in their respective countries." He was sure that "distinguished Americans would be willing to serve on such a commission." If proper steps were taken, "the avenues of American helpfulness cannot fail to open hopefully."

This was a strong statement, coming from the chief representative of a nation which had just abjured all European entanglements, though even its suggestion of loans to Germany could be said to fall within the isolationist formula: "In political matters, isolation; in all others, business as usual." But lest the Senate bridle at the boldness of his appeal, Hughes emphasized that:

> The economic conditions of Europe give us the greatest concern. They have long received the earnest consideration of the administration. It is idle to say that we are not interested in these problems, for we are deeply interested from an economic standpoint, as our credits and markets are involved, and also from a humanitarian standpoint. . . . We cannot dispose of these problems by calling them European, for they are world problems and we cannot escape the injurious consequences of a failure to settle them. They are, however, European problems in the sense that they cannot be solved without the consent of European Governments. We cannot consent for them. The key to the settlement is in their hands, not in ours. The crux of the European situation lies in the settlement of reparations. There will be no adjustment of other needs, however pressing, until a definite and accepted basis for the discharge of reparation claims has been fixed.

The advice was sound; it was well meant, and it stemmed from a valid national interest. But coming unofficially from a government which France regarded as having repudiated the obligations of two signed treaties, after persuading France to make an inconclusive peace, it could not have much weight. As Hughes said, the key was not in our hands. In the French view we had forfeited all right to send advice to the council chamber.

The Ruhr Occupied. Thirteen days after the Hughes plea, French and Belgian troops started marching into the Ruhr Valley, that vast forest of smokestacks from which originated three-fourths of Germany's heavy products and railway traffic. The Germans could not resist by arms, but neither could bayonets force them to operate the mines, factories, railways, telephones, telegraphs, or other aids to the Allied occupation. They could be put in jail, as thousands were, but that moved no coal to France. They could be deported or stirred to voluntary exile, to a total of 147,000, without creating any revenue, for the German Government supported the passive resistance by financial aid to those ousted and by decrees placing a penalty upon any who aided the invaders.

Yet none of these measures could keep the industrial paralysis from spreading out of the Ruhr across Germany and, to a painful degree, over the British Isles and all Europe. American commerce with the entire continental area was necessarily hurt. Nor was it improved by the angry effort of the occupying forces to operate the Ruhr mines and industries themselves. In spite of great strikes, they managed to send just enough materials back to France to enable a nominal paper profit to be claimed on the first year of occupation. The French countered, too, by encouraging separatist movements which enlisted little support.

One thing only was accomplished with total success—the extinction of the mark. All hands aided in that tragedy. Money to replace the government's sinking revenues, and to finance the passive war in the Ruhr, poured from the German presses in an ever-widening torrent, sweeping away the savings of the middle classes and bringing to poverty all who could not manage to get hold of some physical property. Within a month the mark had dropped from 8,000 to the dollar to 50,000. In June a dollar would buy 100,000 marks; thirty days later, 200,000; and by August, 5,000,000.

Germany was prostrate. She could resist no longer. The Cuno Cabinet fell and Stresemann came in to negotiate terms of surrender. First German offers, on May 2, had been rejected. On June 7, more definite proposals went to both the Allies and to the United States, listing important German assets which might be mortgaged for reparations and reviving the Hughes proposal that a committee of experts be appointed to investigate Germany's capacity to pay. Formal abandonment of passive resistance followed on September 26 but found France still disinclined to submit the problem to the experts. Yet it was clear that reparations could not be collected by force and the rapid sinking of the franc led to the decision to appoint the Dawes Committee.

The Dawes Plan. Officially constituted by the Reparations Commission on November 30, 1923, the Committee consisted of two representatives from the United States and two from each of the four Allies.[41] It began its labors January 14, 1924, and submitted its report on April 9, based upon the principle that since the war "victors" were paying taxes to the limit of their capacity, Germany should do likewise. She was basically strong in resources, in industrial and transportation equipment, and, if set upon her feet financially by her creditors, could with advantage to herself assist them to recuperate.

Germany's state railways could supply, from bond issues and revenues, $237,000,000 a year for reparations, and her industries a blanket mortgage that would yield $75,000,000. Other revenues were good for $312,000,000 annually, but reparations payments were to begin at $250,000,000, rising to a full $625,000,000 only at the end of four years. Even then an "index of prosperity" should guard Germany from undue draining. Safeguards were set up to handle the transfer of funds to the Allies and to prevent undue upsets in foreign exchange by withholding, if necessary, the full sums due the Allies. An organization representing the Allies would supervise the collection of reparations revenues from the railways and other controlled revenues and oversee a new Bank of Issue, to which the German Government would surrender its power to print money. An Agent General of Reparations was to head the control organization. Later a young American, Mr. Parker T. Gilbert, was appointed to this post.

In return, Germany was to receive a gold loan of $200,000,000 upon which to found a new currency, the evacuation of the Ruhr,

[41] Charles G. Dawes and Owen D. Young were the American delegates, assisted by Henry W. Robinson. Mr. Young, Sir Josiah Stamp, of England, and Sir Arthur Salter, of the League of Nations Secretariat, were the principal authors of the Dawes Plan. Buell, *Europe: A History of Ten Years,* p. 80.

and, impliedly, an agreement on the part of France not to undertake forcible sanctions on account of reparations in the future. The Reparations Commission, Germany, Great Britain, Italy, and Belgium promptly accepted the report. Poincaré delayed, but the French elections of May 11 overthrew him, registering a strong revulsion from his Ruhr policy. Thereafter, a July conference, meeting in London, agreed that any future sanctions against Germany should be taken only after a unanimous vote of the Reparations Commission, the United States participating.[42]

To a considerable degree, therefore, the United States returned to hold the scales in the administration of one of the most important parts of the Versailles Treaty. The suggestion of her Secretary of State supplied the basis of settlement which was eventually used. Her citizens led in the framing of the new peace and they supplied 55 per cent of the $200,000,000 German restoration loan. An American was to sit in Berlin, exercising vast powers over the entire economic life of Germany, and, finally, the vote of the United States could thereafter prevent sanctions against Germany.

By these devices the most intricate affairs of our former allies and enemies were composed and regulated—entirely without any entanglement on our part, the prophets of normalcy soon said with pride. It only remained to conclude the funding of the war debts, during the next two years. Then the great world prosperity, which came with Coolidge, unfolded. Everyone began to pay everybody, by a simple yet remarkable process which will be traced in a later chapter, and the United States settled down to that carefree buying and selling in every market on the globe which characterized the great boom.

The policy of Borah and Johnson had triumphed. The United States enjoyed all the advantages of living in a world community without bearing any responsibility for the maintenance of order in it. Normalcy was in full swing.

[42] Benns, *Europe since 1914*, p. 276.

CHAPTER VII

ENDING THE WAR

THE GREAT WAR did not end at 11 A. M. on November 11, 1918. Though it was halted at its center, some time was required for so vast a disturbance to subside, even in the military sense. With long-established authority destroyed in the four great empires of Europe and Near Asia, it was certain to be some time before equilibrium could be restored. The continuance of fighting attendant upon the establishment of new governments was to be expected, especially after the communist success in Russia. Two communist revolts in Berlin, in January and March, 1919, were put down, each claiming more than a thousand lives, but the violence in Germany and Austria was surprisingly small.

Continuing Wars. Hungary and Poland were not so fortunate. In the former, the four-month Red dictatorship of Bela Kun ended in a military offensive against Rumanian troops in Transylvania, which led to an occupation and looting of Hungary by the Rumanian army during August-November, 1919, professedly in retaliation for the stripping of Rumania during the war. In the spring of 1920, the Poles also undertook a similar adventure, invading the Russian Ukraine only to be defeated and hurled back to Warsaw, where a French military mission of six hundred officers reorganized and saved them, thus creating a strong Franco-Polish alliance.[1]

Russian Campaigns. It was in Russia that the greatest post-war conflicts took place. In addition to the Polish invasion, the new communist regime was assailed by no less than seven invasions of Tsarist armies, supported and supplied by Allied troops. In the spring of 1918 the Allies, including the United States, occu-

[1] An alliance which was greatly strengthened by the refusal of Germany to allow a munitions ship to go through the Kiel Canal and the refusal of Danzig authorities to permit munitions to be unloaded in their harbor.

pied Vladivostok in the Far East and the Archangel-Murmansk region in the far north, ostensibly to prevent huge stores landed earlier in these regions for the Russian armies from falling into the hands of the Germans. Serious fighting soon developed from Murmansk, while the French occupied Odessa and the French and the British supported expeditions from the west and the south. Trotsky's Red Guards, however, successively expelled the French from Odessa, defeated an army of 350,000 led by Admiral Kolchak in Western Siberia, drove General Denikin's hardly less formidable host out of South Russia, routed the Poles in a major war, turned back two determined thrusts of General Yudenitch from Estonia toward Petrograd and hurled Baron Wrangel's last remnant of 130,000 men into the Black Sea. In all more than a million men had taken part in the various invasions. Against these formidable forces the communist defenders could hardly have prevailed had not the White armies invariably stirred intense fear and hatred by the vengeance which they took upon the peasants for seizing the land. Their attempted restorations and severe punishments, aside from much looting, stirred the Russian masses to effective support of the Red troops in the wars which lasted throughout 1919 and 1920.[2]

Greco-Turkish Conflict. The Russian wars had hardly subsided when the Greek occupation of Western Anatolia (in accordance with the Treaty of Sèvres) began to encounter severe Turkish resistance. The Turkish leader Kemal's forces also defeated the French in Cilicia, near Syria. This discouragement, coupled with resentment at the return of King Constantine to Greece and distaste for England's predominance in the Straits region, led France to withdraw support from the Greeks and later to come to terms with the Turks, on October 20, 1921.

In May of the same year the Greeks, against the advice of the Allied Supreme Council, had decided to try to break the

[2] F. Lee Benns, *Europe since 1914*, New York, 1934, pp. 540-44; James H. Powers, *Years of Tumult*, New York, 1932, pp. 74-81; George Seldes, *World Panorama: 1918-1933*, Boston, 1933, pp. 114-20.

Turkish resistance. But after one long advance toward Angora and a year of stalemate their forces disintegrated and they were driven pellmell into the sea at Smyrna, in September, 1922.[3]

Against these bloody wars, as well as other conflicts in the Baltic States and Finland, the young League of Nations was powerless, a fact which its opponents in the United States constantly and scornfully proclaimed.

Post-War Conferences

In attempting to cope with the train of wars and disturbances which followed the war, and to execute the peace treaties, the Allies were in almost perpetual conference. Toynbee has listed twenty-four conferences in the four years 1920-1923, when Poincaré, determined to enforce reparations from Germany, stopped attending conferences. Many of these gatherings were meetings of the Allied Supreme Council, consisting of the Allied Prime Ministers. Other interested Powers might be invited. Germany first came on a footing of formal equality to the Spa Conference, July 5-16, 1920, although only to be compelled to sign new dictated terms concerning her disarmament and coal deliveries.

Germany attended, also, the important conference at Cannes, January 6-13, 1922, which called the Genoa Economic Conference. This gathering, devoted principally to opening up economic relations with Soviet Russia, was attended by delegates of twenty-nine European states and the British Dominions. The conference could not agree with the Russians on the recognition of the debts of the Czarist Government or upon compensation for foreign property nationalized in Russia. It was, in fact, disrupted by the signature of the Treaty of Rapallo between Russia and Germany, whereby the latter waived her claims for debts and compensation and granted full recognition of the Soviet Government.

Throughout this period of many conferences, and especially

[3] W. C. Langsam, *The World since 1914*, New York, 1933, pp. 576-78.

after its close in the Genoa fiasco, the Allied Conference of Ambassadors regulated boundary questions and other conflicts. This body was composed of the Allied Ambassadors at Paris. It was set up early in 1920 to hear reports from, and to supervise, the numerous commissions set up by the peace treaties.[4]

The Conference of Ambassadors was the designated agency for the administration of the Treaty of Peace. Even if this had not been the case, the continued existence of the League of Nations was too much in doubt to enable it to seize hold of the frightful train of wars which followed the Armistice. Yet as the newly born organs of the League sought to begin life in the midst of so much disorder, they did manage to compose several disturbing controversies arising from the settling of the new boundaries. The word "compose" is used advisedly, for to magnify unduly the League's early efforts in the settlement of disputes is as useless as to see no value in each of its attempts.

The Aaland Islands Dispute

The controversy over the Aaland Islands was the first important clash to be adjusted by the League. The people of this archipelago, lying between Sweden and Finland, were Swedish. Taken by Russia in 1909, along with Finland, they now wished to be rejoined to Sweden, whose Government did not take up their claims until the Finnish Government had forcibly asserted its authority in the islands, at which point Great Britain brought the case before the League Council.

Finland, while not yet a member of the League, accepted its jurisdiction but contended that the difficulty was only a domestic matter. A commission of jurists held the Council competent to act and, after a commission of inquiry had conducted an extended investigation in the islands, the Council adopted a settlement on June 24, 1921. Its proposals, accepted by Sweden and Finland, conceded sovereignty to Finland, but on condition that the

[4] A. J. Toynbee, *Survey of International Affairs, 1920-1923*, London, 1925, Chapter I.

Aalanders should not be subject to any compulsory teaching of Finnish and that the sale of land should remain under their control. They were further protected by a five-year residence requirement for voting and by the right to have a governor approved by their Assembly, all these guarantees to be subject to League supervision. An international agreement for the neutralization and demilitarization of the islands was also specified.[5]

This adjustment was not ideal. It overrode the wishes of the inhabitants, ninety-seven per cent of whom had petitioned for union with Sweden. No frontier problem would have been created, either, by their transfer to Sweden under non-militarization guarantees. On the other side, Finland's legal claims were strong and the precedent of detaching dissatisfied minorities from recognized nations was one to be made with caution, especially in the then confused state of affairs. The compromise arrived at sought to give the islanders full safeguards for their Swedish culture and it did allay very high feeling in two nations.

Upper Silesia

Some six weeks after this adjustment, the League Council had a far greater burden laid upon it and again it made a settlement which no one could extol as a model of abstract justice. The great German industrial district in Upper Silesia was a prize which the new Poland coveted in the Peace Conference, on the ground that its inhabitants were predominantly Polish.

This was true, according to the German census of 1910, which enumerated 1,245,000 Poles to 672,000 Germans, but the "Wasserpolaks" had been ruled by Germans for seven centuries. Their dialect had grown unintelligible to the Poles of Poland, their

[5] League of Nations, *Official Journal*, 1st Year, pp. 248-50, 394-96; 2d Year, pp. 151, 699; J. S. Bassett, *The League of Nations*, New York, 1928, pp. 52-68; Erik Achorn, *European Politics and Civilization since 1815*, New York, 1934, pp. 662-63.

The commission of inquiry sent to the islands included Hon. Abram I. Elkus, former American Ambassador to Turkey. Sweden's case was plead by Hjalmar Branting. A. J. Balfour was the Council's *rapporteur* in the early stages. He was succeeded by H. A. L. Fisher.

blood very mixed, and the Polish nationalistic revival was much weaker among them than elsewhere. In short, the Upper Silesians had become as much a people in themselves as the Alsatians are.

Germany contended also in the Peace Conference that not only was the immense investment in the district hers, but that she could never pay reparations without it. She perforce yielded eventually to Lloyd George's suggestion of a plebiscite, feeling confident that control would be maintained by a large majority.

Germany Won Plebiscite. The German majority was large—707,605 to 479,359. Large numbers of predominantly Slavic natives clearly preferred to remain in defeated Germany, though many had been persuaded that reparations would ruin them if they did and had voted Polish. But Poland demanded a division of the area and Korfanty, a Pole, seized much of the district with the acquiescence of a large body of French plebiscite troops. Korfanty was disavowed, but his bands, armed and equipped from Polish stores, held sway until four battalions of British troops could hastily be sent.

Then the French and British representatives on the Supreme Council could not agree. Sir Cecil Hurst argued forcibly for the indivisibility of the great industrial area, even at the cost of keeping the Polish thirty per cent in Germany. The dividing line advocated by France gave most of the district to Poland. The French line was passionately advocated by the French press, which throughout a long deadlock stubbornly took the attitude that France had agreed to the plebiscite only because of the Treaty of Guarantee signed by Wilson and Lloyd George. Now that this treaty had been repudiated, they could still deprive Germany of the coal, iron, and zinc of Upper Silesia, which would otherwise go into her future munitions. If France was left to achieve her security alone, others must not interfere. She would weaken Germany while she could.[6]

[6] Harold W. V. Temperley, *The Second Year of the League*, London, 1922, p. 110. The facts used above are obtained mainly from his first-hand account of the Silesian dispute (pp. 105-27). See also League of Nations, *Information Section Pamphlets*, Vol. I, pp. 24-26.

Against this argument, the British member of the Supreme Council could not make headway. Nor could Colonel George Harvey—the American "observer" and the chief architect of the defeat in the Senate of the League Covenant and of France's Treaty of Guarantee—if it is to be presumed that he tried. When at length the representatives of the four Allies pledged themselves, on August 21, 1921, to accept without reserve a decision of the League Council, Harvey, of course, quickly dissociated himself from the proceedings.

The division among the Allies drove public feeling to such heights in France and Poland, in Britain and Germany, that the quarrel was turned over to the League Council for lack of another way out. The Council referred the imbroglio to four of its members who had no direct interest in it. Da Cunha (Brazil), Wellington Koo (China), Quiñones de León (Spain) and Paul Hymans (Belgium) considered the testimony of witnesses and evidence from Upper Silesia, but in the high state of tension existing did not summon representatives of Poland and Germany. Their decision was sent to the Supreme Council on October 12, 1921.

The District Divided. The report divided the great industrial triangle on a line between the earlier proposals of the French and the British in a way which served the cause of self-determination better than either but gave the great bulk of the mines and industries to Poland. The blow to German industrial strength was terrific, and to German emotions even more devastating. An immense coal supply was taken from the German market which needed it and given to the new Poland, which could use it only by a policy of forced exportation, injurious to other coal exporters, especially the British.

The impact of the change was softened by elaborate provisions devised by the Council committee for preserving during fifteen years the economic unity of the sundered industrial empire. The principles laid down were eventually expanded into a book of regulations running to 606 pages and were administered by a Mixed Commission, with the assistance of an Arbitration Tribunal, for the settlement of resulting disputes between private parties.[7]

The best thing to be said for the Silesian settlement is that it was a settlement. In the circumstances of the time that is not an empty tribute. Violence on a large scale had raged over the Silesian region. The deepest passions were still inflamed, and more dangerous still was the high tension between Britain and France. Neither could find a way out of an explosive situation which could not be allowed to continue much longer. "The whole machinery of agreement, carefully and painfully built up during half a dozen years of comradeship, collapsed. The Supreme Council had failed, and had failed lamentably. Yet where it failed, the League Council succeeded. By interposing the elements of time and impartial investigation, the League Council worked out a decision which both France and Great Britain could accept with honor. This was not its only service. The Council did actually compose a conflict the continuance of which would have worked like a festering wound in the body politic of Europe."[8]

While the League allayed successfully the extreme danger caused by the Silesian sore, it is not yet certain that it will finally heal.

[7] League of Nations, *Official Journal*, 2d Year, pp. 1220, 1225-27.

Accounts of the Silesian struggle from the German viewpoint may be found in Lieut. Col. Graham Seton Hutchinson, *Silesia Revisited*, London, 1919; René Martel, *The Eastern Frontiers of Germany*, London, 1930, pp. 132-39; Emil Lengyel, *The Cauldron Boils*, London, 1932, pp. 207-46

Lengyel estimated that the Germans still retained, in 1932, four-fifths of the capital in Polish Silesia, but cited many evidences that the German population was losing ground. After a survey of the region in June, 1937, Otto Tolischus, financial expert of the *New York Times*, reported that during 1936 German capital decreased from 57.7 per cent to 42.5 per cent and was believed to have fallen to 30 per cent in the first half of 1937. Similarly, the German minority had declined from 250,000 to half that figure, and a mass exodus still continued. *New York Times*, June 30, 1937.

[8] Temperley, *The Second Year of the League*, p. 127.

The procedure adopted during the Silesian dispute was devised by Viscount Ishii, of Japan, who prolonged his Presidency of the Council in order to put it into execution. See Bassett, *The League of Nations*, pp. 115-17.

Albania's Boundaries

For the people of Albania the League was able to perform a clearer service. That small Balkan state, set up precariously after the Balkan wars of 1912-1913, had been virtually without government during the war. Afterwards the Peace Conference left the delimitation of Albania's boundaries to the Allies. They let two years pass without action. During that time the Serbs fostered a so-called Mirdite republic in the North and the Greeks supported agitation for the separation of districts in the South and also increased their armed forces in the adjacent areas. Apparently no one desired to preserve Albania. In the first League Assembly, the Committee on Admission of New States, Great Britain concurring, rejected Albania's application for admission. But Lord Cecil championed the Albanians on the floor of the Assembly and won their entry into the League on December 17, 1920.

Their condition was still pitiful, 40,000 having fled from the Serbs in the North. An appeal to the Council in May, 1921, did lead to the appointment of a boundary commission by the Allied Conference of Ambassadors which seemed to agree upon Albania's frontiers during the summer. When the Assembly met, Lord Cecil criticized the Powers severely for the many delays, saying that they had no right to leave such questions undecided while all interested parties agitated for conflicting solutions, "no right to play with the lives and happiness of the people in order to serve the methods of the Old World diplomacy." Cecil moved and secured the sending by the Assembly of a commission to Albania, to observe and report.

Then the Assembly adjourned and an army of 12,000 Serbs marched into Albania, to accomplish what previous irregular bands had failed to do. Italy, already driven out of Avlona (excepting the island of Sassino) by the Albanians, was strongly aroused and contemplated a counter move. But Lloyd George now acted with speed. On November 7, 1921, he called for a

Boesch

VISCOUNT CECIL OF CHELWOOD

The statesman who was the stanchest and most effective supporter of the League of Nations and of its ideals during the critical decades, 1918–1938.

special meeting of the Council to consider the application to Jugoslavia of the economic blockade provided in Article 16. Two days later the Conference of Ambassadors at last announced that it had fixed the boundaries and ordered the invading troops out. The threat of economic sanctions led Jugoslavia's exchange to fall and her loans in London to become unnegotiable. Her troops were retiring before the Council met in Paris on November 16. It empowered the already authorized League commission to supervise the evacuation and pacification of the country and Albania, now quickly recognized by the Powers in rapid succession, became a state with substantially the boundaries for which she asked.

She owed her existence quite clearly to the League. It had first staved off her dissolution by admitting her to its membership, helped to keep her alive through its visiting commission, trumpeted her wrongs to all the world throughout the Second Assembly, compelled the Powers to fix her boundaries, and secured these frontiers by threat of Article 16 while supervising the evacuation of foreign troops. Considering the fact that the Conference of Ambassadors had primary legal jurisdiction over Albania, this was not a small accomplishment.[9]

VILNA

It cannot be said that the League was able to achieve as much for Lithuania in the Vilna dispute. Vilna had been the ancient Lithuanian capital until Lithuania and Poland were united by marriage in the fourteenth century. Then during four centuries Vilna became a center of Polish culture. At the close of the Great War the city was occupied by the Lithuanians, who had made a treaty with Russia, July 12, 1920, by which Vilna was ceded to Lithuania. Poland, not yet certain of victory in her war

[9] *Official Journal*, 2d Year, pp. 474-83, 724, 1196-1210; Temperley, *The Second Year of the League*, pp. 129-63; League of Nations, *Information Section Pamphlets*, Vol. I, pp. 26-28; Bassett, *The League of Nations*, pp. 121-30.

with Russia and fearful of Lithuanian intervention, appealed to the League Council, September 5, 1920.

Lithuania, though not yet a member of the League, accepted its jurisdiction and was represented at the meeting of the Council in Paris, September 16, by Professor Voldemaris. Poland, then under a somewhat liberal government, sent Paderewski.

As *rapporteur,* Paul Hymans reported that Lithuanian troops had occupied land assigned to Poland provisionally by the Supreme Council's demarkation, but included within the area ceded to them by Russia. The Council's first task was to get the Russians to evacuate Lithuania, which they did under a guarantee of Lithuania's neutrality by Poland, and then to get the Lithuanians to withdraw back behind the Supreme Council line. A military commission, dispatched at once by the Council, succeeded in stopping the fighting between the Poles and Lithuanians and, by its continued presence, in preventing a renewal. Peace seemed assured as the two Governments were persuaded to sign, on October 7, an agreement accepting provisionally a boundary which still left Vilna in Lithuania. The agreement was to become effective October 10.

By this time, however, Russia's resistance to Poland had collapsed and she was about to sign, October 12, the Treaty of Riga, by which she ceded to Poland the territory she had signed over to Lithuania on July 12. Poland's military victory also put her army leaders into the ascendancy. They were resentful that Lithuania had made friendly terms with the Russian troops, instead of making a flank attack as the Poles desired. On October 9, therefore, the day before the Suwalki agreement was to go into force, a Polish General, Zeligowski, copied the device of the Italian poet D'Annunzio, who had successfully defied the Allies by seizing Fiume. The Polish irregular took possession of Vilna and was duly disavowed by his Government, which also refused to permit him to be driven out. He soon received many armored cars, tanks, and other military supplies from Poland, together with plentiful recruits, and established himself. His act was popular in Poland and as the Polish Government argued in Geneva, "created a new situation." The procedure to be followed later by the Japanese in Manchuria and the Italians in Ethiopa was clearly foreshadowed. The movement of armed men, however commanded, created "new situations" which must then be accepted.

The new conditions created by Zeligowski inclined the Polish leaders to agree to a plebiscite, of which Lithuania had also spoken. The Council then made plans for sending a broadly international force of 1,500 men to supervise the voting and received the word of General Pilsudski that the last of Zeligowski's force would leave Vilna as the League's contingents marched in. Thereupon the Lithuanians became convinced that they would lose the plebiscite, or that it would be operated against them, and withdrew their consent, talking of the advantages of arbitration. Their obstructive tactics multiplied until the Council, speaking through Léon Bourgeois, on March 4, 1921, threatened to wash its hands of the affair.[10]

As a last effort, Arthur Balfour proposed that the two parties meet in Brussels, under the presidency of Hymans. This savored of arbitration and Lithuania accepted. Poland gave up reluctantly the idea of a plebiscite held under the authority of her friends, but agreed. At the conference, Hymans eventually proposed a loose federation between the two countries, only to find that they could not agree upon its terms. The Council adopted his proposal, but the Polish delegate, Askenazy, was affected neither by a famous rebuke which Balfour administered to him for his intransigence in the Council on September 3, 1921, nor by a powerful speech by Hymans in the Assembly on the 24th. Everyone else was moved, but the only effect upon Askenazy was to induce him, at last, to mention the existence of Zeligowski, whom he defended.

Polish Putsch Legalized. No sign of Polish acceptance of Hyman's plan was ever indicated, and the Lithuanian parliament

[10] Bassett, *The League of Nations*, pp. 78-83. Chapter II, pp. 69-90, contains a good account of the entire controversy.

rejected it by a small majority. Two years later, February 3, 1923, the Council surrendered, recognizing Zeligowski's conquest by approving provisionally a line between the opposing forces as they then stood, and shortly afterward the Allied Council of Ambassadors made final the same boundary line. Lithuania then declared herself in "a state of war," closing the boundary, but eventually, during a fresh crisis in 1927, Voldemaris met Marshal Pilsudski in Geneva, December 10, 1927, and was compelled to say that Lithuania was no longer at war with Poland.[11]

The record of the League in the Vilna conflict was not brilliant, yet it was notably better than that of the Conference of Ambassadors. The League stopped armed conflict, prevented its renewal, and gave a moral verdict to Lithuania though the basic claims were not completely one-sided. According to the Russian census of 1897, the last reliable evidence of racial claims, neither the Poles nor the Lithuanians had a right to Vilna on grounds of self-determination. In the province of Vilna, including the city, 56 per cent of the people were White Russians, 17.59 per cent Lithuanians and but 8.18 per cent Poles. In the city alone, the percentages were: Jewish 40, Polish 31, Russian 21, and Lithuanian 2. Thus the province was Russian and the city Jewish.

Lithuania's ethnic claim to Vilna was unfounded. Poland's was far stronger. Juridically, Lithuania's case was much better. By the treaty of July 12, 1920, she had received title to Vilna from Russia, which had been incontestably the last sovereign over it, though the existing Russian Government had not yet been recognized by the Allies *de jure*. The Polish case rested too heavily upon an act of freebootery, legalized by the Conference of Ambassadors under the Treaty of Versailles. Actually, as Toynbee points out, the Allies, as in the case of Bessarabia, were making over to a third party former Russian territory, of which they had no apparent right to dispose.[12]

[11] *Official Journal*, 1st Year, pp. 397-400; 2d Year, pp. 181-82, 272-76; 770; 9th Year, pp. 144, 177; Temperley, *The Second Year of the League*, pp. 92-104.

[12] A. Toynbee, *Survey of International Affairs, 1920-1925*, p. 256. This author believes the Russian census figures quoted to have been free from intended bias.

Memel. Arbitrary violence is unfortunately contagious, especially when successful. Lithuania's reply to the seizure of Vilna, acquiesced in by all, was to send some irregulars to drive the French troops out of the German city of Memel, on the Baltic, which was being held by an Allied high commission, ostensibly for Lithuania. The Lithuanians thus solved, in January, 1923, Allied doubts as to whether or not it would be better to leave Memel a free city, like Danzig. The Conference of Ambassadors, finding the Lithuanians stubborn in negotiation, abdicated, asking the League Council to arrange a settlement. The Council appointed a commission, headed by Norman H. Davis, former Under Secretary of State of the United States, which visited Memel and elaborated a convention transferring sovereignty to Lithuania, internationalizing the port to protect Polish traffic, and establishing safeguards for the cultural rights of the Germans who formed the overwhelming majority of the population.[13]

The only justification for detaching the Memel territory from Germany had been to provide a port for the still inchoate Lithuania. It was unfortunate that she had to resort to illegal violence to get her port.

Corfu

The Memel difficulty, growing out of the Vilna disturbance, was hardly adjusted before a new crisis developed out of the settlement of the Albanian frontiers. On August 27, 1923, the Italian members of a mission, engaged under the authority of the Conference of Ambassadors in making preliminary surveys of Albania's southern boundary, were murdered. Four Italians, including a general and a major, and also an Albanian chauffeur, were massacred. The crime was committed in Greece, after the Greek population had evinced resentment at the southward movement of the mission.

[13] Official Journal, 5th Year, pp. 122, 363-64, 440; Denys P. Myers, *Yearbook of the League of Nations,* Boston, 1928, p. 212; Toynbee, *Survey of International Affairs, 1920-1925,* pp. 256-61.

Ultimatum. The crime was serious and under pre-League precedents entitled the Italian Government to demand redress and apology from Greece.[14] This the Italian dictator, Mussolini, proceeded to do in an eight-point, twenty-four-hour ultimatum which called for: an official apology; a formal memorial service and military honors for the victims; honors to the Italian flag; capital punishment for the murderers; an inquiry within five days in the presence of an Italian military attaché; and an indemnity of 50,000,000 lire, about $2,500,000.

These demands were as harsh as the Austrian ultimatum to Serbia in July 1914, and with much less justification. Greek agitation was no peril to the Italian State, as Serb propaganda had been to the Hapsburg Empire, and the military officers murdered were not as important to Italy as Austria's Crown Prince had been to her. The 1923 ultimatum indicated that in Mussolini's view nothing had been changed or proved by the Great War. It was evidence that he did not attach the slightest importance to the League of Nations, the first purpose of which was to replace the ultimatum method of settling disputes. Even more than to express the indignation of the Italians against Greece, he was determined to notify the Allies that Italy considered herself aggrieved by the peace settlements and would hereafter promote her interests in defiance of everyone.[15]

Corfu Seized. The reply of Greece, like that of Serbia in 1914, accepted the demands except those which were believed to be an infringement of sovereignty, particularly the Italian demand for participation in the administration of justice. The reply objected to the size of the indemnity demanded and suggested an appeal to the League.

[14] The British had occupied Corinto in Nicaragua (1895) to enforce payment of $15,500 for certain injuries. France had occupied the island of Mytilene (1901) to compel the Turkish Government to carry out some commercial agreements. The United States had occupied Vera Cruz (1914) to avenge the arrest of American sailors. A. Lawrence Lowell, *World Peace Foundation Pamphlets*, Vol. VI, pp. 170-71.

[15] Dino Grandi, in *The Foreign Policy of the Powers*, Council on Foreign Relations, New York, 1935, pp. 82-84.

On receiving this answer, Mussolini promptly ordered the occupation of Corfu, one of the most strategically situated islands in the Mediterranean, and one over which the Greeks had feared the murdered Italian mission would impair their control. His action was more precipitate than had been Berchtold's in 1914. His fleet met with no resistance, but some obsolete forts were nevertheless shelled, some fifteen women and children refugees housed in them were killed and nearly a hundred others were wounded. The Greek statement later filed with the League alleged that an Italian officer, landing to demand surrender, was warned of the presence of the refugees and told by the prefect that no resistance would be offered.[16]

The Italians denied knowledge that the forts were in fact hospitals and refused to concede any jurisdiction over the affair to the League Council. On September 1, the Italian representative on the Council, Salandra, was without instructions and pleaded for delay. On September 4, he was still without orders, though he had sent one of his colleagues to Rome to get them. He asked adjournment, but Lord Cecil insisted upon an open session. The next day the Council received word from the Conference of Ambassadors that it was deliberating on the case and heard Salandra deny again that the Council could do so. The occupation of Corfu was only a pledge, not a hostile act. Whereupon Cecil had Articles 10, 12 and 15 of the Covenant read aloud and the Council adjourned.

On the following day Quiñones de León, of Spain, proposed a modification of Italy's demands, which was forwarded to the Conference of Ambassadors, without formal adoption. It was suggested that the Greek investigation be participated in by representatives of the three Conference-of-Ambassadors Powers and that the 50,000,000 lire demanded should be deposited in a Swiss bank, pending a decision as to the indemnity by the Permanent Court of International Justice (the World Court).

[16] C. 598, 1923, VII.

Indemnity Delivered. The Conference of Ambassadors at once accepted these suggestions and added that the Greek salutes should be given to vessels of the three Powers and returned gun for gun. A week later, however, after Italy's promise to evacuate Corfu on September 27 had been obtained, new minutes were adopted which foreshadowed the turning over to Italy of the full 50,000,000 lire, and on September 26 the Ambassadors found that Greece had not been active enough in pursuing the assassins and gave Italy the fifty millions.[17]

The report of the Ambassadors' investigating committee, which was the basis for turning the indemnity over to Italy, said that the commission was unable to decide whether the apparent shortcomings of the Greek authorities were due to negligence or to imperfect means of criminal investigation. For the moment, the Italian commissioner, "for reasons more particularly of a moral order," inclined to the first view, and the other three to the latter. The final report of the same commission was not only as inconclusive as the first but also brought out that the Greeks had not been able to conduct an effective inquiry without the cooperation of Albania.[18]

The Corfu incident was not quite a complete victory for Mussolini's policy of force "with the League, without the League or against the League" as he later phrased it in seizing Ethiopia. He had first declared that the Corfu trouble was purely an Italian question. Then, as indignation ran high at Geneva and in the world's press everywhere, he retreated to Salandra's position that the Ambassadors but not the League might consider the case, at the same time indicating that he would keep Corfu and resign from the League if that body persisted. In the Conference of

[17] The best account of the Corfu Affair is contained in Manley O. Hudson, *The Council of the League of Nations and Corfu,* Boston, 1923. See also: *Official Journal,* November, 1923, pp. 1276-85, 1287-90, 1294-1301; Achorn, *European Politics and Civilization since 1815,* pp. 665-67; Ion S. Munro, *Through Fascism to World Power,* London, 1933, pp. 168-71; Max Beer, *The League on Trial,* Boston, 1933, pp. 276-78; League of Nations, *Information Section Pamphlets,* Vol. I, pp. 35-37.

[18] Toynbee, *Survey of International Affairs, 1920-1923,* pp. 353-54; Achorn, *European Politics and Civilization since 1815,* pp. 666-67.

Ambassadors he carried all before him, except for some mitigation of the obeisance required of Greece. The wholly reasonable and proper suggestion of the League Council that the World Court assess the indemnity was laid aside and a sum far in excess of what was reasonable surrendered to him. It was strongly indicated that violent diplomacy could achieve good dividends, even against world opposition, if backed by a resolute will. Yet in the opinion of a veteran observer "the adventure of Corfu was a moral disaster without the smallest compensation in prestige." [19]

Corfu Returned. It is also not to be forgotten that Corfu was evacuated, when nothing in the Italian dictator's rise to power, or in his subsequent conduct, would have indicated that result. For Greece, bitter as was her punishment, that recovery was no small salvage. Quite probably this result was obtained by stern notice from the masters of the British navy that the island must be returned.

In all likelihood, too, this notice made the dictator determined to take control of the Mediterranean later. Yet the indignation expressed by the smaller Powers at Geneva, especially by France's allies, Belgium, Poland, and the Little Entente, had, in the judgment of A. J. Toynbee, "a profound effect upon the policy of France, and so, both directly and indirectly upon that of Italy." [20]

The League Council could assuredly claim no laurels from the crisis. At best it had influenced the decision to a very moderate degree. It had not been able to prevent a Great Power from resorting to force to settle the kind of dispute which the Council had been expressly created to handle. Its authority was flouted throughout. On the credit side it may be said that the Council's business was not to assert its authority as such and it quite plainly did not have clear jurisdiction over the dispute, especially since Greece had promised the Conference of Ambassadors, on Septem-

[19] F. H. Simonds, *Can Europe Keep the Peace?* London, 1932, p. 215. In his *Through Fascism to World Power,* Ion S. Munro states that the 50,000,000 lire were handed back "for distribution among the Armenian and other refugees of Asia Minor" (p. 171).

[20] Toynbee, *Survey of International Affairs, 1920-1923,* p. 350.

ber 2, to accept any settlement which it proposed. The murder of the Italian officers was a direct offense against the Conference of Ambassadors. Its right to take action could only be modified by the League's right to protect its members against acts of war. The occupation of Corfu was a violation of the whole spirit of the Covenant, but the return of the island and the quiet termination of the conflict prevented a state of war from arising.

At all events, the Powers were still responsible for the adjudication of the new boundaries. They were also still unable to believe in the permanence of the League. Italy was unwilling to believe. And the smaller nations, with the aid of League supporters in Britain and France, were not strong enough to do more than give the League organs a modest growth and the League ideas some development, while a technique for investigating and adjusting international clashes was gradually worked out.

The League Council, too, had at least made a better record for energy, impartiality, and constructive effort than the Conference of Ambassadors.

The Greco-Bulgarian Clash

What the League, when backed by the Great Powers, could do to prevent war between small nations, was demonstrated in the Greco-Bulgarian frontier clash of 1925. Occurring a year after Premiers MacDonald and Herriot had given the League the full benefit of their personal attendance and support, this clash showed at their best the Council's methods for dealing with sudden emergencies.

The new boundary between Greece and Bulgaria was one of the most irksome of the post-war frontiers. It cut Bulgaria off from the Aegean sea and divided the very turbulent Macedonian area. Civilians on both sides were armed and the border was watched by isolated posts of raw troops, some of whom exchanged shots about noon on October 19, 1925. A Greek soldier was killed on the Bulgarian side of the line and a Greek officer bearing a small white flag was slain some hours later—unintentionally the Bulgars claimed—while attempting to establish a truce. Fighting continued for two days, though with few casualties, and was dying out when the Greek army, stimulated by exaggerated reports reaching Athens, began an invasion of Bulgaria, early on the 22d, and had soon occupied about seventy square miles. Bulgaria offered only slight resistance.

Proposals of the Bulgarian Government for a mixed commission of inquiry having been ignored in Athens, and strong demands made by Greece, the Bulgarian Government telegraphed to the Secretary-General of the League, invoking Articles 10 and 11 and asking for an early meeting of the Council. Within a few hours of the receipt of this message, early on the 23d, Briand, as President of the Council, telegraphed both parties urging withdrawal of troops and summoning them to a meeting of the Council on the 26th. This request was reinforced by a resolution, adopted by the Council as its first step, asking both states to report within sixty hours that all troops had been withdrawn. Military attachés of France, Great Britain, and Italy were sent from Belgrade to report on the execution of these directions, which were carried out on schedule.

The Council then appointed, October 29, a commission of inquiry headed by the British Ambassador to Spain, Sir Horace Rumbold, a French general and an Italian general, a Swedish diplomat, and a member of the Netherlands parliament. This body, after visiting the scene of the trouble and the two capitals, reported, November 28, that there was no premeditation on either side. It noted extenuating circumstances for the drastic action taken by Greece, but felt that its extent called for indemnity to Bulgaria, after subtracting something for Greek losses. Greece was required to pay $220,000, one third of which was for moral damage suffered by Bulgaria, the balance to indemnify the loss of lives and property during the fighting and occupation. This award was accepted by the Council December 3, 1925, and the indemnity was paid in full, on March 1, 1926, after the Council had strongly supported the principle that the violation of territory justified reparations even though provocative incidents had occurred.[21]

To guard against future incidents a mission of Swedish military officers was arranged for, which reorganized the frontier guards on both sides and contributed to the growth of better feeling between the two nations after the incident.

The affair of 1925 established a standard which would reduce the risks of sudden war to a minimum, if accepted by the Great Powers. Unfortunately such was not the case with some of the Powers. Whether intentionally or not, Greece was only applying the lesson which Mussolini had taught her by his seizure of Corfu. She was the stronger militarily. In the killing of Captain Vassiliades under a flag of truce, she had emotional provocation comparable to the Italian state of mind after the Janina murders. Italy had then seized territory and extorted an excessive indemnity. Why should Greece not proceed likewise? There was no reason, except that the Powers were more disposed to enforce the Covenant in 1925.

When Greece justified her invasion of Bulgaria as a pledge for the exaction of satisfaction for the killing of her sentry and her captain, just as Italy had done, Briand made a speech strongly deprecating the taking of such sudden and drastic steps "under the pretext of legitimate self defense" and all the other members of the Council joined in condemning such action. Even the Italian delegate, Scialoja, ventured to associate himself entirely with the declarations of his colleagues. As a member of the commission which had drafted the Covenant, he was "happy to note that the League of Nations was working perfectly in conformity with the intention of its founders." [22]

[21] *Official Journal*, 6th Year, pp. 1676-1700, 1711-12; 7th Year, pp. 172-75, 199-200, 205-7; C. A. Macartney, *Survey of International Affairs, 1925*, London, 1928, Vol. II, pp. 299-309; League Secretariat, *Ten Years of World Cooperation*, pp. 31-34.

[22] *Minutes of the Council*, 36th Session (Extraordinary), pp. 1706-9.

It was well that these utterances should be made as soon as possible after the Corfu affair, though they could not counteract all the damage done then. There was encouragement also in the fact that one of the defeated and disarmed nations, even though a small one, had received prompt and impartial justice when attacked. It was possible, too, that a few precedents of this character might lead to the disciplining of a Great Power engaged in some headstrong violation of frontiers.

Mosul

Eleven days after settling the Greco-Bulgarian incident the Council also disposed of the long-contested dispute over the vilayet of Mosul, one of the most troublesome disputes to come before the League and one of which much use has been made by its critics. In this case the decision went entirely against one of the defeated powers and in favor of the most powerful member of the League. There was oil in Mosul, also, and, especially to Americans but lately accustomed to the scandals surrounding the filching of the United States navy's reserve oil lands, the presence of oil tended strongly to arouse questions in any situation with which it was associated. If there was oil in the Mosul affair, Americans were quite ready to believe that the whole thing was a British reach for the all-powerful fluid and that the League had weakly allowed itself to be used as a pawn.

The method by which Britain obtained control of the area, too, tended to substantiate these charges. When Turkey capitulated in the Armistice of Mudros, on October 30, 1918, British troops were rapidly moving northwards beyond Bagdad into the Mosul vilayet, of which they had occupied less than a third. The armistice, however, provided for the surrender of the Turkish garrison and contained a somewhat elastic clause under which the Allies might occupy any strategic point in case they felt their security threatened. Under these terms, the British commanders promptly consolidated their security by advancing another hundred miles north, occupying the important city of Mosul and the remainder of the Mosul vilayet. The League commission of inquiry later reported that this action was covered by the terms of the armistice.[23]

Quite probably the armistice was so drawn as to justify considerable extensions of authority. There seems to be little question about the intent of the British authorities to round out the borders of Mesopotamia, which they intended to separate from Turkey along with the remainder of her Arab possessions. The Mosul vilayet was an extension of the Tigris valley and it had mountain frontiers on the north. It was clearly a part of Mesopotamia geographically and economically.

That there was oil in the region was known. A Turkish petroleum company had secured from the Turkish Government, in June, 1914, a written promise of an oil concession covering the vilayets of Bagdad and Mosul. In this company the Anglo-Persian Oil Company, in which the British Government had a controlling interest, had an important holding. British interests therefore had a pre-war claim to develop Mosul oil.

Racial Complications. In completing their occupation of Mosul the British found a very mixed population. Though in a minority, the Kurds were the leading element, some 500,000, one-sixth of the Kurdish race, living in the district. Except for one center of activity, the Kurds had no nationalistic feeling, one-half of their race being still in Turkey and a quarter in Persia. Their dialects were very different and they were a minority of the whole population, which contained Turks, Arabs, Satan-worshiping tribes, and representatives of two sects of Christians, both of which were to have an important influence on the future disputes between Great Britain and Turkey. The League Commission was later convinced that Mosul city, a city of 100,000, the only considerable town in the vilayet, was undoubtedly Arab in character.[24]

[23] *Commission of Inquiry Report,* p. 84.

[24] The above statements as to population are all taken from the Commission's Report.

British administrators found at once a perplexing problem in the presence of some 35,000 Assyrian Christian refugees who had been drifting about for four years after revolting against the Turks at the instigation of Russia in 1915. These pauperized people had been promised homes under a benevolent government and they were a drain on the British treasury. After efforts to clear a district for their housing led to the murder of several of the few British officers in the district, the offer of one of the chiefs to lead them to a new home on the Turco-Persian frontier was accepted. This trek degenerated into a raid upon all in its path, in the spring of 1920, and was thrown back. Eventually, in 1921, the majority of the Assyrians were returned to their original homes, just north of the Mosul vilayet boundary line. They were loath to return to Turkish jurisdiction and appear to have had some assurances from the local British authorities that the Iraq frontier would be drawn to include them. The men who had the urgent task of getting these wretched people off their hands were doubtless somewhat too optimistic about the future boundaries of the new state.

Turkey Resurgent. This solution of the Assyrian problem had been possible in 1921 because the power of Turkey was still at low ebb, but in the same year it began to revive, under the nationalist government of Mustapha Kemal, and to send small parties to reassert authority on the boundaries of Mosul. The Turkish National Pact of January 28, 1920, had asserted claim to all former Turkish territories not inhabited by Arab majorities, partly with the purpose of regaining control of the Kurds of Mosul, whose culture was so primitive that the Turks believed they could Westernize and assimilate them into their new state. They particularly objected to so large a body of Kurds escaping their jurisdiction, lest a focus for a possible Kurdish nationalistic movement be set up which would draw the main body of Turkish Kurds toward it. That would be a very serious development for the new Turkey. That the British had given one Kurdish sanjak in Mosul a large degree of autonomy, employing Kurdish officials and soldiers and recognizing the Kurdish language, was not reassuring to the Turks.

Because of this feeling on their part, no settlement of Mosul's future could be arrived at in the Lausanne Treaty of 1923, which registered the victory of the resurgent Turks over the Allies at practically every other point. Deadlock having been reached on Mosul, Lord Curzon appealed to the League Council under Article 11, but at the request of Ismet Pasha, suspended his appeal for one year to permit negotiations. This arrangement was recorded in the Treaty of Lausanne with the proviso that: "In the event of no agreement being reached between the two Governments within the time mentioned [nine months] the dispute shall be referred to the Council of the League of Nations." In the meantime the *status quo* was to be rigidly respected.

The negotiations soon broke down, the Turks demanding the restoration of Mosul and the British asking for the extension of its boundaries to include the resettled Assyrians. The Turks maintained that the British were raising a demand not envisaged by the Lausanne Treaty, that it was inequitable that the interests of the Assyrian minority should determine the fate of the additional territory demanded, and that the Assyrians had brought their troubles upon their own heads by revolting—contentions in which they were later sustained by the League Commission of Inquiry. On the main issue, the disposal of Mosul, the Turks could not prevent the British from appealing to the League Council on August 6, 1924.

Council Jurisdiction Accepted. Turkey sent a representative to the Council session of August 29 and after some hesitation matched the British pledge to accept the final award of the Council. The British retreated from their position that the disposal of Mosul was a settled question and agreed that the Council might fix the line at any point it saw fit. Thereupon the Council appointed a commission of inquiry which consisted of (1) M. de Wirsen, the Swedish Minister at Bucharest, (2) Count Paul Teleke, a distinguished geographer and former Prime Minister of Hungary, and (3) Colonel Paulis, a retired officer of the Belgian army. The commission was perfectly balanced from the standpoint of occupational qualifications. That all of its members came from small nations was not unfavorable to Turkey. One of Turkey's ex-allies sat alongside one of Britain's and the chairman came from the neutral state which had been most sympathetic to the Central Powers. The Council's *rapporteur* on the dispute was also a Swede, Hjalmar Branting.[25]

Before the Commission could begin its work there was an outbreak of bad feeling on both sides concerning the *status quo*. The British were progressively taking over the Mosul sanjak which had been left largely under Kurdish control, the Turks protesting at every step. Simultaneously, the Turks were attempting to reassert their control over the northern area in which the British had restored the Assyrians. In spite of being bombed by British planes on five days in the middle of September, 1924, a Turkish column reached the Assyrians, plundered and burned their villages, and sent 8,000 of them flying back within the Anglo-Iraq lines.

The Brussels Line. These events led to strong Turkish protests and to a British ultimatum, on October 9, demanding that the Turks withdraw within forty-eight hours from the northern area from which the Assyrians had been expelled. Turkey then appealed directly to the League. The Council hastily assembled in Brussels on October 27, and a committee of three, headed by Branting, drew a compromise line between the conflicting claims of the parties, behind which both agreed to withdraw, and both honored that promise by November 15, the date set.

The League Commission could then begin its work. It assembled in Geneva, visited London, Constantinople, Angora, and Bagdad, arriving in Mosul January 27, 1925. For the next three

[25] On the entire dispute see A. J. Toynbee, *Survey of International Affairs, 1925*, London, 1927, Vol. I, pp. 471-531; *Report Submitted to the Council by the Commission Instituted by the Council Resolutions of September 30, 1924*, League of Nations Document, C. 400, M. 147, 1925, VII; Bassett, *The League of Nations*, pp. 277-99; Beer, *The League on Trial*, pp. 280-82.

months its members traveled separately over the disputed territory by motor, airplane, horseback, and on foot. They were hampered at the start by the usual stupid efforts of local officials to control the movements of a League Commission. The Turks had sent as assistants to the Turkish assessor two men who had been expelled from Mosul by the British for pro-Turkish activity. These men were first isolated behind barbed wire in Bagdad to "protect" them from the natives and the natives from their contaminating influence. The Commission indignantly secured from the British Ambassador different quarters for the Turks, only to find in Mosul that their uniforms led to a pro-Turkish demonstration which the police broke up. Afterwards the Commissioners were notified that for their protection it would be necessary to send a police escort with them constantly.

After this new effort to "protect" them was rejected by the Commission with equal indignation, the British High Commissioner appeared, made charges against some of the natives employed as interpreters and tried to keep the Commission from separating, on the ground that some of them might be unduly influenced and led to divide in writing their report. He urged that the people be consulted through the local authorities. The Commission, however, rejected all these efforts to circumscribe its activity and was thenceforth allowed complete freedom of movement, unimpeded by popular demonstrations in favor of Iraq.

The Commission's Report. In their report the Commission agreed that sovereignty rested in Turkey. If the Council attempted to decide what was best for the vilayet, it would first be necessary to know whether Great Britain would extend her mandate over Iraq for a term of twenty-five years. Otherwise Turkish administration would be better. No Iraq national feeling of importance was found, but it was felt that on the whole the majority of the people were "more in favor of Iraq than of Turkey." If the Council desired to divide the territory, several possible lines were suggested. The Commission felt that for geographic and economic reasons it would be better not to divide the area and it suggested awarding to Iraq the "Brussels line," subject to the guarantee of the usual cultural rights to the Kurds.

Before the Council, which began its session September 3, 1925, the British representative accepted the report of the Commission so far as it went, but still contended for the zone which the Brussels line had left largely to Turkey. The Turks, stressing the fact that sovereignty still resided in Turkey, would give no assurance of special rights for the Kurds and failed to renew their pledge that they would accept the decision of the Council.

The Council's Jurisdiction Denied. To the Council's committee, consisting of the representatives of Sweden, Spain and Uruguay, the Turks soon denied the Council's jurisdiction, claiming that Article 3 of the Treaty of Lausanne did no more than make the Council a mediator. They now took the position that it could decide nothing without the vote of the Turkish representative. To cover the withdrawal of their previous agreement to accept the Council's decision as final, they alleged that the Turkish National Assembly could not be bound by any acts which it had not ratified and that at all events the Turkish pledge had been given under an assurance offered by Lord Curzon, during the Lausanne Conference. In arguing for the reference of the dispute to the Council, Curzon had said that "Article 5 of the Covenant provides that the decision of the Council, upon which the Turkish Government will be represented, will have to be unanimous, so that no decision can be arrived at without its consent."

Confronted by this denial of its ability to proceed, the Council, on September 19, 1925, requested the Permanent Court of International Justice for an advisory opinion as to whether (1) the Treaty of Lausanne provided for "an arbitral award, a recommendation or a simple mediation" by the Council and (2) whether the decision must be unanimous, or by a majority and whether the interested parties might vote. The Court gave as its opinion, November 21, 1925, that the decision of the Council would be binding and should be given by a unanimous vote, the votes of the disputing parties not being counted. But at a meeting of the Council on December 8, the Turkish representative rejected the Court's opinion and continued to maintain that nothing could be decided without his vote.

Fresh Disturbances. At this juncture another report from the disturbed area along the Brussels line reached Geneva. While the first League Commission had been in Mosul an extensive revolt of the Kurds in Turkey had occurred, entailing the establishment of martial law in thirteen vilayets and severe campaigning. Its source appears to have been the repugnance of certain Kurdish notables to the centralizing and Westernizing campaign of the new Turkish regime, which foreshadowed the loss of their power and privileges. The revolt was sternly repressed and the vengeance of the Turks carried into the area of the Brussels line. These fresh disturbances in the zone covered by previous assurances to the Council led the Council to send, September 24, 1925, a new mission to Mosul, consisting of General F. Laidoner, of Estonia, assisted by a Czechoslovak officer and a Spanish diplomat. After a month spent on the Iraq side of the Brussels line, beyond which he was not permitted to go, General Laidoner reported that the raids and turmoils were due to several causes, among which were the facts that the Brussels line was not a natural frontier and that the long postponement of a final settlement was unsettling.

The most serious disturbance had been caused by the deportation of Christians from the region north of the Brussels line, claimed by the British since the Assyrians had been resettled there in 1921. As one aftermath of the Kurdish revolt, the Turkish 62nd Infantry Regiment had descended upon a community of about 8,000 Chaldean Christians, about a hundred miles west of the resettled Assyrians. These people had never taken up arms against the Turks, yet the atrocities committed upon them were equal to those perpetrated upon the Armenians in 1915. After repeated visits in which the Turks exacted first money, then cattle, and finally women, killing the men who interfered, the Chaldean villagers were rounded up and taken on a journey lasting a week or more, without food, during which the indignities and the killings continued. It was from this fate that some 3,000 of the Chaldeans had escaped into Mosul, providing General Laidoner with detailed evidence of what had occurred.

Mosul Awarded to Iraq. At the moment when the Council was faced with the final denial of its jurisdiction by the Turks, General Laidoner arrived in Geneva and read his report to the Council, on December 10. Up to this moment Unden, the Swedish *rapporteur* who had succeeded Branting on the latter's death, had been credited with favoring a compromise decision, mainly on the ground that it would be unfortunate for the League to give a decision wholly in favor of a Great Power within the League against a small one outside it. His committee did in fact give the Council a choice between dividing Mosul on the line of the Lesser Zab River and awarding the Brussels line to Iraq, but no one voted for division. If the Brussels line was not a natural frontier it was much better from Iraq's standpoint than any which could be drawn south of it. A more southern line, cutting across the plain, would scarcely be defensible, and in the light of what was occurring north of the Brussels line defense seemed an important matter. The news brought by the Chaldeans had stirred the fears not only of the Christians of Mosul but also of all the Arabs who had favored joining Iraq.

The Council's decision of December 16, 1925, was naturally accepted at once by the British Government, which had considerable difficulty with its home opinion because of widespread concern about the financial and military commitments involved. The Government, having succeeded in convincing Parliament that Britain was already committed by other agreements to see Iraq through to nationhood, then turned to negotiations with the Turks to persuade them to accept the settlement. This the Turks did in a surprisingly short time, in a treaty of June 5, 1926, which contained elaborate provisions for coping with tribal raids across the new frontier and conceded to Turkey for twenty-five years 10 per cent of all royalties to be received by the Iraq Government from the Turkish Petroleum Company. The latter had received a limited concession from the Iraq Government, on March 14, 1925, to exploit 192 square miles divided into 24 areas.

The Oil Factor. Was oil the motive power behind the whole dispute? Sir Austen Chamberlain denied the charge in the House of Commons, February 18, 1926. He declared that in March, 1925, he had rejected an offer of the Turkish Government of concessions covering all the oil in Mosul, pipe lines, half a dozen ports, and 3,000 miles of railways, in return for the Mosul vilayet. While such an offer could hardly have been accepted at that late date, the proposal was evidence that the Turks attached more importance to regaining control of the Kurds of Mosul than they did to all the oil which might be involved. The story of the whole controversy indicates, moreover, that political considerations weighed more heavily with the British and Iraq Governments than their future hopes of oil profits. Certainly the political factors absorbed their energies during much of the time, however important the hidden wealth may have been in the back of their minds.

In any event, United States oil interests secured a division of Mosul's oil. After the Anglo-French oil agreement of April 24, 1920, which transferred to France the one-quarter interest in the Turkish Petroleum Company formerly held by German interests, our oil men asked for a share and were supported by the Harding Administration, under the claim that the Open Door was being violated in a mandated territory. This controversy continued until the Anglo-Persian Oil Company offered half of its holding in the Turkish company to the Standard Oil and other American companies. This conversion was completed in principle in the spring of 1923.

On the merits of the Mosul dispute, it would seem to be difficult to convict the League Council of acting throughout as the obedient cat's-paw of Great Britain. The Council during the long continuance of the quarrel kept it in the hands of men of ability and integrity who were nationals of small countries. It is possible for opinions to differ as to whether the Treaty of Lausanne made the Council the court of last resort when it "referred" the issue to the Council if negotiations could not settle it. If the Council was not so intended, additional procedure should have been indicated. Certainly it would be difficult to allege that the representatives of the League, who spent many months on the problem, did not intend to do justice to the people in Mosul as well as to those in Iraq proper. Justice to Turkey in the long run may have demanded a division of the Mosul vilayet, but there was not much to justify such a conclusion at the time.

Granting that exact justice was seldom achieved in the series of settlements just reviewed, two questions remain to be answered. Would fresh appeals to force have settled all or any of them more equitably? And would any other arbitral agency have done better?

If the League worked imperfectly in some cases, there was open opportunity to every one to strive for better operation in the future.

CHAPTER VIII

THE SEARCH FOR SECURITY

BY 1925 the acute issues growing out of the new frontiers had been adjusted. The Dawes Plan had also shelved the reparations issue for a time. These settlements prepared the way for the general peace of Locarno and the entry of Germany into the League of Nations.

Before that beneficent truce could be reached, the many conflagrations left by the war had to be extinguished, or at least brought under control. Simultaneously, also, a prolonged search for national security passed through many stages. This effort centered around the French fear of Germany, an emotion so acute that up to the advent of Herriot in 1924 the security offered by the League Covenant seemed wholly inadequate. The fact that the League was untested dictated to Frenchmen the taking of other measures.

While the shock of the war and of the German occupation was still acute it is not certain that even the guarantee of the two great Anglo-Saxon Powers would have set France at ease concerning the future. Certainly nothing less could. A careful historian of the period states that: "Even more staggering than the loss of her former Russian ally in 1917 was the blow which fell upon France when her new and compensating alliance with the English-speaking powers failed to materialize." [1] After this development, France not unnaturally refused absolutely to disarm at the request of the Anglo-Saxons. She quickly narrowed the possible achievements of the Washington Conference of 1922 down to a small field by refusing to discuss land disarmament or the limitation of submarines.

French Alliances. Immediately after the Treaty of Versailles had been first defeated in the United States Senate, on November

[1] F. Lee Benns, *Europe since 1914*, New York, 1934, p. 308.

19, 1919, France had returned quickly to the policy of encircling Germany. Negotiations begun in January, 1920, for a military alliance with Belgium were concluded on September 7, and the ensuing outcry led only to registration with the League of notes which did not reveal the terms of the treaty. A defensive alliance with Poland, signed February 19, 1921, was registered at Geneva.[2] Then on January 25, 1924, after the occupation of the Ruhr had lost France many friends and given new hostages to the future, a treaty was signed with Czechoslovakia, January 25, 1924. This pact, not quite so definitely a military alliance, called for consultation and concerted action against any effort to upset the peace settlements. It was followed by a similar treaty with Rumania, signed June 10, 1926, and another with Jugoslavia, November 11, 1927.[3]

The Little Entente. France was then closely linked with the four principal succession states of Central Europe. These new nations had themselves drawn together to ward off the perils which beset them. Their most immediate danger was a Hapsburg restoration in Hungary. Benes, the Czechoslovak Minister of Foreign Affairs, forestalled this risk by approaching Rumania and Jugoslavia early in 1920. He concluded a defensive alliance with Jugoslavia, August 14, 1920,[4] and after the first attempt of the ex-Emperor Karl to regain his throne in Budapest, late in March, 1921, identical treaties of alliance were signed between Czechoslovakia and Rumania, April 21, 1921, and between Jugoslavia and Rumania, June 7, 1921. The "Little Entente" was then ready to meet the second reappearance of Karl in Hungary, October 20, 1921, with such vigorous action that Hungary at once surren-

[2] No. 449 in the *Treaty Series.* Published also in J. W. Wheeler-Bennett and Langerman, *Information on the Problem of Security (1917-1926)*, London, 1927, p. 233.

[3] Wheeler-Bennett and Langerman, *Information on the Problem of Security*, pp. 40-47; J. W. Wheeler-Bennett, *Disarmament and Security since Locarno, 1925-1931*, London, 1932, Chapter I.

[4] Promptly registered with the League of Nations as No. 209 in the *Treaty Series.* The alliance provided for the negotiation of military agreements.

dered Karl to the Conference of Ambassadors and hastily deposed the whole Hapsburg dynasty.

The Little Entente, however, developed its solidarity steadily, not only as a permanent watch upon Hungarian revisionism, but also to oppose the movement for Austro-German *Anschluss* and the activities of the Hapsburgs in both Austria and Hungary. A common fear that Russia might attempt to recover some of her former territories led to a Polish-Rumanian alliance of March 8, 1921, which, however, did not bring Poland into the Little Entente.[5]

Franco-British Security Negotiations. Alliances with Belgium and the secondary powers beyond Germany gave France some reassurance. Yet they brought a new danger. If a resurgent Germany should at some time go to war with Poland the combined strength of the French alliances might easily be insufficient. Knowing this full well and realizing that something was necessary to reduce the suspicion caused in British minds by France's policy at the Washington Conference, Briand began new negotiations, December 5, 1921, for a security pact with Great Britain. Lloyd George soon told him, however, that the British people would still approve "a plain guarantee to France against invasion," but that they were little interested in what happened on Germany's eastern frontier. This was disappointing to France, but eventually a draft treaty was agreed upon by the French and British Premiers during the conference at Cannes, January 12, 1922. In addition to an unequivocal guarantee of France against "unprovoked aggression against the soil of France" it reasserted the common interest of the parties in Articles 42-44 of the Treaty, dealing with the demilitarization of the Rhineland, and bound them to consult together should any breach of these Articles be threatened. The case of a German-Polish war was covered only by a

[5] Wheeler-Bennett and Langerman, *Information on the Problem of Security*, pp. 187-99.

vague agreement to "concert together" in the event of any German military measures which were inconsistent with the Treaty.

Fearing that Poland was being deserted, the French Chamber quickly recalled Briand from Cannes and overthrew him. Thereafter Poincaré demanded a military agreement and a term of twenty or thirty years for the treaty, instead of ten years. These terms were refused, and negotiations dragged on into the impasse between the two countries over the occupation of the Ruhr.

A German Offer. Before this decisive step was taken the German Chancellor, Dr. Cuno, had made a proposal which was to change thought on the subject of security rapidly in England, and more slowly elsewhere. Realizing that Germany was defenseless and in danger of an attempt by France to crush her and also that France was moved by a deep-seated fear of Germany, Cuno sent an offer to France, through Secretary Hughes in Washington, proposing that Germany, France, Great Britain, and Italy should not make war against each other for a given period without a popular vote in each country involved. This promise was to be given to the United States as a sort of trustee.

Cuno's initiative was brushed aside by Poincaré as a mere political maneuver. The invasion of the Ruhr went forward at once. But the idea of getting enemies into one alliance instead of two was to be heard from again. It was, after all, the basic principle of the League Covenant. It had also been elaborated most cogently with reference to the Franco-German problem by H. G. Wells in connection with the Washington Conference, two years before the Cuno offer.[6]

[6] *Ibid.*, pp. 48-60. "The only security for a modern State," wrote Wells, "is a *binding and mutually satisfactory* alliance with the Power or Powers that might otherwise attack. The only real security for France against a German revenge is a generous and complete understanding between the French and German Republics so that they will have a mutual interest in each other's prosperity. . . . Other Powers may come into such a treaty as guarantors, but the essential thing for peace between France and Germany is peace made good and clear between them, a cessation of mutual injuries and hostile preparations."—H. G. Wells, *Washington and the Hope of Peace*, London, 1922, pp. 88-89.

Article 10 Attacked

While the nations most nervous about their future were contracting alliances to protect it, the other members of the League were also examining their obligations under the Covenant, in the light of the non-membership of the United States and of the new race for allies. It was a cold light. The power of the United States was so overshadowing that her rejection of the obligations of Articles 10 and 16 of the Covenant could not but have a chilling effect. With the enormous authority of the United States back of the League the possibility that the League might be defied by any important lawbreaker had seemed small and not to be dreaded should the event occur. This did not mean, as Wilson's opponents so often alleged, that the United States would be expected to shoulder the brunt of every disturbance of the peace on every continent; it meant that in a crisis no nation's contribution to the restoration of peace would be excessive.

With the United States aloof from the League the probabilities appeared to many geographically protected nations to be quite different. Might they not have to give to the League more than they received? This unexpected doubt was reinforced by the natural reaction that may come after any pledge to high endeavor. The instinct of the League's proponents in getting the Covenant adopted while the war was fresh in mind was sound, but the abrupt termination of American leadership made the recoil especially keen. And although it was generally believed that the Senate had rejected the Covenant principally for reasons of domestic politics, the grounds for doing so were certain to be adopted by conservative-minded people in other countries.[7]

Canadian Objections. Especially was this true of Canada, which had objected to Article 10 during the peace conference.

[7] "It may be that the political situation at Washington was such that, no matter what happened, the Treaty of Versailles could not have been approved. We do know that, so far as the Treaty was discussed on its merits, one of the strongest objections was to Article 10."—Hon. William S. Fielding, of Canada, at the Third Assembly of the League. *Official Journal*, 1922, p. 217.

Both Sir Robert Borden and C. J. Doherty had questioned the wisdom of a guaranty of frontiers and the fairness of asking the small nations to underwrite the settlements then being made by the Great Powers. They thought that the lesser states which were not benefiting by the peace settlements might be excused from becoming responsible for them.[8]

Debate in the Canadian Parliament on the ratification of the Treaty also centered on Article 10. Quite in the style of Senator Lodge, the leader of the opposition declared that if Great Britain declared war on Uruguay, Canada would have to fight Great Britain. Honorable gentlemen might smile but that was the position. He was supported also by several speakers who quoted from speeches and articles current in the United States. As in the Senate, also, it was claimed that the right of Parliament to control the making of war was infringed.[9]

In reply other speakers, notably Mowat, McGibben, Stacey, and Lemiux, agreed that Article 10 took away the liberty of the choice about entering a European war but contended that, if it didn't, "the Covenant would not be worth the paper it was written on." They held this condition to be the price of peace. Both Newton D. Rowell and C. J. Doherty denied that the League could come between the Parliament and people of Canada, raising troops and ordering them out of the country. Not a man or a dollar could be so taken. Canada retained full power to act upon the advice of the League Council that Article 10 be applied. To Lieut. Col. Cyrus W. Peck, V. C., the partisan character of some speeches was deeply deplorable. Remembering the long siege of the war and the great army of comrades left behind him, he could not understand how party prejudice could blind a man to "the fact that in taking part in this great business he is involved, no matter in how humble a way, in the greatest and most

[8] Bruce Williams, *State Security and the League of Nations*, Baltimore, 1927, pp. 88-90.

[9] Canada, *House of Commons Debates*, Second Session, 1919, Vol. I, pp. 80, 91, 95-96.

significant event that has occurred in the world since Christ was born." [10]

The debate indicated clearly that the principal objection to the Treaty came from Quebec, which feared to lose its highly safeguarded position in the Canadian Federation if Canada assumed full nationhood and took part in the League. Many French members opposed the whole idea that Canada was a nation. They wanted nothing done which might modify the British North America Act. "It satisfies me," said L. J. Gauthier, "it is the safeguard of my privileges and my liberties and I want to keep it." He had "confidence in no other" safeguard, a sentiment shared by Mr. Grose Parent, who was one of several to reiterate that "Canada is not a nation; we are a colony." They not only protested against Canada's signing the Treaty but argued that it should not have been presented to Parliament at all. They wanted to have nothing whatever to do with it.[11]

Repeal Proposed. In addition to its own reasoned convictions, the Canadian Government therefore had strong reasons of domestic politics for proposing to the First Assembly of the League that Article 10 be struck out of the Covenant. Mr. Doherty, who moved the amendment, had specifically asked the opposition in

[10] *Ibid.*, pp. 100, 103, 153, 157, 129, 198-99, 219-20. A reservation to say that the powers of Parliament were not impaired was defeated by a vote of 102 to 70. In considering it the government leaders rejected flatly the view that Parliament could make reservations to a treaty after the manner of the United States Senate. Mr. Doherty held that a reservation "either involves an amendment or it is absolutely worthless" and Mr. Rowell that "once the treaty is signed it cannot be amended. It is quite true that the letter 'i' cannot be dotted or a 't' crossed, without the consent of the other party." It was "not anomalous that this Treaty should be brought before the House and that the House should not be able to amend it."

The probable result of unilateral amendments to the Treaty, emanating from the parliament of one signatory, was suggested by Mr. Cockshutt when he asked if all the amendments passed in the Senate would not have to come before the Canadian Parliament for action. He objected to the Article in the Covenant concerning the Monroe Doctrine, which had been inserted as "a kind of mental reservation placed there for the purpose of appeasing an outcry that was being made by our neighbors to the South" (pp. 118, 168, 202).

[11] Canada, *House of Commons Debates*, Second Session, 1919, Vol. I, pp. 190-91, 218, 230-32, 239.

the Canadian Parliament to withdraw its proposed reservation and trust to amendment later.

The Second Assembly received two reports on the proposed amendment.[12] A committee of jurists ruled that Article 10 did not unreservedly confirm the territorial *status quo* or oblige the members of the League to take part in any military action. The Council's Committee on Amendments, on the other hand, thought that by the Article members had contracted "an absolute obligation to put their forces at the disposal of the Council, which may use them in any part of the world where aggression occurs," though it added: "Political and geographical considerations will influence the nature of the recommendations addressed to each member."

Doherty objected to a proposed interpretation of Article 10, arguing that it was impossible to justify a provision which imposed an obligation on all the nations of the world alike. He consented to a postponement to the Third Assembly and at this session a new Canadian Government gave up the attempt to expunge the Article. Instead it proposed an amendment specifically recognizing the rights of parliaments in applying Article 10.

Interpretation Secured. The Council asked for comments from the governments on this proposal and received twenty-five replies, but six of which were favorable. Only four governments (Albania, Greece, Poland, and Finland) expressed the opinion that the parliaments were bound by the ratification of the Covenant. Most of the others held to the view that the advice of the Council was not mandatory. But since there was some dissent, Canada continued to press her amendment in the Fourth Assembly and after a long debate in the First Committee secured approval, by a vote of 26 to 4, to an interpretative resolution containing the following three points:

The Assembly, desirous of defining the scope of the obligations contained in Article 10 of the Covenant so far as regards the points raised by the Canadian Delegation, adopts the following resolution:

1. It is in conformity with the spirit of Article 10 that, in the

[12] A 24 (1) 1921 V [A. C. 40 (a)].

event of the Council considering it to be its duty to recommend the application of military measures in consequence of an aggression, or danger or threat of aggression, the Council shall be bound to take account, more particularly, of the geographical situation and of the special conditions of each state.

2. It is for the constitutional authorities of each Member to decide, in reference to the obligation of preserving the independence and the integrity of the territory of Members, in what degree the Member is bound to assure the execution of this obligation by employment of its military forces.

3. The recommendation made by the Council shall be regarded as being of the highest importance and shall be taken into consideration by all the Members of the League with the desire to execute their engagements in good faith.

This interpretation failed of adoption in the Assembly because of the negative vote of Persia. It was supported by 29 states, with 22 abstaining. Although declared neither adopted nor rejected, the resolution stood as an authoritative interpretation of Article 10 and one of a character to give reassurance to states feeling themselves distant from centers of trouble. The majority of the members of the League agreed that in recommending military measures to restrain aggression the Council was bound to take account of "the geographical situation and of the special conditions of each state." It would be the duty of the constitutional authorities in each state to decide "in what degree" it should employ its military forces, but the obligation to regard the Council's call for action as "of the highest importance" was reaffirmed.[13]

These interpretations were but the deductions which common sense would derive from any universal agreement to support the common peace. Contributions to the repression of any war of aggression could not but be affected strongly by proximity to the struggle and material interest in it. Nor could any League be ef-

[13] Williams, *State Security and the League of Nations*, pp. 63-119. This extensive discussion, with many excerpts from Assembly debates, is supplemented by the statement of fifteen governments, mostly in strong support of Article 10, as the heart of the Covenant, pp. 252-56. See also, *Records of the First Assembly*, p. 279, *Third Assembly*, pp. 215, 217; *Fourth Assembly*, p. 87.

fective unless all of its members felt bound to take action in some degree to resist aggression anywhere.

Article 16 Interpreted

In a similar fashion Article 16, the section providing for financial, economic, and military sanctions, was early subjected to close scrutiny, with a view to lessening the obligations under it of some of the smaller nations. This time it was the Scandinavian states which were nervous. Their objection was not that they were too far away to be expected to take a full part in controlling aggressive states in Europe, but that they were too close. Most acute on this score were the fears of Denmark, bound as she was to Germany by geography, without possibility of escape. She was afraid that her full participation in the sanctions of Article 16 against Germany might easily lead to her destruction.

Accordingly, supported by Norway and Sweden, she had proposed, March 20, 1919, before the Covenant was finally adopted, that in calling for economic and military sanctions account should be taken of the military and geographic situation of states. As reinsurance she further proposed that each state should decide for itself whether it should take part in sanctions at all and, to make safety doubly certain, that those "states which, by their history and pacific policy, could offer guarantees of impartiality, should have the privilege of declaring their permanent neutrality." [14]

This arrangement would give Denmark, and perhaps other small European neutrals, all the advantages of a League of Nations without their incurring any risks in its behalf. From this too ideal position the Scandinavian states retreated somewhat in the amendment to the first paragraph of Article 16 which they offered to the First Assembly. It was then proposed that: "At the request of a member for whom the application of the above provisions

[14] Williams, *State Security and the League of Nations*, p. 126. See all of Chapter III, pp. 120-50, for a full account of the efforts to modify and interpret Article 16.

might entail serious danger, the Council may authorize this member to maintain intercourse, in such measure as the Council shall decide, with the Covenant-breaking state." [15]

In support of this amendment it was contended by the Swedish Government that even the application of economic sanctions by a small state might lead her great neighbor to occupy her territory. This view was conceded by the Second Assembly, in one of a series of amendments to Article 16 placed before the governments, only to the extent of agreeing that the Council should have authority to suspend the immediate application of sanctions by especially exposed states.[16]

Anticipating considerable delay in the ratification of the amendments and desiring also to implement the sanctions Article, the Second Assembly simultaneously voted an interpretative resolution (which contained nineteen sections) concerning the application of economic sanctions. These interpretations of 1921 remained the guidepost until 1935, when the League did eventually apply economic sanctions against Italy's Ethiopian conquest. Several of the more important principles laid down are quoted below.[17] The stipulation in point number four, that each member

[15] First Assembly, *Minutes, First Committee*, p. 68.

[16] Second Assembly, *Minutes, Third Committee*, p. 381. The first of four proposed amendments sought to remove objections to paragraph one, whereby the nationals of a Covenant-breaking state residing within another member's own territory might have to be boycotted.

[17] "The unilateral action of the defaulting State cannot create a state of war: it merely entitles the other Members of the League to resort to acts of war or to declare themselves in a state of war with the Covenant-breaking State; but it is in accordance with the spirit of the Covenant that the League of Nations should attempt, at least at the outset, to avoid war, and to restore peace by economic pressure.

"It is the duty of each Member of the League to decide for itself whether a breach of the Covenant has been committed. The fulfilment of their duties under Article 16 is required from Members of the League by the express terms of the Covenant, and they cannot neglect them without breach of their Treaty obligations.

"All States must be treated alike as regards the application of the measures of economic pressure, with the following reservations:

"(a) It may be necessary to recommend the execution of special measures by certain States;

"(b) If it is thought desirable to postpone, wholly or partially, in the case of certain States, the effective application of the economic sanctions laid down

should decide for itself whether a breach of the Covenant has been committed, did not prove to be important when the Italian invasion of Ethiopia occurred. The breach of the Covenant was too clear for anyone to deny it. But in the years after 1921 this agreement seemed to give all reluctant states the loophole which they desired for avoiding any expensive support of the Covenant. Nevertheless, as in the case of Article 10, no other interpretation of the Covenant was tenable. The League not being a superstate, each member would have to be trusted on its honor to support the Covenant in each case to the degree which it felt the circumstances required. If there was not sufficient honor among the nations, they would have to take their chances again with the uncontrolled ravages of private wars.

The Draft Treaty of Mutual Assistance

Necessary as the foregoing assurances were to some small states, they could not but make more uneasy still the many nations which felt that the League must become strong enough to give security to its members, if it was to justify itself.

The security issue came to a head in 1922 for two additional

in Article 16, such postponement shall not be permitted except in so far as it is desirable for the success of the common plan of action, or reduces to a minimum the losses and embarrassments which may be entailed in the case of certain Members of the League by the application of the sanctions.

"It is not possible to decide beforehand, and in detail, the various measures of an economic, commercial and financial nature to be taken in each case where economic pressure is to be applied.

"When the case arises, the Council shall recommend to the Members of the League a plan for joint action.

"For the purposes of the severance of relations between persons belonging to the Covenant-breaking State and persons belonging to other States Members of the League, the test shall be residence and not nationality.

"In cases of prolonged application of economic pressure, measures of increasing stringency may be taken. The cutting off of the food supplies of the civil population of the defaulting state shall be regarded as an extremely drastic measure which shall only be applied if the other measures available are clearly inadequate.

"In special circumstances and in support of economic measures to be taken, it may become advisable: (a) to establish an effective blockade of the seaboard of the Covenant-breaking State; (b) to entrust to some Members of the League the execution of the blockade operations."—Second Assembly, *Minutes, Third Committee*, pp. 387-88.

reasons. The Anglo-French negotiations on the subject had broken down and it had at length become apparent that disarmament could not be achieved while nations continued to feel insecure. This impassable psychological barrier had not been seen in the first years of disarmament discussions. It was then felt that disarmament would naturally follow the organization of the League. The Council appointed a Permanent Advisory Commission, composed of military and naval experts, in May, 1920, and in the following February created a Temporary Mixed Commission of twenty members, composed of economic and political experts together with some military men. These bodies considered disarmament largely as a technical problem, in the early stages, and were confirmed in this tendency by the success of a mathematical formula in limiting battleships at Washington. It took some time to discover that none of the conditions which had made a limited mathematical solution feasible at the Washington Conference existed with reference to land armaments.

Resolution XIV. It was not until July, 1922, that Lord Cecil proposed to the Temporary Mixed Commission his famous resolutions recognizing the interlocking of security and disarmament. He proposed a general defensive arrangement subject to two conditions: that the obligation to render military assistance should be "limited in principle to those countries situated in the same part of the globe" and conditional upon a reduction of armaments.

This scheme for mutual assistance was debated throughout the Third Assembly. It naturally alarmed the Canadian and Scandinavian delegates anew, seeming to imperil all the whittling down which they had been able to do. They opposed it throughout, only to see it adopted as Resolution XIV, in a form suggesting the detailed prearrangement of measures for the assistance of states in special danger of attack.[18]

The Temporary Mixed Commission worked on the proposed

[18] Third Assembly, *Minutes, Third Committee*, pp. 15-17, 35-38, 69. For the text of Resolution XIV, see Fourth Assembly, *Minutes, Third Committee*, p. 15. Williams, *State Security and the League of Nations*, pp. 151-64 (text, 164); A. J. Toynbee, *Survey of International Affairs, 1924*, London, 1926, p. 18.

treaty during 1924 and received communications from the various Governments. Those from the Netherlands and the Scandinavian states vigorously opposed the idea of partial alliances for the protection of some states, fearing it meant a return to the old system of competitive alliances. They did not, however, come forward with offers to assume guarantees of security themselves. Instead they argued for the elaboration of means of settling disputes by arbitration or court procedure. France and Belgium, however, were strongly for limited security agreements.

After much labor the Temporary Commission combined a draft of a Treaty of Mutual Assistance which Lord Cecil had submitted with one proposed by Colonel Requin of the French delegation. The result was submitted to the Fourth Assembly in September, 1923, and after the Third Committee had debated it for another month, the Assembly voted to submit it to the Governments.

Security Guarantees. The Draft Treaty provided that the signatories would go immediately to the assistance of any state attacked, the Council being bound to name the aggressor within four days of the outbreak of any hostilities. To obviate the dangers of even this short delay and to make certain that some troops at least would march to the relief of the attacked state instantly, limited alliances were to be permitted, but their terms must be approved by the Council and published in advance of trouble. Moreover, the emergency action of these special alliances was subject to review by the Council, which might hold the alliance the aggressor if its action was not clearly defensive. No state, either, could claim the benefits of the treaty unless it had reduced its armaments to a degree approved by the Council.

Thus, in the words of Lord Cecil, there could be no limitation of arms without security, but no security without limitation.[19] The scheme harmonized strictly defensive alliances with the chief purpose of the League, making them "no more than one special

[19] *League of Nations Union Pamphlet*, No. 142, p. 4.

means of rapidly applying a general system of security."[20] The Draft Treaty represented "the furthest advance of the efforts of the League toward constructing a system of state security based primarily upon material guarantees."[21]

The Governments Divided. The verdict of the Governments upon this effort to achieve disarmament and security at one stroke was mixed. Sixteen states accepted it in principle. They included all the states of Eastern Europe except Greece—even Bulgaria; also France, Italy, Japan, Siam, and Uruguay, which was the only Latin American State to reply. The others felt too safe to consider the matter. Hungary and Austria were likewise silent, for a different reason. Germany found that the treaty increased her helplessness and danger as a disarmed state. The United States and Russia joined the European neutrals and English-speaking countries in rejecting it. Of the twelve countries which refused the Draft Treaty only Jugoslavia was in an exposed position. She found its guarantees insufficient to justify her disarmament.[22]

British Objections. The British reply strongly supported Jugoslavia on this point and reinforced the objection of the Scandinavians to strengthening the power of the Council. Great Britain thought that neither the Council nor the states could agree rapidly enough to provide the automatic security desired but feared that there would be conflict between the limited alliances sanctioned and the Council. Since naval forces were highly mobile, the British Government argued that the obligations of the treaty would necessitate a large increase in British naval armament. It advanced, in short, every reason for rejecting the treaty except the two which were most vital to Britain.

Of these the first was the impact of the Draft Treaty upon the British Commonwealth. The theory of limiting military obligations to continents meant that one part of the Empire might be at war and the others at peace—a thing which the British statesmen

[20] Philip Noel-Baker, *The Geneva Protocol*, London, 1925, p. 148.

[21] Williams, *State Security and the League of Nations*, pp. 178, 165-82.

[22] Wheeler-Bennett and Langerman, *Information on the Problems of Security*, pp. 99-100.

of the time could not envisage. Or if the Empire continued to fight as a unit it would have to bear the unique burden of helping to put out fires in all continents. Certainly the British navy could not be localized. In any case an acute sharpening of constitutional issues within the Commonwealth was indicated.

Behind this weighty objection was the still deeper one that both Britain and the Dominions wanted to minimize the guarantees of the Covenant, not to stiffen or expand them. The flight from the Covenant begun in Washington was continuing. A school of thought was rapidly growing up in the British countries which held that the League was useful as a place of consultation and as a means of developing an international public opinion but that the guarantees against aggression were out. "The most vital factor in bringing about this change was, no doubt, the withdrawal of the United States." [23] The Americans had escaped all responsibility for the peace of other countries and had demanded a navy equal to the British. Why should others continue to incur the risks which were thus made much heavier?

Yet the "very ubiquity of British interests, which tended to raise to a prohibitive figure the premium demanded from the Commonwealth collectively by any insurance scheme, had also the effect of making world peace and British interests identical; and there was a real danger that while the members of the Commonwealth were exhaustively discussing exactly what premiums they would be prepared to pay, and what should be their respective contributions, they might see their scattered premises caught in a fresh conflagration." [24] In the debate on the Draft Treaty in the House of Lords, Lord Grey warned that: "What public opinion in this country does not realize is that, under modern conditions, a policy of isolation and drift is the risk of certain catastrophe." [25]

[23] G. M. Gathorne-Hardy, *A Short History of International Affairs*, London, 1934, pp. 56-57.

[24] Toynbee, *Survey of International Affairs, 1924*, p. 36.

[25] *Ibid.* Grey spoke from his experience as British Foreign Secretary in the period before the Great War.

The Geneva Protocol

The United Kingdom, at least, could not put the issue by lightly. At this moment, also, elections occurred in Great Britain and France which gave the League its first whole-hearted support from those two Great Powers, indeed from any major power. In Britain Ramsay MacDonald headed the first British Labor Government, and in France liberal Edouard Herriot succeeded the unbending nationalist, Poincaré. Both the new leaders agreed to make the League the center of their foreign policy and signalized their intention by heading their respective delegations to the 1924 Assembly. The advent of the leading Prime Ministers to Geneva brought others, and an increasing number of foreign ministers took their seats in the Assembly, making it an annual diplomatic gathering of great importance.

It was thus a notable gathering which surveyed the wreckage of the Draft Treaty. What could be done? In their opening addresses both MacDonald and Herriot called for a return to the Covenant. Arbitration was the test, said MacDonald, and Herriot welcomed emphasis upon it as one of an inseparable trinity: arbitration, security, and disarmament. Their addresses were followed by two remarkable speeches from Eduard Benes, of Czechoslovakia, and Nicholas Politis, of Greece, in which they surveyed exhaustively the previous efforts to achieve security and the implications of adding a system of arbitral procedure to the foundations of disarmament.

As *rapporteurs* of the First and Third Committees, Benes and Politis were entrusted with the framing of a "Protocol for the Pacific Settlement of International Disputes." They were aided at the start by a "Draft Treaty of Disarmament and Security" which was submitted by a large, unofficial committee of distinguished Americans, headed by Professor James T. Shotwell and including Dr. David Hunter Miller and General Tasker H. Bliss. The American scheme provided the basis of the Geneva Protocol, particularly on the vital point of how to identify an aggressor, a difficulty which had seemed real to many heretofore.[26]

Three Objectives. The Shotwell plan attempted three great tasks, the first of which was the creation of a complete system of compulsory arbitration. All disputes of a legal nature, those recognized as such in the obligatory clause of the statute of the Permanent Court of International Justice, had to be submitted to that Court. For the great field of "political" disputes, out of which wars commonly grow, an elaborate system of arbitration was provided, under which the Council first tried to conciliate a dispute, then to persuade the parties to agree upon arbitration. If they would not agree, the Council could appoint arbitrators at the request of one side; if neither side wished arbitration, then the Council became the tribunal, unanimity being required for decision. Failing unanimity, the Council would, as a last resort, appoint arbitrators, and their ruling would be obligatory.

The Protocol definition of the aggressor was not new, but it laid down specific rules for automatically indentifying the aggressor, thus obviating the common objection to the Draft Treaty which gave the Council that power. A state would label itself as the aggressor if it committed acts of war either (1) without using the arbitral machinery provided, or (2) in defiance of a verdict, or (3) by refusing an order of the Council to halt its forces. Only a unanimous vote of the Council could keep any one of these acts from constituting aggression.

Against the contingency of aggression the Protocol sought to achieve its second object by binding all its signatories into a firm defensive alliance, within which the lesser defensive alliances already existing could function only at the call of the Council upon all the signatories of the Protocol to apply sanctions. When the Council did issue such a call, the signatories were bound not only to apply the sanctions in Article 16 of the Covenant, but

[26] The text of the Shotwell draft may be found in: Fifth Assembly, *Minutes of the Third Committee*, Annex 4; also in D. H. Miller, *The Geneva Protocol*, New York, 1925, pp. 263-70. The latter monograph is the best exposition of the Protocol, by one who had a major hand in the drafting of the Covenant.

also to cooperate loyally and effectively "in resistance to any act of aggression." This was a distinct stiffening of the Covenant and in Miller's judgment it was not qualified but emphasized by the added words, "in the degree which its geographical position and its situation as regards armaments allow." [27] The obligation to join in all sanctions in some degree was made definite. The apparent right enjoyed under the Covenant to decide not to cooperate at all was eliminated. States could still decide how much they would do, but not whether they should join in sanctions.[28]

The third outstanding feature of the Protocol was its defense of the *status quo*. Any lingering doubts as to whether Article 10 of the Covenant had made the changing of boundaries by force illegal were completely removed. It is most remarkable, therefore, that the Protocol was accepted by Count Apponyi, Hungary's veteran statesman. Nor was there any protest from Austria, Bulgaria, or Lithuania. Germany was not present, but no outcry was made in the German press. Since 1918 the war had come home to the vanquished as it had come home to others while the Germans fought on the soil of the "victors." The neutrals, too, accepted the Protocol without protest. Loudon of the Netherlands, Lange of Norway, and Branting of Sweden all welcomed it. In the autumn of 1924, no European nation considered war as a proper method of improving the *status quo*.[29]

[27] Miller, *The Geneva Protocol*, pp. 77-78.

[28] In his excellent book, *The Geneva Protocol*, London, 1925, Professor Philip Noel-Baker held to the general view that the sanctions already provided in the Covenant were not increased. Even if there was some stiffening in the Protocol, he believed that Britain was already strongly committed to Article 16, since "the published documents prove beyond dispute that Article 16 was, in its origin, in every sense an entirely British proposal" (p. 141).

[29] Toynbee, *Survey of International Affairs, 1924*, pp. 59-61.

Miller's book contains the most penetrating discussion of the *status quo* which I have encountered. He challenges the view that "whatever is is wrong"; shows that every frontier tends simply by existing to become right, to some extent; makes clear that all new changes are disrupting, that in most disputed areas there are two sides; and denies most cogently that better frontiers can be created by new wars of aggression which are certain to follow no principle of right. Showing that plebiscites, even, are uncertain guides to exact justice, he rejects any tribunal with power to change boundaries and denies that political control of raw materials is anything like so important as "access to the market on an equal footing." Peaceful changes of boundaries had often been made and should be encouraged, but not at the cost of perpetual unsettlement. Miller, *The Geneva*

British Nations Demur. The Protocol was accepted with acclaim by the representatives of the nations in the Fifth Assembly during the autumn of 1925. No state voted against it, but its fate was forecast by the distinct note of reserve which the Canadian delegate sounded. Mr. Dandurand observed that in this association of mutual insurance against fire, the risks assumed by the different states were not equal. "We live," he said, "in a fire-proof house, far from inflammable materials." [30] This proved to be the attitude of his Government and of the other British Dominions toward the Protocol. The new British Government headed by Conservative Stanley Baldwin also felt the same way. The flight from the Covenant was still on. The League, said the British Government, "is not the League designed by the framers of the Covenant." They had not forseen that the United States of America would not be a member. Rigid provisions for sanctions should not be adopted, wrote Canada, for one reason, because of "the effect of the non-participation of the United States upon the attempt to enforce sanctions." The progressive incorporation of the powerful nations outside the League "should precede and not follow the assumption of greater obligations," added Australia. It was generally agreed, reported South Africa, that with America, Germany, and Russia standing aloof, the League "cannot over any length of time achieve its great and primary object," and nothing should be done to make it more difficult for these nations, notably America, to become members. This conclusion was stated also by the Irish Free State, which felt that "as long as some of the more powerful States refrain from participation in the League of Nations the feeling of uneasiness and distrust will continue." [31]

Protocol, Chapter VII, pp. 28-45. In the Protocol even the aggressor was protected from loss of territory, though he was made liable to pay the full costs, public or private, of aggression.

[30] Toynbee, *Survey of International Affairs, 1924,* p. 63.

[31] Williams, *State Security and the League of Nations,* pp. 306-20. The reports of the Dominions to the British Government (in the case of Ireland, a statement to the Dail) are reprinted here from "Protocol for the Pacific Settlement of International Disputes, Correspondence Relating to the Position of the Dominions," Great Britain, *Parliamentary Papers,* Cmd. 2458.

More Gradual Advance Necessary. The sincerity of the importance which the British countries attached to the absence of the United States from the circle of League states need not be questioned. Yet it was clear that, apart from our absence, the statesmen of the Empire regarded the pace of the Protocol as too rapid. "The gradual strengthening of the Covenant in these directions where it reveals weakness should be the aim" was the final observation of the government of Australia. David Hunter Miller had also reached the conclusion that what was attempted was the work of two or three generations of development, a judgment in which all of the relatively safe states concurred. Only seventeen exposed states signed the Protocol and but one ratified it.

The Protocol had attempted to settle the whole problem of peace and war at one stroke. The task could not be done so quickly, particularly when the outlying states probably would not have undertaken the lesser obligations of the Covenant if they had been able to choose in 1924. Woodrow Wilson's inspired insistence had secured their adhesion to the Covenant before the inevitable tendency to trust to future luck and to become absorbed in daily cares had asserted itself. Now they were distinctly not ready to join an ideally perfect league of nations, aside from its lack of universality. Most probably they would not have been ready if the three Great Powers outside of the League had been. Centuries of regarding the will of a nation as beyond any legal restraint could not be overcome in four years. Aggressive war would have to be actually repressed in at least one or two important cases before the fact of its passing could be really believed, and before the technique of suppressing it could begin to be firmly established. Meanwhile, the machinery of peaceful change would have to begin to operate.

In 1924, no nation was in peril. Britain and her daughters could not foresee that within twelve years they would be glad to rally to the Covenant, to cope with an Italian war of conquest in Africa which threatened to endanger every corner of the Empire, unless it be Canada and perhaps the Irish Free State.

Certainly Russia could not foresee that within the same decade she would be glad to cease ridiculing the League and seek the shelter of its Articles 10 and 16.

A Constructive Failure. Yet the failure of the Geneva Protocol was a great landmark in the story of human endeavor. It caused more hard thinking on the world's inescapable problem than had taken place in generations before the League of Nations was born. It compelled the statesmen of fifty nations to wrestle with the issue and many nations to debate whether or not to join in the new effort. The immediate effect seems to have been to cause the public in many nations to discover what vows they had already taken and to shrink from them. But with knowledge there could come in the ensuing years a real allegiance to the League and a readiness to rally to it, when that degree of safety which had been snatched from the disasters of the war was about to be lost.

In the immediate future, too, the great effort which culminated in the Protocol was not totally frustrated. Before rejecting it, the British Government had concluded that vows just as binding could and should be taken with the nations living on what had become Britain's Rhineland frontier. Thus Locarno was taken from the dying body of the Protocol, while its spirit remained to stimulate the thinking of a long future.

Locarno

If the five years of earnest negotiations which culminated in the Protocol had done nothing else, they had proved that the feeling of insecurity in Europe was deep and universal. No nation felt safe and the ex-enemy states all felt highly insecure. A fresh struggle greatly damaging Europe had just been fought in the Ruhr and others might follow. While fear dominated the continent, there could be no real recovery of confidence and of prosperity, in which Great Britain had a deep interest.

It was therefore a statesmanlike hint which the new Foreign

Secretary, Sir Austen Chamberlain, dropped in Berlin to the effect that the time seemed to be ripe for Germany to renew the Cuno offer.[32] The suggestion was accepted, and on February 9, 1925, the German Ambassador to Paris proposed to Herriot the conclusion of a Rhine security pact, to be supplemented by arbitration treaties and deposited with the Government of the United States as trustee. This memorandum began a long negotiation, often interrupted, as by the fall of Herriot and by the election of Marshal von Hindenburg as President in Germany. But Stresemann's hold on German foreign policy proved to be firm and Briand's control of French policy extensive. The latter's reply to the German offer, made on June 16, after many conferences with the British, proposed several conditions, among them the inclusion of Belgium in the guaranteed area and the entry of Germany into the League.

The real difficulties were much more formidable. France was bound to the two nations on Germany's eastern frontiers and Germany was not willing to recognize their boundaries. Poland, particularly, was suspicious of the undertaking. French nationalists feared a German peace offensive, while German nationalists opposed the renunciation of Alsace-Lorraine and drove their Government into injecting the war-guilt question into the negotiations, thus incurring a sharp rebuff from London and Paris. The Sixth Assembly, however, brought the statesmen again to Geneva and led to many informal talks which greatly improved the atmosphere, while the Assembly speeches in behalf of the rejected Protocol added some stimulus to the negotiations.

The Locarno conference met in a small Swiss town on Lake Maggiore on October 4, 1925, and, aided again by intimate talks in small groups and in excursions about the lake, eventually resulted in the nine agreements which together constitute the Locarno achievement.[33] Of these the most important was the

[32] See index for earlier reference.

[33] C. A. Macartney is of the opinion that the Locarno agreements could never have been arrived at by negotiations between capitals. The meeting and gauging

Treaty of Mutual Guarantee, whereby Great Britain, Italy, France, Germany, and Belgium guaranteed both Germany's western frontiers and the demilitarization of the Rhineland for fifty kilometers beyond the Rhine. The three neighbors forswore all acts of invasion or of war, unless in case of a flagrant breach of the demilitarization of the Rhineland, or unless in response to action taken in enforcement of the League Covenant, self defense against outright invasion always being taken for granted.

Article 16. Possible action of the League under Article 16 was the hardest thing for the Germans to accept, because they feared that in case of another war between Poland and Russia they would have to permit French troops to march across Germany. To ward off the unpredictable consequence of this contingency they fought long for a special status under Article 16, alleging their disarmed state as a reason for non-participation in military sanctions.

This vital difficulty was finally solved by resorting, as in many other instances, to the terms of the Geneva Protocol. Germany accepted the obligations of the Covenant without reservation, but the other states represented at the conference agreed to announce as their own interpretation of Article 16 the one contained in Article 11, paragraph 2, of the Protocol, which required each state to cooperate in the sanctions of Article 16 "in the degree which its geographical position and its particular situation as regards armaments allows." This satisfied the Germans that they could refuse the passage or contribution of troops without incurring moral isolation within the League.[34]

Throughout the discussions Germany refused to accept formally, or to guarantee, her Eastern frontiers. She did, however, sign with Poland, Czechoslovakia, France, and Belgium identical

of personalities under favorable surroundings was essential. See his *Survey of International Affairs, 1925*, London, 1928, Vol. II, p. 50.

The resentment of Germany at the inclusion of Poland and Czechoslovakia in the agreements was somewhat softened by having their Foreign Ministers arrive four days late. Mussolini joined the conference on October 15.

[34] Chancellor Hans Luther to the Reichstag, *Deutsche allgemeine Zeitung*, November 24, 1925.

bilateral arbitration treaties in which the parties bound themselves to settle "all disputes of every kind" by peaceful means. These treaties have all the completeness of the Protocol, providing for the successive use of a permanent conciliation commission or the League Council, then of arbitration or the World Court, with safeguards at all stages against any aggravation of a dispute. The treaties between Germany and France's two Eastern allies were guaranteed by France only, by means of bilateral treaties with Poland and Czechoslovakia in which the parties promised mutual assistance should non-observance of the treaties be accompanied by unprovoked recourse to arms.[35]

The settlement in the East was not as firmly guaranteed as in the West. Yet it went a long way. Germany retained the right to agitate for a change, to bargain for it, applying diplomatic pressure, or to campaign for revision of her frontiers within Articles 11 or 19 of the Covenant. But she did renounce the right to attempt a forcible change. That was a real renunciation, beyond which she could not reasonably be expected to go.

German Gains. In return for this sacrifice of future warlike action against settlements deeply distasteful to her, and in return for the permanent surrender of Alsace-Lorraine, Germany received the evacuation of the Cologne area by Allied troops in advance of the Treaty date and assurance of an atmosphere in which the disarmament of the former Allies might be expected to begin. Of more importance still, she removed any dangers of renewed occupation of her territory on reparations account, which might have survived the Dawes settlement, and she closed the door to the efforts of French militarists to achieve the coveted Rhine frontier. In addition, Germany received assurance of a permanent seat in the League of Nations, with the recognition of full status which accompanied it and the opportunity for championing her interests which Geneva afforded. And not least,

[35] Complete accounts of the Locarno negotiations and treaties are given in Wheeler-Bennett and Langerman, *Information on the Problem of Security*, pp. 115-56; Macartney, *Survey of International Affairs, 1925*, Vol. II, pp. 25-65; Williams, *State Security and the League of Nations*, pp. 206-26.

she was given a chance to breathe and live, along with the other nations of Europe, in the good feeling created by Locarno. Fear of a deadly future was allayed, for a time at least.

In this great gain France also shared. Diplomatically, she had also achieved almost everything which she had sought so constantly since 1918, while Great Britain had assumed a heavy obligation with no tangible return. Yet the sacrifice of Britain was more apparent than real. Her foreign office knew that for centuries she had fought to prevent the Low Countries from falling into the hands of a strong power, and that the reasons for doing so were growing ever more imperative, not less. The Rhine was her frontier, so why not give everybody firm notice that she would defend it? By so doing, another war, facilitated by doubts as to what she would do, might well be averted.[36]

While Poland was cool to the Locarno treaties, only one nation opposed them with all the resources of its diplomacy. Russia, fearing to lose her only friend in Europe, sent her Foreign Minister to Warsaw and then to Berlin in an effort to prevent the agreements. "Russia had affected from the first to look on the League as an organization of predatory, capitalist states, who with Machiavellian hypocrisy had chosen this innocent-seeming method of ensuring their ill-gotten gains." [37] Now the Soviet Government did not like the idea of being the only European power outside the League.

Entry of Germany into the League

The signing of the Locarno accords (1925) was an event of immense significance in the history of international relations. It did not achieve the total solution at which the Geneva Protocol aimed, but it took the principles of the Protocol and applied them to the sorest spot in the world.

Locarno could not have been achieved without the great labor

[36] See the remarkable memorandum, "Britain and the Low Countries," submitted to the British Foreign Office by one of its high officials, Sir James Headlam-Morley, *Studies in Diplomatic History*, London, 1930, pp. 176-86.

[37] Macartney, *Survey of International Affairs, 1925*, Vol. II, p. 63.

and the accumulated yearning for a more secure future which had gone into the Protocol. Yet the Locarno truce was an even greater triumph for the Covenant. The Locarno treaties were founded solidly on the central idea of the Covenant—that rival nations must be got into one alliance for their mutual protection, not two armed camps for their eventual extermination. To accomplish this imperative objective, the Covenant relied upon two basic and complementary principles, a guarantee of territorial integrity and a guaranteed process of arbitration.[38] These were the foundation stones of Locarno.

Yet the hour in which the Covenant was deliberately and voluntarily accepted by the principal ex-belligerents as the cornerstone of their future relations was swiftly followed by a crisis within the League which dangerously imperiled the Locarno structure and threatened the collapse of the League itself. The League met in Special Assembly, in March, 1926, to receive Germany into the League and failed, because several other nations demanded that they receive permanent seats on the Council along with Germany and one of them persisted in the demand.

To the world at large it looked as if Spain, Poland, and Brazil were quite willing to defeat the Locarno promise of real peace in Europe and to disrupt the League if their private ambitions were not humored. France and Britain seemed involved, also, in secret promises to these Powers which appeared to whittle away their bargain with Germany. To the newspaper reader, the selfishness of all peoples and the futility of their trying to cooperate was apparent. Even the conservative *New York Herald Tribune* headlined the news, "League Faces Wreck as It Bars Germany Now."[39]

Had the League suffered a moral collapse, if not an actual one? Undoubtedly the Germans had not expected that other states would be admitted to the Council with them, much less to receive permanent seats. When they had received assurances of a perma-

[38] Williams, *State Security and the League of Nations,* p. 219.
[39] March 18, 1926.

nent seat nothing had been said of other seats being created. The Germans understood, as did everyone else, that permanent seats were for the Great Powers only. Not having followed League politics as closely as member states, they were not aware that there had been much unrest over Council seats from the beginning.[40]

Spanish and Brazilian Candidacies Well Developed. The Council as originally created had consisted of the five principal Allied and Associated Powers sitting permanently, and four other seats to be filled by election from the smaller members of the League. To start the Council, the Covenant had designated Belgium, Brazil, Greece, and Spain to hold the elective seats temporarily. These states had been agreed upon quite quickly one afternoon during the Peace Conference by David Hunter Miller and Lord Cecil.[41]

The framers of the Covenant seem to have thought of all the nations as either Great Powers or as small ones. That had been the situation before the War. In Europe only Spain had been neither one nor the other and Spain had not counted heavily in international affairs, particularly after the Spanish-American War. With the creation of the League, however, and after her comparatively fortunate status as a neutral, Spain began to remember her former greatness and to recall that she was still the mother of many nations, more than a dozen of which were now members of the League. Being an important state in her own right, why should she not sit permanently in the Council as the eldest member of the great Spanish speaking family?

[40] The following account is based upon the very complete and thoughtful chapter, "The Admission of Germany to membership in the League and the composition of the League Council," in the Royal Institute of International Affairs Survey for 1926. See A. J. Toynbee, *Survey of International Affairs, 1926*, London, 1928, pp. 1-78. See also the excellent Chapters 10 and 11 on the composition and evolution of the Council in Felix Morley, *The Society of Nations*, Washington, 1932 (on these events, pp. 356-67), and W. H. Kelchner, *Latin American Relations with the League of Nations*, Boston, 1929, pp. 65-72; J. S. Bassett, *The League of Nations*, New York, 1928, pp. 300-335.

[41] D. H. Miller, *The Drafting of the Covenant*, New York and London, 1928, Vol. I, p. 477.

Of the original members of the Council, Brazil also did not look upon her own exit from that body as a settled matter. She too was no longer a small nation, even in population. In territory she was immense, larger than the United States. If not clearly superior to Argentina in South America, she regarded herself as the leading state on that continent. She was certainly the greatest of the Portuguese countries. And finally, was not the Western Hemisphere entitled to one permanent voice on the Council? Since the United States had rejected that role, why should Brazil not assume it?

These considerations probably did not concern the Brazilian people greatly, but to the Brazilian Government of the day they seemed valid, especially after Brazil and Spain had retained their seats by re-election during the early years of the League. Both had been re-elected for one year by the First Assembly, after prolonged discussion as to the principles on which the non-permanent seats should be filled.

Rotation Long Demanded. In the Second Assembly (1921) Agustín Edwards of Chile proposed the addition of one non-permanent member to the Council and the creation of permanent seats for Spain and Brazil, thus formally launching the candidacies of these states for permanent representation. This Assembly approved the principle that a system of rotation of the non-permanent seats should be adopted, but, because of disagreement as to whether the question should be decided by a majority vote or by unanimity, it merely confirmed the sitting members for another year. To settle the issue it proposed an amendment to the Covenant stating that the matter of Council seats should be regulated by a two-thirds vote of the Assembly. Since amendments to the Covenant require the assent of all members of the Council (plus a majority of the Assembly members), Spain, supported by France, was able to block the proposed amendment for years. Its adoption would remove her from the Council, unless she could gain a permanent seat, for it made every non-permanent member ineligible for three years after having served a three-year term. Spain had failed to get a permanent seat in 1921, because Brazil would not agree unless her own election was also approved. Accordingly, Spain would go off the Council if the amendment passed, whereas under the existing situation she could count on a practically permanent tenure from the votes of her daughters and friends.

The resulting delay did not prevent the Third Assembly (1922) from revising the number of non-permanent seats from four to six, Brazil and Spain being re-elected. China had replaced Greece in 1920, but she failed of re-election in 1923, giving way to Czechoslovakia.[42]

The Fourth Assembly was unable to take further action, except to urge the ratification of the delayed amendment to the Covenant. In its First Committee, however, Edwards once again proposed that the seats of Spain and Brazil be made permanent. The Fourth and Fifth Assemblies still could do nothing to establish the system of rotation which the great majority of the lesser states wanted, but the latter Assembly adopted, in 1925, a warning resolution that the election of 1926 should be subject to the principle of rotation. This action was taken on the motion of Zumeta, of Venezuela, after the delegates of the Latin American nations had held a private conference during which they had served notice on Brazil that the two seats occupied by South American countries should be rotated. In order to make sure of her re-election at that time (1925) Brazil was obliged to agree not to be a candidate in 1926.[43]

Poland's Claim Added. This, then, was the state of affairs when the Locarno powers made their bargain, which included a permanent seat for Germany. The general dissatisfaction over the allocation of Council seats was due to come to a head in the 1926

[42] Partly out of deference to China's arguments, the general standard was set up that the non-permanent members should be selected "with due consideration for the main geographical divisions of the world, the great ethnical groups, the different religious traditions, the various types of civilization and the chief sources of wealth." *Verbatim Record, Third Assembly*, September 29, 1922, p. 11.

[43] J. C. de Macedo Soares, *Brazil and the League of Nations*, Paris, 1928, p. 99.

Assembly. While the successive Assemblies waited for a regular system of rotation to be established they had continued to re-elect the sitting members, with only the two exceptions mentioned above. Offense had thus been avoided, but relatively few states had a chance to be represented. On the other hand, Spain and Brazil had got quite used to sitting permanently, and other intermediate states had developed a feeling that they might as well belong to the world's board of directors. The fact was that natural growth and the War had created a group of middle-sized nations which were not small states. Neither were they Great Powers, but they were large enough to think themselves on the way to becoming such, or at least to know that they had greater interests to watch than the little nations. Of this group Spain, Brazil, and China have been mentioned. The three states of the Little Entente secured representation on the Council in 1923 through Czechoslovakia. Poland, however, the strongest and most aggressive of all the intermediate nations, was still on the outside at the moment when Germany, her bitterest enemy, was about to enter the League and the Council without having surrendered the right to champion strongly the German minorities in Poland and to campaign for a revision of her Polish boundaries. The Poles feared especially that the comprehensive Locarno arbitration treaty which they had signed with Germany might enable the latter to force a revision of their boundaries by arbitration. With the admission of Germany, Poland would also be the only one of the Locarno powers not represented on the Council as it then stood.

Made uneasy by this prospect, Poland now raised during the month preceding the Special Assembly—March, 1926—a determined claim to a permanent seat on the Council, alleging that she must be there to defend herself against Germany. Poland's ally, France, supported her and Great Britain agreed, "under suitable circumstances," to renew her earlier support of Spain's claim. Sweden, representing the small nations on the Council, was publicly and completely opposed to any nation's riding into a permanent seat along with Germany. Dr. Unden announced that Sweden would veto giving a permanent seat to Poland.[44]

Opinion in Germany concerning the proposed creation of new seats can readily be imagined, and in all the other Locarno countries public interest was acute. Polish and French sentiment was all but unanimous for the elevation of Poland and Spain.

In Great Britain the Government was disposed to agree to the enlargement of the Council, citing the growth of business and the need to increase the Council's moral authority. But the British public was overwhelmingly opposed. "Indeed the strength of the public interest and public feeling aroused resembled that which was usual in the party struggles of internal party politics." [45] The public protests, led by Lord Grey, culminated in a debate in the House of Commons, March 4, 1926, in which the Government defended its right to go to Geneva formally uninstructed, but knowing what the nation demanded.

The Assembly Deadlocked. The Special Assembly which met in Geneva March 8 to 17, 1926, transacted only formal business.[46] The issue of the permanent seats was the subject of almost innumerable private discussions, especially among the Locarno powers, all of which produced no result. Luther refused to accept a compromise plan admitting Poland to a non-permanent seat, which came to be the real object of Polish diplomacy. Then Unden, fearing that France might block Germany if he vetoed Poland, reluctantly offered to resign the Swedish seat to Poland, and

[44] China renewed her demand in terms which quite eclipsed the claims of the other intermediate states. If population was the test, China had a quarter of all humanity; if area was the criterion, she occupied the greatest spot on the greatest continent; if antiquity of civilization counted, China was impelled to believe that "its traditional culture could but enhance the efficacy of the League of Nations."

[45] Toynbee, *Survey of International Affairs, 1926*, p. 34.

Ramsay MacDonald declared that he had never known a situation which had so united the nation. The issue was the occasion for one of those remarkable series of letters from public figures to the *Times*, February 12 to 26, 1926, through which the British sense of fair play and support of signed agreements is expressed in a crisis. This expression is comparable to the much greater outpouring of significant statements which occurred in August and September, 1935, in support of the League during the Italo-Ethiopian crisis.

[46] *Cmd.* 2648 of 1926.

Benes and Vandervelde suggested that they would give up the Czechoslovak and Belgian seats to Spain and Brazil. But Mello Franco, of Brazil, had indicated, at a gathering of the Council members for tea on March 10, that he might have to veto Germany's entry unless Brazil was given a permanent seat. A week of further negotiations failed to move his determination. He received positive instructions on the 15th to veto Germany's entry. The Council appealed to his Government, and the delegates of ten Latin American states adopted a resolution that a matter so vital to Europe should not be blocked by a South American state, but neither this resolution nor another adopted by them on the 16th had any effect on Mello Franco. On March 17, "in the dead silence of the Assembly, pale, trembling, in tears even," he made his statement announcing that Brazil would not yield." [47]

The Assembly was thereupon adjourned, after the Council had put the problem into the hands of a committee consisting of representatives of the states which were members of the Council and five others. This committee, after two long sessions in May and August, elaborated a way out proposed by Lord Cecil. It provided that the number of non-permanent members on the Council be increased from six to nine, three of which might be declared eligible for re-election by a two-thirds vote of the Assembly. This solution was achieved through the withdrawal of Spanish opposition to the long-delayed amendment to the Covenant which permitted two-thirds of the Assembly to regulate the matter of Council seats.

Two Resignations. Spain's ratification of the amendment was made possible, the Spanish delegate reported, by the fact that she was withdrawing from the League. While compelled "to take a dignified refuge in a proud abstention," Spain gave her notices

[47] Macedo Soares, *Brazil and the League of Nations*, p. 136.

Before the Assembly adjourned, the representatives of Germany, Belgium, France, England, and Italy signed a joint statement reaffirming their adherence to the Locarno accords and expressing their conviction that agreement on the questions arising out of Germany's entry into the League would be reached in the September Assembly. See the account of the March session in Wheeler-Bennett and Langerman, *Information on the Problem of Security*, pp. 151-56.

of withdrawal, September 4 and 8, with many expressions of thanks for past honors and of good will to the League's future. Before her two years' notice period was up, Spain canceled her resignation. She had presented it three months after Mello Franco had taken Brazil from the League, June 10 and 14, with greater formality and less grace. He had insisted to the end that the New World was entitled to a permanent seat and that Brazil should have it. Unable to claim to represent Latin America, he was compelled to fall back upon the fact that Brazil's frontiers at least touched all South American states except two, and upon a "continental" claim.[48] At the very least, Brazil contended, she should have the permanent seat allotted to the United States until the latter should decide to occupy it.[49]

The principal explanation of Brazil's extreme stand appears to be found in the needs of President Arthur Bernardes, who was nearing the close of a term of dictatorial rule during which his capital had been under martial law for forty-two months out of forty-eight. With little popularity left, and yet with all means of informing public opinion under his control, he seems to have thought that either the dramatic seizure of a permanent seat on the Council or a spectacular resignation from the League would rally patriotic sentiment to him.[50]

[48] In his valedictory, July 10, 1926, the Brazilian delegate said: "It is necessary, therefore, to sweep away all ambiguities and to affirm categorically that the object of the Brazilian claim was essentially continental in character . . . without there being any question of a political representation of the other states of the continent."—*Official Journal*, VII, 1926, pp. 888-89.

[49] "*Confidential Memorandum* of July, 1925, from the Brazilian Government to the states members of the Council," Geneva, 1926, p. 11. Quoted in Macedo Soares, *Brazil and the League of Nations*, p. 132.

[50] This is the view of Macedo Soares, one of Bernardes's opponents, who says: "The Brazilian Government delivered its claim as an ultimatum to the nations over the head of its own ambassador. It took a strong line because it thought it would thereby enhance its own prestige at home. It cared little whether its claim were granted or not. It would not treat or plead or negotiate. . . . Instead of putting forward a clear-cut diplomatic problem to solve, a modest and reasonable claim to be decided, we forced our demands through by insensate willfulness."—Macedo Soares, *Brazil and the League of Nations*, pp. 11, 106.

The same author observes that: "From the continental point of view it is hard to see how the presence of Salvador or Nicaragua or the Dominican Republic can add to the prestige of America on the League Council" (p. 101).

On the other hand, others have noted that the atmosphere of private discussion and intrigue which dominated the Special Assembly naturally stimulated Spain and Brazil to take strong positions. Both were outside the Locarno circle, around which everything revolved, and Brazil did not have a Great Power to back her candidacy, as Spain did. This situation facilitated the taking of strong stands—especially by dictatorial governments—from which they could hardly retreat. It does not appear that any serious effort was made to placate Brazil until after her threat of veto.[51] All attention was centered on Poland for days.

The Brazilian method, on the other hand, was not likely to accomplish anything other than a probable stirring of Brazilian national pride. A protest against a too-strong centering of the League upon European problems might have been in order. But after Brazilian leaders had held high positions of honor in the League from its birth, such protest might be expected to have some restraint.[52] The course pursued left the League no choice but to reject the right of any state to block its most important processes, especially when the state was not vitally involved. The League could not continue to operate under the whip of ultimatums.[53] The ultimatum method, too, left Brazil no choice but to withdraw. After she had blocked the will of all the other members of the League to admit Germany she was quite sure not to be re-elected to the Council in September, whereas if she had curbed her pride she would have been practically certain of one of the non-permanent seats soon to be created. Spain

[51] Kelchner, *Latin American Relations with the League of Nations*, pp. 65-66.

[52] The Brazilian jurist Raul Fernandes had had a very prominent and useful part in drawing the World Court statute. First Barbosa and then Pessoa sat on the Court. Brazilians had been president of the Council and had held high positions in the Assembly.

[53] "It is inconceivable," said Briand, "that a great organization like the League should again suffer such a humiliating paralysis." *Verbatim Records of the Special Session of the Assembly*, March, 1926, p. 26.

The report in the *Diaro Official* (Rio de Janeiro, June 12, 1926, p. 11970) that the United States Minister had congratulated President Bernardes "on Brazil's recent attitude in regard to the League" was denied by the United States consul at Geneva, according to the *Journal de Genève*, June 17 and *Le Temps*, June 19, 1926. See Macedo Soares, *Brazil and the League of Nations*, p. 142.

was soon to be re-elected by a vote of 46 out of 50 and Brazil might have been similarly rewarded had her President at the time been less intractable.[54]

Naturally, some popular support could be won in answer to the question: "Was not Brazil great enough to demand the recognition of a permanent seat?" How Brazil's interests could be served by withdrawing from the Council and the Assembly altogether, her people would have to discover in the course of time. It was remarkable, to say the least, that Brazil's position and interests which had been so important as to demand constant attendance at the Council table should now be safeguarded by never appearing at the Council at all.

Germany Brought In. If perchance the Brazilian rulers enhanced their position at home, they made that of the German leaders precarious enough. During the six-month deadlock the German Nationalists had a free field on which to justify their predictions that the League was only a trap into which Germany's conquerors were trying to lure her. That they did not succeed in preventing the consummation of Locarno is a tribute alike to the good sense of the German people and to the patience and tact of Luther and Stresemann under the most trying of circumstances. The unopposed entry of Germany into the League at the opening of the Seventh Assembly, September 10, 1926, was but partial compensation for the ordeal of her leaders in March and afterwards.

The September ceremony was one of the most notable in the life of the League. The speeches of Stresemann and Briand, testifying in terms of earnestness and high eloquence to the reconciliation of two ancient foes, made an unforgettable impression upon a crowded Assembly and spread in some degree through many nations.

While the Germans had won prestige by their conduct, the League had suffered severely from its failure to air the March

[54] The succeeding regime declined an invitation of the Council to withdraw its resignation in a note written in cordial terms. *Official Journal*, IX, p. 778.

tangle in the Assembly. The smaller states may be censured perhaps for not compelling an open discussion of the issue, but the chief responsibility was clearly upon the Great Powers. The Powers came out worst of all from the impasse, their moral authority seriously diminished. The absence of the chief among them was increasingly important. Their numbers were decreased by the casualties of the war, which had not in itself argued for their right to command. The addition of the United States to their ranks would have closed the gap considerably—in the present instance, perhaps decisively. It does not appear to be probable that Brazil would have asserted her claims so long and stubbornly if the United States had been continuously asserting her immense influence and authority in the League Council.

Nevertheless, the lesser states could no longer be left out of serious account. They were now too numerous and important ever to be relegated to insignificance again. A democracy of nations had come into existence, even if some of the nations did surrender occasionally to dictatorships. The fifty smaller peoples had hereafter to be conceded importance. At the very least their collective weight was real, and it had been given means of expression in the League.

The crisis over Germany's entry, too, did lead to a long-delayed recognition of the new balance of forces in the League Council. Of fourteen members the small states were assured of chances at six, and the middle-sized powers were fairly certain to hold three, though the Assembly kept the right to control all of the nine non-permanent seats. It also asserted a right of recall by holding at any time a new election for all the elective seats, only a two-thirds vote being required to precipitate such election.

Together the smaller nations represented on the Council could outvote the five Great Powers, or the seven, if the United States and Russia were included. This did not mean that they would do so, or that they would often use their veto intransigently, the example of Brazil to the contrary. It was already clear that the dramatic assertion of vetoes, or the lining up of majorities in the

Boesch

ARISTIDE BRIAND

Boesch

GUSTAV STRESEMANN

Boesch

SIR AUSTEN CHAMBERLAIN

Wide World

RAMSAY MACDONALD

Wide World

EDOUARD HERRIOT

Underwood & Underwood

SIR JOHN SIMON

PREMIERS AND FOREIGN MINISTERS OF THE GREAT POWERS WHO PLAYED ACTIVE PARTS IN THE LEAGUE OF NATIONS

Assembly, was much less important than the League's opponents in the United States had predicted. Nothing could prevent the Great Powers from controlling most matters. But the lesser nations had henceforth to be considered and conceded some share in policy making. And occasionally their collective will would be asserted successfully.

The League in Control

The upheaval which accompanied Germany's entry into the League was severe, but it did not conceal the arrival of the League as the real center of European politics. The evidence of the great distance traveled from the days of the League's early impotence to its unchallenged sway after 1926 is nowhere more strikingly described than in the record of a veteran American observer, Frank H. Simonds. In his book, *How Europe Made Peace without America*, he traced in unforgettable words "the bankruptcy of Nationalism." In the closing months of 1923 there was "nowhere any surviving illusion of victory." The occupation of the Ruhr "seemed to disclose, not merely the bankruptcy of European statesmanship, but the prelude to a decline of European civilization itself." Europe had moved steadily toward political and economic disintegration. It "was now filled with the evidences of the incapacity of that nationalism which had failed in every single effort to restore order. No political groups had ever been allowed greater latitude in the application of their ideas than was bestowed upon the respective leaders of various countries between 1919 and 1924." Yet those leaders had failed.

Finding that the League was in existence and was holding up at least some feeble torches of sanity, the liberal groups in all countries—except in Italy, where they were suppressed—had turned to Geneva. Despite temporary reactions, too, continued Simonds, "it is not merely patent that liberalism is gaining ground in Europe, but also that nationalism finds itself, even in periods of temporary success, unable to reverse the movement toward

Geneva." Liberalism in all countries "and all parties in small countries have decided to adopt the idea of the League as the basis of foreign policy."

Beneath this movement was a perception that another war meant the probable extinction of European civilization. International compromise was the single alternative. Hence Europe accepted the idea of compromise and Geneva as the place to meet. No one, of course, could foretell the outcome, but it was clear to the observer that "the single conceivable basis of hope for the future, which has emerged from the catastrophe of our own time, is the idea which is instinct in the popular conception of the meaning of the League of Nations. Geneva may fail, but the experiment of European peace is to be made there and nowhere else."

To Simonds the periodic contact between the statesmen and journalists of Europe was "a fact of enormous importance." Those who made policies met not only each other but also those who made opinions in many other countries. It was a cross section of Europe which met in Geneva each September.

Had Our Fears Materialized? Thus, said Simonds, "it must be perceived how little of all that is most important in the achievement, not primarily of the League, but because of the League, relates to those phases which were the bases of the American political debate. As an institution the League of Nations has evolved slowly and, after all, slightly, but as an idea and a place its expansion has been well-nigh incredible."

"Only in the United States," he added, "does the opposition to the League of Nations successfully hold its ground." [55]

[55] F. H. Simonds, *How Europe Made Peace without America*, New York, 1927, pp. 267, 373-74, 376-80, 386. Disturbed by a widening gulf of non-understanding between the United States and the new Europe, the author concluded, on his last page: "In recent years, it has never been quite possible to escape the disquieting suspicion that, while the American government continues to cherish the eagle as a domestic symbol, it is to the ostrich that it turns instinctively for an example in all questions of foreign policy" (p. 401).

CHAPTER IX

NORMALCY

WHILE peace was gradually being restored in Europe, in the midst of a constant search for security, the attitude of the Harding Administration toward the League perceptibly softened. Communications from the League were answered promptly. The State Department would not reply to the Secretary-General of the League in the first person, using the form of address which is used by the executive of one government when writing to another. Instead, replies were usually sent unsigned and in the third person through the American Legation at Berne or the Consulate in Geneva. This was the indirect method of communication used by the State Department in addressing foreign institutions, and the Department insisted that no discourtesy was meant. "No other government treated the League as just another institution set up somewhere in Switzerland, and in the course of time the United States dropped the practice. When in 1924 Sir Eric Drummond sent a copy of the Geneva Protocol to Secretary Hughes, the latter acknowledged receipt and promised consideration over his own signature." [1]

Cooperation with the League

"Unofficial Observers." Long before 1924 it had become evident that the League could not be regarded with complete indifference. It was tackling a whole succession of problems in which the United States had an interest, and some way of participating in these activities had to be found. The device hit upon was the "unofficial observer," a man who upon his arrival at a League conference announced that he had come only to listen and observe, that he could not take any part in the proceedings or vote. His position was, of course, quite anomalous. He was

[1] J. S. Bassett, *The League of Nations*, New York, 1928, pp. 339-40.

something between a guest and a spy in a gathering called and financed by an organization which his Government considered too dangerous to approach except with the most extreme caution.

Nevertheless, he was present; he represented in some fashion the most powerful government on the globe; and he frequently ended up by taking a quite prominent if irresponsible part in the proceedings. As early as 1922 the "American observer," silent at the Genoa Conference in April, was freely discussing questions raised at the Lausanne Conference for the framing of peace with Turkey in the summer, and by the close of the year the remarks of Observer R. W. Boyden to the Reparations Commission on the unworkability of the Versailles Treaty attracted much attention.[2]

This underground method of protecting its interests and asserting its influence was a strange one for a great government to use. Its one virtue was that it evaded the Senate. Though members of that body were aware of it and resented the practice, they could do nothing effective about it. Senator Borah frequently alleged that the unofficial observers represented us in everything except name. This was far from true,[3] for our semi-clandestine delegates could seldom make a proposal that would involve expense—as many a constructive proposal would—since their Government was not contributing. Nor could they venture leadership

[2] *Annual Register*, London, 1922, p. 284.

[3] As late as January 8, 1934, Borah expressed his resentment at the "unofficial observer."

After "that shambling, unequivocal policy which found expression in a multitude of reservations," said Borah to the Council on Foreign Relations, "there came into international affairs a strange figure known as the 'unofficial observer,' a kind of international spy, going about over the continents listening in on other peoples' business. I say 'other peoples' business' because had it been our business, we should have been there in the person of a duly appointed and authorized agent of the government assuming full responsibility with all participants. This practice brought discredit to our government, impeached before the world our sincerity, and had a tendency at least to degrade the revered policy of Washington to the level of the fugitive discretion or whims of an international interloper.

"Whatever happens in the future, let's be rid once and for all of this un-American and humiliating policy, if you may call that a policy, which policy has none. Wherever we go or wherever we disclose an interest, let's go as full participants and assume full responsibility."—*New York Times*, January 9, 1934.

of any kind, with a hostile Senate in their rear. They had to be constantly mindful of the fact that they represented a government which was divided within itself by the conflict of two independent bodies for the control of foreign policy. Such a contest had just led to a complete breakdown, and another fight might be precipitated at any moment by something said by an American representative at Geneva. In these circumstances American leadership could be exercised only fitfully at best.[4]

Arms-Traffic Regulations. The advent of an American observer was not unlikely to have a distinctly chilling effect upon a League gathering. Thus when in 1924 the League again took up the subject of arms traffic regulation, upon which it had been unable to secure any cooperation from Secretary Hughes from 1921 to 1923,[5] its persistence was finally rewarded by an admission from Washington that the subject was of such importance that the United States ought at least to know what was being proposed. The American Minister to Switzerland, Joseph C. Grew, accordingly appeared at the opening meeting of the Temporary Mixed Commission in Geneva, in February, 1924, armored by a statement, which he read as follows: "I have been instructed to attend the meetings of this Commission, in accordance with the invitation extended to my Government in December last, for the purpose of being fully advised as to any proposals that may be made and particularly to receive information respecting any draft convention which may be considered by the Commission." [6] Grew added that he was without authority to bind his government in any way to the conclusions which might be reached.

Thawing Recognition. In this manner was the Committee informed that the United States would listen to what they had to

[4] A recent historian says: "The factor that contributed the most to undermine the effectiveness of the League was the attitude of the United States—the power which by reason of strength and disinterestedness could have exercised a greater influence than any other."—Erik Achorn, *European Politics and Civilization since 1815*, New York, 1934, p. 651.

[5] See Chapter IV, above.

[6] *Monthly Summary of the League of Nations*, Vol. IV, No. 2, p. 32.

say but would not promise to contribute anything.[7] In spite of such instructions, however, the members of the Berne legation and the Geneva consulate came to cooperate personally with League organs on cordial terms. The interests of the United States had to be looked after, in one way or another, and the men on the ground soon came to see that much earnest effort to accomplish worthy objectives was being expended in Geneva. For that matter, officials in the State Department were corresponding with League officials on terms of cordiality for years without the Senators responsible for the official American attitude being aware of it. For the men on Capitol Hill the admission that their cry, "The League is dead!" was not true was one which they could not soon or easily make.[8]

Greek Refugee Settlement. First one American interest and then another suggested using the League. American generosity had been keeping alive great numbers of Greek refugees, cast up by the war and the Greco-Turkish conflict. By 1923 the American organizations saw that some constructive solution of this huge problem must be devised and the suggestion was made that the League should arrange an international loan for the settlement of the refugees. This led the United States Government to send Colonel James A. Logan, the American observer on the Reparations Commission, and Mr. F. C. Dolbeare to assist in the arrangements. These gentlemen appeared without invitation from the Council and saw the matter through. Colonel Logan actually

[7] A suspicion that Grew was not quite so frigid as his introduction is suggested by Hughes's refusal to follow into the Third Committee of the Assembly the draft treaty which resulted. In correspondence published September 3, 1924, he notified the League that our views had been "fully explained" and "that they could not usefully be amplified."

[8] Philip Gibbs has described the persistence of the belief that the League must be dead or dying as portrayed to him by Louis Mallett: "Solemnly or exultantly, prayerfully or profanely, earnestly or indifferently, one has heard it proclaimed in America every day since Harding was elected. Those who desired the League's death have announced the consummation of their wish so frequently that they have come to believe it true."—Philip Gibbs, *More That Must Be Told*, New York, 1921, p. 357.

attended a private meeting of the Council itself at which the loan protocol was approved.[9]

Backed by an international loan of $48,000,000, the Greek Refugee Settlement Commission restored 1,400,000 homeless, destitute people to productive livelihood. In the course of three years 150,000 families were settled on the land and, among other large endeavors, 16,700 urban dwellings were constructed. The Settlement Commission was headed first by former Ambassador Henry Morgenthau and later by two other Americans.[10]

The Illicit Traffics

Opium. The control of the opium traffic was a subject in which the United States could not avoid taking an interest, in self defense. Before the war an International Opium Conference had been called by the United States at Shanghai in 1909, largely through the efforts of Dr. Hamilton Wright. It was succeeded by another conference at the Hague in 1912, which drew up an opium control treaty. This treaty, however, was not ratified by many nations until incorporated into the peace treaties and then some of the chief producing states held out.

The State Department refused to recognize the transfer of the administration of the 1912 treaty from the Netherlands Government to the League of Nations, insisting upon addressing that government, even though all other governments, including that at the Hague, had turned to Geneva.[11]

This attitude made it impossible for the League to go ahead with any practical control of the opium traffic, since the United States was one of the richest markets for the drug traffic. Accordingly, the Second and Third Assemblies renewed the earnest plea

[9] C. A. Berdahl, "Relations of the United States with the Council of the League of Nations," *American Political Science Review*, June, 1932, Vol. 26, p. 499; *Official Journal*, 1923, IV, pp. 903-4, 1014.

[10] See Henry Morgenthau, *I Was Sent to Athens*, Garden City, 1929. A short account of the immense human and economic rehabilitation involved is found in: Wallace McClure, *World Prosperity as Sought through the Economic Work of the League of Nations*, New York, 1933, pp. 321-24. It is a thrilling story.

[11] See index for reference to account in earlier chapter.

of the First Assembly for cooperation. The Council also sent an urgent invitation which was finally accepted by Secretary Hughes, December 6, 1922, and Dr. Rupert Blue was designated "to cooperate in an unofficial and consultative capacity" with the League's Advisory Committee on Opium, which he did in January, 1923.[12]

The Porter Mission. The drug evil was one in which the United States could not avoid interesting itself. The drug habit was well rooted in the United States and in the two years during which Secretary Hughes refused to speak to the League about opium, it was estimated that the number of drug addicts in the United States had increased to one million persons. There was every reason why Dr. Blue's sitting with the Advisory Committee should be followed by the attendance at its next session, May, 1923, of a delegation headed by Chairman Stephen G. Porter, of the House Committee on Foreign Affairs, and including Bishop Charles H. Brent, who had presided over the 1909 Opium Conference. Dr. Blue and Edwin L. Neville of the State Department were the remaining delegates. The arrival of this imposing group, unexpected and almost unannounced, surprised Geneva and galvanized the Advisory Committee immediately.[13] The League had been working on the hypothesis, embodied in an Assembly resolution of 1922, that the drug traffic would have to be stamped out by slow degrees. Representative Porter came fortified with a resolution of Congress which he had sponsored and which stated that "the effective control of these drugs can be obtained only by limiting the production thereof to the quantity required for strictly medicinal and scientific purposes." [14]

From the standpoint of the United States, the problem was

[12] C. A. Berdahl, "The Relations of the United States with the Assembly of the League of Nations," *American Political Science Review*, February, 1932, Vol. 26, p. 102.

[13] The Americans found the other delegations headed only by experts, and when this continued to be largely true in the succeeding opium conferences they came to feel that American cooperation was not wanted unless for some selfish European end.

[14] *Congressional Record*, Vol. 64, Pt. 5, p. 4709.

simple. We did not produce opiates but consumed them illicitly in large quantities. Other countries produced them, for the sake of profits and revenue, in much greater amounts than the world could legitimately use. All that was needed, therefore, was for these countries to cut their production to medicinal needs and our problem would be solved. The poison which was debauching our people would be scotched at its source. A little might escape from proper channels, but it would not amount to much.

Prohibition at Source Demanded. Mr. Porter laid down this principle in a letter to the Secretary-General on his arrival, with a request that he have an opportunity of explaining to the Advisory Committee what the United States had done under "the regulation of the Hague Opium Conference." On May 25, Porter and Bishop Brent made speeches to the Committee concerning the American principle and the moral evils of the traffic. When, after pursuing its regular order of procedure for several sittings, the Committee came to discuss the American principle, Porter and his colleagues, "acting on motives of delicacy," gravely walked out of the room, to the consternation of the Committee, saying that if further explanation was desired the delegates could be found at their hotel.

This was notice to the Committee that the Americans did not consider themselves as members of it but as a body of equal rank. They had not come to sit in conference as one of many nations interested in a common problem but to negotiate with the League Powers as a whole, or perhaps with "the League" as an entity in itself. Throughout his stay in Geneva Porter carefully stood on the Hague treaty of 1912, to avoid getting League ground under his feet.[15]

This method of negotiation was practically certain to break down. Yet considering that Porter had been strongly anti-League, he did well to go to Geneva, even though impelled by an urgent need. There had been so much talk of an all-devouring League in Washington, too, that it was not unnatural that Porter should

[15] Bassett, *The League of Nations*, pp. 344-49.

expect to find in Geneva an entity to be dealt with, and of which to beware. Having set himself to the task, he persisted. After the Advisory Committee had accepted his principle of opium control "in principle" only, he hinted that if invited to be present before the Fifth Committee of the Assembly, which would receive the Committee's report, the invitation would be accepted. The invitation was extended and the Porter delegation was the first to establish United States cooperation with the League Assembly. Our representatives sat with the Assembly's Fifth Committee, September 18-22, 1923.

In the Fifth Committee. Porter this time took an active and conciliatory part in the Committee's discussion, explaining in detail our point of view and urging not only that a new opium conference be called, but also that it be a League conference. He observed that "the conference could no doubt be convened by some state acting independently, but, in his opinion, it would conduce to the success of a conference if it were convened by the League of Nations and consequently supported by the prestige of the League." It is to be assumed that Porter was more concerned with the utility of the organization which he had found in Geneva than with the League's prestige. In any event, he saw his proposals adopted by the Fifth Committee and later by the Assembly with a completeness that could not have been achieved without representation on the spot.

For American delegates to go so far as to "sit with" an Assembly committee, though only "in a consultative capacity," was of course to tempt the lions of the Senate to roar alarmingly. The acceptance of the invitation and authorization of our attendance do not appear to have been announced from Washington. Later, Washington dispatches consistently gave the impression that the delegation was proceeding to work with the same "opium commission" with which it had previously collaborated. No reference was made to the Assembly or an Assembly Committee and it was explained that "the American representatives have not sat, and will not sit in the future, as members of the commission. Their status is that of advocates permitted by the courtesy of the nations represented on the commission to argue the American case." The contamination of American "observers" by contact with one of the "political" organs of the League thus escaped public attention. Even the *New York Times* gave the event but meager notice.[16]

The Geneva Opium Conference. This was not true of the subsequent activity of the Porter delegation in the opium conferences which the Fourth Assembly had called. The Assembly had decided to call two conferences, one of the Far Eastern countries to wrestle with the evil of opium smoking, and another of all nations to consider the other phases of the opium problem. The First Conference met in Geneva, November 3, 1924, and got nowhere, keeping the Second Conference in suspense for a month. In the latter body Porter introduced a draft treaty covering the question of "prepared opium," with which the First Conference was still dealing, and proposing a ten per cent annual reduction (for ten years) in the production of prepared opium. This drive being blocked on the ground that it exceeded the jurisdiction of the conference, Porter read from his instructions paragraphs which he held forbade him to sign any less comprehensive agreement, and withdrew with his delegation from the conference, February 6, 1925. A joint Congressional resolution of May 15, 1924, insisting upon the limitation of production, was also cited as binding the American delegates.[17]

Congressional Diplomacy. From the standpoint of our Congress, the suppression of the production of opiates was the thing at which to aim. To the countries of the Far East, the American

[16] C. A. Berdahl, "The Relations of the United States with the Assembly of the League of Nations," *American Political Science Review*, Vol. 26, pp. 102-105. See also his detailed footnotes, pp. 101, 102, 104.

The 1923 precedent was not followed in 1924 when the work of the Temporary Mixed Commission for the Reduction of Armaments, which our Minister to Switzerland had observed, was to report to the Assembly's Third Committee. The President of the Council again secured the telegraphed consent of its members to invite our representatives to be present, but the invitation was declined (p. 107).

[17] China, being dissatisfied with the decisions of the First Conference committee on opium smoking, withdrew from the conferences on the same day.

plan for reducing the production of opium to small limits threatened grave economic difficulties. They refused to go so fast. Viewed through our eyes, this reluctance was wicked. Yet nothing was so clearly a purely domestic question as the control of agricultural production, and the United States Congress was the most touchy body in the world concerning the control of domestic questions. It was even nervous in 1920 about League interference in the American white-slave traffic. Number four of the Lodge reservations had sternly declared that the United States reserved to itself exclusively the right to decide what questions were within its domestic jurisdiction and had proceeded to enumerate several subjects including "the suppression of traffic in women and children and in opium and other dangerous drugs" as "solely within the jurisdiction of the United States" and not "to be submitted in any way either to arbitration or to the consideration of the Council or of the Assembly of the League of Nations, or any agency thereof, or to the decision or recommendation of any other Power."

Four years later, the Congress was laying down fiats to the forty-one nations represented in the Second Opium Conference concerning what they should not grow in their fields. Furthermore, our legislative body was attempting to determine in advance what the conference should decide. This was political isolation with a vengeance.

It brought forth from Loudon, head of the Dutch delegation to the Opium Conference, the declaration that "an international conference pre-supposed the possibility of reciprocal concession and of true and real exchanges of opinion, and of good will." A conference, he added, was "doomed to failure if one of the parties has imperative instructions to impose its will upon others under pain of leaving the conference."

Subsequent Progress. Yet, notwithstanding the inevitable failure of the Congressional method of negotiation, Porter's work in Geneva was not a failure. He stirred the issue and stimulated some lukewarm and laggard governments to take a more advanced stand than they would have. Some even desired to bury the opium question. His aim of a definite and progressive solution was a good one and his leadership rallied the delegates of many nations to support his position.[18] The League, too, went ahead with the control of opium from the time the United States resumed its rightful place in the anti-drug crusade. The Second Opium Conference was paralyzed for a time by the American withdrawal, but it gathered itself together and produced the Geneva Opium Convention of 1925. The United States and China maintained that the new treaty was no advance over the Hague Convention of 1912 and that for several reasons it was a backward step. Many other countries felt that it was an advance and accepted it.[19]

The subsequent story of the League's campaign to control the drug traffic would require a volume to describe in adequate detail.[20] It is an absorbing story of slow pressure and steady advance, with a great measure of success sometimes achieved. The 1925 treaty provided for a Permanent Opium Control Board, consisting of eight members, around which the struggle against the traffic has since turned. Following the break with the 1925 Conference, the United States refused to participate in the nominations for this board. Secretary Kellogg rebuffed the Council's invitation sharply on October 1, 1928, severely criticising the 1925 treaty, then coming into force. The Council replied to these criticisms in detail and itself elected an American, Mr. Herbert L. May, to the Opium Board. As a sign of continued displeasure, the United States persisted in sending her reports to the Board through the Netherlands Government,[21] but these reports became full and

[18] The Government of India soon acceded to the American demand by agreeing to cut its exports of opium for smoking by ten per cent annually for ten years. League Secretariat, *Ten Years of World Cooperation*, p. 307.

[19] The reasons advanced by the two groups of nations are given at length in League Secretariat, *Ten Years of World Cooperation*, Geneva, 1930, pp. 304-5. They are succinctly stated in Ursula P. Hubbard's *The Cooperation of the United States with the League of Nations*, International Conciliation, No. 274, November, 1931, p. 733. Miss Hubbard's section on opium, pp. 729-38 is an excellent account of our relations to the League's opium campaign.

[20] Some references on the subject are: John Palmer Gavit, *Opium*, New York, 1927; Kathleen Gibberd, *The League in Our Time*, London, 1933, pp. 125-44.

[21] See Chapter IV, above.

regular. American observers have also continued to attend the Opium Advisory Committee regularly since 1923.[22] In May, 1931, another Opium Conference was held in Geneva which resulted in a third convention dealing with the manufacture of narcotic drugs. The United States was officially represented at this conference and its delegates cooperated fully in the work of the conference, as well as in the preliminary Conference of Opium Manufacturing Nations which was held in London in December, 1930. The treaty which resulted was pronounced by Stuart A. Fuller, of the State Department, "the biggest advance in the matter of the control of dangerous narcotics developed so far. It embodies most of the ideas of this department." [23]

The achievements in the war against the drug traffic are heartening. The system of export-import certificates gives many clues to the sources of offense. The nations are gradually being induced to establish enforcement agencies. The traffic can no longer get insurance and it can no longer be carried legitimately in the ships of most nations, Japanese and Chinese ships remaining the principal carriers. The steady pressure of the opium-control organization in Geneva stimulates the governments of offending nations to greater activity in repressing the traffic and the seizures of outlaw drugs grow in volume. Information and experience are being accumulated.

A Perpetual Conflict. Progress is undeniable, but it gives no ground for complacency. The peril of the drug habit is still acute for the whole of humanity. Large quantities of drugs and opium are being smuggled into the United States and Canada. "Cocaine is streaming into India, Burma and other regions from centers of

[22] An American, Mr. Frederic L. Delano, headed a League Commission of Inquiry to Persia in 1926 to study the substitution of other crops for the poppy. Other support, both moral and material, was rendered by Americans previous to 1931.

[23] Hubbard, *The Cooperation of the United States with the League of Nations,* International Conciliation, No. 274, November, 1931, p. 766. *New York Times,* July 18, 1931. Contrasting with the story of 1925, the report of A. E. Blanco, of the Anti-Opium Bureau, was that the American delegation in 1930 "could have led the Conference and obtained a perfect Convention but accepted a secondary role; lacked fighting spirit" (Hubbard, p. 738).

distribution which at present are only partially known. Egypt is being flooded with drugs to such a degree that the number of addicts is estimated by the Egyptian Government to reach a total of 500,000 out of a population of 14,000,000. The illicit traffic still remains enormous, involving tons of drugs and hundreds of thousands of pounds." [24]

The interest of the United States in this deadly traffic is permanent. With her many thousands of miles of frontiers she cannot defend herself adequately from the degradation of a half-dozen deadly drugs unless the war on the dope business is world-wide and incessantly prosecuted. World cooperation is required to keep our prisons, asylums, and almshouses, not to speak of our festering slums, from filling with dangerous drug derelicts to an appalling degree—a statement which is equally true of many countries. If the League of Nations should cease to exist to-morrow, another league would have to be organized soon for the express purpose of combating the drug menace. It is hardly possible to cope with a global traffic which its victims will do anything to support without any central organization or unified command.

The White-Slave Traffic. In lesser degree the same conclusion should apply to the League's Health Organization and to its drives against the traffic in women, in obscene publications, and in slaves. But in none of these fields can it be recorded that the support of the United States has been as important as in the case of the drug traffic. Miss Grace Abbott attended a session of the Permanent Advisory Committee on the traffic in women, March 22-27, 1923. She was the first of all the unofficial observers. She returned to Geneva in 1924 and 1925, but was kept at home thereafter. The treaty on the Suppression of the Traffic in Women and Children was drawn up in Geneva in the absence of a United States delegate, the League's invitation having miscarried in the State Department. The treaty was not signed by the United States later on the ground that it required our adhesion to an earlier

[24] League Secretariat, *Ten Years of World Cooperation*, p. 310.

treaty of May 4, 1910, which necessitated enforcement measures that only our forty-eight state governments could fulfill.

Obscenity and Slavery. An American observer attended the 1923 Conference for the Suppression of Obscene Publications and the resultant treaty was signed but not ratified by the Senate. The same fate befell the Anti-Slavery Convention of 1925, during the negotiation of which the State Department contented itself with informing the League that slavery had been abolished the United States.

Later, the scandal of slavery in Liberia, and of the slave trade between Liberia and the Spanish Island of Fernando Po, compelled the attention of the United States Government to the delinquencies of the Afro-Americans who now rule Liberia. After direct protest to the Liberian Government, the United States accepted membership on an investigating committee which Liberia asked the League Council to appoint. Mr. Samuel Reber, Jr., represented the United States. The commission amply verified the reports of slavery but held that Liberia would require economic and political assistance to end it.

A new League committee formed in 1931 to work out the necessary aid was unable to reconcile the Liberian Government with two American corporations which largely dominated the country, the Firestone Plantations Company and the Finance Corporation of America, the latter being the holder of Liberia's public debt. After two years of proposals and counter proposals, the League Council was obliged to abandon the effort to reorganize Liberia and bring its chapter of modern slavery to a close. Our Government likewise found itself unable to insist upon such a compromise between the claims of the Liberian Government and the American companies as would have put the projected reforms into effect.[25]

[25] Benjamin Williams, *American Diplomacy*, New York, 1936, pp. 279-84; William J. Koren, "Liberia, the League and the United States," *Foreign Policy Reports*, November 21, 1934, Vol. X, No. 19.

Health

Toward the very great work of the League Health Organization, the official contribution of the United States has been small. The blunt refusal of Secretary Hughes to permit the nations to turn over to the League the International Public Health Office in Paris has already been noted. This attitude delayed the formation of the Health Organization, but did not prevent the temporary Epidemics Commission from rendering exceptionally notable service in combating the typhus and cholera epidemics which followed the war and the succeeding Polish and Greek wars. Since then two Epidemiological Intelligence Centers for the constant telegraphic reporting of data on epidemic diseases have been developed, one at Geneva, the other in Singapore. The latter was founded at the suggestion of the Japanese Government and enables it, along with many others, to take timely measures against contagious ships while avoiding useless quarantine expense for all other vessels. Whether the Singapore station can control the plagues growing out of the current war remains to be seen.

The multitude of other activities performed by the League Health Organization includes: publication of information on the health equipment of ports and the fumigation of vessels; coordination of simultaneous investigations in several countries; acting as an exchange center for laboratories; standardization of the international morbidity and mortality statistics; special investigations of epidemic focal points; preparatory monographs on the public health services of various countries; organization of international study tours of health officials; researches by a Malaria Commission which has made secondary products of quinine, having an equal curative value, available to the poor; special malaria courses; a survey of sleeping sickness in Equatorial Africa; a conference on tuberculosis vaccines; wide surveys by a cancer commission and similar studies of smallpox vaccination, leprosy, rabies, infant mortality, child welfare and the protection of the blind; standardization of sera; organization of cooperation between the public health authorities of many countries.[26]

A Continuous Campaign. No topical enumeration can measure adequately the achievements of the Health Organization. Disease is not national. Many nations cannot defend themselves single-handed against contagious disease; all are in need of the discoveries and methods which have been worked out in other lands. No nation wants to be known as squalid and disease-ridden. In comparative reports officials can find out how backward their country is or take pride in her leadership. There is much truth in the observation of Sir Eric Drummond that as regards health "the governments were not opposed to progress." The need of the United States for the League's health service is for the moment less than that of many other countries. Perhaps it is little enough to justify the very small amount of official recognition accorded it. Yet the Surgeons General of the United States have usually sat on the Health Committee, and they no longer have to do so ostensibly as accredited to the International Public Health Office in Paris. Our government officials have also taken part in many phases of the health program, and there is now only friendly interest in it on their part.

It is, however, from private institutions that the League has received its greatest American aid. Distinguished members of the medical schools of Harvard, Yale, and Columbia Universities have cooperated, and the Rockefeller Foundation has supported the Health Organization powerfully from the start. This Foundation's financial contributions now exceed $1,000,000 spent for many purposes, and it has not been a matter of giving money alone.[27]

It would be difficult for the health authorities of many countries to conceive of the disappearance of the Health Organization, with its steady streams of vital information and helpful service.

[26] League Secretariat, *Ten Years of World Cooperation*, pp. 232-60.

[27] Miss Hubbard's account contains the names of more than a dozen leading American doctors who have served with the Health Organization. She states that the Rockefeller Foundation contributions had reached $941,000 in 1931.—*The Cooperation of the United States with the League of Nations*, International Conciliation, No. 274, November, 1931, pp. 722-25.

OUTSTANDING OFFICIALS OF THE LEAGUE OF NATIONS SECRETARIAT

Top, left to right: Sir Arthur Salter (British), Director of the Economic and Financial Section, 1922–1930; Salvador de Madariaga (Spanish), Director of the Disarmament Section, 1922–1928, representative in the League of Nations Council, 1931–1936; M. R. Haas (French), Director of the Communications and Transit Section, 1920–1935.

Bottom, left to right: Dr. Ludwik Rajchman (Polish), Director of the Health Section since 1921; Paul Mantoux (French), Director of the Political Section, 1920–1927; Sir Herbert Ames (Canadian), Financial Director, 1919–1926.

Pictures of Madariaga by Wide World, of Mantoux by Boesch, of Ames by Notman; other pictures from the Information Section of the Secretariat.

It would be especially deplorable for the Organization to be destroyed by new wars, which would bring famine and pestilence in their train.

Labor

With the League's greatest effort to improve conditions of life and labor the United States was not associated at all during Normalcy. The International Labor Organization had developed as a semiautonomous wing of the League until it was one of the largest and most active international agencies in existence. Its annual conferences had recommended, up to 1931, some 31 treaties aimed at improving labor conditions by international agreement. The number of ratifications of these treaties by individual nations had mounted to 628. The staff of approximately 400 people maintained at the Geneva office of the I. L. O. gathered, systematized, and published a wealth of material on labor and economic conditions which could be found nowhere else. The I. L. O. library and files comprised a storehouse of information such as had never existed before. Here every nation could see how its own economic conditions compared with those in other countries. Here every advanced nation could aid in lifting, by slow degrees, the labor standards of the more backward nations.

Originally, too, Samuel Gompers, President of the American Federation of Labor, had presided at the Paris Peace Conference over the creation of the I. L. O. Under the cautionings of Professor James T. Shotwell and others, the whole organization had been molded to permit the United States, with her federal system, to have a part. The first conference of the I. L. O. was held in Washington and was presided over by our Secretary of Labor, William B. Wilson. After 1920, however, the I. L. O. was shunned as something connected with the League. American labor lost interest in it during the days of prosperity. American employers regarded it as somewhat socialistic. The great gain to ourselves from any raising of labor standards among our competitors was not appreciated.[28] Nor was there any serious concern because the efforts of the I. L. O. were continually negatived by the fact that the most powerful industrial country in the world would accept none of the treaties proposed. The United States went her way, ignoring the charges of economic imperialism leveled against her, until her share of world-wide economic ruin gave a new perspective.[29]

World Court Entry Proposed

The extent to which the opposition to the League persisted in the United States, at least among the Senators who had defeated our entry, was freshly illustrated by their attitude toward the effort of the Harding-Hughes Administration to adhere to the World Court.

A Development Long Supported. For more than a century the United States had justly claimed to be a leading advocate of the peaceable settlement of international disputes, if not the leader. The mixed commissions of the Jay Treaty of 1794 with great Britain had "marked the advent of modern arbitration as a means of settling international disputes." Between that date and 1900, the United States had participated in fifty-six arbitrations. Both Houses of Congress had repeatedly endorsed the practice and our jurists and statesmen had been foremost in the movement to establish a permanent court. In the First Hague Conference, 1899, they had led a strong fight for such a court and had secured it—in name only (the Permanent Court of Arbitration).[30]

In the Second Hague Conference our leaders had been equally active in behalf of a real court and when, early in 1920, the

[28] See Williams, *American Diplomacy*, pp. 284-88, and Charles W. Pipkin, "Relations of the I. L. O. with the League of Nations," *Annals of the American Academy of Political and Social Science*, March, 1933, Vol. 166, pp. 124-34. The fullest account of the American origins of the I. L. O. is to be found in the two volume work edited by Professor James T. Shotwell, ed. *The Origins of the International Labor Organization*, New York, 1934.

[29] The United States accepted membership in the I. L. O. in August, 1934.

[30] See H. Lauterpacht, in A. J. Toynbee, *Survey of International Affairs, 1926*, London, 1928, p. 82-83.

League of Nations had proceeded to organize the Permanent Court of International Justice, two Americans, Elihu Root and James Brown Scott, had taken a leading part in drafting the Court's governing statute. It was, in fact, Root who solved the deadlock of the Hague Conferences by pointing out to the League committee in charge that the means were now at hand for solving the quarrel between the large states and the small ones as to how the judges should be elected. Let the League Council and Assembly both take part in the balloting, said Root. Then neither the Powers nor the lesser states can dominate the elections, yet both will have a veto on every candidate.[31]

Since Root was the chief attorney for the Republican Senators in their campaign against the League in the Senate, it might have been supposed that his advocacy of the World Court would take the League taint from it enough to permit our long advocacy of the judicial settlement of disputes to bear fruit. And in the campaign of 1920 there had been some indications that his influence would prevail. Republican leaders gradually developed the idea that their party continued to stand for the "judicial" method of settling disputes as opposed to Wilson's "political" league. Harding himself hinted that his proposed substitute for the League might be built around the new Court.[32]

Search for an "Association of Nations." After the election a prospectus of the new Association of Nations which centered around a world court was issued, on January 12, 1921, and on May 31 a semi-official White House statement indicated that the Administration was negotiating for a "gradual development of the (Allied) Supreme Council, coupled with the creation of an international court of justice." [33]

It was hoped that the Washington Conference would enable the Harding Government to gather the powers around the treaties

[31] This calculation was based upon continued control of the Council by the Great Powers. Their loss of a voting majority in the Council has not, however, created any difficulties in the election of judges.

[32] C. A. Berdahl, *The Policy of the United States with Respect to the League of Nations*, Geneva, 1932, pp. 75-76, 83.

[33] *New York Times*, January 12, June 1, 1921.

signed there and, with some provision for a continuing series of world conferences plus a world court, would cause the League of Nations to be abandoned. These hints were given out in an official White House statement in November.[34] But it was found that these proposals did not tempt our former Allies, while they definitely displeased the Irreconcilables. Consequently, H. G. Wells was soon able to state from Washington that Senator Johnson had received "positive assurances from President Harding that no further steps towards a definite organization of an association of nations were to be taken for the present." [35]

Thereafter, little was heard of the promised association of nations. But the pro-League majority in the Republican party was restless.[36] The President's inaugural address had promised flatly that we "would gladly join" in a world court, and the reputable members of the Harding Cabinet could not accept a total negation of the tremendous rebellion of the American people in the war years against the tragic absurdity of a world of nations at the mercy of any warmaker. Though in the main these men bowed their heads to the fury of the storm which the Senate had stirred up, it seemed incredible to some of Harding's advisors, as to countless others, that nothing whatever would result from the unprecedented amount of clear-sighted, hard thinking which American leaders of every rank had done on the subject of war prevention while the pitiful but colossal folly of the war was before their eyes. They knew that the solutions agreed upon so universally before the Armistice could not be utterly false im-

[34] Berdahl, *The Policy of the United States with Respect to the League of Nations*, p. 26; *New York Times*, November 19 and 26, 1921.

[35] *Chicago Tribune*, December 9 and November 28, 1921.

[36] In his autobiography, Calvin Coolidge says concerning the situation as the campaign of 1920 opened: "Many Republicans did not like the uncertain tone of the platform concerning the League of Nations. Though it was generally conceded that the bitter-enders had dictated the platform there were some who felt it was not explicit enough in denouncing the League with all its works and everything foreign, and *a much larger body of Republicans were disappointed* that it did not declare in favor of ratifying the treaty with reservations."—Calvin Coolidge, *The Autobiography of Calvin Coolidge*, New York, 1929, pp. 148-49. Italics mine.

mediately afterwards, and that the probability of our regaining a carefree isolation was small.

When to these convictions was added the knowledge that the pro-League Republicans would go to the polls again in 1924 it would have been strange if the Harding Administration had not concluded that something tangible must be done to reunite the United States with the cooperative effort being made through the League to supplant war as a means of settling disputes. It would have been strange indeed if Harding had not plucked up the courage to recommend to the Senate, February 24, 1923, that the United States adhere to the World Court. He made no empty assertion in saying: "Our deliberate public opinion of today is overwhelmingly in favor of our full participation." The statement was true, as every subsequent test of the nation's judgment for several years proved, but the Senate leaders could never admit the fact.[37]

The Hughes Reservations. With the hope of placating them, Secretary Hughes himself had proposed four reservations: (1) that adhesion to the Court should not involve any legal relation to the League or the assumption of any obligations under its Covenant; (2) that the United States should participate in "all proceedings of either the Council or the Assembly for the election of Judges;" (3) that we should pay a fair share of the Court's expenses, a share to be determined by Congress; and (4) that the Court's governing statute should not be amended without our consent.

The first of these reservations was politically inevitable and the remaining three were necessary to give us, as a non-member of the League, a working membership in the Court. But these stipulations did nothing to reassure the Republican Senate leaders. Nor were they alarmed. They knew that by their control of the Senate machinery they could defeat any treaty proposal that might be laid before them, no matter how reasonable or how

[37] See D. F. Fleming, *The Treaty Veto of the American Senate*, New York, 1930, Chapters 9 and 10. On the reaction of the country, see especially pp. 185-89.

strongly supported. The experience of 1919 was too fresh in mind to give them a moment's uneasiness. The Committee on Foreign Relations was still dominated by the bitter-enders, placed there for the handling of Wilson's League. The Committee was further packed, and its members began to brand the Court before the country as "a League court." It was a vague objection and for the time being they had no specifications for it, but they felt confident that it would be sufficient, if urged long enough.

The Court's proponents were nervous. Remembering the flames of hatred which had been roused until they consumed Wilson and his League, they proceeded to argue that it was not a League court. This was true to the extent that the Court was now an independent entity, operating under its own statute. It was even possible that if the League went under, the Court might still continue to function. But it had been created by the League, had the same members, and if the League disintegrated or was smashed by a new holocaust there was small reason to think that the Court would survive.

The Smallest Possible Step. Secretary Herbert Hoover, of the Commerce Department, speaking in Des Moines on April 11, 1923, held that the connection with the League was remote, but he did utter two truths which have permanent validity. "The Court," he said, "is not the total solution of international cooperation for peace, for the great field of political action as distinguished from judicial action remains unsolved, but this step is sound and sure. It is the minimum possible step in eliminating the causes of war." [38]

[38] *New York Times,* April 12, 1923. In an address in New York, April 23, 1923, President Harding stressed that the Court was to be a substitute for the League, of which he said: "In compliance with its pledges, the new Administration which came into power in March, 1921, definitely and decisively put aside all thought of the United States entering the League of Nations. It doesn't propose to enter now by the side door, the back door or the cellar door."—*New York Tribune,* April 24, 1923. In making this statement the President ignored the fifty per cent of his campaign utterances which had looked toward the League.

Shortly afterward, on June 22, 1923, in order to further placate his pained friends and creators in the Senate, Harding proposed a new plan for entering

Hoover rightly had "no confidence in the continuity of our civilization unless preventive safeguards can be established." Then as now the future of civilization rested with the political machinery of the League, not with its judicial arm, the Court. The enthronement of the Court was the eventual aim, but no man of reason could expect it ever to have a chance unless over a long period the League prevented other and deadlier wars. Joining the Court was the "minimum possible step" that the United States could take. As a non-member of the Court we were already privileged to submit our disputes to it if we chose, and by formally accepting membership in it we bound ourselves to nothing additional.

As a practical measure to meet a deadly world peril, from which we had just suffered and which, if the League failed, would certainly recur again and again, adherence to the Court was the smallest conceivable step that could be taken. As a sign that we had not permanently separated ourselves from the society of nations, joining the Court would have very great moral value. But unless it led to our support of the League before or when its hour struck, the step would have no permanent importance.

Obstruction and Delay. The best friends of the League and its strongest opponents both understood the issue. But for some time the Senate clique could only cry "Unclean!" Their logical position was hardly defensible, so they asked for long explanations about this strange court, of which they had apparently not heard. Ten months passed. Then Senator Lenroot gravely introduced a resolution, December 10, 1923, proposing to create two new electoral bodies, almost exact duplicates of the League Council and Assembly, in order that we might not be contaminated by occasionally sitting in those bodies for an hour. In other specifications he called upon the forty-four members of the

---

the Court, which was "so impossible of acceptance that Senator Borah promptly indicated his willingness to accept it," while the President's more responsible advisers ignored it. C. A. Berdahl, *The Policy of the United States with Respect to the League of Nations*, p. 92; *New York Times*, June 22, 1923.

League to stultify themselves by cutting the Court away from all connection with the League.[39]

Meanwhile, the Senators were campaigning in the country to rouse the old passions which had defeated the League. Senator Borah explained to a New York audience, March 19, 1923, that he was strongly for *a* court, but not this one. With his usual all-embracing and confusing generosity he offered to support it if the nations would accept the compulsory jurisdiction proposed for the Court by Elihu Root—an offer which he well knew he would never need to fulfill. Borah saw eye to eye with Senator Lodge, who was "thoroughly in favor" of a "true" world court. Lodge yearned for a "genuine" court.[40]

After he had succeeded Harding, President Coolidge urged the Senate to approve the Court proposal, December 3, 1923, but Mr. Lodge's committee was too busy to conduct a first hearing until compelled by public demands to do so on April 30, 1924. Then Bishop Brent, Chief Chaplain of the A. E. F., uttered a pregnant and prophetic warning. "Unless our Government," he said, "provides a moral substitute for war, as far as in it lies, a vast proportion of our citizenry are presently going to find themselves in the predicament of being opposed to war as an arbiter in international disputes, but without any provision being made for an adequate substitute of a peaceful and orderly character." [41]

A Democrat, Senator Claude Swanson, at last introduced a resolution proposing to adhere to the Court on the Harding-Hughes terms. The campaign of 1924 was approaching. Something was necessary to tide over that emergency. Senator Pepper of Pennsylvania, a member of the Committee, stepped forward, May 22, 1924, with a plan for divorcing the Court from the League more painlessly and elaborately. His plan even permitted the Council and the Assembly to continue as the electoral bodies of the Court, if only they were called to order for this purpose by an official of the Court. Bluntly or subtly the nations would

[39] *Congressional Record*, Vol. 65, Pt. 1, p. 151.
[40] *New York Times*, March 20, and December 14, 1923.
[41] *New York Times*, May 1, 1924.

be asked to confess that there was something sinister, or at least hardly respectable, in the relationship between the League and the Court. But to make his demand certain of rejection, Mr. Pepper nailed it down with six substantive specifications, in the form of amendments to the Court's statute, and ten formal changes.[42]

A Danger Discovered. So far the Committee's obstruction and delay had been too transparent to deceive anyone. But at last the portentous danger which they had long sought was discovered. The Court gave advisory opinions to the League Council and Assembly on matters of law, as do the supreme courts of eleven states of the United States. Couldn't the Council embarrass the United States some time by asking the Court if the war debts should be paid on the terms agreed? Or couldn't the Court be told to drag out the old skeleton of our repudiated state bonds and rattle it? Wouldn't the Court be sure to listen to Japanese complaints about the total exclusion from the United States of Japanese immigrants? All Japan was writhing under the blow of the exclusion law which had recently been passed by Congress. Wouldn't she certainly persuade the Council to ask the Court a question which would embarrass us?

No more could be alleged. An advisory opinion was binding upon no one. The most that it could do would be to make us feel ill at ease. The practical prospect, too, that the members of the League Council, representing all kinds of nations in all parts of the world, would gang together to make things uncomfortable for the United States was very small. It was true that we had not been too sociable since the war and that our creditor position did not bring us great popularity, but the utility of baiting the world's creditor with pin pricks administered deftly by the Council through the Court was hard to discover, particularly if the League powers were all bent upon ensnaring the United States into League membership. If that was their purpose there would

42 *Congressional Record,* Vol. 65, Pt. 8, p. 7904.

be neither rhyme nor reason in alarming us by sly attacks through the Court which would keep us out of the League permanently.

Yet the ensnarement argument broke down equally if we were "inveigled" into the League by way of the Court, for then we could protect ourselves against the asking of any advisory opinions by the Council which we thought might embarrass us. Moreover, bolting from the League back to the "safety" of political isolation would always be open to us. The whole advisory-opinion bogey was self-annihilating, again, for the reason that if the full cooperation of the United States was not valuable to the Court or the League, they would not desire it, and if they obtained it, they could not afford to destroy it.

Moreover, the Court itself had established a protective precedent, July 23, 1923, in refusing to give an advisory opinion in the Eastern Carelia case because Russia did not accept the Court's jurisdiction. It was, said the Court, "well established in international law that no state can without its consent be compelled to submit its disputes with other states either to mediation or to arbitration or to any other kind of pacific settlement." [43] If the Court would not try to embarrass Russia, then a pariah among nations with no prospect of ever tolerating Court or League, the danger of the Court's changing a precedent which protected its own future in order to displease the United States was remote, to say the least. Nor did the reservation made by the Council to the Court's refusal of an opinion in the Eastern Carelia case point to peril for the United States. The Council recorded that it could not "exclude the possibility of resort by the Council to any action, including a request for an advisory opinion from the Court, on a matter in which a State a non-member of the League and unwilling to give information is involved, if the circumstances should make such action necessary to enable the Council to fulfill its functions under the Covenant of the League in the interests

[43] For a full discussion of the advisory function of the Court, see Manley O. Hudson, *The Permanent Court of International Justice*, New York, 1934, Chapter 22, pp. 450-471. This book is the leading authority on all phases of the Court's activity and history.

of peace." [44] If there was danger to the United States in this, she already stood under it and could only protect herself by taking her place in the Council and the Assembly. As a non-member of both the Court and the League the United States was, and is today, in the greatest possible jeopardy from any perils which may exist in the advisory-opinion function. Both as a signatory of the Court's statute and as a member of the League, she could defend herself by voice, vote, and the use of her tremendous influence against the supposed hazards of surreptitious condemnations by the Court.

As a non-member of both Court and League the United States is utterly defenseless against the alleged dangers.

A reservation aimed at these assumed perils was, however, inevitable as soon as they were set up. Acting upon the Senate's settled maxim—that if a reservation is not necessary it won't hurt anything to add it anyway—other Senators were sure to rally to those who desired a nullifying reservation. As early as May 23, 1924, it was decided in the Committee on Foreign Relations that a reservation on advisory opinions must be added.[45] Otherwise, Japanese emigrants might invade the country by way of The Hague. The lawyers of the Senate could easily be persuaded that nothing must be left to the good sense of the judges of the Court, that everything must be made safe for all time by another added sentence or two.

The Committee finally let the Court proposal escape to the Senate, May 24, 1924, after it had been loaded down with the Pepper plan (later discarded), a few days before the Republican National Convention endorsed the Court.[46] After the election it therefore had the endorsement of a huge Republican electoral majority and the renewed support of President Coolidge. Yet

[44] *Ibid.*, p. 458.

[45] *New York Times*, May 23 and 24, 1924.

[46] Senator Lodge had withdrawn his plan, which ignored the existing World Court entirely and called on the President to summon a Third Hague Conference to set up an entirely new court, on the basis of Lodge's sixty-seven-article plan. *Senate Joint Resolutions*, No. 122, Senate Document No. 107, 68th Congress, 1st Session.

another full year elapsed before the question was permitted to come up for action in the Senate. Lodge had died, but Borah had inherited his chairmanship of the Committee and his threats prevented action until December, 1925. During this time, Borah was continuing his campaign to arouse the country, without appreciable success. With but few exceptions all the great national organizations, both lay and religious, stood for the Court. Scores of state or regional associations and four-fifths of the press did likewise. The country refused to be stampeded again. The old cries were distinctly less terrifying. Only the Ku Klux Klan and the Irish organizations responded to them.[47]

A Fifth Reservation. As the debate began in the Senate, December 17, 1925, Senator Swanson introduced the expected fifth reservation, which said that the United States should be "in no manner bound" by any advisory opinion "not rendered pursuant to a request in which it, the United States, shall expressly join." This after all, was fairly harmless. No one could object to it. And therefore it was an unsatisfactory reservation. Unless it could be stiffened the members of the Court would accept it.

Accordingly, while Borah and others thundered in the Senate about the Court's connection with the League and the peril to the Monroe Doctrine, a new Pepper plan was elaborated, in which it was demanded: (1) that we should pledge all the members of the Court to make forever binding the principle laid down in the Eastern Carelia case, that no advisory opinion should be given when one of the parties refused to accept the jurisdiction of the Court; and (2) instead of merely declaring that we would not be bound by any advisory opinion which we had not joined in submitting, we should bind the Court never to *give* an advisory opinion on any matter affecting the United States unless we had "consented that the Court take jurisdiction."

These demands would plainly accomplish the purpose sought. They required the nations who were members of the League and the Court to proclaim publicly that they were not to be trusted,

[47] Fleming, *The Treaty Veto of the American Senate*, pp. 185-89.

that they were likely at any time to engineer the reversal of a sound precedent and to conspire in the making of a propaganda attack upon the morals of some aspect of United States policy. Of course, no self-respecting government could make such an admission. The formula had been discovered which would make impossible the cooperation of the United States in support of the Court.

This formula also had the double advantage of securing from the Court's proponents in the Senate, if they could be induced to accept it, admission that they were really seeking to put the United States at the mercy of a nest of blackmailers—the League Council—and that the Court could never be trusted to defend itself against conspiracies, in which case, no hope remained of its attaining the only kind of authority it could expect to have for generations, a high moral standing throughout the world.

To put the advocates of the Court in this position, the handful of permanent opponents of the League in the Senate could rely upon the long-proved willingness of the lawyers in the Senate to increase the advantage of the United States (or to make assurance doubly sure) by the addition of another sentence or two to a treaty or a reservation. To ensure success in early 1926, the embattled dozen were able to confront the pro-Court leaders with nothing less than support for their position from the American who had been sitting as a judge on the World Court since its opening in 1922.

Judge Moore Enlisted. Never friendly toward the League, Judge John Bassett Moore had not approved at the start of giving advisory opinions to the Council or to the Assembly.[48] He had later supported the establishment of the same full and open procedure for the consideration of advisory opinions as for the cases in which judgments were to be given,[49] and in 1923 he had opposed ably and effectively a proposal of Judge Altamira for

[48] Series D, No. 2, pp. 383-98.
[49] *Ibid.*, p. 160.

secret procedure in giving advisory opinions.[50] In the Eastern Carelia case, in the same year, Judge Moore had been a leading member of the majority and had noted that four of the eleven judges dissented from the finding of the Court that an advisory opinion could not be given when a state concerned refused to appear before the Court.

Judge Moore was known as the greatest living American authority on international law and as a man of very impressive personality and appearance. When, therefore, he appeared in Washington one evening before a group of some twenty Senators and advised that it would be wise for them to insist that the United States have an absolute veto upon the hearing of all advisory opinions that might come before the Court, there were none to say him nay. The Democratic leaders acquiesced, especially when Moore's advice was supported by a memorandum presented by Senator Borah to the Senate, January 18, 1926. Borah did not say that Moore wrote the memorandum. He said: "I regret that I am not at liberty to use the name of the author, who is well known as an international jurist, because he is in official life and I have not permission to do so, though I hope to get permission later." It may be added that the description "a well known international jurist . . . in official life" applied to very few, if any, Americans other than Judge Moore.

The memorandum stressed that the Eastern Carelia precedent had been set "only by a majority of 7 to 4, so that a difference of two votes would have turned the scale the other way. Such a difference might easily occur in another case. Wholly apart from the possibilities of two of the majority judges shifting their position, the absence of two of them and the substitution of two deputies might produce the same result." The implication was strong that the judges could not be trusted. On any day they might upset the wholesome Eastern Carelia precedent. Nor was this all, continues the memorandum: "When we consider the

[50] Series D, No. 2 (Add.), pp. 293-96; Hudson, *The Permanent Court of International Justice*, p. 212.

formal reservation made by the Council and what has since occurred,[51] it must be admitted that the action taken by the Court in that case, two years ago, cannot now be accepted as a sufficient safeguard for the future.

"Nor could it ever have been so accepted by any prudent statesman." Evidently, the State Department had been most careless. The issue at stake was "too vital, too far-reaching, too profound." It was "simply whether the United States, which is not a member of the League of Nations, shall, in adhering to the court, put itself in a position of national inferiority, by omitting to assure to itself a right of self-protection similar to that which other great powers, members of the league, possess."

The original form of the Fifth Reservation, continued the international jurist, was "worse than useless," because it admitted the right of the Court to give advisory opinions in which we were concerned. The four Great Powers on the Council could block the submission of questions to the Court. On what principle was the United States to "renounce the right of self-protection in like circumstances?" Plainly, the mere Senators who had framed the Fifth Reservation had been guilty of something close to treason. "Strange as it may seem," chided the memorandum severely, "the proposal to denude the United States of this right of self-protection is made solely in the United States. There is not the slightest reason to suppose that any other country would have the hardihood either to propose to the United States such an act of self-immolation, or to deny the request of the United States to be treated as an equal."

After hearing this from the highest authority it would have been stranger still if the Senators had not hastened to pull the United States out of this position of dangerous inferiority in which they had left her. They had evidently been most remiss. For once the Senate had been negligent in the art of reservation making. The oversight was, however, easily reparable, for they were positively assured that there was "not the slightest reason"

[51] The reference is probably to the Mosul advisory opinion.

to anticipate any objection from any country to the proposed achievement of equality for the United States. Certainly, no Senator could fail to accomplish that objective, especially when assured that it was "in the interest of the Court as well as in the interest of all concerned."

Then, after a long paragraph on the dangers of the Court's giving secret advice, there followed a suggested reservation to give the United States its due equality in really effective fashion. The draft read:

That, in acting upon requests for advisory opinions, the court shall not, under any circumstances, depart from the essential rules guiding its activity as a judicial tribunal but shall give notice and open hearings to all interested parties, and shall in such case freely determine, in the exercise of its own judgment, whether it can, in keeping with its judicial character, properly answer the question put to it, and what shall be the nature and form of its response; that in no case shall the court give any confidential advice but shall announce its opinions publicly, together with the opinions of dissenting judges; that the court shall not give an opinion on a question to which the United States is a party without the consent of the United States; and that the United States disclaims all responsibility for any opinion on any question to the submission of which the United States was not a party.[52]

There was nothing in this draft that was not desirable. All the rules of procedure demanded of the Court were necessary and proper. They had all been adopted, too, under Judge Moore's able championing, perhaps largely because of it. But for a new member state coming into the Court to insist that they be bound tightly upon the Court was a different matter. The implication was plain that the Court was a highly risky experiment; that its members could not be trusted to follow sound and established precedents. If the United States could not safely venture to give the Court the advantage of its nominal membership without solemn promises from the forty-eight nations who were members of the Court that its good behavior was guaranteed, the Court

[52] *Congressional Record,* Vol. 67, Pt. 2, pp. 2293-94.

Wide World

WILLIAM E. BORAH

Underwood & Underwood

HIRAM JOHNSON

Underwood & Underwood

WILLIAM RANDOLPH HEARST

Underwood & Underwood

JOHN BASSETT MOORE

Underwood & Underwood

EDWIN M. BORCHARD

Underwood & Underwood

GEORGE HOLDEN TINKHAM

LEADING OPPONENTS OF AMERICAN MEMBERSHIP IN THE LEAGUE OF NATIONS

was indeed not a safe place into which to venture. And if it was as risky an institution as the specifications of the international jurist maintained, the nations which had set it up could not thus formally admit the failure of their efforts. They were no more likely to admit that the United States could not be safe from their machinations unless these bonds for good behavior were given.

The Fifth Reservation Expanded. In his zeal to rivet the chains of rectitude upon the Court, the international jurist had done so much more than seize equality for the United States that even the Senators felt that they would have to be content with less. Judge Moore's assistance was therefore enlisted and the fifth reservation was expanded to say simply that the Court should not "without the consent of the United States entertain any request for an advisory opinion touching any dispute or question in which the United States has or claims an interest." [53]

The expanded reservation was offered in the Senate by Senator Swanson, January 23, 1926. Senator Overman, of North Carolina,

[53] *Congressional Record*, Vol. 67, Pt. 3, pp. 2656-57; *New York Times*, January 28, 1926. The *Times* said in a box on page one: "Washington, January 27.–It was made known today by pro-court Senators that John Bassett Moore, Judge of the World Court, had assisted in the preparation of the new reservations to the enabling resolution offered in the Senate Saturday by Senator Swanson. Judge Moore came to Washington from Wilmington, Delaware, it was said, and helped Senator Swanson and Senator Walsh to draft the new reservations, which are supplementary to those comprised in the so-called Harding-Hughes-Coolidge plan of American adherence.

"After this work was completed, Senator Lenroot, in charge of the World Court contest for the court's proponents, Senator Willis and several others were called in and gave their approval to the new reservations. All of these new reservations were adopted by the Senate yesterday without change."

Senator George Moses, of New Hampshire, leading irreconcilable, said on the 23rd of September, 1926, after an interview with President Coolidge: "Any one who knows the origin of the fifth reservation, and who is acquainted with its parentage, both real and putative, knows it will not be changed. No reservation drawn by John Bassett Moore and presented to the Senate jointly by Claude Swanson and Thomas Walsh is going to suffer much from changing."–*United States Daily*, September 24, 1926.

It might have seemed that Judge Moore's opinion of the trustworthiness of the Court was such as to justify his resignation, especially after the memorandum of the international jurist had been published and after the fifth reservation had kept the United States out of the Court. He did not, however, quit the World Court bench until April 11, 1928.

followed with a reservation which would bar the Court from considering without our consent "the question of the alleged indebtedness or moneyed obligation of any state of the United States or of immigration or of the Monroe Doctrine." This reservation was to be called up only in case the amended Fifth Reservation failed. The latter reservation was thus assured of the support of the Southern Democrats, because of the repudiated state bonds of eight states held abroad by foreign citizens. About $75,000,000 of "carpet bag" bonds were involved, on which about $300,000,000 of interest would now be due.

It was quite in vain that Senator Gillett, Republican, of Massachusetts, warned, on January 26, that the supposed dangers against which the reservation legislated were exceedingly remote. The Senate proposed our adhesion to the Court under it the next day by a vote of 76 to 17. Most Senators still assumed that any terms laid down by the United States would be accepted by all the other nations. Those who engineered the reservation knew better, but they had convinced the majority that the new Fifth Reservation was necessary to give the United States equality with the members of the League Council. Advisory opinions had always been requested of the Court by unanimous vote of the Council. Any member of the Council could therefore block the asking of an opinion by voting against the request. The United States should have the same right. Hence the reservation asserted a right on our part to block any advisory opinion proceeding in which "the United States has or *claims* an interest."

Would Equality Result? In practical operation, however, the free veto demanded by the Senate might put the United States in a position superior to that of the Council. The latter, when some legal angle of a dispute was blocking a settlement, would be familiar with all the details. Having wrestled with the case, perhaps repeatedly, each member of the Council could be depended on not to block an appeal to the Court unless some real interest of his nation was seriously and visibly menaced by what the Court might say. With the responsibilities of League and

Council membership resting upon him, a Council member could not block the solution of a dispute by any light objection to an appeal to the Court, even if some minor or supposed interest of his nation might turn out to be involved. And if a real interest should clearly be imperiled—which would very seldom be the case—he would exert himself privately to prevent the necessity of a public veto in the Council.

The United States, aloof from the urgency of advancing the settlement of the world's disputes, could act in each case only by sending, after the Council had acted, a formal notice to the Court ordering it to abandon hearing on the question submitted to it. This would be true unless the United States kept in such close touch with the Council's problems and deliberations as almost to be a member, a development which would be the last thing desired by the authors of the fifth reservation. In practice, again, our government would be likely to go very slowly in vetoing a request of the Council by asserting a claim of interest. The chances of our ever becoming alarmed about any proposed advisory opinion were very small. Yet the members of the League had to remember that the isolationist tail of the Senate not only motivated that body into sending ultimatums to them repeatedly, as in the case in point, but also dominated and overawed the President and the State Department. A government so controlled could certainly exercise a veto over the securing of an advisory opinion more irresponsibly than could the fourteen governments represented in the Council, representing as they did, directly or indirectly, the other members of the League. If the United States was to proclaim from the housetops her suspicion of each and every other nation, at the same time repeatedly repudiating or nullifying the signature of her Chief Executive to great treaties, she could not complain if other nations wondered whether she could always be trusted with a free and irresponsible veto over an important function of the Couucil.

Was Unanimous Consent Necessary and Advisable? Even more important was the serious doubt which the Senate precipitated as to whether any one nation, even a member of the Council, should be guaranteed an all-time right to block the Council's pacific functions on any day that it chose. Unanimous consent had been the rule followed, but the Covenant provides that matters of procedure may be settled by a majority vote. Some held that the asking of an advisory opinion was a matter of procedure, not of substance, and the argument for this view was strong. It was unlikely that a change of practice to avoid the stoppage of Council action by the captious opposition of one or two governments would be necessary. Still, the League was young, and when asked by the United States, in effect, to fix permanently the requesting of advisory opinions by unanimous vote, many people felt that it was not well to settle a debatable question so soon. The very moment when Brazil was bringing the League almost to the point of disruption by her lone veto of Germany's entry into the League was certainly not the time to congeal the unanimity rule. Aside from the convulsion through which the League was passing, there was a growing feeling that the success of the League might depend on weakening of the unanimity rule, instead of strengthening it.

Would Forty-Eight Nations Agree? The manner in which the Senate demanded the acceptance of its terms was also not calculated to make the nations conclude that they could safely strengthen the unanimity rule by giving the Senate-controlled United States a free veto over advisory opinions. The Senate had specified that the signature of the United States to the Court protocol should "not be affixed until the signatory powers to such protocol shall have indicated, through an exchange of notes, their acceptance of the foregoing reservations and understandings."

No discussion of the Fifth Reservation was to be permitted, and no acceptance with reservations. Only the Senate could do that. The forty-eight members of the Court were each to send an unconditional acceptance to Washington. To some Senators, accustomed to settling everything by legislative fiat, this may have appeared to be a sober proceeding. To those intent upon defeating our adhesion to the Court it must have been the cause of many chortles of glee. To expect fifty busy governments scattered over the globe to return, without a word of protest or qualification, fifty acceptances of the Senate's remarkable demand that they all promise they would never slyly pick the pockets of the United States was to expect what was most improbable, to say the least. To expect a dozen individual men to return by mail a single word, "Yes," in answer to a complicated proposition affecting their interests to an extent not easily calculable would have been naïve indeed; to assume that four dozen governments would do so was a supposition which only the United States Senate, from the depths of the mental and factual isolation from world affairs in which it operated, could make.

After the hit-and-run policy which the Senate had pursued at the close of the war, the nations might be expected to view its next approach with at least the degree of caution which they evinced. Five small states did indicate, in the course of six months, that they would be willing to trust the Senate to use with discretion the defensive weapon which it demanded. Six much more important states, including two of the great British Dominions whose formal entry into the family of nations the Senate had so gravely deplored, did not reply at all.[54] Sixteen nations simply acknowledged the American proposal without indicating whether they thought it acceptable or not. That such replies should be received to any questionable proposition from a third of the governments was not strange, yet the Senate's communication required the simple assent of the forty-eight. One failure to agree positively and unreservedly would keep us out of the Court.

The chances of our adhesion to the Court were not as good as 48 to 1, unless the representatives of the governments could be gathered together and some sort of agreement secured. Accordingly, on March 18, 1926, at the close of the Council session which

[54] Brazil, Bulgaria, Canada, Chile, Hungary, and New Zealand. The states which accepted the Senate's terms were: Cuba, Greece, Liberia, Albania, and Luxembourg. *United States Daily*, December 31, 1927.

had been made dangerously abortive by Brazil's free use of her Council veto, Sir Austen Chamberlain proposed a conference of the members of the Court, to meet September 1, 1926, in order to discuss the implications of the Senate's proposals.

Upon receipt of this news the Irreconcilables were properly amazed. Borah announced that the United States would have to go through with it and "sit with" the League.[55] But the State Department knew that it could not venture to discuss the Senate's last word with anyone. To an invitation to attend the September Conference, Secretary Kellogg replied that no "useful purpose could be served" by attending the conference. The reservations were "plain and unequivocal," and "according to their terms they must be accepted by an exchange of votes between the United States and each of the forty-eight States." He even went so far as to "see no difficulty in the way of securing the assent of each signatory by direct exchange of notes, as provided by the Senate" and to "regret if the Council should do anything to create the impression that there are substantial difficulties in the way of such communication." In this brusque manner did Kellogg avoid a conference in which he could neither sit as a legal equal nor afford to appear as anything less.

The conference was attended by the representatives of twenty-two nations. It deliberated in a careful and conciliatory manner through the month of September, solely on the provisos added by the Senate to the Hughes reservations. To Secretary Hughes's fourth reservation, saying that the Court's statute should not be amended without our consent, the Senate had added that we could withdraw our adhesion at any time.

A Counter Reservation Adopted. To this provision the conference made no objection, but since none of the members of the Court had reserved a right of withdrawal, the conference felt that: "In order to assure equality of treatment, it seems natural that the signatory states, acting together and by not less than a majority of two-thirds, should possess the corresponding

[55] *New York Times*, March 19 and 20, 1926.

right to withdraw their acceptance of the special conditions attached by the United States to its adherence to the said Protocol in the Second part of the fourth reservation and in the fifth reservation. In this way the *status quo ante* could be re-established if it were found that the arrangement agreed upon was not yielding satisfactory results." [56]

This reservation doubtless seemed to the United States Senators quite unnecessary. But in view of the attitude of the Senate no one could say it was illogical or unjustified. The Senate had balked American membership in the League by reservations which no other nation had put forward. Again it was setting up conditions which no other nation had thought necessary. That it would play a similar role in the future was to be expected. To be sure, there was party politics in the affair of 1920, but there might be soon again.

The impossibility of telling when some fraction of the all wise Senate would demand the stoppage of an advisory-opinion proceeding was one of the things which the conference had to consider in pondering Reservation Five. Who would decide when the United States veto was to be exercised? Was it to be the Senate, or the Executive? And how should it be done? If the Senate was not in session, could the Council venture to refer a critical legal point in a dispute to the Court before the Senate assembled?

Negotiation Invited. The conference did not know. Nor could anybody supply the information. It was therefore proposed that "the manner in which the consent provided for in the second part of the fifth reservation is to be given, will be the subject of an understanding to be reached by the Government of the United States with the Council of the League of Nations." An agreement might thus be worked out which would permit the United States to feel comfortable as a member of the Court, without disorganizing one of the Court's most useful functions.

[56] *The Final Act of the Conference*, Publications de la Société des Nations, V. Questions Juridiques, 1926, V. 24, p. 6.

The conference did not reject the Fifth Reservation, but accepted it in principle, freely admitting the right of the United States to an equal position. The Final Act said: "The Conference understands the object of the United States to be to assure to itself a position of equality with states represented either on the Council or in the Assembly of the League of Nations. This principle should be agreed to." And again: "In any event the United States should be guaranteed a position of equality." How this position of equality should be vouchsafed in working terms to a non-member of the League, distant and suspicious, was a subject for negotiation and accommodation.

Discussion Declined. It is difficult to see what other reasonable conclusion could have been reached, but the reply of the principal members of the Court to the Senate's ultimatum, forwarded by the conference powers in twenty-two separate notes, as the Senate required, found no response in Washington. President Coolidge, who had repeatedly advocated adhering to the Court, did not seize the opportunity to press the negotiations rapidly to a conclusion. The Executive had not sponsored the reservations which had complicated the situation. It was common knowledge that the majority of the Senators had been convinced that the expanded reservations would only give us equality with the League members. The bulk of the Senators had not intended to ask for more and the Senate was in adjournment for three months.[57]

But it did not occur to Coolidge to risk the thunders of the terrible dozen in the Senate by promptly advancing a solution of the imbroglio which they had caused. Instead, he took umbrage at the temerity which the nations had displayed in venturing to analyze the Senate's offer and joined the Irreconcilables. The reply of the Powers went unanswered until, in an Armistice Day speech six weeks later, the President announced that he "did not intend to ask the Senate to modify its position." The address was correctly headlined as "World Court Entry Only On Our Own

[57] See Berdahl, *The Policy of the United States with Respect to the League of Nations*, pp. 92-94. For an excellent account of this entire episode see pp. 81-95.

Terms." [58] After advising us against any national spirit of suspicious distrust and hatred, a "form of luxury" in which "the Old World had for generations indulged itself," the President explained acidly that: "We are a creditor nation. We are more prosperous than some others. This means that our interests have come within the European circle where distrust and suspicion, if nothing more have been altogether too common. To turn such attention to us indicates at least that we are not ignored." Then, with lofty condescension, he bespoke, for the unfortunate "others," our "patience, our sympathy and such help as we believe will enable them to be restored to a sound and prosperous condition."

"Normalcy" was in full swing. At the top of its stride in the material conquest of the four-cornered earth it was able to look out over the nations and announce complacently: "At least we are not ignored!"

Normalcy

No review of the foreign affairs of the United States in the period succeeding the political demolition of Woodrow Wilson and "Wilson's League" could be complete without at least a brief description of the character of the regime which ruled the United States after the election of 1920. Just as the personality of Wilson dominated the war era, so did those of his successors set the tone of the period of Normalcy.

Harding Made President. The drive to destroy Wilson and all his works was conducted by men far abler than Warren G. Harding, but it suited their purposes perfectly to set him in Wilson's place. Amiable, "regular," impressive in appearance, without any strong views, a Senator, he could be depended upon to go along without disturbing either the political or economic powers-that-be by reforms, either international or national. The day after his nomination, the *New York Times* said in a front-page editorial that it would be received with astonishment and dismay. Harding was "a very respectable Ohio politician of the

[58] *Kansas City Star,* November 12, 1926.

second class." Never a leader of men or a director of policies, his Washington record had been "faint and colorless. He was an undistinguished and indistinguishable unit in the ruck of Republican Senators who obediently followed Mr. Lodge in the twistings and turnings of that statesman's forays upon the Treaty and the Covenant." His nomination was "the fine and perfect flower of the cowardice and imbecility of the Senatorial cabal." [59]

This was a strong condemnation, but it did not disturb the backers of Harding. They were too interested in what was ahead. "In 1920," says the outstanding chronicler of the period of Normalcy, "the American people, impatient of the rigid morality of Woodrow Wilson, turned instinctively to the Republican Party as the historic vehicle for the satisfaction of their predatory desires." [60] Harding's slogan, "A Return to Normalcy," adds William Allen White, "meant the return to respectability of those capitalist forces of greed and cunning in American life which Roosevelt had routed and Wilson civilized." The "bars were down and the hungry herd of capitalism came raging into the green pastures when Harding began to rule." [61]

In the forefront of the herd were the oil barons, led by Jake Hamon of Oklahoma City, who aspired to be Secretary of the Interior and thus to control the extensive public lands of the United States. Hamon, who made many boasts of his financial responsibility for Harding's nomination, was killed by his alleged mistress shortly after the election of 1920.[62]

[59] *New York Times*, June 13, 1920.

[60] M. R. Werner, *Privileged Characters*, New York, 1935, p. 3. Werner has obtained the bulk of the astonishing array of evidence which he presents from the many volumes of testimony by Congressional committees. His careful exposé is as compelling reading as a powerful drama. The sordid tragedy which he recounts is relieved by a deft use of comic elements.

For a sympathetic and palliative account of the Harding scandals, see Mark Sullivan, *Our Times*, New York, Vol. VI, 1935, pp. 221-372. A small book by M. E. Ravage, *The Story of Teapot Dome*, New York, 1924, is a keen description of the oil scandals, simply told. For an excellent short account of these events, see Frederick Lewis Allen's *Only Yesterday*, New York, 1931, Chap. 6.

[61] William Allen White, *Masks in a Pageant*, New York, 1930, p. 419.

[62] Werner, *Privileged Characters*, pp. 7-11. Harry Daugherty, Harding's campaign manager, later wrote that Hamon "had more influence among the delegates than any other one man in the convention" (p. 11).

Albert B. Fall Installed. Others no less ambitious survived him. Among them was Senator Albert B. Fall, of New Mexico. As a stern Irreconcilable, he had offered fifty amendments to the Treaty of Versailles purporting to divorce it from the League Covenant. It was therefore highly fitting that he should sit in the Harding Cabinet and that when his name was presented to the Senate for confirmation as Secretary of the Interior Senator Lodge should rise and secure its approval by acclamation, without reference to committee, as a special mark of approbation. It was fitting also that Fall should thereafter stand as a symbol of the triumph of the Senate cabal.[63]

The appointment of Secretary Fall was highly satisfactory to the oil men as well as to the Senate. Since 1909 the Navy Department had been entrusted with three very valuable tracts of reserve oil lands, to safeguard its future sources of motive power against a time of scarcity and emergency. As the price of oil rose during the war, Secretary Daniels and his Assistant Secretary, Franklin D. Roosevelt, had vigilantly fought off the efforts of oil companies to get control of the naval oil reserves.[64]

With the advent of Fall, the oil men began to frequent Washington. Fall started talking oil to Congressmen and reached for control of the naval oil reserves as well as of the national forests and of the rich resources of Alaska. His task with reference to oil was made easy by Harding's appointment of Edwin Denby, a mediocre politician from Michigan, as Secretary of the Navy.

Navy's Oil Reserves Turned Over to Fall. Less than a month after assuming office, Denby confessed to Rear Admiral R. S. Griffin, who as chief of the Naval Engineering Bureau was guardian of the Navy's oil reserves, that they were to be transferred to Fall's control. It was President Harding's wish, and

[63] Harding had wanted to appoint Fall Secretary of State, but that was too much even for Fall's fellow Irreconcilables. Senators Moses, McCormick, and Knox protested so strongly that he was given the Interior Department instead. Sullivan, *Our Times*, Vol. VI, pp. 146-47.

[64] *Congressional Record*, Vol. 62, p. 5792. At one time both men watched all night at the Capitol, during the closing hours of a session of Congress.

Denby also was in favor of it, so much so that he soon forwarded a draft of an executive order which Secretary Fall had written for Harding's signature. After he had failed to induce Fall to approve a safeguarding clause proposed by Admiral Griffin, Assistant Secretary of the Navy Theodore Roosevelt, Jr., carried the document to the White House, May 31, 1921, and secured the President's signature.[65]

In October, 1921, Denby removed Admiral Griffin from his post; abolished the Naval Fuel Oil Board, which Secretary Daniels had created to conserve the Navy's oil supply; and transferred all these functions to Admiral John K. Robison, a man who had been vastly impressed by hearing from a great oil magnate, Edward L. Doheny, that one of the Navy's oil reserves had already been drained away.[66]

Mr. Doheny was also an old friend of Secretary Fall. They were so intimate, in fact, that on November 28, 1921, a month after the appointment of Robison, Doheny wrote to Fall offering to construct storage tanks for the Navy at Pearl Harbor, Hawaii, in exchange for oil to be taken out of the Navy's oil reserves. From this deal Doheny expected to make $100,000,000.[67] He therefore could afford to honor promptly, the day after his letter of November 28, a request of Fall for a loan of $100,000 which was delivered to Fall in bills.

The Continental Trading Company Formed. In the same month a still more remarkable transaction occurred. November 17, 1921, four oil men gathered in the Vanderbilt Hotel in New York.[68] The four men proceeded to buy 33,333,333 barrels of oil

[65] Werner, *Privileged Characters*, p. 53; Ravage, *The Story of Teapot Dome*, p. 31.

[66] Three other naval officers who persisted in opposing the looting of the Navy's oil were shipped from Washington. Werner, *Privileged Characters*, p. 54. Robison was eventually retired as a Captain instead of a Rear Admiral and went into Harry Sinclair's employ (p. 188).

[67] Werner, *Privileged Characters*, p. 142.

[68] They were Col. Robert M. Stewart, chairman of the board of the Standard Oil Company of Indiana; H. M. Blackmer, president of the Midwest Refinery Company, a Standard subsidiary; James E. O'Neil, president of the Prairie Oil and Gas Company, another Rockefeller company; and Harry F. Sinclair, presi-

from Colonel A. E. Humphreys, of Mexia, Texas, at $1.50 per barrel. The oil, however, was delivered to a dummy concern, the Continental Trading Company of Toronto, which turned it over at $1.75 a barrel to the oil companies represented by the four. The difference of $8,000,000 was to be split among the four conspirators, in the form of United States liberty bonds. It was a part of his share of this loot which Harry F. Sinclair later gave to Fall, carelessly forgetting that the numbers of the bonds might have been registered in Canada. They were.

The Oil Leases Effected. Sinclair obtained the lease to the Teapot Dome oil reserves in Wyoming, April 7, 1922, and Fall received from Sinclair $233,000 in liberty bonds, besides other sums in cash.[69] Sinclair then organized the Mammoth Oil Company, with 2,000,000 non-voting shares to 5,000 voting shares, and gave it the Teapot Dome lease. With this as its only asset, Sinclair thought, before any scandal arose, that the Mammoth Oil Company was worth $100,000,000. In any event, he made $17,059,700 in dealing in its shares, for which a market was "organized." Insiders bought the stock at $17.00 a share while the public was paying from $50.00 to $90.00.[70]

Meanwhile, Doheny had been securing control, by degrees, of the Navy's valuable oil reserves in California. His task was complicated by laws requiring public bidding, but in a series of contracts signed between April 15 and December 11, 1922, he achieved his objective. The Doheny transactions had been somewhat delayed by the La Follette Senate resolution of April 29, calling for an investigation of the whole business. This led President Harding to issue a statement, June 8, 1922, giving his full

---

dent of the Sinclair Crude Oil Purchasing Company, of which Blackmer and Stewart also shared the control.

69 Werner, *Privileged Characters*, pp. 70-71, 83.

70 When Col. James G. Darden started to drill upon his own land in the Teapot Dome area, Fall raged to President Harding until the latter gave his consent to the sending of marines to stop this iniquity. Theodore Roosevelt, Jr., arranged the expedition and when it returned added his congratulations to those which Fall gave to the commanding officer, Captain Shuler. Fall preferred strong-arm tactics to any airing of lease titles in the courts. Werner, *Privileged Characters*, pp. 89-97.

approval to the leases and taking full responsibility for the acts of his officers.

Fall Retired with Honors. On January 9, 1923, it was given out that Fall would resign on March 4, 1923. He had then signed the last contract with Doheny and concluded a sale of Shipping-Board oil to Sinclair. Harding announced that he had offered to appoint Fall a Justice of the Supreme Court, but Fall wished to look after his long-neglected private affairs. It was true. Fall was transforming into a show place his ranch at Three Rivers, New Mexico. He wanted to retire, not to repair his private fortunes as suggested, but to enjoy the spending of his bribes from the oil men. To further adorn his retreat, he took with him the elegant Jacobean office furniture from his office in the Department of the Interior, after he had transferred it to a Treasury Department committee and had given the committee a small check covering a minor fraction of the value. After him went a note from Herbert Hoover, Secretary of Commerce, voicing the "deep regret" of the vast majority of our people. In Hoover's recollection the Department of the Interior had "never had so constructive and legal a headship." Hoover trusted that Fall's private affairs would enable him to return to public life.

They never did. Fall lived a haunted and hunted life, always playing a bold and brazen game, until he finally went to prison in July, 1931, after being convicted on October 25, 1929. His fine was $100,000. Hoover, then President, refused to pardon him and he served five months. For the first time in the nation's history a Cabinet officer had been imprisoned.[71]

The Oil Chiefs Escaped Conviction. Fall's millionaire playfellows were more fortunate. The Supreme Court canceled the

[71] Edwin Denby, Secretary of the Navy, who had turned over the Navy's oil to Fall, quickly resigned when the storm broke. "Poor Denby," says Mark Sullivan, "was hounded."—*Our Times,* Vol. 6, p. 340. But M. E. Ravage refuses to pity him. "Mr. Denby," he says, "is neither a martyr nor a scoundrel. He was dismissed, not because he corruptly betrayed his trust, not because an aroused people demanded a scapegoat, but purely and simply on his record. His record demonstrated him to be ludicrously unfit for the post. The man merited neither tears nor prosecution."—*The Story of Teapot Dome,* p. 176.

Doheny leases, ordering reimbursement for all oil taken, and, on October 10, 1927, it declared unanimously that the Sinclair lease on Teapot Dome was made with fraud and corruption, branding Fall as a "faithless public officer." But the juries of Normalcy could not believe that men so wealthy as the oil barons could be guilty. Both Doheny and Fall were acquitted of conspiracy in Washington. Sinclair was convicted of contempt of the Senate in March, 1927, and sentenced to three months in jail, a penalty which did not daunt him. When his trial with Fall for criminal conspiracy came up in October, he had hired the Burns detective agency to put a man on every juror. Then the juror who decided to hang the jury talked too much, and after another trial lasting three months, Sinclair was sentenced to a further six months in prison. Both his terms were served. But on the conspiracy charge both he and Fall were acquitted, April 21, 1928, and after one jury had convicted Fall of taking a bribe from Doheny, another quickly decided that Doheny was not guilty of giving a bribe to Fall. It was only on his incidental offenses that Sinclair could be convicted.

To avoid their share of the reckoning, two of the four clandestine oil dealers, Blackmer and O'Neil, fled abroad and remained. Colonel Stewart narrowly escaped contempt of the Senate on a technicality. Later he was ousted as the head of the Standard Oil Company of Indiana by John D. Rockefeller, Jr. The grateful stockholders then voted him a pension of $75,000 a year, after he and others had made restitution of the twenty-five-cents-per-barrel liberty bonds to their companies.[72]

[72] No account of the oil exposures should overlook the indispensable and decisive part played by Senator Thomas J. Walsh, of Montana. As chairman of the Senate investigating committee, his industry was prodigious and his persistence never failing.

Senator Walsh received more censure for his activity at the time than the culprits he was uncovering. Leading New York papers called him and his colleague Senator Burton K. Wheeler "the Montana scandal-mongers," "mud-gunners" and "assassins of character." Elsewhere, the investigations were termed "poison-tongued partisanship, pure malice and twittering hysteria."—Allen, *Only Yesterday*, pp. 154-55.

Those who had voted for Normalcy wanted nothing done to disturb it. Besides, was not business doing well?

The Republican Party Financed. Some $185,000 in bonds had been given to Will Hays by Sinclair to help pay off the Republican campaign deficit. Sinclair had contributed $75,000 originally. After the investigations into the oil leases began, Hays was somewhat embarrassed by these bonds. He decided to peddle them out to prominent Republicans for cash. Some were disposed of in Chicago. Secretary of War John W. Weeks accepted others. Secretary of the Treasury Andrew W. Mellon was too canny; he was too wise to act as a fence for the disposal of goods of doubtful origin. Mellon's knowledge of the bonds, however, was not revealed until it was extorted, and his Department made no effort to collect income tax on the Continental bonds for three years after discovering their existence.

The Riot with Veterans Funds. While the Secretary of the Interior played for big stakes, others were not idle. Harding had placed one of his good-fellow friends in charge of the war veterans. Like Fall, Colonel Charles R. Forbes desired to have his domain extended. On April 29, 1922, the control of all veterans hospitals and of the huge supply depot in Perryville, Maryland, was transferred to the new chief of the Veterans Bureau. Six months later the Perryville depot was raided for train loads of goods, which were sent to the Thomson and Kelly Company of Boston at a price of twenty cents on the dollar. Twice Harding was roused to order the shipments stopped, but the first time Forbes talked him out of it and on the second occasion he was ignored.[73]

Veterans hospital sites were purchased and hospitals built in the same spirit. One was completed without a laundry, another without a kitchen. All over the land money was spilled out until, when the reckoning time came, more than 1,300 lawyers, physicians, and others assisted in the investigation as volunteers. It was

[73] Some 85,000 unused bed sheets, which had cost $1.00 each, went at 20 cents each. While these sheets were going out of one end of the warehouse others purchased by Forbes for the veterans' hospitals at $1.03 each were coming in at the other end. Other articles to the value of $6,000,000 were given away in a similar manner, with great haste and determination. See also Allen, *Only Yesterday*, p. 150.

estimated by a Senate Investigating Committee that the Forbes riot of waste and misconduct had cost the government $200,000,000. Colonel Forbes was convicted in 1924 of taking a bribe and sentenced to two years in prison.[74]

The Shipping Fleet Dispersed. The zeal of Colonel Forbes to dissipate valuable government property was exceeded, if possible, by Albert D. Lasker as head of the Shipping Board. Lasker's chief aim was to get out of the hands of the government the great merchant fleet built during the war. He made himself master of the Board, stopped the keeping of its minutes, declared the records of ship sales "private," and sold $20,000,000 worth of ships at $30.00 a ton, buyers to take their pick.[75] Lasker lobbied persistently for a huge ship-subsidy law and as steadily exaggerated the losses incurred by the Government-operated ships.[76]

Justice under Daugherty. In the Department of Justice, Harding had installed as Attorney General the man who had engineered his nomination. Harry Daugherty brought with him from Ohio, as bodyguard and confidant, Jess Smith. Among many others who came also was Howard Mannington. Smith and Mannington became the principal agents of a wholesale business in selling medicinal-liquor permits to drug companies, which in most cases received $1.00 a case for the use of their names but did not get the liquor. It went direct to bootleggers, after the collection of $14.00 a case for the withdrawal permits. This trade netted the ring about $750,000 in New York alone.[77]

[74] Werner, *Privileged Characters*, pp. 193-228. As the storm broke, one of his confederates in the Veterans' Bureau, Charles F. Cramer, shot himself.

[75] R. S. Dollar of the Dollar Line did so well in selecting 17 ships that his company paid him $635,493 in commissions for his services, in addition to his salaries and expenses. Werner, *Privileged Characters*, pp. 332.

[76] Werner, *Privileged Characters*, pp. 339-343. One ship-company lobbyist drew $332,000 from his companies for "Washington expenses" in 1928, in addition to a salary of $125,000 (p. 340).

[77] Werner, *Privileged Characters*, pp. 267-72. As convenient Washington headquarters, Daugherty's business men were supplied with two small houses. One at 1509 H Street was turned over to him by Edward B. McLean, along with two servants, for the use of Daugherty and Jess Smith. Mr. McLean's mansion had been a rendezvous for the bitter-enders while they were planning their campaign against the League, and it now became the social headquarters of the

The profits from liquor graft were large. But Daugherty and his friends also controlled the war-fraud and land-fraud cases. After turning the Department of Justice into the den of a ward politician, Daugherty was not interested in prosecuting violation of the antitrust laws. Restraint of trade ran riot and large price-fixing associations developed. The Department's investigators were used as a private spy system in an endeavor to "get something" on the Congressmen who pushed for investigations of Daugherty's conduct and proposed his impeachment. Small business men had little chance of securing redress and the alien owners of nearly $500,000,000 worth of property, still in the hands of the Alien Property Custodian, were in a worse plight.[78] In the American Metals Case, tried in 1926, Daugherty's defense admitted that $200,000 had gone to Jess Smith, in an effort to secure control of certain property. Everything was blamed on Smith, then dead. Daugherty, refusing to testify, escaped conviction. Colonel Thomas W. Miller, the Alien Property Custodian, was sentenced to eighteen months in prison.

The Carnival Ended by Death. For many Washington figures it was well that Jess Smith was found shot to death, May 30, 1923. Smith had so much to fear that he had lived in mortal terror

Harding regime. McLean was in charge of Harding's inauguration, and in place of the inaugural ball which Wilson had discontinued, "all Washington" went to his home and "revelled throughout the night." Alice Longworth, *Crowded Hours,* New York, 1933, p. 323.

In the Little Green House at 1625 K Street, Mannington and P. Kraffmiller were installed. This house became a favorite rendezvous of the Harding officials. William A. Orr, the New York head of the bootleg ring, arrived regularly with suitcases full of whisky and departed with permits for the withdrawal of liquor. But soon the Wells Fargo Express Company was delivering twenty cases of liquor at a time to the Little Green House. So many of the Harding officials called that small supplies would not do. Werner, *Privileged Characters,* pp. 22, 255-56, 267.

[78] The dope traffic flourished in the Atlanta and Leavenworth penitentiaries. When the Atlanta warden, J. E. Dyche, attempted to stop it, Heber Votaw, brother-in-law of President Harding, who had been appointed Superintendent of Prisons, blocked the attempt. Daugherty also reprimanded Dyche. The prisons became schools of the dope habit, to the joint profit of prison officials and the underworld.

In the prisons the few big bootleggers who could not be kept out were given private apartments and their meals served privately in the chapel from the official's mess. Werner, *Privileged Characters,* pp. 277-78.

for weeks before his death. By that time also, Harding himself was gravely troubled. He had turned a large part of the nation's government over to thieves and had made the White House into a night club. There, says one Republican recorder, crooks and grafters "burned incense before him. With them he drank, played poker and relaxed." But "always there must have been, in the dark periphery of his consciousness, cackling ribald voices: Daugherty's voice, Fall's voice, drunken voices, raucous in debauch; the high tensioned giggle of women pursued; the voices of men whispering in the greedy lechery of political intrigue; cynical voices crackling like the flames of the pit in scurrilous derision of the booming presidential rhetoric, Harding's highfaluting yearnings. This was his hell; the hell which he could escape only by sinking further into it." [79]

In poor health and oppressed by the charges already made against his Administration, Harding went to Alaska in the summer of 1923, where he fell seriously ill. On the return journey he died at San Francisco, August 2, 1923. "The exact cause of his death was not satisfactorily established," says a recent historian, "but there was reason to believe that it might have been brought about, directly or indirectly, by certain deeds of official corruption in the years 1921 to 1923 which eclipsed even the notorious happenings of the Grant administrations." [80]

[79] White, *Masks in a Pageant*, pp. 420-21, 425.

Alice Longworth, the daughter of Theodore Roosevelt, has described what occurred during the public receptions at the White House, as follows: "Though violation of the Eighteenth Amendment was a matter of course in Washington, it was rather shocking to see the way Harding disregarded the Constitution he was sworn to uphold. . . . While the big official receptions were going on, I don't think the people had any idea what was taking place in the rooms above. One evening while one was in progress, a friend of the Hardings asked me if I would like to go up to the study. I had heard rumors and was curious to see for myself what truth was in them. No rumor could have exceeded the reality; the study was filled with cronies, Daugherty, Jess Smith, Alec Moore, and others, the air was heavy with tobacco smoke, trays with bottles containing every imaginable brand of whisky stood about, cards and poker chips ready at hand—a general atmosphere of waistcoat unbuttoned, feet on the desk, and the spittoon alongside."—Longworth, *Crowded Hours*, p. 324.

[80] W. C. Langsam, *The World since 1914*, New York, 1933, p. 629.

Harding's Farewell. Shortly before Harding's death, an address on foreign affairs, which he had prepared to deliver in San Francisco, was published. In it he rationalized and justified the separate peace with Germany and the attitude of his Administration toward the League as follows: "If our people are ever to decide upon war they will choose to decide according to our own national conscience at the time and in the constitutional manner without advance commitment, or the advice and consent of any other power. To revive the old controversy in any phase would have been disastrous. We do not challenge the utility of the League of Nations to others; we wish it more power in every righteous exercise of its functions; but it is clearly not for us as presented in the Versailles Covenant."

Still assuming that membership in the League meant war, refusing to distinguish between war and the collective restraint of aggression, he confirmed the wisdom of the Senate in opposing the League. The League was not for us. Yet that was not quite all, for, after an interval, he continued: "Out of the inevitable Presidential contacts with the World War's havoc and destruction and the measureless sorrows which attended and has followed, I would be insensible to duty and violate all the sentiments of my heart and all my convictions if I failed to urge American support of the Permanent Court of International Justice. I do not know that such a court will be unfailing in the avoidance of war, but I know it is a step in the right direction." [81]

To his last utterance the prophet of Normalcy was able to condemn the League, for the benefit of one wing of his party, and yet yearn for what only the League could give, for the sake of the other half of his following. Harding's final statement, too, was a confession of the bankruptcy of his policy toward the greatest of all issues. For the most urgent of all world needs, what was offered? Membership in a world court which had no prospect of handling the world's serious disputes for the predictable future. Only as a step away from the League, according to Harding, was

[81] *New York Tribune*, August 1, 1923.

entry into the court "a step in the right direction." How could it be, when the havoc and devastation and measureless sorrow of which the President spoke could be prevented from returning only by the success of the League in the next crisis? Upon the League would hinge the world's fate, and any steps which led away from it would be as futile as all previous efforts of the Harding Administration to evolve a substitute for it had been.

Wilson's Last Word. Harding's final word and the last public utterance of Woodrow Wilson, soon afterward, left the issue sharply outlined for their successors. Wilson delivered a brief Armistice Day message to the American people in the following November. He spoke over the radio—that new miracle which had come just too late to enable him to carry his appeal for the League to the people without the breakdown which had sent him back from the West four years before, a broken man. On November 10, 1923, the remnant of Wilson's strength was scarcely sufficient to permit him to speak five minutes from his home. It was five minutes after he was introduced before he could utter a word. Then his sentences were halting, at times high-pitched and hoarse, but the fire of his spirit still flickered through his tones and even more through his words. There was no touch of equivocation in his charge that the triumphs of the war, fought on "high levels of vision and achievement," were "forever marred and embittered for us by the shameful fact that when the victory was won we turned our backs upon our associates and refused to bear any responsible part in the administration of peace, or the firm and permanent establishment of the results of the war—won at so terrible a cost of life and treasure—and withdrew into a sullen and selfish isolation which is deeply ignoble because manifestly cowardly and dishonorable."

His flail was merciless, more so than any considerations of expediency could justify. It was the last postscript of his appeal to history, the final expression of his abiding faith that what was right must eventually prevail. "We shall," he said, "inevitably be forced by the moral obligations of freedom and honor to retrieve that fatal error and assume more of the role of courage, self-respect, and helpfulness which every true American must wish and believe to be our true part in the affairs of the world." [82]

How long it would be before the United States would have a leader with the will and the political ability to exert a strong world leadership, Wilson could not know. Regarding Harding as the tool of the ruling Senate clique, he bore him no ill will. He used a little of his meager strength to ride in Harding's funeral procession.

His own end came less than three months after his final affirmation of belief that keeping the peace is a collective undertaking. In the larger sense, death was not kind to Wilson, as it had been to Lincoln, also up against the fury of post-war passions, and to Harding, faced with the exposure of his corrupt regime. Wilson missed narrowly the martyrdom which might have made his cause immediately or much more quickly triumphant. Yet he lived to see at least the capital city, and to a lesser extent the nation, look to him again as one who never broke faith, either with the greatest objectives or with lesser things.[83] He missed the powerfully moving effects of death in battle and of a transcontinental funeral journey, but the moment of his passing shook the millions whom he had stirred to high endeavor as no other event could have, and left those who had hated him in no mood to breathe more freely.

In New York City a false report of his death was spread on February 1, which resulted in a deluge of inquiries to the news-

[82] Speaking as he did at the close of the disastrous struggle in the Ruhr, Wilson continued: "That we should have done a great wrong to civilization, and in one of the most critical turning points in the history of mankind, is the more to be deplored because every anxious year that has followed has made the exceeding need for such services as we might have given more and more manifest and more pressing, as demoralizing circumstances which we might have controlled have gone from bad to worse until now, as if to furnish a sort of sinister climax, France and Italy between them have made waste-paper of the Treaty of Versailles and the whole field of international relationships is in perilous confusion."

[83] "In the picture theaters of Washington when Harding's likeness was shown there was a scattering handclap, but when Wilson's picture was shown there was always a deafening roar of applause. The thing was so pronounced that the President and the former President were never shown on the same screen together."—*New York Tribune*, February 4, 1924.

papers. The telephones of the Republican *Tribune* "rang constantly all afternoon. Hundreds of persons, agitated and tearful, demanded to know if the reports were true." [84] Elsewhere, the tremor of his going moved many in all lands who had known the justice of his demand that world war must not happen again. Only in Germany, newly embittered and again prostrate, did hatred overcome all emotions as they remembered his Fourteen Points, from which so little alleviation of their fate had seemed to come.[85]

For Wilson, death was as peaceful as possible. In the midst of a succession of tragic deaths among those who had supplanted him, Wilson went quietly.[86] Four days before, without a dissenting vote, the Senate had called on the President to bring criminal proceedings and institute civil suits to recover the Navy's oil reserves. Within two weeks Denby was out of the cabinet and two months later Daugherty had at last been ousted.

Republican Control Unimpaired. The regime imposed upon the nation by the Senate cabal of 1919 had already been proved the most shameless and corrupt in the entire history of the nation.

[84] *New York Tribune*, February 2, 1924. When the report reached a meeting of the New York City Federation of Women's Clubs in the Hotel Astor, "a groan swept through the hall and dozens of women burst into tears."

In Washington, a crowd stood in the snow before his home for two days and nights. Sometimes kneeling in prayer, these sentinels of his greater following included the poor and the crippled as well as the more fortunate.

[85] The German Government refused to permit the flag of its embassy in Washington to be half-staffed during the mourning for Wilson.

[86] During the next year death took two of his most bitter and choleric enemies in the Senate. Senator Frank B. Brandegee, most implacable of all, who had invented the Round Robin of March 4, 1919, as a means of blocking Wilson, killed himself in his Washington home, October 14, 1924. It was in his house that the Senate cabal of bitter-enders had had its "accustomed meeting place" in 1919. After his death, Secretary of War John W. Weeks announced authoritatively that it was due to financial losses from dealing in Washington real estate. This was doubted by his associates in New London, Connecticut, who replied that he could have realized $250,000 on a quick sale of his Connecticut holdings.

Other reports said that he had been in ill health for some time. That was certainly true of Senator Medill McCormick, of Illinois, who "had long suffered from indigestion and stomach trouble." One of the most caustic of the bitter-enders, McCormick died alone in a Washington hotel, February 25, 1925. He had recently been defeated for renomination in Illinois by Charles S. Deneen. *New York Herald Tribune*, October 15, 1924; February 26, 1925; George Harvey, *Henry Clay Frick the Man*, New York, 1928, pp. 325-26.

The evidence then available should have been amply sufficient to sweep the Republican Party from power in 1924. If ever a party deserved to be ousted for malfeasance in office, the Republican Party stood in that position. Its record, however, did not appear to damage it in the slightest. The good fortune of Harding's death led to an immense amount of national sympathy for him and to much systematic extolling of him as a kindly man. Moreover, the lax Harding was succeeded by the puritan Coolidge. That fact, to most Republicans, absolved them entirely. They would not admit that the party was in any way responsible for the acts of its elected and appointed officials.

Anyway, did not Coolidge cleanse the temple? "All the courtier thieves, Rasputins, drunkards, harem favorites guarding the intrigues of plunder, all of the owlish soothsayers of the high temple of politics—the whole mess of trash in the White House—Coolidge banished forthwith." [87]

"Forthwith" could hardly describe Coolidge's sweeping out of the Department of Justice, where Daugherty was allowed to hang on for eight months. Coolidge was most reluctant to offend him. The President ignored a resolution introduced into the Senate, January 29, calling for the ousting of the Attorney General. On the night of February 17, Senator Borah labored at the White House with both Coolidge and Daugherty for the good of the party, but fruitlessly. Then Senators Lodge and Pepper called on Coolidge in the interest of the party and Borah went again, but in vain.

Coolidge did call Daugherty in three times at the close of February, but he could not persuade him to resign. Then, on February 29, the Senate passed its resolution setting up an investigation of the Attorney General, and as the time for public testimony approached, panic grew among the Republican politicians. Still Coolidge could not bring himself to oust Daugherty. On March 12, the testimony began. "A succession of bootleggers, go-betweens, detectives and businessmen were heard, and every day

[87] White, *Masks in a Pageant,* p. 448.

the revelations established more clearly the nature of the Department of Justice under Daugherty." After two weeks of this, the President at last dismissed Daugherty, March 27, 1924.[88]

Coolidge Triumphantly Elected. Then all was well. The Democrats threw away whatever chances they had in a record-breaking convention deadlock between William G. McAdoo and Alfred E. Smith. This stalemate gave the nomination to John W. Davis, one of the best-qualified men ever to receive a presidential nomination. He was, however, conservative and was opposed also by Senator Robert M. La Follette, Sr. on a Progressive party ticket. This enabled the Republicans to allege that a three-cornered split of the vote might throw the election into the House of Representatives, thus causing great uncertainty to business. The threat influenced many, but it, too, was not necessary. The country cared only for prosperity, which was synonymous with Republican rule. Coolidge received more votes than both his rivals and 8,000,000 more than Davis.

The latter stood loyally for the League of Nations in his campaign, after his party had attempted to dispose of that issue by warmly endorsing the League and calling for a separate referendum on the question, which no one knew how to conduct. The Republicans declared strongly against the League but were in favor of the World Court. In point of fact, neither question was conspicuous in the campaign of 1924. Formally, the great Republican victory was a defeat for the League and a triumph for the Court, with results that have already been recorded above.

Having been successfully liquidated, "Normalcy" remained in secure control of the nation's policies, both foreign and domestic. Its post-war record was described, on December 29, 1929, by the most distinguished elder statesman of the Republican Party in terms as sharp as any disciple of Wilson might have chosen.

[88] Werner, *Privileged Characters*, pp. 239-41.

The testimony of Mark Sullivan is that Daugherty came to Washington to protect Harding, that he wanted no office for "corrupt advantage" and "went about Washington quietly alert-eyed, too busy to think much about himself, and with a modesty that was more than modesty, an insight which told him the danger of lack of modesty."—*Our Times*, Vol. VI, pp. 149-52, 229.

Acknowledging an award of $25,000 by the Woodrow Wilson Foundation, in recognition of his fatherhood of the World Court, Elihu Root recalled that when the war ended President Wilson was "our negotiator; he was our agent; he was the only one to whom the nations of Europe could look to ascertain what would be satisfactory to the people of the United States."

Then we rejected the organization of peace to which the President agreed, as we had a constitutional right to do. But when "Europe was left with an incomplete organization, left without the support of the most populous and richest and most potentially powerful nation whose name was written into the covenant . . . What did we do?" Did we admit soon that a mistake had been made, or at least wish the League Godspeed? "Has there," asked Root, "ever been an exhibition by America of friendship or sympathy with its work?" "Unfortunately," he replied to his own question, "the controversy which resulted in our determining not to enter the League was violent and bitter feelings were aroused. These feelings came to be carried over to the League itself and it came to be a common thing that we would read in the newspapers and hear in speech and conversation expressions of expectation that the League would fail, and evident pleasure when it seemed that it might fail." Those same feelings were "also extended to the Court."

Nor was this all, continued Root relentlessly. "Not only did we forget the demands of honorable obligation resting upon old association and fellowship and the expectations raised by our own representative, but consider the service that was rendered by the League and by the Court. For these years the League in the political field and the Court in the judicial field have been rendering the best service in the cause of peace known to the history of civilization; incomparably the best."

While the League and the Court were teaching the peoples of Europe to think of conference instead of war, to practice peace, "we, the great peace loving people, what have we done to help in this wonderful new work? No sympathy, no moral support, no brotherhood—No! . . . We have allowed insensate prejudice, camouflaged by futile phrases to appear, but falsely to appear to represent the true heart of the American people, with all its idealism, with its breadth of human sympathy, with its strong desire that our country should do its share for peace and happiness and noble life in all the world."

These, concluded Root, "are some of the evils visited upon us by a hateful and contentious spirit," from which he prayed that we might be delivered.[89] A few days later Dr. Nicholas Murray Butler rendered a verdict no less stringent when he said, before the League of Nations Association: "The policies—or perhaps lack of policies—as to international affairs, that have been pursued since the Armistice have made this nation of ours a dangerous derelict afloat across the path of every ship that sails laden with the precious cargo of international friendship and accord."[90]

[89] *New York Times*, December 29, 1926. Root at once turned the Wilson award over to the Council on Foreign Relations.

[90] *Saturday Review of Literature*, 1930, Vol. 6, p. 618.

CHAPTER X

PROSPERITY

THE AMOUNT of wealth consumed by the Great War is beyond all human imagination. The quantity of labor which went into the making of the instruments of destruction used in it would have performed miracles in the production of homes, schools, and other usable goods. If the many thousands of shiploads of war supplies which went from the United States to Europe could have been used for useful construction, Europe, if not the world itself, would have been transformed. Instead, Europe was in great danger of mass starvation when the war ended. Factories had been destroyed or diverted to war uses, farms had run down in fertility and care, livestock had disappeared over large areas. Whole regions were in a state of famine panic. Farmers hoarded food against the towns, the towns against the cities, nations against each other. Hardly a nation was able to survive the terrible winter of 1919 without help, and few had any credit with which to purchase it. Some 400,000,000 people were threatened with disaster.

The War's Ravages Stemmed

The Terrible Winter. For this emergency the great economic machinery of the United States was available. It was already geared up to an undreamed-of pitch of productivity and it was used to furnish food and clothing to all. From Ireland to Siberia and from Finland to Armenia supplies were received from the United States approximately in proportion to the need. Ten million tons of American foodstuffs and supplies were shipped and distributed. Those who had any credit left were required to pledge it, to the extent of some $500,000,000. To those who had no credit we advanced it from the United States Treasury, to finance an additional $2,000,000,000 worth of supplies. Medical aid costing $35,000,000 was supplied by the American Red Cross and other agencies.[1]

The role of the United States in tiding over the post-war crisis was decisive. It was, to be sure, best for us that the great quantities of food and supplies heaped up by forced production to win the war should not remain in the country to cause a sudden crash in prices and a rise in unemployment. Nevertheless, our share in pulling the world out of the worst of the war's devastation was magnificent, and it should be remembered in calculating what part of the war debts ought to be paid.

The League's Contribution. The part which the League of Nations played in the slower process of reconstruction was more modest. Its work in rehabilitating the 1,400,000 Greek refugees has been noted above. During the Russian famine the League stimulated the governments to make contributions and to send old war stocks for Russian relief. Its Epidemic Commission was also set to work in Russia. Meanwhile the League had organized, under Dr. Fridtjof Nansen, the repatriation of 427,000 prisoners of war of 27 different nationalities. Most of them were soldiers of the defeated powers left stranded in Russia. This task well advanced, Dr. Nansen was put in charge of the more permanent problem of alleviating the lot of more than 1,500,000 Russian refugees and some 300,000 Armenians, scattered over Europe. The famous Nansen certificates, enabling them to travel, were accepted by the Governments, and work was found for nearly 500,000 in various parts of the world.

While millions of individuals were being succored by the League's activities, the whole of the new Austrian nation needed to be rescued. Its capital city too large for its small agricultural

[1] An address of October 24, 1924, by President Coolidge. *New York Times*, October 25, 1924. The President estimated that the $950,000,000 expended by the Belgian Relief Commission, largely contributed here, had saved 10,000,000 people in the occupied regions during the war.

In 1922, when famine followed the post-war disturbances in Russia, the American Relief Association expended $70,000,000, including a Congressional appropriation of $24,000,000, in Russian relief. Some 12,000,000 people were kept alive.

body, Austria subsisted from 1919 to 1921 on foreign loans amounting to $125,000,000 and upon charitable donations one-third as large. Early in 1921, the League was asked to propose a general scheme of reconstruction. The Financial Committee complied and evolved a plan whereby the Governments would release all prior claims for reparations and other liens. All agreed promptly except the United States, where there was a year's delay in Congress.[2] By that time the Austrian currency had collapsed completely and the bankers generally were wary of any further loans. During the 1922 Assembly, however, a detailed plan for guaranteeing the control of Austria's currency and balancing her budget was agreed upon and a gold loan of $170,000,000 was guaranteed by the Governments of ten nations, though not by the United States. The loan served as a basis for a new currency and under the guidance of Dr. Alfred Zimmerman, of Holland, as Commissioner-General for the League, the Austrian situation was quickly reversed. Capital rushed back to Vienna. In June, 1926, League control ended and Austria remained solvent until the world depression was well under way.[3]

The rehabilitation of Austria set the pattern for the Dawes Plan reconstruction of Germany. It also led to a League loan of $50,000,000 to Hungary, which was administered from May, 1924, to June, 1926, by Mr. Jeremiah Smith of Boston with simi-

[2] See the letter of Sarah Wambaugh in the *New York Times*, November 2, 1924. Miss Wambaugh explains that all of the former allies, except ourselves, agreed in March, 1921, while Austria's credit was reasonably good, to relieve her from all prior liens during a period of twenty years. Then for months American individuals and groups sent letters to Senator Lodge, asking that our consent be given to salvaging Austria. No action resulted. Many vital months passed. On December 15, 1921, the Federal Council of Churches of Christ sent a petition to Congress. Still no attention was paid to Austria's worsening plight. A new appeal was sent by Edward A. Filene on March 15, 1922. At last the necessary waiver was adopted by Congress and signed on April 6, 1922. But in the meantime Austrian credit had disappeared entirely. See also the *Report of the Financial Committee of the League to the Second Assembly*, September 28, 1921, p. 9.

[3] From the day of the Austrian loan, said President Coolidge in 1924, Austria "has become an outpost of confidence and reassurance in Middle Europe."—*New York Times*, October 25, 1924. See also Wallace McClure, *World Prosperity as Sought through the Economic Work of the League of Nations*, New York, 1933, pp. 487-91.

lar success. In 1926, Bulgaria received a League-sponsored loan of $11,250,000, with which about 200,000 refugees were settled under the supervision of a League Commissioner.

The United States the World's Banker

To all these loans American bankers had subscribed the heavy quotas allotted to them and had thus played an important part in the success of these measures of reconstruction in Europe.

Our own post-war difficulties were acute but short-lived. While we were revictualing Europe the war boom continued, even reaching new heights under the optimism released by victory. This inflationary period, monetary and mental, collapsed in 1921, in "the most violent commodity slump in our history." From July, 1921, to June, 1922, said the report of the Secretary of Commerce, "both prices and manufacturing production, outside of foodstuffs, fell by roughly forty per cent and in consequence some 4,000,000 to 5,000,000 were unemployed." Recovery, however, was "marvellously rapid," for within sixteen months unemployment was practically extinguished and production was almost restored.[4]

Unequal Deflation. There was one difficulty about this rapid recovery. As Secretary Hoover noted, the readjustments were still unequal between wage earners and farmers. The index for crop prices dropped from 284 in 1920 to 107 in 1921 and recovered to 118 in 1922 (119 for livestock). The farmers' sale prices were quickly deflated, but they were left subject to the numerous mortgages which they had incurred while both money and prices were inflated. But the prices of the things which they must buy did not fall so low. The index of clothing prices fell from 300 in 1920 to 172 in 1921 and rose to 180 in 1922. In the same years the figures for building materials were 269 and 160 and 170; likewise for household furnishings, 275 and 180 and 173. The prices of industrial securities responded accordingly, 25 selected stocks

[4] *Tenth Annual Report of the Secretary of Commerce*, 1922, p. 15.

sinking from 191 to 127 and rebounding to 171 in 1922. There was no such resurgence in the $500-an-acre land values upon which the mortgages of 1918 and 1920 had been placed in the corn belt.[5]

The great prosperity which began in 1922 was thus supported by two legs of distinctly uneven length. The industrial leg was as brawny and powerful as ever. For seven years, indeed, it kept growing in all dimensions while the agricultural leg, shortened by the paralysis of 1920-21, had difficulty in securing enough nourishment to prevent its shrinking further. In this situation the body of Normalcy, untrammelled and free, had to have an artificial support. A crutch was ready at hand and it was used, unconsciously by the nation.

Huge Foreign Investments. The war had been financed and won by loans. Prosperity might be similarly promoted. The credit resources of the earth, including ours in part, had been poured into the war. Now the nations wanted credits and it suited our purposes to give them. In 1922, our private loans to foreigners aggregated a billion dollars and this figure was maintained, on the average, until 1930. The rewards were attractive: beautifully lettered bonds of foreign cities and states which promised high interest returns; shares in foreign industries which seemed to be comparable to our own industrial giants; the physical ownership and control of thousands of factories and other businesses running in value to seven billions of dollars.

These things appealed to individuals, while the bankers enjoyed the large fees and commissions which came from promoting the sale of the foreign securities to the public. The National City Company earned $24,757,002.47 in this manner from 1919 to 1930.[6] No land was too far distant or too poorly governed for the

[5] *Ibid.*, pp. 38-42. The same report for 1923 says that taking all agricultural products together, they fell from 247 in January, 1920, to 114 in June, 1921, while other commodities, including manufacturers' goods which are much affected by farmers' prices, fell from the same maximum to a minimum of 154 (p. 4).

[6] M. R. Werner, *Privileged Characters*, New York, 1935, p. 453. The same company floated directly issues totaling $1,171,955,000 and participated in issues totaling $3,260,000,000.

United States to buy shares in it. From Lands End to the borders of Russia, American bond buyers plied to and fro, obliging eager cities, or persuading reluctant ones to borrow money.

Germany Rebuilt. After the Dawes Plan had stabilized Germany for a time, the Germans especially did not need much persuading. German industrialists underwent a mass conversion to American "rationalization" methods. They were quite willing to accept funds with which to rebuild their plants and equip them with the latest expensive machinery. There were some outcries against this new "enslavement" of Germany, protests which evoked whispered replies that these debts might prove to be uncollectable. In any event, Germany would have a fine industrial plant. The German city councils, largely Socialist, saw to it also that additional comforts were provided for the German workers. To accommodate the eager American investors, they paved streets, built new power plants, huge apartment houses, stadia, and swimming pools. If debts passed away, these things would remain.

The American Agent General for Reparations warned in 1926 that the theory of American bankers that their loans would take precedence over reparations was not reliable, and in 1927 he issued a solemn warning that Germany had overborrowed, but he did not stop the flood of American loans. Among the bankers, Thomas W. Lamont, of J. P. Morgan and Company, added his voice in the same year to the warnings against "rash and excessive lending," but without result.[7] Prosperity was rampant, and no one worried about the most intimate entanglement in the affairs of other nations which was taking place. Our politicians had told us so often that we were isolated only in the political sense that we bought stock heavily and gaily in all the nations, knowing that it was only political entanglement which was taboo.

The nations, too, reacted in bitterness and hatred to the excessively rapid purchase of their countries by the Americans. Especially in those continental nations which suffered either complete

[7] *Ibid.*, pp. 454-55.

or almost complete collapse of their currencies, was resentment keen at the manner in which the Americans picked up properties for a slight fraction of their value. Soon it was alleged Americans would own everything everywhere. European politicians and industrialists warned that we were about to secure control not only of European industry, but also of European policy.[8] Americans would contribute nothing to governing the world, but they didn't mind owning it.

Latin America Mortgaged. Eventually, the cry went up from Latin America also that the financial invasion of the Yankees must be halted or their marines, already in Haiti and Nicaragua, would be occupying other countries. The representatives of American banking houses ranged from the Rio Grande to Cape Horn, competing "on the almost violent scale" of which Lamont spoke, for the chance to sell foreign bonds to their countrymen, from Cape Cod to Hollywood. A syndicate headed by J. and W. Seligman and Company floated a loan of $15,000,000 for the Republic of Peru March 1, 1927. The bonds promised seven per cent interest and the bankers reaped a handsome profit, so handsome that they could afford to pay the son of the Peruvian dictator $415,000 in commissions during the next two years, besides $117,000 to others.

This loan so improved the credit of Peru that another Seligman syndicate was able to float a new issue of $50,000,000 for Peru at only six per cent, though the bonds sold at 91.5 to the public. This issue of December 21, 1927, was taken up so rapidly that still another $25,000,000 of Peruvian bonds was floated in October, 1928, by a Seligman syndicate. The demand had been kept up by "rigging the market" before each new issue until at last $90,000,000 had been transferred to a military dictator, who squandered the money as he saw fit. Needless to say all of these bonds went into default when the crash came.

During the period in which these handsome loans were floated, O. C. Townshend, United States commercial attaché in Peru, had

[8] Sisley Huddleston, "Europe's Distrust of America," *New Republic,* August 25, 1926.

constantly warned the Bureau of Foreign and Domestic Commerce of the weakness of Peruvian finance, only—as he testified later—to be severely reprimanded for his pessimism. Dr. Julius Klein, the head of the Bureau, was consistently preaching optimism. The State Department, which had a chance to object to all loans issued, though it never positively approved of any, did not act as a noticeable brake upon the huge transactions of which the Peruvian bonds were only a small fraction.[9] It was not inappropriate that while we were being recklessly and unscrupulously entangled in Peru to the embitterment and disgust of both nations, the American embassy there should be presided over by Miles Poindexter. As a Senator from the state of Washington, Mr. Poindexter had been one of the most rigid and unbending of the bitter-enders of 1919. He would stand for no entanglements whatever.

No Entanglements. None of the prophets of Normalcy intended to entangle their country in the affairs of the entire world so thoroughly that when collapse came all would go down together. Yet none of them did anything to prevent the catastrophe. They obstructed a constructive attempt to regulate the world's affairs and then let the world drift where it would. Insofar as the more responsible leaders of the time attempted to justify rationally the policies of the period, they felt that American capitalism was expanding normally. The constant foreign loans kept American trade moving, particularly our manufactures. The surpluses of our factories poured outward on an ascending scale, thus removing the brakes both from rising production and from mounting profits. Nothing mattered much beyond that. Many appreciated that a creditor country could hardly retain a large export surplus of goods without giving something to compensate. Fewer understood that the stream of American loans was financing the payment of German reparations, the installments coming to us on the war debts, and a large part of the returns from abroad on all our private investments in foreign lands. Fewer still believed that the

[9] Werner, *Privileged Characters*, pp. 456-64.

prosperity and trade of the world itself was being financed, too furiously, by the United States. The rank-and-file champions of America Unentangled knew only that all supposed economic laws were repealed. It was being demonstrated daily that we could have high tariffs and a large export surplus of goods and collect our debts, public and private, all at the same time. What else mattered? [10]

The First World Economic Conference

Naturally, also, the repeal of economic laws was not confined to the United States. The peace treaties had greatly lengthened, unavoidably in the main, the tariff frontiers of Europe. With peace came currency depreciation which led to the swift raising of tariffs, both in the afflicted countries and among their neighbors, as a means of defense. Fears for future security fostered attempts at a high degree of self-sufficiency. Industries inflated during the war sought tariffs, and unemployed labor seemed to argue for the preservation of uneconomic industries, while war-inflamed nationalism supported rises in tariffs for any alleged reason.

Thus by 1925 the world's production of raw materials and foodstuffs had increased by sixteen to eighteen per cent, but the

[10] Our export surplus of commodities 1912-1931 inclusive, was $28,723,313,000. For the years 1914-1920 inclusive it was $18,555,944,000; 1923-1929, $4,976,000,000.

In the latter period our tourist and immigrant remittances distinctly exceeded the commodity surplus, and equaled substantially the amount of our foreign loans. Foreign investments in the United States were also nearly as large in value as the commodity surplus, though most of this was a reinvestment in our short-term money market of funds loaned to foreigners on long-term account.

The *net* movement of private long-term investments abroad was therefore much smaller than the gross movement. The Bureau of Foreign and Domestic Commerce estimated in 1932 that over the period 1922-1932 our net long-term investment abroad was about $329,000,000 each year, after all items in the balance of payments had been considered.

These compensating factors did not, however, do much to mitigate the violence of the outthrust of our loans at the rate of a billion dollars a year. Without excessive and unproductive loans, other items in our balance of payments, both debit and credit, would also have been distinctly smaller.

See Department of Commerce, *Trade Information Bulletin*, No. 814, pp. 32-33; George N. Peek, *Letter to the President on Foreign Trade*, May 23, 1934, p. 5; *World Almanac, 1933*, p. 378.

volume of international trade had barely kept pace with the increase of population. Each was five per cent. In Europe, international commerce had actually decreased ten per cent in spite of the increase in the number of nations from twenty to twenty-seven.

This situation led the Economic Organization of the League to convoke a World Economic Conference in Geneva. The League's invitation brought together, May 4 to 23, 1927, a gathering of one hundred and ninety-four delegates and one hundred and fifty-seven experts from fifty different countries.[11] The delegates attended as individuals and were consequently free to express their judgment without official restraints. Most of them were in fact chosen by their governments, though a considerable number represented international organizations. The results of their deliberations were expressed in a final report, unanimously adopted, the keynote of which was that prosperity cannot be enjoyed in small compartments. In this conclusion the American delegates concurred. "Our experience," said Henry M. Robinson, "has taught us to consider prosperity as a whole." [12]

Tariff Peace Urged. To this end the conference declared "that the time has come to put an end to the increase in tariffs and move in the opposite direction." Since "excessive protection, which reduces national production and purchasing power, in the end defeats its own object," the conference urged that: "Governments should immediately prepare plans for removing and diminishing by successive stages those barriers that gravely hamper trade." Long-term commercial treaties containing the unconditional most-favored-nation clause were especially recommended. It was stressed that this clause "should be of the widest and most liberal

[11] The United States delegates were: Henry M. Robinson, President of the First National Bank of Los Angeles and member of the Dawes Commission; Norman H. Davis, formerly Assistant Secretary of the Treasury and Under Secretary of State; John W. O'Leary, President of the United States Chamber of Commerce; Alonzo E. Taylor, Director of the Food Research Institute, Stanford University; and Julius Klein, Director of the Bureau of Foreign and Domestic Commerce, United States Department of Commerce. Ten experts from various Government departments assisted the delegation.

[12] *Minutes,* C. 356. M 129, 1927, II.

character and that it should not be weakened or narrowed either by express provisions or by interpretation." [13]

The final report of the conference was universally acclaimed but was not accepted in practice. It appeared to halt the rise in tariffs during 1928. But each nation was afraid to lead in reductions, and efforts to arrive at multilateral treaties covering particular commodities resulted only in a treaty on hides and bones. Early in 1929 the United States Smoot-Hawley Tariff Act ended the truce decisively, by sharply raising our tariffs again. Thereafter, the world depression halted all efforts toward tariff reduction.[14]

The Second Naval Conference

While economic disarmament made no progress it was not to be wondered that naval disarmament should lag. The race in constructing cruisers was embarrassing to the Coolidge Administra-

[13] League Secretariat, *Ten Years of World Cooperation* suggests that one of the chief reasons for the failure of the efforts to reduce tariffs was the fact that the conversion of the United States to the unconditional most-favored-nation system in 1922 upset the calculations upon which it was intended to work. Instead of operating between economic equals with tariffs of substantially the same level, the smaller nations now had to grant automatically all concessions to a country which had very high tariff walls behind which were the greatest natural resources and the largest consuming markets in the world (pp. 200-201).

The campaign of Secretary Hull for lower tariffs through reciprocity treaties based firmly on the unconditional most-favored-nation clause should do something to reduce this difficulty.

[14] The 1927 Conference led to other more limited conferences. The United States was represented at a Conference on Economic Statistics, November 26, 1928, but did not sign the treaty drafted. A Conference on the Abolition of Export and Import Prohibitions agreed upon a treaty condemning such prohibitions, though many reservations were made. This treaty was signed and ratified by the United States. Senator Borah listed 38 important products which we might sell more freely if the treaty succeeded. Since we had only one prohibition in force, helium, this was a treaty which would have been entirely to the advantage of the United States. Our delegates attended two later conferences, the second of which produced a supplementary agreement, in order to get the treaty into force.

This was a different attitude than that of 1923 when the United States refused to attend a Conference on the Simplification of Customs Formalities because "it would be impracticable to make the United States customs formalities the subject of an international convention."—Ursula P. Hubbard, *The Cooperation of the United States with the League of Nations*, International Conciliation, No. 274, November, 1931, pp. 708-11.

tion, which would soon be compelled to agree to a large building program for cruisers, unless an agreement to limit their number could be reached. Japan and Great Britain were developing their cruiser strength and there was much demand in the United States that we should do likewise. There was no special reason why we needed a large cruiser fleet, except to achieve parity with Great Britain. Large expenditures for cruisers were also distasteful to the Coolidge Government, the chief aim of which was economy and the lowering of income taxes. These reasons for a fresh effort at naval agreement were reinforced by the need of the Republican party for an achievement in foreign affairs. The Washington Conference had atoned to a degree for our failure to enter the League. Perhaps a new naval limitation agreement would divert attention from the World Court fiasco.

President Coolidge's invitation of February 10, 1927, was addressed to Great Britain, Japan, France, and Italy. It asked that the delegates of these countries to the forthcoming session of the League's Preparatory Commission on Disarmament consider, apart from their regular work, an extension of the 5-5-3 ratio to all naval categories. Remembering her unpleasant time at the Washington Conference, France promptly declined, alleging that the authority of the Preparatory Commission was endangered and that the naval issues could not be isolated from the whole disarmament problem. Italy, intent only on attaining parity with France, also stayed away.

The remaining three powers met in Geneva, June 20, 1927, and at once fell into deadlock. The chief British delegate, Mr. Bridgeman, proposed that the 5-5-3 ratio be applied to cruisers of 10,000 tons, but Britain desired to build a large number of 7,500 ton cruisers limited to six-inch guns. Hugh Gibson explained that the United States did not want small cruisers, feeling that it must have larger range vessels to compensate for its lack of naval bases. The British insisted, however, that they must have seventy cruisers, including fifty-five small ones, to protect their world-wide commerce lanes. This ran the total tonnage of cruisers which the United States would have to build, to achieve parity, up to such a high figure as to defeat totally our purpose in calling the conference and led Gibson to question both the practicality and the wisdom of trying to prepare in time of peace for all possible contingencies in time of war. He was unable to see how the British six-inch-gun cruisers could be classed as defensive weapons when to be useful they would have to deny the seas to others in time of war.

The fact was that a section of the British Cabinet was not willing to concede parity to the United States in all categories and the conference broke up August 4, 1927, leaving matters much worse than before. Public opinion in the United States was inflamed and opinion was badly divided in Great Britain. Lord Cecil resigned from the Conservative Cabinet and launched, through the League of Nations Union, a great campaign for disarmament.[15]

The Franco-British Agreement. This campaign was greatly stimulated by the revelation of a secret agreement made by the British and French Governments in the spring of 1928. The British took the initiative and soon received an offer from the French to support the British position on small cruisers, if the British would withdraw their opposition to the exclusion of trained army reserves from the proposed Draft Disarmament Convention. The latter half of the bargain was not revealed when it was cautiously announced to the public. However, William Randolph Hearst managed to obtain in Paris a copy of a French Foreign Office letter to its representatives abroad in which the nature of the deal was revealed, and published it in his *New York American*, September 21, 1928.[16] The French Government then tried to secure

[15] J. W. Wheeler-Bennett, *Disarmament and Security since Locarno, 1925-1931*, London, 1932, pp. 102-27. One of the principal reasons for the failure of the conference was its inadequate diplomatic preparation. The simple extension of the Washington Conference ratio was not feasible. The gulf between what the British and the American navies considered their needs to be was apparently not narrowed at all before the conference met. Perhaps it couldn't have been at that moment by any amount of preliminary negotiation, but this fact might have been ascertained before the conference was called.

[16] The French Government arrested and deported the Paris representative of the Hearst papers and two years later had the temerity to deport Hearst himself as "an enemy of the Republic."

the publication of the full texts of the notes exchanged and, when London demurred, forced Britain's hand by publishing, on October 5, full summaries, which led to complete publication October 22.

While these revelations were in progress, resentment in the United States mounted to hot indignation and the demand for twenty-five heavy cruisers, already raised in Congress, was with difficulty held down to fifteen and one aircraft carrier, with an appropriation of $274,000,000 in the law of February 13, 1929.[17]

In Great Britain public condemnation had been visited decisively upon the Anglo-French naval compromise and the defeat of the Conservative Government in the election of May 30, 1929, was largely due to its handling of the naval negotiations. Nevertheless, the strongly aroused dislike of Britain in the United States was cordially returned by a large section of the British public. The "unthinkable" war was very much thought about on both sides.[18]

War Outlawed

But within a year practically every nation in the world signed a new treaty, sponsored by the United States, "outlawing" war.

It was remarkable enough that the United States should lead in a new renunciation of war less than ten years after her failure to enter the League. That the nations should follow again so soon was a tribute to her immense power. That the United States Senate should bless the Pact, led by Senator Borah, was stranger still.

Like the creation of the League itself, the making of the Pact of Paris was due to a combination of strong leadership, mass support, and political necessity. The leadership came from three different directions. To escape from a completely negative posi-

[17] This appropriation helped to lift the total army and navy expenditures of the United States to $692,399,804 in 1929, an increase of 161.4 per cent over 1913. In the same year Japan's bill was up 151.1 per cent to $242,667,310. Our nearest rival in dollar expenditure was Great Britain, whose total was $560,421,275. Her war bill had increased 57.3 per cent over 1913, and that of France 43.2 per cent to $432,552,400. James H. Powers, *Years of Tumult*, New York, 1932, p. 309.

[18] Wheeler-Bennett, *Disarmament and Security since Locarno*, pp. 127-42.

tion a small school of American isolationists had developed a burning allegiance to the "outlawry" of war. Samuel O. Levinson, a successful lawyer of Chicago, had conceived the idea in 1919, while his Irreconcilable friends in the Senate were organizing the defeat of the League. Levinson was amazed to discover that war, for any purpose, was a perfectly legal and proper undertaking so far as international law was concerned. That struck him, not unnaturally, as an anachronistic state of affairs about which something ought to be done. He could see no reason why a law should not be passed against war. Surely the greatest enemy of humanity ought to be outlawed.

He was in favor at first not only of passing the law, but of creating a sheriff to enforce it. Finding soon that Senators Borah and Knox would not agree to that, he fell back upon Madison's argument that only public opinion should govern the relations of states.[19]

Without believing that a simple statute could deter powerful nations from war, Professor James T. Shotwell, of Columbia University, was equally convinced that great nations could not continue to use war as an instrument of national policy. Nor could he believe that the United States could remain indefinitely out of all relation to the keeping of world peace. His talks with Briand, Foreign Minister of France, in the spring of 1927, sought a basis upon which the United States might cooperate with the League for peace. The Locarno treaties, then a fresh achievement, suggested to both that if a small circle of heavier obligations could be established within the League, now weakened both by events and by interpretation, a universal circle of all the nations sharing minimum obligations might be formed to strengthen collective security on its outer circumference.[20]

Briand's Overture. From these Briand-Shotwell discussions came the Briand proposal of April 6, 1927, suggesting that

[19] Drew Pearson and Constantine Brown, *The American Diplomatic Game*, New York, 1935, p. 13.

[20] James T. Shotwell, *On the Rim of the Abyss*, New York, 1936, pp. 132-36.

Underwood & Underwood

NICHOLAS MURRAY BUTLER

Kazanjian

JAMES T. SHOTWELL

Wide World

NEWTON D BAKER

Underwood & Underwood

WILLIAM E. DODD

Underwood & Underwood

MANLEY O. HUDSON

LEADING AMERICAN ADVOCATES OF INTERNATIONAL ORGANIZATION

"France would be willing to subscribe publicly with the United States to any mutual engagement tending 'to outlaw war,' "—to use an American expression—between these two countries. The renunciation of war as an instrument of national policy, continued Briand, "is a conception already familiar to the signatories of the Covenant of the League of Nations and of the Treaties of Locarno." [21]

This mention of outlawing war sent Levinson posthaste to Paris, to camp on the doorstep of the French Foreign Office until something came of it, while Shotwell returned to the United States. President Nicholas Murray Butler, of Columbia University, called attention to the importance of the proposal in the *New York Times* of April 25, 1927.[22] Borah supported the idea of a multilateral antiwar treaty in an address at Cleveland, May 9,[23] and a powerful public opinion began to form back of the proposal.

Washington, however, did not warm to the idea. President Coolidge had been persuaded by Raymond Robbins to mention outlawry in his acceptance speech, but in April, 1927, Robbins found him irritated by the French proposal and by Briand's boycott of his Geneva Naval Conference. In a press conference, Coolidge icily referred to the State Department "certain individuals, particularly in New York—including Professor Shotwell of Columbia—" who were "preparing proposals for treaties between this government and other countries" for outlawing war.[24] Three times in the next four days the Secretary of State, former Senator Frank B. Kellogg, informed his press hecklers tartly that he was too busy to look into the matter.

[21] James T. Shotwell, *War as an Instrument of National Policy*, New York, 1929, p. 41. In the previous citation, the fullest statement he has made, Shotwell vigorously clears Briand of the charge that he was aiming to form a disguised alliance with the United States. Their conversations had had a far broader basis.

[22] "The offer of France and the challenge of Dr. Butler passed once more to the news columns, not only in the metropolitan press, but of the newspapers of the smaller cities and towns throughout the whole country." Shotwell, *War as an Instrument of National Policy*, p. 44.

[23] Pearson and Brown, *The American Diplomatic Game*, p. 19.

[24] *Ibid.*, pp. 21-22.

A Text Proposed. It was no wonder that Levinson had some difficulty before he succeeded in persuading the Quai d'Orsay to make a formal inquiry as to our willingness to outlaw war, especially after Ambassador Herrick had omitted to pass on one informal question to Washington. When formally queried, the State Department could hardly say "No," and on June 20, 1927, Briand submitted the following treaty:

Article 1. The High Contracting Powers solemnly declare, in the name of the French people and the people of the United States of America, that they condemn recourse to war and renounce it respectively as an instrument of their national policy towards each other.

Article 2. The settlement or the solution of all disputes or conflicts, of whatever nature or of whatever origin they may be, which may arise between France and the United States of America, shall never be sought by either side except by pacific means.[25]

Six months passed, during which Kellogg was too busy to go into the question of outlawry. On November 25, President Coolidge was still coldly of the opinion that: "There is no short cut to peace or any other kind of salvation. The matter must be worked out with fear and trembling." Secretary Kellogg agreed with him the next day, declaring rather petulantly that: "Some people might think it was very simple. And perhaps it is. But I do not wish to discuss it." [26] He was similarly disposed when he happened to confer with Senator Borah's Foreign Relations Committee on December 22. The meeting was to consider a new treaty of arbitration with France, containing a reference to outlawing war which apparently both the State Department and the older heads of the French Foreign Office hoped would give the impression that outlawry had been achieved. But Borah insisted on polling the Committee on the desirability of proposing a world outlawry treaty to Briand. All agreed, even Senator George Moses, of

[25] Most of this text is said to have been written originally on the back of an envelope by Levinson. Pearson and Brown, *The American Diplomatic Game*, p. 25.

[26] *Ibid.*, pp. 26-27.

Irreconcilable fame, who growled that that was the best way to get rid of the thing.

Six days later Kellogg yielded to his Senatorial mentors and to a growing public opinion, still ably led by Dr. Nicholas Murray Butler. On December 28, 1927, Kellogg despatched to Briand the proposal to make outlawry multilateral. From then on, Kellogg pushed the treaty single-mindedly, resisting all efforts to change it. His chief assistant, Spencer Phenix, pointed out at once that some plan for consultation whenever war threatened should be included, but Kellogg remembered what had happened to the League Covenant and demurred. He must have something that the Senate would ratify. At every stage, too, Senator Borah and the advocates of outlawry resisted all efforts to set up any machinery for consultation. They would have no "teeth" put in it. Only the public opinion of mankind should support it.[27]

The Pact Signed. Accordingly, the text which Briand had intended merely as a preliminary for negotiations was signed in Paris on August 27, 1928, by the representatives of fifteen nations, without the slightest substantive change.[28] Yet this triumph of simplicity and of faith in world opinion did not soothe the embattled fears of the right-wing Irreconcilables. The adhesion of forty-four additional states to the treaty by the time it was submitted to the Senate, December 4, 1928, only increased their alarm. They found no comfort even in President Coolidge's rally to the Pact, expressed with unaccustomed abandon in his statement that "the observance of this covenant, so simple and so straightforward, promises more for the peace of the world than any other agreement ever negotiated among the nations."

[27] *Ibid.*, p. 34; Shotwell, *On the Rim of the Abyss*, pp. 126-27.

[28] Article I: The High Contracting Parties solemnly declare in the names of their respective peoples that they condemn recourse to war for the solution of international controversies, and renounce it as an instrument of national policy in their relations with one another.

Article II: The High Contracting Parties agree that the settlement or solution of all disputes or conflicts, of whatever nature or of whatever origin they may be, which may arise among them shall never be sought except by pacific means.

Reservations Pressed. Senators Moses, of New Hampshire, and Reed, of Missouri, at once asked the Senate to exercise its customary caution by listing all the things which the treaty did not mean. Their proposal of December 14 resolved:

(1) That the treaty imposes no obligation on the United States to resort to coercive or punitive measures against any offending nation.

(2) That the treaty does not impose any limitations upon the Monroe Doctrine or the traditional policies of the United States.

(3) That the treaty does not impair the right of the United States to defend its territory, possessions, trade or interests.

(4) That the treaty does not obligate the United States to the conditions of any treaty to which the United States is not a party.[29]

These reservations would have robbed the Pact of any suspicion of effectiveness even more completely than the reservations of 1919 had weakened the Covenant, but this time the advocates of the treaty controlled the Senate Foreign Relations Committee. As its Chairman, Senator Borah defended the treaty from all assaults. Against the claim that the members of the League and the World Court could decide questions to our disadvantage "by pacific means," he replied that this could be done without this treaty. He resisted, by deflating the Monroe Doctrine of the high pretensions of 1919, the allegation that it was being bartered away. He denied that self defense could be surrendered by this treaty or any other. The lack of a definition of self defense was a weakness, but an inevitable one. Even the British reservations, and others made during the negotiations, fazed Borah not at all. They had no legal effect whatever, neither adding anything to the treaty nor taking anything away from it.[30]

This heresy from the cult of reservation-making left its true devotees aghast. Their discomfort was increased by Borah's solicitude for the effect of their efforts upon other governments. He was not "willing at any time to do anything which could be construed into a change of the treaty or constitute a reservation."

[29] *Congressional Record*, Vol. 70, p. 623.
[30] *Ibid.*, pp. 1145, 1218, 1267-89.

Nor was he "willing to do that which could be represented abroad as a change or reservation." The threat of such a thing had "produced a serious situation" in Europe.[31] It began to appear that the failure of the nations to accept the Senate's World Court reservations had registered in the Senate.

Faced with Borah's stern insistence that the feelings of other nations really had to be taken into account, that the Senate could not emasculate even the shortest and most general treaty ever presented to it, the objectors were compelled to retreat steadily. First they offered to accept a statement of their reservations to be adopted by the Senate and forwarded to the signatories as a separate document. This less binding form of qualification being rejected, they at last agreed to be satisfied if the Senate would merely adopt a reservationist report, without sending it to the other signatories. But even this was opposed. Neither Secretary Kellogg nor President Coolidge could see why this peace treaty should be reserved and amended. A surprising blow at the practice of trying to make every important treaty suit every vocal Senator in every particular was struck by Senator George Norris, of Nebraska, a former Irreconcilable. "Would there not," he asked, "be just as much dispute about what the committee meant as there is about what this treaty means? We cannot do anything that will prevent men from disagreeing, and honestly so, as to what certain words mean, and if there is a disagreement as to what the treaty means now, there would be a disagreement as to what the Foreign Relations Committee meant if they undertook to re-write the treaty."[32]

A Committee Report Conceded. It was well that the friends of outlawry defended the Briand-Kellogg treaty against the Senate's perfectionists, for some sixty nations were watching closely to see whether the Senate would operate on the Pact in the same manner in which it had the Covenant and the Court. Naturally, this mat-

[31] *Ibid.*, pp. 1717-19.

[32] *Ibid.*, p. 1537. Senator Fess, of Ohio, added his belief that "if anybody hopes that any statement can be made in language sufficiently clear that 96 senators will agree to it, I think it is a vain hope" (p. 1724).

tered not to the emasculationists. They signed again a round robin, though this time it was not published and the necessary thirty-three signatures were not claimed very confidently. But when a group of Senators object to a treaty, they must have something to show for it, if only a committee report brought into the Senate and read but not adopted. Practically all of the Senators had privately promised not to move the adoption of the report which was presented January 15, 1929. No one did, and the treaty was at once approved by a vote of eighty-five to one.[33]

Achievement or Delusion? Senator Blaine, of Wisconsin, alone dissented in the vote on the treaty. In his view it was "not even a truce."[34] Senator Glass, also, was not willing for anybody in Virginia to think that he placed much dependence on it. He thought it "one of the many devices that have been contrived to solace the awakened conscience of some people who kept us out of the League of Nations; and whether it was so intended or not it is going to confuse the minds of many good and pious people who think that peace may be secured by polite professions of brotherly love." No peace would amount to anything that did not have behind it the potential use of the military power of the nations combined.[35]

Senator Johnson, of California, had about the same degree of faith in the Pact. He thought it had been analyzed by its proponents practically into disintegration. He remembered that when war comes the first casualty is truth and that a nation seeking to coerce another always insisted it was acting in self defense.[36] Senator Bruce, of Maryland, believed that trust in the mere enlightened self interest of a country was an unreliable thing, but he welcomed the treaty as a step toward our entry into the League and the Court. He agreed that it was a difficult thing to police international peace but held that it was "an idle dream to believe

[33] I have given a more extended account of the proceedings in the Senate in my *Treaty Veto of the American Senate,* Chapter 11.
[34] *Congressional Record,* Vol. 70, p. 1467.
[35] *Ibid.,* p. 1781.
[36] *Ibid.*

that the peace of cities has to be policed, that the peace of a single state of the Union has to be policed, that the peace of the United States has to be policed, but that the peace of the world need not be policed." He voted for the treaty under the belief that it would have some appreciable influence in ushering in the day when war would at least be sternly kept within very narrow bounds by the united efforts of the nations.[37]

Senator Swanson also reached the conclusion that the treaty was a friendly gesture toward peace. As a peace pact it would be found ineffective and disappointing. No nation could rely on it for protection; the restraints it placed on the strong arm of war were too feeble. It spoke with the voice of peace, however, and he was unwilling to silence that voice however faintly raised.[38]

Senator McLean, following Swanson, thought it was "well to bear in mind that neither peace leagues nor world courts nor modifications of international law can abolish wars or rumors of wars without the aid of an international army and navy, operated in obedience to international decrees, delivered in sealed envelopes to international generals and admirals. International wars and crimes and misdemeanors must be abolished as the domestic varieties are abolished by superior force." [39]

Senator Wagner, of New York, considered it to be obvious that the treaty did not provide for either old-fashioned peace machinery or the new-fashioned outlawry of war. Senator Gillett, also, in a sober, well-balanced speech concluded that the treaty did not quite live up to the happy and expressive phrase "to outlaw war." "Outlawry," he said, "seems to carry with it a little more resolute, militant, punitive spirit of hostility than renunciation; it means not only abandonment and a condemnation by public opinion, but it means positive activity to run it down and suppress and exterminate it. It is more virile and less pacific than

[37] *Ibid.*, pp. 1284, 1392.

[38] *Ibid.*, p. 1216. Like other Senators, he could hardly recall a war that had not been fought ostensibly in self defense.

[39] *Congressional Record*, Vol. 70, p. 1219. Senator McLean was not, of course, advocating the establishment of a superstate.

renunciation. It implies sanctions as well as aversions. Perhaps some time in the future that will come among all nations." Public opinion might be found to be an adequate sanction. In any case, Briand had wisely said, "Such a treaty means a beginning, not an end." [40]

Both Gillett and Senator Walsh, of Montana, felt it to be a splendid first step. The latter emphasized the great moral value of reversing the legal situation with reference to war. Instead of engaging in a perfectly legal, respectable activity the war-maker would now become a lawbreaker, guilty of an international crime. The frantic efforts of the belligerents in the war to establish the rectitude of their course left no room for doubt about the importance of world opinion in such a crisis. The treaty must act as a powerful deterrent upon a nation bent on war. Nobody doubted that the plighted word of individuals generally exercised a restraining influence over them, yet the innumerable treaties which were scrupulously kept were ignored in stressing the few that had been broken.[41]

Were We Morally Involved? Naturally most speakers were interested in what would probably happen when the treaty was broken. All agreed that no legal obligation to do anything about an infraction could possibly be read into the treaty, yet there was a general feeling that in case of violation a moral obligation to determine and deal with the guilty nation would be felt.

How the line between self defense and aggression would be drawn was indicated by Senator Borah himself in his opening discussion. "No government," he said, "refusing to come into conference, or refusing to make an effort for peaceful settlement, could, in my judgment, ever afterwards successfully claim that it was in good faith acting in self-defense. It would have great difficulty in satisfying the public opinion of the world that it was acting in good faith. It would indeed be violating the treaty. Here is a method and a means by which to test any government

[40] *Congressional Record,* Vol. 70, pp. 1398, 1404.
[41] *Ibid.,* p. 1773.

which might be acting not in good faith under the treaty, and to place it in a position before the world where it would be practically impossible to defend its course or conduct." [42]

The same development was forecast by Senator Gillett. Since we are all agreed to settle our disputes by pacific means, he said, "if one party to a quarrel offers such a resort and the other refuses, it is plain who has broken the treaty and who is the aggressor," and no nation, he thought, would want to make war in the face of the outraged public opinion of the world.[43]

No duty was prescribed for the United States States, or for any nation, when other signatories approached a breach of the treaty, or actually engaged in war. We would legally be free to take any action we saw fit. That we could hardly be so free morally was pointedly demonstrated by Senator James A. Reed. "If we ratify this treaty," he scoffed, "and a nation breaks it, no matter how grossly, we are under no obligation to stand by or assist in any way the nation that is injured. We are at perfect liberty to open our ports and our commerce to the wicked and offending nation just the same as though we had never made this pact of peace." Did we mean to say, he demanded, that "if fifty nations sign this treaty, the object being to maintain the peace of the world, and one of them wrongfully assails another, we are to let that nation stand out and take the brunt of the whole matter, it alone to suffer, and the rest of us at perfect liberty to deal with the offending nation exactly as with the injured nation?" [44]

A Treaty with the League? We might consider ourselves free to pursue such a course, but, Senator Hiram Johnson pointed out early in the debate, the other signers would not be. A breach of this treaty would also be a breach of the Covenant of the League and "all the nations except the United States under the covenant of the league would then endeavor to enforce the obligation that rests upon them and against the party that was guilty of the breach. The United States then would stand aloof, the

[42] *Ibid.*, p. 1269.
[43] *Ibid.*, p. 1404.
[44] *Ibid.*, pp. 1540-41.

only nation on the face of the earth that was a party to the same breach in a different treaty, doing nothing at all, with no obligation either express or implied." [45] Johnson, of course, was not contending that the United States should shoulder a portion of the duties and risks of membership in the League. He was merely registering his conviction that the Pact bound us morally to support the League in its handling of breaches of the peace.

Senator Reed, too, seemed as convinced that further controversies between nations which brought them to the point of war would be settled by the League, though he too relished the prospect not at all. While enumerating the wars that were still legal under the Pact, he explained that the Covenant "leaves fifty nations or more, practically every nation except ourselves, having solemnly agreed to maintain the status quo, having solemnly agreed that any war or threat of war by any nation anywhere shall be justiciable by the league, and that the league may take such action as it seems proper. It leaves to the council of the league, or some of its bodies, the decision as to who is right and who is wrong, just as the Locarno pact leaves to the council of the League of Nations the decision as to who is right and who is wrong. The decision having been rendered, provision is made for imposing the conditions of the decision on the nation adversely decided against, and those provisions, as we all know, are provisions for war; not war in defense of a country's territory, not war in defense of a country's trade, not war in defense of a country's nationals, but war in defense of the status quo. Take that away from your treaty, and will somebody tell me what you have left? What have you left?" [46]

Returning to the point again, Senator Johnson quoted from David Hunter Miller, who helped to draft the League Covenant and continues to be the leading American authority on its meaning, to show what the situation would be in the event of a simultaneous breach of the Covenant and of the Pact. Miller con-

[45] *Ibid.*, p. 1270.
[46] *Ibid.*, p. 1585.

sidered it quite impossible to suppose that the United States would stand wholly aloof, issue the usual proclamation of neutrality, and treat the power that had broken our treaty like any other friendly nation. Various steps short of war, such as the breaking of relations with the violator or a policy of benevolent neutrality toward the other side might be taken, but an attitude of supine indifference to our own treaty was unimaginable.

Further than that, continued Miller, "the treaty links the United States to the League of Nations as a guardian of the peace. It is, in effect, a treaty between the United States and the League, and, in the largest sense it makes the aim of the League and of our foreign policy identical. Textually it is correct enough to say that the Pact has no sanctions, no means of enforcement back of it, but its conjunction with the Covenant means that the sanctions of Article 16 of the Covenant have behind them the moral acquiescence of the United States." The attitude of the United States toward a power that flouts its promise, unexpressed, but potential, is a "very true sanction." [47]

Very similar conclusions were quoted by Senator Bingham from Professor Edwin M. Borchard, of Yale, a consistent opponent of the League. The relation of the Pact to the Covenant and the Locarno treaties seemed to him "the most significant part of the whole treaty. The treaty does in practical effect, as Europe has made clear, tie us up to the decisions of the League of Nations on any subject." The alleged violations of the Covenant would be certain to be called a violation of the Pact, and unless we made it clear that we were not bound by League decisions we were certain to invite the most bitter recriminations in a future crisis when other nations would ask us to support our treaty.[48]

Thus for a second time within five years the Senate was confronted with the fact that all roads to peace seemed to lead to Geneva. Moreover, disclaimers that we would not be bound by League decisions did not seem to be much protection against the

[47] *Ibid.*, p. 1532. For a full commentary on the Pact see: D. H. Miller, *The Pact of Paris*, New York, 1928.

[48] *Congressional Record,* Vol. 70, p. 1532.

probable weight of world opinion likely to be behind those decisions. Did even the greatest nation dare flout that opinion as organized in the League? And after all did we not really want to back the efforts of the League instead of opposing them? The intervening years had mellowed somewhat the feelings aroused against the League in 1919 and had brought an even clearer realization of the necessity of controlling war.

The denunciations of war were not so impassioned and so bitter in 1929, but they were, in some respects, even more deadly. There was not so much emphasis upon war as a brutal, sinful bloodletting, but there was more stress upon it as a destruction of life and wealth which didn't pay. Senators stated and reiterated all through the debate the conviction that modern war destroyed victor and vanquished alike and that it would do so in increasing degree in the future. That is the basic reason why Senator Dill, of Washington, declared that: "The peace movement is in politics in this world as it has never been previously in history." [49] Modern war has not only the power of religion and morals enlisted against it; it has aroused the deepest instinct we have—the instinct of self-preservation.

Had these great forces triumphed in the signature and ratification of the Pact? Had the obligation of Wilson's conquerors to provide some other "association of nations" been met at last—and without costing anything? Joining the World Court was a substitute for entering the League. Was the Pact now a substitute for entering the Court? Now that a law against war had been solemnly passed, could it not be hoped that the great public which believed that something should be done to buttress the peace had been pacified finally? [50]

[49] *Ibid.*, p. 1726. "Make no mistake about it," warned Senator Dill, "science had made the nations neighbors and war both contagious and uncontrollable. When once it is started it almost surely will become world wide."

[50] In 1929 there was still reason for taking seriously the prophetic warning of Samuel Colcord that "What pro-League Republicans and the people in general in our own country and throughout the world would not tolerate and would not forgive, would be a falling back into doing nothing—continued isolation which would mean destruction of our own financial, commercial and

Was that all? Or had the United States taken a step from which she could never turn back entirely? Had she committed herself by the clearest kind of implication to the defense of collective security? Had we become bound ourselves to scrutinize military aggression wherever it should occur and to resist it in some degree, in cooperation with others? Was our collaboration with the League in times of crisis now inevitable, if not our eventual entry into the League?

The War in the Gran Chaco Postponed. The answer to these divergent interpretations and hopes could not be made soon. Yet it began to take shape almost immediately. During the same month in which Kellogg signed the Pact of Paris, his Assistant Secretary of State for Latin American affairs, Francis White, approved a new loan of $23,000,000 to Bolivia by Dillon Read and Company. Of this sum, $5,060,000 was to pay for munitions already ordered in England and $1,500,000 was to go into military roads directed toward Paraguay. The remaining $14,000,000 was earmarked to refund a previous loan of the same amount, made in 1927, which the bankers argued would be defaulted if not refunded.

By December 10 the war for the Gran Chaco had begun, the day before a Pan American Conference was due to meet in Washington to formulate arbitration and conciliation treaties of far reaching scope. The coincidence was fortunate in the extreme for the Pact's American godfather. For once a Pan American conference tackled a political question and seized it boldly. Paraguay soon yielded and eventually Bolivia accepted a mediation which was to postpone the war for two years. She did not accept it, however, until the pressure of Pan American public opinion became unendurable. In the Peace Pact's first test it had an instrument ready at hand through which public opinion could express itself. A conference of eighteen nations was in session and it wanted to mediate the dispute. Why, asked the newspapers of these nations, more caustically every day, does not Bolivia yield

industrial prosperity, destruction to the world in which we must be inextricably involved and the end of hope for world peace."—Samuel Colcord, *The Great Deception,* New York, 1921, p. 37.

to our mediation? Eventually, she was compelled to yield.[51] But it did not follow that, without any means of making itself felt, public opinion would be of much use in preventing the next violation of the Pact.

The necessity of giving public opinion organization and institutions through which to operate was never made more plain than by Elihu Root in 1925. He wrote: "Public opinion cannot make itself affirmatively effective except by the creation of institutions adapted to give it effect. Mere verbal expressions of opinion get nowhere. . . . There is no reasonable doubt that the majority of the people of most civilized nations are strongly opposed to involving themselves in war, and the question inevitably arises, 'How is it that nations composed of people who don't want war are continually fighting?' The answer is that the opinion against war has been without adequate institutions to give it effect. War is an international affair; and to prevent it there must be international opinion, and international action upon that opinion, and international institutions to give effect to that opinion." [52]

[51] Pearson and Brown, *The American Diplomatic Game*, pp. 42-50.

[52] Elihu Root, "Steps toward Preserving Peace," *Foreign Affairs*, April, 1925, Vol. 3, p. 353. In the same article Root rebuked, in a paragraph which attracted wide attention, the constantly reiterated assertion that world peace and organization did not concern us. He said: "Another consideration which should be kept in mind is that our people really do desire to contribute towards the preservation of peace and the progress of civilization throughout the world. We do not wish to be selfish and cynical and indifferent about the welfare of the rest of the world. We do not think we are and we do not wish to be thought so. We really have ideals about human progress and we wish to stand for them. We have long professed them and we do not wish anybody to put us in the position of appearing to be hypocrites and humbugs. If there be any project of international cooperation proposed which will really be for the benefit of civilization, we do not wish to have it treated as something that somebody else wants and is trying to get us into. If it is real, we want it to succeed just as much as anybody else can want it to succeed; and we wish to be counted in as supporting it unless there is some real obstacle in the way which cannot be removed. And by real obstacle we mean something substantial, not any fanciful or trivial difference of opinion about non-essential things. No two men ever devised plans of action to accomplish a particular object without finding that there were differences in their plans. This is particularly the case in international affairs. A real desire to accomplish the object will brush aside all the non-essential differences. That is the way in which we wish proposals for our cooperation in projects for the benefit of mankind to be treated" (p. 352).

World Court Entry Revived

Immediately after the Senate had approved the Kellogg Pact, Root made another effort to open up one blocked channel through which our public opinion for international order might express itself. Senator Gillett, of Massachusetts, had introduced a resolution into the Senate on February 6, 1928, calling upon the President to conduct the exchange of views for which the World Court Conference of September, 1926, had asked.[53]

A score of leading newspapers joined in support of the Gillett resolution and it mustered strength enough to be scheduled for discussion in the Senate in December, 1928. Shortly before debate on it opened, the President expressed a willingness to reopen negotiations and the debate was not held. On February 20, 1929, Secretary Kellogg made public a note which he had just sent to each of the nations belonging to the Court. The note was frank and cordial. It admitted that the Senate's terms had received unconditional acceptances from but five of forty-eight states, disclaimed any intention to interfere with the work of the League Council, "doubtless often perplexing and difficult," and suggested that an informal exchange of views ought to produce some formula that would protect our rights in unobjectionable form.[54]

The 1928 Assembly of the League (and Council) had elected former Secretary of State Charles Evans Hughes to the vacancy on the World Court bench caused by the resignation of Judge John Bassett Moore, and his subsequently active part in the campaign of 1928 had prepared the public, at least indirectly, for a reopening of the Court negotiations. This was facilitated by a

[53] *Congressional Record,* Vol. 69, Pt. 3, p. 2503. A nation-wide petition had been presented to President Coolidge in December, 1927, praying a renewal of negotiations. On this occasion the Scripps-Howard newspapers had reminded the President, in an editorial of December 14, 1927, that in acting upon the World Court the Senate had deliberately thrown his recommendations to the winds and had "indulged in so many refinements of logic, sophistries and subterfuges that we were finally finessed out of the Court." These reservations were "more sounding than sound" and one of the most useful acts the President could perform before leaving the White House would be to tell the Senate so.

[54] *United States Daily,* February 20, 1929.

further action of the Assembly in creating a commission to review the statute of the World Court, prior to the approaching general election of judges. It was appropriate that Elihu Root, more than any other man the father of the Court, should sit on this commission and that he should propose a plan for reconciling the Senate's reservations with the desire of the nations to preserve the advisory opinion function of the Court. It was fitting that Root, already famous for efforts to compromise the American schism over the League, should try to resolve the impasse over the Court.

The Root Formula. His solution was to reaffirm the Senate's claim to a veto over any and all advisory opinions and then lay down rules for its exercise. He believed that in practice no difficulty would arise, but in order to satisfy the Senate he proposed that the United States have a right to halt an advisory-opinion proceeding, either before a request was made to the Court or at any later time while the Court had the matter under consideration. To provide for the bare possibility, or rather what he considered the near impossibility, that agreement could not be reached, his plan provided for our withdrawal from the Court "naturally and without any imputation of unfriendliness or unwillingness to cooperate generally for peace and good will." [55]

This plan was accepted by the jurists' committee and later embodied in a protocol, the signing of which President Hoover authorized in December, 1929, after he had already supported the Court strongly in his inaugural address. The way seemed at last open for the United States to lend its moral weight to the Court. Under the Root plan we did not have a legal right to veto outright the asking of an advisory opinion. That could be acquired only by membership on the League Council. But we gained the right to stop an advisory-opinion proceeding at any stage and thus to throw the full weight of the most powerful nation against it. Under these terms adherence to the Court appeared to be at least as safe as membership in the army of nations which had just outlawed war.

[55] *New York Times*, March 7, 1929.

The Pact Invoked in Manchuria

Though the signatures on the Pact of Paris made it an almost universal pronouncement, the Pact had not yet been officially promulgated. This ceremony was set for July 24, 1929, in Washington.

But on July 10 a grave dispute was precipitated between China and Russia over the Chinese Eastern Railway in North Manchuria. The Soviet Government had been the first to give up extraterritorial rights in China, but in 1924 it had recovered a half interest in the valuable short-cut railroad which the Tsarist government had built across Manchuria. Chiang Kai-shek's break with his Soviet advisers in 1927 soon altered the situation and led to the expulsion of the Russian ambassador from China.

Two years later, May 27, 1929, four Soviet consulates in Manchuria were raided and evidence of subversive activities alleged. Then on July 10, while the ruler of Manchuria, Chang Hsueh-liang, was conferring in Peking with Chiang Kai-shek, two hundred Russian officials of the Chinese Eastern Railway were arrested, sixty of whom were deported. The railway telegraph administration was also seized and a systematic liquidation of all Russian economic agencies begun.

On July 13, the Soviet Government delivered a three-day ultimatum demanding a restoration of the *status quo* and a conference. When the Chinese demurred, on July 17, Russia severed all railway and diplomatic intercourse and brought up troops. Nanking replied in kind, July 20, and Germany became the diplomatic intermediary between them.

The United States Acts. Two days earlier Hoover's Secretary of State, Henry L. Stimson, had decided that the United States, as the sponsor of the Pact of Paris, must take some steps to uphold it. On July 18, he called in the Chinese Minister to remind him of China's signature to the Pact. Since the United States had no relations with Russia, France was asked to speak to Russia. Stimson conferred also with the Ambassadors of the Great Powers and soon received their approval of his initiative.[56] The Pact was put into full force, as planned, on July 24.

The next day Secretary Stimson called in the representatives of the Powers and proposed a neutral commission of inquiry, a withdrawal of forces and a temporary administration for the disputed railway.[57] His sense of diplomatic politeness, however, led him to make the mistake of withholding the plan from the public which had applauded his first move generously and now had nothing to do, while the plan leaked out through Vienna, two weeks later, in a garbled form which made Russia highly suspicious. It even appeared, falsely enough, that Stimson had been intriguing to get control of the Chinese Eastern Railway.

Military Pressure. Then for several weeks the Russians exerted a steadily increasing military pressure on the Manchurian border. Their policy appears to have been one of "restricting the use of military force within the narrowest possible limits" [58] to achieve their diplomatic aim. The Soviets would show that they did not behave like the capitalist powers, seizing all convenient occasions to carve out protectorates, but that they knew how to defend their rights. Border raids came first, gradually increasing in intensity from one end of the long Manchurian frontier to the other. When the Chinese retaliated by interning a large number of Soviet citizens, the Soviet forces seized both Manchouli and Jalia Nor, on November 17. Only three thousand strictly disciplined troops were used. The Chinese troops looted and fled. The Soviet air force rescued Hailar, on the railroad a hundred miles from the border, from a Chinese force which was out of hand and carried air raids much further into the interior. No private property was seized, and the conduct of the Russian troops was exemplary.[59]

The Russian offensive brought a quick capitulation from

[56] A. J. Toynbee, *Survey of International Affairs, 1929*, London, 1930, pp. 344-69.

[57] Russell Cooper, *American Consultation in World Affairs*, New York, 1934, pp. 92-93; Pearson and Brown, *The American Diplomatic Game*, pp. 54-58.

[58] Toynbee, *Survey of International Affairs, 1929*, pp. 359-60.

[59] *Ibid.*, pp. 362-63.

Chang Hsueh-liang, on November 21, 1929. Russia's terms, requiring a return to the *status quo*, were accepted November 26 and embodied in a preliminary agreement December 3, all Russian troops being withdrawn.[60]

The Pact Formally Cited. Meanwhile, the Russian offensive had alarmed the foreign offices, and appeals from Manchuria, recounting Soviet atrocities, had disturbed the American Government.[61] There was sustained consultation between the principal capitals, ending in the dispatch of identic notes to Russia and China on December 2, by the governments of the United States, Great Britain, France, and Italy. The statement recalled the earlier *démarche*, quoted Article 2 of the Pact and stated that: "The American Government feels that the respect with which China and Russia will hereafter be held in the good opinion of the world will necessarily in great measure depend upon the way in which they carry out these most sacred promises." [62]

Stimson asked all the signatories of the Pact to take similar action, and announced later that thirty-seven of them had, though in most cases they had waited a few days. Germany did not send a note, saying that she sympathized with the appeal but was the intermediary between the disputants. Japan did not participate and refrained from approving the appeal. Russia rejected it outright. Litvinoff's reply, relayed through Paris, was that since the two governments were already agreeing upon terms, the note of the four powers was "unjustifiable pressure on the negotiations, and cannot therefore be taken as a friendly act." He declared that the dispute could be settled only by direct negotiations and expressed "amazement that the Government of the United States, which by its own will has no official relations with the Soviet, deems it possible to apply to it with advice and counsel." The Soviet Government further stated "that the Paris pact does not

60 Pearson and Brown, *The American Diplomatic Game*, p. 61.

61 Cooper, *American Consultation in World Affairs*, pp. 95-96.

62 For the full text see Cooper, *American Consultation in World Affairs*, p. 99, or Department of State, *Press Release*, December 3, 1929, pp. 83-84.

give any single State or group of States the function of protector of this pact." [63]

This sharp rejoinder led to much public condemnation and defense of Secretary Stimson's effort to invoke the Pact. Former Secretary Kellogg came to Stimson's aid with an address in which he asserted the right of any signatory of the Pact to call the attention of other powers to its provisions. Moreover, it appeared to him to be a duty on all the signatories to help adjust difficulties and prevent war. "It was certainly the business of the United States to do everything it could to prevent the violation of a treaty which it and the other nations had signed." Consultation, too, Kellogg believed to be "inherent in the treaty." [64]

Defective Procedure? The Sino-Russian dispute had demonstrated that our Government had not signed the Pact as a gesture only. It was what its terms purported to be, a sober effort to get rid of war. Yet the 1929 incident showed clearly that, if the Pact was to live, some better way of invoking it had to be discovered. No one nation could be its guardian, not even its original sponsor. Yet quick action was necessary. Diplomatic consultation between several capitals was better than none, but it was slow and clumsy. Also all the signatories had an equal right to take part in the consultation; it was not a matter for a few large nations. And finally, consultation could not achieve proper results unless it rested on adequate, impartial information. In the 1929 case the news had come too exclusively from Chinese sources.[65]

The whole affair pointed to the need of the machinery which the League of Nations already provided. The League was left to one side during the dispute, apparently to give full sway to the initiative of the United States and the Pact of Paris. Our Government accepted the responsibility and learned quickly that no one nation is the world's guardian. It appeared that collective action in defense of the peace was much safer than for one nation to attempt to mobilize the nations. When still more serious

[63] *New York Times*, December 4, 1929.
[64] Department of State, *Press Release*, December 4, 1929.
[65] See Cooper, *American Consultation in World Affairs*, pp. 105-8.

trouble soon arose in Manchuria, we were far more ready to use the machinery of the League.

Closer Cooperation with Geneva

By 1929, the cooperation of the United States with the ordinary activities of the League was constant and cordial. An official of the Secretariat could say readily that "communications go back and forth quickly. There is the utmost courtesy and friendliness and the Washington Government cooperates about as far as possible, given existing circumstances." [66] The United States participated in the Third Conference on Communications and Transit, in 1926, in three Conferences on the Abolition of Import and Export Prohibitions in 1927 and in the Conference of Experts on Double Taxation and Fiscal Evasions in 1928.[67]

During slightly more than twelve months in 1929-30 we took part in twelve League conferences, three of them officially.[68] By February, 1931, Professor Ellery C. Stowell was able to compile a list of two hundred and twelve persons officially appointed to represent the United States in League conferences.[69] We had traveled far from the time when an American diplomat who wished to see a document at the League Secretariat in Geneva waited on the sidewalk outside while it was brought out to him, for fear that a report of his visiting the premises of the League

[66] *New York Times*, March 28, 1927.

[67] R. L. Buell, "The United States and the League of Nations," *Foreign Policy Association Information Service*, 1930, Vol. 6, p. 173.

[68] Besides sending delegates to a Conference on Economic Statistics, a Conference on Counterfeiting Currency, and a Conference on the Codification of International Law, representatives in an expert or advisory capacity were sent to six assemblages: the International Conference on the Treatment of Foreigners (November 5-December 4, 1929); Committee of Experts on Unification of Transport Statistics (December 9-29, 1929); Advisory Committee on Opium (January 20-February 14, 1930); Preliminary Conference for Concerted Economic Activity (February 17-March 24, 1930); Conference on Bills of Exchange (May 12-June 7, 1930); a Committee set up in connection with Investigation into Traffic in Women and Children in the East (August 21, 1930). *United States Daily*, September 5, 1930, p. 2075.

[69] American University Graduate School, *Cumulative Digest of International Law and Relations*, February 9, 1931, Bulletins No. 28 and 29. See also *New York Times*, February 10, 1931.

might hurt his standing in Washington.[70] The distance traveled was summarized by Parker T. Moon, of Columbia University, as the substitution of straightforward, official cooperation for side-window observation and back-stairs diplomacy.[71]

The change was attested by the creation of a greatly enlarged consular staff in Geneva, Consul Prentiss Gilbert being assigned especially to League affairs in June, 1930, and later given several assistants.

Little Progress in Treaty Making. In putting the treaties negotiated in these conferences to work the record of the United States had not been as cooperative. Of thirty non-political treaties drawn up, the United States had signed or adhered to nine, of which but two had been ratified.[72] In concluding arbitration treaties the record of the United States was far worse. Of one hundred and sixty bilateral arbitration treaties ratified in the world between 1910 and 1926, the United States was a party to only two. Stimulated by Article 12 of the League Covenant, the other nations had gone ahead, concluding even more far-reaching and more binding arbitration agreements, but under the non-political-association complex developed in the campaign of 1920 the United States surrendered its century-old place of leadership for arbitration and during nine years did not lift a finger in its behalf.[73] The United States, in the measured words of Manley O. Hudson, of Harvard University, had "lost her share of the leadership in the movement for international arbitration." [74]

To remedy this lamentable lapse, Secretary Kellogg negotiated a new series of arbitration and conciliation treaties, but they con-

[70] J. S. Bassett, *The League of Nations,* New York, 1928, p. 337.

[71] Parker T. Moon, "The League Survives," *New Republic,* January 22, 1930, p. 242. In the words of H. V. Kaltenborn, "Each year the United States has cooperated in the League's work more willingly, more largely, and more effectively."—*Current History,* January, 1930, Vol. 31, p. 653.

[72] R. L. Buell, "The United States and the League of Nations," *Foreign Policy Association Information Service,* 1930, Vol. 6, p. 172.

[73] F. B. Sayre, "America at the Crossroads," *Atlantic Monthly,* July, 1929, Vol. 144, p. 4.

[74] Manley O. Hudson, "The New Arbitration Treaty with France," *American Journal of International Law,* 1928, Vol. 22, p. 373.

Wide World

RAYMOND B.
FOSDICK
Under Secretary General, 1919–1920

Shelburne

ARTHUR
SWEETSER
Assistant Director, Information Section, 1918–1934; Director attached to principal Officers of the Secretariat since 1934

WHITNEY H.
SHEPARDSON
Assistant to the Under Secretary General, 1919

BENJAMIN
GERIG
Member of the Information Section since 1930

HOWARD
HUSTON
Establishment Officer, 1920–1930

AMERICAN MEMBERS OF THE
LEAGUE SECRETARIAT

Mr. Huntington Gilchrist was chief of the Department of Administrative Commissions, 1920–1924, and Assistant Director of the Mandates Section, 1924–1928.

tained so many exceptions that John B. Whitton, of Princeton University, concluded that they constituted "little advance over the Root treaties of twenty years ago—long before the lessons of the war and the modern swing toward veritable obligatory obligation." [75] In December, 1928, delegates of twenty American nations drew up in Washington a far-reaching conciliation treaty, providing for the submission of *all* disputes, without exception, to a two-year investigation, with hostilities ruled out. This treaty was ratified by the United States Senate February 20, 1929,[76] but the Pan American Arbitration Treaty, framed at the same time, was emasculated by the addition of that hoary reservation which requires the *compromis* of each and every arbitration to be submitted to the Senate for its approval, thus nullifying completely the object of the treaty that arbitration should be certainly provided for.[77] The Pan American treaty did, however, secure the qualified agreement of the United States to arbitrate the same four categories of juridical disputes which are enumerated in the optional clause of the World Court statute, now in force among the principal powers and nearly all of the smaller ones.[78]

League Membership Dismissed. Politically, the nation turned further away from the League. The Republican platform of 1928 dismissed League membership in three lines: "This government has definitely refused membership in the League of Nations and to assume any obligations under the Covenant of the League. On this we stand." The Democratic platform also dropped all mention of the League and talked instead of "freedom from entangling political alliances with foreign nations." Alfred E.

75. Address to the National Council for Prevention of War, Washington, October 30, 1929.

76 *Congressional Record,* Vol. 70, pp. 3852-54.

77 *Congressional Record,* Vol. 75, pp. 2240-48. The treaty was ratified January 19, 1922. On this reservation and others attached to the same treaty, see the editorial by James W. Garner, *The American Journal of International Law,* 1932, Vol. 26, pp. 333-36.

78 (a) The interpretation of a treaty; (b) any question of international law; (c) the existence of any fact which, if established, would constitute a breach of an international obligation; (d) the nature and extent of the reparation to be made for the breach of an international obligation.

Smith, the Democratic candidate for President, said: "Any time fifty-five men are going to consider matters that may affect my business I like to sit in," [79] but the League figured in the campaign almost not at all.

After his election, President Hoover put aside his 1920 championship of the League and rationalized our attitude in accordance with his Quaker faith. On Armistice Day, 1929, he said: "The European nations have by the Covenant of the League of Nations, agreed that if nations fail to settle their differences peaceably, then force should be applied by other nations to compel them to be reasonable. We have refused to travel this road. We are confident that at least in the Western Hemisphere that public opinion will suffice to check violence. This is the road we propose to travel." [80]

This pronouncement preceded the Russian thrust in Manchuria on November 17. It came before the public opinion of the Western and Eastern Hemispheres had failed to stop the long, bloody war in the Chaco and, needless to say, before it had failed to deter Japan in Manchuria and Italy in Ethiopia. But in the full bloom of Hoover prosperity and Coolidge outlawry it seemed enough to leave the world's peace to "public opinion," and to the inspiration of the moment.

[79] Quoted by John Palmer Gavit in *Saturday Review of Literature*, 1930, Vol. 6, p. 619.

[80] *Current History*, January, 1930, Vol. 31, p. 676. On April 14, 1930, he repeated that "the instinct of the vast majority of our people is that our contribution is not to be based upon commitments to use force to maintain peace." R. L. Buell, "The United States and the League of Nations," *Foreign Policy Information Service*, 1930, Vol. 6, p. 173.

CHAPTER XI

COLLAPSE

BY THE summer of 1928 prosperity was permanent and it was completely Republicanized. The Republican claim to prosperity was well established in earlier years. Cleveland had been unfortunate enough to preside over the panic of 1893. Wilson had had no panic, except for a brief war flurry in 1914, but the Republicans had thoroughly convinced themselves that business would have gone to smash under him if the war had not intervened. In any event, the Harding-Coolidge era had demonstrated beyond the possibility of disbelief that prosperity and Republican rule were one and the same.

It was useless for the Democrats to put a leading spirit of the New York Stock Exchange, John J. Raskob, in charge of their campaign in 1928 and equally idle for him to try to make the Democrats as protectionist as the Republicans. Protectionism was the great Republican dogma. The majority of Americans had been born to it and took it as a matter of religion. It was a system, too—or a racket—which was unbeatable. It conquered all opposition by sharing the tariff spoils with all and sundry. All that anyone of any importance needed to do was to ask for a tariff. Those producers who didn't ask were persuaded that a little dose of the tariff medicine would make all things right. It was an infallible remedy.

None knew this better than Herbert Hoover, successful engineer, distinguished war administrator and Republican choice for President in 1928. As Secretary of Commerce during the whole period of Normalcy Mr. Hoover knew that the magic of the tariff had made the country so wealthy that poverty was about to be abolished for all those who would work. In his acceptance speech he admitted that the goal had not yet been reached, but the poorhouse was "vanishing from among us" and "given a chance to go forward with the policies of the last eight years, we shall soon, with the help of God, be in sight of the day when poverty will be banished from this nation." [1]

Farmers' Subsidies Rejected

There was, to be sure, one very weak spot in the national economic body. Hoover knew that the agricultural half of the nation had been depressed since 1920 and that it was falling into a state of permanent decay. He knew, also, that the great world of business which he represented would not permit the farmers to be subsidized. That matter had been settled. The distressed farmers had cried out for aid eight years before. For their relief they had been cordially invited to come bodily into the tariff temple. Up to that time they had served the nation by building up industry. Now they should have heavy tariffs of their very own. The Tariff of 1922 granted liberal duties on all the great crops of which we had a surplus—duties which could not be otherwise than ineffective in preventing the farmers' products from selling, at home and abroad, at the world price. When the United States sold abroad 700,000,000 pounds of lard, as in 1927, the effect of the lard duty on imports of 5,052 pounds, or upon any other pounds of lard that might want to slip from abroad into our kitchens, was not perceptible.[2] With exports of 37,972,894 bushels of barley the tariff collected on 713 bushels of imports had a truly microscopic effect upon the sale price of our total crop of 265,882,000 bushels.

McNary-Haugen Bill Defeated. Nevertheless, when the farmers worked out a scheme for making the tariff on the great surplus crops mean something, it was greeted with horror as interfering with the sacred laws of economics. The McNary-Haugen Bill, first presented in 1924, frankly proposed to do just what the tariff

[1] *New York Times*, August 12, 1928.

[2] United States Tariff Commission, *Comparison of Imports and Consumption*, Washington, 1930.

did for industry, that is, to enable the farmers to get a higher price in the home market than abroad. The farmers had been taught for decades what a fine thing it would be to have a great protected "home market" right at their doors. Now they wanted actually to take possession of that home market. Their method could not be as simple and silent as the tariff, but it would do the same thing. An equalization fee would be collected from the growers of each staple, sufficient to cover the losses of marketing the large minor fraction of these staples abroad. The price of the bulk of these products, sold at home, would then be raised to a level with the prices of tariff-protected industry.

This outrageous scheme for doing publicly what the tariff did so quietly was soundly defeated in the House of Representatives in June, 1924, by a vote of 223 to 153, and again in May, 1926. The Senate turned it down in 1924 by a smaller margin, 45 to 39. In February, 1927, the bill passed both houses and was firmly vetoed by President Coolidge. Again it won both Houses in April, 1928, and again it was vetoed. President Coolidge branded it as "a regime of futile, delusive experiments with price fixing . . . of intolerable espionage and tax collection." He called it a sales tax on the whole nation—unaware, probably, that every tariff duty was a sales tax and a price-fixing device. His successful vetoes were sagely applauded by all the beneficiaries of the tariff.[3]

The Export Debenture Plan Smothered. Then the agricultural interests brought forward another plan, perfected by Dr. Charles Stewart, of the University of Illinois. Coolidge had sensed bureaucracy in the McNary-Haugen Bill. The Export Debenture Plan avoided this objection and others. It proposed to pay export bounties on the farm surpluses sold abroad by issuing negotiable instruments called debentures which would be receivable in payment of tariff duties. This scheme would not even take money out of

[3] L. M. Hacker and B. B. Kendrick, *The United States since 1865*, New York, 1932, pp. 645-47.

the Treasury, though it would keep money from going into it, exactly as every protective tariff duty does, for no tariff duty can be protective without keeping some goods from entering the country, goods which, if admitted, would pay duties into the Treasury. The Export Debenture Plan was as like the tariff as any scheme could be without being identically the same thing. It was also carefully limited to prevent the home prices of farm products from going too high. This new twin brother of the tariff, however, was never able to pass either branch of Congress in the Coolidge era.

President Hoover did not espouse it, either, in his acceptance speech. He recognized that "The most urgent economic problem in our nation today is in agriculture." He declared: "It must be solved. We have pledged ourselves to find a solution." The solution was not proposed. Hoover had heard, however, of the tiny trickles of lard, barley, and other surplus crops which came in from abroad. "The tariff on some products," he said, "is proving inadequate to protect him [the farmer] from imports abroad." Out of his wide knowledge acquired as Secretary of Commerce he asserted that "an adequate tariff is the foundation of farm relief" and promised solemnly that: "I would use my office and influence to give the farmer the full benefit of our historic tariff policy." Yet when the Senate later voted for the Export Debenture Plan, Hoover used his full influence to defeat it in the House.[4] To have permitted the farmers really to come under the tariff tent would have taken away a large part of the pleasurable profits enjoyed by those already there. But in July, 1928, Hoover was serenely sure that "there is no selfishness in this defense of our standard of living," by which he meant the standard of living of those already enjoying tariff favors. "A general reduction of the tariff," he prophesied, "would fill our streets with idle workers." He did not know how soon the streets would be black with tariff-protected workers turned loose to drift dully into huge bread lines.

[4] Hacker and Kendrick, *The United States since 1865*, p. 647.

Tariffs Lifted Higher

If Hoover had had any doubt as to the potency of the tariff elixir to calm the farmers, if it did not relieve them, Senator Borah removed that doubt. Borah was a power in the Hoover campaign and a firm believer in the magic of protectionism. His promptings were sufficient to induce Hoover to promise, late in October before the election, a limited revision of the tariff for the benefit of agriculture.[5]

This limited revision took the natural and inevitable course. The House Committee on Ways and Means began to hold public hearings January 7, 1929. All who desired protection were welcomed and the already protected manufacturers came in quantity. Before the Committee they received the most sympathetic treatment, on one condition only—that they refrain from taking the Committee's time. Day after day they filed by, exhorted constantly to be brief in presenting their demands. Five minutes was an age to the Committee. Minutes were doled out by the chairman as if an era of insufficient protection were rushing to a close on a day inexorably fixed. Some petitioners were lucky to get three minutes—two minutes. But it was enough if they would only leave the rates they wanted in writing—as little writing as possible.[6]

Swift Procession. Some representatives of important industries had, of course, to be granted more time. They were questioned most deferentially by the Republican members of the Committee and hostile questions from Democratic members were suppressed. The Republicans felt it was most indelicate to ask the protected industries questions about their profits. That was their own private affair. Witnesses found it easy to evade searching questions by professing ignorance and even by refusing to answer. The business

[5] *New York Times*, October 28, 1928.

[6] The 20,000 pages of testimony collected by the two committees has been analyzed in penetrating fashion by E. E. Shattschneider in his *Politics, Pressures and the Tariff, a Study of Free Private Enterprise in Pressure Policies as Shown in the 1929-1930 Revision of the Tariff*, New York, 1935. This is the most illuminating study yet made of the way in which tariffs were made prior to 1934. No one who would understand the process should fail to consult it.

was expedited, for, as Schattschneider comments, agreements may be reached in a friendly proceeding "when every major premise of the petitioners is conceded in advance." No attempt was made to check briefs, to requisition accounts, or to reach persons able to verify disputed testimony. The Committee plunged ahead on its minute schedule, made out far in advance. At one time a crisis arose because only 118 witnesses out of a listed total of 184 had been heard in four days; at another the Committee actually "heard" 127 in four days, "nor was this performance unusual." To drive them through faster, various kinds of closure were adopted. The bankruptcy of the proceedings was openly confessed by cutting off witnesses who had more to say and were struggling to say it.

"Cost of Production." Yet the moral and physical collapse of Congressional tariff making was not as complete as the bankruptcy of the "principle" under which the system operated. As in 1922, the tariff makers solemnly sat to determine the difference in the costs of production of tens of thousands of articles produced in sixty different nations. Even the Democratic platform of 1928 had plumped for this ancient article of faith, saying that "actual difference of cost of production at home and abroad, with adequate safeguard for the wage of the American laborer, must be the extreme measure of every tariff rate." Who could fail to subscribe to this great aim? And who could apply it? Hoover's Commerce Department had tried to spy out the costs of production of industries abroad, but without much success. The foreign manufacturers had ideas about the privacy of their businesses. The physical impossibility of determining costs of production for even a fraction of the articles produced in many lands under many conditions was manifest. And if it could have been done, the results would have been unreliable when completed because of the rapidity with which conditions change. The equalizing-costs-of-production theory was, moreover, a contradiction in itself. A tariff rate which barely equalizes the costs of production is not protective unless it is high enough to keep the

foreign article out. Yet if it keeps foreign goods out, competition is destroyed, not preserved as is pretended.

As a screen for extending protection to all and sundry the formula is perfect, though it breeds its own death by spreading "protection" so widely that finally it will tend eventually to become valueless to all. Protection is real and valuable only if it takes money from the national income and gives it to a relative few. When everyone can take money from the national purse then this practice is sure to lose its attractions to the original protectionists. If the farmers were really admitted, the system would probably be killed, as their leaders know, though they believe that the farmers can survive only by imitating the tariff beneficiaries, not by combating them. Yet as a camouflage, "equalizing costs" was an enormous success. Behind its large symbols of patriotism and nationalism the minority interests which profit from the tariff periodically marched rapidly past the House and Senate tariff committees in endless review, filing, as they passed, the new rates of protection which they desired—without arousing the vast slumbrous majorities.

To these hearings those who paid did not come. The huge mass of consumers was inert. The farmers were given many high and empty duties. Even the rank and file of the industries which would be injured by the new rates were seldom aroused until too late. Then they would be too weakened to fight the next time. A few interests opposed to increasing rates did appear to contest them. They were appeased with compensatory duties, that is, with duties on manufactured articles, the raw materials of which are taxed. Importers could be counted on to oppose higher duties but they were waved aside as traitors trying to smuggle articles of value in for the use of the American people.[7]

[7] It is not to be wondered at that the Republicans of 1936 bitterly opposed the continuation of Secretary Cordell Hull's method of changing tariff rates by negotiating tariff agreements with individual nations, under unconditional most-favored-nation treatment. The executive method draws into its hearings many more interests which would be injured by rate increases or which would profit from decreases. The Executive can break the vast tariff problem down into small fragments and take time to examine them. It can conduct several hearings

Rates Based on Rumor and Assertion. Not even those demanding higher rates pretended to know what the production costs of their foreign competitors were. In dozens of cases they frankly said so,[8] and their admissions troubled the Committeemen not at all. The Committee listened gravely, instead, to completely unsubstantiated rumors as to the dire things foreign competitors were thought to be plotting. Day by day it heard without demur protective duties claimed as a matter of established right.[9] For forty-three days the House Committee sat. Then it rose and banished its Democratic members, as was its right, and drafted the tariff act of 1930 so successfully that the House passed the bill May 28, 1929, three weeks after it had been reported. Then the Finance Committee of the Senate held hearings from June 13 to July 18, after which it revised the bill extensively and reported it on September 4, 1929. The desire of the Republican organization was still for haste, to avoid arousing the great aggregate of quiescent groups which could defeat the legislation if once aroused. There were in fact enough stirrings of interest in the bill to hold it in the closely balanced Senate until June 13, 1930, when it passed the Senate by a vote of 44 to 42, with eleven Republicans against it and five Democrats for it. The inevitable log-rolling process had finally whittled away what had been a Senate majority against the bill, a majority which had stood firm for months until eventually an oil-lumber-cement combination started the usual stampede to gain favors for local interests.

Even then the decisive vote was close, but it was eminently satisfactory to the protected interests. The high rates of the Act of 1922 went higher in the Smoot-Hawley Act of 1930. The duty on sugar advanced from 67 to 77 per cent, on cotton manufactures

simultaneously, if necessary. The executive officials can better resist the lobbyists and inquire into their claims. Above all they can keep the national interest in mind and oppose it to the specious claims of lesser interests.

[8] Schattschneider, *Politics, Pressures and the Tariff*, pp. 68-70. "The procedure under which the hearings were managed was thus a failure measured in its own terms, and talk of tariffs written on the costs formula is no more than an elaborate sham and bluff" (p. 84).

[9] *Ibid.*, pp. 88-92. At times it was even hinted that the Constitution guaranteed established tariff privileges (p. 92).

from 40 to 46 per cent, on wool and its manufactures from 49 to 59 per cent. Manufacturers of automobiles who wanted their product on the free list were compelled to accept a duty of 10 per cent.[10] Without knowing what it had done, otherwise than to lift the rates, Congress had levied duties on hundreds of thousands of items of commerce. Not all of these rates were enumerated in the 200 pages which comprised the statute. There were 264 "basket" clauses in the law, one of which alone (paragraph 360) covered 10,000 items carried in the catalogues of one Chicago firm.[11]

Economic War. The Tariff Act of 1930 was a declaration of economic war by the strongest economic power against the whole of the civilized world. It was notice to the other nations that retaliatory tariffs, quotas, and embargoes against American goods were in order. Protests from scores of foreign trade associations poured in while the bill was in preparation and the tariff rises in other countries which it provoked began to be passed as soon as it was adopted. The act was notice to our war debtors that the dollar exchange with which they might make their payments to us would not be available. Our campaign of frantic lending abroad had already ended—suddenly. Now credits due to others for goods imported by us were to be sharply curtailed. The law proclaimed to our legions of new private debtors on every continent that they too could expect a shortage of dollar funds. It was a plain warning to all domestic growers of staple crops and to many manufacturers that their markets abroad would soon be curtailed further; these markets had already begun to shrink before the law was passed. It was a notice to all producers that the myriads of people now dependent on foreign investments and foreign trade would soon have less with which to buy; it was an edict to all consumers that they could expect to enjoy

[10] Hacker and Kendrick, *The United States since 1865*, p. 568.

[11] David J. Lewis, former member of the Tariff Commission and of the House Committee on Ways and Means. Schattschneider, *Politics, Pressures and the Tariff*, pp. 16-17.

less foreign goods and to see the prices of many domestic goods rise or be held up artificially.

In view of all these ominous though elementary considerations, did the businessman who now sat in the White House promptly veto the Smoot-Hawley Bill, as a threat to the economic life of the nation and of many nations? Hoover did not issue a ringing veto; he signed. He put his name to the bill with full knowledge of what it involved. He had had before him for six weeks the most remarkable protest against an American tariff bill ever filed.[12]

A Thousand Economists Warn. On May 5, 1930, there was published throughout the country a message to Congress and to the President signed by 1,028 economists, members of the American Economic Association. This plea from the bulk of the nation's students of economics urged that any general upward revision of tariff rates be rejected by Congress, or, if passed, vetoed by the President. They warned that increased restrictive duties would not only increase prices but "encourage concerns with higher costs to undertake production, thus causing the community to subsidize waste and inefficiency in industry and force it to pay higher rates of profit to established firms."

The economists attempted to rally, for once, some of the great groups of inert people whose interests were adversely affected, continuing: "Few people could hope to gain from such a change. Miners, construction, transportation and public utility workers, professional people and those employed in banks, hotels and newspaper offices, in the wholesale and retail trades and scores of other occupations would clearly lose, since they produce no product which could be specially favored by tariff barriers." Likewise the

[12] It has been charged by the correspondent of the *New York Herald Tribune* that Hoover's secretaries carefully culled the press comments on the Smoot-Hawley Bill, withholding a large body of hostile editorials from him. The suggested explanation for this dangerous kind of censorship, that the secretaries were trying to protect Hoover's health, seems inadequate. See John T. Whitaker, *And Fear Came*, New York, 1936, p. 58.

Mr. Whitaker was later to witness in Europe how the Smoot-Hawley Tariff started the stampede toward economic nationalism, which slowly strangled international trade and cleared the way for Hitler.

vast majority of the farmers would lose, but doubly, through higher prices for what they bought and through restriction of their markets abroad. The same losses would be faced by exporting manufacturers of such things as copper, automobiles, typewriters, and agricultural machinery.

The economists said flatly that they did "not believe that American manufacturers, in general, needed higher tariffs." The report of the President's Committee on Recent Economic Changes had "shown that industrial efficiency has increased, that costs have fallen, that profits have grown with amazing rapidity since the end of the World War." Already our factories supplied our people with "96 per cent of the manufactures which they consume" and our producers looked to foreign markets to absorb the increasing output of their machines. "Further barriers to trade would serve them not well, but ill."

After pointing out that unemployment would increase and a cloud be thrown over some thirteen billions of private investment abroad, not to mention the war debts, the manifesto continued: "Finally, we would urge our government to consider the bitterness which a policy of higher tariffs would inevitably inject into our foreign relations." But it was in vain that the economists recalled the resolution of the World Economic Conference that "the time has come to put an end to the increase in tariffs and move in the opposite direction." The country had been taught so long that protective tariff makers could do no wrong that it could not be sufficiently aroused.[13]

Wall Street Collapse

Sinking and Soaring Land Values. Eight months before the Smoot-Hawley Tariff was enacted, too, prosperity had cracked wide open. Before the stock market catastrophe of October, 1929,

[13] The 1,028 economists included most of the staffs of the great universities, East and West alike. Originally drawn by seven leading Eastern economists, the protest was signed by men from: Columbia, 28; Cornell, 18; Harvard, 25; Yale, 14; Princeton, 17; Dartmouth, 24; Chicago, 26; Wisconsin, 23; Illinois, 14; Minnesota, 15; and California, 11.

there had been more than a few warning signals. The distress flag of the farmers had flapped to tatters in the western winds. The plight of the farmers was advertised year in and year out by failing banks: 678 in 1923, 776 in 1924, 612 in 1925, 956 in 1926, 662 in 1927, 491 in 1928, and 642 in 1929.[14] During the years of the great prosperity no less than 4,817 banks had failed. But while the too heavily mortgaged owners of the best land in the nation struggled in vain against a price structure weighted against them, the golden streamers of real estate speculators waved over all parts of the country. Every town of any size must have its skyscrapers and suburban developments. The desire to get rich quickly through real estate speculation merely reached its fantastic height in Florida. There, sand-lots were sold from blueprints in great quantities and prices soared to incredible heights. Bank clearings in Miami leaped to $1,066,528,000 in 1925 and then sank swiftly to one-sixth of that sum in 1928, as the boom burst.

Strange New Corporations. No banners waved over the towering corporate structures which were piled one on the other, until the Samuel Insull public-utility pyramid, dizziest of all, was seven or eight stories high. Yet by 1928 it was already clear that a maze of corporate relationships had been created which defied understanding or control. The only certain thing about these mysterious monsters was that each layer of companies sucked the cream of profits from the layers below, along with new funds from fresh investors' pockets, preferably small investors who would

[14] Frederick Lewis Allen, *The Lords of Creation,* New York, 1935, p. 308. For the facts used in the remainder of this chapter I have drawn heavily upon three of the excellent yearly studies compiled by the research staff of the Council on Foreign Relations and edited by Walter Lippmann. These volumes, published under the title *The United States in World Affairs,* review in thorough fashion the economic and political developments of the year, both domestic and foreign. They are based upon wide research in economic statistics and contain valuable statistical appendices.

I have also used extensively two penetrating surveys by Frederick Lewis Allen, *Only Yesterday,* New York, 1931, and *The Lords of Creation,* and *The Wreck of Reparations* by John W. Wheeler-Bennett, New York, 1933. The latter is an account, by one who was in close personal touch with the events described, of the European phases of the world depression from 1929 to 1933. This chronicle is centered, as the title suggests, on the final struggle over reparations.

hold their little stocks and keep quiet. The small investor was the quarry also of the investment trusts, a new kind of corporation that could be born, live, and die in Wall Street. All they needed to do was to buy and sell stocks, including their own. The investment trusts, too, had their intricacies, different classes of stock, some of which netted the insiders large sums and carried control of the "trust." Beginning in 1927, hundreds of these expensive excrescences sprang up annually.

And while the spectators and insiders required more and more profits, the income of the "small investors" and the consuming wage earners was insufficient to keep the ever-growing flood of manufactured goods moving. Then it was that the pennants of the installment salesmen were raised in every city block, visible and universal warnings of trouble ahead.

These warnings that the riotous, heedless pursuit of gain might end in national disaster were striking enough, but they were not more ominous than the black flag of anarchy which flew perpetually over the foreign trade of the United States. A nation which had become a creditor on a colossal scale stubbornly insisted that it would continue to pour out into the laps of other peoples more goods than it received, come what might. Never would we permit others to send us more to eat and wear than we shipped to them, if we had to lend them the surplus to the end of time.

A Bull Market. The storm signals were many, but the clearest of all evidence that too great a proportion of the nation's income was being siphoned away from the consuming public was supplied by the steadily mounting excesses of the New York Stock Exchange. The Exchange had long served an indispensable need as a market for investments, as well as a gambling place, but as the gospel of Coolidge prosperity spread, the speculators seized greater and greater control of the market until at last the nation's market place became a huge casino in which the savings of the nation and its future were staked with ever-increasing abandon.

The big bull market was under way early in 1927. It was featured throughout by persistent inflation of the value of common stocks. For their own gain, market optimists preached that the profits of particular corporations, and of all companies in general, were due to rise to unheard-of heights. Soon hundreds of thousands of people believed them. The prices of stocks lost all relation to earnings. Not only was the future discounted "but the hereafter itself." During the week of December 3, 1927, all records for trading were broken and broker's loans had increased $739,794,000—indicating plainly that a vast number of people were buying stocks by paying a minor percentage of the sale price down (a margin), the broker supplying the rest of the money and reserving the right to sell the stock on the market to get his money should the price fall. Yet the spread of this dangerous practice was encouraged in Washington. The bull market was the visible sign and testimony of the wisdom with which Coolidge and Mellon ruled. They were proud of it and nursed it with fatherly care. In January, 1928, the President took the totally unheard-of and equally unwise step of saying publicly that he did not consider brokers' loans too high. Whenever "confidence" lagged a little, he or his Secretary of the Treasury was always ready with a reassuring statement designed to start the market up again.[15] Coolidge and Mellon, living in the faith that businessmen must be free from interference, still saw no harm in helping them along.

As 1928 opened, this official optimism was not shared by the mercantile world or the business forecasters. Uncertainty lingered for three months, until a powerful ring of speculators opened, on March 3, a drive to boost General Motors stocks. On the basis of its five-per-cent dividend this stock was already selling at 140, high above its value. Soon it was above 150. Then Radio Corporation of America stock had a ride, gaining 12 points a day, then 18 points, then 21. A stock-exchange record of 3,875,910 shares traded was soon lifted to 4,760,000. The public was in. Everybody knew of someone who had just made a fortune. The market boiled up and down like a mighty geyser until June, when several units of the resplendent empire which A. P. Giannini had

[15] Allen, *Only Yesterday*, p. 291.

been building in the Far West, with incredibly rapid success, fell down, several of his stocks losing from 80 to 100 points on June 11, 1928. The collapse in Wall Street the next day was terrific. On the following day Herbert Hoover was nominated to succeed Coolidge. The market rallied and rose with him until his election in November, when it went into a frenzy. "Four more years of prosperity" were now assured. Who could doubt it?

Hoover Boom. Nor did Hoover lift a hand to halt the uncontrolled orgy in his honor. What did it matter if Montgomery Ward stock had climbed, during the general rise, from 200 to 440, on November 30, or that call money was at nine per cent and broker's loans still rising? It was more than dangerous that Radio Corporation stock, worth on its earnings about 100, should be selling at 363, yet the Federal Reserve Board feared that to raise the discount rate above five per cent would precipitate a market smash. Other and quieter means of pressure were tried, and with such success that call money rates advanced in March, 1929, as high as twenty per cent, accelerating the rush of funds from foreign nations into the market, and precipitating a bad break in the prices of stocks.

But the end was not yet. The nation's largest bank, The National City Bank, was headed by Charles E. Mitchell, who had gained its presidency as a supersalesman of stocks through the bank's affiliate, the National City Company. He did not propose to see the great game ended. His bank threw $25,000,000 into the market on March 26 and the panic was averted. Mitchell was a hero. The great corporations emulated his example and loaned huge sums on the call-money market. The rate of interest was high and the prices of their own stocks were supported.

Prices recovered and fresh lambs leaped into the market; corporations changed their bonds into common stocks. They split the shares of stocks repeatedly and every time a share was decreased in value its market price increased. It was "sheer corporate megalomania. Every rumor of a merger or a split up or an issue of rights was the automatic signal for a leap in the prices of the stocks affected." [16] Broker's loans climbed to a new high on October 2, 1929, reaching $6,804,000,000. "Confidence" continued. Mitchell asserted that "our credit situation is in no way critical." [17] But at last the inverted pyramid of dreams and fantasies could not bear its own weight. It started to sag, and when it reached a certain point no power on earth could stop its fall.

Collapse. On October 23, multitudes of margin holders were sold out in a hurricane of liquidation which struck terror in hundreds of towns and buried the Stock Exchange so deeply under the debris that it lost all ability even to tell the world how bad the news was. The ticker was four hours late in recording the 12,894,650 shares sold. Among the items on it appeared Radio Corporation at 44½ and Montgomery Ward at 50, prices which later were to seem high. Not even the statement of Hoover that business was "on a sound and prosperous basis" could stop the collapse. October 29 was a day of madness in which the *New York Times* index fell 40 points, while 16,410,030 shares were dumped, often without finding any buyers at all. Some thirty billion dollars of make-believe money, which the prophets of Normalcy had floated under the benevolent aegis of Coolidge prosperity, disappeared as magically as they had come, to be followed by many other billions before the bottom was reached. Here was the first fruit borne by the philosophy that a great nation could make itself as rich as it desired to be through seeking its own gain by any and all means.[18]

A World Crisis

For a time the watchwords of the Coolidge era resounded anew. We had been assured that we were "entering a whole new

[16] *Ibid.*, p. 312.

[17] *Ibid.*, p. 324.

[18] It should be recorded that some men in positions of responsibility issued warnings of what was ahead. Paul M. Warburg had shown his awareness of the dangers of the bull market. The editor of the *Commercial and Financial Chronicle* and the financial editor of the *New York Times*, Alexander Dana Noyes, had issued warnings. Allen, *Only Yesterday*, p. 322; *The Lords of Creation*, p. 315.

plateau of values." Then when the market plunged off another precipice, and the solid plateau of values proved to be as substantial as the values of Florida swamps in 1926, additional reassuring words poured forth: "Fundamentally sound"; "wholesome liquidation"; "the bottom has been reached." [19] But prices sank after five successive flurries until the panic levels of October, 1929, were remembered as high indeed. While the stocks declined, very high corporation dividends were still paid in 1930, the bulk of which went to the insiders who had lost the most in the Wall Street crash. Great salaries and huge bonuses also continued to be paid to many corporation executives.[20] Drastic savings were made at the point where they were easiest—by cutting labor costs. More and more men were discharged, to lose their consuming power and thus lead to the dropping of additional men, from the small executives on down. The nation's economic life moved downward in a cruelly vicious spiral—catastrophic in the case of farm prices. The highly organized industries could not prevent their prices from falling, but in the main production was reduced three or four times as much. The production of agricultural implements declined by 80 per cent but their price by only 6 per cent.[21]

Disastrous Decline in Farm Prices. Not so the prices of farm products. Hoover had insisted that the millions of individualist farmers must work out their salvation by cooperative marketing. Yet when the prices of the great agricultural commodities began to tumble, the Hoover Farm Board began in December, 1929, to lend money to farmers' cooperatives at 16 cents a pound for cotton and at $1.25 a bushel for wheat. And when this venture in price-fixing failed, the Farm Board went into the open market, beginning in February, 1930, to buy wheat and cotton. By May, 1931, it had bought 1,300,000 bales of cotton and 250,000,000

[19] Stuart Chase, *Prosperity: Fact or Myth*, New York, 1929, pp. 10-11.

[20] See the columns of salaries and bonuses published in the *New York Times* throughout the months of April and May, 1935 and 1936.

[21] Allen, *The Lords of Creation*, p. 407. The total amount of dividends paid out in 1930 was but three per cent less than in 1929 (p. 400).

bushels of wheat, without accomplishing more than to retard the drop in prices. With the Board's support removed, cotton fell to 8½ cents in June, 1931, and wheat to 56 cents. Even then the bottom had not been reached. Cotton sold below 5 cents in June, 1932, wheat at 50 cents and corn at 31 cents.[22] The heavy surpluses held off the market by the Farm Board still hung threateningly over it, while the Board was reduced to imploring the farmers not to plant so much. Hearing this advice and borne down by a constantly shrinking income, they concluded it was a good time to plant more and during the depression years nature blessed them with large yields, thus adding to the surpluses which could not be sold at a profit. Industry might cut production drastically and ride out the storm behind the shelter of its tariff walls. Agriculture was denied any artificial protection against the tax gatherer and the mortgage holder. Forced sales of land multiplied until at last the farmers halted them by violence and intimidation in many parts of the Middle West.

For a year the Administration could not believe that the tide could not be turned by a determined show of confidence. Between November 4, 1929, and December 31, 1930, Secretary of Commerce Robert P. Lamont issued ten confident predictions. Dr. Julius Klein, Assistant Secretary of Commerce, was even more persistent. In the early months President Hoover made no reference in his addresses to world conditions, appearing to believe that the crisis was a local result of the Wall Street crash. It was not until September, 1930, that he declared the depression was world-wide, resulting largely from the overproduction of raw materials.[23]

Streams of Capital Reversed. The world-wide effects of the overproduction of speculative values in the stock market had been felt as early as 1928. The wild inflation in Wall Street had two important effects upon the structure of world prosperity,

[22] Walter Lippmann and W. O. Scroggs, *The United States in World Affairs, 1931*, New York, 1932, p. 20; *1932*, New York, 1933, p. 39.

[23] Lippmann and Scroggs, *The United States in World Affairs, 1931*, pp. 8-10.

which rested on American loans. The first effect was to curtail the loans. With such fabulous returns to be had at home, either in buying skyrocketing stocks or in enjoying high call-money rates, there was no reason why one should pursue a paltry seven per cent in Peruvian bonds. Even in Germany, long-term investments by foreigners increased but little in 1929, though her short-term borrowings continued at a perilous rate. American long-term investments abroad declined from a peak of $1,195,000,000 in 1928 to $765,000,000 in 1929, then to $345,000,000 in 1930. In 1931, the flow of long-term funds had been reversed and $165,000,000 more came into the United States than was sent out of it.[24] The stream of American investments abroad began to dry up before the top of the stock-market boom had been reached and ceased altogether soon afterward, when they were desperately needed to help the deranged economic machinery of the world operating.

The second effect of the bull market had been to attract funds from all parts of Europe to share in the winnings. This migration of credits both decreased the long-term loans of foreigners abroad and put a strain on the currency systems of many countries, a strain which became serious as soon as the New York market had collapsed, consuming a part of the foreign funds used in it.

The derangement of international lending and the breakdown of confidence both accelerated the abnormal movement of gold. In 1930 and 1931 gold in large quantities persisted in flowing uphill, that is, out of countries with high discount rates and into others with low interest rates. The United States, France, and the small neighbors of Germany were the gainers. Wealth was nervous, flying hither and yon, responding especially to political movements. The gain of six million votes by extremist parties in the German elections of September, 1930, made necessary a New York syndicate loan of $125,000,000 to check the flight of gold from Germany.

[24] *Ibid.*, p. 135; United States Department of Commerce, *Trade Information Bulletin*, No. 803.

These gold movements only accentuated the maldistribution of gold which our policies, and those of France, had produced. Refusing to accept payment in goods for the vast debts owed us, or for our huge merchandise exports, we had already compelled the world's traders to send gold to us until we had 42 per cent of the world's monetary gold. This oversupply promoted both our own inflation and painful deflation in other countries, both movements helping to precipitate the Wall Street crash.[25]

Austro-German Customs Union. The alarming gains of the National Socialists in the September election also had much to do with producing a German move, the wisdom of which cannot be explained except in terms of internal politics. On March 21, 1931, a proposal for an Austro-German customs union was published. Austria by this time was again sadly in need of outside support, but the proposed remedy violently aroused the worst fears of the creditors of both countries. A customs union had preceded the creation of the German Empire; another Zollverein seemed to presage certainly the formation of a greater Germany than had existed in 1914. It was therefore attacked on legal grounds as violating articles 88 and 220 of the Treaty of Saint-Germain, as well as the League of Nations loan protocols of October 4, 1922, which had attempted to safeguard Austria's independence, both political and economic. While Dr. Benes, of Czechoslovakia, argued exhaustively that the proposed customs union would benefit neither Austria nor Germany, enough pressure was brought to bear on Germany to make her agree that the legal questions involved should be referred by the League Council to the World Court for an advisory opinion. This action was taken on May 19, 1931.

By a vote of 8 to 7 the Court advised, September 5, 1931, that the proposal was in conflict with the protocol of 1922. Seven of the eight judges were willing to rule that it violated the treaty of peace also. The majority observed that Austria's existence as

[25] Eugene J. Young, *Powerful America*, New York, 1936, p. 351. Mr. Young believes that the panic was started by the sudden withdrawal of large amounts of gold and credits by French interests (p. 174).

an independent state is "an essential feature of the present political settlement" and concluded that it was difficult to maintain that the proposed regime would not "threaten the economic independence of Austria." This conclusion was denied by the seven dissenting judges, who argued that a political union between Austria and Germany would not necessarily follow, that Austria had means of warding off this result, and that anyway it was a contingency too remote to be reasonably foreseen.[26]

Panic in Vienna. Germany and Austria had, however, already been compelled, by the downfall of their financial systems and the pressure of France and her allies, to abandon the customs-union project. Their surrender was recorded publicly at Geneva September 3, 1931, two days before the Court returned its opinion. The attempt to gain a success in foreign affairs, with which to combat the Nazis, had only advanced disaster. The weakest link in the European financial chain had snapped in Vienna on May

[26] Manley O. Hudson, *The World Court, 1921-1934,* Boston, 1934, pp. 13, 128-32.

The fact that the Court had frankly taken political considerations into account enabled its opponents in the United States to charge that it was "a political court." The seven dissenting judges were said to represent the view of the neutral world. The nationalities of the dissenters were as follows: Adatci (Japanese), Van Eysinga (Dutch), Hurst (British), Kellogg (American), Rolin-Jaequemyns (Belgian), Schücking (German) and Wang (Chinese).

Conversely, the majority were labeled as the tools of France. These judges were: Altamira (Spain), Bustamante (Cuba), Fromageot (France), Guerrero (Salvador), Negulesco (Rumania), Rostworowski (Poland), Urrutía (Colombia) and Anzilotti (Italy). Without doubting that political considerations influenced some of the judges as much as the social and economic beliefs of members of the United States Supreme Court determine their verdicts, particularly in close decisions, it may be observed that if the decisions in this case had been wholly partisan the Belgian judge would have voted with the majority, instead of with the minority. The Chinese judge might also have differed with his Japanese colleague, instead of agreeing with him. There is no reason to suppose, either, that the three Latin American judges were motivated solely by political and partisan motives in joining the majority. Their homes were all far from the scene of dispute. Also, a first reading of the treaties involved reveals plenty of room for honest difference of opinion.

In any event, it could hardly be contended that any national supreme court makes all of its decisions without regard to the crucial issues of the day and time. It is not to be expected that both sides of any hotly contested issue will accept the decision with equal relish. The vital thing is that imperfect decisions shall continue to be made, and accepted, as a means of preventing disastrous appeals to force.

11, with the announcement that the Kredit Anstalt Bank had suffered losses of $19,600,000 during 1930. This bank had been one of the great financial institutions of Europe since its foundation by the Rothschilds in 1855. It had even succeeded in maintaining its empire in Central Europe after the breakup of the Hapsburg Monarchy. It had been weakened by taking over the assets of its chief Viennese rival in 1929, under heavy pressure from the Government. Now it controlled two-thirds of Austria's economic life and had large interests in all surrounding countries.

The fall of the Kredit Anstalt would spread disaster in a wide circle. The Austrian Government and the Rothschilds poured $22,400,000 of new capital into the bank. Nevertheless, Austrians began to withdraw their funds and send them out of the country, depleting seriously the supplies of foreign exchange. To stop this drain, a consortium of eleven central banks, including the Bank for International Settlements and the American Federal Reserve Banks, advanced $14,000,000 on May 29. Americans had $25,000,000 of short-term money in the bank and the British a like sum. Both were indisposed to help further when an Austrian loan of $21,000,000 was soon needed. France, able to provide the money, would not unless the customs-union project should be abandoned. While France was being denounced in Austria and Germany as a political blackmailer, both Great Britain and the United States decided to move to the relief of the Teutonic countries. The Bank of England advanced the $21,000,000 to Vienna on June 16. Four days later the Hoover moratorium was launched.[27]

The two Anglo-Saxon powers sought to prevent a world financial panic, the one by saving Austria, the other Germany. The position of Germany had become desperate and her revolt against the payment of reparations ominous. The adjustment of Europe's most dangerous problems by the quiet, unofficial action of American capitalists was in imminent danger of failure.

[27] Lippmann and Scroggs, *The United States in World Affairs, 1931*, pp. 123-31.

The Young Plan Dead. The Young Committee, headed by Owen D. Young, of New York, had settled the reparations issue. The final sum which Germany was to pay had at last been fixed at about $26,000,000,000, payable in sixty annual installments. Beginning with an installment of $406,000,000 in 1930-31, Germany would continue to remit until the good year 1988, when her debt to the Allies would be extinguished. The settlement was final, no provision being made in it for revision.

The Young Plan had been built upon the assumption that world trade would continue its upward rise, and that Germany would have an increasing share in it. No other means had ever been found whereby she could carry permanently the great load laid upon her, though in the Coolidge years the intergovernmental debts had been kept moving by American lending to Germany. We had not at first loaned Germany the money with which to pay. She had begun to pay, and then the vacuum created had sucked in foreign capital. The governments had created a regime which could operate only if their own private investors kept it going. This they did by rebuilding Germany from end to end and by supplying her with working capital. In the seven years ending June 30, 1931, $2,272,000,000 had been loaned to Germany on long-term account, of which we supplied 55 per cent. Short-term loans, of which our share was estimated to be $925,000,000, were larger, bringing the foreign investments in Germany up to six billion dollars.

A World Run on Germany. These billions now sought to save themselves by flight from Germany. In the first week of June, $21,000,000 in gold left Germany. By the end of the third week, the loss was $227,000,000. In another week, all of Germany's gold reserves would be gone. But if collapse came, how could the panicky American creditors get the remainder of their billions?

The situation was doubly disturbing to all Germany's creditors because of the weakness of her government finances. Germany's budget had not been balanced since 1925. The accumulated deficit was by 1930 above $300,000,000.[28] Something had to be done, and when the Reichstag refused to pass a budget for the fiscal year beginning April 1, 1930, Chancellor Brüning took the drastic, and for the Republic the dangerous, step of resorting to the emergency-decree powers of the President. The first emergency decree, of July 26, 1930, imposed various taxes and economies—savings which were swallowed up in unemployment relief while revenues declined still further. A second emergency decree, issued December 1, 1930, compelled still heavier taxes and greater economies without closing the widening gap between income and outgo. By June, 1931, the German position was so desperate that a third decree, published June 5, again slashed salaries, pensions, and relief, boosting taxes still higher. This decree was accompanied by a manifesto saying that the limits of the privations imposed upon the German people had been reached and that Germany must have "relief from the unbearable burden of reparations obligations."

The burden of reparations had become unbearable, not because of its size but because of the improvidence of Germany during the boom and the great drop in her foreign trade which came with the depression. The problem of transferring so large a sum over a long term of years was, to be sure, always beyond solution. But it was not reparations which ruined Germany. Her original ruin was sealed when she expanded her industries and armaments so rapidly before the war that she was never able to achieve financial independence of London and Paris. The war blockade then deprived her of her very lifeblood, the immense foreign trade which had fed and clothed her people. To win the war she spent more prodigally than ever—160,000,000,000 gold marks—and when her war effort died, everything was gone. Then it was that the immense void of lost world markets, filled for a time by war activity, engulfed the German people. Beginning again after 1924 with new supplies of borrowed capital, the Germans over-

[28] The Constitution of the German Republic contained a serious flaw in the requirement that fixed percentages of all revenues collected must be turned over to the states and cities, thus subsidizing their extravagance.

built again and failed to husband enough of the imported capital to ward off a quick collapse when their regained foreign markets once more started to disappear rapidly. The resulting unemployment turned loose myriads of miserable people to listen to Hitler and his orators tell them that all their ills were due to the Treaty of Versailles and especially to reparations.[29]

That reparations, among other debts, had become unbearable was true. Yet little was gained, apart from sympathy, when Chancellor Brüning and Foreign Minister Curtius went to England, on the day following the June 5 emergency decrees, further advertising Germany's plight and antagonizing France. The British could not help Germany, though they still risked one magnificent bluff on June 16 by throwing their $21,000,000 loan into Vienna. These events, together with the presence of Secretary Andrew W. Mellon in London had already convinced the French that their vital interests in reparations and security were being disposed of, before the Hoover moratorium suddenly struck them on June 20.

The Hoover Year

A Moratorium on All Intergovernmental Debts. As early as June 5 President Hoover had been considering emergency action in Germany's behalf. Traveling to Indianapolis on June 14 for an address, he found much evidence of American distress. His speech to the Republican Editorial Association was phrased in terms of the doctrine of self-containment. The shrinkage of our foreign trade amounted to "only two or three per cent of our total productivity." The main trouble must be at home.

Arriving back in Washington on June 18, the President was at once convinced that something must be done to stop the panic

[29] See the penetrating article by Bernard L. Cohen, "Is the Versailles Treaty Responsible?" *University of Toronto Quarterly*, April, 1936, Vol. 5, pp. 334-47. After dropping from 26,000,000,000 marks in 1929 to 15,000,000,000 marks in 1931, Germany's foreign trade still gave employment to "29 per cent of the working population." Hitler's appeal declined with prosperity and rose again with want. It was not until hunger and uncertainty came in force that he was able to arouse great bitterness over such items of the Treaty as the "war guilt lie."

of Germany's creditors, chiefly Americans. Secretary Mellon's report was sufficient. The crisis was beyond Germany's control. She could get no help under the Young Plan. Ninety days would be required to operate its provisions and then only partial relief, from the conditional annuities, could be obtained. Yet something had to be done in hours, not months. And if complete collapse came in Germany, important financial houses in New York would be gravely threatened. The President consulted many Congressional leaders of both parties by telephone and in person and issued, Saturday afternoon, June 20, his call for a year's moratorium on all intergovernmental debts.

The effort of Normalcy to collect war debts without taking them in the form of goods had collapsed, along with the contention that there was no connection between war debts and reparations. Germany had to have relief in June, 1931, from the huge reparations charge, and relief could come only from the great creditor of her creditors. Speed was as essential as the agreement of France was necessary.

France Demurs. Perhaps France had not been consulted because of Anglo-Saxon indignation at her use of financial power to coerce Austria. Frank Simonds believed that Hoover remembered all the European countries as he had left them in 1919, when France was weak.[30] But France was no longer prostrate. She was the strongest power in Europe in every respect, and as Germany's chief creditor her consent to the moratorium had to be obtained. It was slow in coming. The great burst of enthusiasm which greeted the moratorium did not extend to France and her allies. Debates in the Chamber of Deputies revealed that France felt that, having saved herself by thrift, she was now being asked to save Germany from the consequences of her extravagances. It was

[30] "As a consequence the President's delusion that France could either be ignored or coerced led straight to the ruin of all his larger undertakings, of the Five Power Conference in London in 1930, of the Moratorium in 1931, and finally of his address to the Arms Conference in Geneva in 1932." Frank Simonds, *Can America Stay at Home?* New York, 1932, p. 231.

argued that if reparations were canceled the funds released would soon go into arms or economic dumping. The Chamber demanded that France cling to her last remaining guarantee, the unconditional annuities of the Young Plan.[31]

Followed sixteen days of hectic negotiations, in which the transatlantic telephone played an important part. Eventually, on July 6, it was agreed that the unconditional annuities should be paid into the Bank for International Settlements during the moratorium, to be loaned back to the German railways in exchange for government-guaranteed bonds of the railways.

By this time the chief purpose of the moratorium, the stoppage of the run on Germany, had been largely frustrated. The panic revived and soon led to the closing of the important German Danat Bank on July 13. All German financial institutions were at once closed for two days. The Reichsbank raised the discount rate from seven to ten per cent. On July 17 American and British banks were compelled to agree to the renewal of their short-term credits in Germany as they matured. Fresh alarm spread throughout Europe. Secretary Stimson had arrived in Europe to see what could be done. Dr. Luther, President of the Reichsbank, further advertised his nation's plight by flying spectacularly to London for help and then, with Governor Norman of the Bank of England, to Paris. But the French still demanded political guarantees which the Germans felt themselves too weak at home to grant.

A conference between the chief cabinet ministers of the United States and the other principal creditor powers assembled in London, July 20, deliberating in great secrecy for three days with small result. All that could be agreed upon was a renewal of the Central Bank consortium loan of $100,000,000 to Germany. It was recommended that "concerted measures should be taken by the financial institutions of the different countries with a view to maintaining the volume of credits they have already extended to

[31] Wheeler-Bennett, *The Wreck of Reparations*, p. 60.

Germany" and that the Bank for International Settlements should set up a committee to examine Germany's further credit needs.[32]

The Wiggin Committee's Appeal. This committee was composed of the representatives of the central banks. It sat in Basle from August 8 to 18, under the chairmanship of Albert H. Wiggin, Chairman of the Chase National Bank of New York. The committee surveyed Germany's economy minutely. It found the normal conditions favoring long-term loans to Germany still present but discovered no way around the reparations dilemma. The reparations payments involved either a continuous increase in Germany's foreign debt or such an excess of exports as would threaten the prosperity of other countries. Either alternative was alarming to the investors, new and old. Yet Germany was a large and essential part of a world economy. It was vital that she should not be too badly crippled.

The final report of the Committee, drafted principally by Sir Walter Layton, was a stirring appeal to the governments to make political peace and establish order. "Time is short," said the report. "The body of the world's commerce—whose vitality is already low—has suffered a severe shock in one of its chief members. This has resulted in a partial paralysis which can only be cured by restoring the free circulation of money and goods." Only the governments could establish a basis for mutual confidence and decide "that the international payments to be made by Germany will not be such as to imperil the maintenance of her financial stability." The world could not regain its financial balance while it developed "an international financial system which involves the annual payment of large sums by debtor countries to creditor countries, while at the same time putting obstacles in the way of the free movement of goods." To enable "the normal process of investment of fresh capital" to be resumed, the Wiggin Committee concluded "by urging most earnestly upon all Governments concerned that they lose no time in taking the necessary measures for bringing about such conditions as will allow financial

[32] *Ibid.*, pp. 72-80.

operations to bring to Germany—and thereby to the world—sorely needed assistance." [33]

London Besieged. Far from taking the sweeping remedial action for which the bankers prayed, the Governments were not able even to stop the spread of the financial panic. Already Great Britain, the citadel of world finance, was on the defensive. Her economic position had been unfavorable since the war. Her share of world exports was declining, due in part to internal causes. These were, according to the view of creditor interests: (1) the huge internal war debt; (2) obsolete equipment and management in the older industries; and (3) high wages, held up by powerful trade unions and by the cushion of the dole to the unemployed. In Great Britain, one school held that the trouble arose out of stabilizing the pound at too high a gold point, an argument not reassuring to foreign creditors. It was not so disturbing, however, as the report of the Macmillan Committee, issued inopportunely in June, 1931. This official committee had been studying Britain's economic ills for some months. According to British custom, the Macmillan Report mercilessly analyzed—and advertised—Britain's economic woes, seeming to lean toward some sort of world inflation to stop the world crisis. Close on the heels of this disturbing document came, too, on July 31, another from the Treasury Committee headed by Sir George May. It predicted a budget deficit of $600,000,000 in 1932 and advised a cut in the social services.

The next day a joint credit of $250,000,000 was advanced to the Bank of England by the Federal Reserve Bank and the Bank of France, to check the run on London which had developed out of the German panic. By July 17 it was clear that the enormous short-term loans in Germany were "frozen." With these huge sums lost for an indefinite time, if not forever, creditors read in the Macmillan Report that Britain held uncovered short-term loans frozen in Central Europe to the amount of $1,850,000,000. With Britain short to that extent, it was known that several finan-

[33] J. W. Wheeler-Bennett, ed., *Documents on International Affairs*, London, 1931, p. 133.

cial institutions in London must be involved. A run on London took $155,000,000 in gold in late July, bringing Britain's gold reserves for the currency below minimum. Raising the discount rate from 2½ to 4½ and negotiating the Paris-New York loan checked the outflow momentarily. The removal of the "cushion" of the dole from underneath British wages was now the test of British solvency, upon which the concern of the world's creditor classes centered. An attempt was made to allay the storm by reducing the dole. But this proposal caused Labor Prime Minister Ramsay MacDonald to be denounced by his party, by a vote of 274 to 6, and a National Government headed by him was formed to impose the necessary cuts and taxes.

Britain Abandons Gold. Four days later, August 28, a joint loan of $400,000,000 was granted direct to the British Treasury by private banking interests in New York and Paris. The French supplied $200,000,000, half of which was taken up by public subscription. If the French had helped start the run on London they were now anxious enough to stop it.

Still the flight from sterling continued. Were not the Laborites still obstreperous and the trade unions too strong? The run continued until September 15, when it was announced that there had been a mutiny in the British fleet—because, it developed, of pay cuts imposed hastily and unequally without previous warning. Though the scope of the mutiny was greatly exaggerated, that it had occurred at all knocked the last leg out from under creditor confidence. The fleet in mutiny! Britain was indeed done! Within four days the $400,000,000 credit advanced from New York and Paris had rolled out again. A full billion dollars had fled from London since the middle of July. Soon what gold remained would be gone. The British had contracted $750,000,000 in new debts to Paris and New York without avail. On September 20, the new National Cabinet gave up the struggle and suspended the gold standard. During the next month seventeen nations followed suit.[34]

[34] Bolivia, Canada, Denmark, Egypt, Estonia, Finland, India, Irish Free State, Japan, Norway, Rhodesia, Salvador, and Sweden formally suspended payments

THE INTERNATIONAL LABOR OFFICE BUILDING IN FOREGROUND

First international public edifice built by public funds. Completed 1926. Cost $650,000. League Palace in background.

THE NEW LEAGUE OF NATIONS LIBRARY

Built from a gift of $2,000,000 made by John D. Rockefeller, Jr. One half of this sum was reserved for endowment. An American, Miss Alice Bartlett, is one of the Librarians.

A Run on New York. The crisis was racing around the earth like a virulent epidemic. During 1930 and 1931 it was the primary, though not the sole, cause of eleven revolutions in Latin America. These revolutions increased the economic difficulties, and during 1932 there were several additional revolts. Economic conditions everywhere affected political conditions and vice versa. The great delusion upon which Normalcy had been built, that the great world of economics could operate without reference to political stability, was utterly shattered. From Vienna the panic of 1931 leaped to Berlin, stirring myriads of jumpy American dollars to attempted flight. Naturally, most of them were not able to take off from the factories and houses into which they had disappeared, or from the tills of businesses in which they were finding employment. British pounds were also caught. A cloud of creditors descended upon London and devoured her gold. Then they flew for New York. New York had much money tied up in Germany. French, Swiss, and Dutch speculators launched an attack on the dollar, in which some London papers took part. In the month after London's fall, $665,000,000 in gold left the United States. By that time only French balances remained in New York in quantity. Spurred by Federal Reserve authorities, the French government had put a stop to the public campaign of the French bears on the dollar, thus easing American resentment somewhat.

Panic Conditions in the United States. The American financial system had more than enough gold to meet the world's claims on it without endangering the gold coverage of the currency, even though in a year of business stagnation the money in circulation had increased by a billion dollars. "A silent nation-wide run on the American banking system" was taking place, for which there was reason enough inside the country. In the third quarter of 1931, bank failures totaled 456 and commercial failures 5,863; in the fourth quarter 1,055 banks gave way and 7,316 businesses

---

in gold. Bulgaria, Czechoslovakia, Latvia, and Jugoslavia achieved the same result by exchange regulations. Lippmann and Scroggs, *The United States in World Affairs, 1932*, pp. 284-85.

acknowledged bankruptcy.[35] It was this internal situation which the foreign run on New York might make catastrophic. Runs on domestic banks might become universal.

Laval Comes to Washington. Could the two nations which had three-fourths of the world's gold stop the steady spread of economic paralysis and financial panic? This was surely a moment to try. At the peak of the British crisis the leading financial newspaper of Paris, *L'Information,* had suggested a visit of the French Premier to Washington. In less than a week he had been invited. On October 22, 1931, Laval arrived in New York and until October 25 he conferred with President Hoover and other officials.

When Laval arrived, his objectives appeared to be: (1) to gain a pledge by the United States that she would not abandon the gold standard; (2) to arrive at some understanding about the intergovernmental debts, securing, if possible, a reconsideration of the war debts, and, in any event, assurance that no sudden move affecting reparations would be made from Washington in the future. Both of these aims appeared to be achieved in the joint communiqué which was issued on October 25. The necessity of "the gold standard in France and the United States" was quietly stated, and with reference to the intergovernmental debts it was assumed that at the end of the Hoover year "some agreement regarding them may be necessary covering the period of the business depression." Neither Government committed itself as to what should be done, but the communiqué said significantly: "The initiative in this matter should be taken at an early date by the European powers principally concerned within the framework of the agreements existing prior to July 1, 1931." [36]

This statement appeared to imply a revision of all the debts and seemed to constitute a considerable triumph for Laval. Yet, by giving him the initiative, it in reality separated war debts from

[35] *Ibid.,* p. 41. Commercial failures from January 1, 1931, to October 1, 1932, reached the enormous total of 47,721. During 1931 nineteen railroads with a capitalization of $432,151,526 were placed in receivership.

[36] *New York Times,* October 26, 1931.

reparations again and left France to settle the European political tangle before revision of the war debts would be taken up. The communiqué opened the way for Germany to invoke the Young Plan, which she did November 19, 1931, by asking for an investigation of her capacity to pay.

Germany's Plight Desperate. The Bank for International Settlements at once assembled a distinguished committee of eleven, representing as many nations, which sat December 8 to 23, 1931.[37] On the day the committee convened the German Government issued a fourth emergency decree which the Basle committee later described as "including measures without parallel in modern legislation." The decree cut prices, freight, postal, and utility rates, rents, wages, salaries, pensions, and interest charges. Interest rates had risen to twelve per cent; a quarter of Germany's workers were unemployed and a third of her economic life had stopped. Examining the extent of her paralysis, the December committee unanimously agreed that she could not continue the unconditional reparations payments and indicated that if the committee had been permitted it would have ruled out the conditional payments also. The report agreed that transfers upsetting the balance of payments could only accentuate the chaos; that merely releasing debtors might place too heavy a burden on the creditors; and that the readjustment of all intergovernmental debts was "the only lasting step capable of re-establishing confidence, which is the very condition of economic stability and real peace."[38]

Continued Deterioration in the Period of Postponement. Spurred by the report, the British Government at once issued invitations for a conference on reparations to meet January 18, 1932. It soon developed, however, that Laval was unable to take advantage of the initiative which he had regained. Hoover's effort to resolve the world crisis had failed because a decade of political isolation had led his administration to underestimate the political difficulties involved in ending reparations. Now he was to discover

[37] The American member, Dr. Walter W. Stewart, this time refused the chair.
[38] *New York Times*, December 24, 1931.

that while he was concentrating on the world crisis a gulf had opened between himself and the Congress. For nine months the Congressmen had been at home, subject to the full force of the domestic crisis. They came back to Washington in December in no mood to approve either the scaling-down of war debts or co-operation with Europe, particularly since the Administration desired to avoid appropriations for relief, to cut expenditures, and to increase taxes. Demands that the United States quit meddling in European affairs and look after its own people were soon loudly raised.[39] The Hoover moratorium was grudgingly approved but the President's request that the World War debt funding commission be reconstituted was summarily rejected and the refusal clinched by a Congressional declaration that "It is hereby expressly declared to be against the policy of Congress that any of the indebtedness of foreign countries to the United States should be in any manner canceled or reduced and nothing in this joint resolution shall be construed as indicating a contrary policy, or as implying that favorable consideration will be given at any time to a change in the policy hereby declared."

With the door thus slammed against revision of the war debts on December 23, Laval was confronted, on January 9, with a declaration by Chancellor Brüning that Germany's position made it "impossible for her to continue political payments." It seems that Brüning had not originally intended to declare the end of reparations in this fashion, but statements of quite variable intensity, made singly to the ambassadors of the Allied powers, had leaked out and had made a public statement necessary. Now there was nothing for the projected Lausanne Conference to meet about and, since impending elections in France and Germany offered a good excuse, the conference was postponed until June, 1932, the end of the Hoover year.

In Germany, the Presidential elections of April, 1932, revealed that the National Socialists were able to poll 13,417,460 votes and presaged the fall of both Chancellor Brüning and the German

[39] *Congressional Record*, Vol. 75, Pt. 1, p. 536.

Republic. Soon a palace *camarilla* persuaded the aged President von Hindenburg that the Chancellor's proposal to break up one-sixth of the many-times-bankrupt estates in East Prussia was pure bolshevism and Brüning resigned on May 28, to be succeeded by a Cabinet of nationalists headed by Captain von Papen. In France Laval was succeeded by Tardieu in a ministerial shuffle on February 16 and both were swept out of power by the May elections. Herriot came in again to head a France now beginning to have bank runs and seriously disordered finances. In March a severe struggle between Germany's short-term creditors and the Bank of France ended in a new "standstill" agreement which gave the private creditors the power to outwait the Governments. In April a French effort to organize a loose Danubian customs union was defeated by Italian and German opposition. Everywhere the crisis deepened and suffering increased. Everywhere the statesmen found themselves powerless before publics which clung to outdated slogans they had been taught during the post-war decade.

Reparations Ended at Lausanne. It was not until June 16, 1932, that the long-postponed conference on reparations opened at Lausanne. As chairman, Premier MacDonald reminded the six hundred delegates present that they were not there to consider policies but to deal with a world catastrophe in which there was "no France, no Germany, no America, no Great Britain apart from the rest of the nations of the world." MacDonald began bravely and he eventually carried the conference through many storms to an agreement. Chancellor von Papen almost lost his position by an interview given to the Paris *Matin*, in which he seemed to the German nationalists to be too yielding. German opinion was shocked, too, by his admission that Germany might pay something. Later, Von Papen almost wrecked the conference by a public statement demanding that the discriminations of the Versailles Treaty be removed. But this time France would not consent to mixing financial and political questions.

Eventually, debate settled upon the amount of the final sum which Germany should pay, after MacDonald had piloted the conference determinedly into committee and out again and through private three-power meetings, six-power consultations, and many other groupings. The final agreement called for a last payment by Germany of $714,000,000 in the form of five per cent bonds, guaranteed by the Reich, to be paid into a fund administered by the Bank of International Settlements "for European reconstruction." The bonds were not to be issued, however, until German Government securities were on a five per cent basis or better and then only at a rate which, in the judgment of the Bank for International Settlements, would not disturb normal economic relations or disturb Germany's credit. Being interpreted, this agreement meant that reparations were ended forever. A formula had been found which masked from the French people the passing of reparations. Yet on German opinion the effect was chilling. The revival of reparations, even in imaginary form, could not but be depressing, notwithstanding the fact that Germany had at least managed to equip herself splendidly as a vast workshop during the reparations period. Germany's leaders, and all others, knew that reparations were finished.

Two Other Lausanne Accords. There remained the war debts, about which strong hopes of cancellation or revision downward had been aroused before the rebellion of Congress. If no promises had been made, at least Europe had been given to understand that war debts could not be scaled down until the reparations tangle had been unsnarled. But would not the American Government now be unable to revise the debts? To provide against that contingency, the delegates at Lausanne representing Germany's creditors initialed a gentleman's agreement saying that ratification of the Lausanne agreement would not be "effected until a satisfactory settlement has been reached between them and their own creditors."[40] While this precaution may have seemed natural enough to our European debtors, it provoked violent criticism in the United States, particularly since it had been kept secret for two weeks. Something suspiciously like a "united front" of our

[40] Lippmann and Scroggs, *The United States in World Affairs, 1932*, p. 145.

debtors seemed to have been formed. Soon the gentleman's agreement was being interpreted differently by the French and British Governments. It was viewed with satisfaction by the French press and strongly condemned by London papers of various political hues.

On July 13, the day before President Hoover issued a letter to Senator Borah strongly frowning upon the affair,[41] another "Accord of Confidence," signed at Lausanne by MacDonald and Herriot, was made public in London. It was an agreement of the two Governments to work closely together, especially in finding a solution of the disarmament question and in preparing for the proposed World Economic Conference. Although other countries were invited to adhere to this accord, it caused chagrin in Germany and led to the resignation of the Italian foreign minister, Grandi.

Revision of War Debts Asked. The chief political result of the Lausanne Conference was the re-establishment of closer cooperation between Great Britain and France. This renewed cooperation did not prevent Great Britain from making one more semi-annual war debt payment to the United States on December 15, 1932, $95,550,000 being remitted in gold. Czechoslovakia, Italy, Finland, Latvia, and Lithuania also paid, while France, Poland, Belgium, Estonia, and Hungary deferred payment.[42] The Herriot Cabinet resigned in France when its stand in behalf of payment was overruled by the Chamber of Deputies on December 13, 402 to 187.

Shortly after the November election in the United States notes from the debtor states began to arrive in Washington, asking for suspension of payment and reconsideration of the debts. The British argued that the burden of the war debts must be judged by comparing it not with a nation's internal revenues, but with its international trade balances. The French contended that if the Hoover moratorium had not acknowledged the relationship

[41] *New York Times*, July 15, 1931.
[42] Greece had already defaulted in October.

between reparations and war debts it had certainly ended entirely Germany's will to pay. To all and sundry the State Department replied that the two kinds of debts were not connected, that each case must be dealt with singly, and that it had no authority to ease payments. To France the reply was shorter and less sympathetic than to Britain.

The Debts Defaulted. President-elect Roosevelt rejected Hoover's plea for a new Congressional debt funding commission and continued the negotiations through diplomatic channels. Further discussions, including an unexpected debate in the World Economic Conference in May, 1933, produced no agreement. In June, 1933, the British remitted $10,000,000 in silver as an acknowledgment of the validity of the debt. Italy, Czechoslovakia, Rumania, Lithuania, and Latvia also made token payments. This small trickle brought war-debt payments to the United States to a close, with the exception of the tiny rivulet which the Government of Finland kept flowing regularly.

In the United States the overwhelming feeling was one of resentment. The average citizen knew little of the commodity transactions which had given rise to the war debts and nothing about the excess-profits taxes which the Government had collected on these transactions. He could not understand the complexities of international exchange and balances of trade. He only knew, with Coolidge, that the foreigners had hired a lot of American money, which they now refused to pay. What did it matter if American tariffs prevented payment in goods? What did we want with their goods? Let them send the money.

Some sentiment for revision or cancellation had developed prior to the onslaught of the depression. Newton D. Baker had been the first to issue a carefully reasoned plea for revision, in August, 1926.[43] Since the debts "could only be paid in goods or the proceeds from the sale of goods," he termed the settlement with England "a magnificent disaster," instead of a magnificent achievement. Baker received only condemnation at home and the

[43] *New York Times,* August 30, 1936.

forty-two members of the Faculty of Political Science of Columbia University, who signed a protest, published December 20, 1926, fared little better. They condemned the "capacity to pay" principle on which the debts had been funded as one which could not be justly applied. Capacity to pay would rise and fall frequently in every country concerned during the three generations covered by the debt agreements. Instead of an attempt to measure the capacities of many nations to pay, the Columbia men called for a policy based on the promotion of present peace and the future prosperity of the world.[44]

Later, a number of influential bodies asked for a reopening of the debt question,[45] but the yawning emptiness of the Government's own purse prevented the masses from thinking of anything except the "dollars" defaulted.

Financial Paralysis

The American citizen and taxpayer could not have much sympathy for the appeals to him of powerful foreign governments for debt relief because he was so terribly in debt himself. The prophets of Normalcy had told him to go ahead and multiply. The restraints of the Wilson Government against certain kinds of business activity were off. "No interference with business" was the new law and it was given full play. Business multiplied, not only by the splitting of stocks, the building of huge holding company pyramids, and the begetting of a new investment trust every minute; money was borrowed for legitimate, if mistaken, plant expansions; industrial exports were aggressively forced into the world's markets in total disregard of the towering creditor position

[44] In 1932, with prices down 40 to 50 per cent below wartime levels the indictment by the Columbia men of the capacity-to-pay principle gained proportionate weight. The derangement of the currencies also undermined this principle radically. With the British pound off gold and depreciated to $3.22 in December, 1932, the British Government was compelled to spend 3 pounds to purchase the dollars which 2 pounds would have bought before.

[45] The General Conference of the Methodist Episcopal Church, The National Association of Mutual Savings Banks, the head of the National Grange, and a committee of the Railway Brotherhoods. *New York Times*, May 14, 21, 24, November 7, 1932.

of the United States. Loans would keep all of these artificial activities moving.

Prosperity Built upon Debt. Loans did. Loans financed everything—additional land for many farmers who were not already overmortgaged; the purchase of the golden sands of Florida and a stake in a thousand other real-estate booms; shares in "America Incorporated and Inflated" which could be bought by anyone on a little "margin"; and finally the new car, radio, furniture, and the very clothing on the borrower's back. During the seven fat years from 1922 to 1929, long-term debts had increased in the United States by one-third, to the awe-inspiring sum of $154,000,000,000.[46] Not only was world prosperity dependent upon the continuance of the stream of American loans abroad, a stream which turned into the stock market in 1929 and disappeared in the vortex, but American prosperity itself could be kept going only by furiously mortgaging what was left of the future.

Day of Reckoning. Now, in 1932, the future had come. Some mountains of debt, indeed, fell down, but other great peaks stood firm. Mortgages and taxes remained. State and local debts, already at towering heights, had to go higher. The national debt, reduced some nine billion dollars during the boom, began to mount again, while revenues dried up. By September, 1931, the budget was unbalanced by $1,278,000,000, and no one, it developed, wanted to finance the deficit. The Administration proposed excise taxes but the industries affected could not bear the thought. Then Congress turned to a small sales tax and a revolt in the House decisively defeated that, on March 24, 1932, 223 to 153. A long struggle ensued before the budget was brought into purely theoretical balance.

Meanwhile, the Reconstruction Finance Corporation, a huge government bank proposed by President Hoover, was baling out banks and railroads by putting them further in debt. This venture into state socialism was the most far-reaching ever attempted in

[46] National Industrial Conference Board estimate. Quoted in Walter Lippmann and W. O. Scroggs, *The United States in World Affairs, 1933,* New York, 1934, p. 4.

the United States. It rapidly multiplied government ownership and control in many large economic units, yet the descent downward was only retarded a little. By July 1, 1932, the *New York Times* Business Activity Index had fallen fifty per cent and from twelve to fifteen million people were unemployed, their condition becoming more and more desperate. Some hope returned in the summer of 1932, along with a sharp gain in the prices of livestock and the final repatriation of foreign gold stocks held in the United States. The hoarding of currency decreased and the stock market rushed at once to register "the return of confidence." Stocks rose from an average price of 34 in June to 58 in September. Bond prices also advanced.[47] In September and October, when the business indices reflected only slight recovery, stock prices lost a large part of the summer's gains.

Republican Rule Ended. In November, President Hoover was defeated for re-election by Franklin D. Roosevelt. Roosevelt received an electoral vote of 472 and carried 42 states. Only four New England states, Delaware, and Pennsylvania remained in the Republican column. The popular vote recorded 22,821,857 for Roosevelt and 15,761,841 for Hoover, or 39.6 per cent, the lowest percentage polled by a Republican candidate in fifty years, the 1912 schism excepted. Roosevelt's 57.5 per cent gave his party a new high record for the same period.[48] In the newly elected House of Representatives only 117 Republicans faced an army of 313 Democrats. Even in the slower-moving Senate the Republicans retained but 36 Senators and were to sink to a minority of 25 out of 96 in 1934. Only eight states elected Republican governors in 1932 and 1934. In the latter year even Pennsylvania went Democratic, and in 1936 only Maine and Vermont remained Republican.

The catastrophe which had overwhelmed the Republicans seemed complete in 1932. But Republican misfortune was in-

[47] Standard Statistics Company estimate, quoted in Lippmann and Scroggs, *The United States in World Affairs, 1932*, p. 156.

[48] In 1928 Hoover had polled 21,392,190 popular votes and received 444 in the electoral college. Smith received 15,016,443 votes.

creased during that winter by the survival of a provision of the Constitution which had enabled early Congressmen to journey leisurely to Washington by stagecoach. A rebel Republican senator, George W. Norris, of Nebraska, had already fathered a constitutional amendment which would soon end this anachronism, but from November, 1932, to March, 1933, there was one more interregnum during which no effective action was possible to forestall a complete financial paralysis. Probably no action could have been taken in this period which would have warded off the final denouement of the Republican regime. During 1932 prices had declined another 8.7 per cent, factory employment 11.6 per cent, factory pay rolls 26.7 per cent, freight-car loadings 16 per cent, and department-store sales 23.4 per cent. Railway revenues were the smallest in fifteen years and steel production the lowest in twice that period. Under conditions such as these a copper smelter had to produce three and one-half times as much copper to pay mortgage charges and the cotton and wheat farmers crops two and one-half times larger than before.[49] The pressure of the debts which had been incurred during the boom was so terrific that only

[49] Lippmann and Scroggs, *The United States in World Affairs, 1933*, p. 3.

In his speech accepting the Vice-Presidential nomination of the Republican party at Chicago on July 30, 1936, Colonel Frank Knox declared that: "The present Administration in the winter of 1933 had just one immediate responsibility to meet. That responsibility was to promote the little flame of recovery that had begun to burn in the summer of 1932." Knox predicted also "that with the election of a new administration next November the dammed up forces of recovery will burst forth in a magnificent prosperity."

On the same day, an investigation conducted by the Securities and Exchange Commission brought out the fact that an investment trust called the Interstate Equities Corporation of New York had sustained losses totalling $20,566,527 between September, 1929, and May, 1932. Of this sum $5,044,840 represented losses from syndicate operations the true nature of which was not disclosed in any reports made by the corporation to its stockholders.

The investigation indicated that since 1932 the investment trusts had invaded the fields of banking, savings banks, and insurance, actively selling through the country installment contracts whereby the small purchaser bound himself to pay premiums over a long term of years. These "policies" did not even call for the eventual return of all of the money invested, but held out the hint of possible returns above the normal rate through stock-market operations.

It was estimated by George E. Anderson in the *New York Herald Tribune* on August 2, 1936, that upwards of $4,000,000,000 had been drawn into this dubious type of "investment," a field still not under any adequate regulation. See also the *New York Times*, August 1, 1936.

the most heroic measures could halt a complete breakdown of the nation's financial system. The Hoover Administration, too, could take no such steps. It could only sit in an agony of suspense, while the financial foundations cracked around it, hoping that the final collapse might not come in its time.

The Banks Give Way. The hope was vain. The nation's business was conducted in bank money—still $42,000,000,000 in volume—not in currency or gold. Yet individuals could attempt to save themselves only by withdrawing currency or gold from the banks, and confidence in the banks was approaching zero. A bank panic in any important center was bound to spread, and it would be a miracle if no one of the shaky citadels of debt erected on the Coolidge boom gave way. It was not remarkable, either, that the greatest boom town of all, the world capital of installment buying, should give the signal for the final panic. Nor was it strange that the Union Guardian Trust Company of Detroit should precipitate the crash. This bank was dominated by one of the crowning glories of the era of Normalcy, a holding company. This holding company controlled also nineteen other banks, seven security companies, and a variety of other financial enterprises. If the Union Guardian went under, would there not be runs on all the children of the "parent" company? Repeatedly the Reconstruction Finance Corporation had pumped loans, finally totaling $12,500,000, into the Union Guardian. Now, as March, 1933, drew near much more was needed, and quickly. A conference of many interests in Detroit, on the night of February 13-14, broke up in dispute and the Governor of Michigan raced in his automobile to the state capital before daylight to issue a proclamation closing all banks in Michigan for eight days.[50]

The end had come. Detroit factories were compelled to draw on their balances in other states to meet pay rolls. The area of money stringency spread naturally—all too naturally. Banks everywhere began to complete their fortifications by calling home their deposits in reserve cities. During February a billion dollars left

[50] Allen, *The Lords of Creation*, pp. 423-26.

New York banks for the smaller cities. Bonds were sold, dragging bond prices still lower. Corporations and individuals in all parts of the nation drew out deposits from the banks.

On February 24, Governor Ritchie was compelled to close the banks of Maryland. From then on other governors swiftly issued their proclamations until only the great banks of New York and Chicago held out. At last, at 4:30 in the morning of March 4, the governors of New York and Illinois issued virtually simultaneous bank holiday proclamations.[51] At noon Herbert Hoover rode down to the Capitol to end the period of Normalcy. An immense crowd awaited him. It was a grim, silent throng, almost too frightened to cheer the ringing declaration of the new President that he would drive the money-changers out of the temple.[52] Elsewhere, a nation stricken with complete financial paralysis, and with its economic life almost as impotent, waited in fear and hunger and bewilderment for a new era to begin.

Twelve years of Normalcy had ended in a disaster without parallel in the life of any modern industrial nation. Yet at that moment the greatest nation was but one of many whose sufferings were as acute, though less enormous in bulk.

[51] *Ibid.*

[52] The writer watched the crowds on the Capitol grounds for hours without detecting a cheerful word or expression.

CHAPTER XII

DISARMAMENT

IN THE preceding chapter an account has been given of the effort of the Hoover Government to modify the policy of the preceding administrations with respect to the war debts. The Hoover moratorium was a confession that the international lending policy of the post-war era had broken down. All war debts and reparations were suspended in an effort to save American private debts and to prevent the spread of financial panic to our own shores. In two other important respects, also, the Hoover Administration tried to reverse the steps of its predecessors. Perceiving that economic collapse and political instability were inseparably entangled, Washington made a sustained effort to promote world disarmament and supported the League strongly, if spasmodically, in its effort to deal with the Manchurian crisis.

The London Naval Conference

One of President Hoover's first concerns was the negotiation of an agreement with Great Britain concerning cruisers. The failure of the Geneva Naval Conference in 1927 had left bad feeling between the British and American peoples, without doing anything to enable the United States to economize on naval building. The achievement of a navy equal to Great Britain's was proving to be a costly process and it would be much more so if the British would not agree to limit their cruiser fleet. Like Coolidge, Hoover did not find spending large sums for warships compatible with the economy program, which was his first concern. We wanted parity with Britain, but on as inexpensive a level as possible.

Hoover discussed this dilemma with the veteran London correspondent of the *Chicago Daily News*, Edward Price Bell, while the President-elect was returning by sea from his pre-inauguration tour of South America, and Mr. Bell was commissioned informally to see what he could do in London to forward agreement. A visit by Premier Stanley Baldwin to Washington seems to have been envisaged. Baldwin's government was defeated, however, in the elections of May 30, 1929, and Ramsay MacDonald, who had campaigned for a naval agreement with the United States, became Prime Minister. He was very willing to go to Washington, but his trip was delayed until October, 1929, while the admirals and foreign offices of the two countries hammered out the details of a naval agreement, cruisers alone excepted.[1]

MacDonald's visit created much good feeling in the United States, even though what was said when the Premier and President Hoover sat together on a log at the latter's Rapidan camp was only surmised.[2] The visit consolidated the understanding between the United States and Great Britain. After all, there was no political disagreement between the Americans and the British. The British people showed plainly in the electoral campaign of 1929 their understanding that the American desire for naval parity carried no threat to them and that it was likely to be achieved, with or without their consent. About Europe the British felt very differently. In Europe they believed it vital to maintain a navy as strong as that of any two others. The two others, in 1930, were France and Italy.

Deadlock in the Mediterranean. The British, like the Americans, were desirous of attaining their standard in the Mediterranean as cheaply as possible. So was Italy. She was poor but was also bent upon obtaining naval parity with France. The parity business was already contagious and destined to spread soon into

[1] Drew Pearson and Constantine Brown, *The American Diplomatic Game*, New York, 1935, pp. 65-95. See the excellently documented account of the Conference in Russell Cooper, *American Consultation in World Affairs*, New York, 1934, pp. 35-53; also A. J. Toynbee, *Survey of International Affairs, 1930*, London, 1931, pp. 31-82; and C. P. Howland, *Survey of American Foreign Relations, 1930*, New Haven, 1930, pp. 317-431.

[2] It appears that MacDonald advanced the idea of dismantling all of Britain's Naval bases in American waters, only to have the idea rejected the next day by both the United States Navy Department and MacDonald's colleagues at home. Pearson and Brown, *The American Diplomatic Game*, pp. 103-8.

Japanese-American relations. France had no idea of conceding parity to Italy, whose desire to possess Tunis, Corsica, and Nice was so strong as to be avowed publicly and often in the Fascist press. France could accept an equal Italian navy and preserve the safety of her African empire only if granted a firm promise of support by Great Britain, covering the Mediterranean on the Locarno model. Then she could accept a theoretical or even an actual naval parity with Italy, thus allowing the Americans and the British to attain their economy objectives.

But, for the British, the extension of these hard and fast agreements to the Mediterranean was a new burden which they felt able to undertake only if the Americans were willing to agree to come to conference in case Britain should have to aid France. Once again the success of an important conference depended on a political understanding, and the Hoover Government was not prepared to grant such an understanding. The opposition of the Senate, of the jingo press, and of a broad public opinion was certain. Moreover, the concession did not seem necessary. France would be isolated in the London Conference. It was keenly realized that the Geneva Naval Conference had failed for lack of preparation, and months of negotiation with Great Britain had remedied that difficulty so successfully that Secretary Stimson went to the London Conference confident of success.[3]

The conference opened January 21, 1930, and did not close until April 22. The three months interval was used up in an effort to change the position of France. The Five Power Conference could not succeed without a political agreement, just as the Washington Conference could not have succeeded without the political agreement that no islands within a vast radius of Japan should be further fortified, or without the Nine Power Treaty and the Four Power Treaty. Since both Kellogg and Stimson had moved strongly in the direction of consultation when the

[3] The American delegation consisted of Secretary Stimson, Secretary of the Navy Charles Francis Adams, Ambassador Dwight W. Morrow, Senator David Reed, of Pennsylvania, and Senator Joseph M. Robinson, of Arkansas.

Chaco and Manchurian conflicts threatened the Kellogg Pact, there was no logical reason why Stimson should now decline to consult in other quarters covered by the Pact. But he did not believe it was necessary and carly in the conference repudiated reports that he was considering a consultative agreement.[4] Dwight Morrow, who had long known the French Premier, André Tardieu, understood the precariousness of the latter's political position in France and the necessity of a political agreement if success was to be achieved. He could not, however, make headway, particularly after an upset which occurred early in the Conference.

British-American Accord. To postpone consideration of the troublesome European angle, the British and Americans had proceeded to discuss the single remaining difficulty between them, whether the United States should have 21 crusiers with eight-inch guns or only 18. Inside the American delegation the debate between the naval officers over the efficacy of eight- and six-inch guns was finally won, for the time being, by the advocates of the smaller gun, and an agreement was arrived at with the British whereby the United States might build "either eighteen eight-inch-gun cruisers plus 143,520 tons of six-inch-gun vessels, or the alternative of fifteen eight-inch-gun cruisers plus 189,000 tons of six-inch-gun vessels." [5]

This agreement preserved the possibility of some economy in cruiser building, but it was prematurely disclosed to Arthur Sears Henning, of the *Chicago Tribune*, who had been criticizing Secretary Stimson vigorously. This leak caused a hurried release of the British-American agreement, without notice to the French

[4] Pearson and Brown, *The American Diplomatic Game*, p. 121. The American delegation ignored the suggestion of an Atlantic Pact on February 3. By February 19 some of the delegation were reported as favoring a reconsideration of the political agreement issue. Three days later it was understood that the delegates had decided adversely. On March 3 the Willard Straight Post of the American Legion in New York City telegraphed the conference urging support of consultation when the Kellogg Pact was violated. On March 12 the United States delegation took a strong stand against a consultative pact. *New York Times*, February 3, 19 and 22, March 3 and 12, 1930.

[5] Howland, *Survey of American Foreign Relations, 1930*, pp. 355-56.

delegation. Convinced that they were confronted with a firm Anglo-Saxon bloc, the French remained adamant, even on the question of humanizing submarine warfare. They had ten cruisers and 100,000 tons of submarines provided for and meant to build them. Italy was at the moment in the process of capturing Sahara territory claimed by France. Eventually, therefore, on February 17, Secretary Stimson suggested to the press that there was no reason why the United States should not enter into a consultative agreement modeled on the Four Power Pact signed at the Washington Conference.[6]

Japan's Claims Conceded. The essential move having been made, the French Cabinet fell on the same day, and it was seventeen days before Tardieu could set up another and get Foreign Minister Briand back to London. During this interval the conference made no headway, not even in persuading the Japanese to drop their demand for a 10-7 ratio of auxiliary vessels (including cruisers), instead of the 10-6 ratio to the American and British navies conceded to them in Washington. Yet the signature of the Japanese to a three-power treaty was indispensable if a five-power treaty could not be obtained. Both Hoover and MacDonald had staked too much on the conference to let it fail entirely. Accordingly, the Japanese eventually won. They were conceded parity with Britain and the United States in submarines, a 10-7 ratio in destroyers and six-inch-gun cruisers and a 10-6 ratio in eight-inch-gun cruisers. In practice the Japanese gained the 10-7 ratio even in big cruisers, since it was agreed that the last three American cruisers of this type already appropriated should not be completed until after the London Treaty expired in 1936.[7]

Consultation Reconsidered. Meanwhile Briand, on his return to the conference on March 6, had made it clear that French

[6] Pearson and Brown, *The American Diplomatic Game,* p. 133.

[7] Toynbee, *Survey of International Affairs, 1930,* p. 59. A leak to the press concerning the nominal abandonment of the 10-7 ratio for large cruisers caused such an explosion of protest in Japan that the final agreement on this point hung fire for some weeks.

signature to the treaty depended on a Mediterranean pact. But by that time Secretary Stimson had received word from Washington that any treaty mentioning "consultation" would have very hard sledding in the Senate. Senators Johnson, of California, Fess, of Ohio, and Walsh, of Massachusetts, were strongly opposed to the idea. Senator George H. Moses, of New Hampshire, one of the most intransigent of the Irreconcilables, supported the proposal, saying that he still stood by the Knox resolution of June 10, 1919, which he had helped to frame as a substitute for the League of Nations. This resolution proposed:

That finally, it shall be the declared policy of our government, in order to meet fully and fairly our obligations to ourselves and to the world, that the freedom and peace of Europe being threatened by any power or combination of powers, the United States will regard such a situation with grave concern as a menace to its own peace and freedom, will consult with other powers affected with a view to devising means for the removal of such menace, and will, the necessity arising in the future, carry out the same complete accord and cooperation with our chief co-belligerents for the defense of civilization.

In 1930 Senator Moses was still unable to "see why we should be afraid of this proposal as a general principle." [8] He was in such a minority, however, that on March 11, two days after Briand had put the consultative pact into the headlines again, Stimson explained to the press that the United States could not enter such an agreement because it implied a moral obligation to use armed force against an aggressor should consultation fail.[9] Briand

[8] *New York Times,* March 7, 8, 10 and 11, 1930; *Congressional Record,* Vol. 58, p. 894.

[9] *New York Times,* March 12, 1930. Why an agreement to consult would be any more of an entanglement with France than the Four Power Treaty of 1922 was with Britain has never been explained. The agreement of Britain and Japan to limit their navies was reached and the Anglo-Japanese Alliance was abrogated only after the Four Power Pact had been agreed upon. The treaties were all related to each other, as Secretary Stimson later reminded Japan in his open letter of February 24, 1932, to Senator Borah.

Perhaps the objection was raised in 1930 because in the intervening years the controversy over the origins of the war had brought out the fact that Britain was bound to France in 1914 more effectively by informal understandings than by articles of alliance. No doubt, too, even a vague commitment to France was considered more dangerous by the Senators than a similar one to Great Britain.

threatened to go home, and deadlock ensued until March 21, when Dwight Morrow's able assistant, George Rublee, convinced Morrow that a consultative agreement was essential, not only to compose the Mediterranean impasse but also to give the British assurance that the United States fleet would not be used against them if they moved to enforce Article 16 of the League Covenant.

It took Morrow two or three days to reconvert Stimson and the other members of the American delegation. Then they remembered that President Hoover believed there was political dynamite in consultation and sought to inform him of the new move in that direction. He had already heard of it through the press and through the Foreign Policy Association, which had urged his support, and he was in no mood to support the venture by the time full details of it arrived. On the contrary, he killed the idea decisively in his press conference of March 25, saying that no security or consultative pact had been either suggested or considered at any time during the conference and that none would be of any avail in reducing naval tonnage unless it contained military guarantees. The United States would not make such an agreement.[10]

Before this broadside struck the conference, Stimson had been

[10] Pearson and Brown, *The American Diplomatic Game*, p. 160. Senator Borah at once ridiculed the idea of a consultative pact as a "pious fraud" unless we were ready to go ahead and do what the consultants found necessary. No plan not backed by military force would satisfy France. Senator Shipstead, of Minnesota, joined in the criticism and Senator George, of Georgia, was quite as much opposed to the idea as Borah. He expressed the "view that even though a consultative pact might carry no military sanctions some senators would fear that, in time of crisis, American obligations might be misinterpreted by other nations and thus involve the United States in war."

Another Democratic Senator, Swanson of Virginia, was, after consultation with Borah, against the proposal on all grounds. It was a special alliance, against which both Washington and Wilson had warned. It would be far better to join the League where all nations could meet and consult. *New York Times*, March 28 and 29, 1930.

The same issue of the *Times* carried an account of a great demonstration at Calais, France, against the new American tariff on laces, which was regarded as prohibitive. Some 20,000 workers marched silently through streets on which all shops were closed as on a day of mourning.

The lace manufacturers of Nottinghamshire in England also foresaw the end of their struggling industry.

compelled by a story published in the *London Daily Herald* to give a guarded admission that consultation was in the foreground again. He repeated a former statement that there was "no objection to entering a consultative pact as such," since the United States was already a party to such treaties, but we would not enter into any treaty involving military assistance to another nation as a *quid-pro-quo* for naval reduction. "If, however, this demand for security could be satisfied in some other way, then the danger of misunderstanding a consultative pact would be eliminated and the question would be approached from an entirely different standpoint. In such a case the Americans would consider the matter with an entirely open mind." [11]

No Political Accord. This statement electrified the conference and opened a period of vacillation on the part of Premier MacDonald which was as violent as that from which Stimson had suffered. The "some other way" to which Stimson referred was the proposed Mediterranean Locarno, which Britain would underwrite. But the British public had had nearly three months to become nervous about any new commitments on the Continent. MacDonald was dependent on Liberal support and the Liberals were as critical as the part of his own Labour following in the Cabinet which was led by Philip Snowden. For this reason MacDonald on April 1 inspired a reassuring statement to the British public, which upset the negotiations.[12] It was with the greatest reluctance that he was persuaded to approve a reaffirmation of the interpretation of Britain's obligations under Article 16 of the League Covenant, which was contained in the Locarno Treaty. This interpretation was safe enough, since it contained the saving clause promising to resist aggression "to the extent which is compatible with its military situation and takes its geographical position into account."

Yet British willingness to reaffirm even this mild admission of responsibility on the Continent was reassuring to France and

[11] *New York Herald Tribune*, March 26, 1930.
[12] Toynbee, *Survey of International Affairs, 1930*, p. 58.

created so much good feeling that the French Cabinet gave its friendly blessing to a three-power treaty and promised to resume negotiations with Italy looking to the later entry of the two Latin nations into the treaty. This led to the insertion in the treaty between Britain, the United States, and Japan of an "escalator" clause, permitting Britain to build to higher levels if French and Italian naval rivalry continued. A treaty had become possible because of the willingness of the United States and Great Britain to discuss political questions, even if nothing tangible had resulted from the discussion.

The main lesson of the conference, that success in disarmament depends on the removal of political obstacles, was obscured in the United States by satisfaction at the final achievement of parity with Great Britain at a not too excessive cost. Yet the realization that actual parity would mean a bill for construction approximating a billion dollars somewhat tempered enthusiasm over the achievement. For France and Italy, the conference had had only bad results, exacerbating an already high state of feeling between them. There the roles were reversed. The poorer nation was the aspirant for parity and had no means of enforcing it.[13]

Senate Opinion Controlling. The London Naval Conference had failed to do more than advance agreement between the United States and Great Britain because the Administration would not risk a clash with the Senate. As a matter of constitutional law the Executive had the power to agree to consult without the permission of the Senate. Professor Lindsay Rogers clarified the point at the opening of the 1930 conference by recalling that: "The most important foreign policy that the United States has—the Monroe Doctrine—was put forward by Executive action alone." There could similarly be a Hoover Doctrine, which would "declare the desire of the United States to consult instantly with Great Britain and the other principal Powers whenever any viola-

[13] Throughout the year 1929 the French and Italian armed forces had been practically on a war footing. Frank Simonds, *Can America Stay at Home?* New York, 1932, p. 244. See also the account of the Five-Power Conference, pp. 239-52.

tion of the Kellogg Pact seemed possible and then to consider what its future course should be." [14] This policy could, of course, become established only if successive administrations adhered to it.

Even the separate enunciation of such a policy would, no doubt, have made certain a hard struggle over the London Naval Treaty in the Senate. The abortive discussions about consultation at London caused a reservation to be attached to the treaty in the Senate. Senator Norris sponsored the reservation saying that the Senate gave its approval "with the distinct and explicit understanding that there are no secret files, documents, letters, understandings, or agreements which in any way, directly or indirectly, modify, change, add to, or take away from any of the stipulations, agreements, or statements in said treaty." [15]

This extreme precaution mirrored the firm belief of Senators that the United States would not be rushed into another world war by the tremendous issues precipitated by the war itself. If the most powerful magnifying glass could not find extant anything remotely suggesting a positive obligation on the part of the United States, all would be well.

A Movement for a Consultative Pact. The executive authorities could not be so completely confident. Especially after the shock of the world depression and their experiences at London, they knew that as long as fear and insecurity dominated Europe American life was also insecure. President Hoover himself soon admitted, in an address of April 14, 1930, "the clear need of some method of mobilizing public opinion against the violation of the Kellogg Pact" and of "appropriate agencies for regular,

[14] Lindsay Rogers, "The United States, Parity and Neutrality," *Contemporary Review,* February, 1930, Vol. 137, p. 163.

[15] *Congressional Record,* Vol. 73, pp. 368, 378. Among several reservations defeated by substantially the same vote was one by Senator Johnson, of California, which proposed: "That this treaty shall be null and void if and when the United States enters the League of Nations by the ratification of its covenant or allies itself with the League of Nations by adhering to the protocol of the International Court of Justice, or in any other way accepts membership in the League of Nations or in any of its subsidiary organizations." The vote was 8 for and 58 against (p. 375).

methodical disposal and solution of controversies."[16] Again on Armistice Day of the same year Hoover cautiously brought up the subject of consultation in similar terms saying, "I do not say that some such further step may not some day come about." Ten days later admission was made that the Administration was willing to discuss a consultative pact.[17] No new negotiations, however, developed from these feelers. The economic crisis developed apace, and within a year the Japanese conquest of Manchuria made it clear that consultation and action alike were feasible only through the League of Nations.[18]

The World Disarmament Conference

Post-War Statutes. Virtually since 1920 the organs of the League of Nations had been engaged in preparation for a disarmament conference. The fourth of President Wilson's Fourteen Points, upon which Germany accepted the Armistice, had called for "adequate guarantees given and taken that national armaments will be reduced to the lowest point consistent with domestic safety." In Article 8 of the Covenant this obligation had been considerably watered down by substituting "national" safety for domestic, but the obligation remained in substantial form and the Council was made responsible for formulating disarmament plans.[19]

16 *New York Times,* April 15, 1930.

17 *New York Times,* November 12 and 25, 1930.

A distinguished committee of the Twentieth Century Fund, headed by Dr. Nicholas Murray Butler, urged the Government to call a conference of the signatories of the Pact to draw up a supplemental protocol providing means of upholding the Pact. For this report see Evans Clark, *Boycotts and Peace,* New York, 1932, pp. 7-9.

18 For a full account of the movement toward a consultative pact which succeeded the London Naval Conference, see Cooper, *American Consultation in World Affairs,* pp. 53-59. His lists of the Congressional resolutions favoring consultation and sanctions and of the private initiatives in the same direction are especially impressive. See pp. 56-57.

19 Article 8 also recognized that "the manufacture by private enterprise of munitions and implements of war is open to grave objections" and required the Council to "devise how the evil effects of such manufacture can be prevented, due regard being had to the necessities of those members of the League which

The former Allied Powers were also bound by the preamble to Part V of the Treaty of Versailles which had obliged Germany to observe the military, naval, and air clauses of the treaty "in order to render possible the initiation of a general limitation of the armaments of all nations." This pledge was made more definite in the reply of the Allied and Associated Powers of June 16, 1919, to the protests of the Germans. In this note the disarmament of Germany was described as "the first steps toward that general reduction and limitation of armaments which they seek to bring about as one of the most fruitful preventives of war, and which it will be one of the first duties of the League of Nations to promote." [20]

Early Explorations. The First Assembly of the League debated the problem and discovered that disarmament must be based on security. It requested the creation of a special commission to survey the whole field and the Temporary Mixed Commission was set up on February 25, 1921.[21] The Second Assembly debated the subject still more extensively. During 1922-1923 efforts were centered on the preparation of the Draft Treaty of Mutual Assistance, and thereafter disarmament was merged in the security discussion until 1926. The Geneva Protocol was to have led to the disarmament conference. Since the Protocol was abortive, a Preparatory Commission for a disarmament conference was set up in

are not able to manufacture the munitions and implements of war necessary for their safety."

Article 8 further required the members of the League "to exchange full and frank information as to the scale of their armaments, their military, naval and air programs," etc. This provision resulted in the publication of the huge annual *Armaments Yearbook*. Unfortunately, however, the Governments robbed this compilation of much of its value by submitting figures covering only men and material in commission, refusing to reveal their reserves.

[20] The most complete account of the struggle over disarmament is to be found in the three books by J. W. Wheeler-Bennett: *The Reduction of Armaments*, London, 1925; *Disarmament and Security since Locarno*, London, 1932; and *The Pipe Dream of Peace*, New York, 1935. The last is a much more scholarly account of the disarmament conference than its title would indicate. See also A. J. Toynbee, *Survey of International Affairs, 1932*, London, 1933, pp. 173-201.

[21] This Commission worked with the Permanent Advisory Commission for Military, Naval and Air Questions, which had been constituted May 17, 1920. See League Secretariat, *Ten Years of World Cooperation*, pp. 49-54.

1926 upon which three non-members of the League—Russia, Turkey, and the United States—accepted membership. Hugh Gibson, Ambassador to Belgium, and Hugh Wilson, Minister to Switzerland, represented the United States.

American Cooperation, 1926-1931. The deliberations of the Preparatory Commission continued through six sessions held at intervals over four years; the last opened December 9, 1930, and formulated a draft convention for the disarmament conference. In 1926, at the start of the period, the American delegates were still unable to do business with the League's Permanent Advisory Commission, or with the Joint Commission of Economic Experts which had succeeded the Temporary Mixed Commission. The names of these two bodies had accordingly to be changed to Sub-Commission A and Sub-Commission B.[22] Toward the close of the period the United States received September 19, 1931, an invitation to take part in a consultative capacity in the discussion concerning a truce in arms building which would be held in the Third Committee of the League Assembly. Two days later the State Department published the invitation with an announcement that it had been accepted.[23]

The world economic crisis accounted in part for this change of attitude toward the League. More important still had been the greater knowledge of the whole problem of arms and security which the American diplomatic service had gained from the constant discussion of disarmament problems. They had learned that the technical issues involved in disarmament were unbelievably complex and that the political issues were almost impossible of solution. On the issue whether the trained reserves of conscript armies should be counted in fixing the size of the armies the United States had first stood with Great Britain and Germany in favor of counting them. Later, after Great Britain had accepted the French thesis as a part of the Anglo-French naval compromise, the United States did likewise. Similarly, on the question

[22] Salvador de Madariaga, *Disarmament,* New York, 1929, p. 155.

[23] Walter Lippmann and W. O. Scroggs, *The United States in World Affairs, 1931,* New York, 1932, p. 243.

of trying to check armament indirectly by budgetary limitation our Government long opposed the method, feeling that our higher costs and some constitutional limitations prevented its acceptance. But in 1932, after it had been agreed that a military budget should be compared only with its predecessor, not with the budgets of other nations, opposition to the method was withdrawn. Also, in the matter of supervising the enforcement of the proposed disarmament treaty our delegates long opposed supervision, contending that the execution of the treaty must rest on good faith alone. Yet eventually they joined in recommending the creation of a Permanent Disarmament Commission to watch the application of the treaty and report regularly on it. Even on consultation the Hoover Administration accepted the broad provisions of Article 50 of the Draft Convention, which bound the signatories to advise together promptly if any signatory feared that its security was menaced. A comparison of Article 50 with a similar article in the London Naval Treaty indicated also that the League was now intended and accepted as the vehicle of consultation.[24]

Issues Technical and Political. Time had brought appreciation in Washington that if the peace was to be kept it would be done through the League, but the years of discussion about disarmament had brought out more difficulties than solutions. There was, for example, the question of war potential, that is of the industrial power of a nation. Obviously, the great industrial powers could rearm quickly if they chose, whereas weaker ones could be overwhelmed unless they had great stores of prepared weapons. Particularly would this be true of aerochemical warfare. Nations with great chemical and civil aviation industries could rapidly turn the instruments of peace into the deadliest engines of war, and on a huge scale. This did not mean that differences in industrial capacity could ever be equalized, but it did mean that if disarmament ever became a reality it would have to be accompanied by such a strengthening of the League as would prevent individual nations from coercing their neighbors.

[24] *Ibid.*, pp. 234, 237, 241.

The issue, of course, centered around France and Germany. The Germans were determined that their unequal status should end. They ascribed most of their troubles to the lack of armed force and, after the depression came, condemned all moves at Geneva which did not look to the removal of their inequality. Yet not many steps were taken in that direction. France and her allies could not rid themselves of the fear of Germany. France had lost, or had seen watered down, the treaty guarantees which in 1919 she thought would give her security. By 1932 she believed she had made herself secure by arms, alliances, and money. She would not surrender her superiority unless she received real guarantees in exchange. She had to consider, moreover, not only Germany, but Italy. The latter under Fascism was the most intransigent and openly avaricious power in Europe. For a decade there had been tension between France and Italy. Germany and Italy were also potential allies, even if Austrian and Tyrol questions divided them. France had to be prepared to fight a war on two fronts. And as the German Nazis grew in power, France felt increasingly greater fear of Germany, when less apprehension was required if agreement was to be reached.

France Firm for Security. When the Disarmament Conference finally met on February 2, 1932, the Japanese had supplied France with every argument for maintaining her position. For nearly five months they had been ignoring and defying the League of Nations while they made war on China. From Manchuria the conflict had spread to Shanghai, a great section of which was being hammered to dust by Japanese artillery and bombing planes on the day the conference met. In this atmosphere it was not remarkable that France should immediately confront the conference with proposals for the internationalization of civil aviation, an international police force, compulsory arbitration, a strict definition of aggression, and close international supervision of any agreements made.[25]

[25] At the opening session of the conference, huge samples of the tons of petitions gathered by women's organizations the world over, but chiefly in the English speaking countries, were presented. More than 8,000,000 signatures were affixed to these prayers for disarmament and peace.

The other leading powers presented plans stressing the importance of limiting the weapons which they feared most and the opening speeches continued until February 25, under the chairmanship of Arthur Henderson, recently Foreign Minister of Great Britain in the Labor Government.[26] Early in March it was necessary to give way to a special session of the League Assembly, called to deliberate on the undeclared war in China. On March 19, the conference took an Easter recess without having done more than equip itself with an abundance of committees.

German Impatience Rising. For Chancellor Brüning and the German Republic the delay was deadly. Brüning's appeal at the opening of the conference that the nations follow Germany's enforced example had elicited no action. After having forced a republic upon Germany the Allies had continued to treat her as if she were still ruled by the Prussian Junkers. In large measure this was true, since the Republic left the servants of the old regime in control of the courts and civil service and allowed them to rebuild the army as a power above and beyond the state. But now when speed in disarmament and other agreements was vitally necessary if the Republic was to be saved, no headway was being made. At bottom the economic suffering attendant upon the world depression, and not peculiar to Germany, was responsible for the rapid slide of the German people into the Nazi and Communist parties. Yet that only increased the urgency of the German Government's need for some success at the Disarmament Conference with which to disarm the Nazi campaign. The deep passions of the Hitler movement were concentrated on the demand for

[26] Belying the claims of many Americans that our representatives can never hold their own in international politics, Hugh Gibson led two successive moves to keep the machinery of the conference out of the hands of the French bloc. To prevent Benes and Politis, the Vice-President and the *rapporteur* of the conference from becoming the chairmen of the Bureau, or steering committee, and of the General Commission, respectively, Gibson moved and carried the election of Arthur Henderson, the President, to both posts. Later, when the French secured the creation of a Political Committee to deal with security issues, Gibson led in obtaining the chairmanship of this body also for Henderson. Walter Lippmann and W. O. Scroggs, *The United States in World Affairs, 1932*, New York, 1933, pp. 231-32.

arms equal to those in the hands of any nation. In reality Germany's plight was due chiefly to the terrific economic losses inseparable from her four years of war and to the fact that she had lived far beyond her means during the years of the Coolidge boom, but the German Government could not contradict the bitter cry of the Nazis that it was all due to the Versailles "Dictat" and especially to Germany's disarmed condition. It could only impose heavier taxes and more drastic economies in decree after decree, without any success at Geneva to make the pinch bearable.

The day before the conference reassembled, on March 11, the vote for Hitler in the Presidential runoff had increased two millions, ascending to thirteen millions. There was not much time left. Hugh Gibson, for the American delegation, tried to spur the reassembled conference to an immediate discussion of abolishing the offensive weapons which are designed to attack land defenses. The abolition of these weapons would remove fear, he argued, and would provide security.[27] It would also go a long way toward giving equality to Germany, which did not have the great engines of attack. French opposition, however, soon blocked that line of approach [28] and on April 24 elections in the German states registered enormous advances for the National Socialists.

April Negotiations. Chancellor Brüning decided to go at once to Geneva. Secretary Stimson and Ambassador-at-Large Norman H. Davis were there.[29] They were joined by Premier MacDonald in conversations with Brüning, in which the Chancellor proposed

[27] The American delegation to the Disarmament Conference consisted of Hugh Gibson, Norman H. Davis, Claude A. Swanson, and Mary E. Woolley. Hugh R. Wilson was alternate.

[28] The General Commission did adopt three resolutions between April 19 and 22. They were: (1) that the reduction of armaments should be continued by successive revisions after the existing conference had done what it could; (2) that arms should be reduced as much as was compatible with national security and the execution of international obligations; and (3) that certain classes of weapons should be banned to all states. Wheeler-Bennett, *The Pipe Dream of Peace*, p. 30.

[29] Secretary Stimson was the first American Secretary of State to sit in a League conference. He appeared quietly on April 18, soon disappearing into a leased villa for private conversations with the other heads of state. According to one account, he desired to talk about Manchuria, while his visitors insisted on discussing Europe. Pearson and Brown, *The American Diplomatic Game*, p. 201.

that Germany should be allowed to reduce the twelve-year period of Reichswehr service to five years and to enlist another 100,000 men in a militia, Germany to have the right to "samples" of all weapons. He asked also that the new agreement replace Part V of the Treaty of Versailles. The Chancellor's terms were moderate, but were not accepted by France. Tardieu was away campaigning in one of the series of national elections which continually interrupted the conference, and when he received word from the *camarilla* in Berlin which was plotting Brüning's overthrow that they were near to success, he allowed his laryngitis to keep him away from Geneva. Bruning went back empty handed to his fall, on May 30, four days after the General Commission had adjourned to allow the committees to complete their work. Tardieu also fell, and the committees wrangled over the size of the land guns and the kinds of warships which could be considered as offensive until the Lausanne Conference on reparations monopolized attention. No agreement could be reached that any weapon was offensive. To the British and the Americans huge battleships were defensive and the submarine horribly offensive. To the French and others the reverse was true. Nor could the exact width of a gun's mouth which would make it offensive ever be determined.

The Hoover Plan. The conference was getting nowhere and could never progress while it discussed technical issues alone. The American Government therefore determined to make another effort to secure disarmament by appealing to the peoples over the heads of their governments. The Hoover Plan for breaking the deadlock struck the conference even more suddenly than the Hoover moratorium had hit the creditors of Germany. The General Commission was called without warning on June 21, 1932, to meet the next day. When it assembled, the Hoover Plan calling for a reduction of all land armies by one-third was laid before it. The plan promoted equality for Germany by taking her permitted force of 100,000 men as a police component and calculating the police needs of all powers on it as a basis. The one-third reduction was also to apply to all battleships and submarines, other types of warships to be reduced one-fourth. All tanks, large mobile guns, bombing planes, and chemical-warfare weapons were to be abolished.[30]

The mathematical bombshell method of attack had succeeded in the Washington Conference. Perhaps it would win at Geneva. Since the plan would reduce the relative strength of France, Italy at once accepted it enthusiastically. Russia welcomed it as warmly, and the German delegation was pleased. Some thirty of the smaller nations endorsed it strongly in sessions of the General Commission July 7 and 8.[31] But the key delegations praised the spirit of the plan without agreeing to its substance. The British Admiralty, which had been most reluctant to accept the cruiser limitations of the London Naval Treaty, was not disposed to cut its forces steeply again. MacDonald quickly came to terms with Herriot on both arms and reparations. Japan was alarmed lest the balance of armed forces, by which she was holding the Far East in her grip, should be upset. It was believed that the Hoover cuts would strengthen the United States fleet relatively to that of Japan. France naturally looked askance at another proposed reduction of her forces which carried no guarantees of aid in case she was attacked. Her policy was no less pacific than that of the United States but her distrust of her neighbors was infinitely greater.

The United States thus found itself supported by all the governments except the two or three whose cooperation was indispensable, and it was decided to forsake the many for the collaboration of the few. A month of secret conversations between the American, British, and French delegations ensued, which greatly irked the smaller powers and the representatives of American organizations in Geneva. Mussolini was also so displeased that Grandi resigned as Italian Foreign Minister and General Balbo flew to Geneva in a great seaplane to express his chief's disapproval of the resolution which the Western powers finally agreed

[30] *New York Times*, June 23, 1932.
[31] Conf. D./C. G./P. V. 22.

upon. Russia likewise cooled toward the result, and the Germans concluded that their special problems were not receiving enough attention.[32] All three voted against the resolution of July 23, 1932, which, under the prodding of eight of the lesser nations, attempted to record the progress of the conference to date.

The July Resolution. The strongest part of the resolution was its preamble. Here the best of intentions were firmly expressed in the lucid style of Sir John Simon. The progress recorded was less inspiring. It was agreed that air attack against civilians should be absolutely prohibited, though "civilian" was not defined. Restriction of military aircraft and international control of civil aviation were favored. Limits on the size of land guns and tanks would be fixed, and chemical, biological, or incendiary warfare prohibited. A permanent disarmament commission would supervise the promised treaty.[33]

When the resolution was presented to the conference Gibson spoke first in its defense. He could only thank the many delegations which had supported the Hoover plan, saying indirectly that the Americans had decided that they must work with the British and the French. Doubtless this was a wise decision, though the United States was not yet prepared for a degree of collaboration which would consolidate the peace.

For Germany, the July resolution was another severe defeat. Nadolny warned the conference again that further German collaboration was possible only "on the basis of a clear and definite recognition of the principle of equality of rights." Nor was the hardening determination of Germany soothed by a plea in behalf of the French budget which was made in the Chamber of Deputies the next day. The huge expenditures on France's Maginot line of fortresses, said the *rapporteur* for the budget, had given France

[32] For the best account of Russia's part in the Disarmament Conference, see Kathryn W. Davis, *The Soviets at Geneva*, Geneva, 1934, pp. 131-97. While this volume was written before Russia entered the League, it contains the full background for that step.

[33] IX Disarmament 1932. IX. 51. The resolution contained a page of plans and instructions for the future work of the conference.

the security which she had long sought. This could not be allowed to pass in Germany, and when the German Minister of Defense, General von Schleicher, enlarged upon the theme in a radio address, the French press was much alarmed and was confirmed in its opinion that disarmament should proceed very slowly.[34] On July 31, the Nazis increased their voting total slightly in new elections to the Reichstag. Polling nearly 14,000,000 votes, they raised their number of seats from 107 to 226. The democratic parties still held a precarious majority.

"*Consultation Inevitable.*" On August 8, Secretary Stimson took a long step in the direction of bridging the gap between the secure and the insecure nations. Supported by the recent declaration in both of the 1932 party platforms in favor of consultation when the Kellogg Pact should be violated, Stimson made an important address to the Council on Foreign Relations, in which he declared that: "Consultation between the signatories of the pact when faced with the threat of its violation becomes inevitable." Dwelling upon the Pact's mission in the mobilization of world opinion, he concluded that: "Any effective invocation of the power of world opinion postulates discussion and consultation." More significant still was his virtual admission that neutrality had become impractical. He recalled that tangible proof had been given during the Great War of "the impossibility of confining war within any narrow limits." The Pact itself, Stimson held, had made war illegal. "Hereafter," he said, "when two nations engage in armed conflict, either one or both must be wrong-doers–violators of this general treaty law. No longer do we draw a circle about them and treat them with the punctiliousness of the duellists' code. We denounce them instead as lawbreakers." Unless some such steps were taken, "modern civilization would be doomed." He completely refuted the criticism that the Pact was "the mere declaration of a pious purpose." "If such

[34] Toynbee, *Survey of International Affairs, 1932,* pp. 258-59. Von Schleicher repeated, in two newspaper articles of August 31 and September 1, his threat that Germany meant to carry out the reorganization of her forces with or without permission (p. 261).

an interpretation were correct," he said, "it would reduce the Pact to a mere gesture. If its promises conferred no rights as between the signatories it would be a sham. It would be worse than a nullity, for its failure would carry down the faith of the world in other efforts for peace." [35]

Germany Withdraws. This clear statement that the League of Nations was vital to the future peace made it plain also that the United States had not sponsored another world peace treaty merely as a gesture of idle sentimentality. The "Stimson doctrine" strongly roused French hopes, but it had little appeal to the German Government, which submitted a note to France three weeks later, on August 29, withdrawing from the Disarmament Conference but stating that if an equal right to arms was granted to Germany she would be satisfied with less than equality in fact during the term of the first treaty.

The thesis that Germany must have equal rights had been long recognized by the American negotiators. Norman H. Davis had agreed to it publicly.[36] Nor did the French deny it, though they mistrusted the capacity of the Germans to be satisfied with an inequality in fact. The German Cabinet of barons was in French eyes a plain revival of the old militaristic regime in Germany. Herriot had agreed to end reparations only six weeks before and now felt that he should not be asked so soon to quash the arms provisions of the Treaty of Versailles. His political position was also precarious. Yet the sympathy of the other powers for Germany's equality demand was so strong that France risked isolation.

The Herriot Plan. To extricate himself from this dilemma, Herriot on November 14 presented to the Disarmament Conference a new French plan which registered one important advance toward a solution of the disarmament tangle. It proposed that the home-defense forces of the continental European states on land should be reduced to a uniform type, "that of a national

[35] *New York Times*, August 9, 1932.
[36] Lippmann and Scroggs, *The United States in World Affairs, 1932*, p. 247.

short-service army with limited effectiveness—not adapted to a sudden offensive." The defensive militias would not be equipped with any powerful mobile weapons. These would be given to small contingents of long-service troops which would be at the command of a majority of the League Council should an aggression occur. While these League forces would remain in their home territories, a true international air force, armed with superior machines and stationed at Geneva, was suggested.

The entire Herriot plan, of which only the chief elements have been indicated, was founded upon the acceptance of three principles (based upon the Kellogg Pact), which France evidently thought should follow from Secretary Stimson's August address. The principles were that every breach of the Paris Pact or threat of it should lead to prompt consultation, that all financial and economic relations with the aggressor, direct or indirect, should be severed, and that in each case the signatories of the Pact would at once refuse to recognize any situation brought about by violating an international undertaking.[37]

December Formula. Meanwhile, Norman H. Davis had visited London, Rome, and Paris to see what might be done, and a series of conversations among the four Western European powers and the United States continued. The object which Mr. Davis had in view was a short-term treaty, which would register a beginning and give time for the reconsideration of security with equality. The result of the December conversations, which followed in Geneva, was a Five-Power Declaration signed on December 11, 1932, which laid down the principle that Germany and the other disarmed powers should have "equality of rights in a system which would promise security for all nations," it being "clearly understood that the methods of application of such equality of rights will be discussed by the Conference."[38] Germany thereupon agreed to return to the conference. She had just undergone

[37] IX Disarmament 1932. IX. 58.

[38] Lippmann and Scroggs, *The United States in World Affairs, 1932*, pp. 255-56.

another palace revolution, Captain von Papen being ousted as Chancellor by General von Schleicher, a bold general who proved to have no plans or policies and who was in turn overthrown by the final intrigue around the aged President von Hindenburg which turned the German Government over to Hitler on January 30, 1933.[39]

February Session. On February 2, 1933, three days after the man who had long been the most passionate advocate of upsetting the entire Versailles settlement came to power in Germany, the Disarmament Conference was doomed to meet again. The anniversary of its first session also found the Japanese army gathering for the invasion of Jehol, after having conquered all of Manchuria. It also came at the height of the Hirtenberg arms affair, which convinced the *status-quo* powers that Italy was arming Hungary by way of Austria. There was far less reason to believe that arms could be restricted than there had been a year ago. The conference opened by discussing the Herriot plan, but only France's allies endorsed it. Italy and Germany were opposed, especially to the proposal for new mutual-assistance treaties. They found practical objections to the international-police provisions of the plan. The British called attention to the already numerous treaty guarantees and to their inability to sign others. The Americans indicated that they could not discuss the details of the plan, and it was soon acknowledged to be dead.

Then, in their turn, the French found many inadequacies in the British proposal that the European states forswear all "resort to force," though this renunciation was eventually approved by a vote of half the delegations present. In the Air Commission there was deadlock, the French holding out for the internation-

[39] Von Schleicher's threat to expose the *Osthilfe* scandals roused the 13,000 *Junker* families en masse. The Nazi party, having lost 2,000,000 votes in the November elections, was bankrupt in every sense of the word. Von Papen's hope to tame it was therefore not totally impossible, though his strategy in giving the Nazis control of nothing except the Chancellorship and the armed forces was sadly defective. A report that Von Schleicher was marching on Berlin with the Potsdam garrison stampeded both the Nazi chiefs and the palace into a final agreement which seemed to leave the substance of power in the hands of the Nationalists, but actually gave it to the Nazis.

alization of aviation, the Germans and Italians for the total abolition of fighting aircraft. The stalemate was so complete that the British Government belatedly decided to exercise some leadership. Another plan was drawn up and MacDonald hurried to Geneva to lay it on the table on March 16, 1933. MacDonald berated the delegates in such language as to lead one of the closest students of the conference to term his address "a shocking impropriety, a dreadful vulgarity,"[40] but he found no British arms which needed limiting—on land or sea—and he balked at restrictions on civil aviation.

British Plan. The draft set definite figures for the proposed short-service army of each European nation. France, Germany, Italy, and Poland were put down for 200,000 home troops each, with France allowed another 200,000 overseas. The plan covered every other item just as definitely and laid down security proposals (based on the Pact of Paris), which appeared to ensure a conference of the signatories in the event of conflict, though any conclusions reached would have to be concurred in by the representatives of all of the seven Great Powers and a majority of the others represented[41]—a provision which appeared finally to take away from Article 16 all of its automatic character.

The British plan was an advance over all others in definiteness, but it came far too late. The fears aroused by the Nazi revolution in Germany grew during the summer of 1933 and hardened into a decision of the former Allied and Associated Powers that Germany would have to accept a probationary period of four years, during which the short-term militias would be organized and their supervision established, before the heavily armed powers began to disarm. This decision led to the final resignation of Germany from the conference on October 14, 1933, and from the League of Nations. From that moment rearmament, not disarmament, absorbed all energies.

[40] John T. Whitaker, *And Fear Came*, New York, 1936, p. 135.
[41] Wheeler-Bennett, *The Pipe Dream of Peace*, p. 109.

Too Late. The effort to disarm Europe had come too late. It had never been a practical proposal, unless the Anglo-Saxon Powers would assume some degree of responsibility for world order. "The American rejection of the Treaty of Versailles had resulted in the complete disorganization of the whole system of international peace and order founded upon the League of Nations." [42] Neither in 1932 nor in any other year was it possible for us to induce the *status-quo* powers to equalize their armies with the revisionist nations by pleading that arms were wasteful and dangerous. It was not a moral issue, but a matter of life and death to nations new and old, and of self-respect and future power to the disarmed peoples. The nations which had present military security were fully within their rights in asking something in exchange for it. "Effectively to promote disarmament in Europe, the United States had to join the League of Nations and subscribe to all the engagements of the Covenant." [43] If this course was not feasible, the definite implementation of the Kellogg Pact was an alternative. And if this treaty covered too much territory, the United States "had only to revive the Treaty of Guarantee which Wilson had given to Clemenceau." [44]

"Every student of disarmament knew," said one of the American newspaper correspondents on the scene, "that there could never be disarmament without security, and that there could never be security without a strong League of Nations, where every country, great or small, could be sure that the navies of the United States and Great Britain were not instruments of national policy, but the policemen of an organized world community." [45] As a leading British publicist put it: "Disarmament must be impracticable until international security against war has been provided by the renunciation of neutrality towards a war-

[42] Simonds, *Can America Stay at Home?* p. 226.

[43] Frank Simonds, *American Foreign Policy in the Post War Years*, Baltimore, 1935, p. 105.

[44] *Ibid.*, p. 107.

[45] Whitaker, *And Fear Came*, p. 127.

making state." [46] The responsible leaders of the American people knew that this was true, but they were never willing to tell the people so.

The price which we had to pay to get disarmament was not considered that seriously. The Hoover Administration attempted to regulate Europe from the outside. While Wilson had compromised with Europe to advance world organization and peace, Hoover would not, though compromise was essential. Instead, disarmament became a moral crusade in the United States. The people applauded the President's efforts to drive the blind Europeans to do what was best for them, and when the effort failed, there was great resentment and disillusionment. It appeared that the Europeans would not be saved. Yet the United States had been as stanch as any in defense of the weapons in which she believed and had regarded her armaments as of no significance to others, because her motives were wholly pacifist. It was not perceived by the American people that the French people were still more pacific than they. The education of the French in the terrors of war had been infinitely more thorough. It was not appreciated in the United States, either, that the Europeans had grounds for believing that President Hoover desperately needed a success in foreign affairs to bolster his political position at home, even as the fate of German and French leaders depended on the turn of events in the Disarmament Conference.

There was failure enough to give all the leaders their portion. The French, British, and German leaders deserved their share, along with the Americans. It was to the Hoover Administration's credit, also, that it had recognized that Normalcy had done nothing to forestall another armed crash as deadly to civilization as the economic crash which post-war American policy had promoted. Something had been gained in attempting to repair the damage by strenuous if irresponsible cooperation. But more was essential if the sequence of world catastrophes was to be interrupted. The ten crucial years which had been squandered could

[46] Henry Wickham Steed, *Vital Peace*, New York, 1936, p. 209.

not be regained. The ground lost could not be recovered by half-hearted efforts at the eleventh hour. Only a leadership that would call upon the American people to accept international responsibility commensurate with their wealth, their power, and their good intentions could halt the downward plunge of a new armaments race.

The League Repudiated by Roosevelt. The Hoover Administration could not decide to propose a course so risky politically. In defense of the Administration it is fair to remember that on the very day the Disarmament Conference first met, February 2, 1932, the League of Nations itself was repudiated by Franklin D. Roosevelt, the outstanding leader who was practically certain to receive the Democratic Presidential nomination. After having been hammered by the Hearst Press for some time, Roosevelt deserted the League outright, showing that he considered sponsoring it to be politically impossible. As events afterwards developed, it became clear that he would have been nominated and elected without so sweeping a renunciation and without the support of William Randolph Hearst, who was soon enough to desert him. But at the moment Roosevelt could not be certain and he chose to jettison the League in the following paragraphs:

> In common with millions of my fellow-countrymen, I worked and spoke, in 1920, in behalf of American participation in a League of Nations, conceived in the highest spirit of world friendship for the great object of preventing a return of world war. For that course I have no apology to make.
>
> If today I believed that the same or even similar factors entered into the argument, I would still favor America's entry into the League; and I would go so far as to seek to win over the overwhelming opposition which exists in this country today.
>
> But the League of Nations today is not the League conceived by Woodrow Wilson. It might have been had the United States joined. Too often, through these years, its major function has been not the broad overwhelming purpose of world peace, but rather a mere meeting place for the political discussion of strictly European political national difficulties. In these the United States should have no part.
>
> The fact remains that we did not join the League. The League

has not developed through these years along the course contemplated by its founder, nor have the principal members shown a disposition to divert the huge sums spent on armament into the channels of legitimate trade, balanced budgets and payment of obligations.

American participation in the League would not serve the highest purpose of the prevention of war and a settlement of international difficulties in accordance with fundamental American ideals. Because of these facts, therefore, I do not favor American participation.

What the world needs most today is a national policy which will make us an example of national honor to other nations."[47]

If the United States was to be nothing more in the world than a shining example of virtue, all hope of her being a positive influence in world affairs was gone. To say that the League developed into "a mere meeting place for the political discussion of strictly European political national difficulties" was only to state what one of its original and inevitable purposes had been. Europe was the center of Western civilization, and Europe would continue in that capacity, or plunge toward extinction according as it was or was not the center of new world wars. That our abstention had sharply accentuated the European character of the League was only too true, but to suggest that the League should have spent its time pondering "the broad overwhelming purpose of world peace," and "in the highest spirit of world friendship," was to indicate that Roosevelt was hopelessly Utopian, instead of being the eminently practical politician that he was.

His repeated enunciation of the word "political" in his disclaimer was a complete obeisance to the Harding myth that, while national politics were clean enough, all world politics were bad and dangerous. His insistence, developed at length later in his address, that the payment of the war debts should take precedence over national armaments also perpetuated the legend of Normalcy that international economic relations were on a higher plane than politics, on a level which politics could and should keep clear of. If the myths of the dying Republican era were still so powerful

[47] *New York Times*, February 3, 1932.

that an opposition Presidential candidate, who was certain to be backed by a tidal wave of domestic discontent, must do obeisance to them, it is not strange that the expiring Republican statesmanship did not have the courage to reverse altogether its derelict course.

The Many Dominated by Fear of the Few. After coming to power, the Roosevelt Administration did take soon an important forward step toward that lessening of the fear of conquest without which all disarmament is impossible. Shortly before this initiative was taken, widespread fear arose that in a much-advertised speech set for May 17, 1933, Chancellor Hitler would precipitate a European crisis. To forestall this danger, President Roosevelt himself sent, on May 16, a remarkable letter to the heads of more than fifty nations, in which he revealed with great clearness his awareness of the extent to which a very few nations were destroying the security of the many. Said Roosevelt: "If we ask what are the reasons for armaments, which, in spite of the lessons and tragedies of the world war, are today a greater burden on the peoples of the earth than ever before, it becomes clear that they are two-fold: first, the desire, disclosed or hidden, on the part of Governments to enlarge their territories at the expense of a sister nation. I believe that only a small minority of Governments or of peoples harbor such a purpose. Second, the fear of nations that they will be invaded. I believe that the overwhelming majority of peoples feel obliged to retain excessive armaments because they fear some act of aggression against them and not because they themselves seek to be aggressive." [48]

The Davis Declaration of May 24, 1933. Within ten days this pregnant description of the world's key problem was followed by a statement at Geneva which went far toward removing the United States from the position of promoting aggression by its aloofness. On May 24, 1933, Norman H. Davis, Ambassador-at-Large in both the Hoover and Roosevelt Administrations, stated to the Disarmament Conference that:

[48] *New York Times,* May 17, 1933.

Underwood & Underwood

NORMAN H. DAVIS
Ambassador-at-Large

Boesch

STEPHEN G. PORTER
Opium Conference Delegate

Underwood & Underwood

HUGH WILSON
Minister to Switzerland

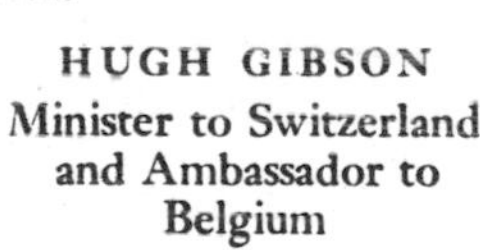

Boesch

HUGH GIBSON
Minister to Switzerland and Ambassador to Belgium

Underwood & Underwood

PRENTISS GILBERT
Consul at Geneva

PRINCIPAL NEGOTIATORS FOR THE UNITED STATES AT GENEVA

Recognizing that any breach or threat of breach of the Pact of Paris (the Briand-Kellogg Pact) is a matter of concern to all the signatories thereto, the Government of the United States of America declares that, in the event of a breach or threat of breach of this Pact, it will be prepared to confer with a view to the maintenance of peace in the event that consultation for such purpose is arranged pursuant to Articles . . . and . . . of Part I of the Disarmament Convention. In the event that a decision is taken by a conference of the Powers in consultation in determining the aggressor with which, on the basis of its independent judgment, the Government of the United States is agreed, the Government of the United States will undertake to refrain from any action and to withhold protection from its citizens if engaged in activities which would tend to defeat the collective effort which the States in consultation might have decided upon against the aggressor.[49]

This declaration was conditioned upon the creation of a disarmament treaty, and since none was concluded, it has no legal force. It is nevertheless a disavowal to which the American people can hardly avoid recurring in the future. The Davis statement promises nothing except consultation, which in every crisis is inevitable in some form, probably in some ineffective form as matters now stand. But the declaration does contain the all-important pledge not to aid aggression when it is committed. It does not go so far as to say we will help to suppress the aggressor, if we agree in identifying him, but it promises definitely not to take any positive action which would aid him and to withdraw protection from any of our private citizens who do.

This renunciation falls far short of assuming a full share in the repression of international lawlessness, but it removes from the many nations who live in fear of wars of conquest the paralyzing prospect of the world's most powerful nation's acting to protect its trade with all and sundry during any future outbreak. It is true enough that some British Conservatives have used the danger of an American challenge to a League blockade as a screen to cover their own desire to whittle away the League's

[49] IX Disarmament, 1933. IX. 10. pp. 495-96.

authority, and to cover their inclination to play power politics according to the ancient formulae.[50] It is a measure of the small courage and lack of faith of British statesmen, too, that they did not lead vigorously the many nations willing to follow them after our defection and trust that the sound sense of the American people would prevent the United States from delivering the final blow to the League when its first great test should come.

Yet the risk that we would continue to stand on the old concept of neutral rights, for which we fought Germany in 1917 and Britain in 1812, was such as to give British leaders excuse for retreating, especially when the violence of the American reaction in 1919 and the many subsequent evidences of small spirit are remembered. The Davis pledge was the indispensable step toward laying the specter of our taking retrogressive action and toward withdrawing us from alliance with those who would break the peace.

The statement of May 24, 1933, did not come into binding force, but it must become a guiding principle of our conduct toward peace-breakers and peace-defenders. For self-preservation against world wars and their frightful aftermaths, the American people cannot afford to stand in the way of any collective effort to restrain aggression. Surely this is the least that can be said. If we will not put our incomparable economic power decisively on the side of law and order, we must at least refrain from active aid to aggressors and from interfering with those who do resist them. A lesser role for the greatest nation on a rapidly shrinking planet cannot be seriously imagined.[51]

[50] See Steed, *Vital Peace*, pp. 310-11; Whitaker, *And Fear Came*, pp. 116, 260.

[51] "The Covenant, moreover, was written on the assumption that the United States would be a signatory. When Senator Lodge and his band of irreconcilable isolationists refused ratification of the Versailles Treaty, they torpedoed the Covenant almost beyond recovery. With the United States a League member, sanctions could absolutely outlaw and isolate an errant state. But American withdrawal from the League system made effective sanctions all but impossible, because America, by insisting on its neutral right of trading with an aggressor, could frustrate any League blockade. The British Navy, necessarily the chief instrument of a blockade, would not risk conflict with the United States." John Gunther, *Inside Europe*, New York, 1937, p. 395.

CHAPTER XIII

MANCHURIA

IT WAS the misfortune of the League that the first great test of its power to prevent aggression should come in the autumn of 1931, just after the world financial panic had swept across Europe, headed for the United States.

MANCHURIA

Another clash had been maturing in Manchuria for some time. The first modern struggle of interest to the outside world to occur in that vast land had been the Sino-Japanese War of 1894-95, the South Manchurian fruits of which had been taken from Japan by Russia, Germany, and France, only to be turned over to Russia by China. The Russo-Japanese War of 1904-1905 had thrust Russia back into Northern Manchuria and had left her properties in South Manchuria, notably the South Manchurian Railway, securely in Japanese hands. Thereafter, the Japanese regarded Manchuria as having been paid for by their blood and money.

They sought at once to secure a monopoly position for the South Manchurian Railway. After a conference with the Chinese at Peking in December, 1905, they continually alleged that the Chinese had promised not to build any "parallel lines" to the South Manchurian, or any branch lines which might injure it—a contention which the Chinese always denied. Eventually, the Lytton Commission established that this agreement was contained in the Sino-Japanese conference minutes of December 4, 1905, but not embodied in a formal treaty.[1] The understanding was definite enough, however, to enable the Japanese to keep other foreign capital out of Manchurian railway construction and to dominate

[1] The *Report* of the Lytton Commission which investigated for the League of Nations the Japanese conquest of Manchuria. C. 663. M. 320. 1932. VII. p. 44.

the economic life of South Manchuria by means of their own road, which engaged profitably in all sorts of business undertakings. It was also protected by 15,000 Japanese troops.

Japan's Position Undermined. After the Chinese Nationalists established themselves in the Yangtse Valley in 1927, and after the young Manchurian dictator had joined forces with them in 1928, the domination of the South Manchurian Railway was gradually undermined. Having discovered in 1929 that they could not eject Russia by force from North Manchuria, the Chinese concentrated on economic measures against the Japanese. Earlier they had accepted Japanese capital to finance several railroads which would feed the South Manchurian. Now they built new lines financed by Chinese capital and revenues. Between 1926 and 1931 some 800 miles of such lines were constructed, over Japanese protest, on both sides of the South Manchurian. By 1930, these roads were beginning to be joined effectively into a unified system which could throttle the South Manchurian and its port of Darien. A new Chinese harbor terminus at Hulutao was well under way. Pending its completion, rates were cut and traffic routed out through the port of Newchwang so successfully that the South Manchurian had to cut its rates more than 40 per cent and reduce its dividends for 1930-31 from 11 per cent to 8. Net profit fell more than 100 per cent, while the gross profit of the Chinese lines actually increased about 50 per cent from $21,613,489 to $32,256,543.[2]

Along with heavy development of other industries by Chinese capital the Chinese had found a way to destroy the monopoly of the Japanese in South Manchuria and probably to make their position untenable. Perhaps for this reason a railway conference in the spring of 1931 had no results, both sides having been responsible for postponements until hostilities began.[3] In 1915, at

[2] T. A. Bisson, "Railway Rivalries in Manchuria," *Foreign Policy Reports*, April 13, 1932, pp. 30-41. See also the Lytton *Report*, pp. 42-49.

[3] The experts attached to the Lytton Commission came to this conclusion after probing repeatedly the reasons for the failure of the conference. See the *Supplementary Documents* to the Lytton *Report*, C. 663. M. 320. 1932. VII. Annexes, pp. 42-45.

the most critical point in the World War, Japan had compelled China, without any *quid pro quo*, to renew the leases by which she held the South Manchurian, the Kwangtung Peninsula, and other properties, extending the leases from expiration dates, which were but a few years off, ninety-nine years. Rights to lease land and to do business in the interior of Manchuria were also extracted as a part of the the famous Fifteen Demands. Now Chinese nationalism was finding ways to nullify all of these "rights."

Militarist-Capitalist Rivalry in Japan. At the same time a struggle developed in Japan between the capitalists, who had increasingly controlled the government through the parties after 1925, and a military party which was rising from the ranks of the poorer classes. The militarists attacked the party system, advocated state socialism, and assailed especially the conciliatory policies of the Foreign Minister, Baron Shidehara. A coup in Manchuria would enable the militarists to dominate the government through the aroused patriotic fervor of the people, whereas the continuance of party government was likely to relegate the army permanently to the role which it occupies in democratic nations.[4]

"Incidents" Stir Feeling. A succession of incidents served to arouse the Japanese army and people. Japanese police backed a group of Koreans in enforcing a questionable land lease at Waupaoshan, which involved the damming of a river, the inundation of much land, and the cutting of an irrigation ditch for several miles through many Chinese farms. When this project was resisted, though without casualties, exaggerated reports were spread throughout Korea with such effect that a massacre of Chinese began on July 3, during which 127 Chinese were killed, 393 wounded, and large amounts of property destroyed. The riots lasted three days and aroused such indignation in China that a strong anti-Japanese trade boycott spread rapidly.[5] A Japanese, Captain Nakamura, was also killed in North Manchuria, June 27,

[4] T. A. Bisson, "The Trend toward Dictatorship in Japan," *Foreign Policy Reports*, February 13, 1935, pp. 318-28.

[5] Lytton *Report*, pp. 61-63.

1931, while traveling as an agricultural expert, and his murder was used as a means of crystallizing Japanese feeling in favor of forcible action in Manchuria.

September 18. Frequent night maneuvers of the Japanese army accustomed the people of Mukden to night firing and put the Japanese troops in position to seize the capital of Manchuria and other cities on the night of September 18, 1931. As justification it was alleged that some Chinese soldiers had tried to blow up the track of the South Manchurian Railway north of Mukden. A section of one rail, thirty-one inches long, was said to have been dislodged, though a fast train passed over the spot a few minutes later without mishap. A large nearby barracks of the Manchurian army was, however, attacked at once and by morning Mukden, Changchun, and other cities were in Japanese hands.[6]

When the "incident" of September 18 initiated far-reaching events in Manchuria, the Assembly of the League of Nations was in session. It had just elected China to the Council, which met September 19 to hear its Japanese member give a brief report of the outbreak. Mr. Yoshizawa said that he spoke by request of the Council's President, Señor Lerroux of Spain, and reported that "the Japanese Government had taken all the measures possible to prevent this local incident from leading to undesirable complications." Since up to this time, the Japanese Government had been a helpful and exemplary member of the League, there was no cause for especial alarm, until it became clear that a wide occupation had occurred and was spreading.

Article 11 Invoked. On September 21, Dr. Sze formally invoked Article 11 of the Covenant in China's behalf.[7] In the

[6] Lytton *Report*, p. 71. The Commission was unconvinced that any attacks upon the railroad ever occurred. Ben Dorfman, who was in Mukden at the time, compared notes with a number of responsible foreigners who had investigated the incident without finding anyone who believed that the alleged attack had happened. See his article, "The Manchurian Incident of 1931," *Harper's Magazine*, September, 1934, Vol. 169, pp. 449-62.

[7] By far the most exhaustive account of the Manchurian crisis is to be found in W. W. Willoughby *The Sino-Japanese Controversy and the League of*

Council on September 22 Yoshizawa maintained that the Japanese troops had acted in a defensive manner, that the incident was a local one, and that his Government had issued a formal order to its troops to take the necessary steps to prevent the trouble from spreading. He also warned that: "Premature intervention in the circumstances would only have the deplorable result of needlessly exciting Japanese public opinion." The issues should be settled by direct negotiation between Japan and China, a proposal which Sze indignantly rejected, but which Lord Cecil supported for Great Britain. China urged instead the appointment of an impartial committee of inquiry, according to well-tested League procedure.

By this time the foreign offices had begun to give credence to an apparent cleavage in the Japanese Government and to believe that the civilians wanted to restrain the outburst of the military. The Japanese diplomats seemed surprised and sincerely anxious to quell the disturbance.[8] There was some disposition throughout the critical period to moderate the action of the League for fear of weakening the Japanese Cabinet. The British argued also that there must be time to concert action with the United States. Probably their opposition to sending a commission to Manchuria was decisive. Nevertheless, many on the Council favored the same kind of quick inquiry which had settled the Greco-Bulgarian dispute of 1925, and it was so strongly urged upon the Japanese that they weakened in their opposition.

Washington Opposes a Commission of Inquiry. Then on September 23 the Japanese suddenly stiffened, saying that they had received word from their Washington Ambassador that Secretary

Nations, Baltimore, 1936. This immense volume contains a vast amount of source material. It has been used extensively throughout the following account.

Article 11 was appealed to because the Council preferred it and had well-established procedure for working under it. China was assured that Japan's vote would be required for any action under Article 10. She did not wish to give Japan full belligerent rights by invoking Article 16 and avoided Article 15 because it calls for report only and, if the report is not unanimous, frees the members of the League to "take such action as they shall consider necessary" (pp. 36-46).

[8] The writer heard Lord Cecil say a year later that he did not doubt the sincerity of the Japanese in Geneva when they maintained at this stage that they were trying to handle the outbreak and believed they could succeed.

Stimson, in discussing the situation with him, "had opposed the commission and criticized the Council's tactics." That evening Minister Hugh Wilson confirmed the report after a telephone conversation with Secretary Stimson. The State Department was unwilling either to approve a commission of inquiry or to agree that the Kellogg Pact had been violated.[9] Ambassador Debuchi had convinced Stimson that any pressure would only weaken the civilians in the Japanese Cabinet.[10]

For his decision Stimson was warmly commended by the London *Times* of September 26. In Geneva the event was regarded as a catastrophe. Its effect was described by Clarence K. Streit, Geneva correspondent of the *New York Times* as follows:

> No one on the inside is likely ever to forget the deep gloom and bitter disillusionment that overwhelmed League officials then, while the Japanese grew arrogant. Apparently frantic messages that night convinced Washington it must try to undo the mistake, for Mr. Stimson rushed into print with a note expressing "whole-hearted" sympathy with League efforts. The American public, seeing only this note, never got the impression that Washington had faltered, but looking backward behind the scenes Geneva finds it came too late—irremediable psychological harm had already been done and the favorable moment had gone forever.[11]

A grave mistake had been made by the State Department, not because of any lack of good will but because of its lack of experience at Geneva. Had the State Department experienced close contact with the League in its consideration of previous disputes, it would have realized the crucial importance of swift, united action at the start, and especially of finding out at once and by impartial inquiry what the facts were. This, of course, was just the kind of experience from which the United States had carefully insulated itself for ten years. The abhorred "political" activity of the League had been shunned as if it were leprous.

[9] Russell M. Cooper, *American Consultation in World Affairs*, New York, 1934, pp. 200-201. Chapter 5 (pp. 192-284) is a thorough account of our own contact with the crisis.

[10] *New York Times*, September 26, 1931.

[11] *New York Times*, September 18, 1932.

Now when the United States earnestly wished to back up the League it did not know how to do so effectively.[12]

The American note of September 22 to Japan was even stronger than that of the President of the Council. The latter had addressed an urgent appeal to both parties to "refrain from any act which might aggravate the situation" and had asked for conferences to arrange for the withdrawal of troops. The State Department's note of the same date said plainly that "The actual situation is that an arm of the Japanese Government is in complete control of South Manchuria." After mentioning the Kellogg Pact and the Nine Power Treaty it observed that "It would seem that the responsibility for determining the course of events with regard to the liquidation of this situation rests largely upon Japan, for the simple reason that Japanese armed forces have seized and are exercising *de facto* control in South Manchuria." After suggesting that there be "no further application of force," the note ended by saying: "What has occurred has already shaken the confidence of the public with regard to the stability of conditions in Manchuria, and it is believed that the crystallization of a situation suggesting the necessity for an indefinite continuance of military occupation would further undermine that confidence."[13]

The Problem of Liaison. This American note and the shorter one of September 24 addressed to both belligerents but intended for Japan, were both doubtless designed to bolster the authority of Baron Shidehara and that of the League. The United States acted promptly and strongly, but the Japanese military leaders knew that the United States would not be able to concert strongly with the League to restrain them. If the United States and Russia, Japan's great neighbors, had been able to exert their full power

[12] In Secretary Stimson's words, "the effective influence of the Kellogg-Briand Pact" had only recently promoted "the emergence of the United States from the accentuated isolationism which had marked its attitude towards the League of Nations since the Great War." Henry L. Stimson, *The Far Eastern Crisis*, New York, 1936, p. 100.

[13] *Conditions in Manchuria*, Senate Document No. 65, 72d Congress, 1st Session, p. 5.

through the League, events in Manchuria would have taken a different course, but neither could do so.

The United States tried fitfully to maintain liaison. During the first days of the crisis, Minister Hugh Wilson was a frequent visitor to the office of the League's Secretary-General and he sat in the anteroom while the Council's Committee of Five (representing Britain, France, Germany, Italy, and Spain) wrestled with the dispute.[14] When, too, the Council unanimously agreed on September 22 to forward the documents in the case to the United States, the American Government promptly replied the next day with assurance of its "whole hearted sympathy with the attitude of the League of Nations." [15]

Japanese Assurances Accepted in September 30 Resolution. On September 25, Yoshizawa read to the Council parts of an official statement issued by his government the day before, after an extraordinary Cabinet meeting, in which the dire peril of the Japanese troops on the night of September 18 was portrayed. After the troops had protected themselves "our soldiers were mostly withdrawn within the railway zone." There still remained "some detachments in Mukden and Kirin and a small number of men in a few other places. But nowhere does a state of military occupation as such exist." The Cabinet evidently felt that additional explanation was needed for the occupation of Kirin, some seventy-five miles west of the northern end of the South Manchurian Railway. This far-flung operation was described as "not with a view to military occupation" but only for the purpose of removing "the menace" to the South Manchurian Railway "on flank." Furthermore, "as soon as that object has been attained the bulk of our detachment will be withdrawn."

It was not too reassuring that the Japanese troops could strike out a long distance from their railway at any supposed "menace . . . on flank" and leave a detachment. However, the Japanese

[14] C. A. Berdahl, "Relations of the United States with the Council of the League of Nations," *American Political Science Review*, June, 1932, Vol. 26, p. 504.

[15] Senate Document No. 55, 72d Congress, 1st Session, pp. 4-5.

Cabinet thought it "superfluous to repeat that the Japanese Government harbors no territorial designs in Manchuria," [16] an assurance which was reiterated by Yoshizawa at the fifth meeting of the Council on September 28.

Two days later the Council decided to put these protestations on record and to trust the Japanese Government to carry them out. Its resolution of September 30 noted that the Japanese Government would "continue, as rapidly as possible, the withdrawal of its troops, which has already been begun, into the railway zone in proportion as the safety of the lives and property of Japanese nationals is effectively assured" and adjourned to October 14, 1931.[17]

"Pressure and Authority" Urged by the United States. This action of the Council was heartily approved by the American Government in a note of October 5 to the Council which strongly urged the League to stand by its guns. The note said: "It is most desirable that the League in no way relax its vigilance and in no way fail to assert all the pressure and authority within its competence toward regulating the action of China and Japan in the premises." On its part the American Government acting through its diplomatic representatives would "endeavor to enforce what the League does." It would remind the disputants of the Kellogg Pact and the Nine Power Treaty, "when it should seem advisable." By this course we would "avoid any danger of embarrassing the League in the course to which it is now committed." [18] By this course, also, the American Government, uncommitted to joint action of any kind, would annoy the Japanese without deterring them.

It was only three days later, October 8, that Yoshizawa sent a letter to the Council complaining that anti-Japanese feeling had developed in all parts of China, though it did not allege that any Japanese had been killed. Far from giving the Chinese credit for

[16] *Ibid.*, pp. 8-9.
[17] *Official Journal*, December, 1931, p. 2307.
[18] Senate Document No. 55, 72d Congress, 1st Session, p. 14.

normal human reactions, it alleged that the "anti-Japanese movement in China is conducted as an instrument of national policy under direction of the Nationalist Party," the party in control of the Nanking Government.[19]

Chinchow Bombing Protested. The Chinese had more tangible charges to add to the record. On October 3, Japanese airplanes had bombed the city of Tungliao, 100 miles east of their railway, and on October 9, they bombed the city of Chinchow, far down the non-Japanese railway to Peiping, after dropping leaflets denouncing Marshal Chang Hsueh-liang and announcing that all Manchuria was under the rule of Japanese troops. It was plainly indicated that the Japanese army intended to drive the Manchurian Government, which had retreated to Chinchow, entirely out of Manchuria. About the same time, also, the general staff in Tokyo announced that the banditry and the atrocities committed by the defeated Chinese troops in Manchuria made it impossible to withdraw the Japanese army to their original stations or even to contiguous territory.[20]

On receipt of the news from Chinchow, the President of the Council sent an appeal to both parties "to refrain from any action which would aggravate the situation" and called the Council to meet October 13. On October 11, Secretary Stimson notified the Japanese Foreign Minister that he could not "understand how the bombing of Chinchow can be minimized or how it [could] be said to be of no importance." The explanation given by the Japanese military authorities seemed "quite inadequate." Bombing an unfortified, unwarned town was "one of the most extreme of military actions, deprecated even in war time." It was "quite at variance" with the commitments undertaken by the Japanese Government in respect to the Council's resolution of September 30.[21]

[19] Willoughby, *The Sino-Japanese Controversy*, pp. 76-78. To this charge the Chinese replied, citing their Government's decree imposing the strictest discipline on all Chinese, an order which had been universally obeyed. The Chinese felt it should be "a matter of surprise to the world that popular indignation in China has limited itself to the mere refusal to purchase Japanese goods."

[20] Senate Document No. 55, 72d Congress, 1st Session, p. 14.

[21] *Ibid.*, p. 17.

On October 12, the reply of the Japanese Government to the telegram from the President of the Council could explain the bombing of Chinchow only by "the atmosphere of over-excitement" and the necessity of taking "meticulous measures of precaution." In the Council, on October 13, Yoshizawa alluded repeatedly to certain "fundamental points" which would have to be settled, but the early part of the October session of the Council was used up in an effort to coordinate the forces of the League and the United States in order to deal with the grave crisis which had evidently developed. As early as September 24, Consul Prentiss Gilbert had been authorized by Secretary Stimson to sit with the Council in a consultative capacity. On the same day Yoshizawa objected to the presence of an American observer, unless it was understood that a new rule was being established for all future emergencies.[22] This was a condition to which the United States could neither agree readily nor object in principle.

The United States at the Council's Table. During October 15 and 16 Japan pressed her objections in secret meetings of the Committee of Five and of the Council. Five questions were addressed formally to M. Briand, who had been advanced to the Presidency of the Council in the hope that his great skill and experience might be of avail. The Japanese questions inquired whether the interest of a non-member sitting with the Council ought not to be established, and whether the invitation to him did not require unanimous consent.[23] The President replied that it was a question of procedure which could be decided by majority vote, reminding Yoshizawa that it had been agreed at the outset that the United States should be kept informed. This decision was adhered to by the Council, on the evening of October 15, over the protest and vote of Japan. While compelled to object on legal grounds, what she feared, of course, was the political effect of a united front of the powers opposed to her course. Yet her

[22] Felix Morley, *The Society of Nations,* Washington, 1932, p. 447. Morley's Chapters 12 and 14 tell the story of the Manchurian case before both the Council and the Assembly.

[23] *Official Journal,* 1931, p. 2323.

strenuous legal objections were well founded and were necessarily reflected somewhat in the Council's invitation to the United States and in our acceptance. Mr. Gilbert was invited to sit "at" the Council table and was instructed by the Department of State to participate in its discussions only "when they relate to the possible application of the Kellogg-Briand Pact." [24]

In practice, Gilbert only listened to the four meetings of the Council which he attended, speaking only twice, and then to acknowledge courteous references to himself. He was there, it soon developed, only to secure the invocation of the Kellogg Pact. The Pact was "invoked" by six of the leading governments represented on the Council in separate notes sent to the two parties on October 17. This time the United States followed suit three days later. Then having invoked a treaty which had no enforcement machinery behind it, the United States relapsed into inactivity.[25]

The Resolution of October 24 Demands Withdrawal. The October session of the Council centered upon an effort to fix a date for the withdrawal of the Japanese troops to the South Man-

[24] Senate Document No. 55, 72d Congress, 1st Session, p. 18. The debate in the Council over the invitation to the United States was long and tense. Yoshizawa suggested by implication that if Russia asked to sit at the Council table it would be awkward to refuse. He asked that the question be referred to a committee of jurists but repeatedly refused to say that he would accept its decision, if one were constituted.

[25] While the majority of the newspapers supported the sending of Gilbert to the Council, Secretary Stimson was belabored heavily by the Hearst press, by the Curtis newspapers in Philadelphia (*Public Ledger*) and New York (*Post*), and by the papers owned by the McCormick family in Chicago (*Tribune*) and the McLean family in Washington (*Post*). The *New York Sun* and the *Hartford Courant* joined in the criticism, the *New York Telegram* and *Brooklyn Eagle* also raising some questions at the start.

Newspapers which supported Stimson were: *New York Times*, *New York Herald Tribune*, *Detroit Free Press*, *Boston Herald*, *Philadelphia Enquirer*, *Baltimore Sun*, *Cleveland Plain Dealer*, *St. Paul Pioneer Press*, *Portland Oregonian*, *San Francisco Chronicle*, *Los Angeles Times*, *Dallas News*, *St. Louis Post-Dispatch*, *Pittsburgh Post*, *Richmond News*, *Richmond Times*, *Raleigh News*, *Worcester Telegram* and *Chicago Daily News*. A survey of newspapers in the Middle West showed 202 favoring and 28 opposing American participation in the Council. The majority of the papers surveyed by the *Literary Digest* also favored the policy. See "The League and Manchuria, Second Phase," *Geneva Special Studies*, October, 1931, Vol. II, No. 11, pp. 40, 42, 43, 46, 54, 59; *Literary Digest*, October 24, 1931, p. 6.

churian Railway zone. On this point no agreement could be reached. Yoshizawa maintained that the withdrawal had already begun and that the Japanese Government had a "firm intention to bring them back." There was "no question of our attempting to wrest concessions or privileges from China," but it was "not possible to fix a definite date by which the last men will be brought back." When comparatively weak drafts providing for withdrawal were rejected by Japan, the Council at length stiffened and voted in its resolution of October 24 to call "upon the Japanese Government to begin immediately and to proceed progressively with the withdrawal of its troops into the railway zone, so that the total withdrawal may be effected before the date fixed for the next meeting," which was November 16.[26] The resolution carried by a vote of 13 to 1, but under Article 11 the negative of Japan prevented it from having any legal effect.

Fundamental Points Raised by Japan. During the debates preceding the vote, on October 23 and 24, the question of Japan's fundamental points figured largely. Both Lord Cecil and M. Briand asked directly what they were. How could the Council agree that they should be first disposed of without knowing what they were? Aside from referring to the safety of Japanese lives and property Yoshizawa could give no reply, even after the President had repeatedly urged a definition. It was not until October 26, two days after the Council adjourned, that the Japanese Government transmitted a statement of its fundamental points. They were prefaced by renewed statements that "the whole Manchurian affair was occasioned solely by violent and provocative attack launched by the Chinese Army on the railway zone." Certain "small contingents" still outside the zone were "urgently needed" and their withdrawal "would create an intolerable situation." Nothing was "further from the thoughts of Japan than to

[26] Willoughby, *The Sino-Japanese Controversy*, pp. 114, 116, 122. Other points in the resolution recalled the previous promises of Japan to withdraw her troops as rapidly as possible, not to aggravate the situation, and to respect the territorial integrity of China. China was called upon to assume responsibility for the safety of the lives and property of Japanese nationals.

bring armed pressure to bear upon China in these negotiations." It was even alleged that "the presence of such a limited number of troops is quite incapable of being represented as a means of dictating to China Japan's terms for the settlement of the present difficulties."

With this introduction, Japan's fundamental points were stated as follows:

(1) Mutual repudiation of aggressive policy and conduct.
(2) Respect for China's territorial integrity.
(3) Complete suppression of all organized movements interfering with freedom of trade and stirring up international hatred.
(4) Effective protection throughout Manchuria of all peaceful pursuits undertaken by Japanese subjects.
(5) Respect for treaty rights of Japan in Manchuria.[27]

In reply, Briand endeavored to show that these points were already covered by the resolution of September 20 and by specific assurances just received from China, which he quoted. Japan, however, replied on November 7, refusing to accept this solution and announcing "regretfully" that she was unable to withdraw her troops.

Two days earlier, on November 5, the American Government delivered a note to Japan urging: "First, the peaceful solution of the present unfortunate situation in Manchuria, and, second, a solution through direct negotiation of the various matters at issue between Japan and China." Our Government had "noted with regret and concern" that at the recent meeting of the Council Japan had insisted that the broader matters be settled before she withdrew her troops. It was confidently hoped that both Japan and China would be guided by the spirit of the two resolutions of the Council.[28]

[27] *Official Journal*, December, 1931, p. 2514.

[28] Senate Document No. 55, 72d Congress, 1st Session, pp. 30-32. In its rejoinder of November 9, the Japanese Government had "no intention of insisting on the final adjustment of the whole series of their controversies with China as a condition precedent." Yet the withdrawal of troops could not take place. If the Chinese troops came back, "violent hostile agitation against Japan under the auspices, overt or covert, of the Chinese authorities would be set to

North Manchuria Invaded. At the moment this note was delivered, the Japanese troops were extending their sway into Northern Manchuria. In a fight between two Chinese forces, the Nonni River bridge on one of the railways financed by Japanese capital was destroyed. The line being important strategically and economically and the Japanese funds invested in it in default, Japanese troops advanced to repair the bridge and engaged in a three-day battle with the troops of General Ma Chan-Shan, November 4 to 6, 1931. This engagement led Briand to address another appeal to the two parties. Simultaneously, China reported that the salt revenues were being seized and turned over to puppet governing bodies and that $2,600,000 belonging to two Chinese banks had been removed forcibly from a bank in Changchun.

The situation which confronted the Council when it met on November 16 was thus much worse than when it adjourned in October. Far from withdrawing her troops, Japan had extended their occupation and was rapidly destroying the last vestiges of Chinese administration. What would the Council and the United States do? The latter had cooled markedly since October 5 when it had urged the League "to assert all the pressure and authority within its competence." Our representatives had sat "at" the Council but had remained silent even when the Council voted, on October 24, to demand Japanese evacuation before November 16. Here was courageous action, but the American Government disapproved of it as too likely to make Japan still more intransigent. It was two weeks before the United States sent its supporting note of November 5, and when the Council met in Paris, on November 16, no American appeared to sit with it.

Dawes in Paris. The American Ambassador to Great Britain, General Charles G. Dawes, was ordered to go to Paris. While he had authority to sit with the Council, Secretary Stimson announced to the press, on November 11, that it was not anticipated

work in Manchuria as in other parts of China." From this it appeared that Japan could not permit the restoration of Chinese authority in Manchuria. Nevertheless, it was solemnly stated that "Japan cannot justly be accused of any intention of exerting military pressure on China" (pp. 36-38).

that he would find it necessary to do so. The sending of a man of Dawes's rank would have been reassuring to the Council had it not developed that he would not be supported by either Hugh Wilson or Prentiss Gilbert, the Americans who knew most about the League and about the controversy. Everything was left to Dawes's discretion, perhaps in order to reassure the Senate. But Dawes was so discreet that his cooperation was abortive. Installed in the Hotel Ritz across the river Seine from the Quai d'Orsay where the Council met, Dawes set up what was in effect a rival league of his own. Safe in his hotel, he conferred with Briand and Sir John Simon and, after much persuasion, with Madariaga of Spain, but he eschewed the other members of the Council and that "town meeting" itself. While the Council sought to make the Covenant effective, Dawes held court in the interest of the Pact. Matsudira of Japan and Sze of China were frequently called before him and toward the end of nearly a month of discussion on both banks of the Seine, Dawes thought he had about ironed out the differences between them. He therefore proposed to attend the final meeting of the Council and make a speech. This news was received with considerable consternation by the Council, but a chair was made ready for him. As the Council assembled word came that the General would not come after all. He had been in conversation with Secretary Stimson, who thought that the speech had better be omitted, though apparently he did not mean that Dawes should not attend the final session.[29]

[29] C. A. Berdahl, "Relations of the United States with the Council of the League of Nations," *American Political Science Review*, June, 1932, Vol. 26, pp. 515-16; Cooper, *American Consultation in World Affairs*, pp. 221-31; *The League of Nations in Review*, December 1, 1931, Vol. 4, p. 2; *New York Times*, November 12, 13, 15, 16 and 18, 1931. One result of this labored method of collaboration was that rumors of a deal between the United States and Japan arose, which compelled Secretary Stimson to issue strong denials on November 18 and led Dawes to issue a clarifying statement in Paris a day later, in which he explained how inappropriate and embarrassing his attendance at the Council would be. See Department of State, *Press Release*, November 18 and 20, 1931.

The conclusion of the *New York Herald Tribune's* representative in Geneva is that when it was vital for us to impress the Japanese, British, and French representatives with the feeling that we were determined to see China through, General Dawes gave "exactly the opposite impression." John T. Whitaker, *And Fear Came*, New York, 1936, p. 113.

The situation which confronted the Council at Paris was aggravated on November 18 by notice from Japan that her army was taking "purely defensive" action "aimed at striking a decisive blow against the Ma Chan-Shan army." When this objective was achieved, the Japanese forces "would not remain in these districts, but will retire as soon as possible to the south." The next day the Japanese pressed on across the Chinese Eastern Railway zone and occupied Tsitihar, the capital of Heilungkiang province.

The Capture of Chinchow Postponed. A week later, on November 25, an urgent message from China reported that Japanese forces were advancing upon Chinchow and appealed for the establishment of a neutral zone between the Japanese and Chinese forces. This led the President of the Council to notify both parties that it was for them "to give the commanders of their respective forces the strictest orders to refrain from any action which might lead to further engagements." China quickly agreed, but Japan replied on November 27 alleging "the serious threat to our troops constituted by the presence of very large Chinese regular forces in the Chinchow district and by the employment of bands of brigands and soldiers in civilian clothes by the Chinese authorities for the purpose of disturbing order in Manchuria." If China would withdraw her forces south of the Great Wall the Japanese forces would not occupy the zone evacuated, "except in the event of a serious and urgent threat endangering the safety of the lives and property of Japanese nationals in North China and the safety of the Japanese troops stationed there." It thus appeared that the Japanese troops could not be safe so long as any Chinese forces remained in Manchuria and that probably the Japanese forces in North China proper would also soon become insecure. The Powers were so nervous, too, that they urged the Chinese repre-

Secretary Stimson's retrospect upon the phase which was closed by this Paris session was that mankind cannot be expected to use new international machinery skillfully on the first occasion, that the first real cooperation between the United States and the League could hardly be effective, that sanctions could not succeed without us, and that all of the governments went as far as their publics would support them. Stimson, *The Far Eastern Crisis*, pp. 83-84.

sentative in Geneva to accept the one-sided Japanese terms. On November 26, however, Briand notified the two parties that the Governments represented on the Council who could do so proposed to send observers to the Chinchow area instructed to try to establish a neutral zone between the Chinese and Japanese forces.

This *démarche* was supported by a telegram to Baron Shidehara from Secretary Stimson, on November 27, which observed that: "Inasmuch as according to Mr. Yoshizawa's statement to M. Briand there are only some 20,000 Chinese troops in the Chinchow district and north of the Great Wall, and inasmuch as Chinchow is substantially 120 miles by rail from the South Manchurian Railway at Mukden, I am quite unable to see how there can be any serious danger to that railway or any serious danger of a clash between Chinese and Japanese troops unless the latter troops should fail to observe the orders which your excellency assured me had been given."

"Third Parties" Excluded. To the Council's proposal of neutral observers Japan replied by brusquely refusing to tolerate "the interposition of third parties." It was a Japanese policy not to permit such interposition "in disputes capable of direct settlement with China." Replying, Briand maintained that exceptional measures were necessary to cope with a dangerous situation. On November 28 the movement toward Chinchow was stopped and the Japanese troops called back to wait until the Council had adjourned. When it disbanded on December 10, after providing for the Lytton Commission of Inquiry to examine the entire Manchurian situation, the Japanese representative ominously reserved the right to take "such action as may be necessary to provide directly for the protection of the lives and property of Japanese subjects against the activities of bandits and lawless elements rampant in various parts of Manchuria." [30]

[30] Willoughby, *The Sino-Japanese Controversy*, pp. 162-71. The Chinese reply to the charge of banditry was that the destruction of the normal government was bound to give rein to certain lawless elements and that it was not fair to term every opponent of Japanese rule a bandit. They alleged also that the

A Commission of Inquiry Accepted on December 10. The proposal to send a commission of inquiry to the Far East was made by Japan at the eighteenth meeting of the Council on November 21. The Japanese representative thought that it would help to give a clear view of the "realities," both "in Manchuria and in China itself." Was there a suggestion here that the commission would find that China was not a state? That was soon to become a major contention on the part of the Japanese. There may have been some hope, too, that the commission could be induced to approve the Japanese occupation of Manchuria. In any event, while the commission investigated, the Japanese grip on Manchuria would be consolidated, whatever the commission reported. The commission was forbidden by the terms of the resolution of December 10 to "interfere with the military arrangements of either party," or to have anything to do with negotiations between the two parties. Aside from these prohibitions, the commission's terms of reference were very wide.

The resolution was a severe disappointment to China because it dropped all effort to set a limit to Japan's occupation. It aroused grave misgivings also among the small nations. Several of their representatives stressed at the time of adoption that it was not to be taken as a precedent. Matos, of Guatemala, declared it to be inadvisable "that the respect for and execution of treaties between countries can depend on the will of one of the parties." The representative of Peru denied any right of a state to effect the military occupation of another state in order to collect debts or to enforce economic claims. Garay, of Panama, underlined the same thesis. Briand stressed that it was "essential that no further incidents of any kind should take place," not even at Chinchow.

Chinchow Taken. The Council had not been adjourned two weeks before Japan's troops were again moving on Chinchow.

Japanese zones in Manchuria had served as a refuge for criminals and as a channel for the arming of bandits from Japan. See Harry Hussen, *Manchuquo, Things Not Told in the Lytton Report*, a small book published at Port Dover, Ontario, by an assistant of Wellington Koo. The Japanese counter case is enumerated in detail in *China's Challenge in Manchuria* by Takeo Itoh, published by the South Manchurian Railway.

Both France and Great Britain protested, and on December 24 Secretary Stimson sent a strong note to Tokyo saying that the military observers of several nations on the spot saw no evidence of any offensive intent on the part of the Chinese at Chinchow. In its reply of December 27 the Japanese Government again alleged the danger of bandits. On January 3, Chinchow was occupied and Marshal Chang's forces and government driven out of Manchuria.

The Stimson Doctrine of Non-Recognition Enunciated January 7. Since no remonstrances or promises did more than delay a little Japan's onward sweep, the American Government determined to voice emphatically its opposition to her conquest. On January 7, 1932, both China and Japan were notified that the American Government

> can not admit the legality of any situation *de facto* nor does it intend to recognize any treaty or agreement entered into between those governments, or agents thereof, which may impair the treaty rights of the United States or its citizens in China, including those which relate to the sovereignty, the independence, or the territorial and administrative integrity of the Republic of China, or to the international policy relative to China, commonly known as the open-door policy; and that it does not intend to recognize any situation, treaty, or agreement which may be brought about by means contrary to the covenants and obligations of the pact of Paris of August 27, 1928, to which treaty both China and Japan, as well as the United States, are parties.[31]

The Japanese reply of January 16, 1932, opened with pretended gratification that the United States was doing everything in its power "to support Japan's efforts to secure the full and complete fulfillment in every detail" of the Washington Treaty and the Kellogg Pact, and the note closed in the same spirit. In between, the reply alleged that the changes in administrative personnel in Manchuria had been "the necessary act of the local

[31] Senate Document No. 55, 72d Congress, 1st Session, pp. 53-54. There was an important precedent for this step in the Wilson Administration. On May 11, 1915, Secretary Bryan had sent a note to the Japanese Government refusing in terms almost as positive to recognize the validity of changes in China's status which were threatened by Japan's Twenty-One Demands. *United States Foreign Relations*, 1915, p. 146.

population," due to the fact that the local officials "for the most part fled or resigned." This was strange conduct, for the note asserted that the Japanese occupation was not hostile and that Japan did not even have any intention of using improper means to gain a proper end.[32]

The "elegant irony" in Japan's reply was fortified by the cold reception which the British Government gave to the American Declaration. An official communiqué of January 11 not only refused to address a similar note to Japan but refrained from indorsing the principle of non-recognition of unlawful conquest. To make matters still worse the London *Times* published an editorial on the same day, in which it waved aside the apparent fear of the American Government "that the Japanese authorities would set up a virtually independent administration in Manchuria which would favor Japanese interests to the detriment of the commerce of other nations." After this large exhibition of calmness and of confidence in Japan's good intentions, the *Times* went so far as to observe: "Nor does it seem to be the immediate business of the Foreign Office to defend the 'administrative integrity' of China until that integrity is something more than an ideal. It did not exist in 1922 and it does not exist today."

This justification of Japan's course helped to embolden her soon to raise the claim that China was not a state, a position from which she never budged thereafter. Both London and Tokyo forsook the purpose avowed in the Nine Power Treaty to give China time to become a modern nation, and both ignored the undoubted progress toward unity which the Chinese were making, though that very progress had been one of the chief reasons for Japan's seizure of Manchuria.

By thus rebuffing the American lead, the British removed the last chance of restraining Japan. If the United States and the British Empire would not stand together in opposition to Japan's career of conquest, no other possible combination of powers could be expected to. The complacency of the "Old China Hands,"

[32] Senate Document No. 55, 72d Congress, 1st Session, pp. 53-55.

in the British Foreign Office, and elsewhere, encouraged the Japanese to plunge ahead until they suddenly delivered a great blow to British interests in Central China, where the British had a billion dollars invested and where they owned a large part of China's greatest city.

Shanghai

Before another month had passed, the Japanese had begun a four-week bombardment of the Chinese section of the great city of Shanghai, far to the south of Manchuria, all in the due exercise of the right of self defense. After four months of war in Manchuria, during which no Japanese citizens in China were killed, some Japanese monks were mobbed in Shanghai on January 18, 1932, and one later died. Strong demands aimed at the suppression of the anti-Japanese boycott movement followed. The boycott was so gravely injuring Japan that she decided to strike that weapon of passive resistance from China's hands, leaving her no choice between militarization or submission.

On January 21 Admiral Kiochi Shiozawa announced in the press that he was "determined to take the necessary steps," and a fleet of nineteen warships arrived in Shanghai, loaded with marines. Further threats culminated in an ultimatum on January 27, requiring compliance with the Japanese demands by 6:00 P.M. the next day. These demands were accepted in full early in the afternoon of the 28th and at 4:00 P.M. the Japanese consul informed the other consuls that the reply was entirely satisfactory.

At this same hour the British and American military contingents in the International Settlement moved out to take up their allotted positions in the defense sectors, in response to a decision of the Municipal Council, which had become alarmed by the many threats uttered by the Japanese against the 30,000 troops of the Chinese Nineteenth Route Army which were known to be quartered in the native Chapei district. There appears to have been an understanding among the foreigners that the Japanese were to extend their lines out into the native city, to include the Hongkew district where many Japanese resided. But the Japanese did not move out promptly, as did the other international forces at 4:00 P.M. They preferred to make another night maneuver, as they had done in Mukden and other Manchurian cities on September 18.

At 11:00 P.M. Admiral Shiozawa notified the Mayor of the Chinese city to withdraw all Chinese troops in a designated section of Chapei. The Mayor received the message at 11:15. At 11:45 the Japanese forces began to move. Shortly after 12:00 the Japanese clashed with the Chinese troops, who could not have withdrawn in the few minutes allowed them had they desired to do so. Stopped dead, Shiozawa proceeded before daylight to bomb the unarmed and helpless native city from the air, incendiary bombs being deliberately used in addition to high explosives. By morning a vast district was ablaze, thousands of innocent people were dead, hundreds of thousands were in flight, and something very like a pogrom was in progress in the Japanese part of the International Settlement.

Then for weeks Shanghai suffered as no great city had during the Great War. Some $300,000,000 worth of property was destroyed while the Japanese vainly tried to drive out the Nineteenth Route Army. It was not until a large army had been brought from Japan that the Chinese were compelled to retreat, in good order.[33]

China Appeals to Articles 10 and 15. The Shanghai tragedy led China at last to invoke Articles 10 and 15 of the Covenant on January 29. Japan opposed China's right to resort to these articles and a long debate extending through two sessions of the Council ensued before the members of the Council wore down the Japanese resistance with irrefutable arguments as to China's rights in the matter. At the Council's meeting of January 26 the Japanese representative, Mr. Sato, abandoned the pretense that the whole trouble had started on the night of September 18, 1931, and made a general defense of the Japanese occupation. It was the most

[33] Stimson, *The Far Eastern Crisis,* pp. 117-32.

reasonable explanation of Japan's course which had yet been made, closing with the usual assurance that "Japan harbours no territorial designs in Manchuria" and adding that she would "uphold the principles of the open door and equal opportunity as well as all existing treaties relating to that territory." [34]

The Great Powers Act Directly. Hardly ever before had world opinion been so strongly aroused by the acts of any nation as it was at the opening of February, 1932. Day by day instantaneous news service brought to the eyes and ears of men everywhere the sequence of horrors at Shanghai, superimposed as they were upon the events in Manchuria. Feeling that the slaughter should stop was strong. If world public opinion had within it any power to halt hostilities, now was the time for it to make its influence known. If the Kellogg Pact, which had staked everything on the power of public opinion, was not to be extinguished gradually on one battlefield after another, now was the time for it to be applied. But neither the Pact nor the Covenant sent any aid to Shanghai. Instead, both Great Britain and the United States, supported by France and Italy, resorted to direct diplomatic action, presenting a five-point peace program, two points of which, dealing with military preparations and neutral participation in peace negotiations, were promptly rejected by Japan—particularly with reference to Manchuria.[35]

[34] Willoughby, *The Sino-Japanese Controversy*, p. 216. Mr. Sato said: "Japan has rights in Manchuria derived from lawfully concluded treaties and agreements and many acquired interests. It is absolutely essential to her existence that her rights and interests should be respected, and that her nationals should be allowed to live and work in peace and safety in this territory. By their campaigns for the unilateral denunciation of treaties, by their anti-foreign agitation and by their systematic violation of undertakings solemnly entered into, the Chinese central authorities and the rulers of Manchuria, particularly Marshal Chang Hsuehliang, have attempted and are still attempting to destroy all the work of the Japanese in Manchuria. For years Japan has suffered and borne, with incredible patience, innumerable vexations and acts of provocation while by this very fact the arrogance of the Chinese authorities has increased."

To this Dr. Yen replied that China could enumerate hundreds of acts objectionable to China which the Japanese had performed.

[35] Although Sato had reverted in the Council on January 29 to the old thesis that "the dispute, if there is one, was originally caused by the destruction of our railway in Manchuria by Chinese soldiers," the Japanese Government was careful to stress in its statement of February 6, and at other times, that the

Britain Speaks for the United States at Geneva. While these events were transpiring, the British representative on the Council, J. H. Thomas, asked the Council to suspend action. It was for this purpose that the opening session of the World Disarmament Conference was postponed an hour while the Council met. At this meeting also Mr. Thomas spoke for the United States, assuring the Council that our Government took "entirely the same view of the situation." At subsequent meetings Sir John Simon continued to caution the Council not to interfere with the Shanghai negotiations. He even went to the length of trying to avert further steps in the Council by asserting, on February 12, that the negotiations were continuing after Hugh Wilson had notified Secretary-General Drummond that they had broken down completely. One effect of this British campaign, doubtless intended, was to make the Council itself reluctant to turn the dispute over to the Assembly within the time limit specified in Article 15. Finally, while the Japanese were preparing for a great offensive at Shanghai, the Council stood by and compelled China herself, at the Council meeting of February 19, to call the Assembly.[36] March 3 was set as the meeting date.

The Twelve Appeal to Japan. Meanwhile Harbin, the center of Russian interests in Manchuria and chief city on the Russian railway, had been occupied by Japanese troops. The American Atlantic fleet had been moved to the Pacific in January. The American and British Far Eastern squadrons had arrived in Shanghai with troops. Fleets of Japanese warships and transports were en route to Shanghai to augment the already large Japanese forces there. In this extremity the members of the Council, exclusive of the two parties, did what they could as individuals. The Twelve

Shanghai affair was not the result of the assault upon the Japanese monks but was due to the broad necessity of protecting Japanese nationals and property. Willoughby, *The Sino-Japanese Controversy*, p. 321.

It should be added that many European and American residents at Shanghai felt that the Japanese were defending all foreigners in China by teaching the Chinese a much-needed lesson.

36 See the excellent account in Cooper, *American Consultation in World Affairs*, pp. 242-47. The Chinese request was made on February 12, but Japanese objections delayed the call a week.

addressed a moving appeal to Japan alone on February 16, 1932, "to recognize the very special responsibilities for forbearance and restraint" which devolved upon her as a Permanent Member of the Council. The Twelve were "far from disregarding the grievances advanced by Japan" and throughout all these months "they had given her the full confidence due to a valued associate of long standing." They could not but regret, however, that Japan had not made full use of the methods for peaceful settlement provided in the Covenant and the Pact, while China had put herself unreservedly in the hands of the League. Japan was reminded of Article 10, and the Twelve added that "no infringement of the territorial integrity and no change in the political independence of any Member of the League brought about in disregard of this article ought to be valid and effectual." Japan had "an incalculable responsibility before the public opinion of the world to be just and restrained in her relations with China." The Twelve appealed to her high sense of honor to recognize the confidence which the nations had placed in her.

"*Manchouquo*" *Declares Independence.* The real reply to the plea of the Council members came two days later. On February 18 a "declaration of independence" was issued for Manchuria by a Japanese-sponsored government. On February 23 the Japanese Government addressed the Twelve, deprecating strongly "these regular and repeated *ex parte* discussions" by select committees, "of whatever composition," which the public was likely to confuse with the Council itself. Moreover, the appeal had been addressed to the wrong party. The Japanese Government could not "understand why an appeal of the twelve powers should be addressed to Japan." It was to "the Chinese as the attacking party" at Shanghai "to whom the appeal might be effectively made." Japan altogether repudiated the stigma "of favoring or desiring war." The reply was a very long one, indicating at least that the Twelve had made a dent in Japanese consciousness. It foreshadowed clearly Japan's later claim to be the arbiter of what occurs in East Asia and formally brought forward the Japanese claim that China had no right to protection by the Covenant, the Pact, or the Nine Power Treaty, because she was not an organized state. No authority in China controlled more than a local area, nor could it "have title" or "extend" its control beyond that local area.[37]

Were China and Japan Responsible States? This was close to saying that Japan would never permit China to become unified. When Japan stressed China's chaos before the Council, on February 19, Dr. Yen replied that Japan did not want to see China united and strong. He charged that year after year Japan had "subsidized and helped one party against the other" in China's civil wars. The enormous people of China was going through a revolutionary period such as every nation sometimes had. But what of Japan? "With her army and navy running amok and out of control of the Government," was she an organized state? After the Japanese earthquake in 1923, said Yen, his people were massacred in Tokyo and more than a hundred Chinese merchants had been killed in the recent pogrom in Korea. Was Japan herself a responsible state?[38]

Stimson's Review of the Treaties on February 23. Probably never before had a nation been under diplomatic pressure as severe as that Japan experienced in February and March, 1932. To the strictures of the Council had been added the appeal of the Twelve. On February 23, Secretary Stimson reviewed the whole basis underlying the Washington treaties, in a letter to Senator Borah. Stimson was driven to this expedient by the refusal of the British to take part in a joint invocation of the Nine Power Treaty. As the Japanese openly prepared for a still greater assault at Shanghai,

[37] Willoughby, *The Sino-Japanese Controversy*, pp. 238-46. In amplifying this charge before the Council on February 19, Japan's representative described "a condition of complete chaos and incredible anarchy" in China and avowed that: "Had such difficulties arisen in another country which had a properly organized and efficient administration, our action would have been different."

[38] He referred to the killings in Korea which followed the Waupaoshan affair described above. Harry Emerson Wildes states that the Tokyo riots following the earthquake were due to emotional rumors broadcast by Japanese police chiefs that ferocious Koreans were about to rise in rebellion. Wildes states that Japanese officials admitted that 500 Koreans were killed in this massacre. See Harry Emerson Wildes, *Japan in Crisis*, New York, 1934, pp. 247-48.

Stimson, at the suggestion of President Hoover, called Sir John Simon by transatlantic telephone on February 11, to hasten, if possible, a decision by the British. On the 12th Stimson telephoned again, cabling his proposed draft in the meantime, and on both the 13th and 15th he repeated his efforts. Four times within six days he talked personally with Sir John, without gaining either consent or refusal to an appeal to the Nine Power Treaty, a treaty of which Stimson has justly suggested that "no human language" could have been more explicitly applicable to the situation at Shanghai and in Manchuria.[39]

Since he was blocked by the continued determination of the British Foreign Office to stay close to Japan, it is to Stimson's credit that he searched for another method of protest until he found it. If the British would trust their commercial future in China to Japan, we could not fail to let the Chinese people know in unmistakable terms that we opposed the course Japan was pursuing. Many decades of American missionary effort had related thousands of our communities to the life and future of China. A large migration of Chinese students to our colleges had similarly given us many links with the coming China. Apart from the immense trade which we might have with a free and united China, it was elemental statesmanship that we should let the 450,000,000 Chinese know that we had not turned against them. The results of our failure to defend democracy by effective international action were beginning to come home to us in a degree that could no longer be ignored. It was not too soon, either, to begin to look forward to the results of a successful piecemeal conquest of all China by Japan. Having antagonized deeply the vast Chinese people, Japan might well find no course open except to keep smashing forward to prevent a powerful China from arising in any part of China's vast domain. Japan's course would promote Chinese unity as nothing else could and thus accelerate the need of Japan's militarists for further conquests.

[39] Stimson, *The Far Eastern Crisis*, pp. 159, 162-66. For the text of the Nine Power Treaty see Chapter V above.

In his letter to Senator Borah, the Secretary of State recalled that the "Open Door" had been invoked in 1899 to save China's future as well as to prevent dangerous rivalry over China. In 1922 this policy had been crystallized in the Nine Power Treaty, intended expressly to guarantee "the sovereignty, the independence and the territorial and administrative integrity of China." China was to have "the fullest and most unembarrassed opportunity" to develop a stable government. The treaty was made because it was known that many years would be required for China to achieve order and stability. China was "entitled to the time necessary to accomplish her development."

Furthermore, the Washington treaties were all tied together. "The willingness of the American Government to surrender its then commanding lead in battleship construction and to leave its positions at Guam and in the Philippines without further fortification was predicated upon, among other things, the self-denying covenants contained in the Nine Power Treaty." If that treaty was to be invalidated the premises upon which it was based would have to be reconsidered.[40]

Irregular Teamwork between Washington and Geneva. The State Department had been considerably disappointed by the slowness of the governments to endorse the Stimson declaration of January 7 refusing to recognize the fruits of conquest. This far-reaching declaration had struck the foreign offices almost without warning, and they had been slow to take it up. Downing Street had in fact moved contrariwise by announcing itself satisfied with Japan's pledge to respect the Open Door. Copies of the Stimson declaration had also been forwarded to the signatories of the Nine Power Treaty, without result. Efforts in the Council to endorse the Stimson lead had been sidetracked. The letter to Borah therefore openly invited concurrence again.[41] A few weeks later Mr. Stimson's perseverance was to be rewarded.

For the moment, the failure of the nations to rally to the

[40] *New York Times*, February 24, 1932.
[41] Cooper, *American Consultation in World Affairs*, pp. 236-38.

American lead probably had something to do with the State Department's discovery that it could not designate a member of the Consular Committee at Shanghai, set up by Sir Eric Drummond under Article 15 to report to him what was occurring there. Consul General Edwin S. Cunningham therefore collaborated closely "with" the other consuls at Shanghai, though he could not sit "in" with them. Mr. Cunningham's difficulties in keeping within the limits of "with," while avoiding the dangers of "in," delayed the first report of the Consular Committee and raised further doubts in Geneva as to the dependability of American co-operation. Then the scene changed, and when a League commission representing six nations was appointed in May to wind up the war in Shanghai, Cunningham was elected as chairman of this much more important body and headed it without any nice distinctions being made in Washington as to whether he was "on" the committee or merely "with" it.[42]

Throughout the seizure of Manchuria and the assault upon Shanghai it was impossible to preserve consistent teamwork between Washington and Geneva. When one led the other lagged. Both wanted the same thing, but each felt that it could not depend on the other. Washington regarded itself as a power co-ordinate with Geneva and acted accordingly. Yet, to be effective, action had to be truly collective and it had to be organized. Neither goal could be obtained. The United States was outside the League and could neither lead it successfully from the outside nor assume the responsibilities which rested on the members of the League. Repeatedly the voice of the United States was heard emphatically at the Council table, but always through the mouth of the British member of the Council. Thus on February 29, Minister Hugh Wilson sat in the diplomatic gallery while Sir John Simon voiced the willingness of the United States "to instruct its representatives in the Shanghai area to co-operate with us who are members of the League to the fullest measure in carrying out

[42] *Ibid.*, p. 254.

the proposals" for a truce at Shanghai.[43] Two days earlier Sir John had succored the Japanese by declaring in the House of Commons that "in no circumstance will this government authorize this country to be a party to this dispute." [44]

Japan Loses in Shanghai. By the end of February Japan had had enough of the conflict at Shanghai. The Japanese navy, which apparently had been anxious to duplicate the feats of the army, its rival for public esteem, had had more than enough. The resistance of the Chinese Nineteenth Route Army in Shanghai was so stubborn that the Japanese army was compelled to take command. Reinforcements had to be sent until a great fleet with air armadas and an army exceeding 70,000 men had been assembled at Shanghai. Even then the progress of Japan's mighty power was exceedingly slow. The Chinese were fighting, and all China was discovering that Japan was not invincible. The Chinese forces were eventually driven back far enough to enable Japan to claim a nominal victory, but it had been purchased at a heavy cost in money and in the prestige which is so valued in the Orient, with a casualty list approximating 3000 men, and at an appalling loss of international repute. Twelve members of the League Council had addressed to Japan an unprecedented appeal to her honor, Secretary Stimson had condemned her course unflinchingly in his letter to Senator Borah, and the League Assembly was meeting to voice the indignation of the great rank and file of the smaller and weaker nations. The war in Shanghai had served to distract attention somewhat from the Japanese absorption of Manchuria, but that was more than counterbalanced by the support for the

[43] *Ibid.*, p. 249. This instance of British representation of the United States was the more remarkable since Sir John Simon had pretended to the Council on February 12 that progress was being made in the Shanghai negotiations, whereas Mr. Wilson had officially informed the Secretary-General that they had completely broken down. See C. A. Berdahl, "Relations of the United States with the Council of the League of Nations," *American Political Science Review*, June, 1932, Vol. 26, p. 523.

[44] *New York Herald Tribune*, February 28, 1933. On February 24, Winston Churchill declared that: "We do not want to throw away our old valued friendship with Japan." He saw China as "a strange combination of anarchy and communism" and thought it to everybody's interest that Japan should establish order in North China. *New York Times*, February 25, 1933.

American policy of non-recognition of the Manchurian conquest which the Shanghai holocaust aroused. On all counts the Japanese military mind had blundered into disaster at Shanghai. Even if the Chinese boycott of Japanese goods and services could be smashed temporarily by cannon and bombers the legacy for the future was terrifying.

The Great Powers Also Fail. Among others who had lost face in the long effort to restrain Japanese militarism must unquestionably be numbered the Great Powers and the League Council. The Powers, in and out of the Council, had maneuvered to and fro, more often than not remaining close to dead center. At last they had really bestirred themselves, but only in a tragic side show, not in the real theater of action. For four months now they had been protesting while Japan marched steadily ahead, wrecking their Disarmament Conference before it ever met and undermining the whole treaty structure upon which the very existence of the Western world rested. The Powers, it is true, were sorely stricken by the world depression, but they had yielded up their future without any struggle commensurate with the issues at stake. They had not even maintained a united front.

The Powers had kept the dispute in their hands. When the first guns of the undeclared war were fired they had been careful to hush any outburst of concern or protest in the Twelfth Assembly. The President of the Council had appeared before the Assembly on September 24, 1931, to say that consultations were in progress and that a further statement would be made to the Assembly. The President of the Assembly then spoke briefly for the Assembly in reply, and when the President of the Council appeared again in the last hour before the Assembly disbanded, the Assembly was told once more that discussion was not necessary.[45]

Japan's feelings had been spared. She had not been irritated by the questions or the censure of little nations. And she had progressed from one defiance of world opinion to another until the world disaster in Shanghai had brought her up short. Now that

[45] Willoughby, *The Sino-Japanese Controversy*, pp. 60-61.

all but irreparable damage had been done, the Assembly was coming back to Geneva, not at the call of the Council, which should have had the courage to summon it, but to answer the agonized cry of dismembered China.

The March Assembly Meets. When the Assembly gathered in Geneva on March 3, 1932, it found precise information about the situation in China awaiting it. The Secretary-General's Consular Committee in Shanghai had reported on February 12 that "since 3rd February state of open war exists, any pretense truce being abandoned. Firing continues intermittently, both in Chapei and Woosung area, with the use of artillery and, on the side of Japanese, by aerial bombardment. Offensive is entirely in the hands of Japanese whose declared object is to capture Woosung forts and drive all Chinese troops considerable distance from Shanghai." [46] A third report of the Consular Committee, dated February 20, gave the terms of a one-sided Japanese ultimatum which had been rejected by the Chinese. And, finally, there was the plan accepted by Japan for a peace conference at Shanghai.

When the Assembly met in special session on March 3, fifty nations had delegates present, forty-five of which at once voted to make Paul Hymans, of Belgium, their President. In this opening vote the Assembly could not have said more. Hymans represented

[46] *Ibid.*, p. 327.

The report stated also that: "Japanese naval authorities took complete control Hongkew district, inside Settlement, barricaded streets, disarmed police and paralyzed all other municipal activities of the Settlement authorities, including fire brigade. Police posts were prevented from all communications with their headquarters. Shanghai Municipal Council was forced to evacuate schools and hospitals. Numerous excesses, including summary executions, were committed by marines, reservists and . . . last mentioned, who had not official standing, being actuated probably merely by spirit of revenge against Chinese for earlier anti-Japanese activities. Reign of terror resulted, and almost entire non-Japanese population of area ran away."

The Assembly found further evidence that the immense printing plant of the Shanghai Commercial Press, with its invaluable library, had been destroyed, thus removing one source of many printed utterances distasteful to Japan. There was record also that Japanese planes had on successive days swept low to bomb and machine-gun the camp of the International Flood Relief Commission, on the extreme edge of Chapei, killing some fifty of the 8,000 unfortunate flood refugees and driving the others away. See the outraged protest of Sir John Hope Simpson (p. 330).

a weak nation which had been overridden by a great military power in 1914. He had also been one of the commission which had framed the League Covenant in 1919, specifically to prevent any other great power from overrunning its weak neighbors. He had been the President of the League's first Assembly in 1920 and had seen the League born in a dark hour when the greatest of all the great powers had already disowned it. Personally, too, Hymans was the complete antithesis of the swashbuckling military men who were again demonstrating their prowess. Small and frail of body, with a thin, kindly face and snow-white hair, Hymans looked more like the righteous judge than the courageous and capable leader that he was. Even as his tiny nation had lived, so perhaps the community of lesser nations might still survive.

The Small Nations Overrule Japan. The Assembly gave him a Bureau of eight Vice-Presidents in which the four Great Powers of Europe were balanced by representatives of four small nations, all of whom had opposed the tendencies of the Great Powers in the League.[47] This body at once drafted a resolution which called for the immediate stoppage of hostilities at Shanghai and for negotiations to "regulate the withdrawal of the Japanese forces." This resolution was promptly presented to the Assembly on March 4 and as promptly the representative of Japan arose to continue the obstructive tactics which the Council had tolerated for four months. Mr. Sato desired only to insert three words to make the vital clause read: "and regulate *the conditions of* the withdrawal of the Japanese forces." The Japanese army still demanded a free hand. Would the Assembly also end by yielding it, as the Council had? For all that the Great Powers might do, it would. Their representatives sat silent. But M. Hymans said from the chair that the Bureau had no intention of leaving the "conditions" of withdrawal to Japanese discretion, since that would make possible

[47] Switzerland, Sweden, Mexico, and Persia. See the pungent account of the Special Assembly in Morley, *The Society of Nations,* Chapter 14. An excellent factual survey of this period, with the more relevant documents included, is to be found in the Secretary-General's *Report on the Work of the League Since the Twelfth Session of the Assembly.* Official No. A 6.1932, pp. 15-27.

the raising of questions other than those of a purely technical military character. Sato then made it plain that Japan still hoped to achieve political objectives in Shanghai, "conditions," he said, "on which we must insist before the withdrawal can be carried out."

The issue was joined, and the President asked the Assembly to take a stand. There was a painful silence, during which the delegate of no Great Power arose. Then Motta of Switzerland reminded the Assembly that under Article 15 it did not need the votes of the disputing parties. To insert the word "conditions" would reopen the question of principle. That was inadmissible. He asked that the resolution be adopted as it stood. Benes of Czechoslovakia at once supported this position and added that it would be "highly dangerous to leave anything uncertain, unclear or ambiguous in a document of this kind." It was essential for all concerned to know "exactly where we stand."

Condoning of Japan's Conquest Condemned. It had remained for the representatives of three small nations to tell Japan exactly where the Assembly stood. When that was clear the Japanese representatives accepted the text as it stood. Then for three days the representatives of twenty-nine small nations, coming from every continent, expressed their dissatisfaction with the manner in which the dispute had been handled thus far and their alarm for the future. "The conciliatory action of the Council did not produce the desired results," and "world public opinion expects the League to take appropriate action," said Braadland, of Norway. Possibly the time had not come to designate the aggressor, said Restrepo, of Colombia, "but we should be prepared to do so at any moment." The League should assert as the will of the whole world that "all aggressive intervention should be barred," continued Ortega, of Mexico. "Any attempt to extend the conception of legitimate defense in the manner adopted in the present case would render it impossible to maintain any legal international order," observed the delegate of Sweden. Were we to go back to the old regime in which unlimited force ruled, asked Erich of Finland? The "political opportunism" of the Powers pointed in that direction. The smaller states knew "very well wherein resides the League's real motive power and which States are actually responsible for the official interpretation and the real application of the Covenant," said Erich, and Politis, of Greece, congratulated China on having referred the dispute to the Assembly.

"The first thing to place on record," began Munch, of Denmark, "is that a State will not be acting in conformity with the Covenant and the Pact of Paris merely because it avoids declaring war." A nation no longer had the right to take justice in its own hands, said Benes of Czechoslovakia. "Any weakening with regard to Article 10, and fumbling in its unqualified application, would be a death blow to the League," declared Titulesco of Roumania, and Buero of Uruguay repudiated the idea that the sovereignty of a state might be encroached upon under the pretext that its internal organization was defective. It was "principally in the case of the inadequately organized countries," insisted the representative of Spain, "those which are striving to set up a better organization at home, that it is essential to maintain the international obligations of the Covenant in all their efficacy," to which Sean Lester of the Irish Free State added: "We must not only settle this dispute; we must settle it right." "We have no other name for the state of affairs in China today than that of war," concluded Te Water of South Africa, and after a telling review of the facts in the case, he stated unhesitatingly the opinion "that a *prima facie* case has been made out that Japan has acted in contradiction to what we believe to be the obligations to which, equally with all of us, she is bound." [48]

[48] On the preceding evening Viscount Grey, who had tried vainly as British Foreign Secretary to halt the outbreak of the Great War, spoke to an assembly of 5,000 persons in Albert Hall in the same vein.

"On the merits of the case in Manchuria my sympathies were on the side of Japan," said Lord Grey. "But Japan's error was that, when she found her treaty rights imperiled she courted war instead of taking up the matter immediately with the League. If she had stated her case at Geneva, I am convinced she would have gained the sympathy of all powers, including the United States, and would have reached a settlement far more in her own interests than war has gained for her."

Lord Grey denied that the Far Eastern crisis was a fair test case for the League because of the inability of the Chinese Government to keep its own

Boesch

PAUL HYMANS

Boesch

EDUARD BENES

Boesch

GIUSEPPE MOTTA

Boesch

FRIDTJOF NANSEN

Boesch

NICOLAS POLITIS

Boesch

EAMON DE VALERA

DISTINGUISHED REPRESENTATIVES OF THE SMALLER NATIONS AT GENEVA

Britain and France Involved with Japan. The utterances of the Powers in the March Assembly were far different in tone from those of the lesser countries. It was clear that the smaller nations were ready to proceed to economic sanctions against Japan and to military sanctions if necessary. Knowing that they would have to bear the main burden of either kind of sanctions, the Great Powers steered away from even any mention of Article 16. The British Government, with no secure naval base in the Orient, was panicky at the thought of having to send its fleet to enforce the Covenant against Japan.[49] The Washington Naval Treaties had made their Hongkong base obsolete—and Japan all but unassailable in the Orient, unless indeed the world's navies united against her. She was supported, moreover, by powerful sections of conservative opinion in Great Britain and in the East. The British had suffered from a widespread Chinese boycott in 1927 and had been forced to give up their concession at Hankow. Therefore, to many Tories and to many British business interests the Japanese were but defending all Western commerce. As late as November 28, 1928, also, the British Foreign Minister had announced in the House of Commons an agreement by the British and Japanese Governments to maintain "constant communication and consultation between their Ministers in Peking" regarding "every new problem as it arises," with a view to achieving "a common course of action" or of explaining to each other why the same course was not pursued.[50]

France also had had since 1907 an *entente* with Japan by which the two powers engaged "to support each other for assur-

---

house in order or of the Japanese Government to control its military party. He thought it not just, either, to dismiss what the League had done. "It has been a restraining influence from the beginning," he said. "We do not know what might have happened if there had been no league."

The Albert Hall meeting was held to urge stronger measures against Japan, looking toward economic sanctions, and to enlist British support for the Stimson policy of non-recognition. *New York Times*, March 8, 1932.

[49] A distinguished Briton who went to London to investigate reported privately in Geneva that the Admiralty was "literally in a blue funk" at the prospect of moving against Japan.

[50] Harold S. Quigley, *Chinese Politics Today*, Minneapolis, 1934, p. 26.

ing the peace and security of those regions of the Chinese Empire adjacent to the territories where they have the rights of sovereignty, protection, or occupation." France, likewise, had built a railway from her colony of Indo-China into the heart of Yunnan province, in South China, and that road dominated that province as the South Manchurian Railway did Manchuria. Britain, too, ruled Burma and had lately extended her control over Thibet.[51] Such factors made it difficult for the British and French to defend the Covenant against Japan.

American Action Essential. They would also be unable to attempt even economic sanctions against Japan without the participation of the United States, which had 44 per cent of Japan's trade. In the United States, as in Britain, there was strong sentiment for economic sanctions. A group led by Newton D. Baker and President A. Lawrence Lowell of Harvard University and including 150 leading educators had declared in favor of the principle. A committee of the Twentieth Century Fund, headed by President Nicholas Murray Butler of Columbia University, submitted a report in March, 1932, favoring a conference of signatories of the Pact of Paris to equip it with measures of non-intercourse when a violation occurred. But American isolationists vigorously denounced all suggestions of this kind as "meddling" in other people's affairs and as likely to lead us into war. Official opinion was also opposed to the attempt, in Washington as well as in London and Paris.[52]

[51] *Ibid.*

[52] Walter Lippmann and W. O. Scroggs, *The United States in World Affairs, 1932,* New Haven, 1933, p. 215.

The *New York Times* correspondent, Arthur Krock, reported that when the Baker-Lowell petition was received at the State Department, "It was obvious that it was being handled as dynamite." A canvass of the Senate a few days previous had disclosed only two Senators who were seriously disposed to discuss the application of economic sanctions against Japan. "They preferred not to be quoted."—*New York Times,* February 21, 1931.

Senator Borah promptly issued a blast against the idea of our joining in economic sanctions. Gone was the terrific indignation with which he had viewed the cession of Germany's economic rights in Shantung to Japan. In 1919, no language had been strong enough to express his deep moral wrath at the Shantung settlement. "It is," he fulminated, "indefensible from any standpoint

The Powers Feared to Back Economic Sanctions. There was no blinking the fact, either, that economic sanctions might readily lead to hostilities. That they would be effective against Japan was hardly open to question. She was already gravely injured by the Chinese boycott of her goods. Her commercial life depended upon the purchase of huge amounts of raw cotton, chiefly from the United States; upon its resale abroad as cloth; and upon the disposal of her silk to the United States. Her supplies of iron ore, and of many less bulky minerals vital to industry and to war, were totally inadequate—in many cases non-existent. Of oil she had but a tiny fraction of the amount necessary to keep her immense military and naval machines in operation.

The application of economic sanctions to Japan, with the cooperation of the United States, would be effective. But for the same reason, the Japanese might strike quickly throughout the Orient. Neither Shanghai nor Hongkong nor Manila could be defended against them, unless the entire British and American fleets moved to the Far East at the beginning of the economic embargo. But they would find there only naval bases made obsolete by the Washington Naval Treaties. Barring a most resolute naval concentration by Japan's opponents also, the Japanese road to the Dutch East Indies, with their great supplies of oil, would be open. It was not certain in the autumn of 1931, or later, that

---

of morals or international justice or common decency. It is one of those things so immoral and unrighteous that we wish to approach it with deaf ears and closed eyes. We dread even to think about it. We loathe to be forced to attempt to defend it. It will dishonor and degrade any people who seek to uphold it. War will inevitably follow as the result of an attempt to perpetuate it. It is founded on immorality and revolting injustice. It is outside the pale of respectability even according to ancient standards. It shocks the conscience even of European diplomacy. Naked, hideous, and revolting it looms up before us as a monster from that cruel and shameless world which all had hoped and prayed was forever behind us."—*Congressional Record*, Vol. 58, Pt. 5, p. 4355.

On February 20, 1932, when Japan's army had bombed and burned China's metropolis, in complete disregard of civilian life and property; when the Republican-sponsored Nine Power Treaty and the Kellogg Pact which he had shepherded had both been totally disregarded, Borah was calmly "in favor of the United States retaining friendly relations with both powers (unless the break comes by some act of their own) and doing all that a friendly neutral power can properly do to bring these powers together in a just settlement of their controversy."—*New York Times*, February 21, 1932.

the Japanese militarists would attack all and sundry if confronted with an economic boycott, but their assault upon Shanghai, if it did nothing else, indicated as much to the Great Powers. While the Great Powers of Europe were not disposed to nerve themselves to the ordeal, it would not have been practical for them to do so unless the United States—and probably also Russia—joined in the enforcement of sanctions, and both of Japan's great neighbors were out of the League and not to be depended on for ultimate measures.

The Powers accordingly had little to contribute to the March debate in the Assembly. Sir John Simon stressed that the first duty of the League was mediation, and he indicated that it was also the League's second and third duty. Conciliation by every means in its power was the League's role. The representatives of France, Germany, and Italy merely echoed Sir John's solemn affirmation of the League's general principles. The Italian delegate also asked regard for the "realities," a word often in the mouths of the Japanese and to be uttered frequently by Italians in Geneva when the seizure of Manchuria had prepared the way for the conquest of Ethiopia.

The Resolution of March 11. Then the smaller nations took charge of the task of drafting a resolution covering the whole of the Sino-Japanese imbroglio. To make sure that the Great Powers did not soft-pedal this declaration, Benes moved that anyone who had a resolution to offer should be made automatically a member of the resolutions committee. When this motion was carried, the Powers made no effort to dominate the committee and it drew up in two days the most important resolution yet written during the dispute, a declaration which the Assembly promptly passed.[53]

The resolution of March 11, 1932, considered the provisions of the Covenant as entirely applicable to the dispute—especially "the principle of scrupulous respect for treaties," the undertaking "to respect and preserve as against external aggression the territorial and existing political independence" of all members, and

[53] Morley, *The Society of Nations,* pp. 551-52.

their obligation to submit any dispute to peaceful settlement. The resolution adopted the principles laid down by Briand in his declaration of December 10, recalled the appeal of the Twelve to Japan, proclaimed the binding nature of all these provisions, and declared "that it is incumbent upon the members of the League of Nations not to recognize any situation, treaty or agreement which may be brought about by means contrary to the Covenant of the League of Nations or the Pact of Paris." By this declaration the members of the League were at last brought to the support of Secretary Stimson's non-recognition declaration of January 7. The Council had moved in that direction a time or two but had been diverted, partly by the events in Shanghai. While the Assembly could not bind the members legally, its action promised the success of Stimson's policy and removed the United States from an embarrassing and isolated advance position. The State Department promptly approved the entire Assembly resolution the day after it was passed and expressed especial gratification at the adoption of the non-recognition principle.[54]

The Committee of Nineteen Constituted. The remainder of the March resolution affirmed that it was "contrary to the spirit of the Covenant that the settlement of the Sino-Japanese dispute should be sought under the stress of military pressure"; recalled the Council resolutions of September 30 and December 10, together with the Assembly resolution of March 4; and decided to set up a committee of nineteen members to be headed by President Hymans and to include six members elected by secret ballot, besides representatives of the Council members other than the disputing parties. The prompt election of Switzerland, Czechoslovakia, Colombia, Portugal, Hungary, and Sweden gave the smaller nations a preponderant and vigorous majority of the Nineteen, whose instructions were: to report on the cessation of hostilities; to follow the execution of previous Council resolutions; to prepare any needed request for an advisory opinion of the World

[54] The United States delegation to the Disarmament Conference had been in close touch with the Assembly throughout its session, unofficially but effectively.

Court or any necessary report under Article 15; and to submit a first report of progress not later than May 1, 1932, until which time the Assembly would remain in session.[55]

The Japanese representative was convinced that Japan had "faithfully observed" the provisions of the Covenant and the Pact. She was "resolutely determined always to act in accordance with their principles" and particularly regretted the allegations "that the action she was compelled to take in China was an attack upon the present political or territorial integrity of another country or was an attempt to exercise pressure for the pursuit of any object whatsoever." Once more he repeated that Japan had "no territorial designs" and was only safeguarding "the life and property of her nationals." With this disclaimer he found it possible to abstain from voting and the resolution was unanimously adopted.

Shanghai Evacuated. The Shanghai Conference opened its negotiations on March 24. Hostilities had nearly ceased and the withdrawal of Japanese troops had begun. A formal agreement could not be reached until May 5, because of the desire of the Chinese that a definite date be set for the completion of Japanese evacuation. Japan would not agree to a fixed date, but she did relinquish a demand that the Mayor of Shanghai's capitulation of January 21, containing a pledge to suppress the anti-Japanese movement, be regarded as still binding. Japan thus evacuated Shanghai with less to show diplomatically than when she marched in. The boycott naturally continued and its organization was soon restored to such effectiveness that there was talk of another Japanese demonstration at Shanghai in August, 1932.[56]

In its report to the Assembly on April 29, the Committee of Nineteen proposed an Assembly resolution, which put additional pressure upon the Japanese and which was adopted the next day in the presence of Secretary Stimson.[57] From Shanghai, the

[55] *Official Journal, Special Supplement* 101, pp. 87-88.

[56] A. J. Toynbee, *Survey of International Affairs, 1932*, London, 1933, p. 514.

[57] After the session Stimson told the American newspapermen in Geneva that he had been much impressed by "the immense value accruing to the American

Japanese troops were all withdrawn before May 31, many of them being sent quickly to Manchuria. The desperate resistance of the Nineteenth Route Army at Shanghai had thrilled the opposition to Japan in Manchuria as it had in China proper. In some districts the Japanese found themselves on the defensive and in others making much slower headway.[58] Chinese patriotism had been stimulated all over the world, along with the opposition of other peoples to Japan's course. The Japanese Foreign Office was quoted on May 11 as saying frankly that Shanghai was being evacuated rapidly "to end the world-wide odium which has fallen upon us." [59]

The Lytton Report

Five Months in Preparation. During the summer of 1932, while Japan proceeded with the subjugation of Manchuria and the organization of Manchouquo, the Lytton Commission completed its investigation. Its membership, as finally approved by the Council January 14, 1932, was as follows: The Earl of Lytton, Chairman (British), Count Aldrovandi (Italian), General Henri Claudel (French), Major General Frank R. McCoy (American), and Dr. Heinrich Schnee (German). The Commission took the longer route through the United States—in order that it might have contact with American public opinion—and arrived in Tokyo February 29. After many interviews with Japanese officials it proceeded to Shanghai on March 14, viewed the devastation there, went on to Nanking March 26, and, after visiting several provinces of China, came to Peiping April 9, where the officials and generals of the former Manchurian Government were received. Departure for Manchuria was delayed because of the unwillingness of the Japanese to admit into Manchuria Dr. Wellington Koo,

---

Secretary of State" from the informal discussion with many foreign ministers of vital problems in which the United States was interested. *New York Times*, May, 1, 1932.

[58] Lytton *Report*, p. 87. "Everywhere opinion hardened and the spirit of resistance increased."

[59] *New York Times*, May 12, 1932. A dispatch from Hugh Byas, the Tokyo correspondent of the *Times*.

the Chinese Assessor attached to the Commission. Dr. Koo was a former Prime Minister and Minister of Foreign Affairs of China and a pronounced opponent of Japan's policy. Strong efforts were made to dissuade him from going to Manchuria, on the ground that his safety could not be guaranteed. When the Commission insisted that he accompany them he was kept in the Japanese railway zone and his movements heavily guarded. It was not until the Commission reached the northern end of the railway zone that he was given permission to enter "Manchouquo." It appeared that his presence might imperil the new state.[60]

In Manchuria the Commission traveled for six weeks, meeting all important officials and receiving delegations from the local population, "most of whom were presented by the Japanese or 'Manchouquo' authorities." [61] Many private interviews with individuals, "both Chinese and foreign," were also held before the Commissioners returned to Peiping to analyze the great bulk of documentary material collected. On June 28 they went again to Tokyo, then back to Peiping, where their report was drafted. It was completed September 4, 1932, and forwarded to Geneva. A document of 148 large folio pages, it was supported by 14 maps and a still larger volume of *Supplementary Documents* and special studies made by the experts of the Commission.[62]

The *Report* opened with a survey of recent developments in China, which found that considerable headway in establishing order in China had been made and that further progress was to be expected. Chinese nationalism was normal, though China had been only "hampered by the virulence of the anti-foreign propaganda

[60] Dr. Koo's reports to the Commission stated that every member of his delegation was followed by one or more police agents when they left their hotel in Mukden. He himself was followed from one room to another in the hotel. He stated further that police agents freely entered the rooms of the Chinese to ask them questions at all hours. No Chinese was permitted to call upon them. Willoughby, *The Sino-Japanese Controversy*, p. 415.

[61] Lytton *Report*, p. 11.

[62] C. 663. M. 320. 1932 VII Annexes. The Commission naturally did not print all the evidence which the two parties would have desired. To give their side a full hearing the Chinese have published through the Chinese Cultural Society, 743 Fifth Avenue, New York, two large volumes of *Memoranda Presented to the Lytton Commission*, by Dr. Wellington Koo, Assessor.

Wide World

THE LYTTON COMMISSION OF INQUIRY

Left to right: GENERAL HENRI-ADOUARD CLAUDÈL, France; the EARL OF LYTTON, Great Britain (Chairman); COUNT LUIGI ALDROVANDI-MARESCOTTI, Italy; DR. HEINRICH SCHNEE, Germany; MAJOR GENERAL FRANK C. McCOY, the United States.

which has been pursued" and which had had disturbing effects in the schools. The problem of safeguarding Japanese nationals and property in China was a grave one, but international cooperation offered the best solution.

"Manchouquo" a Japanese State. Chapter II of the *Report* contained an excellent description of Manchuria and of its relations with China and Russia. Chapter III was a careful and extensive exposé of the Manchurian issues between Japan and China before September 18, 1931. Chapter IV traced the events in Manchuria following that date. Chapter V dealt with the conflict at Shanghai, including the Japanese bombardment of Nanking on February 1, 1932. Chapter VI contained a detailed account of the establishment of "Manchouquo," which concluded that the independence movement had never been heard of in Manchuria before September 18; that it would not have been possible without the presence of Japanese troops; that Japanese officials "conceived, organized, and carried through" this movement. No "genuine and spontaneous independence movement" had existed. The Commission had found much difficulty in interviewing the inhabitants, because of excessive police protection. "Interviews were therefore usually arranged with considerable difficulty and in secrecy, and many informed us that it was too dangerous for them to meet us even in this way." Some Chinese who had been brought in with petitions favorable to the new state afterwards let the Commission know that their real feelings were otherwise. Even some of the officials of the new regime sent messages that they were serving under duress as screens for Japanese power. The Commission believed that there was "no general support for the Manchouquo Government, which is regarded by the local Chinese as an instrument of the Japanese."

The Boycott a Reprisal. Chapter VII discussed Japan's economic interests and the Chinese boycott. Japan's grave problems were portrayed and her need of Chinese markets set forth. Modern Chinese boycotts were found to have been eleven in number, the first being directed against the United States in 1905, because of Chinese exclusion, which had just been stated anew in a commercial treaty. One had been waged against Great Britain. The other nine boycotts had been anti-Japanese. In every case they had originated in "a definite fact, event or incident, generally of a political nature and interpreted by China as directed against her material interests or detrimental to her national prestige." An extended description of the methods used to enforce the current boycott left no doubt as to its being highly organized and backed by powerful popular sentiment. Japan required Chinese markets urgently, and China needed Japanese capital greatly. The interdependence of the two countries called for a *rapprochement* which could not occur "so long as the political relations between them are so unsatisfactory as to call forth the use of military force by one and the economic force of the boycott by the other."

The Case of Outer Mongolia Different. After an analysis of the various economic interests in Manchuria, the Commission came to consider the principles and conditions of a just settlement. It believed that "a mere restoration of the *status quo ante* would be no solution" and likewise rejected the maintenance and recognition of "Manchouquo" as equally unsatisfactory. "About the feelings of the people of Manchuria toward the present regime," said the Commission, "there can really be no doubt; and China would not voluntarily accept as a lasting solution the complete separation of her Three Eastern Provinces." The analogy to Outer Mongolia was not pertinent, since that region was not bound to China by any "strong economic or social ties and is sparsely inhabited by a population which is mainly non-Chinese." The situation in Manchuria was "radically different." [63]

[63] "The millions of Chinese farmers now settled permanently on the land have made Manchuria in many respects a simple extension of China south of the Wall. The Three Eastern Provinces have become almost as Chinese in race, culture and national sentiment as the neighbouring Provinces of Hopei and Shantung, from which most of the immigrants came.

"Apart from this, past experience has shown that those who control Manchuria have exercised a considerable influence on the affairs of the rest of China—at least of North China—and possess unquestionable strategic and political advantages. To cut off these provinces from the rest of China, either legally or actually, would be to create for the future a serious irredentist problem which would endanger peace by keeping alive the hostility of China and rendering probable the continued boycott of Japanese goods."

Bases for a Settlement. The real solution was to be found in a *rapprochement* between Japan and China, which would open the whole Chinese market to Japan. Nothing less would serve the interests of the two countries or conserve the important interests of other nations in the Orient. Granting the sovereignty of China in Manchuria, the Commission felt that "a satisfactory regime for the future might be evolved out of the present regime without any violent change." It suggested ten conditions of a satisfactory settlement, as follows: (1) compatibility with the interests of both China and Japan; (2) consideration also for the interests of Russia; (3) conformity with existing multilateral treaties; (4) recognition of Japan's interests in Manchuria; (5) establishment of new treaty relations between China and Japan; (6) effective provision for the settlement of future disputes; (7) Manchurian autonomy, (8) internal order and security against external aggression; (9) encouragement of an economic *rapprochement* between China and Japan; and (10) international cooperation in Chinese reconstruction.

Upon this solid basis the Commission proposed an Advisory Conference composed of four groups: representatives of the Chinese and Japanese Governments and two groups representing the people of Manchuria, one to be selected in a manner prescribed by the Chinese Government and the other by the Japanese. It was suggested that this body report to the Council the bases for four separate agreements: (1) a Declaration by the Government of China constituting a special administration for the Three Eastern Provinces, in the terms recommended by the Advisory Conference; (2) a Sino-Japanese Treaty dealing with Japanese interests; (3) a Sino-Japanese Treaty of Conciliation and Arbitration, Non-Aggression and Mutual Assistance; and (4) a Sino-Japanese Commercial Treaty. Many suggestions were advanced as well as to the nature and the content of each of these instruments.

"Manchouquo" Tied to Japan. The state of "Manchouquo" was formally recognized by Japan on September 15, 1932, and an alliance was concluded with it. This action was intended to

confront the League and the Lytton Commission with a final *fait accompli* before the Lytton *Report* could come up for consideration. Japan's motive was rebuked by the President of the Council, Mr. De Valera, at the meeting of the Council on September 24 which granted Japan six weeks' time to study the report and prepare a reply. He would be lacking in frankness, said De Valera, did he not express the regret of the Council that, even before the publication of the *Report*, Japan had taken steps which could not but be "regarded as calculated to prejudice the settlement of the dispute." For almost a year the Council and the Governments had refrained from judging the dispute because it was *sub judice*.

Japan's Denial. Japanese disappointment with the Lytton *Report* was severe. The Japanese Government prepared an extensive reply covering forty large pages,[64] which regretted the "omissions, inconsistencies and misapprehensions" in the *Report* as inevitable, considering the brief studies of the Commission. The Government was "impressed by the feeling that items of information drawn from unimpeachable sources—e.g., those presented by the representatives of the Japanese Government—have been passed over or disregarded, whilst undue credit has been accorded to information coming from obscure or even unknown quarters." The acceptance of untrustworthy evidence from Chinese sources had led to "a complete misapprehension of the motives which actuated the Japanese armed forces." From this lofty height "Japan, maintaining her old friendly attitude" (toward the Chinese people) looked "forward to ages of prosperous and neighborly cooperation between the two nations."

The Japanese *Observations* insisted that China was not an organized state, reviewed anti-foreign activities in China and the abnormal status of foreigners there, surveyed the situation in Manchuria, and denied that Manchuria was "naturally and necessarily a part of China." Japan's special position in Manchuria was

[64] *The Observations of the Japanese Government on the Report of the Commission of Enquiry*, VII Political 1932. VII. 19.

no restriction on the sovereignty "of the region." The Chinese were "destitute of any strong national feeling." The organization of "Manchouquo" had been the "genuine, spontaneous, popular and natural" act of the Chinese people. That the Nine Power Treaty prevented the signatory powers from impairing the sovereignty of China was true "but irrelevant." The assertion of the *Report* that the activities of Japanese officials were "a most effective" factor in the creation of Manchouquo was "destitute of foundation." The principles suggested by the *Report* were inapplicable, because of the lack of a strong central government in China, and the Commission's concrete proposals for settlement were "of too refined and intricate a nature." They might prove suitable if applied to Europe and America, but would not prove adaptable to the "realities" of the Far East. In the Orient, apparently, only simple solutions, such as Japan had arrived at, would do.[65]

Submitted to the Council in November. The consideration of the Lytton *Report* by the Council, beginning November 21, 1932, was featured by a tense duel in English between Wellington Koo, the Chinese representative, and Yosuke Matsuoka, an American-trained Japanese.[66] The November meetings of the Council were presided over by Mr. De Valera, the President of the Irish Free State. This was the same De Valera who had been a hunted rebel in 1919 and whose followers in the United States had bitterly opposed the League of Nations as a scheme for throttling Ireland. In 1932 De Valera was not only free and the head of a free Gov-

[65] The *Observations* maintained that the *Report* had cut the background of the incident of September 18 adrift, insisted upon "the solid fact" that an explosion did take place, that the Japanese army had to have a plan for defeating the huge Chinese forces in Manchuria if anything happened, and that when an incident occurred the plan had to be put into instant and complete execution in order to save the lives of the 10,000 Japanese troops in Manchuria.

To buttress the right of the Japanese to make their own definition of self defense, the *Observations* quoted at length the reservations in the interest of "self defense" and of special positions made at the time the Kellogg Pact was framed by the United States, Great Britain, and France.

[66] This exchange dealt at length with the authenticity of the "Tanaka memorial" and the alleged continental policy of Japan. The justification of the anti-Japanese boycott was also argued.

ernment in Ireland; his nation had been a member of the League of Nations for years, it had been elected to the Council, and its turn had come to preside over that body at a time when the existence of the League was at stake. President De Valera faced a grave responsibility and discharged it with great credit.

The November meetings witnessed a sustained contest between Mr. Matsuoka and the Council over the personal appearance of Lord Lytton at the Council. It had been the custom of the Council to have a commission of inquiry report to Geneva and say whether, in the light of more recent developments, it wished to change any part of its report. Finding that the Lytton Commission had unanimously opposed Japan's major contentions, Japan was determined that the Commission should not say that, after reading the *Observations* of the Japanese Government in rebuttal, the Commission had not changed its mind. Matsuoka argued that the Commission no longer existed and intimated even that it had no right to make suggestions for a settlement. In any case, he contended that the Commission could not pass an opinion on anything which transpired in the Council, that is, the Japanese reply to its *Report*. If the Commission appeared before the Council, a formal Japanese protest of November 25 threatened, the Japanese representative "might naturally be compelled to start quizzing the members of the Commission" and much time might be required for the cross-examination. "It might take a week or even a month," said Matsuoka to the Council.

Throughout this controversy President De Valera presided with a mild firmness which was a match for Japan's belligerence. He spoke softly but defended the League's procedure constantly until at last Lord Lytton was called on to speak and said that "we do not wish to add anything to what we have said in our report." He did not say that the Commission had not learned anything from the Japanese *Observations* which would lead it to change its mind, but the implication was clear.

Debate in the December Assembly. Since there appeared to be no possibility of reconciling the views of the disputants, the

Council decided to refer the Lytton *Report* to the Special Assembly without discussion. When the Assembly took it up, on December 6, 1932, it became apparent at once that the view of the Japanese that the *Report* was an inadequate document, full of inconsistencies and partiality, was not shared by other nations. Mr. Connoly, of the Irish Free State, opened the discussion with as outspoken an address as could have been written. Every line of the *Report* was "pregnant with relevant detail." It gave a comprehensive picture of the entire controversy. Accepting the *Report* was a vital test for the League, which could achieve its purpose only if it stood "with courage and determination behind the Covenant and its own decisions." If the League faltered or hesitated, then it would not survive and "did not deserve to survive." No one could deny that "within what is admittedly Chinese territory" a new "state" had been set up which could not be recognized.

Benes, of Czechoslovakia, likewise agreed that the *Report* should be adopted. Its two most important findings were that Japan's operations in Manchuria and Shanghai were not acts of legitimate self defense and that the creation of "Manchouquo" had not been spontaneous. The League should condemn China's anti-foreignism, including the boycott, along with the taking of the law into her own hands by Japan. He could not understand the opening arguments of Matsuoka that Japan could not have appealed to the League (1) because her national sentiment would not have brooked outside interference, (2) because the population of Manchuria would have suffered from the League's slow procedure, and (3) because Eastern mentality was different from Western. These allegations implied "a total misapprehension of the fundamental provisions of the Covenant in virtue whereof every controversial question which falls under any article of the Covenant must be brought before the League to be dealt with in its entirety." The League must do "its whole duty." If it compromised on matters of principle that "would mean the bankruptcy and the end of the League."

Many Nations Back the Covenant. For Sweden, Unden agreed that the League could not recognize the plea that national sentiment would not brook outside interference. Article 10 should be applied. Lange, of Norway, agreed that conditions in Manchuria had not justified a unilateral recourse to military force. The League had proceeded with wisdom and with patience, said Madariaga, of Spain, when all knew that there would be injustice in the taking of so much time, "that it would permit the sowing, the ripening and the harvesting of the *fait accompli*." Thus it was not without a certain bitterness that he had heard Matsuoka say that the Japanese Government had not submitted the dispute to the League's jurisdiction because of the delays involved in League procedure. Now it was necessary to re-establish the authority of the League. "The permanent and historical Japan has the right to learn from us that we are in disagreement, at any rate as regards the methods of the Japan of the present." The nations individually tended to be circumspect, but there was also the League, "a growing universal city; this living thing which in itself would be sufficient to render the name of Woodrow Wilson immortal."

Motta, of Switzerland, hailed the *Report* as drawn up "with an entirely open mind and an obvious desire to be impartial." He declared that the reasons given by Japan for not resorting to the League would render its Covenant meaningless.[67] Paul-Boncour, of France, argued also that the Covenant did "not authorize a state, however well founded its grievances against another state to seek redress by methods other than the pacific methods set forth in Article XII." The *Report* he termed "extremely clear, substantial and impartial." He urged especially further study of its conclusions.

Simon Opposes Action. At this point Sir John Simon mounted the tribune to plead with all his power once again for still more

[67] Motta contrasted Matsuoka's statement that Japan had not expected the events of September 18 with his declaration that Japan was dealing with a menacing situation. Greece, Guatemala, and Uruguay joined in asking that the rights of weak states be upheld.

conciliation. He stressed the "really complicated character of the Manchurian problem" as brought out in the *Report* and dwelt at length upon the fact that it did not "give a one-sided account, painting everything black on the one side and presenting it in spotless raiments of white on the other." It made "a measured criticism" of both sides, as was evidenced by the fact that both sides objected to parts of it. It made clear that conditions in China had grown worse since the Washington Conference. He called attention also to the "description of the deplorable condition of Manchuria in Chapter 2 and the objective account of the anti-foreign boycott in Chapter 7." The *Report* had stressed also that the restoration of the *status quo ante* would be no solution. With that conclusion Sir John most heartily agreed. It brought him to the "realities," of which he spoke almost as feelingly as had Matsuoka. He believed that "while we all firmly hold by the principles and the ideals of the League, we sincerely wish to act in this matter as practical men. We must concern ourselves with realities." The "inferences of conciliation" must be drawn. He could see no basis for conciliation other than the *Report*. Using it "in a spirit of friendliness and comradeship we must promote conciliation."

One would have supposed that just a little sweet reasonableness would induce Japan to restore to China her Three Eastern Provinces, through direct negotiations. Repeating his ruse of February 12, Sir John declared he had "heard something said about direct negotiations between the parties." If direct negotiations gave promise of results they should be encouraged "by every means in our power." [68] But "the organs of the League may be able, and I believe they will be able, to assist in the work of conciliation." Japan had been a good and loyal member of the League. His own country also desired to act as a loyal member of the

[68] Mr. Quo Tai-chi observed in a later speech that he did not know where Sir John "had heard reports of direct negotiations." If China had desired direct negotiations with Japan on the basis of the military occupation of her soil, she "need not have troubled the Assembly."—Willoughby, *The Sino-Japanese Controversy*, p. 452.

League. All were bound to sustain the law, but "we must seek a practical solution," practical efforts at conciliation. "Then the responsibility that rests upon our shoulders, if we are trying to conciliate, is tremendous. No one can conciliate who is not conciliatory." And with that Sir John closed by quoting Lincoln's second inaugural address: "with malice toward none; with charity for all." It was clear that the Assembly would never take any action against Japan if Sir John could prevent it.[69]

Some Follow Britain. After the delegates of the Netherlands and of Denmark had spoken in a contrary, though equally sober, vein, Baron Aloisi of Italy also stressed that the League was not based upon force but was "a League for collaboration." Looking backward to Corfu and forward to Ethiopia, he observed that the founders of the League had "desired to make possible that free development of the activity of States without going to extreme measures which the League of Nations would have to take if the Covenant were violated." He too asked for conclusions "founded upon realities." The solutions proposed in the *Report* seemed to him practical if not applied rigidly.

Germany, Baron Neurath emphasized repeatedly, had "always attached particular value to the establishment of a system which would prevent the application of military means for the settlement of differences." It was essential that the League should take

[69] The effect of Sir John Simon's oration upon the Assembly was paralyzing for the moment. His figure, very tall and impressive, his splendid voice, and his unsurpassed skill as a barrister enabled him to dominate his hearers as no one had. No other speaker approached the personal power which Sir John commanded. Though one mistrusted his ears, it actually seemed, as he closed, that the League's one duty was to conciliate the conquering Japanese.

Sir John's apostrophe to conciliation was soberly repeated by the editor of the London *Times,* who deprecated "vague threats of coercive action, which are not warranted by the facts in the case as found in the Lytton Report, and which indeed could only be made effective if public opinion in the other countries were profoundly impressed by the justice of the case of one of the disputants and the injustice of that of the other." From reading the *Times* one would have supposed that public opinion in many nations was really in doubt as to whether the post-war peace treaties had been broken by aggression, and one would never have guessed that the world's chief complaint against Japan was the willful way in which she had vitiated them by taking the law into her own hands. See the *Times,* December 8, 1932.

account of "those living forces that exist" and turn them into pacific channels. The German delegate was not so insistent as the representatives of Turkey, Mexico, and Poland that the principles of the Covenant should be upheld.

At this point in the discussion the representative from Canada, Mr. Cahan, went further than any other speaker in defending Japan by attacking the conduct of China. He questioned whether she fulfilled the requirements of membership in the League and emphasized that the Nine Power Treaty did not terminate any of Japan's rights in China. He suggested that China's acts were "manifestly provocative of emergency action" by Japan and quoted at length the complaints of Sir Austen Chamberlain on February 8, 1927, against the anti-British boycott in China. Japan might "with equal veracity and cogency" have written a similar letter in 1931. Yet it would be impossible "to justify the development, out of its own emergent action, of a permanent occupation of any part of a neighboring state." Cahan hastened to add, however, that Article 10 applied only as against "external aggression," and to say that the Assembly should not wholly disregard the emphatic statement of Matsuoka that the Japanese Government had not been connected with the establishment of "Manchouquo." Any discussion of sanctions was out of place at this stage.[70]

In sequence, the representative of Panama asked for "the safeguarding of the guarantees of law and justice"; the representative of Chile that the League "do its whole duty"; and the delegate of Roumania that there be no compromise with the principles of the Covenant and the Pact. Then Stanley Bruce of Australia spoke on Sir John Simon's theme, sincerely hoping that the Assembly would pass no resolution of censure, "either open or implied." He pleaded very earnestly that this be not done.

[70] In opening his address Cahan said that, owing to the difficulties of communicating fully to his Government the views which had been expressed in the Assembly, "the opinions which I am about to express are more or less personal, but nevertheless, I think they are opinions in which my government will concur." Cahan was, however, soon replaced by Dr. Walter Riddell, who reached Geneva before the Assembly met in February.

Conflicting Definitions of the Realities. The December session of the Assembly was closed after two remarkable addresses by the Chinese and Japanese delegates. To the brilliant work of Koo and Yen the Chinese now added that of Quo Tai-chi, who sought to establish the identity of the much mentioned "realities." The first of these was the common obligation of every nation to play its part in preventing aggressive war. If the Japanese military had their way they would not only establish Japanese hegemony in the East but "force the world to return to the international anarchy from which it is striving to escape." The second reality was the solid resistance of the Chinese people. No conqueror had ever overcome them. While they would regard it as a grave disaster to be forced to militarize their people, they knew their capacity to resist. The third reality, which the Japanese covered up, was that China was bearing the strain of the struggle "far better than Japan." This was natural, for she had "incomparably greater resources and staying power than Japan" could have. As Japan's economic condition grew steadily worse the burden of her adventure on Chinese soil grew greater daily." [71]

Without intending to agree with the Chinese forecast of the eventual outcome in the Far East, Matsuoka declared in his

[71] With reference to the generally accepted right of Japan to maintain troops in the South Manchurian Railway Zone, he cited the statement of the Lytton *Report,* quoting the Sino-Japanese agreement of December 22, 1905, in which it had been provided that "in the event of Russia's agreeing to the withdrawal of her railway guards," Japan agreed "to take similar steps." On this point the *Report* had continued: "It is this article upon which Japan had based her treaty right. Russia, however, long since withdrew her guards and she relinquished her rights to keep them by the Sino-Soviet agreement of 1924."

Following Quo Tai-chi's great speech, perhaps the greatest delivered during all the Manchurian debates, Sir John Simon had the effrontery to call him on the carpet and to threaten the return of his credentials as Chinese Ambassador to Great Britain.

Yet the full measure of Sir John's determination to block the operation of the League was not revealed until January, 1935, when he sat by Secretary-General Avenol while the two refused to permit Ethiopia to invoke Article 15 of the Covenant and literally threw the appeal of a sovereign state to the Covenant into the wastebasket. Whitaker, *And Fear Came,* pp. 118, 247-48.

After Mussolini's intentions were plain enough, but before he had shipped whole armies to Africa, the illegal and dictatorial action of Simon let the League in for a second major defeat. It would not be permitted to do anything to check the revival of lawless imperialism if he could prevent it.

Boesch

THE LEAGUE ASSEMBLY WHICH CONSIDERED THE LYTTON REPORT

Left to right: 1. Herriot, France; 2. Ridell, Canada; 3. Paul-Boncour, France; 4. Matsuoka, Japan; 5. Politis, Greece; 6. Simon, Great Britain; 7. MacDonald, Great Britain; 8. Madariaga, Spain; 9. Cahan, Canada; 10. Quo Tai-chi, Koo, and Yen, China; 11. Von Neurath, Germany; 12. The French and English translators; 13. President Hymans, Belgium.

closing appeal that: "Our nation regards the issue connected with Manchuria as involving the very existence of Japan; she regards it as a question of life and death." The Japanese believed it was "a question of now or never." Believing also that they were right, they would not bow to threats or to sanctions. Could 65,000,000 people standing solidly together be wrong, he asked in effect? Was it to be supposed "that they were all insane"? World opinion might be against Japan now, but it would change. And what would the situation be without Japan? But for Japan's power, "sovietism would spread rapidly and would cover the greater part of China in no time." What would the West prefer? Would the world "weaken Japan, the only hope today in that appalling situation throughout Western Asia, thus bringing more chaos to the Far East?"

The League's Verdict

Seventeen Months of Conciliation. The Assembly then referred the Lytton *Report* to the Committee of Nineteen which submitted two draft resolutions to the disputing parties. The negotiations continued another two months, when it became clear that there could be no agreement between Japan on one side and the League and China on the other.[72] The Special Assembly met February 21, 1933, to recognize this fact. President Hymans noted that for exactly seventeen months the efforts at conciliation had been pursued. Yet "today the Three Eastern Provinces are occupied; Japanese troops have crossed the Great Wall and attacked Shanhaikwan; it is announced that operations are being prepared for the occupation of the province of Jehol" (which were soon carried out). Three days later the Assembly adopted by a unanimous vote, Japan alone dissenting, the Report of the Committee of Nineteen, a document of 15,000 words which reviewed the entire controversy and made recommendations for a settlement. The

[72] Throughout these discussions the Japanese steadily rejected the suggestion made by many of the Assembly speakers that the United States and Russia be invited to join the conciliation proceedings.

entire text was sent out over the League's radio station to all parts of the world at the time of publication.[73]

The Resolution of February 24. The Assembly resolution listed many evidences that Japan had constantly recognized the sovereignty of China over Manchuria up to September, 1931. The autonomy maintained in Manchuria did not destroy this sovereignty or prevent the creation of a serious irredentist problem with Manchuria, with its strong political and strategic influences over North China, in non-Chinese hands. The Assembly rejected also the contention that disorder in China justified the acts of Japan in Manchuria. The vast transition going on in China necessarily involved "political disturbances, social disorder and disruptive tendencies." But a policy of international cooperation, involving technical assistance to China through the League, was the remedy, not force of arms. For the settlement of the disputes outstanding in September, 1931, the methods of diplomacy and of pacific settlement had been by no means exhausted. If Japan had regarded the negotiations as unduly protracted, it was incumbent upon her to bring the matter up in the League, where, the report might have added, her immense prestige and good reputation would have enabled her to receive every possible consideration, even if the small nations had insisted that Chinese rights be safeguarded. The whole series of military measures taken by Japan could not be "regarded as measures of self defense." Moreover, the adoption of such measures did not exempt Japan from complying with Article 12, which requires resort to pacific processes and forbids war during their employment.

Far from following the course to which she was pledged, Japan had continually carried out military movements dictated by "essentially political considerations." A group of her officials had "conceived, organized and carried through" an independence movement and established a state in which the power rested in Japanese hands. The forcible nature of the separation of a large Chinese territory from China was "indisputable," and the use of

[73] A. (Extr.) 22. 1933 VII.

the boycott by China subsequent to the events of September 18, 1931, "fell under the category of reprisals." Its employment previous to that date to express Chinese "indignation at certain incidents or to support certain claims" was deprecated as sure to make "a situation which was already tense still more tense," but the Assembly did not say that the boycott had been unjustified before September 18.

Terms of Settlement Proposed. After invoking the observance of the Covenant, the Pact, and the Nine Power Treaty and after restating the principles for settlement laid down in the Lytton *Report*, the Committee of Nineteen called for: the withdrawal of Japan's troops back into the railway zone; for the organization of an autonomous Chinese regime for the region which would recognize all treaties involved, including those for keeping the peace. The Committee also recommended negotiations between the two parties with the assistance of a committee of the Assembly, to be composed of representatives of Belgium, Great Britain, Canada, Czechoslovakia, France, Germany, the Irish Free State, Italy, the Netherlands, Portugal, Spain, and Turkey. The United States and Russia would each be asked to appoint a member of the committee.

Non-Recognition Reaffirmed. The final section of the Assembly's verdict reaffirmed the Stimson doctrine emphatically, saying that it followed from the adoption of the *Report* that the members of the League would continue not to recognize the existing regime in Manchuria, either *de jure* or *de facto*, and that "they intend to abstain from taking any isolated action" and to concert together with the interested States not members of the League.

Japan Withdraws. In rejecting the verdict, Matsuoka declared that Chinese sovereignty was a fiction, denied that the League could have settled the controversy between China and Japan, and declared that the intervention of the League had only raised false hopes in China and encouraged her "to take an attitude of defiance against Japan." In his closing speech, on December 8, 1932, Matsuoka had given the League credit for rendering "a signal service in connection with the Manchurian question by preventing the Powers from taking sides in this matter." This was "a great service which the League has rendered for peace in the Far East." But in his valedictory in February he declared that the efforts of the League had only resulted in adding confusion to the situation. He ended by begging the Assembly for the sake of the peace of the Far East and the world "to deal with us on our terms and give us your confidence."

In declaring the resolution of February 24 unanimously adopted, President Hymans replied that: "The use of force, far from hastening or facilitating a solution of the dispute, can only prolong and aggravate it. Finally, the world fully realizes that some day an international settlement will have to be reached." A solution which would reconcile the rights and interests of two great nations was essential. The Japanese delegate then read a dignified farewell, in which the Japanese Government declared that it would "make the utmost efforts for the establishment of peace in the Far East," and ostentatiously withdrew with his delegation from the Assembly. The formal notice of Japan's withdrawal from the League followed, on March 27, 1933.[74]

Japan Stakes Her Future upon Force. At the close of seventeen months, as at the beginning, Japan was willing to settle all questions affecting herself and China "on our terms," and on no other basis. She was fully determined to carry through "the establishment of peace in the Far East" by force of arms, compelling China

[74] The American Secretary of State replied to the Assembly resolution of February 24 within twenty-four hours of its issuance, saying that our Government had endeavored to give support to the League "reserving to itself independence of judgment with regard to method and scope." With the Assembly's "measured statement of conclusions" we were in substantial accord. Insofar as was appropriate "under the treaties to which it is a party," the American Government expressed "its general endorsement of the principles thus recommended" and earnestly hoped that the two nations would "conform their policies to the need and the desire of the family of nations that disputes between nations shall be settled by none but pacific means."—Willoughby, *The Sino-Japanese Controversy*, pp. 500-501.

The United States thus emerged from the Manchurian storm, clinging to what was left of its Kellogg pennant and hoping that the League ship under it would not go to pieces.

to accept Japanese police control and economic domination. First Manchuria, then Jehol, then North China must submit. Afterwards, Inner Mongolia and other regions would have to be brought under Japan's sway—down to the Yellow River perhaps. Or would it be the Yangtse? Where could Japan stop in forcing China to be orderly and to trade with Japan? Having staked her existence solely upon the sword, how could she rest until the nearby maritime provinces of Russia were conquered? China is vast, amorphous, and growing in power. The militarization of the minds of her youth is proceeding apace, spurred by Japan's triumphant demonstration that there is no other arbiter. While Chinese armaments grow, those of Russia increase still faster. Japanese power on the mainland must grow without ceasing if the two tremendous peoples which she challenges are to be permanently overawed. Having seized control of Japan's future, is there any point in the domination of East Asia at which the Japanese military can rest, content that it is safe?

What of the League? And the League of Nations? Has not the victory of Japanese arms made its future outlook even more desperate than that of Japan? Having failed to protect China from dismemberment, could the League have any more success when other militarists were ready to extend their borders? While the militarists must continually advance, must the League not perpetually retreat until it is lost in another world war more terrific than the last? Perhaps. Yet the League is unmistakably breaking a new trail. Before 1914 it would have been unthinkable that the acts of a Great Power should be examined by the family of nations, through an organized Assembly in which the voice of every nation could be heard, though somewhat awkwardly in the case of the United States. Only twenty years ago it would have seemed doubtful that the facts in a dispute so remote and complicated could be ascertained. Today that much is settled. No one who reads the Lytton *Report* can doubt the ability of the League to establish the essential facts of any controversy. That we can find out who is the aggressor is no longer open to question.

It is as clear also that world public opinion alone is not sufficient to restrain a powerful aggressor. It is quite probable that in the long run the weight of its disapproval may be sufficient to bring down the aggressor, when he comes into a great crisis in war, but that is no more certain than that the League can last with nothing but moral victories to its credit.

That the League saved its soul by the action of the Assembly in the resolution of February 24, 1933, is true enough. If it could not persuade or control an unruly member, it at least refused to bow to her. Instead, she was virtually expelled from the League by a temperate judgment, which was also so firm that Japan had either to accept it or to leave the League. That it is enough to pass judgment and do nothing more would not be alleged by this writer. But the League did look to the future and the future belongs to the League. The Japanese militarists may trade upon the slender resources of Japan until she sinks suddenly back into the ranks of the small nations. A few militarist nations may be able to plunge the world into another war which will hurl other peoples down with them into a common ruin. But when the destruction of civilization has again been halted, the need for the League, in all its original strength, will be piteously greater, not less. The experience gained by the League up to that time will also be infinitely larger than that which existed in the year 1913.

Washington Defeated with Geneva. Yet no belief in the inevitable necessity of world organization can cover up the pathos and the extent of the failure which was finally registered when Japan withdrew from the League. And no convenient memory can eliminate from the record the failure which came home to the United States. The United States had founded the League. Then she had quickly turned her back upon her own creation, attempting to settle her own urgent security problem by hailing the nations, especially Japan, to Washington. The nations came. Japan was put upon the carpet, sworn to non-interference in China, and sent home with the naval and military control of the Orient securely in her grasp. Then when she proceeded to exercise that control without any serious fear of interruption, the United States suddenly realized that she very much wanted to see the League do just that for which it was founded. We rushed to the League's aid but soon discovered that at the last moment we could not get into the League quickly enough to give it success. The authority and prestige with which we might have endowed the League during the ten years respite before its great test came, could not suddenly be conferred. The belief that the League could not be successfully defied—which our irreplaceable leadership and authority might have established in the minds of militarists everywhere—could not be instantly created in the autumn of 1931. We, therefore, could only advance and retreat from Geneva, trying alternately to push the League and then to lead it, without doing more than to slow up Japanese action momentarily. The world forces which indispensably require law and order among the nations were divided and impotent. And when it became probable that the limitless and persistently recurrent agonies of world war would have to be endured again before the opportunity to establish the peace, which had been lost in 1919 and 1920, could be regained, no people wanted the League to retrieve us all from disaster, if it could still be done, any more than the Americans.

The failure of American statesmanship was disastrous. Not only had the League been cast aside at its birth, but in the years afterward our political leaders had never had the courage to tell our people that membership in it would have great advantages. It is to the credit of the short-sighted Republican era under review that its last Secretary of State did his best to repair the damage done by Normalcy and its men of little vision. He had the good sense not only to try to merge our efforts toward halting Japan with those of the League, but the courage to go to Geneva to do what he could. That proved to be little, but Secretary Stimson did not quit. He struggled manfully to find some way to preserve the collective system and he accomplished more than any one else. Stimson has been ridiculed by many for writing notes which only angered Japan. But at least he was not guilty of seeing the post-war peace machinery broken down without trying to prevent the disaster.[75]

Nor did Stimson let it go at that. He has since published his account of the Manchurian crisis with the avowed purpose of stressing the need for regularizing our relations with the League. In *The Far Eastern Crisis* he repeatedly emphasizes the advantages which the members of the League had in approaching the crisis and the disadvantages under which we labored. We had sponsored the Pact of Paris and the Nine Power Treaty, yet neither provided us any machinery with which to work, while the League members had it ready at hand. "In short," he found, "they lived in a world purporting to be governed by law and its methods. We still lived in what was little better than a world of anarchy, governed by force or the threat of force." Stimson is emphatic, too, in his conviction that, at the very least, those who are willing to lead collective action in defense of the peace must not be hampered by the fear of being "stabbed in the back" by us.[76]

One man could not reverse the mistakes and neglects of a decade, but Stimson has made a courageous and able contribution toward that end.

[75] Similarly, the Irishman Sean Lester did valiant service at Geneva in rallying the small nations in the League.

[76] See Henry L. Stimson, *The Far Eastern Crisis*, New York, 1936, pp. 40, 189, 190, 254. The serious student of American foreign policy will wish to read the whole of the book. Among other important features it has a long-range view of what the League did accomplish.

Underwood & Underwood

HENRY L. STIMSON

CHAPTER XIV

FOR AND AGAINST THE LEAGUE

THE DOMINANT faction of the Republican Party had rejected the League of Nations in 1920 as something which did not concern the United States. It was, said the Irreconcilables, either too strong or too weak and in any event it would cost us more than it could be worth to us. The powerful United States had no need of a League to keep the peace.

Eleven years passed, and the inevitable occurred. A Great Power decided to disregard the League Covenant, along with the American-sponsored Nine Power Treaty and Kellogg Pact. Then for nearly eighteen months the American people watched anxiously the efforts of the League to cope with Japanese aggression, hoping that it might muster enough strength to restrain the aggressor. Some, to be sure, remembering their own responsibility for the abstention of the United States from the League, mocked its efforts and hoped it would fail. Others were inert, as always. But the great majority of those who led public opinion saw all too clearly that aggressive militarism had lifted its head again and realized that successful restraint of it would free the world from the most deadly danger which confronts it. The issue, moreover, was not academic and remote. It centered on our nearest Eastern neighbor, a power which, if unchecked, might reach for dominant control of the Pacific ocean. If the Chinese be excepted, probably no people wanted the League to succeed more than did the Americans of 1932. While still at the bottom of a terrifying economic depression which was closely related to the last war, we had no desire to see the start of other wars which might be followed by equally disastrous results.

In an effort to find out what our feeling toward the League was, the writer made a survey of editorials printed in all parts of the nation immediately after the publication of the League's verdict of February 24 on Japan's course in Manchuria. An effort was made to scan the pages of every important newspaper available in the Congressional Library. The results are presented below. To examine sectional trends, if any, the nation has been divided into four parts, the East, the South, the Midwest and the West.

Eastern Opinion in February, 1933

Not Our Affair. Of the 44 Eastern newspapers which expressed an attitude toward the international restraint of aggression on the occasion of the League's resolution of February 24, two took a definitely hostile position. From the fastnesses of Maine the *Bangor Daily Commercial* of February 25, 1933, was sure that: "There is no general desire in this country to punish Japan and rather a belief that the affair is that of the League to which the United States does not belong." The *Camden Courier-Post* (N. J.) was even more forthright. On February 27, under the title "Washington Was Right" the *Courier-Post* averred that the League might be "right or wrong, but it is none of our affair regardless. . . . We must not take sides. We must keep hands off." The following day the *Courier-Post* questioned still more sharply the cooperation of the United States with the League. It appealed to the verdict rendered in the election of 1920 and asked, "What business is it of ours to meddle over there?" The United States might "well join in an arms embargo against both nations," but no "active form of meddling in the Far East!" [1]

The United States Was Concerned. The *Portsmouth Herald* (N. H.) of the same date was not so sure. Most of the disorders were "remote from Washington yet the American Government must cope with ramifications from all of them." Similarly, the *Concord Daily Monitor* (N. H.) (February 27) thought that the Japanese aggression in China proceeded with "such complete defiance of obvious justice and the complaints of other nations"

[1] No other newspaper examined appealed to the election of 1920 as the governing rule of our conduct in 1932.

that the situation was "ominous" with danger. The *Springfield Republican* (February 25) felt that "collision was therefore inevitable, and, if Japan were bent on following so anti-social a course, the League might have felt obliged to expel it from membership if it had not withdrawn in offended dignity." The *Providence Journal* (February 25) hailed the action of the League Assembly as "a high-water mark of courage and determination," and the *Day* of New London, Connecticut (February 25) assessed it as "a firm and positive stand after months of cautious negotiation." To the *Hartford Courant* it was "an historic event of great importance." Some cooperation with the League was, of course, desirable.

The *New Haven Journal-Courier* (February 27) believed that "Japan, the League and America have crossed the Rubicon." Counseling patience and steadiness, the *Journal-Courier* approved of our association with the new Committee of Twenty-One designed to follow up the Assembly's verdict. "It is difficult," said the *Journal-Courier*, "to see how we could refuse. For this bid amounts to an invitation to wield predominant influence in counsels which will affect us vitally anyhow. The old isolationist dream is spent; by the Stimson doctrine we are precipitated into the thick of the Asian crisis. Our stake is heavy in the Orient and in the Pacific. It is inconceivable that any action taken there can leave us untouched. It would be simple wisdom, then, for us to place ourselves in a position to shape action there."

The League Commended in New York. The *New York Post* (February 25) hoped that "this universal condemnation of what Japan has done may yet bring that country to its senses." The *Buffalo Evening News* (February 27) stated without dissent that "the United States supports the League on the Manchurian question." The *News* concluded that "world opinion is directed against Japan as it never before has been directed against any other nation," and thought that Japan could hardly continue indefinitely warfare that was universally condemned. The *Syracuse Post-Standard* (February 27) was not displeased that our support of the League "makes unanimous world opinion that Japan despite her protestations and withdrawal of her delegates from the League of Nations Assembly, is engaged in fact in a war of unjustified and indefensible aggression." In setting Japan "off in a corner by herself," the *Rochester Democrat and Chronicle* felt that the League had done an impressive thing, the moral weight of which might yet have its effect on the peace-loving element of the Japanese people. The League "must now decide upon the next step." [2]

Action or Retrogression? What that step was to be was not clear to the *New York Herald Tribune* (February 25). In an editorial entitled "The Turning Point," the *Herald Tribune* gauged the League's action as a courageous meeting of the issue presented by Japan. The League statesmen throughout the long controversy had "put forth every effort which they felt their system to be capable of, and now in voting without dissent the unequivocal report of the Committee of Nineteen they have done their utmost. They have faced the basic issue of what the League system may practically be worth, squarely presented to them by Mr. Matsuoka as he stalked defiantly from the hall. They allowed him to go in silence; this was the test, and they accepted it."

But the earnestness of the League's effort only emphasized the slightness of the results achieved, and if non-recognition did not get results the League would have to be recognized as a debating society only, valuable but not the league intended by its authors. "Men will then understand," concluded the *Herald*

[2] The same editorial summed up the case against Japan as follows: "In the early stages of the controversy, Japan commanded a large share of sympathy throughout the world. It was recognized that she had a real case in Manchuria, based upon valid treaty rights, and that her interests had suffered from the chaotic conditions under Chinese rule. The whole situation seemed to be one susceptible of arbitration by the League of Nations. In refusing the persistent and patient offers of the League to compose the quarrel, Japan left herself open to the inevitable inference that what she wanted she intended to take by force. Her excuse of 'preserving order' in Manchuria was weakened by the obvious fact that the policy she pursued was producing, not order, but quite the reverse."

The *Rochester Times Union* of February 28 and March 1 also had thoughtful editorials on the League's action.

Tribune, "that this avenue to universal peace is definitely estopped; the understanding may free their minds to grapple again with the problem of finding a new one." The *Herald Tribune* suggested that there might be a substitute for a league with power enough to keep the peace but it did not essay the task of outlining the substitute. Who, indeed, could?

Firmness Required. In Pennslyvania, the *Lancaster New Era* (February 25) agreeing that the League had "acted as best it could under the circumstances" was unable to see any alternative to the debating society role if the League stopped now. Assessing the occasion as "historic in its importance" the *Philadelphia Public Ledger* held that the problem demanded "the utmost in firmness and patience which world statesmanship can provide." In this great endeavor the part of the United States could not be a small one, thought the *Harrisburg Patriot*.[3] While we had cooperated in the present instance, the regrettable impasse "might have been averted had Uncle Sam been a full fledged member of the League, acting in open concert with the forty other nations." Weakened and incomplete as it was, the League had buried in confusion those critics who had predicted it would never brand a great power. "Man's history never recorded a finer demonstration of world unity and cohesion in behalf of a great principle than when the representatives of forty nations in the League of Nations Assembly voted to condemn Japan for its Manchurian policy of grab. Men who love justice and courage can scarcely fail to be moved by that spectacle. . . . The League of Nations has proved its worth." Likewise, the *Pittsburgh Post-Gazette* (February 25) felt that the League's condemnation of a great power had "an importance that cannot be minimized."

Time for a United Front. "The League will undoubtedly win new converts by its sturdy stand," said the *Hudson Dispatch* (N. J.) (February 25). "A year ago some people were sneering at the League, expecting it to cater to Japan, rather than lose so strong a nation." Yet the League went carefully about its investi-

[3] Quoted in the *York Gazette and Daily* (Pa.), March 2, 1933.

gation. "It refused to be hurried and it refused to be bluffed by Japan. As a result, Japan has lost in public respect, the League has gained." "Japan Stands Alone," agreed the *Trenton State Gazette* (February 28). World opinion faced armed might. One must prevail, and it was "more than possible that Japan will soon learn that isolation is by no means a negative experience and that the pressure which may be exerted through this means may be as distressing as the pressure of force." [4]

"Now is the time for law-abiding nations to stand together," declared the *New York World-Telegram* (February 25). Stressing the menace of war, not only in the Far East but from the anti-treaty powers in Europe, the *World-Telegram* continued: "In this emergency there is only one chance for peace. That is a complete united front by the Powers on the basis of the treaties. In the name of peace the United States at once should declare cooperation with the League of Nations in the Far East and recognize Russia. Without that united front the peace of the world is not worth much."

It was "Time For a United Front," agreed the *Trenton Evening Times* (February 28). "American endorsement of the stand taken by the League of Nations in the Sino-Japanese dispute is extremely gratifying from the standpoint of sane internationalism. . . . This is a good time for nations to stand together in opposition to war. Japan has proved herself to be an international outlaw, and the circumstances plainly call for concerted protest. . . . The factor of supreme importance will be a united front on the part of western nations."

Between right and wrong there can be "No Neutrality of Opinion" argued the *Jersey City Journal* (February 27). "This business of keeping out of entangling alliances is becoming more and more difficult." Even if Stimson had not stated our attitude previously, "there would have been no escaping the issue. . . .

[4] The *Daily Journal* of Elizabeth, N. J., said on February 28: "Japan, in defying world opinion regarding her aggression in China, is deliberately adopting the policy of isolation from the rest of the world. Japan in time may come to realize that it is far from an advantageous policy."

In such a row as that between China and Japan there can be no in-betweens: either the Japanese are to be commended or they are not. Silence, or neutrality of opinion, would mean that we had no strong opinions in favor of China, and therefore assented to the invasion of Japan. The same consideration guaranteed that the league would not be able to assume a hands-off or neutral attitude."

Secretary Stimson's attitude had been amply vindicated, continued the *Journal*, and without encouraging war. The whole episode had exposed the difficulty of our maintaining isolation. It impelled wonder as to "why there should still be such fear in so many places in this country about the idea that the United States ought to join the League of Nations. Surely keeping outside has not avoided international entanglement."

The League Justified. In West Virginia the views of the editors were almost as strong. There could be no doubt of the justice of the League's verdict, said the *Huntington Advertiser* (February 25). If the world is patient, suggested the *Charleston Gazette* (March 1), it will find its opinion "as effective as bombs and bullets." The action of the League is "courageous in the extreme," said the *Bluefield Daily Telegraph* (February 28). "It reestablishes the League's right to respectability. It provides a real reason for the League's existence. It reinvigorates it in a degree that is remarkable when one looks back over the League's record. Beyond a doubt, this action has served to save the League of Nations from disintegration. The League is perfectly safe. Its future is assured. But what about Japan?"

She was, said the *Baltimore Sun* (February 25) at the close of a penetrating review of the great opportunities Japan had had to make a case for herself,

> isolated by the relentless logic of her own conduct which has abashed her apologists and united the timid with the reluctant against her. For the first time a great power has been condemned deliberately and after endless patience by an international body reluctant to condemn her but given no alternative. In eighteen months she has failed to convince

a world, hoping against hope that it could be convinced, of the sincerity of her purposes. After eighteen months of skillful dialectic she mustered one vote—her own—in defense of her action toward China. Her guns argued more persuasively than her diplomats. Her lot now is unenviable, the depth of humiliation and bitterness. Whatever the ultimate consequence to her or the world, it seems unbelievable that another nation will soon elect to stand in her place.

Should Collective Action Follow? It is evident that the editors of the East almost unanimously approved of the League's condemnation of Japan. Most of them understood also that probably no further positive action against the Japanese conquest would be undertaken. There was, however, considerable talk of an arms embargo, occasioned by the short-lived British embargo against both Japan and China. This action of the British, in connection with the League's verdict, did lead some editors to consider further eventualities. Were any of them willing to support joint international action to restrain Japan?

Commenting on the arms embargo proposal, the *Kennebec Journal* (March 1) felt that "the American people will be restive under the implication that their country is not doing her best to curb war, wherever it may be." The *Burlington Free Press and Times* (February 25) found "plenty of good reasons why the United States should not ship munitions to Japan." It favored one international agreement to place "all arms manufacturing in the hands of the governments" and another to forbid the sending of munitions to any nation which has violated an international treaty. The *Lynn Daily Evening Item* (March 1) and the *Boston Globe* (February 28) also agreed that "the private munitions exporters merit no solicitude whatever."

Both the *Troy Times* (February 28) and the *Pawtucket Times* felt that the British arms embargo should have been against Japan alone. The latter could not believe that the British Government really wanted a "peace reached through a course which will give Japan a free hand to crush her helpless victim with the passive aid of other nations." The *Hartford Daily Times* (February 27) considered it natural that the question of an arms embargo against Japan should now come before the League, which was "preparing to take its next step in its customary manner of adequate preliminary preparation and continued effort at conciliation." Similarly the *Newark Evening News* (February 28) considered "particular economic measures against the named belligerent" to be in order. The *Christian Science Monitor* (February 24) reasoned that, since we had urged the League to cooperate in our policy of non-recognition of territorial gains by aggression, we should now be willing to support the League's apparent intention to back our policy by embargoes on arms.

Neutrality Advised. The *Wall Street Journal* (March 2) poured upon such suggestions the cold water of neutrality. An embargo against both Japan and China would be more crippling to the latter, while an embargo against one alone would be "decidedly unneutral." Besides, what was there "among the important commodities not almost indispensable to modern warfare"? Peace would have to be made sometime, and, "a nation now manifesting a decided leaning toward one belligerent or the other will not then have the same influence as one that maintains an absolutely neutral attitude. From that standpoint it appears likely that the United States will accomplish more for the cause of world peace if it refuses to declare an embargo against either or both of the belligerent powers in the Orient."

One would have supposed from the *Journal's* icy impartiality that the United States had not been opposing Japan's headlong course in Manchuria for a year and a half so strenuously that all possibility of our acting as an "honest broker" between the disputants had disappeared long ago. However, the *Journal* added that: "If and when a complete international embargo is under consideration, combined with measures for concerted action to render it effective as a check upon predatory warfare, a different question may well be involved."

United Action Essential. The *Journal* evidently thought that no effective economic embargo could be devised. To the *Passaic*

Herald News (February 25) it appeared otherwise. Writing that Japan had "failed at the great crisis in her life as a nation" the *News* added: "It looks as though there was nothing for the rest of the world to do now but to cut her off economically, a course which, if followed, will reduce her forthwith to absolute misery and impotence."

The *Albany Knickerbocker Press* (March 2) also thought that "there may be a point at which further action becomes necessary." "A complete commercial embargo against Japan might be premature," said the *Worcester Evening Gazette*, but "it is time for the public to realize that a policy of vacillation and uncertainty will only complicate the difficulties of a situation which is rapidly approaching a point where firmness and united action are essential to a peaceful solution of the issue."

Likewise, the issue was clear-cut to the *Pittsburgh Press* (February 25). "If the nations want to salvage the peace machinery they will have to do something much more effective than talk about it. An arms embargo against a treaty-breaking belligerent is one of the easiest and most obvious methods, productive of direct results. . . . To permit munitions profiteers to determine government policy on the embargo question is like calling in a germ-carrier instead of a physician to treat a typhoid patient. For the munitions makers not only keep wars going, they help to start wars." There might be great difficulties in the way of imposing a general boycott of Japanese trade, said the *Philadelphia Inquirer* (February 25), but that was apparently the only practical step left to the League. What was the role and responsibility of the United States? "A general boycott, to be effective, would require the cooperation of the United States and Russia, which are not League members. How can the other Powers be expected to run the risk that these two would continue trading with Japan at their expense? There would have to be some definite assurances on this point. It may reasonably be argued that the United States is bound to back the League to the limit, since its own policy of non-recognition has been adopted." "It is a time," concurred the *Wheeling Register* (March 1), "when all law abiding nations should stand together. In this emergency that is the only chance of restoring peace."

The Reaction of Southern Editors

Virginia Newspapers for Cooperation with the League. "As the League, So America" read a caption in the *Richmond News Leader* (February 28). Quoting the drastic provisions of Article 16 of the League Covenant, the *News Leader* commented: "This is the last resort, but it may be necessary. It will not be safe or wise for America to anticipate further action by the League to this end; but if and when the League does apply sanctions, America must support them. That, at the present time, is the only practical way of maintaining the sanctity of treaties." Not quite so emphatic but of similar import was the judgment of the *Lynchburg News* (March 2) that the policy of the United States is "to await action by the League, meanwhile consulting with and advising with the League." The *Newport News Daily Press* (March 2) was against war with Japan, but doubted that Japan was "going to be fool enough to fight the whole world, for that is what she must do if the League of Nations stands by its guns and the United States stands with the League." The United States must stand with the League, believed the *Virginian-Pilot and the Norfolk Landmark* (February 28). Under the heading "We Call Our Policy Good," the *Landmark* asked:

Having made common cause on the policy of non-recognition of Manchukuo, and associated itself with the League in the main findings of fact on which this policy is based, will the United States now associate itself with the League in the consequential steps growing out of this jointly indorsed policy? That is the commanding question of the hour. Only an affirmative answer to this question seems rational and safe. Whether the next step of the nations that have organized themselves for the preservation of world peace shall be one of doing nothing further about Manchuria or of adopting any of the coercive measures contemplated by Article XVI of the Covenant of the League of Nations, the United States must continue to take counsel and act in harmony with the League nations, for only in a united world is there any hope of arriving at the desired goal and arriving at it safely.

A Joint Responsibility. As the Japanese conquest of Manchuria proceeded, "blithe American apostles of 'Let us mind our own business' scoff at the League of Nations and congratulate their fellow citizens that this nation is not a member of that body," said the *Asheville Times* (February 25), but "the truth is that, in moral responsibility, the Government of the United States faces today the same question that keeps the League members at Geneva in council day and night. Because, for better or worse, this nation has signed solemn treaties guaranteeing China against the war of invasion which Japan, in defiance of the world's moral convictions, is now about to wage."

The *Charlotte Observer* (February 27) outlines the proposed embargo steps sympathetically and the *Greenville News* (February 27) thought that "the United States could hardly do otherwise than express its general accord with the position adopted by the League."

The Southeast Cynical. The *Columbia State* (February 27) scoffed at "the simulated furies of indignation" from Japan's fellows and predicted that soon the "wicked old world will go about its interrupted business of plundering its neighbors of fields and granaries and annexing their lands and twiddling their moral thumbs at any of the band that may be detected in too flagrant an act of international brigandage." The *Charleston News and Courier* (March 1) also ran an almost equally cynical editorial, and the *Miami Herald* (February 27) warned against propaganda designed to get us into the war, if there was one. It credited the League with "one strong action" in morally isolating Japan.[5] The *Macon Telegraph* (February 25) hailed the Assembly resolution of February 24 as "the League's clearest cut expression and one which all the facts in the case indicate is a fair and just stand.

[5] The *Savannah Morning News* (February 25) discussed Japan's moral isolation quite dispassionately.

Now more than ever does Japan endanger the peace of the world. We are glad she has been forcibly warned."

The comment most hostile to the League made by any Southern editor came from the *Augusta Chronicle* (February 25). Americans had much cause for congratulation that the League had lately taken up the game of "baiting" the Japanese. The Japanese seizure of Jehol and other warlike acts were ascribed to "the League's strong-arm tactics" and "blustering." Curiously enough the same editor praised Secretary Stimson's policy as preferable to the "economic warfare which President Lowell and other liberals advocated" and which "would surely have brought us into warfare by arms." Doubtless the League would "cease to be intransigent," but if we did drift into war with Japan, we would not be "exposed alone to the forces of Japan." Continuing the neutralist trend of the Southeast, the *Mobile Register* (February 14) was glad to "let the League and the powers go their way and we will go ours." Yet this did not mean "that Japan could afford to assume an attitude of stubborn aloofness." She could not afford a policy of isolation.

Strong Concert with the League Imperative. Taking a long view, the *Montgomery Advertiser* (February 25) was assured that: "Ideas are irrepressible. They are the most potent influences in the life of the race. The idea that peace has at last become essential to the safety of civilization is now very well implanted in the mind of man. So good an idea as that will not be dislodged, but will grow until it bears fruit." To the *Birmingham News* (February 25), war with Japan was "unthinkable." To avoid it, our government "should use every power at its command, in concert with other world powers" to arrest the Asiatic conflict, but "only through concerted efforts." It was only through international action that Japan could be deterred from further madness." Similarly, the *Birmingham Age-Herald* (February 27) quoted Cordell Hull's strong approval of Secretary Stimson's support of the Assembly resolution of February 24. Repeating Stimson's message to Geneva saying that "the league and the United States are on common ground," the *Age-Herald* held that

This means, if it means anything at all, that America is ready to join with the league in taking measures which may be decided upon in the light of Japanese contumacy. If, for example, the league reaches the conclusion that it should require of its members an embargo on arms to Japan, the United States could hardly refuse to take the same step. Tokyo is now put on notice that the condemnation of Japanese policy in Manchuria registered by the league has the approval of the Roosevelt administration. So far as Washington is concerned, there will be no retreat from the attitude taken by Mr. Stimson toward the erection of the puppet state of Manchukuo.

The *Jackson Daily Clarion Ledger* (February 27) rejoiced that the United States stood foursquare for world peace and that its leaders were trying to achieve the ideals of Woodrow Wilson. The *Shreveport Times* (February 27) also took our endorsement of the League's verdict for granted and the *New Orleans Times-Picayune* (February 25) reported that the Assembly "adopted its stinging report with a promptitude and unanimity that tended to drown earlier criticism."

Tennessee Editors behind the League. Tennessee newspapers strongly approved the League's action. The *Nashville Banner* (February 28) wrote that: "It is apparent that the League has behaved with great patience and restraint throughout." There was nothing for the League to do but condemn Japan's course. If Japan had not chosen to quit the League, the League would have been forced to expel Japan.

The *Nashville Tennessean* (February 25) said that the League's deliberations had come to their "inevitable conclusion." Japan had become the "lone wolf" of nations. She must "go it alone, playing her own game in her own way, opposed by the opinion of every other nation in the world, asking no favors and showing nothing but contempt and force." With Japan outside the League were two great powers, the United States and Russia. "After seventeen months of waiting for the Japanese to recover their balance, the League of Nations has definitely accepted the American policy of non-recognition of the Japanese conquest," observed the Knoxville *News-Sentinel* (February 25). Now was the time for a united front. So it seemed also to the *Memphis Commercial Appeal* (March 1). Questioning whether the set purpose of the Japanese military was not to dominate all China, the *Commercial Appeal* called for "a unity of purpose among the white races." This outstanding newspaper doubted that the world was "aroused to the menace that is contained in this policy of Japanese expansion." There seemed to be "no questioning the fact that Japan intends to dominate the great Pacific Ocean, and this certainly is of importance to the other nations of the world as well as to the United States."

Kentucky and Oklahoma for Further Action. Another nationally known journal, the *Louisville Courier-Journal* (February 19) had already spoken frankly of the possibility of arming China, even in spite of a Japanese blockade, observing that: "For the rest it would be carried on through the economic isolation of Japan." A complete economic boycott of Japan seemed to the *Courier-Journal* to be justified by Japan's defence of world law and opinion. Further belying the general supposition that Americans in the deep interior do not have a broad world outlook, the *Daily Oklahoman* (February 27) applauded the League for taking steps toward an arms embargo. The *Oklahoman* also frankly faced the fact that the arms embargo would not be enough. The "arms embargo should be counted an important first step in teaching Japan that it cannot defy world opinion with impunity. If it fails, the nations may bring economic pressure to bear in a way that will be felt by the Tokyo government. The League must be backed in its effort to curb Japan, if the most hopeful agency for the maintenance of world peace is to survive."

The *Muskogee Daily Phoenix* (February 26) feared that the Japanese departure from the League would leave it only a European organization. The refusal of the American Senate to permit this nation to join the League had been the first blow against President Wilson's magnificent conception that the League should "have enough moral force that no nation in any part of the world would dare to stand against its edict." The withdrawal of Japan was the second blow to the League. Writing under the title "The New Wilsonism," the *Houston Chronicle* (February 24) was more hopeful. It thought that signs were not lacking that "the United States Senate, that stronghold of opposition to things international, is about to experience a change of heart." There were still fifteen Democrats in the Senate who had voted for the League and only one of them had changed his mind. New members of the Senate also favored the League.

Embargoes Favored and Opposed in Texas. The *Galveston Tribune* (February 27) did not shrink from standing behind the League. The Japanese would probably reach their objectives "unless the world acts unyieldingly in showing its disapproval by means other than words. The natural decision for the League and its allies to make would be an arms embargo on Japan, followed possibly by an economic embargo." The *Fort Worth Star-Telegram* (February 25), however, opposed any further action on our part. It agreed that the United States held the key position and that the League would hardly resort to drastic action without us, but the final question was, "Does the United States want a war with Japan? To this question public opinion in the United States returns a vigorous negative. It remains for the government in Washington to reflect this public opinion by refusing either to initiate or participate in a boycott of Japan. It is sufficient to adhere to the Stimson policy of non-recognition of territorial acquisitions resulting from illegal aggression." The *Houston Post* (February 27) also decided that it would be "difficult to bring about embargoes, because of the eagerness of munitions makers in the western powers to dispose of their supplies." [6]

[6] The *San Antonio Express* (February 28) and the *El Paso Times* (February 25) carried informative editorials on the impasse at Geneva.

Toward the League. The *Dallas Morning News* (February 28) vigorously rejected a defeatist attitude. The military leaders of Japan did not appear to realize that "the league, the nine-power treaty, and the Kellogg peace pact all point to a code of fair dealing among nations, avoiding war, preferring peaceable negotiations, and favoring arbitration when serious disputes arise. Japan might have gotten substantially all it wished from China had it displayed during the last forty years a spirit of friendly co-operation with China." Now, "international opinion is at last aroused against Japan, it has become an isolated nation, it has no friends in Eastern Asia, and the lands it has already conquered are without love for their masters and would revolt if a favorable opportunity should arise." But to await that solution and to allow Japan to ravish China would be to set the clock of civilization back to 1914. And "if that was a war to end war, where is the war-ending machinery? If the war-ending machinery be not at Geneva, is it in Washington, where we must pay the bills and arm the Sheriff's posse?"

In a later editorial the *News* (March 1) opposed joining in an arms embargo against both Japan and China. We could not surrender to Japan in this fashion "without stultifying our position of 1914-1916. Had we done then what Britain is doing now, Germany would have Europe under its heel today. If we do now what Great Britain has done, we do Japan a military favor." Refusing to admit that there was no course open to us except to submit to fresh wars of aggression, the *News* stood squarely for collective action as the alternative both to submission and to single-handed action to combat the aggressor. "The logic of the situation," concluded the *News*, "is so strongly toward our entering the League of Nations, so as to enable it to take unified action in the Pacific, that it is difficult not to suspect that we are even now trending in that direction faster than we fully realize. Surely joint pressure on Japan to keep the peace is better for us, better for Japan and better for the world than separate pressure with its great likelihood of a Japanese-American war. We want no such war, and it is silly to think that Japan wants it. Certainly she doesn't want it now."

The Western View

For Pressure on Japan. "The League of Nations is redeeming itself in the eyes of America and the rest of the world by its vigorous attitude on the Manchurian question," said the *Albuquerque Journal* (February 15), which looked forward to "an embargo on Japan, at least in arms and finance, and a severance of diplomatic relations." The rash militarists of Japan might bluster but they could hardly "stand up long against universal ostracism." To the *San Francisco Chronicle* (February 25) it seemed also that "the issue is now joined whether a nation which has solemnly agreed not to use war as an instrument of national policy can do so and hold fast to the profits reaped thereby. The answer to this question depends upon how well the rest of the world, outside Japan, can stick together. If it does stick together, neither Japan, nor any other nation, can hold out against it. Brave as Japan is, she cannot make war against a united world."

By contrast the *Arizona Republic* (February 24) predicted that "the great munition interests would be able to exert sufficient influence in Congress to prevent any action that would stand in the way of their seizure of so rich a plum as a great war in the Far East would offer." This opinion was corroborated by the comment of the *Oakland Tribune* (March 2) that "isolationists and arms manufacturers worked together to prevent our Senate from giving heed to the last message which President Hoover delivered to Congress." The *Tribune* (February 25) accepted the action of the League as putting "the weight of a world opinion against Japan."

War Condoned and Condemned. The *Sacramento Bee* (March 1) protested sharply that "the government of the United States should not permit itself to be drawn into any cooperative action with the League of Nations, if that body decides to apply economic 'sanctions' to the Japanese case. . . . The Japanese should realize that this country has no intention of entering on an expensive and useless war in order to uphold a system of treaties which the average American never believed to have been worth signing, and which the average American now sees clearly to have been worth scarcely the paper they were written on." Totally opposite in spirit was the belief of the *San Diego Union* (February 22): "War as an instrument of policy has been tested by experiment, again and again. The results have been recorded by history. It is this type of war whose futility is attested by the vast preponderance of evidence, beyond the shadow of a doubt. The experiment now undertaken by Japan is a cruel experiment, but its more fundamental defect is that it is utterly useless and unprofitable. The experiment with war as an instrument of policy has reached the stage of certainty. Japan is brewing its own doom."

The *Tacoma Daily Ledger* (February 25) observed derisively: "Just what the League will do about it is problematicial for as yet the only suggestion coming out of Geneva and the European capitals is to offer sympathy to the United States and Russia in any attempts, military or otherwise, to unsnarl the oriental tangle."

Embargoes Favored. More seriously, the *Portland Oregonian* (February 27) reasoned that both the League's censure and our own non-recognition would be but gestures unless followed up by "some action." A general embargo would gravely injure American commerce. The best that could be said for it was that it would be "very much less costly than war." The American people were in no mood for war, but the *Oregonian* believed that: "They will resort to measures short of war with their eyes open to the dangerous contingencies. They have no animosity against the Japanese people, being well aware of Japan's cramped position." To the *Ogden Standard-Examiner* (February 28) it appeared also that: "The nations which have condemned Japan should be disposed to assist China in every legitimate way." The *Rocky Mountain News* (February 25) likewise considered that: "The issue is a practical one. If the nations want to salvage the peace machinery they will have to do something much more effective than talk about it. An arms embargo against a treaty-breaking belligerent is one of the easiest and most obvious methods, productive of direct results." The *Butte Standard* (Mont.) (February 15) concluded, however, that: "While America's policy regarding the non-recognition of Manchukuo is in accord with the findings the league is now preparing to report, it is most unlikely that this country would join in attempting to enforce a world boycott against Japan."

The Verdict of the Midwest

Around the vast circumference of the United States, editorial writers generally applauded the League's effort to restrain Japan and believed that the United States should stand behind the League. What was the view of the editors in the great Midwest area, usually considered to be strongly isolationist?

Divergent Views in Minnesota. "The league has no other course open except to repudiate the Japanese doctrine of force," said the *St. Paul Pioneer Press* (February 16). "The Manchurian aggression is a challenge to the concept which the world has embraced of international cooperation as a substitute for force. The new peace system will be vindicated or again revert to the war system that led to 1914." The League had "vindicated itself in a time of great crisis as something far more than the futile debating society which its unfriendly critics would have liked to believe it." The League's verdict was also "a diplomatic victory of the first magnitude" for the United States Government. The issue was "whether military aggression or peaceful and legal cooperation is to be the inspiring principle of the world. Through the first phase of this test the League has come with flying colors."

Of a far different tone was the comment of the *Minneapolis Tribune* (February 28). The *Tribune* was reluctant to consider a complete embargo and doubtful of the efficacy of an arms embargo. It ended by saying that: "If the powers are consistent this should apply to China as well. If it does not the world aligns itself definitely on the side of China, whereas the only real consideration should be to remain on the side of peace." In the same vein the *Mankato Free Press* (February 25) advised: "Proceed With Caution." American policy certainly could not go much further than to "support the Stimson non-recognition doctrine."

Continuous War against War Required. For its part, the *Sioux City Tribune* (February 27) recalled that: "Americans fought a war firmly believing that they were making the necessary sacrifice to end all war." The fight against it must be kept up. Quoting a prominent Midwest paper on "meddling," the *Des Moines Register* also demanded to know "whether the transportation of shipload after shipload of the materials of warfare from the United States to Japan is or is not 'meddling with events in the Far East,' and if not, why the stoppage of such shipments *would* be 'meddling.' "

Moral Isolation Enough. Many editors had expressed, with the *St. Paul Pioneer Press*, the view that moral disapproval could be "a disastrous force for the Japanese." No newspaper voiced this conviction more powerfully than the *Omaha World Herald* (March 2):

Civilization stands as one unit in stern condemnation. It will continue so to stand, and to maintain its refusal to recognize or deal with the government Japan sets up in conquered territory. It will continue to pillory Japan as a nation perjured and faithless, rendered a pariah by her own conduct.

That is perhaps all that civilization can do, or ought to do, or needs to do. There is talk, indeed, of embargoes, of economic boycotts, of severance of diplomatic relationships. Any or all of these measures might well prove futile. What is certain is that no western nation, least of all our own, will permit itself, by any punitive device, to incur the danger of being drawn into the war that Japan has unleashed. That would be only to spread and magnify the horror, to multiply the number of victims, to compound the awful felony.

But there is something more important, in the end more effective, than sanctions. It is that tremendous, irresistible imponderable that directs itself against the Japanese government from every quarter of the world—the power of an aroused international conscience organized and directed in stern protest.

No man may live to himself alone. No nation can—least of all Japan. No man could endure for long with every neighbor, near and far, pointing at him the finger of indignant scorn, an outcast from all friendly association. No more can a nation. And for the first time in history Japan, as a nation, occupies that unenviable, that unendurable, position.

In just what way world opinion, the world conscience, will soon or late enforce retribution and reparation no one now can say. But it is as certain as that the empire of the spirit is mightier than the empire of the sword.

The same conviction was uttered more tentatively by the *Kansas City Kansan* (February 27), while the *Kansas City Times* (February 27-28) cautioned against spreading the field of violence when natural factors were already acting powerfully against Japan. Our support of the League's resolution was "a foregone conclusion." It was given "with exemplary promptness." [7]

The *Illinois State Journal* (February 27) though it noted that we preferred to hold to the policy of the forefathers, felt that: "When the United States and the League see eye to eye on an international question, a nation out of step may be persuaded to back down." The *Chicago Daily News* was not so sure, urging the "utmost caution" in defining our position "beyond non-recognition of aggressive seizures of territory."

Michigan Hailed the League. Michigan editors viewed the future with courage. The *Grand Rapids Press* (February 28) suggested that the future might well look back upon Friday, February 24, the day on which "the League of Nations took its first definitely positive action to curb warfare," as "one of the most important dates in history." The *Flint Daily Journal* (February 25) felt that Japan's isolation could be altered only by a change of Japanese policy. The *Detroit Free Press* (February 28 and March 1) was sure that: "Japan would not be able to stand against

[7] The *Times* is the morning edition of the *Kansas City Star*.

the world alone, either with arms or with economic weapons." But unless our Government should take "a definite, formal stand against Japan by joining with the League of Nations in a move to discipline her" we should avoid any embargoes against Japan alone.[8]

The *Detroit News* (February 28) believed strongly that something new in human history had occurred.

Something happened on Friday which had never taken place in the history of the world, something that a few years ago would have been regarded as impossible within our time. The representatives of 42 nations, sovereign and independent, sat in judgment upon the acts of a powerful empire, and without a dissenting vote condemned them. The case had been well argued by both sides: the matter had been investigated by a commission; differing statements as to fact had been made, differing interpretations had been heard. Yet without reservation or quibble, 42 nations in effect declared that Japan had offended against the international comity, and demanded that she submit to a plan of settlement.

The vote was not taken in anger but in sorrow. No threats were uttered. No intention was voiced of raising a hand against Japan. She submitted to no penalty save moral condemnation. Yet her statesmen can see the fruits of her military victory turning to ashes.

The world has turned a new corner in its history. "The good old rule" no longer suffices: "The simple plan that they should take who have the power and they should keep who can." It worked very well for a long time: powerful nations took what they wanted, proclaimed the feat and received the acquiescence of their neighbors, who were most of them engaged in the same game. But now there is an international organization in which not only the strong but the weak and small as well have an equal voice; and in this case it was the weak and small who insisted that the League do its duty or confess its futility. Behind them they had not only their own home opinion, but that of the great majority of the larger countries; and it was proven that at last an international popular conscience had developed, which, given an opportunity in the League for expression, could control diplomats and traders and force them to do its will.

[8] Another Michigan daily, the *Bay City Times* (March 24) contained a remarkably well-informed editorial on the provisions of the Covenant dealing with sanctions, detailing especially the efforts to amend and interpret Article 16.

"This," added the *Muskegon Chronicle* (February 28), "is the world 'super-government' of which statesmen in the United States were frantically warning us only a few years ago, when our Senate was deterred from ratification of the covenant of the League on the ground that in so doing the United States would surrender its national sovereignty and its right henceforth to control its national policy in world affairs. The procedure with reference to Japan has been in exact accordance with the covenant. Every effort at conciliation and compromise was made before the Assembly took the decisive step, even, of making a formal pronouncement to the world by which Japan now stands morally condemned." Yet "the 'super-governing' bogey that was waved before our eyes here in the United States" had "all through this troubled period of world readjustment kept us from having any part in the slow, painful but vitally necessary process of saving civilization from self-destruction."

Cooperation Deprecated. The *Indianapolis News* (February 25-28) wondered if Japan's challenge inaugurated a vast campaign of conquest that would establish her supremacy in the Orient. The *News* was not enthusiastic about our membership on the League's advisory committee to observe further developments in Manchuria but agreed that "certainly the United States could not afford to risk an appearance of dissenting from the League's estimate." The contrary was true, according to the *Columbus Dispatch* (February 25, 28). The *Dispatch* was amazed at the amount of war talk. There was "no moral issue at stake. The principles of the League of Nations are certainly not worth fighting for." Most of the great powers, like Japan, only used the League for their own advantage. We must therefore restrain our pro-Chinese feeling and remove from ourselves "the suspicion of aiding China."

Victory at Geneva. Other Ohio editors were deeply moved by the League's verdict. Under the caption "Victory at Geneva" the *Cleveland Plain Dealer* (February 25) recorded that:

The League of Nations fails in the endeavor to halt Japan's war of conquest. And in that failure it wins the greatest victory in its history. For, after having exhausted every resource to bring about conciliation and to establish reasonableness, the League Assembly has voted, with only Japan's voice dissenting, that the Japanese aggression in Manchuria is without justification and that 'independent' Manchukuo is a shallow sham. Such a mustering of world opinion against one of the greatest and proudest nations is indeed a triumph. It is not to be doubted that some of the more powerful members of the League, notably France and Great Britain, have voted on the side of international justice in disregard of their selfish interests.

The *Plain Dealer* granted that Geneva could not enforce its judgment, but: "The League's voice, which is the voice of civilization, is raised in calm but mighty condemnation, and historians of the not remote future will appraise this protest at its just value." "A Jury of the Nations," wrote the *Cincinnati Enquirer* (February 25), "after months of inquiry and deliberation has brought in a verdict of guilty." This action "means first that the League of Nations has restored its waning prestige as an agency for enforcing international law and treaty observance. And it means, secondly, that the world is completely in accord on a policy calculated to isolate Japan until that power adjusts its course of conquest to the public opinion of the world and the spirit of the peace treaties."

"The League Delivers," agreed the *Dayton Daily News* (February 25):

A question which has been hanging over the world for a year and a half has this week its answer. Would the League of Nations, once it was confronted by the lawlessness of one of the mightier nations, stick to its guns? Would the League as definitely condemn great Japan, violating its obligations as a member of the League, as it would little Bolivia or Paraguay when doing the same thing? The skeptics all said no; the League would confront a recalcitrant lamb with a firm face; but let a lion roar, and see it run.

When the League sent its commission into Manchuria to study the situation created by Japan's invasion, that was a sign of the expected weakness. The League, to its critics, was merely playing for time, evading the issue. The commission returned with its report, that most remarkable study of the merits of the case, wholly condemning

Japan. Instead of adopting the report, the League referred it to another commission to seek an adjustment by mediation. This, again, was taken by the cynics as a mark of the inability of the League to face the violence of a great military power. It was one more evasion of the issue." But now for the first time in human history a great nation has been haled to a bar of justice and has heard its guilt proclaimed. The League met the test. It has not evaded the issue. It has set a precedent which, whatever the result in this particular case, will stand as long as human history is written as a pivot point in the progress of the world.

We can be patient with the situation as it is now left. Time seems certain to enforce this verdict as men and munitions could never do. A step, not a long one, perhaps, but a vital step, has been taken toward the evolution of a world ruled less by violence and more by law.

The Chicago Tribune for Japan. Four or five of the editors studied in this survey scoffed at the League and at the possibility of reform in international morals. But in all the vast reaches of the United States, was there not one newspaper which would openly defend Japan's course in Manchuria? Aside from the Hearst press there was in fact one newspaper whose aversion to the League was deep enough to enable it openly to take the Japanese side. In its issue of February 15, the *Chicago Tribune* wrote approvingly that the Japanese Foreign Minister had cabled Yosuke Matsuoka "to take his hat and depart the moment the league undertakes to publish recommendations based upon the conclusions of its Manchurian investigation committee." Under the caption "Stimson Is Worth a Thousand Samurai," the *Tribune* continued:

Thus the activities of our own Henricus Asiaticus, Mr. Stimson of the state department, approach the probability of great good for the Japanese empire. Mr. Stimson, who has come more nearly to a realization of the aspirations of many American leaguists, who has more nearly put the United States in the league than any other leaguist found possible, sends Japan out, or is apparently in a fair way to do so. His Manchurian diplomacy has done his own country the injury of involving it in Geneva's processes and decisions and it has enabled Japan to withdraw itself from the complications its adherence to the league made for it. A handsome statue of Henricus Asiaticus in Tokio would have much to inspire a donor. Some day the Japanese may recognize their friend. Some day the United States may more clearly perceive a mischief maker. Like many another meddlesome Mattie, Wrong Horse Harry had done good where he least expected or intended to do it. . . .

Mr. Kellogg was bitten in his softest susceptibilities by the Wilsonian bug. From him these ideas swarmed on Mr. Stimson, who became inflamed all over. He now seeks to infect the department permanently. American diplomacy has not been afflicted with a worse nuisance or a worse danger in fifty years.

For its part the *Tribune* had not budged an inch since 1919. All other American editors might agree that the League had been born to fill an immeasurable need and that its authority was now in desperate need of vindication; the *Chicago Tribune* was not yet able to wish it well. In perfect tune with the spirit of the Japanese army leaders, who continually talked of the "realities" (forgetting of course some of the greatest), the *Tribune* said on February 21 that: "Japanese statesmanship thinks in terms of the Asiatic realities and is not easily shaken from its purposes by western analogies. It is we who draw conclusions from surface appearances and expect results which do not arrive in oriental conditions, for east is east and west is west." How much pressure could or would be brought upon Japan by the League powers and the United States had "yet to be shown. But nothing transpiring up to this time suggests that it will be strong enough to prevent Japan from pursuing a course which it believes to be essential to Japanese security and prosperity. It is true that Japanese financial and social conditions are not favorable to a long and costly war, but it would seem that the Japanese statesmen feel this to be Japan's hour and have the fortitude to exploit it."

Having thus blessed diminutive Japan's "fortitude" in beginning the conquest of the largest people on the globe, the most fertile and the most tenacious—and having commended Japan's fortitude in alarming the vast power of Soviet Russia—the *Tribune* was naturally opposed on all counts to an economic boycott against Japan. Although admitting that "all observers seem to be agreed that the precipitate decline in the price of Japanese securities which led to the temporary closing of the Japanese stock exchanges had its origin in Geneva" the *Tribune* was confident that "there can be no boycott unless the United States participates in it because the United States is the principal importer of Japanese goods and as long as Japan can import American goods she has no reason to fear a boycott by the other nations. The question arises whether our state department, which has taken the lead in baiting Japan, has not in some fashion committed this country to joining the league in the economic isolation of Japan. . . . To argue that such a possibility is a substitute for war is egregious folly; it would be much nearer the truth to say that the boycott would serve as a logical prelude to war."

A Prophecy. The longer view was best expressed by an American newspaper published in Paris. Said the *New York Herald*, on September 22, 1932: "The cold truth is that Japan is counting upon the apathy and timidity of the western nations. Item by item, hampered by no ponderable obstacle, she proceeds toward her goal. We predict that the time is not far distant when the occidental powers will regret that they did not combine to prevent the seizure of Manchuria, for it will be divulged that the control of Korea, Shanghai and Manchuria by the Island Empire is only a stage in its imperial march." [9]

Hearst and the League

As between the League and Japan, William Randolph Hearst had no difficulty in supporting Japan. On February 16, 1933, his *New York American* published a lengthy interview, which he gave to the Japanese newspaper *Yomiuri Shimbun* of Tokyo. To leading questions Hearst replied (1) that "the American people have not been led by the operations of the League to have any

[9] "Japan dreamed of nothing less than the unification, first, of the Far East under her lordship, and secondly of the whole of Asia, with possibly an attack upon the whole world as an ultimate object."—Victor Margueritte, *The League Fiasco*, London, 1936, p. 187.

higher opinions of its unselfishness or impartiality than they formerly had"; (2) that "we have respect for China's sovereignty, but we think that China should have some respect for her own sovereignty, and should use her own resources for her own development and her own protection, and not dissipate them in civil war and anarchy."

Earlier Tirades against Japan. Hearst's sympathy for Japan in 1933 contrasted strongly with his earlier diatribes against her. While he was campaigning in 1919 to defeat President Wilson, and with Wilson the League of Nations Covenant, Hearst's editors had not been able to find words strong enough to condemn Japan. On May 7, 1919, the *New York American* warned that: "Constant Preparedness is America's only Guaranty against Japanese Danger." Repeating four times the phrase "Japanese autocracy, military caste and diplomats," the *American* charged them (1) with being modeled upon the overthrown autocracy, militarism and diplomacy of Russia, Germany and Austria-Hungary," (2) "with hating America and constantly stirring up hatred against us in Japan, Mexico and South America, planning to launch a sudden and dangerous attack upon our ocean outposts and upon our mainland, whenever the United States has been lulled into another period of unpreparedness and Japan has simultaneously strengthened her armaments and her resources by the covert conquest of China and the secret colonization of Hawaii, Mexico and the Philippines with Japanese reserve soldiers in the disguise of laborers, gardeners, merchants and the like," (3) with conspiring with the Tsar to desert the allies and "to divide China and all the rest of Asia, India included," and (4) with plotting a joint attack of Japan, Mexico, and Germany on the United States.

Filled with indignation by the Shantung compromise which President Wilson had made with Japan, the *American* cried out on August 8, 1919, that: "Decency and Prudence Alike Demand Protest on Shantung." How "futile" it was "to point to an inchoate nation like China and say that the promise of Japan to return political sovereignty to China over the rich province of

Shantung means anything, even if executed, while Japan reserves to herself the right to control the railroads and mines of Shantung." It would be "politically most stupid as well as shameful in morals were the United States, China's one clean-handed friend among the major white nations, to ratify in silence Japan's present atrocious designs upon Shantung." We might not be "ready to fight the Japanese robbers out of the Chinese province which they have marked off for pillage, but we should not be underwriters of their rapacity." We could "at least say plainly what we think of their projected rascality, repudiate any part or parcel in it and assure the Chinese people of our continued good will and friendly sympathy."

The Japanese Peril in 1919 and in 1933. In 1933, when China had really been despoiled by Japan and the League of Nations was trying to defend her, Hearst could muster no anger against Japan. On the contrary, he talked of China's lack of respect for her own sovereignty in being so weak and disorderly. On August 26, 1919, his *American* saw a "'Plain Moral Issue." It lauded Lodge's Committee on Foreign Relations for "repudiating the Shantung outrage" and was sure that: "As to the effect upon our relations with Japan, the risk is infinitely less, in the future, if the enlightened sentiment of mankind is aroused *now* in time to prevent Japan from organizing the economic and military strength of the 450,000,000 people of Eastern Asia under an autocracy even more secretive, unprincipled and grasping than Germany's ever was. Otherwise another generation will see a greater war than the last, with the United States in the front trenches, and Europe merely looking on or, in part, aiding the enemy."

In 1933, when Japan had actually launched upon the organization of China's 450,000,000 people under her military control, Hearst could not produce even an atom of alarm. On May 3, 1919, the *American* exclaimed, concerning Shantung: "What the consequences may be to the world, after one or two generations, if the extension of Japanese power over this fertile, densely populated region, with its police, its schools and all its industries controlled by Japan, staggers imagination." On May 13, 1919, the *American* declared that: "The Japanese conquered Korea by treachery and have ruled the conquered people by ruthless, savage force ever since. . . . The Japanese are not frank and straightforward in their international relations. Their actions speak louder than their words, and are sometimes exactly contrary to their words." In 1933 the *American* was quite willing to see Manchuria go the way of Korea. While campaigning against President Wilson, Hearst had appealed in a signed editorial [10] for a United States of Europe which could combine with the United States of America to protect "Christianity and morality from Oriental depravity." In 1933 when a union of the nations on five continents was opposing Japanese militarism Hearst was for the Japanese militarists.

The League Must Die. In the years after 1919 the Hearst press led the attempt to bury the League alive. On December 7, 1920, the *New York American* carried an article by Senator Borah insisting that the League must disintegrate. An Argentine proposal to increase the number of elective members on the Council went to the heart of the whole scheme. "No small nation can stay in if the amendment is not adopted," declared Borah, "and no great nation will consent to stay in if it is adopted, for the reason that the small nations could always outvote the big ones." Here was the fatal dilemma! "The crumbling process will go on," proclaimed Borah triumphantly.

A few days later Hearst featured a proclamation of the League's death written by Jerome K. Jerome. This obituary said: "Sodden with hereditary disease, with worm eaten body and painted face, it sits propped up in the chair of state at the council table of Geneva. . . . That brainless brat, born amid the abominations of Versailles, whose father was War and whose Mother was Hate, with Sin and Wealth for its godparents, that imp of Satan, nursed by hypocrisy and nourished upon lies, that spawn of Greed and Vengeance decked out by the Big Four in the rags which

[10] *New York American,* August 3, 1919.

they had torn from the bleeding body of peace, thinking to palm it off upon the people as her child, is dead." [11]

Both a Superstate and a Joke. Like other League opponents, Hearst's agents were willing to vary the usual theme that the League was a dreadful superstate by scoffing at its weakness. On September 15, 1921, the *American* protested against the press-agenting of the League. Most of this "stuff" was "pure bunk." The League Council had "no real power"; the Assembly was "a solemn farce." The many reports of activity at Geneva were merely to inveigle the United States into the League. "The League must be dressed up to look important and dignified and more attractive to American eyes than the rag-doll which Mr. Wilson brought home with him, stuffed with rhetorical sawdust and beautified with spangled platitudes." "The Geneva super-government," jeered the *American*, "is a joke." This, however, did not prevent the League from being referred to later, as on September 7, 1925, as "the world's super-government," although the same correspondent, Karl H. von Wiegand, reported four days later that "the league is accomplishing little." [12]

Dissolution Frequently Predicted. To further the campaign to bury the League, Hearst correspondents sent frequent reports that nations were about to resign from the League. On August 21, 1921, Italy would withdraw if France and Great Britain persisted in relegating her to the "second category." In "diplomatic circles" the belief was expressed "that Italy's withdrawal would be the formal step in the dissolution of the league." How difficult it would be later to get Italy out of the League the Hearst organization did not suspect. It was willing, however, to carry an Associated Press dispatch of September 7, 1921, predicting that the

[11] *New York American*, December 12, 1920.

[12] Both on September 7, 1925, and on September 6, 1926, Von Wiegand deplored the "perfect deluge of American requests for admission to the Assembly." These people were "largely individual enthusiasts, who want to spread the League gospel at home, and representatives of pro-league organizations, clubs, societies and churches which believe that American public opinion can be won over to the idea of joining in Europe's miseries."

Bolivian delegation to the Assembly would withdraw if the Tacna-Arica dispute were not considered.[13]

Each crisis at Geneva was likely to be the occasion for predictions of the League's final dissolution. Thus the League's settlement of the Upper Silesian dispute in 1921 would cause Germany and Europe to collapse. "The League was sure to split upon some such rock as this Silesian dispute. . . . Let us be thankful for what the Senate did to Mr. Wilson's stupid and dangerous quack panacea." Again during the Corfu crisis in 1923 Hearst was glad to reproduce a charge by J. L. Garvin that Foreign Minister Curzon and Lord Cecil had ruined the League by attempting to restrain Italy. In 1925, "the moral muddle thickened" under a caption which said, "Moral Issue Stirs Row at League Meet." In March, 1926, during the abortive effort to induct Germany into the League, the "deathblow" to the League was forecast, unless a miracle occurred. A headline from the *New York Herald Tribune* announcing that "The League Faces Wreck" was printed in lieu of the *American's* own headlines, "because they might be colored in opposition to the League, although it is the effort of our paper not to allow its opinions to influence its news columns."[14] This statement was made in an editorial signed by Hearst, who felt certain that the League was now "a wreck. It is like a building tottering and about to fall." "We do not want it to fall on us," he concluded unctuously. "We do not want to be involved in the wreck."[15]

[13] All citations in the remainder of this chapter are from the *New York American* unless otherwise noted. On September 9, 1921, the League was ridiculed in a cartoon above the caption: "Study the futilities of the Assembly of the League of Nations, now meeting in Geneva, and give thanks that your country is still free and sovereign."

[14] *New York American*, October 15, 1921; September 10, 1923; September 25, 1925; March 8, 12, 17, and 20, 1926. It should be said in fairness that in 1923 some articles on the Assembly's work not openly colored did begin to appear. Again in 1924 there were good reports of speeches by MacDonald and Herriot, and on September 11, 1926, an adequate account of Briand's famous welcome to Germany. This dispatch and many other fair ones printed during this month, originated with the Associated Press.

[15] From various dispatches in the *American* it appeared that the League was lax in dealing with the opium traffic, if not actually in collusion with it. A headline of September 20, 1929, announced: "League Adopts American Plan to Curb

Taking the Secretariat Oath Called Treason. The extent to which Hearst was impartial toward the League was illustrated by an editorial which appeared in his papers early in 1931.[16] It was entitled "A Traitor's Oath" and read as follows:

An oath to commit treason, if necessary, against the United States will be exacted by the League of Nations from citizens of the United States who may be employed by the League in the future. Is that statement incredible? Yes, it is absolutely incredible. Is it untrue? No, it is absolutely true. It is the flat, unqualified assertion of an employee of the League who has the effrontery to call himself an American citizen, and who brazenly admits that he is willing to take the oath and live up to it. Let that sink into your minds for a minute, you Americans by birth and by choice, who read this, and when you have thoroughly digested it, read on.

The news of this astounding state of affairs is contained in the following dispatch from Geneva:

"Officials who take the oath of allegiance to the League of Nations owe their first duty to the League, rather than to their own country.

"That is the interpretation placed today on the League's oath by Dr. Benjamin Gerig, an American employed in the Information Section.

"The oath was prescribed at the last meeting. Since it is not retroactive, Gerig does not have to swear to it. He explained:

" 'But if I took the oath, and I am perfectly willing to do so, I would consider that my first duty, in event of a showdown, was to the League, and secondly to my country, the United States.'

"Even a war would not alter conditions, he said. Obligations of the oath, numerous observers here point out, mark the League as setting itself up as a supergovernment."

Presumably Dr. Gerig is a competent witness. He asserts that he is an American citizen, and that assertion has not been challenged. As an American citizen he obtained employment in the Information Sec-

---

Dope." This "triumph came only after vigorous attacks from Latin-American and other victim nations had convinced the League's conservative old guard it was useless to attempt to hold out further against an aroused world opinion." Other headlines of September 16, and 23, 1930, read: "League Flayed for Failure to Curb Dope Evil" and "Evil Gaining Under League: Parley Urged."

[16] *San Francisco Examiner,* January 7; *Chicago Herald and Examiner,* January 8; *New York American,* January 8, 1931.

tion of the League, along with other competent persons who are citizens of other countries.

But there is a far more competent witness than Dr. Gerig that Americans can call to testify, and that is the text of the oath itself. Its exact language as adopted by the League is as follows:

"I solemnly undertake to exercise, in conformity with Article One of the regulations, in all loyalty, discretion and conscience, the functions which have been entrusted to me as an official of the Secretariat of the League of Nations."

Article One mentioned in the oath says:

"The officials of the Secretariat of the League of Nations are exclusively international officials, and their duties are not national, but international. By accepting appointment, they pledge themselves to discharge their functions and to regulate their conduct with the interests of the League alone in view. They are subject to the authority of the Secretary-General, and are responsible to him in the exercise of their functions, as provided in these regulations. They may not seek to receive instructions from any government or other authority external to the Secretariat of the League of Nations."

And there you have it summed up for you, fellow citizens.

There is the writing on the wall. There you see the workings of this supergovernment, stripped of its camouflage, a supergovernment that seeks to rule this nation and all other nations, that demands the peace-time and war-time allegiance of its servants against their own homeland and their own people, that makes a mockery of patriotism and a star spangled joke of the nation's flag.

That is what the League of Nations means, and that is the entangling alliance and supergovernment into which a new attempt is now being made to lure the United States through the back door of the League's Court.

The American people are asked to turn from the leadership of George Washington to the leadership of Benedict Arnold.

No concealment can disguise that fact, no apology can excuse it, and those who try to disguise or excuse it may profit from Benedict Arnold's example.

By implication, the Hearst press denied the right of the League to require the loyalty of its officials. If they pledged themselves to discharge their functions and to regulate their conduct "with the interests of the League alone in view" they were traitors. It was "treason" to agree not "to receive instructions from any government or other authority external to the Secretariat of the League of Nations." Hearst and his editors knew, of course, that treason is very strictly defined in the Constitution of the United States, that it "shall consist only in levying war against them or in adhering to their enemies, giving them aid or comfort." The Hearst executives knew that treason against the United States refers to acts of war, not service in the cause of peace. Nevertheless, the Hearst press did not scruple to attempt a definition of treason which would make any League of Nations forever impossible and brand as traitors any American citizens who enlisted in the service of the League. Behind this charge was, of course, the old forced assumption that, instead of being the servant of the nations, the League was a "supergovernment" seeking to destroy them.

Surreptitious Entry Feared. Hearst's resentment at the apparent approach of the United States to the World Court in 1930 was illustrated by editorial comment on September 23 concerning the effort to amend the Court's statute. Since Cuba was delaying the action of the Assembly, she was a heroine, while the Assembly was "trying to jam through the revision of the Court protocol by a violation of the rules." There was a "bitter exchange of views" between the "political" representative of Greece and the "political" representative of Cuba. On the assumption that people could still be frightened by the proper intonation of the world "political," and especially of "old world politics," the "goings on" at Geneva were described in the following style: "From first to last the whole proceeding reeked with old world politics, old world intrigues, old world jealousies and old world ambitions."

From the beginning the Hearst papers were quick to see the surreptitious dragging of the United States into the League. For this country to accept membership in the Court would be to "sneak" into the League by its back door. Even the Four Power Treaty signed at the Washington Conference was held "to force us to recognize the League of Nations." [17] Naturally when a representative of the United States sat at the Council table, after

[17] *New York American,* September 30, 1930; December 12, 1921.

the Manchurian outbreak in September, 1931, Hearst's ire knew no limits. This was an effort of "old world diplomacy" to unload the whole thing upon the United States. This effort to enmesh the United States in League "politics," it was declared on September 24, 1931, "originates with the Council of the League itself." But by October 15, the editor of the *American* had forgotten this origin in his anger at the Hoover Administration. By that time "the Hoover Administration sent to Geneva an 'unofficial observer' who dallies about the doors of the League tribunal, waiting to poke his nose into an affair that is none of his concern or ours. He tries to force himself upon the League councils, and although Japan growls and resents his intrusion he may get into the mess." By October 17, internationalism had "become a raging obsession with the authorities at Washington." The League of Nations was "a hopeless futility. The hateful lure which it exerts over our Secretary of State is a very irritating fact to Americans." And on October 21 it was "a sorry mess into which our myopic and hapless Secretary of State is doing his best to involve the United States." [18]

From this it was easy to raise the old allegation, on November 12, that we could not boycott either China or Japan because we did not "actually know which is right" and because that "would amount to taking active sides in the war." [19] To the end Hearst dispatches were reporting, as in the *San Francisco Examiner* on September 26, 1933, that: "It was made clear that the League is seeking to draw the United States, on any basis, into the awkward situation created by the clumsiness of the League since 1931, which was climaxed by the withdrawal of the Japanese delegation to the League Assembly."

What the total effect of this kind of constant opposition to the League upon American public opinion has been would be difficult

[18] Quotations are from the *New York American.*

[19] From one year to another Hearst was always insisting that what the old world wanted was "United States money and United States men to pull their chestnuts out of the fire."—*New York American,* November 16, 1931.

to say, but it ought to be taken into account in any appraisal of American attitudes.

That Hearst has had little success in influencing the editors of other newspapers is evident from the preceding survey.

CHAPTER XV

TOWARD THE FUTURE

Shall the military power of any nation or group of nations be suffered to determine the fortunes of peoples over whom they have no right to rule except the right of force?

Shall the strong nations be free to wrong weak nations and make them subject to their purpose and interest?

Shall peoples be ruled and dominated, even in their own internal affairs, by arbitrary and irresponsible force or by their own will and choice?

Shall the assertion of right be haphazard and by casual alliance or shall there be a common concert to oblige the observance of common rights?

—Woodrow Wilson's statement of the issues of the Great War, from his address at the Metropolitan Opera House, New York, September 27, 1918.

THE LAST chapter of this chronicle is written in November, 1937. Since the close of the Japanese conquest of Manchuria the foundations of international law and order have crumbled steadily. Japan had hardly made good her possession of Manchuria before Mussolini decided to duplicate the feat in Ethiopia. After another "incident" had occurred, he poured his military forces into East Africa, during the first nine months of 1935, while nothing was done to stop him until his great war machine was ready to cross the Ethiopian border. Then the League of Nations did resolutely impose economic sanctions against Italy, but the sabotage of the Laval Government of France and the fears of the Baldwin Government in Great Britain prevented the necessary stiffening of the sanctions, and Ethiopia was conquered.

While the fifty members of the League were suffering this second severe defeat, Hitler seized the occasion to denounce the Locarno Treaty and to remilitarize the Rhineland. Since then, with their back door again heavily fortified, the Nazis have been able to concentrate upon their plans for a great German empire in Central and Eastern Europe.

The resistance of Ethiopia had scarcely been overcome before a fascist revolt against the Spanish Republic broke out, in July, 1936, under the tutelage of both Mussolini and Hitler. Each promptly sent arms and men to the Spanish rebels on such a scale as to make the fascist conquest of Spain highly probable. It appears to be established that from 60,000 to 80,000 Italian troops were dispatched to Spain during the first year of the war, and that German intervention, while not so extensive, was powerful.

These events were, of course, not surprising. On the contrary, they were the natural and logical result of the failure of the League to cope decisively with the first great challenge to collective security, the seizure of Manchuria in 1931. After that time Japan went steadily ahead, expanding her aggression below the Great Wall in China. Her pressure took the form of threats, insistence upon puppet governments, wholesale smuggling of Japanese goods, and military action. Meeting with stiffening Chinese resistance, Japan chose to strike again with her whole armed power, during the summer of 1937. Feeling that Italy and Germany had Britain and France immobilized and that Russia was weak internally, Japan's armies swept over North China, while another desperate battle was fought at Shanghai, on a far vaster scale than in 1932. The wholesale bombing of China's great cities, from Canton to Nanking, shocked and aroused the peoples of the free nations until a far higher degree of indignation existed than at any previous time. On October 5, 1937, President Roosevelt denounced the lawlessness of the aggressors in a ringing speech which was timed to stimulate the League's Far Eastern Advisory Committee of Twenty-Three to label Japan as an aggressor. This committee then took the step which the League never ventured to take in 1932, and on the following day our State Department added its endorsement.

This action signified that the world was again brought to the point of deciding whether to resist the ruthless use of force or to give way before it. That humanity will be obliged, against its will, to wrestle with this great central issue until it is decisively settled is all too clear. The men of violence give the nations no choice but to set up an amount of international government sufficient to preserve a tolerable semblance of peace and an acceptable degree of justice.

This volume cannot go into the events since 1933 which have culminated in the crisis of 1937. It is, however, the purpose of this chapter to examine some of the ideas and contentions which have brought the United States to the current crisis shackled by a "neutrality" law which requires the President to apply the severe restrictive measures contained in it to the aggressor and his victim alike. How is it possible for the representatives of the American people to retreat so far as to declare that hereafter we shall be strictly impartial between right and wrong, between brutal conquest and the desperate defense of liberty, between reasonable order and peace on the one hand and perpetual turmoil and disaster on the other?

On November 30, 1937, there appeared in the *New York Times* a two-column editorial which is a plain-spoken description of the position of impotence and danger into which we have fallen. Stating the obvious fact that "the United States has lost its leadership in world affairs," the *Times* places the responsibility squarely where it belongs—upon the isolationists and pacifists in Congress and upon the peace organizations which have been agitating for peace at any price. "Organizing, writing pamphlets and using the *Congressional Record* as their gazette," these elements "gave notice as early as when Japan seized Manchukuo that the fixed future policy of the United States would be to keep out of war abroad, and that it would take no steps to prevent it, however clear the threat to our own institutions." All attempts, in the name of international decency, "to permit aid to nations clearly acting in self-defense against banditry were beaten down in Congress. The world was put upon notice that the United States was out to save its own skin from immediate dangers, and the dictators were informed that the American group controlling policy was prepared to see the world remade on fascist lines without interference and apparently without understanding that this would mean anything dangerous to us at all."

That storm-cellar mentality has paralyzed, for the time being, the power of the United States to prevent or restrain war must be admitted. We are drifting before the storm. We have surrendered our destiny into the hands of the warmakers and passively await the devastations and depressions which are inseparable from their activities. The dictators have received notice that we will not oppose them until they attack our shores, and they are acting accordingly. The world is theirs for the taking. The "greatest" nation on the globe has abandoned all interest in liberty and peace, except for itself alone.[1]

How is it possible for a free, literate people to believe, even temporarily, that it can remain passive and prosperous in a world given over to the savagery of unrestrained wars of conquest?

The Attempt to Reassert Neutrality

It is a difficult thing for a nation, even a free one, to admit that it has made a tremendous mistake. Hence, when it was realized that the United States had won the Great War but lost the peace, it was easier for us to go on to a disavowal of the war itself than courageously to combat the popular belief that, after all, we had no responsibility for collective security.

[1] The "blind" peace organizations to which the *Times* refers are: (1) the National Council for the Prevention of War; (2) The Women's International League for Peace and Freedom; (3) the Fellowship of Reconciliation; (4) World Peaceways; (5) the Committee on Militarism in Education; (6) the Emergency Peace Campaign.

The first two are organizations of some size and intense activity. The last is a temporary offshoot of the same constituents. Before every other consideration they place the preservation of passivity on the part of the United States. They abhor even non-violent sanctions because they might lead to forcible ones. No considerations of right and wrong, of human liberty or of future national safety, move them to abandon the passionate advocacy of passivity. Throughout the autumn of 1937 these six organizations clamorously demanded that President Roosevelt apply the neutrality act to ruthless Japan and crucified China alike. See the *New York Times*, September 3, 4, 9, 20, 23, and 25, 1937.

The Status Quo Is Bad. The Treaty of Versailles was defeated in the United States, not because of its terms, but because it contained the League Covenant. But afterwards, when the full severity of the Treaty became known, it was easy to point to the harshness of the Treaty as a reason why isolation was justified and peace impossible. It became the fashion to praise the peacemakers of 1815 for not taking territory away from France and to allege that the Germans and Hungarians now have legitimate grievances which they will nurse until they can correct them on the battlefield. Hungary did emerge cruelly mutilated from a war which her leaders were reluctantly persuaded to enter only after long argument and much assurance of German backing. At least two or three millions of Hungarians who are now separated from their compatriots should be reunited with them. The necessity of a restoration to Hungary has been recognized by some of her successors and a restitution would be within the outer fringe of practical politics if there were reasonable assurance that this revision of the treaties would not lead to more drastic ones.

Germany, also, has come shorn and humiliated out of a war declared with furious haste in order that the swift lethal blow which alone could preserve and extend the German Empire by war might speedily be struck. Some of her territories have reverted, with sufficient justification, to the peoples from whom they had been taken; others might with greater justice have been left with Germany. It is probable that rectifications should be made in her favor, yet those who extol the map makers of 1815 for their supreme wisdom in refraining from taking any pre-war territory from France overlook the impossibility of avoiding some cessions of German territory in 1919, if France was to be a victor in any sense and if Poland was to be recreated with a chance of survival. The fact that the Congress of Vienna had nothing to its credit other than the non-mutilation of France hardly justifies its elevation above that of Paris.

Austria, source of the decision to strike a heedless blow for the preservation of Germanic rule over the Slavs, and for the extension of its influence southeastward, still lingers helplessly, dependent on the charity of her conquerors, pulled in all directions, living symbol of the necessity of economic union among the new states of the Danubian area. This elementary measure of cooperation for mutual survival is not yet politically possible—nor perhaps will it be while a good chance exists of destroying the new *status quo* by force or by propaganda.

In many parts of Middle Europe large minorities persist, in some cases avoidably, for the most part inevitably. Everywhere there is the economic dislocation and poverty which new boundaries are likely to create and which most people will willingly endure as long as these conditions are plainly the price of political freedom. The new map is far from perfect and its eventual modification is to be taken for granted. But the fact nevertheless remains that it is the best map of Europe that has ever been created. The number of rebellious minorities has been reduced by half and the chance of stability thereby increased in something like the same degree. Whereas the statesmen of the Congress of Vienna have virtually nothing to the credit aside from the non-mutilation of France, the men of 1919 gave full or partial recognition to many repressed nationalities which could not permanently be held in subjection. The liberation of the Czechs and the Poles, the Roumanians and the South Slavs, the Baltic peoples and *Italia Irredenta* may not have been worth a world war. It is a sufficient indictment of the old order that one had to occur before these peoples could be freed.

Neither does there appear to be the slightest hope of peace in the efforts of their former masters to recover sway over them. They may yet have to reach a stable equilibrium among themselves without it following that attempts by the recently defeated peoples to reconquer them will have any constructive end.

Sometime a European *status quo* must be accepted as sufficiently definitive to be preferable to any continental war designed to end it, and we have no present reason to look forward with equanimity to the unending "perfection" of the present map by wholesale slaughter in order that a basis for perfect justice may be established. The one thing that we may expect with greatest certainty is that any smashing of the present map will end in economic chaos, physical devastation, and a welter of war hatreds which will make a just peace impossible. Those who deprecate the lack of benevolence and farsightedness on the part of the men who wrote the "unwise treaties" of 1919 should explain by what process the vindictiveness aroused by the next war could be translated into treaties more wise and more farsighted. Is it to be contended that the triumphant leaders of German militarism, whether past or present, would be more generous and forbearing?

The War Cost Us Too Much. It is not difficult for Anglo-Saxons to sympathize with a defeated enemy. It is easier still for each of several allies in a common war to tell themselves that they paid too much of the bill. Of course the United States paid too much—too many billions, too many men killed, too many lives ruined. So did they all. France with her 1,385,000 dead and 2,675,000 mutilated, with her land devastated and her people mentally wounded and spiritually crucified, with a war debt so great that it could be made bearable only by an 80 per cent inflation of the currency—France paid far too much for the war which was suddenly declared upon her, whatever the long story of its remote origins may have been. Britain likewise, with her 700,000 dead and 2,000,000 men made social liabilities, with her markets gone and still other millions of men unemployed, with her tax rates staggeringly higher than ours—Britain paid far too much for the war which she could not avert. Canada, even, paid far too heavily. With a population one-fifteenth as large as ours she had slightly more of her sons killed. Upon her small resources she placed a war debt of $1,530,000,000. Like most of our allies the Canadians were doomed to live for four interminable years of waiting daily for the news that their men were dead. Surely Canada paid too dearly, along with South Africa, Australia, and New Zealand.

Truly the war cost the United States too much, particularly

since the worst of the bill did not come in until 1929, when our futile effort to re-create a make-believe world collapsed. We do well to recoil from the costs of war.

Our War Aims Failed. Nor did we get anything tangible out of the struggle, except the power to dominate the earth financially and economically for a brief period. Since that adventure came to grief, too, we have been quick to scoff at any possibility of fighting again "to make the world safe for democracy" or "to end war." Inevitably these are sore slogans. But what actually did we do to make the world safe for democracy, aside from feeding the nations during the winter after the Armistice?

Having won the greatest of wars, what, again, did we do "to end war"? It was not those who sought to make that solemn pledge into a living reality who supposed that war would disappear by magic once one great conflict was ended. Nothing was surer than that the new laws against war would be challenged by powerful nations. Nothing was so plain as the need for building a strong League of Nations and doing it quickly. Yet it is not those who have labored to this end for nearly twenty years who now cynically renounce any future wars to end war. This glib renunciation comes instead from those who have put no effort into the immense task of building a world community. When men have spent their lives for generations in intelligent prevention and resolute suppression of the institution of war it will be time to talk of the failure of "the war to end war"—if failure can be admitted without abandoning civilization.

Propaganda Deceived Us. It is easy to say that our great war aims failed—and it is a still greater salve to disturbed complacency to surrender to the new propaganda that propaganda dragged us into the war. It is now said by John Bassett Moore, through the mouth of a Russian Grand Duke, that the United States sent 2,000,000 men across the ocean to "fight for something that did not concern it in the least," while Edwin M. Borchard charges that "the Allied governments in 1917, after an immense propaganda, the like of which had never been seen before, finally succeeded in dragging the United States into a European war it did not understand." [2]

Full justice can be done to the shrewd and effective propaganda of the Allies, as compared with the crude efforts of the Germans, without putting the Americans of April, 1917, upon the same level of intellectual awareness with the Europeans of August, 1914. We had had, after all, more than two years and a half to inform ourselves about the most compelling occurrence that had ever been observed by any except those few who had lived through the Civil War. In this long period of intensive examination of a ceaselessly intriguing phenomenon the acceptance of many propaganda deceits did not prevent us from knowing what the war was about with sufficient accuracy to form a judgment on it. The crucial facts were known then as well as they will ever be.

Who that read the Austrian ultimatum to Serbia did not know that war had been decided upon? If one had doubts, Austria's swift declaration of war removed them. Even in the rush of events, too, there was plenty of time for all who could read to see the demand of Germany that the ring be held while huge Austria-Hungary disposed of Serbia. The invasion of Belgium also, in violation of treaties and of international law, was a fact which no amount of propaganda could cover. Military necessity might be great, but the intention to attack France where she had a right to expect safety was manifest. Above all, it was clear that the political system under which Christian civilization lived had collapsed suddenly and completely—stupidly as well.

Similarly, the long course of our negotiations with Germany over submarine warfare did not escape us, nor was any way to avoid accepting Germany's final challenge suggested. It was perceived by many that the decision arrived at in Berlin was a stroke of desperation, intended to win victory before our strength could

[2] John Bassett Moore, "An Appeal to Reason," *Foreign Affairs*, July, 1933, Vol. 11, p. 585; Edwin M. Borchard, "Dragging America into War," *Current History*, July, 1934, Vol. 40, p. 394.

prevent it, but that did not alter the fact that the war had come to us.

The intervention of the United States on the side of the Allies was determined by facts which were beyond the power of propaganda to cope with. The Austrian descent upon Serbia; the German invasion of Belgium; the submarine campaign climaxed by the sinking of the *Lusitania*—these events determined world opinion as surely as the Japanese attack upon Shanghai in 1932 and the wholesale assault of Japanese bombers on Chinese cities in 1937. It is the decisive events of modern warfare which decide which side world opinion will favor and it is utterly beyond the power of propaganda to keep the manifestations of the militarist mind from determining the attitudes of the free peoples. Never again can the increasing enormities of aggressive war be hidden.

The Bankers Sold Us to the Allies. It now satisfies many to believe that the British persuaded us to fight their war. Yet even this explanation is not simple enough for many, particularly since the British are a vague and distant entity. The multitude ever craves the burning of witches who can be seen and seized. Our own bankers, it is now said, are the culprits who by degrees craftily sold us into the war.

Nor would it be possible to prove with finality that our bankers' loans to the Allies did not have some indirect effect upon our final intervention. Yet all the efforts to show that these loans had any decisive weight upon the political decisions finally made in Berlin and Washington have failed. At the worst the supposed "guilt" of the bankers is but one fractional element in the decision which the American people had already made. Well in advance of our entry into the war we had come to the conclusion that we did not want the Central Powers to win and that it would be worth a good deal of effort to prevent their triumph. We then sensed fully the terrific power, the arrogance, and the vast ambitions which were expressed in German militarism. Had we known that democracy would be inaugurated in all of Central Europe only to be suppressed in most of that region by 1934, it is still to be doubted that we would have welcomed the military rule of Europe by the Hohenzollerns and Hapsburgs. It was an oppressively unpleasant prospect.

Perhaps no war was ever sufficiently understood by a nation in entering it, but when was a war ever understood as completely, or approached as gradually, as the German-American war of 1917?

The American advocates of a "never again" policy toward future world wars have forgotten much of their history. They have failed altogether to visualize that we would now be living in a very different world had German militarism won. Some, it is true, have tried to suggest that the Germans would have made a wise and moderate peace. But the treaties of peace which Germany forced upon Roumania and Russia indicate only too clearly the size of the enormous domain which would today be Prussianized—as it will be tomorrow if the greatest ambition of the Nazis is realized.

If we obtained nothing else from the war we secured a respite from dealing with enormous empires founded and maintained by a ruthless use of force.

The "Have-nots" Must Expand. Another justification for refusing to help enforce the peace is the claim that, after all, the "Have-nots" do have a case. Their territories are small and infertile. They are overpopulated and simply must have additional room. They lack raw materials and cannot be expected to rest until they get them under their own flag. If we were in their place we ourselves would explode.

This is a favorite refuge of our extreme pacifists. It enables them to say that there is at least the morality of necessity on the side of the aggressors. Therefore, we are justified in standing aside. It is even hinted frequently that it would not be right to coerce the aggressors when they attack their neighbors, since the conquerors are poor.

Again it is unquestionable that the political control of large parts of the earth has been a strong factor in the prosperity of

Great Britain and France. But both are far more dependent upon trade with other countries. It is the trade with the United States, Europe, and South America—to mention no other areas—which Britain and France must have, both as markets and as sources of raw materials. When these areas suffer from economic depression, France and Britain suffer in almost the same degree, in spite of all their "colonies." Colonies, too, have a way of maturing and erecting their own tariff barriers.

Nor is there any ground for believing that any of the three challengers can move their surplus populations in any important degree. Japan is not doing it in Manchuria and there is little evidence that the Japanese people will ever brave the Manchurian climate. In order to go to Manchuria, also, they must have more capital-goods equipment than Japan can afford. One of the most careful surveys of Japan's prospects in Manchuria yet made comes to the definite conclusion that Japan is far too weak to succeed in the capitalistic development of Manchuria.[3] Similarly, there is small reason to believe that while standing the heavy drain of holding Ethiopia Italy can find enough capital to develop the country, or to move and equip any considerable fraction of her annual increase in population. Lastly, no one alleges that the return of all of Germany's former colonies would give more than a handful of Germans a new homeland. Since more Germans earned their livelihoods in Paris in 1914 than in all of the German colonies, there is no reason to expect that many Germans could now be sent to these areas.[4]

[3] Nathaniel Peffer, "The Price of Japanese Imperialism," *Foreign Affairs*, October, 1937, Vol. 16, pp. 21-33. Mr. Peffer concludes that if Japan had made her effort a hundred years ago, when conquest was technically simpler, she might have succeeded. Also, if she had developed her own resources for another century before making the effort she might have succeeded. As matters stand now, "she has not been successful and she cannot be successful. All the conditions of her physical and social being are against success. She has overreached herself. She will fail" (p. 33).

[4] One of the most thoughtful studies of the demand of the crowded nations for "room" is that of Grover Clark, *A Place in the Sun*, New York, 1936. After a careful examination of all past migrations to politically controlled lands, Mr. Clark's conclusion is that no amount of blustering by the leaders of Germany, Italy, and Japan can lessen the fallacy that such control can provide outlets for

The return of Germany's colonies would be balm to a wounded prestige. The surrender of all North Africa to Italy would give Italians a glorious feeling, but neither cession would alter sharply the economic problems of Germany and Italy. Nor would such gains appease the ambition of the fascist regimes. No one knows better than the fascist leaders that the acquisition of such colonial territories would not give them the powerful self-sufficiency which they seek. Nothing less than the control of enormous continental areas can assure them the economic and military power which they desire. For Germany, nothing will do short of political control of all Central and Eastern Europe—a vast area into which many nations and parts of nations would be engulfed. For Japan, the aim is frankly to rule East Asia. China, huge as she is, will not suffice.

It is for the seizure of huge areas comparable to the United

---

surplus populations. The leaders of these nations may squander many billions for armaments and kill off great numbers of their people in wars of conquest, but they cannot solve their population problems by migrating to conquered lands (pp. 128, 186).

Clark's conclusions concerning the uselessness of trying to conquer control of raw materials coincide with the study prepared for the International Studies Conference of 1937 by Eugene Staley, *Raw Materials in Peace and War*, New York, 1937. This investigation shows that the raw-material problem is almost solely an armaments problem. "There is no escape from raw material interdependence" and no solution for the efforts of nations to obtain military grasp of raw materials. In this struggle the gain of one must be the loss of another. What will give greater military security to one nation means greater danger to others, whether true security is envisaged or further conquests intended. Such conflicts are "hopelessly insoluble," whereas if struggles for power were put aside and statesmen aimed only at increasing the standard of living of their people, raw-material conflicts would be few in number and subject to trading settlements.

Mr. Staley reasons also that there is no escape for the United States from power wars in "storm cellar" neutrality. He believes that this kind of neutrality could easily bring us into a major war "more quickly than the old policy of neutral rights." A full application of "storm cellar" neutrality in a great war would: (1) generate great explosive power and warlike demands in our economic groups deprived of markets; (2) put us on the side of aggression; and (3) stimulate still more frantic economic nationalism. Even peaceably inclined nations which feared that our products would be denied them in a time of peril would need to form trade connections with nations upon whom they could depend in an emergency. What is required is frank recognition "that a merely negative policy which aims to *avoid* wars is likely to be unsuccessful if wars continue elsewhere in the modern interdependent world" (pp. 44-49, 234-38).

States that the three aggressors are girding themselves. It is for this that they are working with frenzied haste to achieve "autarchy." As things now stand, any real degree of self-sufficiency is for all three an impossible achievement, except as a war measure. They may hope to build their economic fortifications so well that they can endure a world blockade while their military machines are conquering the great self-sufficient areas for which they long. Thus the challengers are strangling themselves, forcing down the standard of living of their people, when it ought to rise with world prosperity, making "poor" peoples poorer by enormous expenditures for unproductive military weapons—all as preparation for the terrific military effort which will relieve them of any future dependence upon the world for raw materials and markets. And should they succeed during another world war in seizing the continents which they covet, the dictatorial regimes would discover that the self-sufficiency of their Gargantuan dreams could not save them from the next world depression. That the United States suffered on a greater scale than any other nation from 1929 to 1933 ought to be sufficient warning to them that they cannot win economic safety by the sword, even if they do not destroy during the war the wealth which they seek.

Nevertheless, many Americans continue to maintain that we ought to stand aside while the three aggressors improve upon the examples set for them by the powers which are now satisfied. Did not "the glory that was Greece and the grandeur that was Rome" flower amid conquest? And would not the carving-out of the present domains of France, Great Britain, and the United States have been impossible without "aggression"? Has not every one of our own wars, down to and including the Spanish War, been characterized by aggressive revolt against constituted authority? Might not Woodrow Wilson himself have been held guilty of "aggression" in pursuing Villa into Mexico and occupying Vera Cruz?

The answer to each of these questions, and many others like them, is necessarily affirmative. But does such affirmative answer really negative the case for the organized restraint of military aggression in the future? There are no more barbarians to be conquered and civilized. They have all been subdued, for the time being at least. There are no more empty lands, loosely held by aborigines, to be occupied. Some African lands or islands of the Orient might, to be sure, pass from one imperial sovereignty to another at the expense of a great war. But who would avow that the exploitation of these lands would be worth the cost of the war, plus the increasing difficulty and expense of ruling the natives? None but the most backward of Africans now fail to aspire strongly toward self-rule.

The day of easy imperialism, if not of imperialism altogether, is over. Soil and minerals and commercial tribute can be seized on a large scale hereafter only from other civilized peoples. They may be taken from peoples not so highly civilized as some nation that has worked itself into a chosen-people complex, but the peoples of lower culture are certainly far enough developed to have every right to push their own way upward.[5]

Even the hitherto respected claim that a nation has a right to expand by uncontrolled or forced breeding must be increasingly challenged. Since Italy and Germany are already "overcrowded" it is the avowed policy of the fascist dictatorships to further increase the population by every kind of pressure—exhortation, mass weddings, bounties and remission of taxes for large families, harsher taxation for bachelors. Mussolini declares to all his determination to have Italy "expand or explode." Hitler conceals from no one that rich areas in Europe must be turned over to the mounting numbers of his pure-blooded Aryans. The rem-

[5] The radio commentator, Boake Carter, is one of the most positive among those who reiterate that we have no right to condemn Japan. His persistent citation of past acts of violence which we have committed does not eliminate the consideration that since 1918 the nations have agreed to a whole series of treaties designed to end decisively the intolerable anarchy of self-help. It may be contended that this world-wide effort was wrong, that since the destruction of cities and seizure of the lands of others was once legal it should always be legal, but it is hardly feasible to contend that the self-willed acts of nations committed before 1918 are on a par with such acts committed after the adoption of the Covenant, the Kellogg Pact, and the Nine Power Treaty.

edy for a lack of natural resources is to increase the overproduction of people until a successful explosion can be set off, or lands extorted out of fear of such an explosion,

Upon what ground of justice, expediency, or decency can such a policy of aggressive breeding be justified? Certainly not on the basis that a nation which stabilizes its population thereby loses the right to its lands. The people which stops the increase of its numbers at a point which will permit all to have a decent livelihood from its own resources is neither decadent nor foolish, unless animal force is to continue to disrupt civilized life perpetually. Far from deserving eviction and subjection, such a people demonstrates its right to live in an international community, a menace to no one and an example to those who would forever unsettle life on a shrinking planet.[6]

The rapid mechanization of all armies, moreover, makes it probable that excess millions of people will become a liability in war rather than an asset. With the cost of expensive war-making machines the limiting factor, we may discover that a wealthy nation of forty millions is more powerful in war than an overcrowded one of twice the population.

The only practical alternative to a policy of adjusting population to home resources lies in industrialization and the cultivation of world markets—in the winning by patient toil of such a place in the sun as Germany had in 1914. There is an element of precariousness in such an expansion, since it cannot be made absolutely safe by any military or naval force which the nation can possess. The defensive power of a great industrial organization is so immense, however, that the dangers of attack upon any large industrial nation are greatly reduced—particularly of attack from trading rivals which are similarly vulnerable to the disrupting

[6] If a people permitted its numbers constantly to shrink to the point of abandoning the utilization of its resources the case might become different, though there is every reason to expect that self-interest would lead it to welcome immigration to the degree that might be necessary to fill any real vacuum that appeared.

effects of war upon the international trade which is their own lifeblood.

The acceptance of a policy of cooperation to maintain the common peace may be difficult for a people taught to believe that all kinds of growth are virtuous and that peaceful expansion abroad must be followed by forcible political consolidation. Yet there does not appear to be any other real choice before the Germans, the Japanese, and the Italians for the reason that the great majority of the nations are disposed to live peaceably within their own boundaries and to defend them, collectively if necessary. They will act together reluctantly but eventually because they must. Those at the greatest distance from the expansion-committed peoples will cooperate with greatest reluctance, but their cultural and commercial ties make them unable to ignore the shattering thrust of major wars, even if they could permit the destruction of weaker nations until their own defenses were reached. The law that neither individuals nor nations can be safe while the weakest among them are imperiled is recognized grudgingly but increasingly. Its eventual acceptance may have to be stimulated by the repeated approach of social chaos, but upon what reasoning are we to doubt that it will ultimately prevail?

Undoubtedly, the so-called "Have" nations have sinned against the "Have-nots" by selfishly raising their tariffs to great heights, regardless of the effect upon the poorer peoples. When, too, the three embattled nations show a disposition to put their threatening armaments aside in favor of a policy of live-and-let-live, it will be urgently necessary for the richer nations to buy and sell more freely. Then the duty of the colonial powers to pursue an Open Door policy will be heavy. When trade with colonial areas is restricted by tariffs it must be expected that others will object. For that matter the Closed Door policy is self-defeating, since it restricts the buying power of the colony.

On the other hand, the land-hungry powers must sometime learn that conquest of territory is not necessary to insure adequate supplies of raw materials, that successful war does not enable a nation to dispose of the surplus that cannot be sold at home, that war is not necessary for the purpose of opening new areas of investment, and that winning a war does not enable a nation to collect its debts. The "Have-nots" must somehow discover, also, "that emigration has never been and can never be anything but a temporary palliative for the population problem." [7]

Unfortunately, there is little present probability that Germany, Japan, or Italy will recognize these intangible bars to successful conquest. By its own deliberate acts each has resigned from the world community, renounced all tolerance, cut its people off from the news and opinions of the world (as far as possible), and reverted to reliance on force alone.

"International Law" Is Sufficient. Yet developments such as these have not prevented some from opposing all international organization on the ground that we can attain nothing beyond the meager alleviations of modern war which international law may secure. It is asserted that by attempting more, in the Covenant and the Pact, we have merely made matters worse and at the same time weakened and injured "the law." [8]

[7] Norman Angell, *Raw Materials, Populations and War,* World Affairs Book No. 14, Boston, 1936, pp. 29-32. An investigation for the Food Research Institute of Stanford University has reached similar conclusions. At the close of his book, *Population Theories and Their Application with Special Reference to Japan* (Palo Alto, 1934), E. F. Penrose writes that there are no blind economic forces which make war inevitable. "Actually," he says, "productive capacity is the one thing which shows no signs of failing," while reproductive capacity is now being rapidly brought under individual control. "It is not, therefore, in the circumstances of the external world but in the minds of men that the mainsprings of violent social conflict lie. Prejudices, narrow provincialism, the pursuit of false ends, mistaken notions of the road to material advantage, the lag of immaterial culture behind material culture, and the defects of world political organization—these and related factors, and not any shortage of natural resources in the world are the stuff out of which wars and other violent social conflicts are made" (pp. 335-36).

[8] John Bassett Moore terms the sanctions provisions of the Covenant "the warlike devices which visionary men in an excited and unsettled time foisted upon those who were wiser and more modest in the estimation of what was practicable and desirable."—"An Appeal to Reason," *Foreign Affairs,* July, 1933, Vol. 11, p. 586. Similarly, Edwin M. Borchard terms the program of enforcing peace by collective sanctions "a purely mental conception" and regrets that it "has had to disparage the existing international law, the product of the centuries,

No one who has any hope of seeing reason prevail over the destructive stupidities which are involved in present-day war should be disposed to reject any help which the usages of international law can give. Yet the attempt to defend international law against the charge that it "legalizes" war indicates the difficulty of relying upon such a "law." It may be agreed that the traditional law merely accepts war as an old institution and tries to regulate it. All those who would rely merely upon "international law" to govern international relations must take that position. The strivings of states for aggrandizement and for power as a means of self-preservation must be taken for granted. War must be accepted as an established, respectable instrument of national policy, a necessary thing which we have had for thousands of years and which in future millenniums we may gradually supplant, in some measure, by more civilized methods of adjusting frictions and disputes.

Indeed, the embattled defenders of international law are without greater hope for humanity as a whole, however much they may expect to develop our present civilization on the North American continent under cover of "neutrality." Moore goes no further than to "modestly pray for peace in my own time" and Borchard aspires only to "return to the time-tested respect for the law which has at least brought us long periods of peace and permitted some advancement in human affairs." [9]

The nostalgia for neutrality is, of course, at odds with the

---

and the usual processes identified with the growth of the law."—"Dragging America into War," *Current History*, July, 1934, Vol. 40, p. 399. Likewise, a conservative Englishman, Sir Edward Grigg, fears "internationalism, with its misty enthusiasms, as a treacherous mirage." He charges that the result of trying to outlaw force has been "the exact converse of what was intended and desired. Instead of ensuring that actual force shall not be used, it has made resort to it inevitable if evolution is not to be entirely throttled. Diplomacy has in consequence been almost completely paralyzed. Both the Manchurian and Abyssinian questions would in all probability have been settled without war, if China and Ethiopia had not been guaranteed against any sacrifice of sovereignty by the League."—*The Faith of an Englishman*, London, 1936, pp. 237, 159.

[9] Moore, "An Appeal to Reason," *Foreign Affairs*, July, 1933, Vol. 11, p. 551; Borchard, "Dragging America into War," *Current History*, July, 1934, Vol. 40, p. 401.

whole effort to suppress war as a practice which kills every prospect of order and law internationally. "The very concept of neutrality," says Felix Morley, editor of the *Washington Post,* "is definitely menacing to most of the constructive work which has been done in the field of trying to ascertain the conditions of peace since the close of the last war." [10] The belief that neutrality has become fundamentally immoral has nowhere been stated more concisely than in Lord Parker's noted address to the House of Lords, on March 19, 1918—when Great Britain, the United States, and the other Allies were bracing themselves to fight together the last great campaign of the war. Said Lord Parker: "The true line of development lies, not in regulating the hateful thing, but in bringing about conditions under which it becomes increasingly difficult and ultimately impossible, not in consulting the welfare of selfish interests of neutrals but in abolishing neutrality. Murders would increase if the murderer could count upon the neutrality of bystanders, and it is the same with war. The neutral, in fact, shirks his share of the burden of humanity." [11]

[10] Felix Morley, "Political Implications of American Neutrality Policy," *Annals of the American Academy of Political and Social Science,* July, 1936, Vol. 186, p. 52.

[11] Henry Wickham Steed, *Vital Peace,* New York, 1936, pp. 225-26. The most convincing defense of the customs of international law encountered in this study is to be found in Philip C. Jessup, *Neutrality: Its History, Economics, and Law,* New York, 1936, Vol. IV, pp. 147-48.

To show that international law has a restraining effect in time of war, Jessup lists several vicious things which belligerents might otherwise do. Yet the best commentary upon the rapid destruction of the customary restraints of international law is to be found in the events which have occurred in the year since Jessup's book was published. He notes that if international law were as useless as is often supposed "a belligerent would be wholly free to use submarines or mines to sink all vessels anywhere on the seas or even in the territorial waters off our coasts." In the summer of 1937, unidentified submarines and planes did cause a reign of terror in the Mediterranean, attacking vessels from the mouth of the Dardanelles to the harbors of Valencia and Barcelona. An international conference had to be held to arrange for a vast international patrol fleet to police all the leading lanes in the Mediterranean Sea.

Again, Jessup observes that in a lawless world the Red Cross would give no protection to hospital ships, and fishing vessels, "which have always enjoyed a favored status during a war," could be destroyed. Here again the reports from the war in China contain serious allegations of violations of the Red Cross by the Japanese, while apparently well-authenticated reports of British ships relate

However much the masses of mankind may long for the chance to abstain from war they can find little hope in renouncing common action to preserve the peace. People simply will not place reliance in a "law" which must yield to the necessities and new weapons of all belligerents or be defended (unsuccessfully in the long run) by the armies of neutrals. We have in the world an affirmative purpose to repress the institution of war, not because of any desire of "shallow dupes" to do "ghost dancing" or to "swing on the trapeze at international performances," [12] but because of a strong conviction that any "law" which hovers impotently around the fringes of a holocaust like the World War needs to be strongly stiffened. It is no consolation to the scores of millions of people whose lives were ended or ruined by the Great War, or to those who will be maimed in the next, to tell them that: "If we would keep men and nations at peace, we must remove the causes of their discontent, elevate their moral sentiments, inculcate a spirit of justice and toleration, and compose and settle their differences." [13] The outlook for the future is dark, indeed, if these millennial tasks must be performed before we can have any assurance of a reasonable degree of international order.

The constantly accelerated pace of modern life forbids any such composed waiting upon perfection. If every community that centered in a small town was essentially self-sufficient; if the Industrial Revolution had never occurred; if the age of steam had never come—and passed into the age of electricity; if advance in

---

that Chinese fishing junks have been wantonly torpedoed, their survivors being rescued by foreign ships.

It appears to be true that the world-wide protests against the indiscriminate destruction of Chinese cities which Japan had begun has distinctly slowed down that ruthless proceeding. Still, the enormities perpetuated in Spain—in the midst of Western, Christian civilization—give little ground for believing that any restraints other than the fear of powerful foreign intervention are any longer operative. There is no valid reason left for believing that totalitarian states will be deterred by any other consideration. By their very nature they must wage totalitarian war. Nothing except the exertion or imminent threat of superior force can have any meaning to them.

[12] Phrases from Moore's article, "An Appeal to Reason," *Foreign Affairs*, July, 1933, Vol. 11, pp. 567, 579.

[13] *Ibid.*, p. 588.

science would let the invention of new implements of warfare stop on some comfortable plane; if wars could be paid for; if they did not destroy the economic and social systems of the world or leave them weakened and diseased for decades to come—if none of these revolutionary developments had occurred, the leisurely accumulation of the customs of international law might have a chance of preventing the collapse of civilization. But with scientific progress requiring the creation of some measure of world government as a first condition of survival, why should the defenders of international law object to such international legislation as the League Covenant and the Kellogg Pact, even though they do not at once bring stability? If the vague customs of "the law" are sacred and indestructible, in spite of perpetual violation, what is to be said of great treaties for peace, written for all men to read and ratified by the governments of some sixty nations? Surely here are elements of law which will not vanish in a twinkling.

The objection to the Kellogg Pact appears to be that it is futile and ridiculous because war has always been "coeval with the history of man" and "human nature has not changed." The Pact, considered as a substitute for the Covenant, might, it is true, become a weakening gesture that would prove to be worse than futile. Unless supported by international organization, the Pact will become a dead letter. It will be some time, however, before the defenders of "the law" can safely pronounce the Pact to be null and void. It has one immeasurable advantage over "the law," the fact that it is so simple in its terms that the masses of mankind can understand and support it, if they will. No learned savants in cloister or court are necessary to convey to the ordinary man the purpose of the Pact. He knows what its purpose is and we cannot be certain that he will not come to support it.

At the worst, the Pact can never exceed the abysmal depth of futility which we witnessed, two decades ago, when six great nations stumbled into war without the possibility even of a single session of their representatives to consider the points in dispute and the consequences of fighting to the death about them. That the Pact will be broken has already been demonstrated; that it may at times sink so low in restraining force as to appear to be extinct is very probable; but that the peoples will be compelled by self-interest and the need of survival to return to it—and to put institutions behind it—is still more to be expected. In any event, the solemn universal renunciation of war which is contained in the Kellogg Pact can hardly be called premature. After the near demolition of civilization in the long-drawn folly of the Great War it was time that the burden of proof be put upon any nation attempting to proclaim itself in the future a law unto itself.

It is said, however, that such a delegalizing of war as the Pact accomplished will be evaded by refusals to declare war. Let that danger be accepted. The fact of war cannot be hidden and the new non-aggression treaties have already shown that restrictive definition of it can keep pace fully with attempts to escape the implications of the Laws of 1920 and 1929.[14]

Why Neutrality Fails

Great Wars Involve All of the Great Powers. No desire is more widespread in the United States than the wish to be exempt from the world's wars. Most of us believe, too, that we have generally escaped from Europe's wars. Lists are frequently made of the European wars in which we have had no part. These lists, however, do not bear analysis. They show indeed that we have remained out of some short wars in which only two or three nations fought, but the record also shows that we have taken part in every general war since Jamestown was settled in 1607. Three times before 1776 we fought in wars which centered in

[14] See Phillips Bradley, *Can We Stay Out of War?* New York, 1936, pp. 236-37, for a statement of the three leading definitions of aggression which have been formulated, *i.e.*, the Geneva Protocol, the Russian, and the Roosevelt definitions. These are so adequate that no others are needed, Bradley feels.

His review of what happened during the last war also leaves him without faith in the restraining power of the rules of international law. If any such rules existed in 1914, "they were not respected by either side." It is illusory to argue that they "have in the past possessed any international sanction" and futile to expect that belligerent interests can be subjected to any rule of law in the future (pp. 36, 42, 45).

Europe. After Independence we said that that kind of business was ended. Yet it was not. We entered both of the world wars which have occurred since. "If there has been any law in our history so far, it seems to have been that America cannot remain at peace when Europe goes to war." [15] The historical basis for expecting that we can avoid the great wars of the future does not exist.

The situation is even worse than that. Professor Quincy Wright has tabulated all the wars in which any great power has engaged since 1600 and he finds that when any war between two great powers lasts more than two years it involves the balance of power and pulls in the other great powers. Only three times during the three centuries has any one of the great powers been able to keep out of a war of the type just defined. "In each case, however, these states became involved in a war very soon after the wars in question were over." [16]

Only, therefore, if the United States is not a part of the balance of power do we have any historical warrant for believing that we can escape participation in any war seriously involving two Great Powers. But, as Professor Wright observes, "participation in the balance of power is a question of fact, not of theory or policy, and the United States is in it." Instead of being on a fringe of the old world, as we have fancied, we are now at the center of the world, between the two great regions where the struggle for world empire is going to be fought out, if we continue to refrain from putting our immense weight behind the collective peace. When the projected wars for supremacy begin, also, if they are not already actually in progress, we shall be compelled to put our weight into the balance. We preferred to prevent a victory by Germany in 1917. In 1937 we are beginning to decide against the establishment of an overmastering Japan in the Orient. So it will ever be, as long as there is nothing better

[15] Christian Gauss, "Can America Live Alone?" *Scribner's Magazine*, August, 1933, Vol. 94, p. 72.

[16] Quincy Wright, "The United States and Neutrality," *University of Chicago Public Policy Pamphlet, No. 17*, Chicago, 1935, pp. 3-4.

than the balance of power to give the world a semblance of government.

Instead of imagining ourselves apart from the balance of power, it would be far more "realistic" to recognize that we *are* the balance. Not only do we sit in the center of the world stage; our economic power is so vast that the world must be forever out of equilibrium until we decide whether our might is to be used to prevent great wars, or merely to end them—leaving us to be engulfed in the backwash. The nation that disposes of a third of all the world's coal and iron and lead, and half of its copper and zinc—together with vast agricultural resources—must decide whether its economic might is to aid or defeat the aggressive war-makers of the future. It is only when control of the oceans is in the hands of our friends that we can afford to indulge in cash-and-carry laws. When the seas are controlled by powers whom we fear, or threaten to be so controlled, we are under the immediate compulsion of deciding whether we shall feed the engines of aggression or not.

War Cannot Be Localized. The hope that somehow someone will circumscribe the wars which do break out is doomed to disappointment. Some small wars may indeed be localized, yet any one of them may prove to be unconfinable. The network of defensive alliances, not to mention a few of offensive intent, which stretches from the Sea of Japan across Eurasia to the North Sea, alone forbids the indefinite continuance of localized wars.

It is true that many powerful Conservatives in Great Britain hope to sacrifice Czechoslovakia and Austria to Germany, without taking part in a general war. This way of escape has been argued at length by Sir Edward Grigg in his book, *The Faith of an Englishman.* The forces which speak from Berlin, he argues (and from Rome and Tokyo), are "too strong to be throttled." They "will burst all control in the end." Hitler must have results "before the emptiness behind the belt brings on internal collapse." Germany's air power is "simply enormous—there is no other word for it." Hence Britain should confine her responsibilities in Europe to defending France, Belgium, and Holland, leaving Germany to do as she wishes in the East.[17]

It will be best, he reasons, "to enable the stronger races which are struggling for power and place each to find its proper sphere of influence and to gather round it a homogeneous group without causing another conflict like 1914-1918." Sir Edward even persuades himself that the threat of Germany's armed power may produce such a reorganization without any violence.[18]

It is noteworthy, however, that Sir Edward does not envisage any expansion of Germany or Japan at the expense of the British Empire. He would "at all costs avoid any course of action which might commit us to conflict with Japan over developments in Northern China, whatever course they may take." "But," he adds, "we do not want her to establish bases in Southern China or elsewhere which would be potential menaces to our imperial security." [19]

For Germany also Sir Edward has several provisos. She must (1) "refrain from another challenge to our sea power," (2) "abandon all aggressive designs upon France, Belgium, Holland and, indeed, Denmark," and (3) concede "parity between the German air force and the British air force which we maintain in these islands." He specifies also that "our trade should not be seriously interrupted, that our markets should not be taken from us, and above all that no power should attain a position of strength and ascendancy in Europe and elsewhere which would place our trade communications at its mercy." [20]

[17] Grigg, *The Faith of an Englishman*, pp. 180, 196, 198-200.

[18] A part of Sir Edward's argument is that the Nazis are, as they maintain, a bulwark against communism, as is Japan. Therefore, and because she also is uncontrollable, Japan should not be opposed. Grigg, *The Faith of an Englishman*, pp. 201, 205, 310.

[19] *Ibid.*, pp. 310, 318.

[20] *Ibid.*, pp. 360, 250. The present tendency of the Chamberlain Government to pursue a half-isolationist policy, confining British responsibility to defense of the Empire and of the Low Countries, is strongly opposed in a recent book edited by E. Thomas Cook, *The Empire in the World*, Oxford, 1937. In the concluding chapters Sir Arthur Willert, former chief of the Press Department of the British Foreign Office, asks if the hesitation of British Ministers to defend the peace is not a conspicuous ingredient of the current madness, about which the

If the demanding nations will leave all British possessions alone, both directly and indirectly, Sir Edward is quite willing that they should seize everything else which is within reach. But it is difficult to believe that the British people will permit such a policy to be applied. It is more difficult to think that the British Empire could escape conquest if the aggressors were given free scope in Europe and Asia. Certainly such a policy of blessing the conquest of others, so long as we ourselves are not attacked, is not feasible for the other European nations. If Germany invades Czechoslovakia, France must decide whether she can survive, without Continental allies, another return of the German flood. Britain's backing may be comforting, but would it be sufficient? Might not the British Tories who would sacrifice the Czechs to Hitler decide to make one more bargain with him? For Russia, too, similar decisions would be imperative. Should she wait until the Germans are at the Ukraine? Will Roumania and Jugoslavia, allies of Czechoslovakia, also decide that there is no course open to them except to submit to German—and Hungarian—domination? Or will they choose to defend the unusually powerful bastion which Czechoslovakia is?

Will the American people, not to speak of the British, harden their hearts at the sight of the small Czech nation attacked by another German juggernaut? Or will they feel that the brilliant success of the Czechs in maintaining liberty and democracy deserves a better fate and commands the support of the remaining free peoples?

If British and American statesmen are even partly "realistic," they will not look forward resignedly to the seizure of Central Europe by the Nazis. The nature of fascism forbids such an easy way out. Fascism has committed itself utterly to force, without any restraint or reservation. Fascism is the most complete incarnation of the will to power which the centuries have been able

---

same Ministers complain. British support is "essential to collective security if only because the forces behind it would be too weak otherwise." To surrender Central Europe to the dictators would expose the Empire to direct attack and lose it the support of the world at large (pp. 266, 306).

to produce. The central idea of the totalitarian state makes the setting of any limit to its power an absurdity. The belief that absolute determination makes defeat impossible is at the heart of all fascist action. Where the will is utterly inflexible, runs the creed, it can create the organization to gain its objectives. Where force cannot prevail for the moment guile and propaganda will be employed with an intensity never attempted before, but force is the final arbiter. That there should be any limits to the will of the fascist regimes to expand their rule is a contradiction of terms, and any hope of making a real settlement with them is illusory. The "general settlement" for which those who fear the fascists plead would at once remove the excuse for fascism to continue. All reason for the high-pressure militarization of the Germans and Italians would be gone; the justification for the rigid autarchies now enforced would cease to exist. Without these things fascism itself would disappear. Hence the dictators will make no general settlement.

Nor will the satisfying of particular demands made by Hitler and Mussolini bring peace. They have placed their nations on a basis of total mobilization for permanent war with the whole of the outside world. To yield this position of irreconcilability would destroy the fascist state. Fascism is war itself. It is wholly incompatible with a state of peace and cannot make peace without destroying itself—for then such things as toleration, adjudication, peaceful enterprise, and the consent of the governed would have to be accepted as the ways and means of life. Should fascism surrender its nuisance value it would sign its own death warrant.[21]

[21] See the article by Walter Lippmann on this subject, in which he concludes that Britain and France will never be able to abandon Czechoslovakia to Hitler. To take this course would "stultify every pretension made by the British and French for the past twenty years" and make these peoples themselves outcasts from the community of nations. No one would ever trust or believe in them again. *Nashville Tennessean*, December 4, 1937.

If in the future Russia should demonstrate the will and the ability to impose communism upon peoples now free, it will be incumbent upon the democracies to stand together against her. Totalitarianism in any form cannot be reconciled with free government.

The present defensive position of Russia may not always continue. The current effort in Russia to move toward the forms, if not the substance, of democracy

Each Conquest Breeds Others. Any expectation that the Nazis would be satisfied with the forcible domination of Central Europe is utterly chimerical. They would be satisfied for the moment to consolidate the greatest area of power on the globe, but only as a means to crushing France and Russia. Both of these powers must be eliminated before Europe can be organized into the world state toward which the Nazis are driving. The hope which comfortable Britons have of quietly enjoying their empire, after approving the first great conquests of the Nazis, is a pure delusion. After the conquest of France's allies in Central Europe, the African and Indian empires of France and Britain would become practical objectives to the triumphant Germans.

The same expanding ambitions guide the conquests of Italy and Japan. Moreover, each new conquest seems to require another, for strategic or economic reasons. Each successful foray also fires the imagination of the conquerors and increases their confidence. There is no reason to doubt that both Italy and Japan will go as far in the direction of creating a new Rome as their physical power permits. But both are operating from an economic base too small to make them a threat as imminent as is to be found in Germany. Should Japan be able to take possession of all East Asia she would still have to find the capital with which to develop an industrial colossus. In Europe there already exists the greatest industrial machine in the world, ready to be unified and employed by German organizing genius. Europe already produces more than twice as much steel as the United States and nearly double the amount of coal and electrical power. Her population is more than four times greater than ours. In German hands Europe would form an engine of offensive power unmatchable elsewhere.

Thrusts for World Supremacy Compel World Federation. These considerations are fully set forth in the remarkable book by Livingston Hartley, *Is America Afraid?* (New York, 1937.)

may be reversed. Up to the present, Russian communism has been anti-imperialistic. Should it become otherwise a different situation would arise. It is the combination of totalitarian ideology with the strongest kind of nationalistic imperialism which has made the fascist regimes the world's public enemies.

The impact of this volume on American thinking should be enormous. Its thesis that the industrial revolution is inexorably compelling the political unification of the world is buttressed by a careful survey of the entire world situation which is as challenging as it is thorough. The issue still to be decided is whether we shall have a world federation of free and autonomous nations or, eventually, a world empire ruled from some imperial capital. Nor is any way open to avoid a choice between the establishment of a world federation and submission to an interminable series of predatory wars waged by the totalitarian states.

With such a cosmic struggle already visibly written on the pages of our daily newspapers, it is blindness indeed for the United States to continue to think of itself as a world apart. There are more than half a billion people on each of the two tips of the Eurasian continents which are now our frontiers. If we permit either of these great power areas to be conquered by Germany or Japan we shall at once face a defensive conflict with the odds enormously against us. The wealth of the Americas is a guarantee of that. It is only the century-long success of the British navy in policing the world which has made the cult of neutrality practical for us. As Walter Lippmann has pointed out, it is already written in the book of fate that Britain is no longer strong enough to exert alone that authority which held the world level and made it a safe place for us to develop in, with the 1914-1918 exception. And "it is also written in that book that our civilization is doomed to another dark age unless that authority can be perpetuated by peoples who intend to live by the same political tradition. There is no alternative—except a century or more of wars fought savagely and indecisively by peoples contending for world supremacy." [22]

This is the pass to which we have been brought by the partisan politicians of 1919 and the reactionary pacifists of recent years. They have killed the influence of the United States for two

[22] Walter Lippmann, "Rough Hew Them How We Will," *Foreign Affairs,* July, 1937, Vol. 15, p. 594.

decades, during which she could have made triumphant the ideals for which she fought and could have secured her future against the deadliest kind of dangers. Raised by the war into incontestably the greatest power on earth, what has the United States done with her strength? She has idled away, in the vain pursuit of unlimited wealth and soft seclusion, the greatest and most urgent opportunity ever presented to a nation.[23] Now it is the men committed to violence without limit who have command of the earth. And as they throttle one free people after another, the democracies can think of nothing more effective than to scold the resolute invaders and retreat before them. The logical result of preventing the world's greatest Power from having a policy is the loss of that power. While our most voluble "patriots" have urged that we do nothing, others have acted. Already the force of their ideas and of their acts is penetrating South America. Should a fascist empire be able to seize the West coast of Africa it would find its work among our Latin neighbors already partly done. And if fascist regimes did not already exist in important South American states, these countries would be subject to invasion from African shores which are 2,000 miles closer than the United States. The defensive power of the scattered South American states, too, could not be depended upon, even if all of them resisted.

[23] The violence of the break with our constructive past which occurred in 1919 has been described in short compass by Manley O. Hudson in one of his lectures at Stanford University, in 1932, as follows: "For twelve years, now, a dead hand has rested over the consideration in the United States of questions relating to international organization. A generation or more ago, we were as ready as any people in the world to consider such questions on their merits, and as a nation we seldom lagged in seizing opportunities to advance those interests which we have in common with other peoples. It was our Government which suggested a postal union in 1862, which stood out against slavery in Africa at the Berlin Conference of 1885, which called a conference in 1889 to deal with rules of the road at sea, which initiated the creation of an International Bureau of the American Republic in 1890, which took the lead in urging permanent organization at the Hague Peace Conferences in 1899 and 1907, and which exercised an energetic influence to preserve a European equilibrium at Algeciras in 1906. For fifty years, at least, we gave encouragement to every effort to escape from international anarchy, and when the thunder of 1914 rumbled over our heads we renewed our determination that such escape should be found." *Progress in International Organization*, Palo Alto, 1932, pp. 103-4.

If reliance is placed upon the revolt of European or Asiatic peoples once conquered, that also is to encourage the triumph of new Romes over world federation, for the reason that the nature of modern weapons precludes successful revolt. The conquered can never hope to have again anything more deadly than some smuggled machine guns and hand grenades. The great fighting tools—bombing planes, artillery, and tanks—are forever beyond them. With fleets of bombers ready to deal swift and crushing reprisal for the slightest resistance, the very possibility of revolt disappears as completely as it has in the fascist states themselves. When fascist power is once established over a region only the most terrific cataclysm, probably from the exterior, can break it.

Even the will to revolt may gradually be lost. Nor is it safe to depend upon the internal economic collapse of the projected empires. If the Germans can once disarm the European peoples and put them into one vast economic unit, the prosperity created would probably exceed anything before experienced. The destruction of tariff boundaries over the whole of the continent would provide the average citizen everywhere with concrete evidence of the advantages of German control. "However bitterly lost causes might be mourned, the average standard of living of Europe would be raised to unimagined heights" [24]—along with the striking power of the imperial air force and navy.

Military Science Forbids Neutrality. No reasonable person would say that a hostile Europe could conquer our Eastern cities today, however much damage might be done to them. But no sensible person would assert that the situation will be the same after fifty years more of development in aviation. If merely the same rate of progress since 1914 is continued, the range and striking power of the aviation arm of any huge industrial power will be enormously increased long before the year 2000 A.D. is reached.

Already the shadow of wholesale death in its most terrible form hangs heavy over every important city in Europe. If any doubt existed in anyone's mind as to what was ahead, the totali-

[24] Livingston Hartley, *Is America Afraid?* New York, 1937, p. 136.

tarian regimes have removed it. For many months General Franco's Italian and German guns and planes have sought without scruple to destroy the capital city of Spain. They have obliterated the smaller city of Guernica and other towns surrounding Bilbao, machine-gunning the farmers in the fields and the people fleeing on the roads for miles around. In China likewise, Japanese planes have spared no city which resisted them. Europe is plainly forewarned that she must expect an enormous mass of heavy bombers to be suddenly launched without warning at Prague, Paris, or London, with the object of paralyzing the nerve center of a nation at one blow—while scores of other cities are being bombed at the same time.

Nor is there much comfort in the usual reply that the defense always manages to keep up with the offense, for that means only that another long-drawn horror of stalemate and mutual decimation must rage again, and over far greater areas than before. The 17,150,000 people who live in our seacoast towns, plus the many millions dwelling in our great inland cities, cannot continue to be safe from attack while the totalitarian killers are free to destroy the cities of other continents without restraint. While continents are to be conquered, by devastating them if necessary, the continent which is the most tempting prize of all cannot live safely in secluded ease.

We cannot continue to assume, either, that our wars will always be safe ones. In all our history we have never had a war of unlimited liability. In 1776, 1812, and 1917 we fought great powers, but they were invariably fighting other great powers besides ourselves. In 1848 and in 1898 we defeated weak nations to whom allies were not available. Always we have had plenty of help or assured superiority. Never have we had to fight for our very lives against an unfettered antagonist as strong or stronger than ourselves. Yet this is precisely the desperate plight which we shall invite if we nurse much longer the illusion of invulnerability while international autocracy overwhelms and organizes Europe or Asia.

No Nation Dares Stand Alone. Already the nation which is willing to stand alone, depending upon its ability to keep neutral in future wars, does not exist. While our impassioned advocates of political isolation defend the ideal, the thing itself has disappeared. The Great War itself should have demonstrated that beyond the necessity of relearning. Since the lesson was not effective, it remained for us to discover that we faced a hostile Japan on one side and a Europe which felt that we had capriciously left her in ruins on the other. Then, far from pursuing the strict logic of the lone hand, we organized a temporary league of nations to deal with the Far Eastern and naval-race issues. The Washington Conference was a living testimony to the impossibility of escaping from world politics.

One Great Power, however, was really isolated. Russia, ringed about with enemies and feared by all nations, scoffed at the idea of collective security and derided the League of Nations. Yet when the League had failed to restrain Japan in 1932 Russia sought the League, and has since been one of the firmest defenders of the Covenant. Huge as she is, Russia did not care to face alone the prospect of a war for existence. She desired allies and friends, even though they be capitalist and democratic.

Our own reaction to the coming of Hitler and to the League's failure in Ethiopia was similar. Instead of seeking only communion with ourselves, we at once attempted to rally all the republics of this hemisphere around us in the Buenos Aires Conference. Our plans for a rudimentary league of American nations were considerably whittled away in that conference, but it was made plain that we considered half a league much better than none.

When the United States and Russia, the two nations which might try to remain isolated with some hope of success, do not care to do so, it becomes clear that no nation on the face of the globe is willing to make the attempt. Even the three aggressors draw together in a Tokyo-Berlin pact, a Rome-Berlin axis, and finally, on November 6, 1937, in a three-power "Anti-Communist" alliance. There is no question of going back to a state of

Boesch

THE NEW HALL OF THE LEAGUE OF NATIONS ASSEMBLY

This central structure has seats for 2,000 people, including 500 for the press and 800 for the public. The Council Chamber and Secretariat wing are out of view on the left, the Library on the right. The memorial to Woodrow Wilson contributed by the Woodrow Wilson Foundation will be placed in the center of the plaza shown above. It will take the form of a large celestial sphere in bronze bas-relief.

About the League's new building, Clarence Streit, the veteran Geneva correspondent of the *New York Times*, wrote, June 21, 1936: "In it the ghosts of all those who through the ages have dreamed an undying dream have at last a common meeting place, a home, their only home on earth. The dream will endure. The only questions are whether the League will survive and whether we shall."

no international organization. Nobody proposes to go further back than the balance of power.

No Substitute for the League Found. It is equally clear, too, that when the League cannot function, because of the absence of key powers, a temporary, *ad hoc* league must at once be invented. This was why the Washington Conference of 1922 had to be held. The same reason explains the strange doings of the present London Non-intervention Committee, which tries weakly and futilely to fulfill the League's function of preventing the conquest of Spain by Italy and Germany. Likewise the Nine Power Conference of 1937, to consider Japan's current invasion of China, enables the United States to participate on a footing of equality. The *ad hoc* leagues, too, stumble as sadly as the League itself, the while they help to weaken it.

The conclusion is plain—that there is no substitute for a League of Nations strong enough to keep the peace, and that none can be invented. In an increasingly interdependent world there is no way out except forward. With all the nations dependent for their prosperity, and most of them for their existence, upon access to the markets of the wide earth, it is inconceivable that they will submit to the restoration of an endless anarchy of private wars. It is intolerable that the family of nations should forever submit to the disruption of wars begun by a few turbulent regimes.[25]

[25] It is to the credit of most American peace organizations, and of a host of the nation's intellectual leaders, that they have never wavered from supporting the inevitable league of the future, even though at times the League's American defenders have been pitied for their firm conviction. Thus Mr. Paul Hutchison, Editor of *Christian Century*, has regretted that after the defeat of the Covenant in the United States our "peace bodies kept right on battling to take the United States into the League" irrespective of the fact that "it would have been at least ten years before the wounds of the treaty fight could have healed sufficiently to make league adherence a wise aim for the peace societies to espouse." This could only give them "a tradition of well-meaning, impractical futility, which, in this land of the success-hunters, is the most damning blight that can fall on man or movement."—Paul Hutchison, "The Collapse of Pacifism," *Scribner's Magazine*, June, 1934, Vol. 95, p. 395.

Nathaniel Peffer has also castigated the friends of international organization for not being "astringently skeptical" and thus preventing "the sabotage of the League and the League idea." Mr. Peffer believes that the League's friends should have been "relentlessly clear-sighted, tough-minded, hard-bitten, worldly wise, incredulous, jaundiced in skepticism of words unsupported by deeds, and deaf

On the closing page of their book, *Neutrality for the United States*,[26] Borchard and Lage advocate as a national policy that we "set the world an example of contented living." They urge that "the cultivation of sagacity in these matters, of detachment, of moderation, of toleration, of the spirit of live and let live, and the renunciation of the psychology and policy of 'enforcing peace' by hostile measures probably present the only tangible hope for preserving peace in broad areas of the world."

A policy of letting what will happen in the outside world might be practical for a people with a high degree of geographical security, if we were not confronted with the total negation of everything for which we have always stood. But the stark fact is that the American example has been wholly repudiated by powerful regimes which have set out to destroy every foundation and principle upon which the American dream is built. Instead of associating with peoples guided by the kindly and moderate virtues which Borchard and Lage extol, we have to deal with nations

---

to mellifluous rhetoric and the glib grandiloquence of easy idealism."—Nathaniel Peffer, "Why Liberalism Is Bankrupt, an Epistle to the Tender Minded," *Harper's Magazine*, August, 1934, Vol. 169, pp. 257-69.

The original champions of the League can afford not to be disturbed by such chidings. The advocates of the League did not support the Harding Administration in its efforts to bury the League quietly. They did not supply hostile newspapers of great circulation with constant evidence that even the friends of the League thought it operated badly. They did not furnish to the governments and peoples who were at least keeping the League alive further evidence of the instability and capriciousness of Americans. The nation that had led in the creation of the League only to be the sole signatory to repudiate it was not the one to save the League by critical dissection of its every move from the outside. If we had occupied the position of leadership and responsibility inside the League that was so long held out to us, our influence in directing its evolution might have been truly decisive.

Instead of being the League's severest critics, the great company of men and women whose clear vision had helped to create the League looked to the future. They remembered that the League had been defeated in the United States by politicians fighting for power, that the nation's non-political leadership had been almost solidly for it, and they sensed that the loose evasions of Normalcy could not continue forever. Hence they continued to stand for the League in the hope that it might receive our indispensable support before it was too late. Those who saw with greatest clearness that national sovereignty, sapped by the inexorable advance of the industrial revolution, had ceased to exist, knew that it would long continue to be asserted.

[26] Edwin Borchard and William Lage, *Neutrality for the United States*, New Haven, 1937, p. 350.

enslaved body, mind, and soul to the limitless ambitions of the militaristic machines which rule them. Nor do these regimes plan some minor rectification of imperfect maps. They are playing for nothing less than the conquest of vast empires equaling or exceeding any on which the sun now rises and sets. The bulk of Europe, the whole of East Asia—these are the first stages of the self-sufficient empires to which the totalitarian regimes look forward.

We or They. The means to these vast empires are also known to all. They have been set forth with stark clearness in the small book by Hamilton Fish Armstrong, *We or They* (New York, 1936). In order to stamp out freedom and toleration and self-government in the lands now inhabited by free peoples, the totalitarian states have trampled under foot every voice and every virtue which might restrain them. "Important is not who is right, but who wins," says Dr. Goebbels. The objective is "to will with cold blood the anarchy of the moral world," says another German "leader." "We do not know of or recognize truth for truth's sake or science for science's sake," says a third. "A handful of force is better than a sackful of justice," adds *Deutsche Justiz.* Peace is "absurd," cries Mussolini, and Hitler preaches a peace "established by the victorious sword of a master nation which leads the world to serve a higher culture." [27]

These are the "principles" which control great nations with absolute ruthlessness, preparatory to extending their sway by military force. "Either the world will be governed by the ideology of modern democracy," says Hitler, "or it will be ruled by the laws of force, when the peoples of brutal determination, not those that show self-restraint, will triumph." Neither of the fascist chiefs leaves us any choice. In Mussolini's words: "The struggle between two worlds can permit of no compromise. . . . Either we or they! Either their ideas or ours! Either our state or theirs!" [28]

These are the ideas which have held the world at bay since

[27] Armstrong, *We or They*, pp. 9, 10, 11, 15, 16.
[28] *Ibid.*, p. 35.

1931. The men who enforce these tenets are still in control of the world situation and will plunge from one war to another indefinitely, unless some combination of free men can overawe them. "We should be under no illusions that a live-and-let-live relationship between democracies and dictatorships can last indefinitely." The struggle is here and "there is no escape, because the aggressive forces have acquired momentum which their leaders could not control even if they would, and because the battle front is world wide." [29]

A Closed World Threatened. What is to be the role of the American people in the struggle which is already under way? Will they ignore the conflict until it is too late? The author of one of the most significant of recent books does not think so. After many years of work in editing foreign news for metropolitan newspapers, Eugene J. Young, in his *Powerful America*, concludes that we shall not "stand aside in futility and let the great work of the coming world change be done by others." It is not only that it is no longer profitable to cash in on other peoples' wars, since they will have nothing but promises of pay to give us. Our younger generations, finding that there is no longer economic security for all within the nation, will insist upon a fair share in the almost limitless opportunities involved in developing the earth's resources. Historically we have always insisted upon the maintenance of the Open Door in all parts of the world. Now when an Open World is of more importance to us than ever we cannot permit the autocratic regimes to seize and close it.[30]

Where the American people will stand finally cannot be in

[29] *Ibid.*, pp. 45, 80. "To boast that we have no interest in the struggle for freedom is to encourage the forces that threaten it—probably to augment them—perhaps to make inevitable 'the last battle of the west'—perhaps in the end to find ourselves fighting it out alone" (p. 83).

[30] Eugene J. Young, *Powerful America*, New York, 1936, pp. 347, 354, 355. The entire book is written from a frankly nationalistic, but not chauvinistic, point of view. In a series of penetrating chapters it surveys fairly the present position of each of the other world powers. The same broad and stimulating outlook will be found in other chapters, especially "Our Sweeping World Policies," "Balance of Power Passing to America," and "Whither is Great America Bound?"

doubt, Mr. Young believes. "As an overloaded and overextended Britain" loses the power to hold great areas which are now enjoying more and more freedom and self-government, "we shall have to decide whether the resources of their vast domains shall be seized by the autocracies and closed to us, or turned against us." Faced with these prospects, both our necessities and our idealisms will overcome the campaigns of the isolationists. They fight a losing battle, because as between submitting to the losses and dangers of military anarchy and accepting a share of world police power we must choose the lesser evil. The policeman's lot is not a happy one. It is risky. "Spoiled Americans would far rather continue comfortably to let others attend to the disorders of the world while they garnered in benefits. But let no American deceive himself—or herself: that time is really gone." [31]

When we are confronted by disruptive forces of enormous power and intensity, there is nothing to be gained by pretending that the calm and quiet of a bygone age can be restored. The choice between international federation and world empire is forced upon us. We cannot escape it if we would. When men of complete resolution, with the full resources of great nations utterly in their power, face peoples who screen themselves behind the passive formulas of a departed time, there can be but one result. Either we shall take the part of a full-grown democracy, joining with other free peoples to defend the common peace and the common right to live in freedom, or we shall see freedom and democracy stamped out in place after place until the tide of autocracy is irresistible.

The Choice before Us

Concerted Effort or World Anarchy. The desperate situation which seventeen years of passive drifting has created was made suddenly clear by President Roosevelt's speech at Chicago, on October 6, 1937, a part of which follows:

[31] Young, *Powerful America*, pp. 367, 372, 373.

Without a declaration of war and without warning or justification of any kind, civilians, including women and children, are being ruthlessly murdered with bombs from the air.

In times of so-called peace, ships are being attacked and sunk by submarines without cause or notice. Nations are fomenting and taking sides in civil warfare in nations that have never done them any harm. Nations claiming freedom for themselves deny it to others.

Innocent peoples and nations are being cruelly sacrificed to a greed for power and supremacy which is devoid of all sense of justice and humane consideration.

To paraphrase a recent author: "Perhaps we foresee a time when men, exultant in the technique of homicide, will rage so hotly over the world that every precious thing will be in danger, every book and picture and harmony, every treasure garnered through two millenniums, the small, the delicate, the defenseless—all will be lost or wrecked or utterly destroyed."

If those things come to pass in other parts of the world, let no one imagine that America will escape, that it may expect mercy, that this Western Hemisphere will not be attacked and that it will continue tranquilly and peacefully to carry on the ethics and the arts of civilization.

If those days come, "there will be no safety by arms, no help from authority, no answer in science. The storm will rage till every flower of culture is trampled and all human beings are leveled in a vast chaos."

If those days are not to come to pass—if we are to have a world in which we can breathe freely and live in amity without fear—the peace-loving nations must make a concerted effort to uphold laws and principles on which alone peace can rest secure.

The peace-loving nations must make a concerted effort in opposition to those violations of treaties and those ignorings of humane instincts which today are creating a state of international anarchy and instability from which there is no escape through mere isolation or neutrality.

Those who cherish their freedom and recognize and respect the equal right of their neighbors to be free and live in peace must work together for the triumph of law and moral principles in order that peace, justice and confidence may prevail in the world.

There must be a return to a belief in the pledged word, in the value of a signed treaty. There must be recognition of the fact that national morality is as vital as private morality.

Nor is it an issue which can be avoided or postponed. "I am compelled," continued President Roosevelt at Chicago, "and you are compelled to look ahead. The peace, the freedom and the security of 90 per cent of the population is being jeopardized by the remaining 10 per cent who are threatening a breakdown of all international law. Surely the 90 per cent who want to live in peace under law and in accordance with moral standards that have received almost universal acceptance through the centuries can and must find some way to make their will prevail."

Surely any President and any Secretary of State who failed to be aroused by the deadly threat of the warmakers to civilization itself would be execrated by all posterity. For it is abundantly clear that the free peoples must defend the peace or suffer unending wars. The dictatorial regimes which have taken the high road to world power cannot be stopped by words. Their leadership has infinitely more courage and tenacity than any democracy has evinced since the dictators rose to power. Throughout the whole sorry spectacle of the fascist conquest of Spain the democracies have proved that they do not have the will to cease retreating. While this retreat continues the dictatorships will proceed from one invasion to another until they have conquered the great continental domains which they seek, or until catastrophe overtakes them. Arrogant autocracy is not only loose again in the world, but it is armed with weapons of organization, propaganda, and military power such as no previous autocracies have ever commanded. Either the free peoples must stand together before it is too late or they will find themselves submitting to conquest or to the suppression of their liberties by internal fascist machines. That is why President Roosevelt's declaration that "we as a nation seek spiritual union with all those who love freedom" is of pregnant importance.[32] If the people of the democracies are devoid of resolution, it is but a question of time until fascist rule will become universal. Nor can the free peoples continue to retreat much longer, lest they find that the prestige and the momentum

[32] *New York Times,* October 12, 1937.

of the fascist machines are too great to be halted. Internal fascist movements may be as paralyzing as the external attack of the fascist empires. To survive, the free peoples must federate themselves into a workable world organization. The alternative to world federation is submission to a new divine-right tyranny more implacable than any which man has been able to invent before.

Police Action vs. War. If, too, a democratic federation modeled on our own American Union is to keep the world in reasonable order, it is imperative that those who favor international law and order shall make, once and for all, the distinction between international police action and war. "War" has been outlawed as effectively as international legislation can ever proscribe it. It is also condemned by the vast majority of mankind. Yet the first justification offered by all those who would take refuge in passivity is the assertion that the use of military force against lawbreakers is "war." Then it is said that to make war to stop war is an absurdity.

Such reasoning, of course, leaves us totally at the mercy of the dictatorial regimes where no such defeatist thinking can be heard. The deliberate confusion of war with international action to restrain it is a counsel of anarchy. It involves a total refusal to recognize the two greatest statutes in the existing law of nations. For if the League Covenant and the Kellogg Pact were legal expressions of the will of the many nations which put them into force—and no one denies that they were—any common action taken under them to deal with their violation cannot be called war in any legal or moral sense. It is true enough that in the last analysis the use of armies and navies on a major scale might result, but such police measures, however large, would not be war. No collective action taken by a preponderance of the nations against an aggressor can hereafter be legally called war, nor be morally considered as war.

That those who are committed to the inevitability of war, or who desire to maintain the use of it as an instrument of national policy, will continue to apply the term "war" to all restrictive action against war is to be expected. Those who see a reasonable chance of establishing the rule of law internationally should be more careful. The habit of thinking all use of force on a large scale to be war is an old one, but it must be firmly broken before a democratic organization of the peace is possible.

Sanctions Inevitable. It does not follow, as is often alleged, that collective action to keep the peace makes every war into a world war. On the contrary, the first essential for the suppression of war is that the nations shall learn to use their economic power to defeat military aggression. It does not avail, either, to contend that the establishment of law means such a freezing of the *status quo* that a nation can then refuse to adjudicate any and all claims against it—thus goading a neighbor into making war. "This contention is open to the strongest criticism. It confuses the merits of the dispute with the form of its settlement. By implication it justifies the use of all means for the prosecution of a just claim and thus justifies the institution of war itself." [33]

Since the totalitarian regimes have been permitted to gain great headway, it may be that there will be no peace until a major power has been restrained by military sanctions. The possibility must also be weighed that an aggressor against whom economic sanctions are courageously applied may lash out against some of the nations participating in the sanctions. Yet if such an ultimate test of the power of the warmakers should come, who shall say that it is better for many nations to be drawn heedlessly and helplessly into a succession of world wars, hatched obscurely and fought without declared objectives until incredible slaughter has occurred, than it would be for a company of nations to spend a fraction of the same amount of blood and treasure in establishing the right of every nation to have its disputes settled by some method that does not bar totally every standard of justice and moderation, of concession and appeasement?

Further experiences with the indescribable stupidities and

[33] The Report of the Committee on Economic Sanctions, *Boycotts and Peace*, New York, 1932, p. 67.

wastes of endeavoring to promote national policy through war may be necessary before we bring ourselves to the point of preferring to face, as a last resource, a regulated use of force to restrain the lawless anarchies of predatory wars. For some time we may flee from applying the first material restraints to a nation run amok, for fear that the ultimate necessity of military control may follow. But, however haltingly, we appear to be fairly certain to take up weapons more powerful than moral condemnation, imponderably strong though that may be alone. Governments will be slow to back up censure with stronger measures, yet they have no alternative unless war is to restore its unchallenged sway over us.

When an aggressive war takes place, every important nation which continues to trade with the aggressor powerfully aids him to succeed. "Neutrality" thus helps actively to diminish the area of freedom and to break down the post-war laws against war. Thus, as this is written, Japan proceeds with the conquest of China, sustained by American and British resources. In his far-sighted letter of October 6, 1937, to the *New York Times*, former Secretary of State Stimson notes that for the year 1935-1936 fully 75 per cent of the oil used by Japan was sold to her by Americans–and 50 per cent of her iron ore and scrap iron. Of cotton Japan purchased 80 per cent from the United States and India and substantially all of her rubber from the Straits Settlement. Of Japanese silk sold in 1936 the United States bought 81 per cent and England the remainder.

Since these are the commodities upon which Japanese economy and fighting power depend, Stimson's conclusion that the United States and Britain are financing the Japanese conquest of China is solidly based. Equally difficult to parry is his challenge: "Does the safety of the American nation and the British Empire require that we go on helping Japan to exterminate . . . the gallant Chinese soldiers with which she is confronted–not to speak of the civilian Chinese population that she is engaged in terrorizing? Is the condition of our statesmanship so pitifully inadequate that we cannot devise the simple means of international cooperation which would stop our participation in the slaughter?"

Questions such as these will not down. They will arise perpetually until the nations decide to exert their economic power against flagrant disturbers of the peace. Since the interest of the great majority of the nations in order and peace is a paramount interest, they must by degrees come to prefer the use of economic sanctions to the alternative of submission to the continual losses and dangers stemming from wars of aggression. Every consideration of statesmanship impels the United States toward participation in sanctions. The thing which we wish to avoid above all others is the sending of great American armies overseas again. But this worst of eventualities cannot be avoided if we wait until Germany or Japan is about to take a firm hold of either of the two great power areas which adjoin us. Therefore our statesmanship must use all lesser means to keep the totalitarian regimes from final triumph. Economic sanctions, the munitioning of France and Britain, the joint action of our navy with others in the Orient, the sending of our air force to aid the European democracies—these are the lesser means which are open to us to avoid the greatest of evils. The American statesmen, too, who refuse to advise the use of the lesser means, and let us in for unlimited participation in future conflicts, will be execrated by posterity even more bitterly than those American "statesmen" who blocked and hamstrung a democratic world organization of the nations in 1919.[34]

The peaceable nations can hardly be diverted from throwing

[34] See Hartley, *Is America Afraid?* p. 257. One school of pacifists argues persistently against economic boycotts of the aggressor nations because such sanctions would injure many innocent people. That is true, but it does not follow that the innocent neighbors of the aggressor regimes ought to suffer violent death or the loss of all liberties, because the people already under the heels of the dictators have been so foolish as to put themselves there. The issue is not whether some innocent people shall suffer, but whether any limits shall be set to crimes against the innocent. If our totalitarian pacifists could have their way, the sweep of the dictators to an iron rule over all the innocents would be unopposed, and the same pacifists would be among the first to be absolutely silenced and controlled. They would soon discover that unlimited force had deprived them of the power to argue against the regulated use of force in behalf of liberty and law.

their economic power against aggression, either, by the plea that sanctions only stimulate efforts toward autarchy. That such is the effect of sanctions upon aggressor nations is not to be doubted, but if sanctions had never been heard of the same nations would still strive with all their might for military autarchy. Yet autarchy in Germany, Italy, or Japan can be maintained only for the projected war period. Unless vast conquests are achieved, the economic problem of these peoples must be solved, not by self-strangulation, but by increased trade, disarmament, and lower birth rates. Lower tariff barriers and full participation in world trade supply the only answer to the economic problem of the "Have-nots" which is tolerable to the remainder of civilization. Here is the great responsibility resting upon the "Haves." They are indeed guilty of raising against the poorer countries the tariff barriers which have contributed greatly to the difficulties of the "Have-nots." Unless, too, the "Haves" are willing to lower their barriers and trade more freely with the poorer countries they cannot expect to live in peace with them.

Yet such is the penalty of drifting for decades that the soundest of all solutions to the present impasse can be applied now only under conditions of great difficulty and danger. At present even the lowering of tariffs for the benefit of the three challengers would merely give them the sinews for fresh wars or further blackmail. Until the dominant regimes in these nations have given solid proofs of their willingness to abandon their plans for conquest, the piling up of arms must go on. This does not mean that the reciprocal lowering of tariffs among the nations committed to peace should not continue, that there should be any baiting of the dictatorships, or that the nations are to be divided into two ideological camps by any action of the democracies. It is the inability of the fascist regimes to avoid using in their international relations the same methods by which they rule internally which creates a universal fear of them. It is not the free peoples which seek to restore war as the arbiter of every nation's destiny.

If Not the League—What? During the period when the issue between world federation and international autocracy is to be decided, what shall be the position of that nation which we like to believe is still the greatest?

It often appears that the American people will not be ready again to assume their share of the common responsibility for world peace until world war and world depression have again swept over the earth. Nevertheless, the extreme gravity of the present crisis makes it all the more essential to consider what the effect upon the nations would be if at this critical moment we should declare as follows:

> We give notice that henceforth our vital interest in world order is to be defended. We do not promise to send our army or navy anywhere, but hereafter our influence will be thrown consistently on the side of law and order. We shall not permit our traders to aid aggression in any quarter and we shall consistently do nothing to interfere with those who are trying to resist it.
>
> With these understandings we propose to enter the League of Nations and to work actively not only against war and conquest, but for peaceful change, for a freer distribution of raw materials, for limited changes of national boundaries in a few troubled areas and for such a world-wide lowering of tariff barriers, along with the voluntary limitation of populations, as will enable all nations to live in reasonable security.

If the United States took counsel with its long future and made such a declaration, what would the effect be? Is it to be supposed that the British Empire, Russia, France, and the United States, united in the League of Nations and backed enthusiastically by fifty small and middle-sized nations, would be defied by any one of the three nations which now threaten everyone's security? Is it to be supposed even that Italy, Germany, and Japan together would insist upon taking the path of blood, separated by distance as they are?

That they will do so unless restrained by a world combination of clearly superior strength is abundantly plain. It is equally evident that they have a close understanding designed to intimidate the democracies each time that any one of the aggressors is engaged in a depredation. Should the expanding empires of the totalitarian states reach great proportions, wars for supremacy between them may be confidently anticipated, but in the early stages of their empire building it is to the interest of each of the three to support the others in his chosen field of expansion. They may be expected also to give each other determined and daring support.

Will the powers which are opposed to a series of world wars be equally alert and courageous? Or will there be a disastrous lack of coordination and unanimity among them? No more important question can be asked. And not even the greatest of powers can supply the answer alone. Nor is it the duty of any single nation to attempt to cope single-handed with the world peril which confronts all. No nation, however great, has any duty itself to police the earth, to bear the heat and burden of every fray. All that is required of any nation is that it carry a fair share of the costs of living in an ordered world. Even the small nations have a duty to the others and must take some risks. But it is the attitude of the four greatest powers which is crucial, and of these the United States is only one. If any one of the other three does not back the collective system, the way is wide open for another and a greater world war. Should Russia renounce Geneva and compose her ideological war with Germany, the world would be disastrously split in two. Should France again aid and abet one of the aggressors, as she did during the conquest of Ethiopia, the League would in all probability suffer another dangerous reverse.

More important still is the role of Great Britain. She, too, is essential if a structure of peace is to be built. Her contribution also is by no means certain. It is within her power to make another world war almost inevitable. Should her Conservative Governments continue to connive at the death of democratic governments in Europe when beset with fascist aggression, then the United States will have little choice except to arm for the defense of North America and to leave Britain to survive if she can. If Britain's ruling elements are so wedded to balance-of-power politics that they can give no real allegiance to genuine collective action, then the abstention of the United States from any constructive role in Europe will be made permanent.

Such a development would promote new wars on a world scale. Europe needs in its politics the active, stabilizing participation of the United States. It is also in our interest to exert our influence in European politics, not only to prevent the outbreak of war in Europe but to secure the cooperation of Europe in preventing unending war in the Orient. It is easy for Americans to be indignant at the failure of Britain and France to back us up in the Far East, but it is illogical to expect our friends to support us in China when we refuse to support them where they are the most vitally interested. We cannot be half-isolated and half in world politics, as may suit our momentary convenience. We too must play the game consistently, on a world scale.

This does not mean that either we or the European democracies must carry the same amount of responsibility in all parts of the world. It must be understood that while the British navy is no longer expected to keep the entire globe in order, the United States assumes no responsibility to send her armies hither and yon. The shipping of great conscript armies overseas is our touchy point. Nor should that heroic remedy be necessary again. Professor James T. Shotwell has amply demonstrated in his recent book, *On the Rim of the Abyss* (New York, 1936), that there must be a gradation of responsibilities for the nations which have a high degree of geographic safety and for those which have not. Whenever war breaks out, the nations which are nearer the fire are endangered most and must bear the heaviest share of the burden of extinguishing it. Those peoples which are remote from the conflict cannot be expected to go always to the ultimate limit of employing military sanctions, especially the sending of huge armies. But it is of supreme importance that they should have some share in the common task. Their essential interest in defending the structure of peace may be conserved by economic sanctions. The great desideratum is that any and all aggressors shall know that they must count upon the opposition, in some degree, of substantially all the nations. The degrees of opposition will vary, but the determination of the world community to defend itself must remain fixed.

This is the spirit of the Joint Resolution for entry into the League of Nations proposed by Senator James P. Pope, of Idaho.

Resolved by the Senate and House of Representatives of the United States of America in Congress assembled, That the President is hereby authorized to notify the appropriate authority of the League of Nations that the United States accepts its membership in the League of Nations on the following terms and understandings:

(1) That the obligation of the Pact of Paris not to resort to war as an instrument of national policy is recognized as the fundamental and guiding principle of the Covenant; and

(2) That the provisions of the Covenant of the League of Nations relating to cooperation in the prevention of war shall not be interpreted as obligating the United States to adopt measures which might involve the use of armed force; and that the decision as to what action shall be taken by the United States in case the peace of nations is threatened or violated shall rest with the Government of the United States acting according to the Constitution.[35]

Justice and Law. Of course it will be said that to stand by the League now is merely to join one alliance. So it would be. In the recent words of Editor John W. Dafoe of the *Winnipeg Free Press:* "Against an alliance of barbarian tyrannies directed against liberty and civilization there would be an alliance of free nations pledged to a single purpose—the outlawing of aggressive war."[36]

Nor is there a negation of justice in world alliance for peace. The processes for peaceable change and the alleviation of national grievances must be built up, if international self-help is to be for-

[35] Senate Joint Resolution 119, 74th Congress, 1st Session, May 7, 1935. *Congressional Record*, Vol. 79, Pt. 7, p. 7042.

[36] *Supplement, Canadian League of Nations Society Monthly News Sheet*, May, 1937, p. 8.

Wide World

SENATOR JAMES P. POPE

bidden finally. But to demand that this constructive side of international government should be fully developed before the destructiveness of modern war is controlled is to surrender to the warmakers. Those who hold to the view that justice must be enthroned before peace can be established should give us some small area of hope to stand upon. To say that the application of sanctions against aggressor nations is responsible for the perpetuation of hatreds, reliance upon armaments and the spirit of force, is to leave us finally to the gentle ministrations of the boldest diplomats and the mightiest armadas. Why should the establishment of world stability wait upon the achievement of a state of utopian justice, through the chance adjustments of an endless chain of wars? The enjoyment of perfect justice in advance of enforcing a reasonable degree of order has assuredly not been had in any other human society. Why should it be demanded internationally? Few things would seem clearer than that the establishment of that degree of order among the nations which is required by the never-ceasing development of the means of production and destruction cannot be long postponed.

Is it not the true view that the buttressing of international law, the rectification of grievances by peaceful processes, and the repression of war must proceed together? "Rigid insistence upon the realization of any one of these objectives prior to taking practical steps to realize the others must indefinitely postpone all progress." [37] Yet if one objective is to be placed first it must be

[37] Albert E. Hindmarsh, *Force in Peace*, Cambridge (Mass.), 1933, p. 179. The 1938 campaign of the National Peace Conference and the peace organizations of Canada is to deal with the subject of peaceful change through economic cooperation. See the Foreign Policy Association Headline Book, *Peaceful Change*, New York, 1937; also Frederick Dunn, *Peaceful Change*, New York, 1937. The last-named investigator found no evidence that the dissatisfied powers could be won over by any gifts of territory unless the cessions were huge enough to give them a superior power position. He notes that many lesser nations have the same raw-material deficiencies from which the three demanding nations rebel, yet the smaller "Have-nots" do not plan to conquer raw materials. They get them by ingenuity.

Mr. Dunn believes that such solutions as the adoption of international codes of fair practice and international administration of colonial areas, perhaps through an internationalized mandate system, would best meet the problem. Thereby the

the suppression of aggressive war. The extreme anarchy of today makes any important steps along the road of peaceful change almost impossible. Every concession made to the dictators only whets their appetites and enlarges the demands they will make tomorrow. Yielding to international blackmail merely increases the power of the blackmailers to demand still greater surrenders.[38] As one of the foremost students of the League of Nations, Sir Alfred Zimmern, has written in *The League of Nations and the Rule of Law* (London, 1936): "The first and major function of the League is to eliminate once and for all the fear of war. Once this has been achieved we shall witness a relaxation of tension which will manifest itself in many forms." And "if this degree of authority is not embodied in the League none of its other activities can be expected to bear fruit." [39]

In a wise and farsighted address delivered on October 22, 1937, at the University of Toronto, Secretary of State Cordell Hull uttered the fundamental maxim around which mankind will be compelled to rally. "The all-embracing preoccupation of all of us may be summed up in one word—order," said Mr. Hull. "Order in international relations is just as vital as it is in the relations within a nation," he continued, and as fundamental to us as is order within a local community. For, "no matter what form it assumes and no matter from what cause it springs, war represents the most complete negation of order in both the internal and international life of nations." [40]

---

complaint of Germany that she is in an unequal position would be removed, without placing her in military control of areas where such control might be dangerous in the future (pp. 6, 131, 139-41).

That the prestige-and-power hunger of the Nazis would permit them to accept such arrangements is highly doubtful, unless the preponderance of military power facing them should prove to be permanently overwhelming. Where the idea of absolute sovereignty has been fully restored the acceptance of international substitutes for sovereign rule will be possible only as a last resort.

[38] "Any practical realization of a better world legal system will require two positive steps forward—extension of the scope of international law by deliberate international legislation, and the elimination of the right of national self-help."—Hindmarsh, *Force in Peace*, p. 146.

[39] Pages 495, 297.

[40] Mr. Hull made clear his belief that the species of order established in the totalitarian states is, in fact, the negation of all law. "We have discovered," he

The relation which the United States shall have to the League of Nations is still the most crucial question confronting the nation and the world. So long as that issue is not settled the international situation may be expected to deteriorate. "There is only one way to go forward to better things and that is the way of the League." [41] There is no other way to secure peace "than by maintaining an international organ of cooperative pacification. The League is that one body. In the midst of perils it will endure if our civilization itself endures." [42] In the measured words of Secretary Hull, "no more than a community or a nation, can the world of today base its existence in part on order and in part on chaos, in part on law and in part on lawlessness. . . . The outraged conscience of mankind will set into motion forces which will create, in the sphere of international relations, unshakable order based upon law." [43]

This is the law of which Woodrow Wilson was the powerful voice in an hour of the world's desperate need. Then for long years this most urgent of all endeavors was pushed aside. Now under the compulsion of the men of violence we are driven back to it. In the words of a wise English scholar, the hands of the clock can never be put back to 1914. "Whatever the oscillations of politics and of single states, politics are already caught in the

---

said, "from long and bitter experience, that only such laws will produce order in the true sense as derive their authority from the consent of the governed and are subject to change only by the will of the majority of the people. Ambitious individuals may usurp that authority and arrogate to themselves an unchallengeable right to impose or alter laws. But such usurpation and arrogation, though they may be accompanied in some instances by an outward semblance of order, are in fact supreme acts of lawlessness."

Likewise, Hull rejected the thesis of the dictatorial regimes that economic security and prosperity can be conquered by internal organization and external aggression. The "basic materials of sustenance and production" are too widely scattered, and the necessity of sharing in the fruits of new inventions and skills in other lands is too imperative for the totalitarian solution to succeed. "Nor can the flowering of science, intellect and the arts attain its highest development and its rounded development when confined within the frontiers of a single nation."—*New York Times*, October 23, 1937.

[41] John W. Dafoe, in *Supplement*, *Canadian League of Nations Society Monthly News Sheet*, May, 1937.

[42] James T. Shotwell, *On the Rim of the Abyss*, New York, 1936, p. 353.

[43] *New York Times*, October 23, 1937.

international machine, and are affected by the ideal of the abolition of war. Once the peoples have entertained this ideal as something possible it can never fade from their minds and hearts." [44] To which a leading student of international law adds: "It is not open to doubt that as a result either of the contemporary situation or its inescapable consequences, the true direction of the current will be resumed. And, when that happens, the Covenant, possibly with deliberate amendments and certainly with developments, will re-establish its claim to the universal attention of mankind." [45]

Toward World Government. The building of a democratic world organization strong enough to keep the peace is an endeavor which will require the best efforts of individuals, groups, and governments for many years to come. The undertaking is immense. Yet what other offers a greater challenge to forward-looking men and women—to youth? Other fields of service require devoted laborers, yet every other kind of human advancement will be blighted or destroyed by the failure of world organization to restrain the warmakers. What other goal is there upon which the sixty organizations in the United States which have peace as an important objective can agree? The peace organizations must continue, and in a few cases return, to support of the only objective that makes all others attainable. They have no other alternative, if they would not confess to extinction of purpose and effectiveness. Around what other standard than a League of Nations strong and universal enough to keep the peace can the masses of people who have had enough of war gather? To what

[44] G. P. Gooch in the introduction to Luigi Sturzo, *The International Community and the Right of War*, New York, 1930, p. 9.

[45] Sir John Fisher Williams, *Some Effects of the Covenant of the League of Nations*, London, 1934. Professor Jessup believes that "the whole trend of international relations since at least the seventeenth century and, more broadly, the whole trend of human society, is in the direction of cooperation and organization." He concludes, therefore, that the United States should consider participation in the collective system, "not as a short cut to the millennium," but as "a step in the direction of a far-distant goal which will be reached only by a progress as painful as the pilgrim's."—Jessup, *Neutrality: Its History, Economics, and Law*, Vol. IV, p. 152.

other haven can governments which are faced with an imminent revival of the war system retreat?

In a world that is compelled to establish a degree of order that will make the continuance and development of civilization feasible, it is hardly to be expected that the effort will fail because of a final attempt on the part of the United States to reassert a neutrality which would restore the right of war to its uncontrollable estate as the supreme arbiter of our destinies—and not ours alone, but those of our children who must pay the penalties of war's blind decisions for generations to come. It is not credible that the American people will consider it a safe or a wise thing to watch the destruction of liberty by violence up to their own shores. It is not reasonable to believe that they will stand by indefinitely while upstart cliques begin world wars which only the United States can stop. In 1938, as in 1918, and as far into the future as we can see, there can be no world stability or dependable peace without strong participation in world government by the world's most powerful nation.

INDEX

Aaland Islands dispute settled, 151-52
Abbott, Grace, first unofficial observer, 231
Achorn, Erik, quoted on effect of American abstention, 221*n*
Advisory opinions of World Court: danger of, alleged, 243 ff.; reservation against, 246; reservation stiffened, 251; status of, in League law, 252-54; on Mosul case, 175-76, Austro-German customs union, 337-38, 337*n*
Aggression, definitions of, 197, 517*n*; defense of, 508-9
Aggressor Powers, dangers of yielding to, 521-23; extent of ambitions of, 523-26; pacts between, 528; invalidity of claims of, 545*n*, 547*n*
Albania, saved by League, 156-57
Albany Knickerbocker Press, quoted, 466
Albuquerque Journal, quoted, 474
Alliances, French, 117-18, enumerated, 181; Little Entente, 181; Polish-Rumanian, 182
Aloisi, Baron, for an elastic League, 446
Ambassadors, Conference of. *See* Conference of Ambassadors
American Metals Case, 268
Angell, Norman, on making war pay, 131-32
Anglo-Japanese Alliance, disliked by U. S., 80, 85, 90; difficulty in terminating, 82-84; share of Premier Meighen in ending, 82*n*
Anschluss, 182, 337-38
Antiwar Treaty, multilateral. *See* Pact of Paris
Apponyi, Count, accepts Geneva protocol, 198
Arabic, sinking of, 9
Arbitration, treaties on, 314
Arizona Republic, quoted, 474
Arms traffic regulation, cooperation of U. S. on, withheld, 67-69; American observer at conference on, 221
Armstrong, Hamilton F., on Fascist objectives, 531-32
Articles 8, 10, 11, 15, and 16 of League Covenant. *See* Covenant
Asheville Times, quoted, 468
Askenazy, Polish delegate, 159
Assembly, League of Nations. *See* League Assembly
"Association of Nations," 43; a league promised by Harding, 45; search for, 237-38
Augusta Chronicle, quoted, 469
Austria, finances reorganized by League, 279-80
Austro-German Customs Union, 336-37
Autarchy and war, 540
Autocracy: and war, 521-23; seriousness of threat by, 526, 533, 535-36, 539, 541-42, 544

Baker, Newton D., statement on war debts, 354; for economic sanctions (1932), 430
Balance of power, and Four Power Treaty, 93-95; and U. S., 519
Balance of trade during Normalcy, 286*n*
Balbo, General, at Geneva, 379
Balfour, Arthur, 159
Baltimore Sun, quoted, 50, 463
Bangor Daily Commercial, quoted, 454
Bank for International Settlements, 1931 Committee on Germany, 349
Banks, statistics on failures of, 328, 347; collapse of, 359
Bay City Times, quoted, 479*n*
Bela Kun, dictatorship of, 148
Bell, Edward P., and London Conference, 361-62
Benes, Eduard, 57; on Draft Treaty, 196; 212; 376*n*; led Assembly at crisis of Manchurian dispute, 427, 428; on Lytton Report, 443
Bernardes, Arthur, President of Brazil, 213
Beveridge, Senator A. J., and plan to defeat League, 19; 19*n*; on political necessity for defeating League, 27
Bills of Exchange, conference on, 313*n*

Birmingham Age-Herald, quoted, 469
Birmingham News, quoted, 469
Blackmer, H. M., oil executive, 262*n*; flees abroad, 265
Bliss, General Tasker H., and Geneva Protocol, 196
Blue, Dr. Rupert, 65*n*; observer at opium committee, 223
Bluefield Daily Telegraph, quoted, 463
Borah, Senator William E.: conference with Lodge on strategy, 26; attack on Crane, 34*n*; opposes treaty of peace with Germany, 50-51; and Reparations Commission, 51; presses for Washington Conference, 81; opposes Four Power Treaty, 94-95; holds Article 10 of Covenant and Article 2 of Four Power Treaty synonymous, 97; on war debts, 120*n*; alarmed by reparations crisis, 138; demands international action, 138-43; defends conferences, 139-41; admits conference might have prevented great war, 140; his ability to confuse opinion, 141-42; opposes World Court, 242; urges dismissal of Daugherty, 274; lists gains to us under one League treaty, 288*n*; and 1930 tariff, 321; ridicules consultation, 367*n*; predicts League's death, 487
Borchard, Edwin M., on Pact of Paris and League, 303; 502; on League sanctions, 512*n*; quoted, 513; on role of U. S., 530-31
Borden, Sir Robert, on Article 10, 185
Boston Globe, quoted, 464
Bourgeois, Léon, 159
Boycott, Chinese, a reprisal, 437-38
Boyden, R. W. observer at Reparations Commission, 220
Bradley, Phillips, on restraining power of international law, 517*n*
Brandegee, Senator Frank B., Irreconcilable, 33-34, 34*n*; moves reservation to Four Power Treaty, 89; death of, 273*n*
Branting, Hjalmar, Swedish delegate, 57; 152*n*; *rapporteur* on Mosul, 173; accepts Geneva Protocol, 198
Brazil, claim of, to permanent Council seat, 206, 208, 212; resignation of, from League, 213-15; role of, in League, 214*n*
Brent, Bishop Charles H., delegate to opium conferences, 224, 225; quoted on frustration of American peace efforts, 242
Briand, Aristide: in Bulgarian crisis, 167; and security negotiations, 182-83; 1926 oration, 215; and Pact of Paris, 292-93; at London Conference, 366; President of Council in Manchurian crisis, 403 ff.; on Japan's fundamental points, 406
Briand-Kellogg Pact. *See* Pact of Paris
British blockade, effects of, 6
British League of Nations Union organized, 14
Bruce, Stanley, Australian delegate, opposes action on Manchuria, 447
Brüning, Chancellor, declares reparations ended, 350; at Disarmament Conference, 376-78
Bryan, William J., note to Japan on non-recognition, 412*n*
Buenos Aires Conference, 528
Buero, delegate of Uruguay, on intervention, 428
Buffalo Evening News, quoted, 459
Burlington Free Press and Times, quoted, 464
Business and government, 355
Butler, Nicholas Murray: favors League with reservations, 35; on danger of drifting policy, 277; advanced Pact of Paris, 293; on non-intercourse with aggressors, 430
Butte Standard, quoted, 476

Cahan, delegate of Canada, deprecates action on Manchuria, 447; recalled, 447*n*
Camden Courier-Post, quoted, 458
Canada, costs of war to, 501
Cannes, conference at, 182
Cannon, Joseph G., on war debts, 120*n*
Caraway, Thaddeus H., on Four Power Treaty, 100
Carelia, Eastern, case of. *See* Eastern Carelia case
Carter, Boake, radio defense of Japan, 509*n*
Cecil, Viscount: and Phillimore Committee, 14; in first Assembly, 57; and Albania's boundaries, 156; action during Corfu crisis, 163; proposed

Resolution XIV, 192; and Draft Treaty, 193; resigned after Geneva Naval Conference, 290; on sincerity of Japanese liberals, 397, 397*n*; 405
Chaco war, 305
Chamberlain, Sir Austen, and Locarno treaties, 201-2; proposed conference on World Court reservation, 256
Chamber of Commerce of U. S., referendum on League, 13
Change, peaceful, 537; and world government, 544-45; campaign of peace organizations for, 545*n*
Chang Hsueh-liang, 309
Charleston Gazette, quoted, 463
Charleston News and Observer, quoted, 468
Charlotte Observer, quoted, 468
Chicago Daily News, quoted, 478
Chicago Tribune, quoted, 482-84
China, claims to Council seat, 211*n*
Chinchow, capture of, postponed, 409; captured, 411
Christians, Assyrian, 171; Chaldean, 176-77
Christian Science Monitor, quoted, 465
Churchill, Winston, pro-Japanese statement, 423
Cincinnati Enquirer, quoted, 481
Clark, Champ, against canal tolls repeal, 5
Clark, Grover, quoted on expansion by war 506*n*
Cleveland Plain Dealer, quoted, 480-81
Colby, Bainbridge, 63
Colcord, Samuel, quoted, 38-39
Collective security. *See* Security, collective
Collier, James W., on war debts, 120*n*
Colombia given damages for canal seizure, 5
Colt, Senator L. B., on reservation to Four Power Treaty, 90; on necessity of political machinery, 101*n*
Columbia State, quoted, 468
Columbia University Faculty, statement on war debts, 355, 355*n*
Columbus Dispatch, quoted, 480
Committee of Nineteen, controlled by small nations, 433; proposes Assembly resolution, 434; report of, 449
Compromis, controlled by Senate, 315
Concord Daily Monitor, quoted, 458
Conference of Ambassadors, 151; and Vilna dispute, 160; and Bessarabia, 160; and Corfu crisis, 161-66; 182
Conferences, post-war, 150-51; Genoa, 150; Cannes, 182; Lausanne, 351-52; Buenos Aires, 528. *See individual entries for various League conferences, e.g.*, Arms traffic regulation, Opium regulation, etc.
Congress, war power of, 97*n*
Connoly, Irish Free State delegate, 443
Conquest, feasibility of, 506-12
Conservatives, British: attitude toward League, 390-91; refuse to concert with U. S. on Shanghai war, 420; and sacrifice of Czechoslovakia and Austria, 519
Consular Committee, Shanghai, 421-23; reports of, 425, 425*n*
Consultation: and Four Power Pact, 84 ff.; on Chaco war, 305-6; on Sino-Russian clash, 309-12; and London Naval Conference, 363-64, 365-70; Moses for, 366; Knox resolution on, 366; various Senators on, 366, 367*n*; and Executive power, 369; 371*n*; held inevitable by Stimson, 381-82; Davis declaration of May 24, 1933, 390-91
Continental Trading Company, organized, 262-63
Contraband, definition of, indefinitely expanded, 6, 8,
Coolidge, Calvin: for League, 35; on majority of Republicans favorable to League, 238*n*; rejects invitation to negotiate on World Court reservation, 258; and dismissal of Daugherty, 274; victory of, in 1924, 275; and Geneva Naval Conference, 288-89, 290*n*; opposes reservations to Pact of Paris, 297; veto of McNary-Haugen Bill, 319; defends bull market, 330
Corfu dispute, 161-66; ultimatum to Greece, 162; island seized, 162-63; indemnity delivered, 164; island returned, 165
Council, League of Nations. *See* League Council
Counterfeiting, conference on, 313*n*
Covenant, League of Nations: origins of, 15; flight from, 184-201; and international law, 516; Pope resolution on adherence to, 544; probability of return to, 546-48
Article 8, 371

Covenant, League of Nations (*Cont.*)
Article 10: and Article 2 of Four Power Treaty, 95-97, 96*n*; effect of American rejection on, 184; Canadian objection to, 185-88; reports to Second Assembly on, 187; interpretation of secured, 187-88; appeal of China under, 415; Titulesco on, 428; backed by Unden, 444
Article 11, reasons for use of, in 1931, 397*n*
Article 15, appeal of China under, 415
Article 16: effect of American rejection on, 184; fears of small neutrals on, 189-90; interpreted in 1921, 190, 190*n*; interpreted in Geneva Protocol, 203; and London Conference, 368
Crane, Senator Murray, favors League, 33-34, 34*n*
Cravath, Paul D., on rejection of Versailles Treaty, 91*n*
Creditors, world panic of, 345-47
Cummins, Albert B., on war debts, 120
Cunningham, Edward S., Chairman, Shanghai Consular Committee, 421-23
Cuno, Chancellor, offer of, 183; offer renewed, 202
Curzon, Lord, and Mosul dispute, 175
Customs Formalities, Conference on, 288*n*

Dafoe, John W., editor, on alliance against aggression, 544; on future of League, 547
Dallas News, quoted, 473
Danat Bank, closing of, 343
Daniels, Josephus, guards Navy's oil reserves, 261
D'Annunzio, Gabriel, 158
Darden, James G., 263*n*
Daugherty, Harry, Attorney General, 267; confidants of, 267; Sullivan on, 275*n*
Davis, Norman H.: Acting Secretary of State, 62; on Four Power Treaty, 99-100, 102; on reparations dilemma, 134; heads Memel Commission, 161; delegate to World Economic Conference, 287*n*; at Disarmament Conference, 377-78, 377*n*; agrees to German equality, 382; evolves December disarmament formula, 383; declaration of May 24, 1933, 390-91
Dawes, Charles G., for League, 35; and December session of Council, 407-8, 408*n*
Dawes Plan, 146-47; authors of, 146*n*
Dayton Daily News, quoted, 481
Debts, internal, 355-56
Debuchi, Japanese ambassador, 398
Declaration of war against Germany repealed, 47
Delano, Frederic L., 230
Democratic Party, drops League in 1928, 315
Denby, Edwin, Secretary of Navy, 261; abolished Fuel Oil Board, 262; dismissed, 264*n*
Denison, J. H., quoted on Wilson in Europe, 23*n*
Depression, of 1921, 281; of 1929, statistics on, 357-58
Des Moines Register, quoted, 477
Detroit Free Press, quoted, 478
Detroit News, quoted, 479
Deutsche Justiz, quoted, 531
De Valera, Eamon, President of Council, 441-42
Dickinson, G. Lowes, on Wilson's achievement, 115-16
Dill, Senator Clarence C., on peace movement in politics, 304
Dillon Read and Company, loans to Bolivia, 305
Diplomats, American, ability of, 376*n*
Disarmament, first efforts at, 192, 372; Geneva Naval Conference, 288-91; London Naval Conference, 361-71; world conference on, 371-92
Disarmament Conference, 371-92; years of preparation for, 372 ff.; and Manchurian war, 375; petitions presented to, 375*n*; officers of, 376, 376*n*; American leadership in, 376*n*; our delegates to, 377*n*; April resolutions, 377*n*; Hoover Plan, 378-80; July resolution, 380; Herriot Plan, 382-83; December formula, 383; February, 1933, session, 384; British Plan, 385; and security, 386-87; American declaration of May 24, 1933, to, made by Norman H. Davis, 390-91
Doheny, Edward L., impresses Admiral Robinson, 262; loans Fall $100,000,

262; acquitted of conspiracy, 265; acquitted of bribery, 265
Doherty, C. J., on Article 10, 185, 186; on reservations, 186*n*
Dolbeare, F. C., 222
Dollar, R. S., commissions to, 267*n*
Double Taxation, conference on, 313
Draft Treaty of Mutual Assistance, 191-95; security guarantees of, 193; governments divided on, 194; rejected by British nations, 194-95; effect of American abstention on, 195; Lord Grey on, 195
Dresel, E. L., negotiates peace with Germany, 48
Drummond, Sir Eric, Secretary-General of the League, 55; chosen by Wilson, 55
Dunn, Frederick, cited on peaceful change, 545*n*
Dyche, J. E., 268*n*

Eastern Carelia case, 242
Economic Statistics, conference on, 288*n*, 313
Editorial opinions, American, on Manchurian crisis, 457-84
Edwards, Augustín, Chilean delegate, 208, 209
Election of 1918, 17-18
Elizabeth Daily Journal, quoted, 462*n*
Elkus, Abram I., 152*n*
Entangling alliances, 101; Lodge on, 13
Erich, delegate of Finland, on the League's motive power, 427-28
Ethiopian war, 495
Europe, condition of in 1919, 278; fears of American financial control, 283-84; new map of, 499-501
Expansion, economic necessity of, 505-12
Export and Import Prohibitions, conference on, 288*n*, 313
Export Debenture Plan, 319-20

Fall, Albert B., Secretary of Interior, 42, 261; leases Navy oil reserves to Sinclair and Doheny, 263; retires with honors, 264; imprisoned, 264; declared faithless officer by Supreme Court, 265
Farmers, effects of unequal deflation on, 281; subsidies for, rejected, 318-20; and tariff of 1922, 318; prices collapse (1931), 333-34
Fascism and war, 521-23, 531
Filene, Edward A., 280
Financial Conference, Brussels, 58*n*
Firestone Company and Liberia, 232
Fitzgerald, John J., on war debts, 119
Flint Daily Journal, quoted, 478
Forbes, Charles R., in Veterans Bureau, 266; and raiding of Perryville depot, 266, 266*n*; imprisoned, 267
Fordney, Joseph W., on war debts, 120*n*
Foreign Relations Committee, Senate: packed with Irreconcilables, 26; seniority rule violated, 26*n*; amendments to Covenant, 28; holds own peace conference, 28; reports reservation to separate treaty with Germany, 50; and reservation to Four Power Treaty, 89-90; obstruction of World Court proposal by, 242-46; files report interpreting Pact of Paris, 297; and reservation to Pan-American Arbitration Treaty, 315
Fort Worth Star-Telegram, quoted, 472
Four Power Treaty, origins of, 81-84; text of, 84-85; ratification of, pleaded by Harding, 86-89; reservation to, adopted, 89-90; debate on, 90-102; Democratic objections to, 102-3; amendment to, proposed, 103; ratified by Democratic votes, 104; reservation to, criticized in France, 106-7
France: opposes amendment to Four Power Treaty, 106-7; attains inconclusive peace, 113; dilemma apropos of Germany, 113; not open to American advice on reparations, 144; occupies Ruhr, 144-45; objects to Hoover moratorium, 342; insistence on security, 1932, 375; dominates Yunnan province, 429-30; costs of war to, 501
Franco, Mello, Brazilian delegate, 212
Franco-British agreement on cruisers (1928), 290; exposed by Hearst, 290
Fraser, Sir John Foster, on American unanimity for League in 1918, 116
French Canadians, objections of, to nationhood, 186
Frick, Henry C., campaign against League financed by, 26
Fuller, Stuart A., on opium treaty, 230

Galveston Tribune, quoted, 472
Garay, delegate of Panama, 411
Garvin, J. L., quoted, 489
Geneva Naval Conference (1927), 288-91; called by Coolidge, 289; Franco-British bargain after, 290; inadequate preparation for, 290*n*
Geneva Protocol, 196-201; Shotwell plan basis of, 196-97; defines aggressor, 197; rejected by British nations, 199; effect of American abstention on, 199; a constructive failure, 201
Gerig, Benjamin, Secretariat official, and Hearst Press, 482
German-Americans against League, 38-39
Germany: war aims of, 10; entry of into League, 205-17; 1930 election in, 335; flight of gold from, 335; foreign investments in, 339; world run on, 339-40; reasons for her collapse in 1931, 340-41; 1932 elections in, 350-51; reasons for failure of Republic, 376; election of March 11 and April 24, 1932, 377; election of July 31, 1932, 381; first withdrawal from Disarmament Conference, 382; Nazis gain control of, 384, 384*n*; withdrawal from League, 385; validity of claims to territorial expansion, 545*n*, 546*n*, 547*n*
Giannini, A. P., 330
Gibbs, Philip, on Wilson, 55; on cry, "The League is dead," 222*n*
Gibson, Hugh, at Geneva Naval Conference, 288-89; in Disarmament Conference, 376*n*
Giddings, Franklin H., quoted, 12
Gilbert, Parker T., Agent General of Reparations, 146
Gillett, Frederick C., doubts dangers in World Court, 252; on Pact of Paris, 299-300
Glass, Carter, deprecates Pact of Paris, 297
Goebbels, Paul Joseph, quoted, 531
Gold, flight of, from Germany, 335; drained to U. S., 336; flight of, from London, 345-46; gold standard abandoned by Great Britain, 346; flight of, from U. S., 347
Gompers, Samuel L., helps create I. L. O., 235
Gooch, G. P., on permanence of the League, 547-48
Government, world, required in future, 541; 544-48. *See also* World federation, World order, *and* World conquest
Graham, George, representations on war debts, 119
Grand Rapids Press, quoted, 478
Grandi, Dino, Italian delegate, 379
Gray, Judge George, 72-73
Great Britain: abandons gold standard, 346; diplomatically involved with Japan, 429; costs of war to, 501; and world order, 524, 532-33, 542-43
Great Powers, cannot avoid great wars, 517-18
Great War, costs of, 501
Greco-Bulgarian clash, 166-69
Greco-Turkish war, 149-50
Greek refugee settlement, 222-23
Green House on K street, 268*n*
Greenville News, quoted, 468
Grew, Joseph C., observer at arms traffic discussion, 221
Grey, Lord, on a policy of drifting, 195; on entry of Germany into League, 211; on Japan's responsibility, 428*n*
Griffin, R. S., 261, 262
Grigg, Sir Edward, on internationalism, 513*n*; on yielding to the three aggressors, 519-20
Guarantee, Treaty of, 386
Gulflight, sinking of, 9
Gulick, Sidney L., quoted, 80*n*
Gunther, John, quoted on effects of American abstention, 392*n*

Hamon, Jake, 260
Harding, Warren G.: selected as candidate, 34, 34*n*, 35; inaugural address, 42-43; rejects the League, 45; pleads for Senate approval of Four Power Treaty, 86-89; gains executive view point, 87; advises entry into World Court, 239; abjures League entirely, 240*n*; characterization of, by *New York Times*, 259-60; vouches for oil leases, 263; White House receptions, 269, 269*n*; death of, 269; last address of, 270
Harrisburg Patroit, quoted, 461
Hartford Courant, quoted, 459

Hartford Daily Times, quoted, 464
Hartley, Livingston, quoted on the developing world crisis, 523-24
Harvey, George: on sentiment for League, 31*n*; dominates Harding, 37; denies high war aims, 60; rebuked by many, 60*n*; Hughes disagrees with, 60; American observer, 154
Have-nots, validity of claims of, 545*n*
Hays, Will H., in 1918 campaign, 18; on Republican Party split, 27; for the League, 27*n*; receives Sinclair bonds for Republican Party, 266
Health Organization, not recognized by U. S., 64; sketch of activities, 233-34; aid of Rockefeller Foundation to, 234
Hearst, William Randolph exposes Franco-British agreement, 290; pressure on Roosevelt to disavow League, 388
Hearst press: and the League, 484-94; attitude of, toward Japan in 1919 and in 1933, 485-87; predictions of League's demise, 488; features Secretariat pledge as a traitor's oath, 490-92
Henderson, Arthur, 376
Henning, Arthur S., at London Conference, 364-65
Herriot, Edouard: gives League prominence, 196, falls from power, 202; returns to power (1932), 351; 379; and German equality, 382; his disarmament plan, 382-83
Hindenburg, Marshal von, elected President of Germany, 202
Hindmarsh, Albert E., on necessity of world government, 546*n*
Hitchcock, Senator Gilbert, on separate peace, 52-53
Hitler, Adolf, on master nation, 531
Hoar, Senator George F., on Senators as negotiators, 88*n*
Holding companies, 359
Hoover, Herbert: for League, 35, 41; congratulates Fall on retirement, 264; refuses to pardon Fall, 264; relies on public opinion to check violence, 316; on abolition of poverty, 317-18; opposes Export Debenture Plan, 319-20; and the tariff, 320; reports to him censored, 326*n*; stock market boom in honor of, 331; moratorium, 341-44; loses control of Congress, 349-50; defeat of, 357; rejects consultation, 367; Disarmament Conference Plan, 378-80; his effort to regulate Europe, 387
House, Colonel E. M., 3
Houston Chronicle, quoted, 472
Houston Post, quoted, 472
Hubbard, Ursula P., quoted on League conferences, 288*n*
Huddleston, Sisley, on Wilson in Europe, 115*n*
Hudson, Manley O., on our loss of leadership, 314, 525*n*
Hudson Dispatch, quoted, 461
Huerta, General, 5
Hughes, Charles E.: for League, 35, 41; quoted, 46; testifies to our war aims, 61; acquiesces in treating League as taboo, 61; refuses to discuss mandates with League, 63; vetoes merging of Paris Health Office with League, 64; refuses to vest opium regulation in League, 65-66; withholds cooperation on arms traffic, 67-69; letters to, from League unanswered, 70-71; restrains nominations to World Court, 72-73; favors League in 1916 campaign, 73-74; proposes reservations, 74-75; repudiates League, 1922, 75-76; campaigns for Lodge, 75-77; 77*n*; New Haven ad dress of, 143; seeks to avert Ruhr occupation, 143-44; signs letter to Secretary-General, 219; proposes reservations to World Court, 239; elected to World Court, 307
Hull, Cordell, author of first income tax law, 4; on indispensability of world order, 546-47
Humphreys, A. E., 263
Huntington Advertiser, quoted, 463
Hurst, Sir Cecil, 153
Hutchison, Paul, editor, on strategy of peace organizations, 529*n*
Hymans, Paul: President of first League Assembly, 57; and Upper Silesia, 154; *rapporteur* on Vilna dispute, 158; President of Special Assembly on Manchuria, 425-26; 525-26; characterization of, 426; asks Assembly to take a stand, 426; on seventeen months of conciliation, 449; final reply to Japan, 452

Illinois State Journal, quoted, 478
Imperialism, feasibility of, 506-12
Indianapolis News, quoted, 480
Inflation, German (1921), 134, 145
International Labor Organization, sketch of activities, 235; American origins of, 235; entry of U. S. into, 236*n*
International Law: codification conference on, 313*n*; as a defense against war, 512-17; ineffectiveness of, 514*n*, 515-16; and the Covenant, 516; and the Pact; 516-17; Bradley on restraints of, 517*n*
Investments, American foreign, 335
Investment trusts, 355, 358*n*
Irish-Americans against the League, 38-39
Irreconcilables: disrupt compromise negotiations, 31; dominate 1920 Convention, 33; names of, 33; control Harding, 37-38; triumph of, 53; force reservation to Four Power Treaty, 89; hope for death of League, 222*n*; amazed at reservation of nations to World Court reservation, 256; John Gunther's comment on, 392*n*
Ishii, Viscount, and Upper Silesian settlement, 155*n*
Isolation, reasons for return to, 112, 112*n*; feared by all Great Powers, 528

Jackson Daily Clarion Ledger, quoted, 470
Japan: naval rivalry with, 80-81; gains at London Conference, 365; entangled irrevocably, 420; defeated at Shanghai, 423; Grey on responsibility of, 428*n*; Observations on Lytton Report, 440-41; withdraws from League, 451; stakes future upon force, 452-53; failure of, predicted, 506, 506*n*; vulnerability to economic sanctions, 538
Jerome, Jerome K., League obituary, 487
Jersey City Journal, quoted, 462
Jessup, Philip, on restraints of international law, 514*n*; on long-time trends, 548*n*
Johnson, Hiram, compares Article 10 of Covenant with Article 2 of Four Power Treaty, 95-96, 96*n*; deprecates Pact of Paris, 297

Kansas City Kansan, quoted, 478
Kansas City Times, quoted, 478
Karl, ex-Emperor, 181-82
Kellogg, Frank B., on reservation to Four Power Treaty, 90; rejects invitation to conference on World Court reservation, 256; and Pact of Paris, 293-95; defends Stimson and Pact, 312
Kellogg Pact. *See* Pact of Paris
Kennebec Journal, quoted, 464
King, William H., 81
Kitchin, Claude, on war debts, 119
Klein, Julius, optimistic statements of, 285; delegate to World Economic Conference, 287*n*; predictions on depression, 334
Knox, Senator Philander C.: plan to postpone League, 20-21; first attack on Covenant, 25; author of Round Robin, 25; renewed demand that treaty be divorced from League, 26; conference with Root, 27; adviser to Harding, 41; resolution on consultation, 366
Knoxville News Sentinel, quoted, 471
Koo, Wellington, 154
Kredit Anstalt, failure of, 337
Kun, Bela. *See* Bela Kun
Kurds, and Mosul dispute, 171-72

LaFollette, Senator Robert M., Sr., in 1924 election, 275
Laidoner, General F., 176, 177
Lamont, Robert P., Secretary of Commerce, predictions on recovery, 334
Lamont, Thomas W., on U. S. and Reparations Commission, 138*n*; warns against rash lending, 283
Lancaster New Era, quoted, 461
Lansing-Ishii agreement, 107*n*
Lasker, Albert D., dissipates U. S. shipping fleet, 267
Lausanne "Accord of Confidence," 353
Lausanne Conference, 351-52
Lauzanne, Stephen, quoted on French dilemma, 113
Laval, Premier Pierre, mission to Washington, 348
Law, international. *See* International law
League Assembly: first session convened by Wilson, 57; annual sessions decided on, 57; deadlock in 1926

Special, 211-12; Special on Manchuria, 425-35
League Conferences. *See individual entries, e.g.*, Arms traffic regulations, Opium regulations, *etc.*
League Council: first session called by Wilson, 56; its agenda, 56; disputes before—Aaland Islands, 151-52, Upper Silesia, 152-55, Albania's boundaries, 156-57, Vilna, 157-60, Memel, 161, Corfu, 161-66, Greco-Bulgarian, 166-68, Mosul, 169-79; rotation of seats on, demanded, 208-9; nations elected to, 207-9; membership increased, 212, 216; U. S. represented at, 403; Britain represented U. S. on, 417, 422, 423*n*
League of Nations: Wilson's advocacy of (1916), 15; strong sentiment for, at adoption of Covenant, 24, 24*n*; campaign against, financed by Frick and Mellon, 26; public opinion for, 31*n*; all invitations to membership in, accepted, 55-56; Secretariat organized, 55; growing membership of, 56, 57; American opponents desire death of, 61-62; jurisdiction of, on mandates rejected by U. S., 63; jurisdiction of, on health not recognized by U. S., 64; jurisdiction of, on opium rejected by U. S., 65-66; receives statistics from U. S. anonymously, 67; U. S. cooperation on arms traffic withheld from, 67-69; action of, on post-war disputes, 151-79; and interpretation of Articles 10 and 16, 184-91; and Draft Treaty of Mutual Assistance, 191-95; and Geneva Protocol, 196-201; and Locarno treaties, 201-5; and entry of Germany, 205-16; and lesser nations, 207-9, 216; in control of Europe, 217-18; work in repatriating war prisoners, 279; Austrian financial reorganization, 279-80; Hungarian reconstruction loan, 280; Bulgarian refugee loan, 281; first World Economic Conference, 286-88; and Pact of Paris, 302-3; repudiated by F. D. Roosevelt, 388-89; attitude of British Conservatives toward, 390-91; withdrawal of Germany from, 385; withdrawal of Japan from, 451; opinions of American editors on, in 1933, 457-84; no substitute for, found, 529; U. S. policy toward proposed, 541; indispensable function of, 546; future of, 547; Gooch and Williams on permanency of, 547-48
League to Enforce Peace, 11; platform of, 11; 1915 conference, 11; Taft, President of, 11; A. L. Lowell and, 12: *Washington Star* comment on, 12; F. H. Giddings and, 12; Oscar S. Straus and, 13; 1918 Convention, 13*n*; size of, 13*n*
Leases, oil. *See* Oil leases
Lenroot, Senator Irvine L., on Four Power Treaty reservation, 90
León, Quiñones de, 154; and Corfu dispute, 163
Lerroux, Spanish delegate, 396
Lesser Powers, overrule Japan, 426-27; control Committee of Nineteen, 433
Lester, Sean, Irish Free State delegate, 428, 456*n*
Levinson, Samuel O., and outlawry of war, 292-93
Liberia, slavery in, 232
Lippmann, Walter, on danger in Central Europe, 522*n*; on U. S. and world order, 524
Little Entente alliances enumerated, 181
Litvinoff, Maxim, reply to Stimson, 1929, 311-12
Lloyd George, David, and Albanian crisis, 156-57; negotiations, 182
Loans, frozen, 345; panic, 345; internal, 355-56
Locarno, treaties of, 201-5; list of, 203-4; Germany's gains from, 204
Lodge, Senator Henry Cabot: on entangling alliances, 13; for League to Enforce Peace, 13-14; his plan to defeat League, 19, 24*n*; conference with Roosevelt, 21; strategy indicated, 22; attempt to undermine Wilson at Paris, 22; and delegation to Peace Conference, 22*n*; conference with Senator Watson, 24*n*; first attack on Covenant, 25; conference with Borah on strategy, 26; letter to Beveridge on strategy, 29; on Wilson's reactions, 30*n*; deserts own reservations, 33-34; announces League dead, 41; for a dictated peace, 47; demands unity with Allies, 48; presents Four Power Treaty, 84, 84*n*; for Four

Lodge, Senator Henry Cabot (*Cont.*) Power Treaty, 90-92; votes against Lodge reservation, 106; opposes world conference (1922), 138-39; 142; favors "a" world court, 242; proposes third Hague Conference, 245*n*; urges dismissal of Daugherty, 274; responsibility of, for League failure, 392*n*

Logan, James A., American observer on Reparations Commission, 222

London, run on, 345

London Naval Conference, 361-71; diplomatic preparation for, 361-62, 363; our delegates to, 363*n*; Senate reservation to, 370, 370*n*

London *Times*, pro-Japanese, 413, 446*n*

Longworth, Alice, on Harding receptions, 269*n*

Longworth, Nicholas, on war debts, 120*n*

Loudon, delegate of Netherlands, accepts Geneva Protocol, 198; quoted, 228

Louisville Courier-Journal, quoted, 471

Lowell, A. Lawrence, quoted, 12; 35; for economic sanctions (1932), 430

Lusitania, sinking of, 9

Luther, Chancellor, 211, 215; flight to London and Paris (1931), 343

Lynchburg News, quoted, 467

Lynn Daily Evening Item, quoted, 464

Lytton, Lord, his appearance before Council opposed by Matsuoka, 442

Lytton Commission, authorized, 411; personnel of, 435; travels of, 436

Lytton Report, 435-49; summarized, 436-40; Japanese Observations in reply to, 440-41; submitted to Council, 441-42; debated in Assembly, 442-49

McAdoo, William G., 275

McCormick, Senator Medill, and 1920 Republican platform, 33-34; death of, 273*n*

MacCracken, Henry N., quoted on war aims, 61*n*

McCumber, Senator Porter J., on Four Power Treaty, 100-101; on Association of Nations, 101*n*

MacDonald, Premier Ramsay, 196; quoted on entry of Germany into League, 211*n*; forms national government, 346; at Lausanne Conference, 351-52; visit of to U. S., 362, 362*n*; and the Disarmament Conference, 377, 379; lecture to Disarmament Conference, 385

McLean, Edward B., loans house to Daugherty and Smith, 267*n*; his mansion social headquarters of Harding regime, 267*n*

McLean, Senator George P., on Pact of Paris, 299

Macmillan Committee, report of on British finances, 345

McNary, Senator Charles, on value of U. S. participation in League, 139*n*

McNary-Haugen Bill, defeat of, 318-19

Macon Telegraph, quoted, 468

Madariaga, Spanish delegate, to the future Japan, 444; on Woodrow Wilson, 444

Madden, Representative Martin B., on war debts, 119

Mammoth Oil Company, 263

Manchouquo, tied to Japan, 439-40

Manchuria: earlier struggles over, 393-94; Japan's position in undermined, 394; incidents preceding seizure of, 395-96, 396*n*; American notes of September 22 and 24, 399; resolution of September 30, 400; U. S. note of October 5 to Council on, 401; bombing of Chinchow, 401; American note of October 11, 402; Japan's fundamental points, 403, 405-6; U. S. represented at Council, 403; resolution of October 24, 404; Japanese disavowals of aggressive intent, 400-401, 405, 409, 416, 434; long view of crisis, 409*n*; U. S. note of November 27, 410; banditry charges, Chinese reply on, 410*n*; Lytton Commission authorized, 411; December resolution, 411; Shanghai war, 414 ff. (*See also* Shanghai war); appeal of China to Articles 10 and 15, 415; U. S. represented by Great Britain, 417; appeal of the Twelve to Japan, 417-18; Manchouquo created, 418; question of responsibility, 419, 419*n*; Stimson's letter to Borah, 419; irregular teamwork between Washington and Geneva, 421-22; March Assembly (1932), 425-35, small nations control, 426-27; resolution of March 11, 1932, on, 432-33; Committee of Nineteen

on, 433-34, 449; Lytton Report on, 435-49; resolution of February 24, 1933, on, 450-51; terms for settlement on proposed, 451; non-recognition reaffirmed, 451; League's verdict on endorsed by U. S., 452*n*; and future of the League, 454; American press opinion concerning, 457-84; survey of Japanese prospects in, 506
Mandates, jurisdiction of League on rejected by U. S., 63
Mankato Free Press, quoted, 477
Mann, Representative James R., on war debts, 120*n*
Manning, Howard, and sale of liquor permits, 267
Marks, German, American speculation in, 135*n*
Matos, delegate of Guatemala, 411
Matsuoka, Yosuke, Japanese delegate, 441-42
May, Herbert L., elected by Council to Opium Board, 229
May, Sir George, report on British finances, 345
Mediation, A-B-C, 5
Mediterranean, Franco-Italian deadlock in, 362-63
Meighen, Premier Arthur, 82*n*
Mellon, Andrew W.: campaign against League financed by, 26; Secretary of Treasury, 42; confidence in permanence of war debt settlement, 122; refuses oil deal bonds, 266; defends bull market, 330; in London (1931), 341
Memel dispute, 161
Memphis Commercial Appeal, quoted, 471
Miami Herald, quoted, 468
Miller, David Hunter, and Geneva Protocol, 196; quoted on Protocol, 198; quoted on *status quo*, 198*n*; quoted on Pact of Paris and League, 302-3
Miller, Thomas W., Alien Property Custodian, imprisoned, 268
Mills, Ogden L., 33
Minneapolis Tribune, quoted, 476
Mitchell, Charles E., banker, supports stock market boom, 331-32
Mobile Register, quoted, 469
Mongolia, Outer, case not analogous to Manchouquo, 438
Monroe Doctrine, expanded in 1919, 26; deflated in 1929, 296
Montague, Representative Andrew, on war debts, 119
Montgomery Advertiser, quoted, 469
Moon, Parker T., quoted, 314
Moore, John Bassett: Judge of World Court, 59*n*, 72; and Eastern Carelia case, 247-48; memorandum on World Court attributed to, 248-51, 251*n*; 502; on League sanctions, 512*n*; quoted, 513
Moratorium, Hoover, 341-44
Morley, Felix, editor, on the menace of neutrality, 514
Morris, Roland S., on Four Power Treaty, 103
Morrow, Dwight L., and consultative agreement, 364
Moses, Senator George H., quoted, 51-52; supports consultative agreement, 366
Mosul dispute, 169-79; importance of oil in, 169, 178; racial factors in, 170-71; advisory opinion on, 175-76
Motta, Giuseppe, Swiss delegate, 57; leads Assembly at crisis of Manchurian dispute, 427
Muskegon Chronicle, quoted, 480
Muskogee Daily Phoenix, quoted, 471
Mussolini, Benito, policy in Corfu dispute, 164-65; and Disarmament Conference, 379; and conquest of Ethiopia, 495; "we or they," 531

Nadolny, German delegate, 380
Nansen, Fridtjof, 57; heads repatriation of war prisoners, 279; travel certificates, 279
Nashville Banner, quoted, 470
Nashville Tennessean, quoted, 470
National City Company, fees on foreign securities, 282
National Council for Prevention of War, 498*n*
Naval Conference, Geneva. *See* Geneva Naval Conference
Neurath, Baron von, on Manchuria, 446-47
Neutrality: failure of, 6; our sympathy for Allies, 6; effect of atrocity stories, 7; effect of submarine warfare on, 7-9; attempt to reassert, 498-517; and *status quo*, 499-501; and re-

Neutrality (*Cont.*)
sentment of war's costs, 501; and propaganda, 502-4; and the bankers, 504-5; and the "Have-nots," 505-12; "storm cellar," 507*n*; Morley on menace of, 514; reasons for failure of, 517-33
Neville, Edwin L., delegate to opium conferences, 224
New, Senator Harry S., on American origin of Four Power Treaty, 93
Newark Evening News, quoted, 465
Newberry, Truman H., 18
New Haven Journal-Courier, quoted, 459
New London Day, quoted, 459
New Orleans Times-Picayune, quoted, 470
Newport News Daily Press, quoted, 467
Newspaper opinion, American, on Manchurian crisis, 457-84
New York American, quoted, 485-93
New York Globe, quoted, 50
New York Herald (Paris), quoted, 484
New York Herald Tribune, quoted, 206, 460, 489
New York Post, quoted, 459
New York Times, quoted, 71, 259, 357; 1937 editorial on lost leadership, 497-98
New York World-Telegram, quoted, 462
Nine Power Treaty, 108-10; text of, 108; refusal of Great Britain to invoke, 420; cited by Stimson, 421
Nineteenth Route Army, 415; its great achievement, 423
Noel-Baker, Philip, quoted on Geneva Protocol, 198*n*
Normalcy: arrival of, 130-31, 147; period of, 259-75; endorsed in 1924, 275; Elihu Root on record of, 275-76; false foundation of, 282, 347; theory of, 285; economic statistics of, 286*n*; and peace, 316; role of loans in, 355-56; and holding companies, 359; end of, 360; failure of, in disarmament, 387; effort of Stimson to repair damage of, 455-56
Norris, Senator George W., on impossibility of making perfect reservations, 297; and lame-duck amendment, 358

Oakland Tribune, quoted, 474
Obscenity, conference on, 232
Ogden Standard-Examiner, quoted, 475
Oil leases, Sinclair and Doheny, 263
Oklahoman, quoted, 471
Omaha World Herald, quoted, 477
O'Neil, James E., oil executive, 262*n*; flees abroad, 265
Open Door, purpose of in China, 421
Opium regulation: jurisdiction of League on, not recognized by U. S., 65-66; 223-31; American initiative in, 223; roundabout communication on, 223; first Geneva Conference, 227; withdrawal of Porter delegation, 227; second Geneva Conference, 229; failure of Congressional diplomacy on, 227-28; advantages of U. S. collaboration on, 228-30; importance of to U. S., 231
Order, world. *See* World order
O'Ryan, John F., quoted on war aims, 61*n*
Osthilfe scandals, 384*n*

Pacifism, reactionary effects of, 524-55
Pact of Paris: origins of, 291-93; advanced by Butler, 293; reservations to, proposed, 296; reservations opposed by Borah, 296-97; approved, 298; deprecated by Glass and Johnson, 298; welcomed by other Senators, 299-300; and League of Nations, 301-3; and Chaco war, 305; and Sino-Russian clash, 309-12; Stimson on, 381; and consultation, 381-82; legal basis for U. S. action in Manchurian crisis, 404
Panama Canal tolls, repeal, 5
Pan American Arbitration Treaty, 315
Pan American Conciliation Treaty, 315
Papen, Franz von, 351-52; 384
Parker, Lord, on immoraltiy of neutrality, 514
Passaic Herald News, quoted, 466
Paulis, Colonel, 173
Pawtucket Times, quoted, 464
Paxson, Frederic L., cited, 4
Peaceful change. *See* Change, peaceful
Peace organizations: isolationist, 498*n*; internationalist, strategy of, criticized by Hutchison and Peffer, 529*n*; campaign of, for peaceful change, 545*n*; goal for united effort, 548

Peace Pact. *See* Pact of Paris
Peck, Cyrus W., quoted on significance of League, 185-86
Peffer, Nathaniel, quoted on Japanese future in Manchuria, 506*n;* criticizes League's friends, 529*n*
Penrose, Senator Boies, on notice to Allies, 25*n*
Penrose, E. F., on economic forces and war, 512*n*
Pepper, Senator George W., 274; proposes divorce of Court from League, 242, 246
Permanent Advisory Commission, created, 192
Permanent Court of International Justice. *See* World Court
Philadelphia Inquirer, quoted, 466
Philadelphia Public Ledger, quoted, 461
Phillimore plan for league, 14
Pilsudski, Marshal, 160
Pittman, Senator Key, on Four Power Treaty, 98-99; proposes a Lodge reservation in 1922, 106
Pittsburgh Gazette, quoted, 461
Pittsburgh Press, quoted, 466
Poincaré, Raymond, and Ruhr occupation, 135, 147; rebuffs Cuno offer, 183
Poindexter, Senator Miles, on war power of Congress and League, 97*n*; and financial entanglement in Peru, 285
Poland, and war with Russia, 148, 158; and Vilna dispute, 157-60; and Locarno treaties, 205, 210; permanent seat on Council claimed, 209-11
Police action, not war, 536-37
Polish-Rumanian Alliance, 182
Politis, Nicholas, Greek delegate, on Draft Treaty, 196; 376*n*; 428
Pope, Senator James P., resolution of, for membership in League, 544
Population, forced expansion of and territorial demands, 509-11
Porter, Representative Stephen G., opium mission of, to Geneva, 224-29
Portland Oregonian, quoted, 475
Portsmouth Herald, quoted, 458
Power, balance of. *See* Balance of power
Prentiss, Gilbert, Consul to League, 314; sits with League Council, 403, 404*n*
Press comments, on Gilbert sitting with Council, 404*n*; on League's handling of Manchurian crisis, 457-84
Protocol, Geneva. *See* Geneva Protocol
Providence Journal, quoted, 459
Pujo Committee, 4, 4*n*

Quo Tai-chi, Chinese delegate, on the "realities," 448; scolded by Simon, 448*n*

Radio Corporation, boom in stocks, 330-31; collapse of boom, 332
Rainey, Representative Henry T., on war debts, 119
Rapallo, treaty of, 150
Raskob, John J., 317
Rathbone, Albert, cited on war debts, 119*n*
Reber, Samuel J., 232
Reconstruction Finance Corporation, 356-57; 359
Reed, Senator James A., on origin of Four Power Treaty, 93; on alleged new balance of power, 93-94, on war power of Congress and League, 97*n*; on Pact of Paris, 301-2
Reparations: basis of, 132; Premiers Hughes and Smuts on, 132; early claims and deliveries, 132-33; dilemma of, 134-35; deadlock on, 135-36; voice of U. S. on, missed, 137-38, 138*n*; Dawes Plan, 146-47; Young Plan, 339; effect of on Germany, 340; Bank for International Settlements Committee, report on (1931), 349; ended by Lausanne Conference, 351-52; Herriot-MacDonald agreement on, 379
Reparations Commission, and Borah, 51; gives authority to seize Ruhr, 136; voice of U. S. on, missed, 137-38, 138*n*; accepts Dawes Plan, 147; U. S. returns to participation in, 147
Republican Party: victory in 1920, 32; straddles League issue, 33; leaders favoring League, 35; size of pro-League wing, 35, 35*n*, 40; statement of Thirty-One, 36; majorities reduced in 1922, 130; majority held by Coolidge favorable to League, 238*n*; financed by oil deal profits, 266; uninjured by Harding scandals, 274-75;

Republican Party (*Cont.*)
victory in 1924 endorsed World Court, 275; on League (1928), 315; and prosperity, 317, 358*n*; and protectionism, 317; and Hull reciprocity agreements, 323*n*; extent of defeat (1932-36), 357
Reservationists, held in line, 29; rebuffed in 1921, 296-97
Reservations: fourteen voted in Senate, 29; failure of compromise on, 30; hold Republican voters in line, 32; to separate treaty with Germany, 50; Wickersham on constitutionality of, 53*n*; to Four Power Treaty, 89-90; Canadian leaders on, 186*n*; Hughes's draft of, to World Court, 239; usual argument for, 245; expanded fifth reservation on World Court, 246-52; on State debts, 252; to Pact of Paris proposed and rejected, 296-97; relatively harmless form of, invented, 297; impossibility of perfection of, 297; to Pan American Arbitration Treaty, 315; to London Naval Treaty, 370, 370*n*
Resolution, Knox, on consultation, text, 366
Resolution XIV, on security and disarmament, 192
Richmond News Leader, quoted, 467
Riga, Treaty of, 158
Ritchie, Governor Albert, 360
Robinson, Henry M., chief delegate to World Economic Conference, 287; on world prosperity, 287
Robinson, Senator Joseph T., on Senators as negotiators, 88*n*; on Four Power Treaty, 98-99; proposed amendment to Four Power Treaty, 103
Robison, John K., 262
Rochester Democrat and Chronicle, quoted, 460
Rocky Mountain News, quoted, 475
Rogers, Lindsay, quoted, 369
Roosevelt, Franklin D.: guards Navy's oil reserves, 261; vote for, 357; statement repudiating League of Nations, 388-89; message to world rulers, 390; Chicago speech, October 6, 1937, 533-35
Roosevelt, Theodore, attacks on Wilson's leadership, 18; cited, 18*n*; notice to the Allies, 19; conference with Lodge on strategy, 22
Roosevelt, Theodore, Jr., and transfer of Navy's oil reserves, 262, 263*n*
Root, Elihu: unifies Republican factions, 27; author of 1920 platform compromise, 33; 35; writes manifesto of Thirty-One, 36; and first nomination of World Court Judges, 72-73; helps organize World Court, 237; on record of Normalcy, 275-77; Woodrow Wilson Foundation award to, 276; on necessity of international institutions, 306; on our interest in world order, 306*n*; negotiates World Court formula, 308
Round Robin, against League, 25
Rowell, Newton D., on Article 10, 185; on reservations, 186*n*
Rublee, George, 367
Ruhr, occupation of, 144-45
Rumbold, Sir Horace, 167
Russia: civil war in, 148-49; at Genoa Conference, 150; and Treaty of Rapallo, 150; and League, 201; opposed to Locarno treaties, 205; famine relief for, 279; and clash with China (1929), 309-12; abandons isolation, 528
Russo-Polish war (1920), 148

Sacramento Bee, quoted, 474
St. Paul Pioneer Press, quoted, 476
Sales tax, rejected, 356
Sanctions: Albert Hall meeting for, 429*n*; Great Powers afraid of, 429; undermined by Washington Naval Treaty, 429; American movement for (1932), 430, 430*n*; supposed inability of Powers to enforce, 431-32; significance of Manchurian crisis and, 454; opinions of many editors upon quoted, 457-84; not war, 536; inevitable, 537; less expensive than war, 537-38; U. S. impelled toward, 539; arguments of pacifists against 498*n*, 539*n*
San Diego Union, quoted, 475
San Francisco Chronicle, quoted, 474
San Francisco Examiner, quoted, 493
Sato, Japanese delegate, defends Japan, 415, 416*n*; attempt to amend resolution of March, 1932, 426-27
Saturday Evening Post, quoted, 18*n*

Schattschneider, E. E., quoted on tariff of 1930, 321-44
Schleicher, General von, 381
Scialoja, Italian delegate, 168
Scott, James Brown, helped organize World Court, 237
Security, collective: and campaign for a league of nations, 16 ff.; collapse of, 20; barred by Hughes, 75; and Four Power Treaty, 84, 95-96, 100; and Nine Power Treaty, 108-10; and France, 113-14, 182; and Borah, 141-42; search for, 180-218; Wells on, 183*n*; and the interpretation of Articles 10 and 16, 187-90; in Draft Treaty of 1923, 193-95; in Geneva Protocol, 197-98; and Locarno treaties, 203-5; and national prosperity, 355-60; in London Conference, 368; in Disarmament Conference, 375, 386-87; and Davis declaration of May 24, 1933, 390-91; effects of Manchurian war on, 453-56; Stimson on, 456; U. S. editorial opinion on, 457-94; deterioration of, 495-97; and *status quo*, 500-501; and costs of war, 501; and forced expansion of population, 509-10; and laws against war, 515-17; and the localization of war, 519-20; coming decisions on, 521; and fascism, 521-22; and conquest, 523; and conquests planned, 523-25; and military science, 526; and the League, 529, 541-42; and Britain, 532-33; Roosevelt on, 534-35; and police action, 536; and sanctions, 536-39; degrees of responsibility for, 543; and the U. S., 547-49
Self-sufficiency, and war, 540
Seligman and Company, loans to Peru, 284-85
Senate, U. S.: adopts reservations to League Covenant, 29; reject Versailles Treaty, 29, 31; adopts reservation to separate treaty with Germany, 50; dominates State Department, 67; adopts reservations to Four Power Treaty, 89-90; rejects reservations to Pact of Paris, 296-97
Senators: Democratic—accept separate peace treaty with Germany, 52, give Four Power Treaty a majority, 104; Republican—unified for reservations to Covenant, 29, solicitude on Shantung, 102, 110; as negotiators, 87, 88*n*, 92
Shanghai war: 414 ff.; aimed at boycott, 414; and Nineteenth Route Army, 415; direct protest against by Great Powers, 416; work of Consular Committee, 422, 425, 425*n*; a defeat for Japan, 423; failure of Great Powers in, 424; end of, 434-35
Shantung question, settlement at Paris, 107-8; agreement at Washington, 108
Sheppard, Senator Morris, 51
Shiozawa, Admiral Kiochi, at Shanghai, 414-15
Shotwell, James T.: provides basis for Geneva Protocol, 196-97; share in organizing I. L. O., 235, 236*n*; and Pact of Paris, 292; quoted on Pact, 293*n*; on varying degrees of responsibility for world order, 543
Shreveport Times, quoted, 470
Silesia, Upper, dispute, 150-55
Simmons, Senator Furnifold M., on tariff of 1922, 129-30
Simon, Sir John: attempts to block League action on Shanghai, 417; refuses to concert with U. S. on Shanghai war, 420, 423*n*; represents U. S. on Council, 422; bars all intervention in Manuchurian dispute, 423; urges conciliation, 432, 445-46, 446*n*; threatens Quo Tai-chi, 448*n*; throws Ethiopian appeal in wastebasket, 448*n*
Simonds, Frank H.: quoted on bankruptcy of nationalism, 217; on expansion of League's influence, 217-18; on American policy toward League, 218, 218*n*; on Hoover's attitude toward France, 342
Sinclair, Harry F.: in Continental Trading Company deal, 262*n*; gives bonds to Fall, 263; buys oil through Fall, 264; acquitted of conspiracy, 265; hires jury shadowed, 265
Sino-Japanese war of 1937, 496
Sioux City Tribune, quoted, 477
Slavery in Liberia, 232
Smith, Alfred E., 275; on our interest in League, 316
Smith, Jeremiah, administered Hungarian reconstruction loan, 280
Smith, Jess: and sale of liquor permits, 267; violent death of, 268
Smoot, Senator Reed, on war debts, 120

Soares, Macedo, quoted on Brazil's resignation from League, 231*n*
Spain, claims permanent seat on Council, 207-8; threatens resignation from League, 212-13
Spanish civil war, 496
Speculation, in real estate, 327-28; in stocks, 328-32
Spencer, Herbert, quoted, 13
Spencer, Senator Selden P., on Four Power Treaty reservation, 89-90
Springfield Republican, quoted, 459
Staley, Eugene, quoted on demands of "Have-nots," 507*n*; on "storm cellar" neutrality, 507*n*
Status quo, Miller's defense of, 198*n*; and neutrality, 499-501
Steffens, Lincoln, quoted on Wilson in Europe, 23
Stewart, Charles L., author of Export Debenture Plan, 319
Stewart, Robert M., oil executive, 262*n*; ousted by John D. Rockefeller, Jr., 265
Stimson, Henry L.: invokes Pact of Paris in Sino-Russian clash, 309-12; trip to Europe (1931), 343; visits Disarmament Conference, 377, 377*n*; August, 1932, speech on consultation, 381-82; opposes Manchurian inquiry, 397-98; on accentuated isolationism of U. S., 399*n*; press comments on sending of Gilbert to Council, 404*n*; on long view of Manchurian crisis, 409*n*; his "doctrine" enunciated January 7, 1932, 412; letter to Borah, 419; telephone calls to Simon, 420; on interrelation of Washington treaties, 421; on value of contacts at Geneva, 434*n*; his non-recognition doctrine formally endorsed, 451; his effort to repair damage of Normalcy, 455-56; long view in his *Far Eastern Crisis*, 456; letter of October 7, 1937, 538
Stimson Doctrine, 412; Japan's reply to, 412; early origins of, 412*n*; cool reception of, in London, 413; supported by resolution of March 11, 1932, 433; formally endorsed by League, 451
Stock market, 1929 crash of, 328-32
Stowell, Ellery C., quoted, 313
Straus, Oscar S., 41, 72-73; quoted, 13
Streit, Clarence K., on our mistake at start of Manchurian crisis, 398
Stresemann, Gustav, on separate peace with the U. S., 53-54; 1926 oration of, 215
Submarine warfare, 7-9
Sussex, sinking of, 9; pledge, 9-10
Swanson, Senator Claude A., proposes World Court resolution, 242; offers expanded fifth reservation, 251; on Pact of Paris, 299; delegate to Disarmament Conference, 377*n*
Switzerland, referendum on League, 57*n*
Syracuse Post-Standard, quoted, 459
Sze, Chinese delegate, 396

Tacoma Daily Ledger, quoted, 475
Taft, William H.: President, League to Enforce Peace, 11; quoted, 12; stands by Wilson after Round Robin, 25; protests against packing of Foreign Relations Committee, 26; favors League, 34*n*, 35; 41
Tardieu, André, quoted, 112*n*; political position of, 364; avoids Disarmament Conference, 378; fall from power of, 378
Tariff: Underwood Tariff Act, 3-4; 1921 bill vetoed by Wilson, 125-27; 1921 Act, 127; Fordney-McCumber Act (1922), 127-31, on farm products, 318; Smoot-Hawley Act (1930), ends tariff truce, 288, 321-27; "cost of production" in, 322-23; a declaration of economic war, 325; 1,028 economists warn against, 326-27; effects of, 326*n*; Calais demonstration against 367*n*; and plight of poor nations, 511; current dilemma on, 540
Teapot Dome lease, 263
Teleke, Count Paul, 172
Temporary Mixed Commission, created, 192; frames Draft Treaty, 193; 221
Te Water, delegate of South Africa, on Japan's guilt, 428
Thirty-One, manifesto of, 36; Root author of, 36
Thomas, J. H., British delegate, speaks for U. S., 417
Thompson and Kelly Company, and Perryville Depot, 266, 266*n*

Three Rivers, Fall's ranch, 264
Titulesco, delegate of Rumania, on Article 10, 428
Townshend, O. C., warns against Peru loans, 284-85
Toynbee, A. J., quoted on Corfu dispute, 165
Transit Conference, Barcelona, 58; invitation to, declined, 62
Transportation Statistics, conference on, 313*n*
Treaties, arbitration, statistics on, 314; Kellogg series, 314-15; Pan American, 315
Treatment of Foreigners, conference on, 313*n*
Treaty of Guarantee, Anglo-American, 153
Treaty of Peace with Germany: first attempts at, 43-44; Knox resolution for, vetoed by Wilson, 44; negotiated by E. L. Dresel, 48; based on Treaty of Versailles, 48-50; terms of, 48-50; reservation to, adopted, 50, 53*n*; opposed by Borah, 50-51; Senator Williams on, 51; criticized by Senator Walsh, 52; approved by Senate, 52
Treaty of Riga, 158
Treaty of Versailles. *See* Versailles, Treaty of,
Trenton Evening Times, quoted, 462
Trenton State Gazette, quoted, 462
Troy Times, quoted, 464
Twentieth Century Fund, report of on sanctions, 430
Two thirds vote on treaties, 31, 53; Harding's fear of, 84-86; 104, 118, 118*n*

Unden, Swedish delegate, 211; backs Article 10, 444
Union Guardian Company, 359
United States: entry into Great War, 10-11; contributes statistics to League anonymously, 67; letters from League not answered by, 67, 70-72; withholds cooperation on arms, traffic, 67-69; effects of intervention in Europe of, 113-14, 116; unanimity of, for League in 1918, 116; effects of abstention of, from League on defeated nations, 116-17; Australian comment on abstention of, from League, 117*n*; creditor position of, 123-25; seeks to avert Ruhr occupation, 142-44; returns to participation in Reparations Commission, 147; demands share of Mosul oil, 178; drops practice of impersonal communication with League, 219; unofficial observers sent to Geneva, 219-21; Achorn on effects of abstention of, 221*n*; sends delegates to opium conferences, 224 ff.; rejects invitation to negotiate on World Court reservation, 258; famine relief of, to Europe (1919), 277; depression of 1921, 281-82; world's banker, 282; loans to Germany, 283; loans to Latin America, 284-85; balance of trade during Normalcy, 286*n*; delegates to World Economic Conference, 287*n*; and most-favored-nation treatment, 288*n*; and various League Conferences, 288*n*; and Geneva Naval Conference, 288-91; increased cooperation with Geneva, 313; leadership in arbitration lost, 314; gold drained to, 336; and London Naval Conference, 361-71; and world disarmament, 372 ff.; leadership in Disarmament Conference, 376*n*; failure of effort of, to disarm Europe, 387; and world politics, 388, 398, 399*n*; effect of abstention of, on League of Nations, 392; and Manchurian crisis, 397 ff.; opposes Manchurian inquiry, 397-98; represented at League Council, 403, 404*n*; represented at Geneva by Great Britain, 417, 422, 423*n*; strong ties with China, 420; irregular teamwork with League, 421-22; League's verdict on Manchuria endorsed by, 452*n*; defeated with League in Manchuria, 454-55; editorial opinions on League in 1933, 457-84; *New York Times* on loss of leadership of, 497-98; costs of war to, 501; why war aims failed, 502; and world balance of power, 519; Hudson on lost leadership, 525*n*; dangers confronting, 524-26; desires companionship, 528; Borchard on role of, 530-31; Young on future of, 532-33, 532*n*; impelled toward sanctions, 537-39; Stimson on policy of (1937), 538; essentials of future pol-

United States (*Cont.*)
icy, 539; policy toward League and world order proposed, 541; action of in world politics required, 543; indispensability of, in world government, 549
Unofficial observers, 219-21; Borah's objection to, 220, 220*n*
Upper Silesia, dispute, 150-55

Vassiliades, Captain, 168
Vera Cruz, occupation of, 5
Versailles, Treaty of, first rejection, 29; second rejection, 31; ratification proposed by President Harding, 45-46; abandoned, 46; Part V, 372
Vilna dispute, 157-60
Virginian-Pilot and the Norfolk Landmark, quoted, 467
Voldemaris, Lithuanian delegate, 160
Votaw, Heber, and dope traffic, 268*n*

Wall Street crash, 327-32
Wall Street Journal, quoted, 465
Walsh, Senator Thomas J., on separate peace, 52; on tariff of 1922, 129-30; as prosecutor of oil scandals, 265*n*; attacks upon, 265*n*; on Pact of Paris, 300
Wambaugh, Sarah, quoted on our slowness in cooperating on Austria, 280*n*
War, Russo-Polish (1920), 148; Russian civil, 148-49; Greco-Turkish, 149-50; outlawry of, 291-92; and Borah, 291; localization of, 519 ff.; and Fascism, 521-23
War debts, 118-23; origins of, 118-19; wartime Congressional leaders on, 119-20, 120*n*, 121*n*; law upon, 121; Funding Commission membership, 121; total of, 121; terms conceded, 121-22; collapse of, 342; revision of, forbidden by Congress, 350; and Lausanne Accord, 352; revision of, asked, 353; defaulted, 354; American resentment on, 354; statement of Newton D. Baker on, 354; statement of Columbia University Faculty on, 355, 355*n*; reopening of urged, 355*n*
Washington Conference, 79-111; pressure for, in Congress, 81-82; nations represented at, 82; our delegates to, 82*n;* supplementary treaties, 105-6; Shantung agreement, 107-8; Nine Power Treaty, 108-10; evacuation of Siberia, 110*n;* naval limitation treaty, 110-11; adverse effect upon sanctions, 429
Washington Star, quoted, 12
Washington Treaties, all related, 421
Watson, Senator James E., and plan to defeat League, 24*n*; on how League was defeated, 29*n*; on how 1920 platform was made, 34*n*; 142
Weeks, Secretary John W., bought oil deal bonds, 266; and death of Brandegee, 273*n*
Wells, H. G., on Franco-German problem, 183*n*; on influence of Irreconcilables, 238
Wheeler, Senator Burton K., 265*n*
Wheeling Register, quoted, 467
White, William Allen, editor, on forces dominating Harding era, 260, 269; on Coolidge cleansing of White House, 274
White-slave traffic, conference concerning, 58; campaign against, 231
Wickersham, George W., 35; on constitutionality of a Senate reservation, 53*n*
Wiegand, Karl H. von, quoted, 488
Wiggin Committee, on Germany's economic condition, 344; report of, 344-45
Willert, Sir Arthur, on danger in Central Europe, 520*n*
Williams, Sir John Fisher, on permanence of League, 548
Williams, Senator John Sharp, on separate peace, 51; on effect of U. S. abstention from League, 142*n*
Wilson, Hugh R., 377*n*, 398, 400, 417; watched Simon represent U. S., 422
Wilson, William B., 235
Wilson Woodrow: Progressive achievements of first term, 4; Mobile address, 5; address to League to Enforce Peace (1916), 14; and League in 1916 campaign, 15; message to Russian people, 16; and Fourteen Points, 17; address of July 4, 1918, 17; and election of 1918, 17-19; appeal for Democratic Senate, 18; reception in Europe, 23, 23*n*; western tour, 28; accepts Hitchcock res-

ervations, 30; expects 1920 victory, 40; chooses Secretary-General, 55; Philip Gibbs on, 55; impact of, on Europe, 115-16; estimate of, by Dickinson, 115-16; Huddleston on, 115*n*; veto of 1921 tariff bill, 125-27; Armistice Day Message (1923), 271, 272*n*; and Harding, 272; death of, 272-73, 273*n*; Madariaga on, 444; statement of the issues of the war, 495

Winnipeg Free Press, editor of, quoted, 544

Wirsen, M. de, 172

Women's International League for Peace and Freedom, 498*n*

Woodrow Wilson Foundation, award to Root, 276

Woolley, Mary E., 377*n*

Worcester Evening Gazette, quoted, 466

World conquest: drive toward, inherent in Fascism, 521-23; thrusts toward, 523; facilitated by modern weapons, 526; or world federation, 533; and democracies, 535-36; Dafoe on alternative to, 544

World Court: organized, 58; share of Root in, 59; nominations to, restrained by Hughes, 72-73; American origins of, 236-37; Hughes reservations to, 239; calls a League court, 240; supported by Hoover, 240-41; proposal held in Senate Committee, 241-42; opposed by Borah, 242; resolution sponsored by Swanson, 242; divorce of, from League proposed, 242; danger in, discovered, 243; fifth reservation to, added by Senate committee, 245; endorsed in 1924 campaign, 245; fifth reservation text, 246; expanded fifth reservation advocated by "international jurist," 248-51, 251*n*; fifth reservation expanded, 251 ff.; action of 48 nations on Senate reservation to, 254-56, conference on, 256 ff.; endorsed by Republican victory of 1924, 275; Gillett resolution on, 307; negotiations on, revived, 307; Hughes elected to World Court, 307; petition for, 307*n*; formula on negotiated by Root, 308; protocol of signed, 308. *See also Advisory* opinions

World Economic Conference, first, 286-88; U. S. delegates to, 287*n*; urged tariff peace, 287-88

World federation: forces compelling, 523-33; or anarchy, 533 ff.; and peaceful change, 544-45; Hindmarsh on necessity for, 546*n*

World order: Root on, 306*n*; Lippmann on, 524; policy of U. S. toward proposed, 541; Shotwell on varying degrees of responsibility for, 543; Hull on, 546; Woodrow Wilson and, 547; challenge of, 548; necessity for, 549

World supremacy, and Fascism, 521-23; thrusts for, 523-36

Wright, Hamilton, 223

Wright, Quincy, on Great Powers and war, 518

Yap, island of, held by Japan, 80

Yen, Dr., Chinese delegate, on Japanese responsibility, 419, 419*n*

Yoshizawa, Japanese delegate, 396 ff.

Young, Eugene J., on role of U. S., 532-33, 532*n*

Young, Owen D., chairman Reparations Committee, 339

Ypiranzi, 5

Zeligowski, General, 158-60

Zimmerman, Dr. Alfred, League Commissioner to Austria, 280

Zimmern, Sir Alfred, on indispensable function of League, 546

Zumeta, delegate of Venezuela, 209